LAST MAN

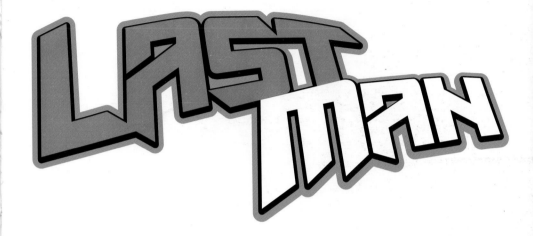

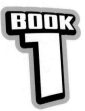

BOOK 1

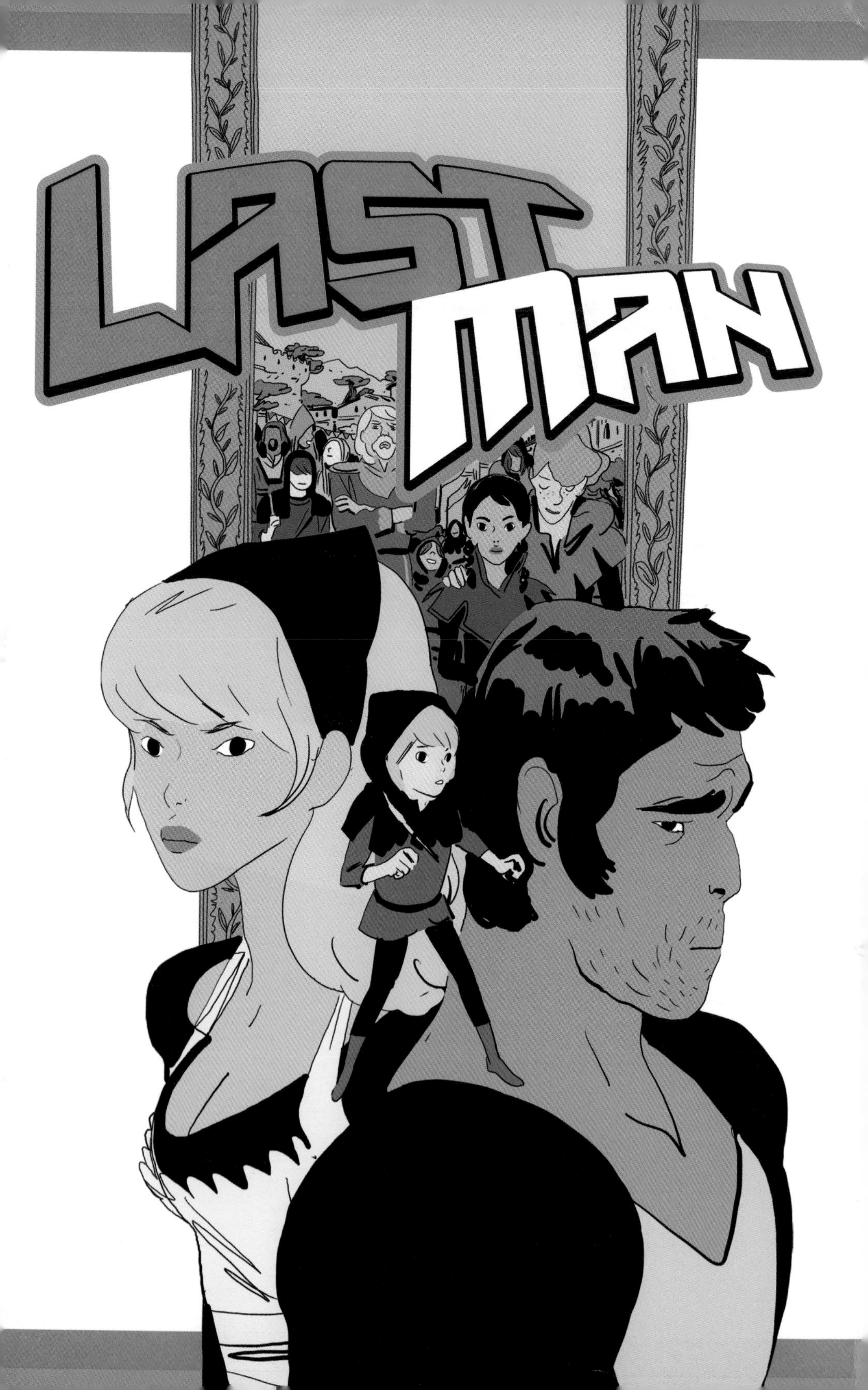
LAST
MAN

WRITTEN BY

MICHAËL SANLAVILLE
BASTIEN VIVÈS
BALAK

ILLUSTRATED BY

BASTIEN VIVÈS
MICHAËL SANLAVILLE

TRANSLATED BY
EDWARD GAUVIN

COLLECTION DESIGN BY
ANDRES JUAREZ

ENGLISH EDITION, EDITED BY
AMANDA LAFRANCO

LETTERED BY
ANDWORLD DESIGN

FRENCH EDITION, EDITED BY
DIDIER BORG

FOR SKYBOUND ENTERTAINMENT

ROBERT KIRKMAN Chairman
DAVID ALPERT CEO
SEAN MACKIEWICZ SVP, Publisher
SHAWN KIRKHAM SVP, Business Development
ANDRES JUAREZ Art Director
ARUNE SINGH Director of Brand, Editorial
SHANNON MEEHAN Public Relations Manager
ALEX ANTONE Editorial Director
AMANDA LAFRANCO Editor
JILLIAN CRAB Graphic Designer
MORGAN PERRY Brand Manager, Editorial
SARAH CLEMENTS Brand Coordinator, Editorial
DAN PETERSEN Sr. Director, Operations & Events

Foreign Rights & Licensing Inquiries:
contact@skybound.com

SKYBOUND.COM

FOR IMAGE COMICS, INC.

ROBERT KIRKMAN Chief Operating Officer
ERIK LARSEN Chief Financial Officer
TODD MCFARLANE President
MARC SILVESTRI Chief Executive Officer
JIM VALENTINO Vice President
ERIC STEPHENSON Publisher / Chief Creative Officer
NICOLE LAPALME Vice President of Finance
LEANNA CAUNTER Accounting Analyst
SUE KORPELA Accounting & HR Manager
MATT PARKINSON
Vice President of Sales & Publishing Planning
LORELEI BUNJES Vice President of Digital Strategy
DIRK WOOD Director of International Sales & Licensing
RYAN BREWER
International Sales & Licensing Manager
ALEX COX Director of Direct Market Sales
CHLOE RAMOS Book Market & Library Sales Manager
EMILIO BAUTISTA Digital Sales Coordinator
JON SCHLAFFMAN Specialty Sales Coordinator
KAT SALAZAR Vice President of PR & Marketing
DEANNA PHELPS Marketing Design Manager
DREW FITZGERALD Marketing Content Associate
HEATHER DOORNINK Vice president of Production
DREW GILL Art Director
HILARY DILORETO Print Manager
TRICIA RAMOS Traffic Manager
MELISSA GIFFORD Content Manager
ERIKA SCHNATZ Senior Production Artist
WESLEY GRIFFITH Production Artist

IMAGECOMICS.COM

LASTMAN BOOK ONE.

FIRST PRINTING.

ISBN: 978-1-5343-2229-5

Published by Image Comics, Inc. Office of publication: PO BOX 14457, Portland, OR 97293. Copyright © Casterman 2022. All rights reserved. Originally published in French by Casterman as LASTMAN Tomes 1-2. Image Comics® and its logos are registered trademarks and copyrights of Image Comics, Inc. All rights reserved. No part of this publication may be reproduced or transmitted in any form or by any means (except for short excerpts for review purposes) without the express written permission of Image Comics, Inc. All names, characters, events and locales in this publication are entirely fictional. Any resemblance to actual persons (living or dead), events or places, without satiric intent, is coincidental. Printed in Canada.

The best thing about comics is that it's a collaborative medium. In the best of cases, making comics is really kind of like hanging out with your friends and doing something fun together. Some people like to go to sporting events, or go camping, or something else people do for fun that I can't really think of. Me? I like making comics.

I've done other things, but comics is the medium I enjoy working in the most. Part of the reason is that there's not a lot of weight on one person's shoulders. Writing a novel? That sounds insane. Thinking of cool things for someone else to draw? Heaven. Absolute heaven. I mean really... why would you write in any other medium? Your story is just going to live as words on a page? Boring. You have to get a bunch of human beings to stand in places and act out your story? Too tedious and SO MANY ways that can go wrong. You want an army of people to draw your story in so many pictures that they can actually move? Well... to be honest, animation is the closest you can get to comics without just making

comics, and it is pretty cool, but right now, we're talking about comics.

In the best cases, the collaboration is so fun, and all parties involved are so energized by working with each other, the joy they're feeling bleeds through on every single page. One such collaboration I can think of that fits that bill is the one you're holding in your hands right now! It's LASTMAN, stupid!

LASTMAN, a collaboration by Michaël Sanlaville, Bastien Vivès, and Balak, is a book that I absolutely fell in love with a few years ago. Coming from France, I knew it was well underway by the time my dumb American brain caught wind of it. So, I was able to plow through many volumes all at once, without any delay. For a story that starts with such humble beginnings, a mother and child, a tournament, a mysterious stranger... you could never in a million years guess where it's going.

Each volume brings you deeper and deeper in the world of LASTMAN and takes you on a journey that is as unique as it is enthralling.

As a comic creator who has been at it a while, the feeling I've come to cherish the most when I read a new comic is UNCONTROLLABLE JEALOUSY. When a book makes me feel completely inadequate as a writer, when it makes me feel like my entire career is a farce, when it makes me want to give up completely because I know I'll never write anything as good, it's just so damn fulfilling. I mean, I wanted to throw my copy of LASTMAN across the room when I was done reading it. How great is that?!

Sanlaville, Vivès, and Balak, three geniuses who have separately created absolute masterworks, have come together like a French Voltron to make one of the most inventive and exciting stories I've ever read. And that's just the writing! How can I ignore the stunning art? Have you seen a comic that has better fight choreography? The gestures and movement achieved in this series are breathtaking. The emotion wrung out of every line,

and masterfully done with so few, brings to life an amazing array of complex and unique characters.

I just love this book so damn much.

That's why, when I learned that LASTMAN was in need of an American publisher, I jumped at the chance. I mean, what is having your own comics company for if you can't help bring books you love to the masses? I'm so proud of how the team at Skybound has rolled their sleeves up and pulled out all the stops for this series... and now it's your chance to fall in love with this book.

So really, what are you reading this boring intro for? There's a whole new world for you to discover a few pages away.

Go on! Get reading!

ROBERT KIRKMAN
Backwoods, California
2022

CHAPTER ONE

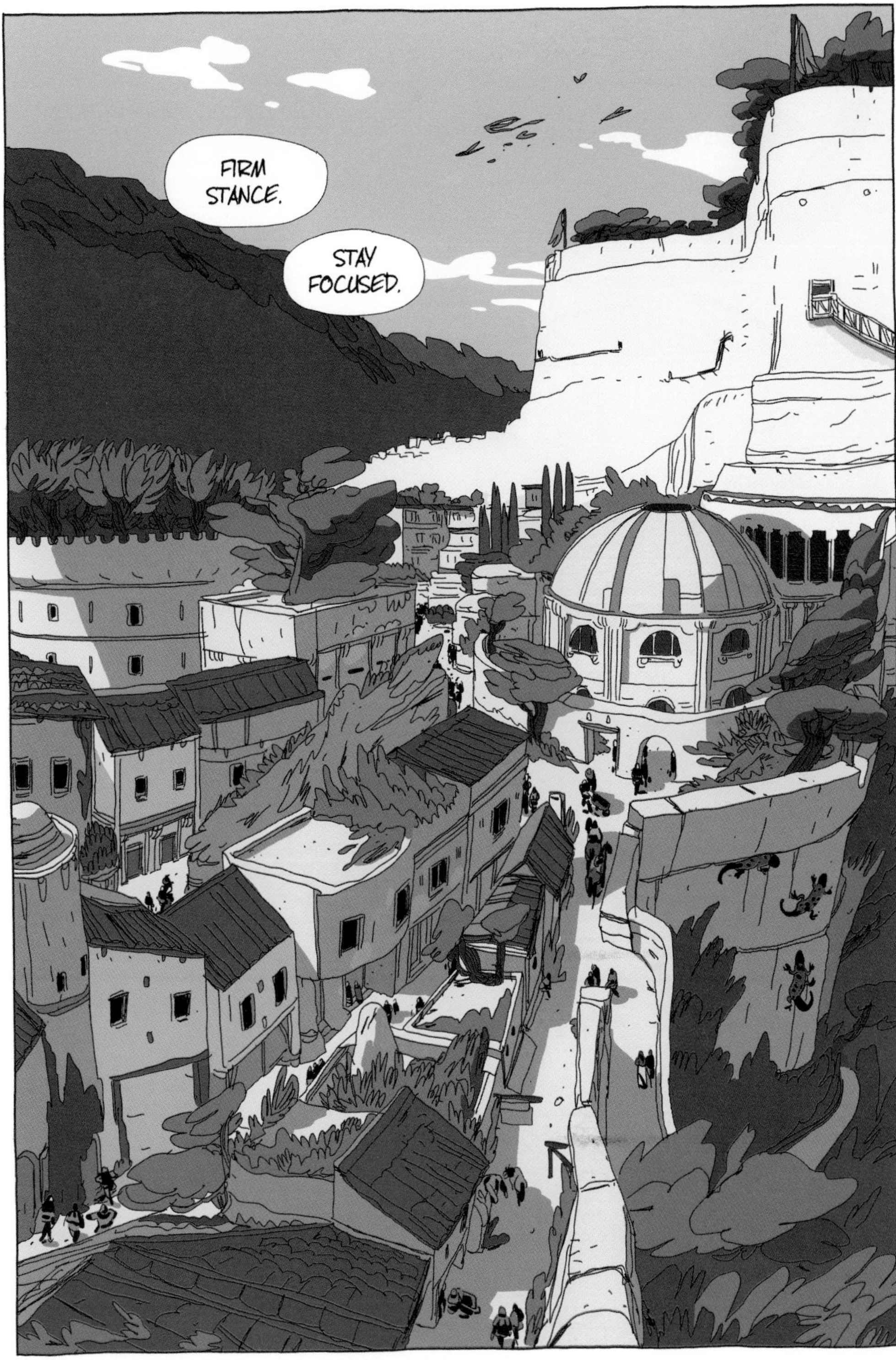
FIRM STANCE.
STAY FOCUSED.

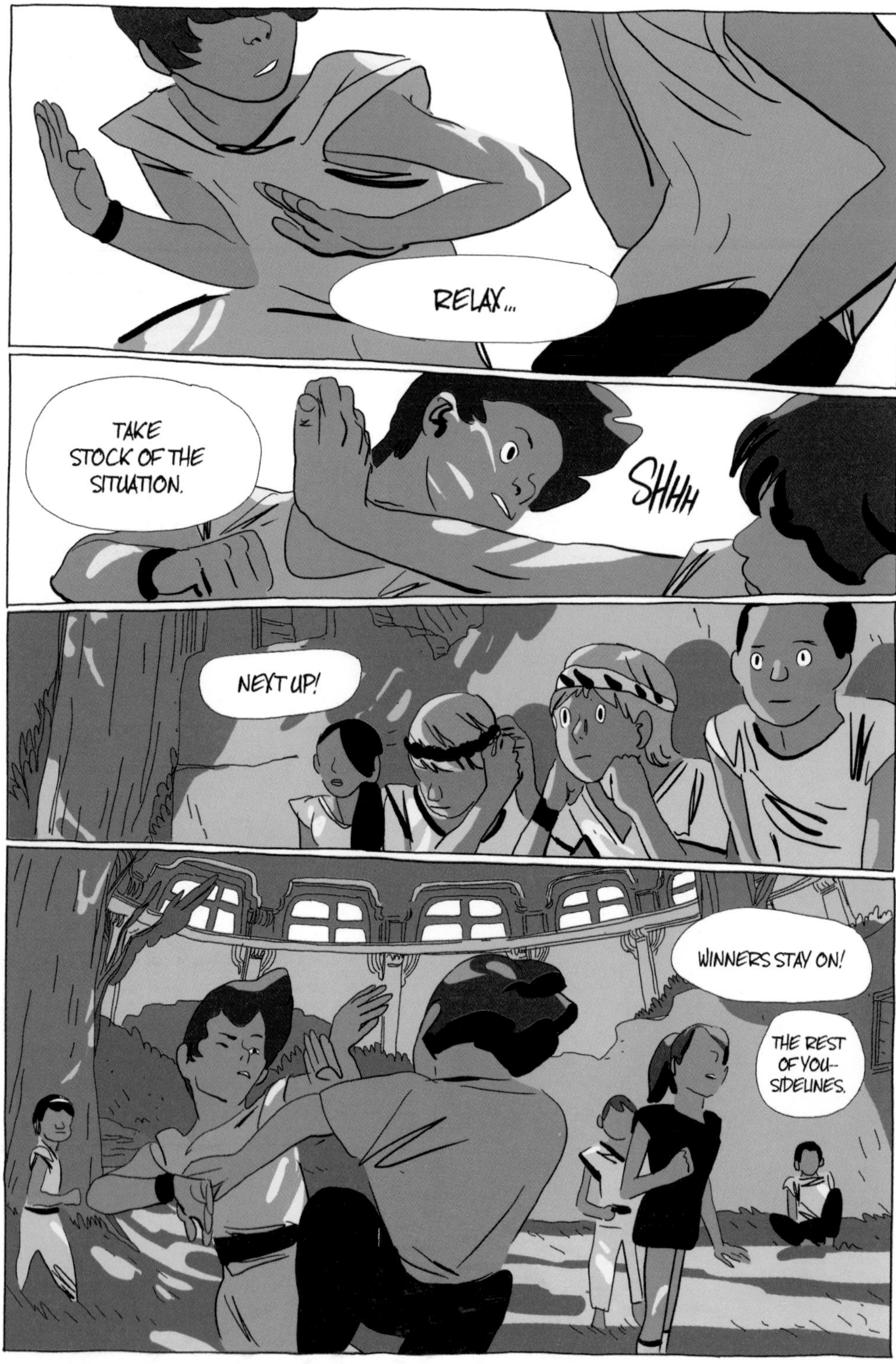
RELAX...
TAKE STOCK OF THE SITUATION.
SHHH
NEXT UP!
WINNERS STAY ON!
THE REST OF YOU-- SIDELINES.

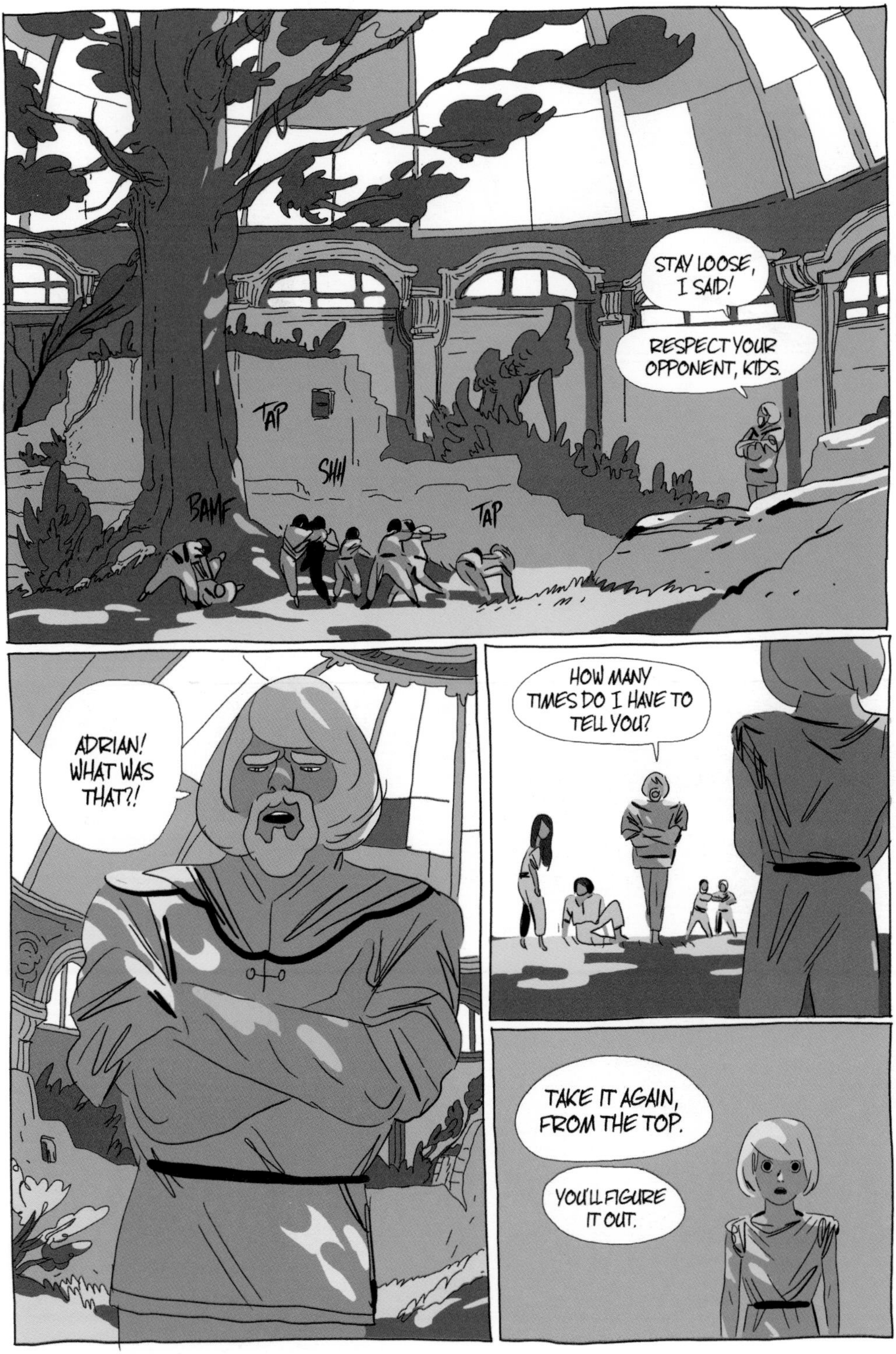
STAY LOOSE, I SAID!
RESPECT YOUR OPPONENT, KIDS.
TAP
SHH
BAMF
TAP
ADRIAN! WHAT WAS THAT?!
HOW MANY TIMES DO I HAVE TO TELL YOU?
TAKE IT AGAIN, FROM THE TOP.
YOU'LL FIGURE IT OUT.

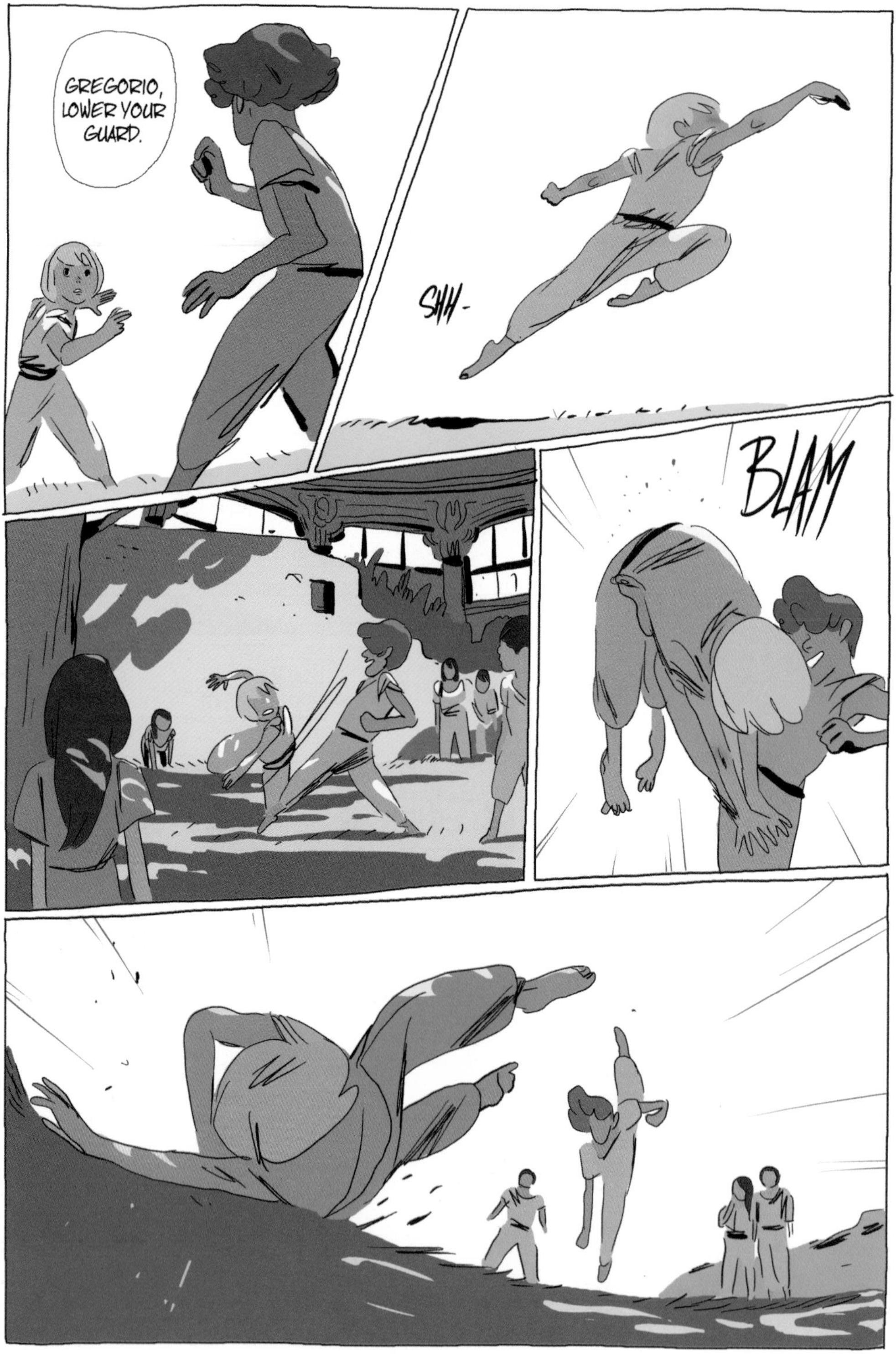
GREGORIO, LOWER YOUR GUARD.
SHH-
BLAM

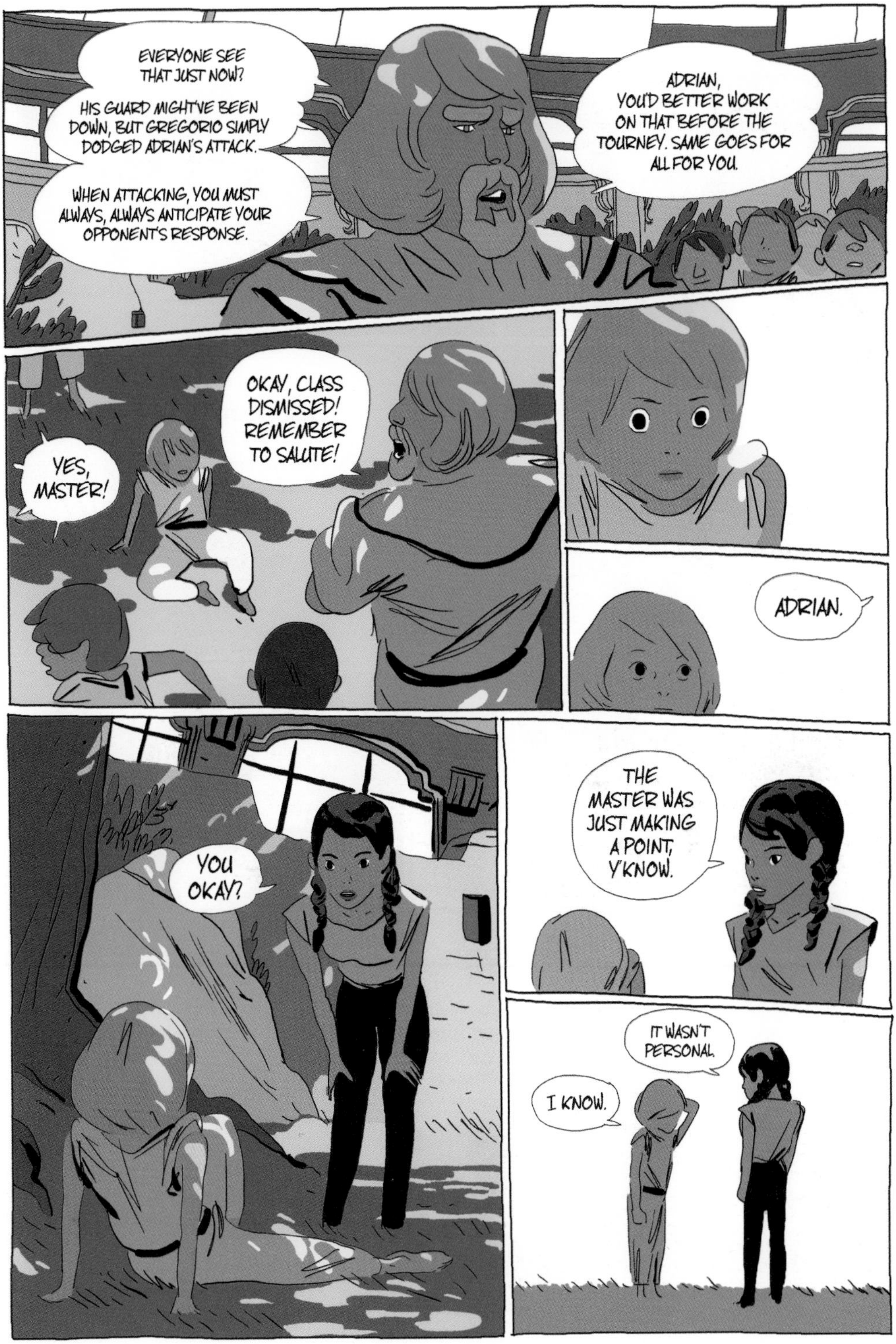
EVERYONE SEE THAT JUST NOW?
HIS GUARD MIGHT'VE BEEN DOWN, BUT GREGORIO SIMPLY DODGED ADRIAN'S ATTACK.
WHEN ATTACKING, YOU MUST ALWAYS, ALWAYS ANTICIPATE YOUR OPPONENT'S RESPONSE.
ADRIAN, YOU'D BETTER WORK ON THAT BEFORE THE TOURNEY. SAME GOES FOR ALL FOR YOU.
OKAY, CLASS DISMISSED! REMEMBER TO SALUTE!
YES, MASTER!
ADRIAN.
YOU OKAY?
THE MASTER WAS JUST MAKING A POINT, Y'KNOW.
IT WASN'T PERSONAL.
I KNOW.

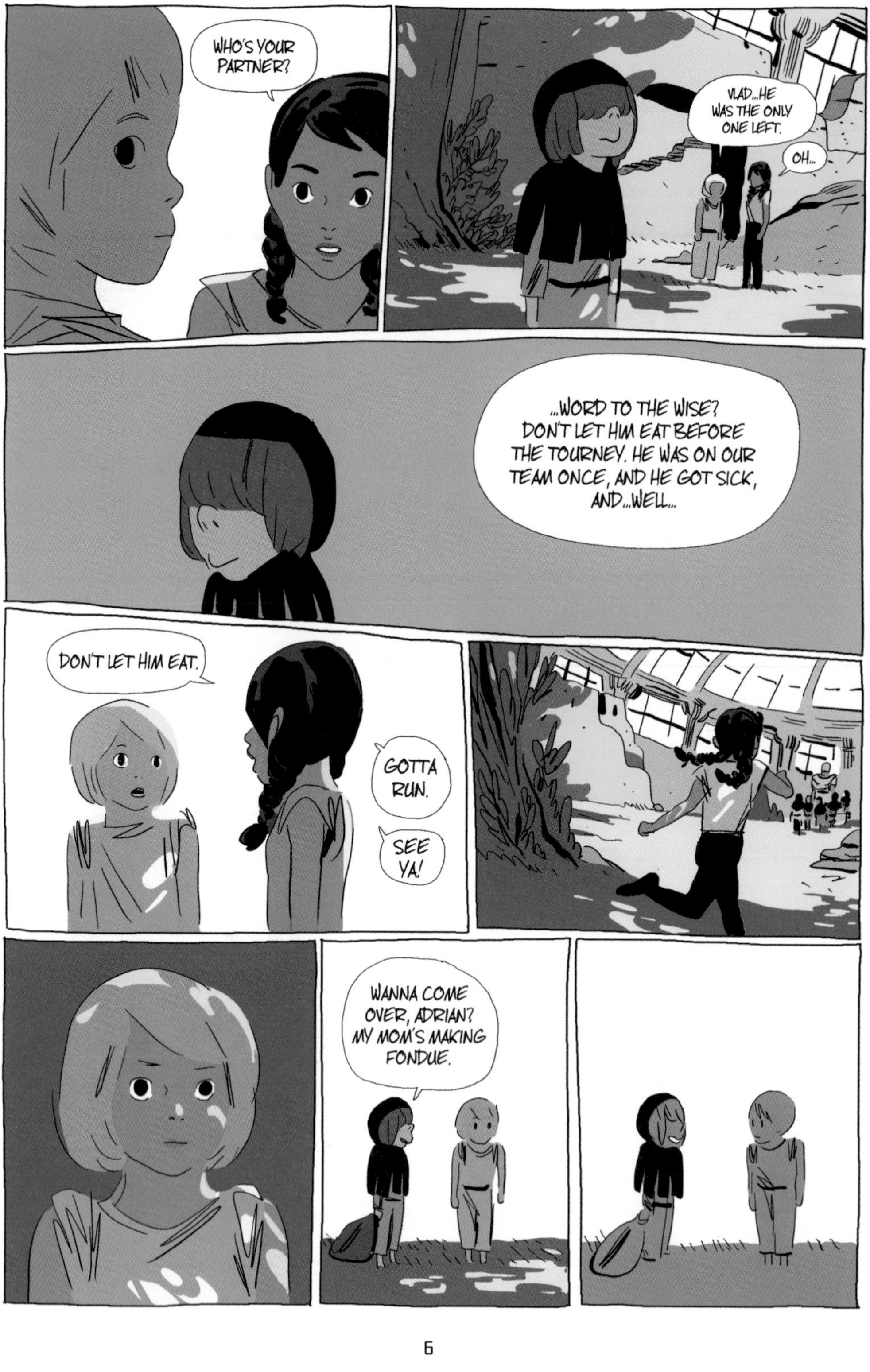
WHO'S YOUR PARTNER?
VLAD...HE WAS THE ONLY ONE LEFT.
OH...
...WORD TO THE WISE? DON'T LET HIM EAT BEFORE THE TOURNEY. HE WAS ON OUR TEAM ONCE, AND HE GOT SICK, AND...WELL...
DON'T LET HIM EAT.
GOTTA RUN.
SEE YA!
WANNA COME OVER, ADRIAN? MY MOM'S MAKING FONDUE.

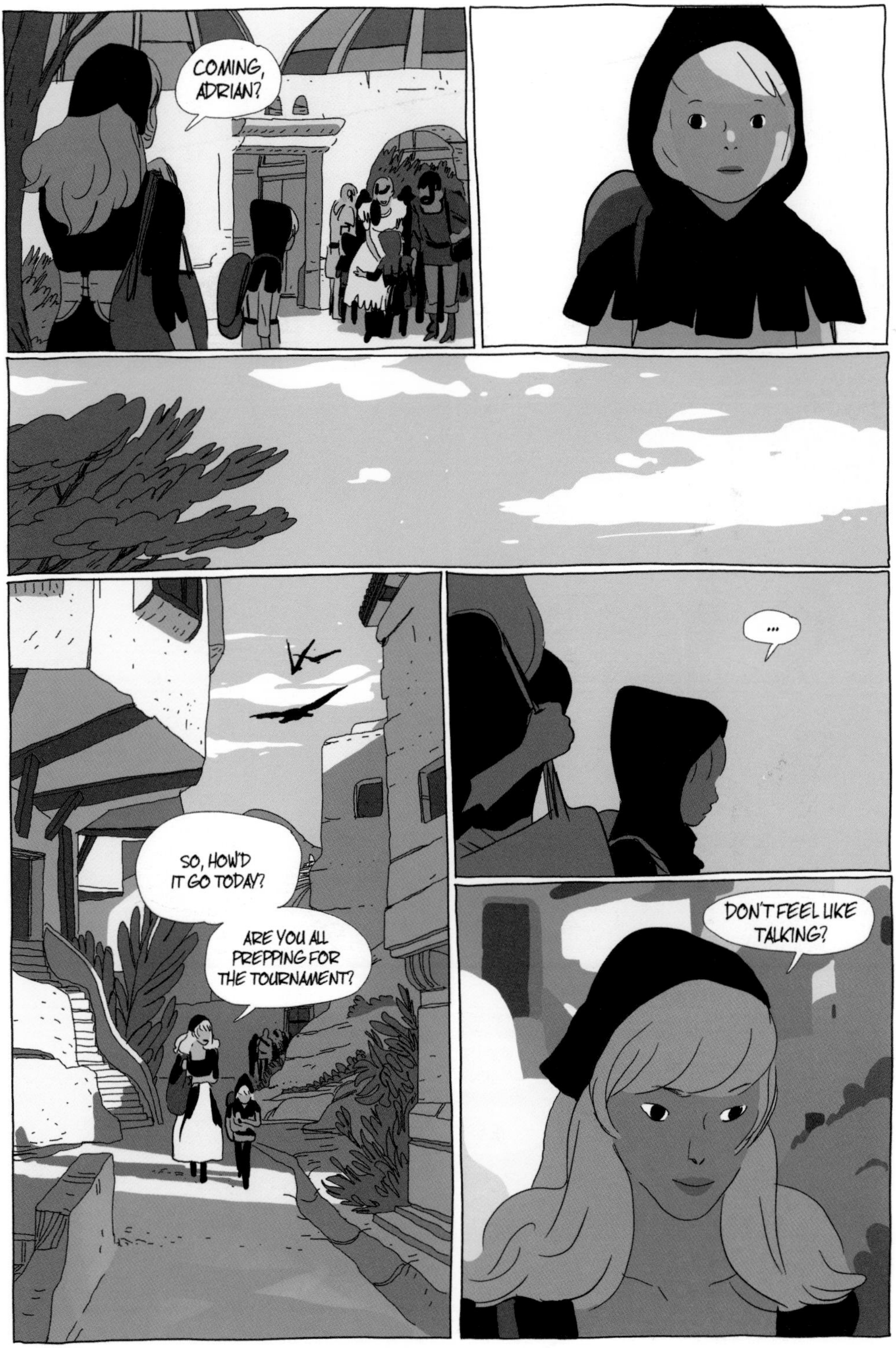
COMING, ADRIAN?
...
SO, HOW'D IT GO TODAY?
ARE YOU ALL PREPPING FOR THE TOURNAMENT?
DON'T FEEL LIKE TALKING?

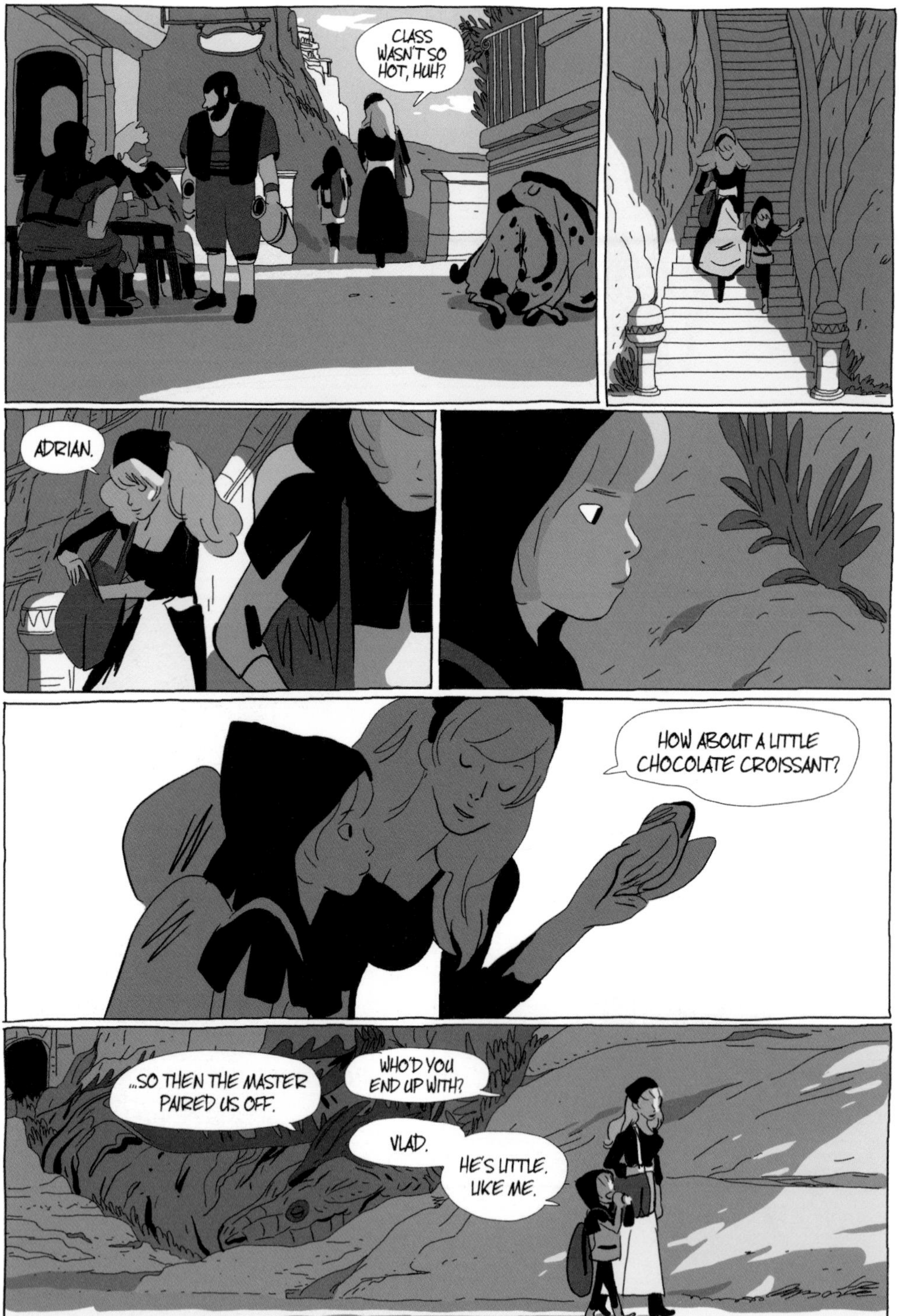
CLASS WASN'T SO HOT, HUH?
ADRIAN.
HOW ABOUT A LITTLE CHOCOLATE CROISSANT?
...SO THEN THE MASTER PAIRED US OFF.
WHO'D YOU END UP WITH?
VLAD.
HE'S LITTLE. LIKE ME.

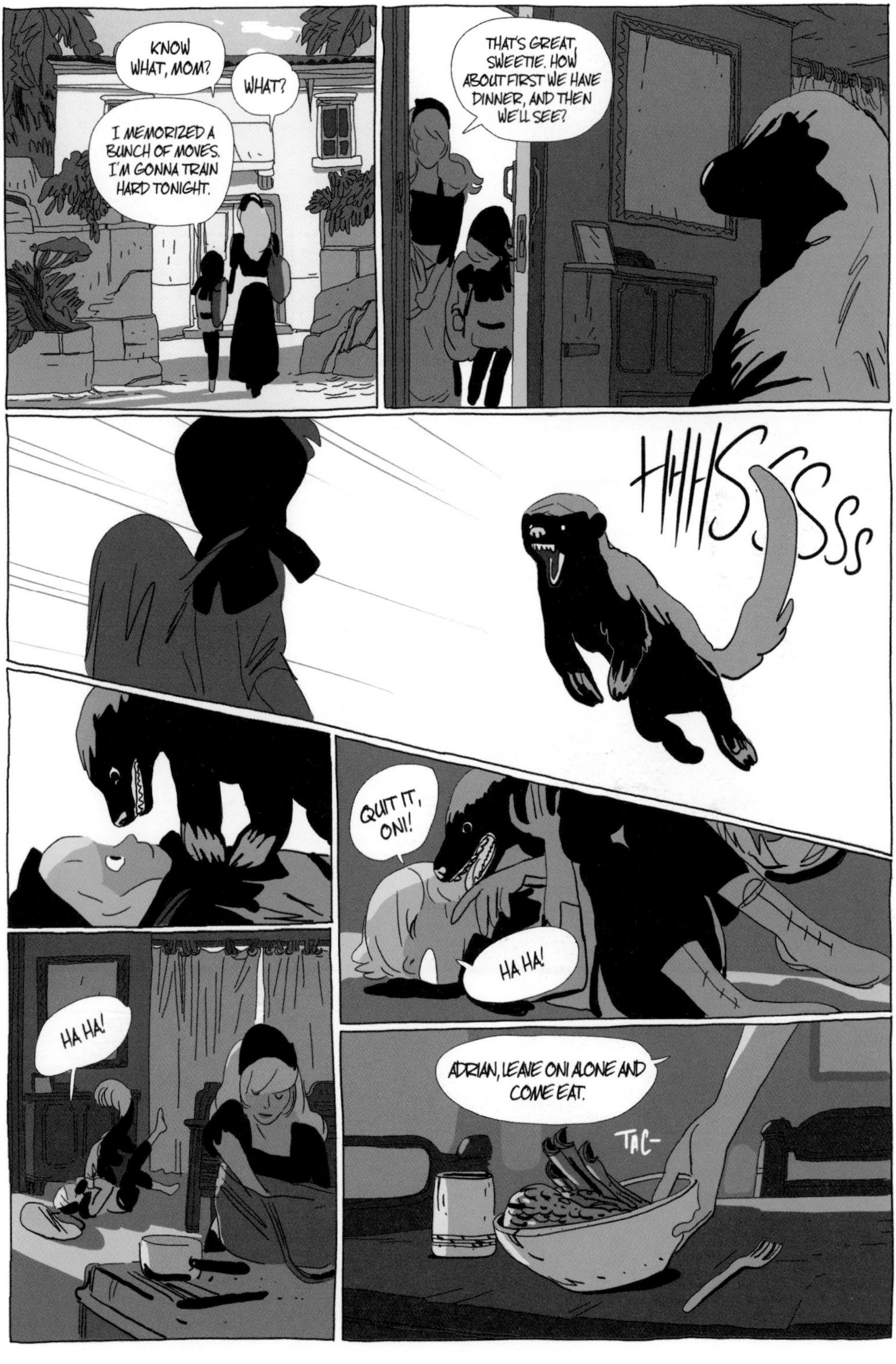
KNOW WHAT, MOM?
WHAT?
I MEMORIZED A BUNCH OF MOVES. I'M GONNA TRAIN HARD TONIGHT.
THAT'S GREAT, SWEETIE. HOW ABOUT FIRST WE HAVE DINNER, AND THEN WE'LL SEE?
HHHSSSSSS
QUIT IT, ONI!
HA HA!
HA HA!
ADRIAN, LEAVE ONI ALONE AND COME EAT.
TAC-

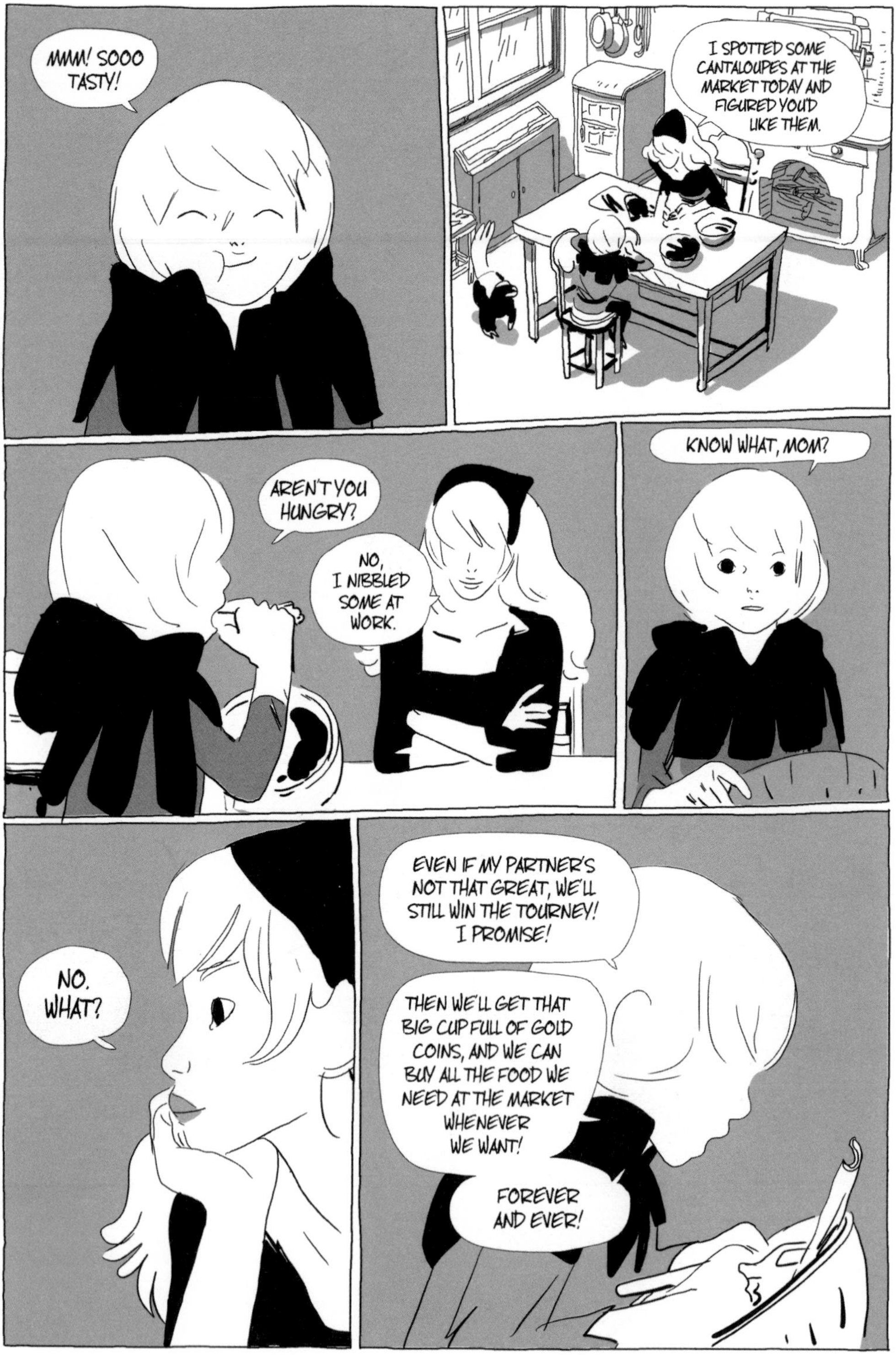
MMM! SOOO TASTY!
I SPOTTED SOME CANTALOUPES AT THE MARKET TODAY AND FIGURED YOU'D LIKE THEM.
AREN'T YOU HUNGRY?
NO, I NIBBLED SOME AT WORK.
KNOW WHAT, MOM?
NO. WHAT?
EVEN IF MY PARTNER'S NOT THAT GREAT, WE'LL STILL WIN THE TOURNEY! I PROMISE!
THEN WE'LL GET THAT BIG CUP FULL OF GOLD COINS, AND WE CAN BUY ALL THE FOOD WE NEED AT THE MARKET WHENEVER WE WANT!
FOREVER AND EVER!

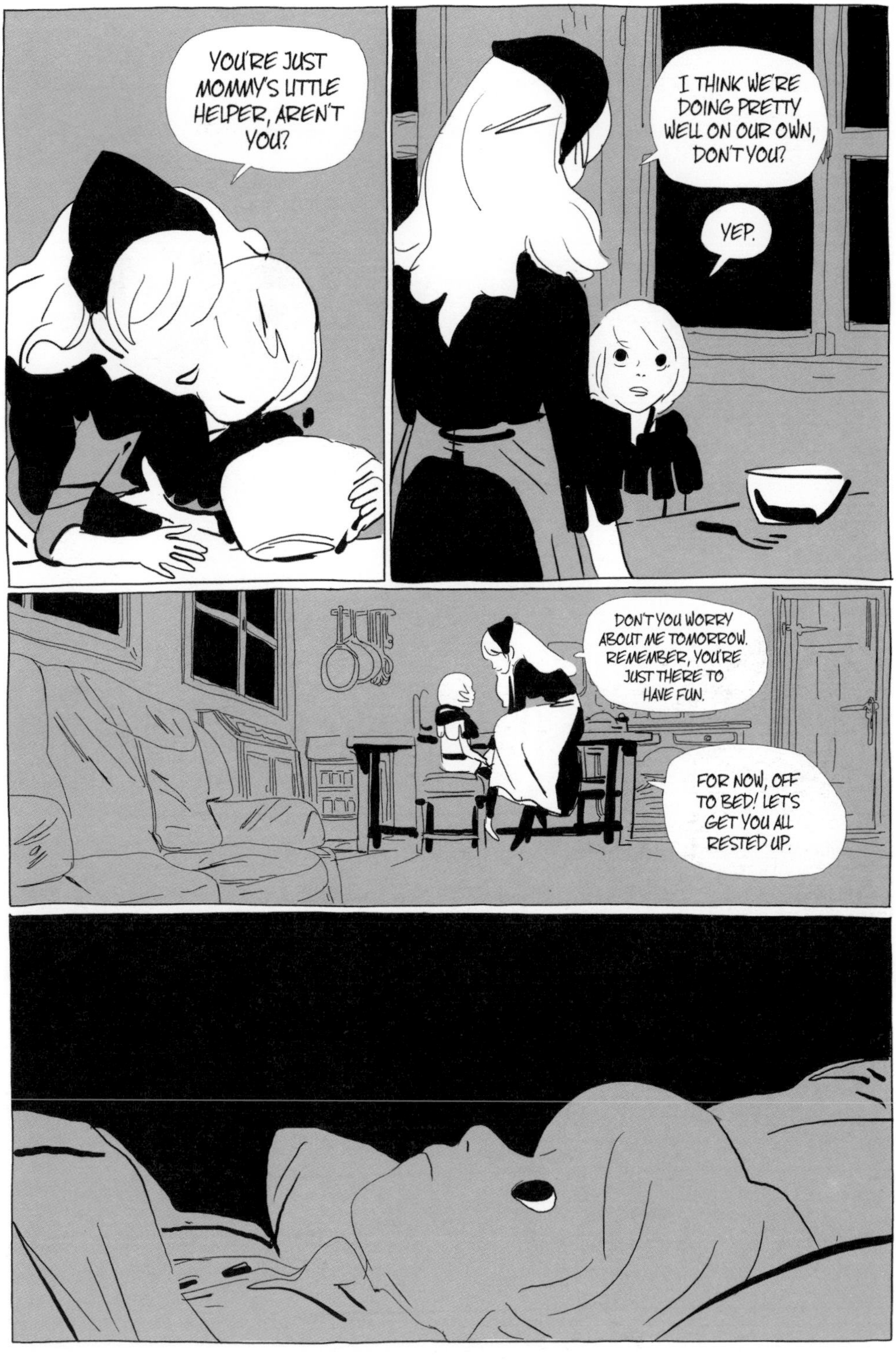
YOU'RE JUST MOMMY'S LITTLE HELPER, AREN'T YOU?
I THINK WE'RE DOING PRETTY WELL ON OUR OWN, DON'T YOU?
YEP.
DON'T YOU WORRY ABOUT ME TOMORROW. REMEMBER, YOU'RE JUST THERE TO HAVE FUN.
FOR NOW, OFF TO BED! LET'S GET YOU ALL RESTED UP.

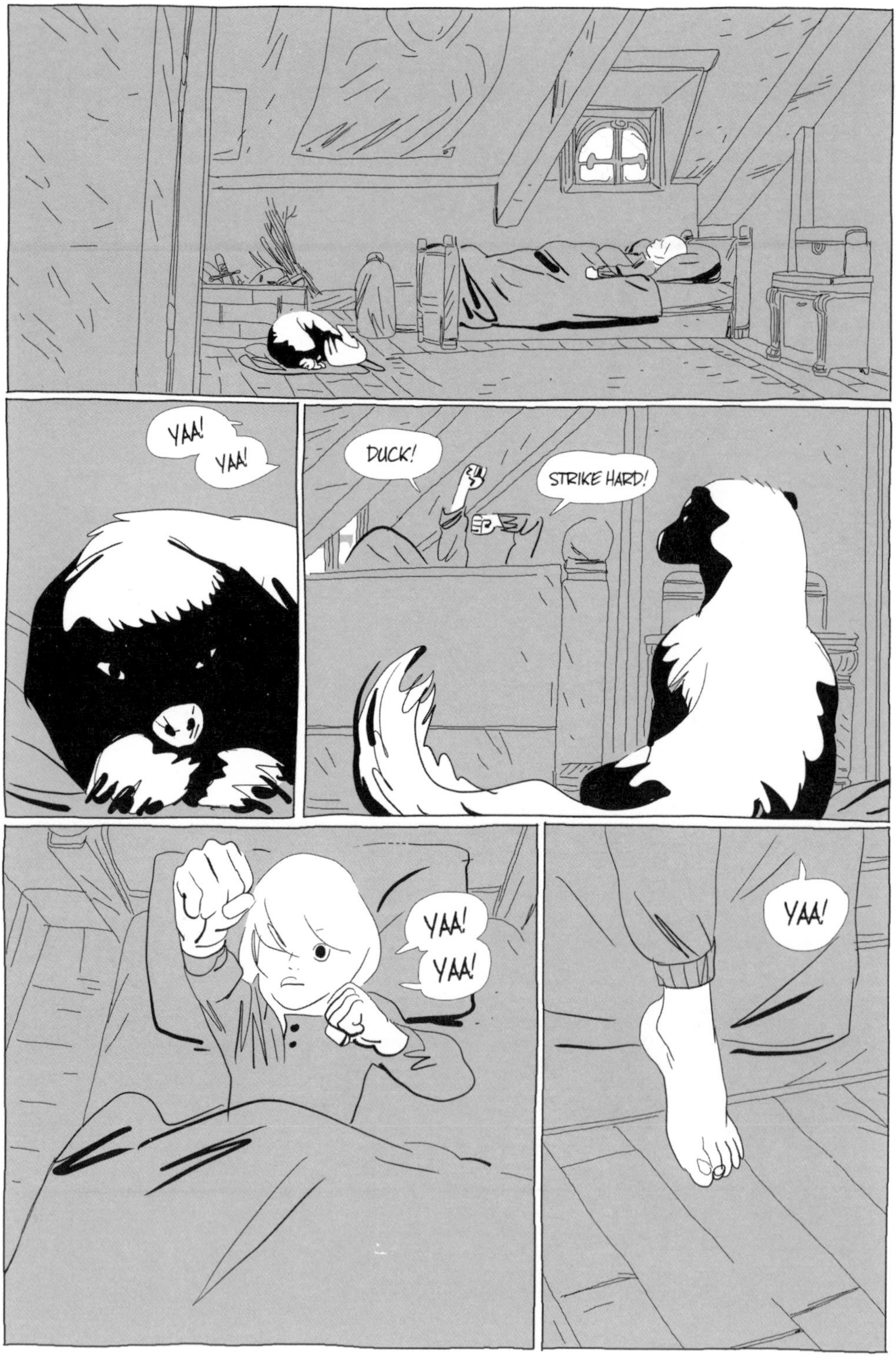
YAA!
YAA!
DUCK!
STRIKE HARD!
YAA!
YAA!
YAA!

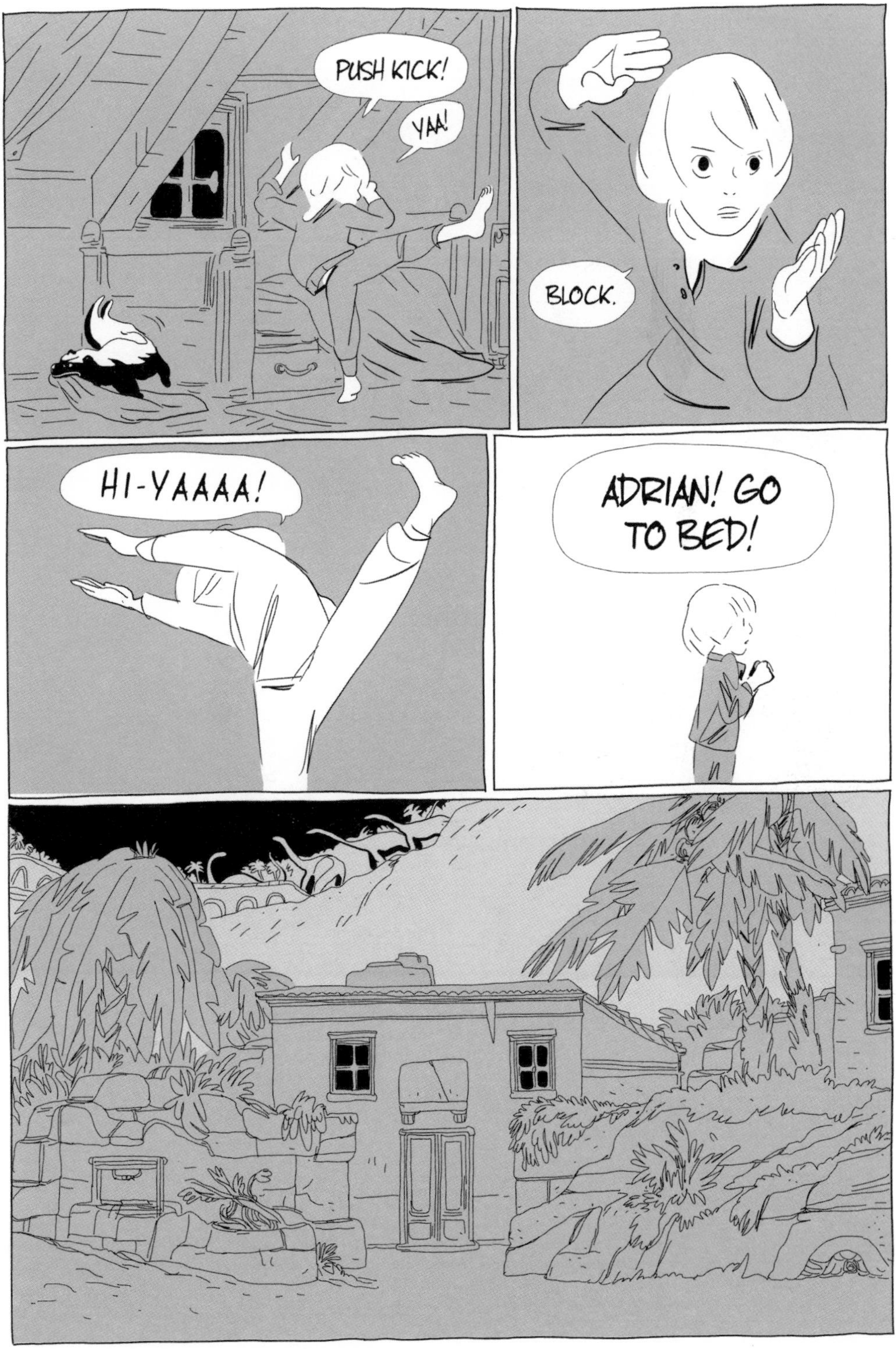
PUSH KICK!
YAA!
BLOCK.
HI-YAAAA!
ADRIAN! GO TO BED!

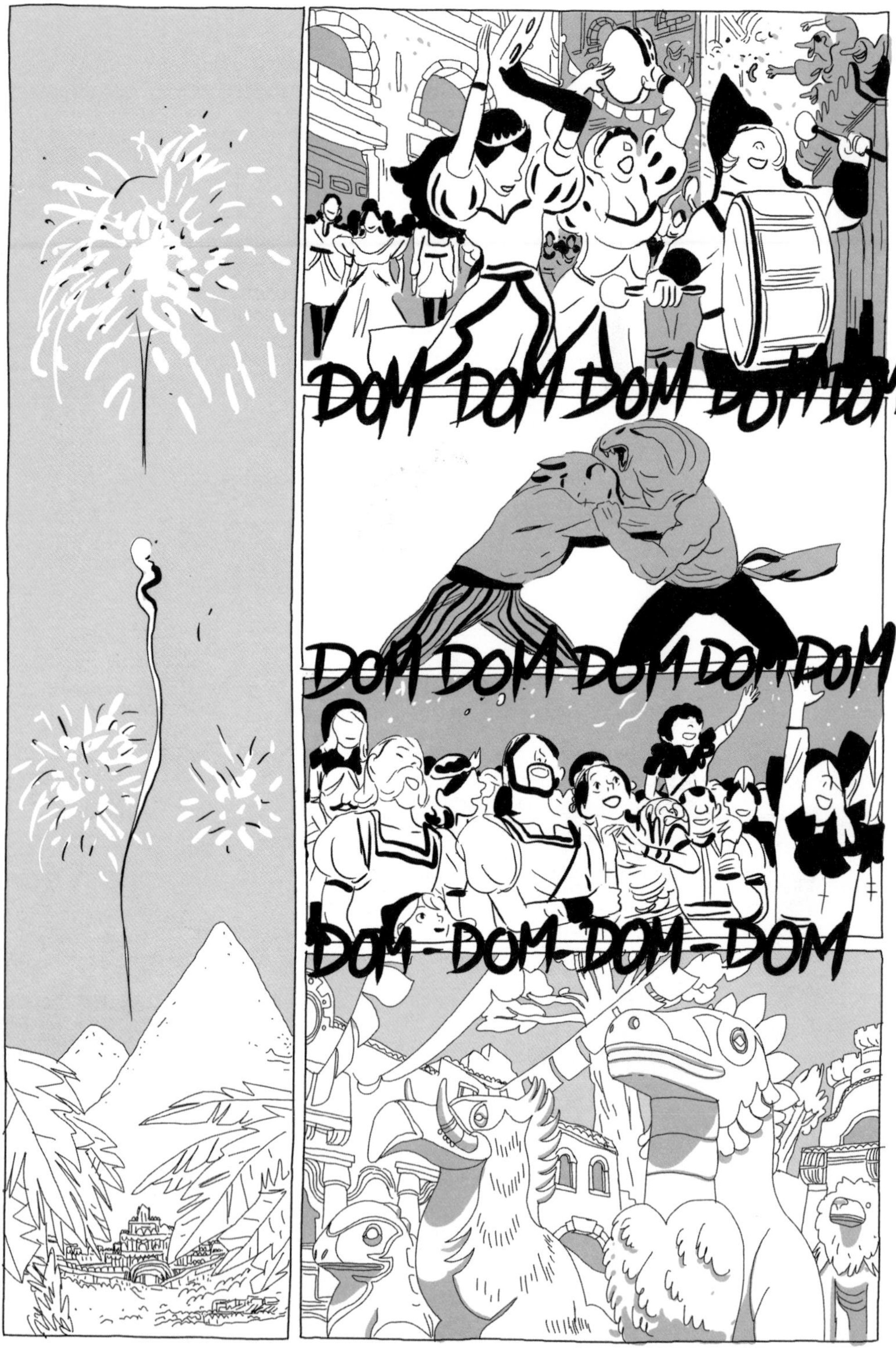
DOM DOM DOM DOM DOM
DOM DOM DOM DOM DOM
DOM-DOM-DOM-DOM

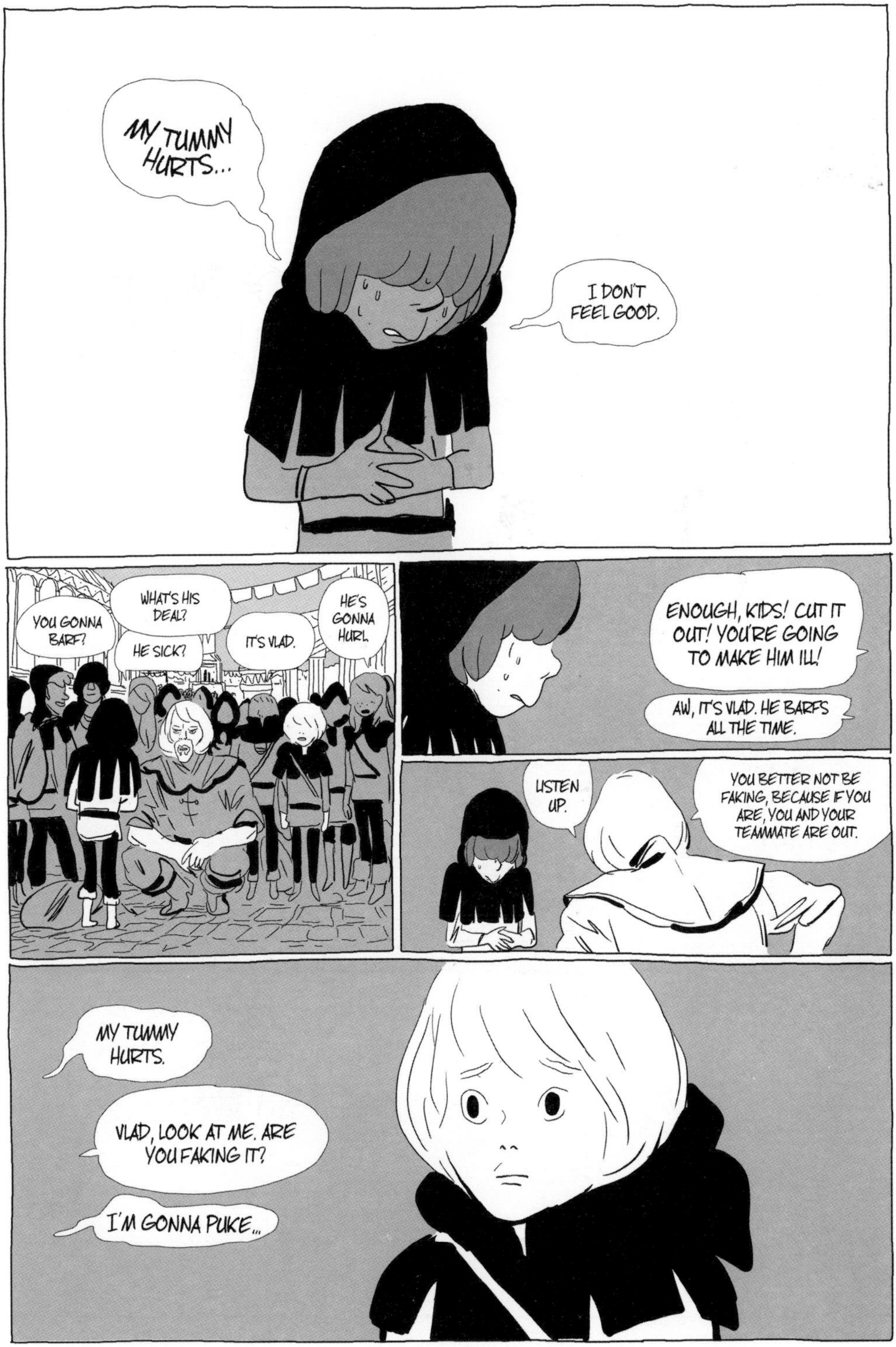
MY TUMMY HURTS...
I DON'T FEEL GOOD.
YOU GONNA BARF?
WHAT'S HIS DEAL?
HE SICK?
IT'S VLAD.
HE'S GONNA HURL.
ENOUGH, KIDS! CUT IT OUT! YOU'RE GOING TO MAKE HIM ILL!
AW, IT'S VLAD. HE BARFS ALL THE TIME.
LISTEN UP.
YOU BETTER NOT BE FAKING, BECAUSE IF YOU ARE, YOU AND YOUR TEAMMATE ARE OUT.
MY TUMMY HURTS.
VLAD, LOOK AT ME. ARE YOU FAKING IT?
I'M GONNA PUKE...

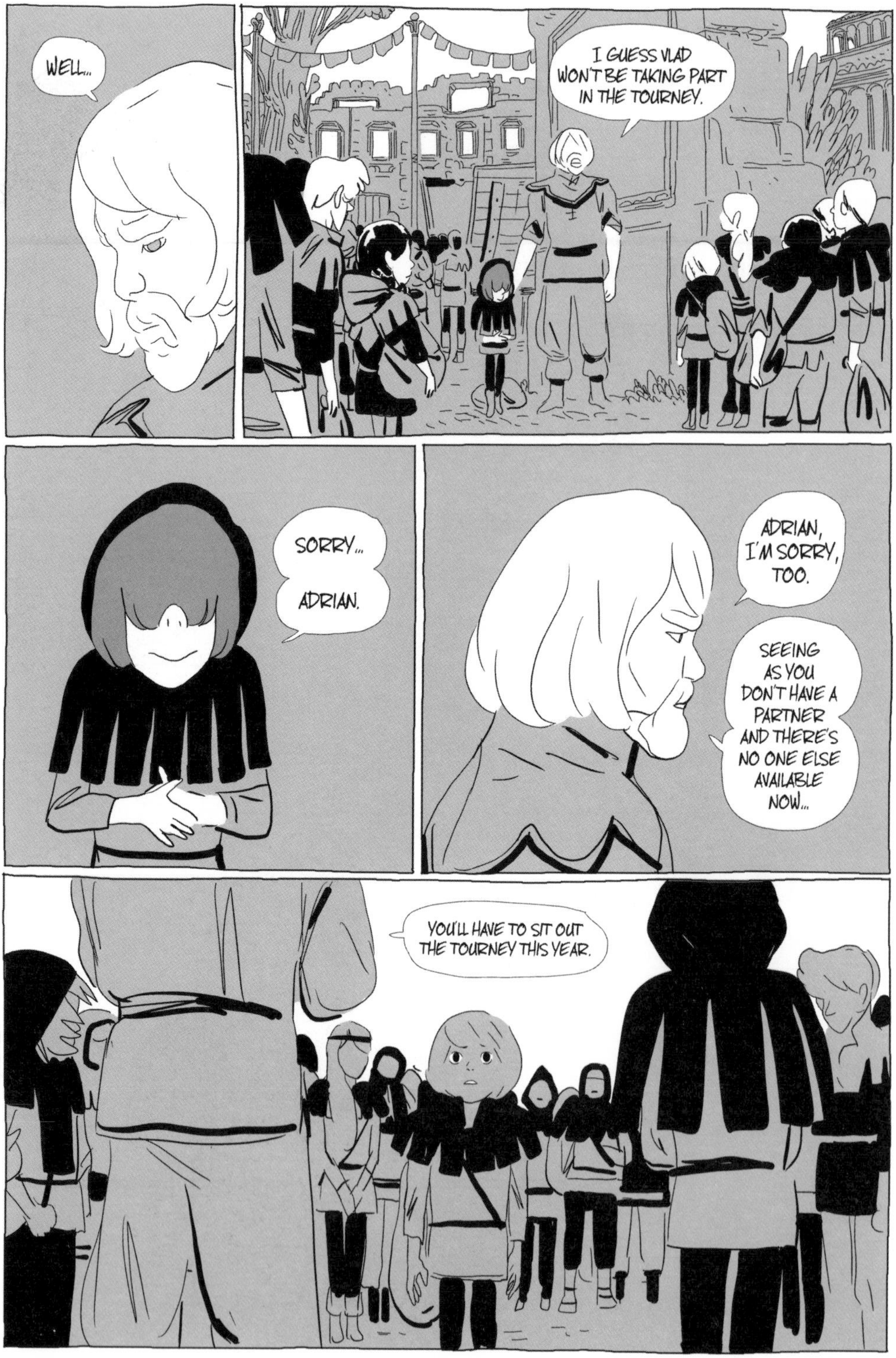
WELL...
I GUESS VLAD WON'T BE TAKING PART IN THE TOURNEY.
SORRY...
ADRIAN.
ADRIAN, I'M SORRY, TOO.
SEEING AS YOU DON'T HAVE A PARTNER AND THERE'S NO ONE ELSE AVAILABLE NOW...
YOU'LL HAVE TO SIT OUT THE TOURNEY THIS YEAR.

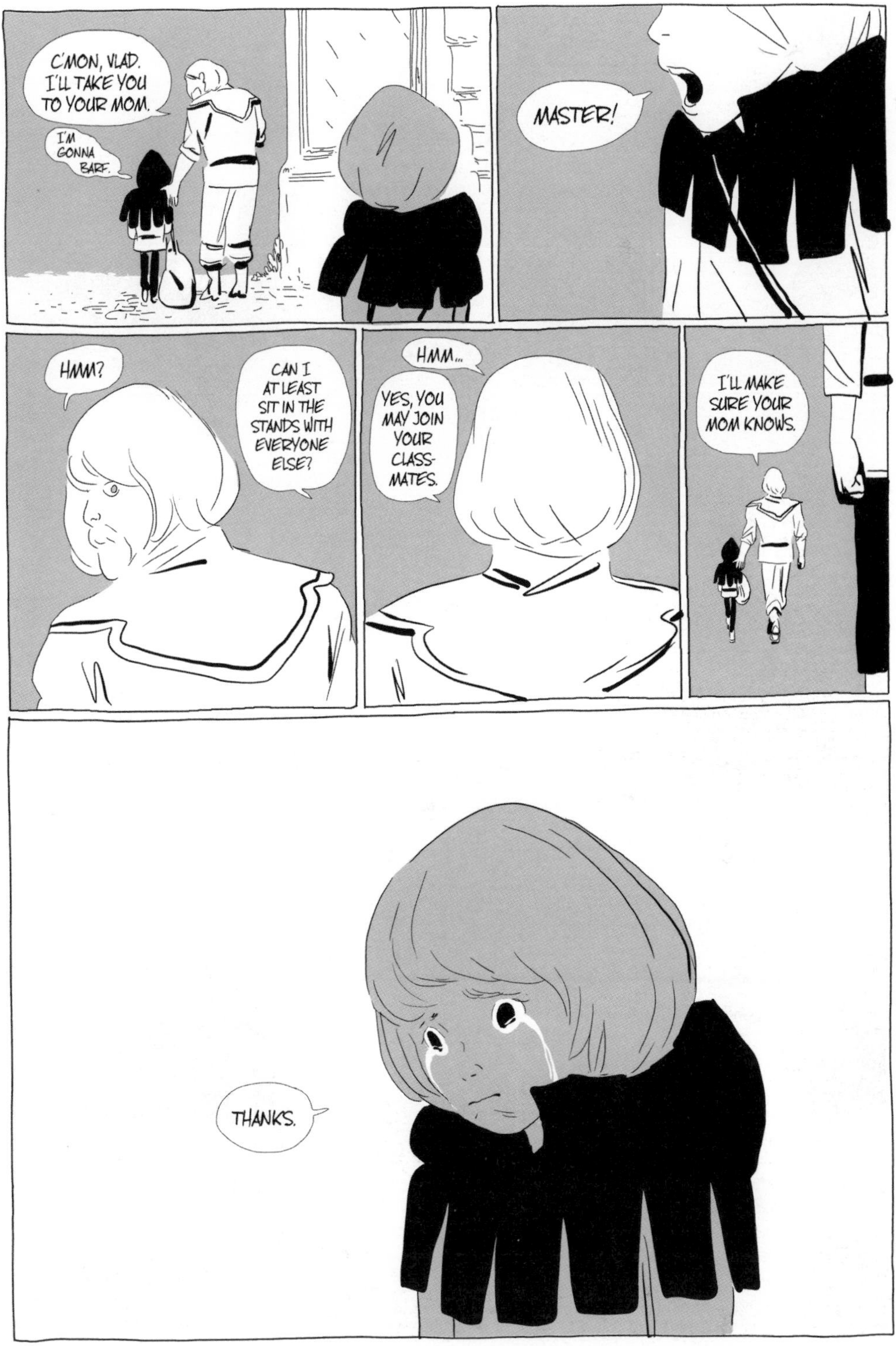
C'MON, VLAD. I'LL TAKE YOU TO YOUR MOM.
I'M GONNA BARF.
MASTER!
HMM?
CAN I AT LEAST SIT IN THE STANDS WITH EVERYONE ELSE?
HMM...
YES, YOU MAY JOIN YOUR CLASS-MATES.
I'LL MAKE SURE YOUR MOM KNOWS.
THANKS.

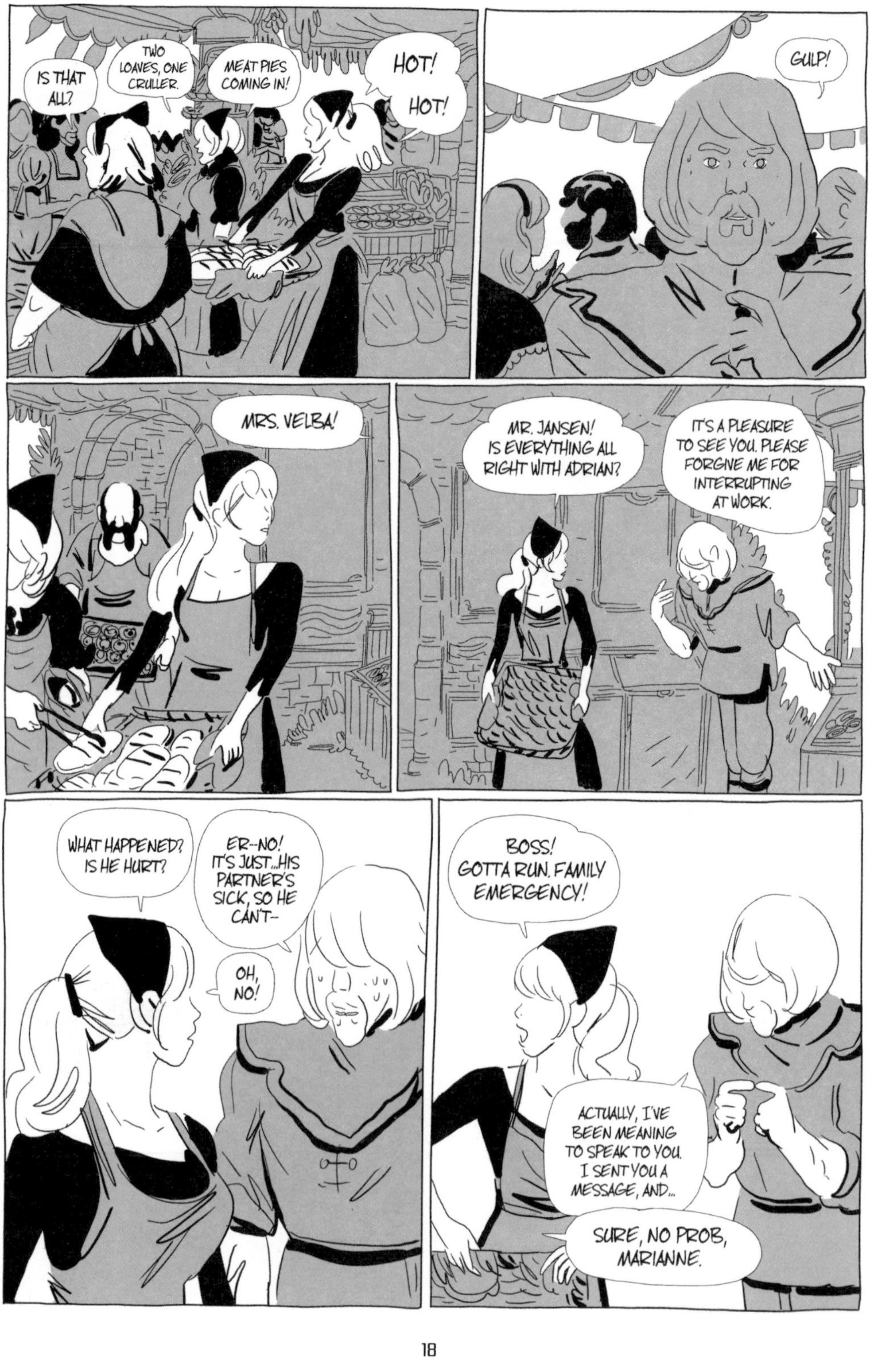
IS THAT ALL?
TWO LOAVES, ONE CRULLER.
MEAT PIES COMING IN!
HOT!
HOT!
GULP!
MRS. VELBA!
MR. JANSEN! IS EVERYTHING ALL RIGHT WITH ADRIAN?
IT'S A PLEASURE TO SEE YOU. PLEASE FORGIVE ME FOR INTERRUPTING AT WORK.
WHAT HAPPENED? IS HE HURT?
ER--NO! IT'S JUST...HIS PARTNER'S SICK, SO HE CAN'T-
OH, NO!
BOSS! GOTTA RUN. FAMILY EMERGENCY!
ACTUALLY, I'VE BEEN MEANING TO SPEAK TO YOU. I SENT YOU A MESSAGE, AND...
SURE, NO PROB, MARIANNE.

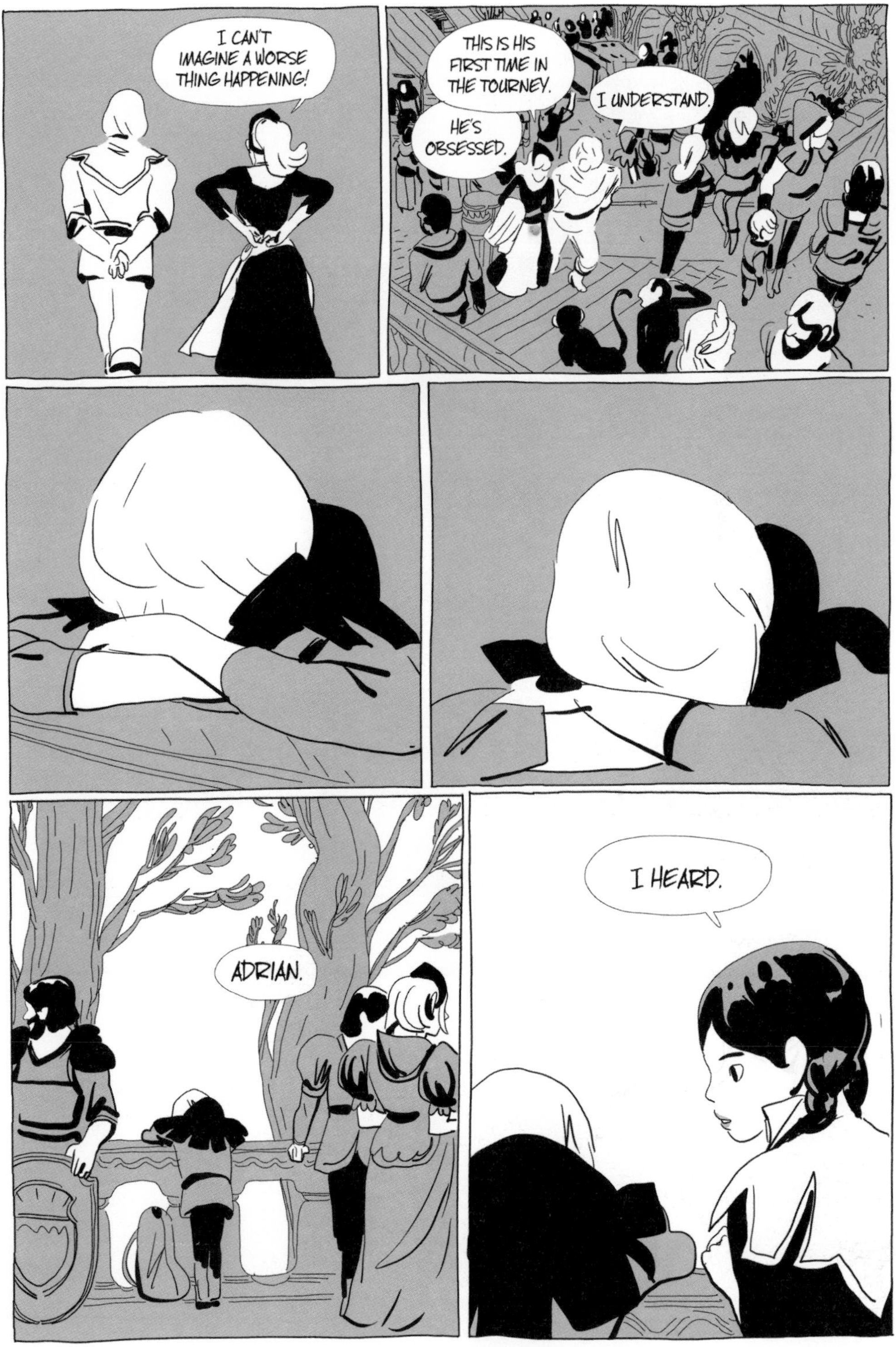
I CAN'T IMAGINE A WORSE THING HAPPENING!
THIS IS HIS FIRST TIME IN THE TOURNEY.
HE'S OBSESSED.
I UNDERSTAND.
ADRIAN.
I HEARD.

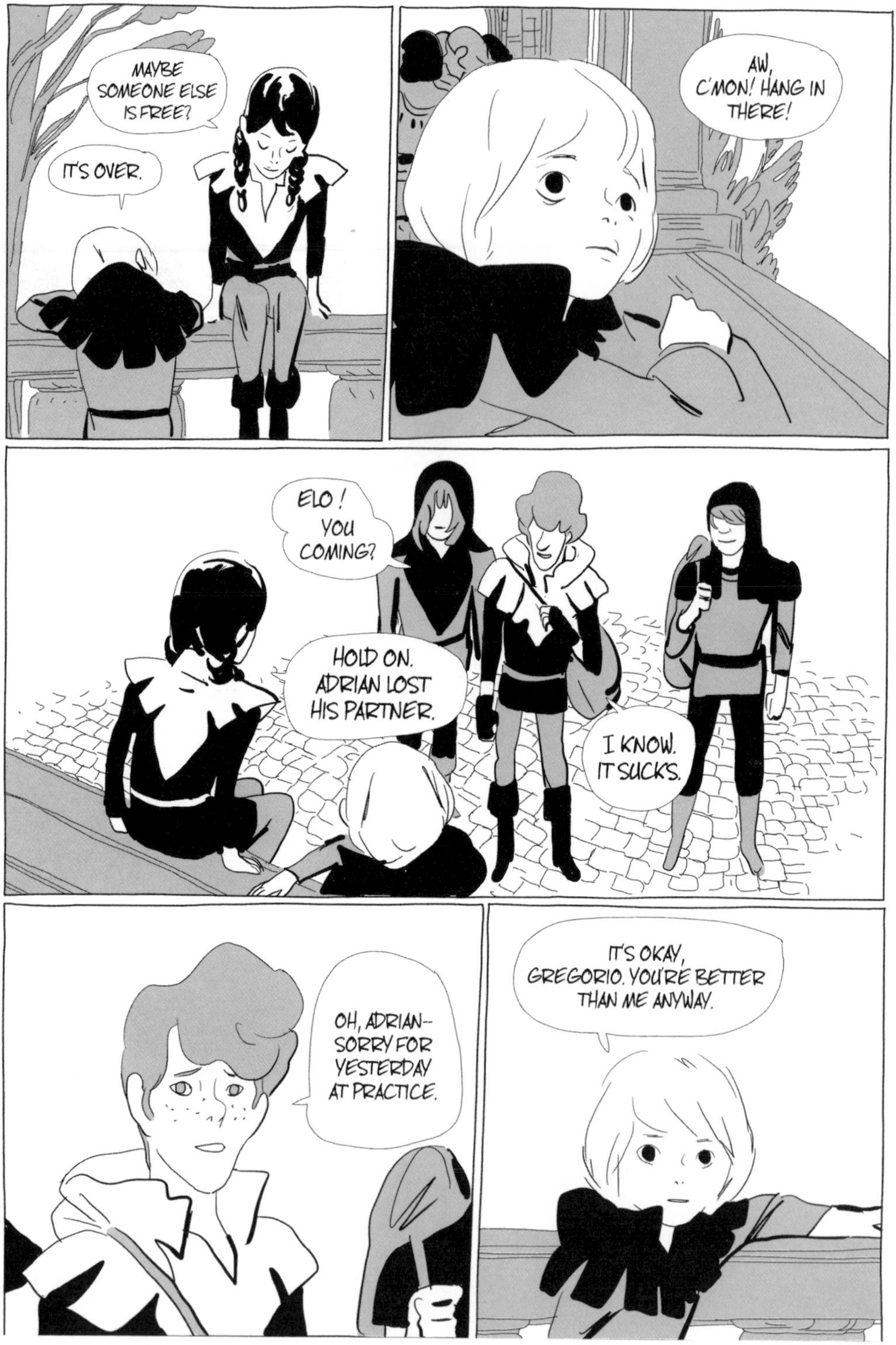
MAYBE SOMEONE ELSE IS FREE?
IT'S OVER.
AW, C'MON! HANG IN THERE!
ELO! YOU COMING?
HOLD ON. ADRIAN LOST HIS PARTNER.
I KNOW. IT SUCKS.
OH, ADRIAN-- SORRY FOR YESTERDAY AT PRACTICE.
IT'S OKAY, GREGORIO. YOU'RE BETTER THAN ME ANYWAY.

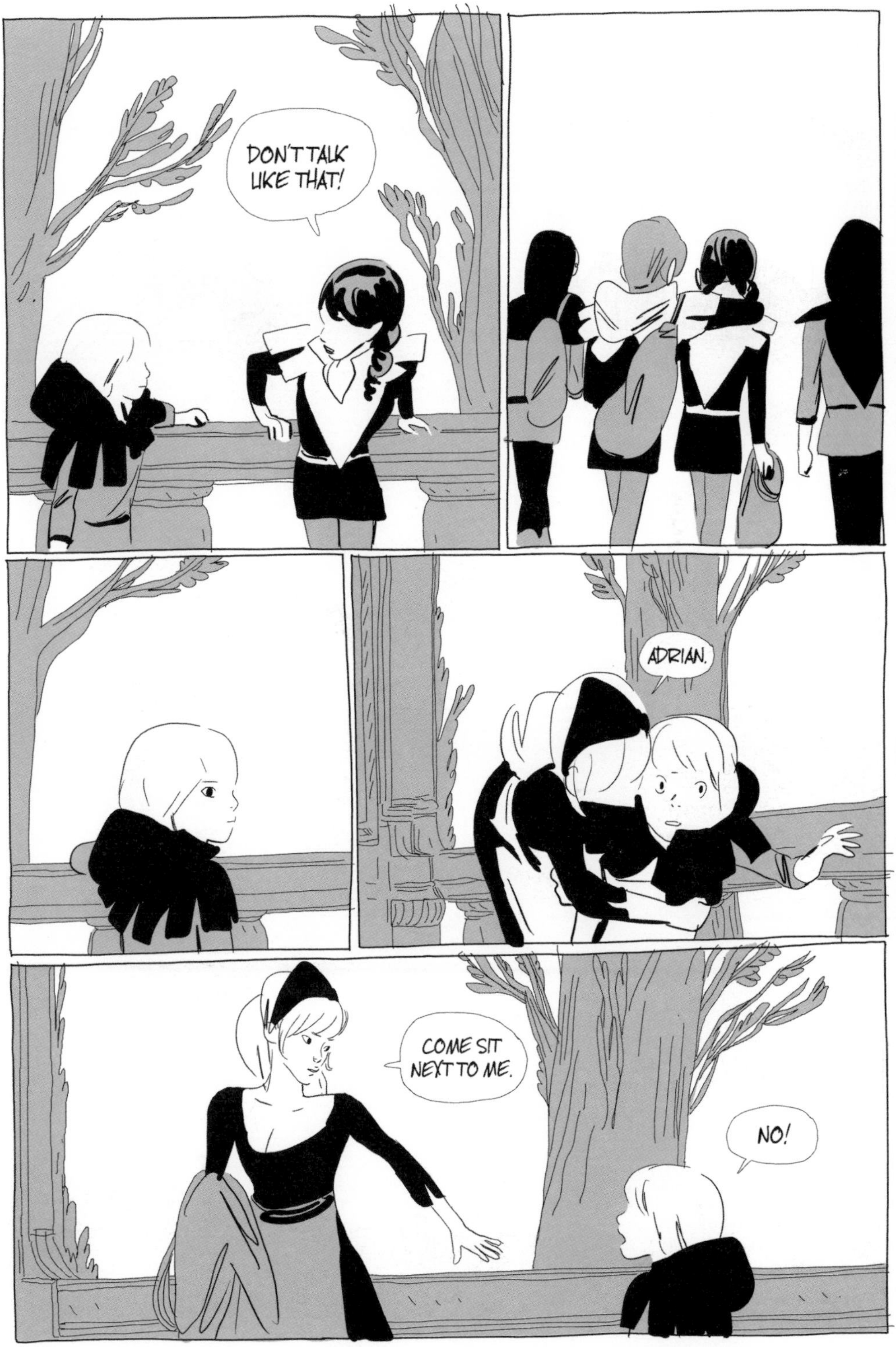
DON'T TALK LIKE THAT!
ADRIAN.
COME SIT NEXT TO ME.
NO!

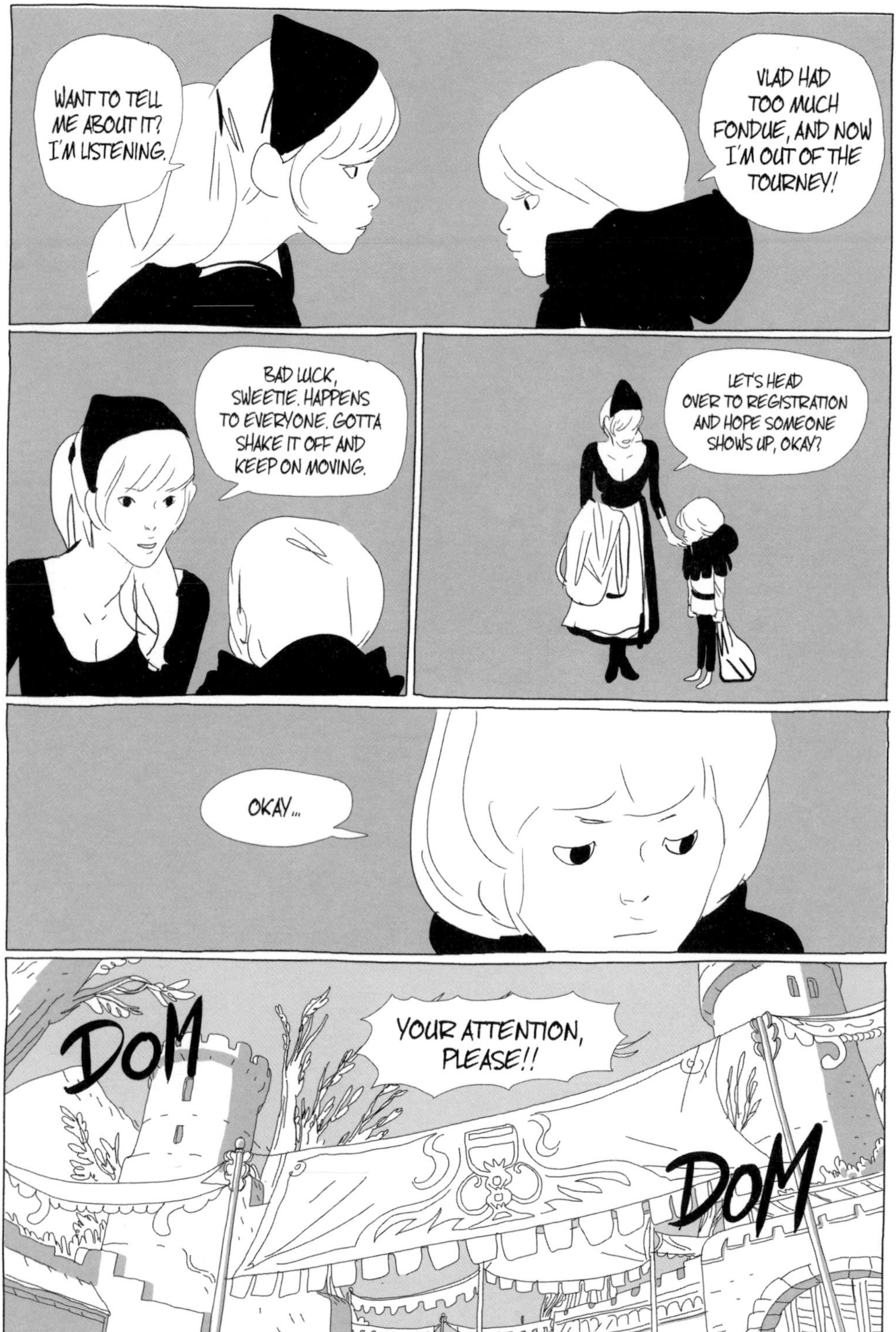
WANT TO TELL ME ABOUT IT? I'M LISTENING.
VLAD HAD TOO MUCH FONDUE, AND NOW I'M OUT OF THE TOURNEY!
BAD LUCK, SWEETIE. HAPPENS TO EVERYONE. GOTTA SHAKE IT OFF AND KEEP ON MOVING.
LET'S HEAD OVER TO REGISTRATION AND HOPE SOMEONE SHOWS UP, OKAY?
OKAY...
DOM
YOUR ATTENTION, PLEASE!!
DOM

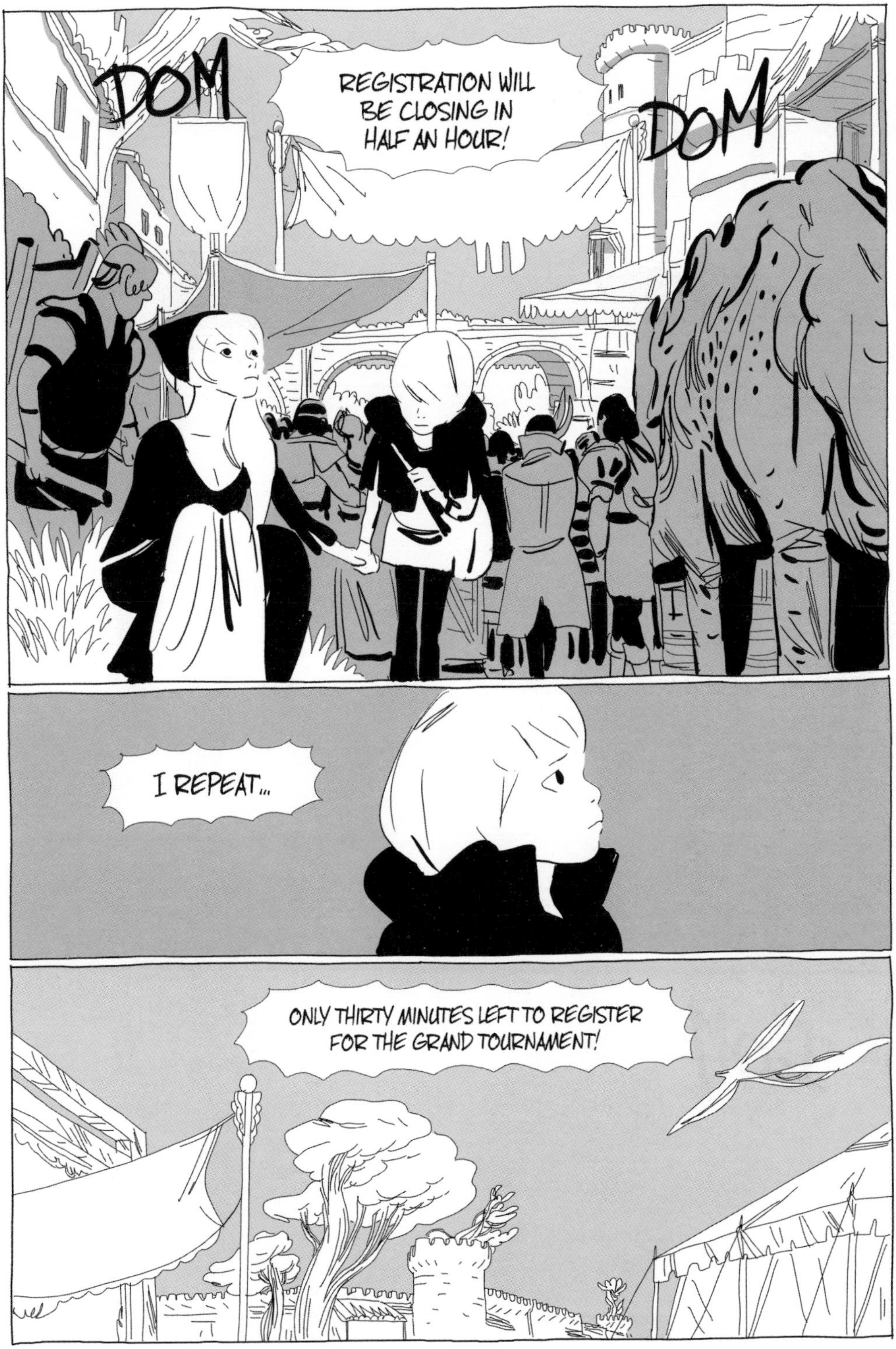
DOM
REGISTRATION WILL BE CLOSING IN HALF AN HOUR!
DOM
I REPEAT...
ONLY THIRTY MINUTES LEFT TO REGISTER FOR THE GRAND TOURNAMENT!

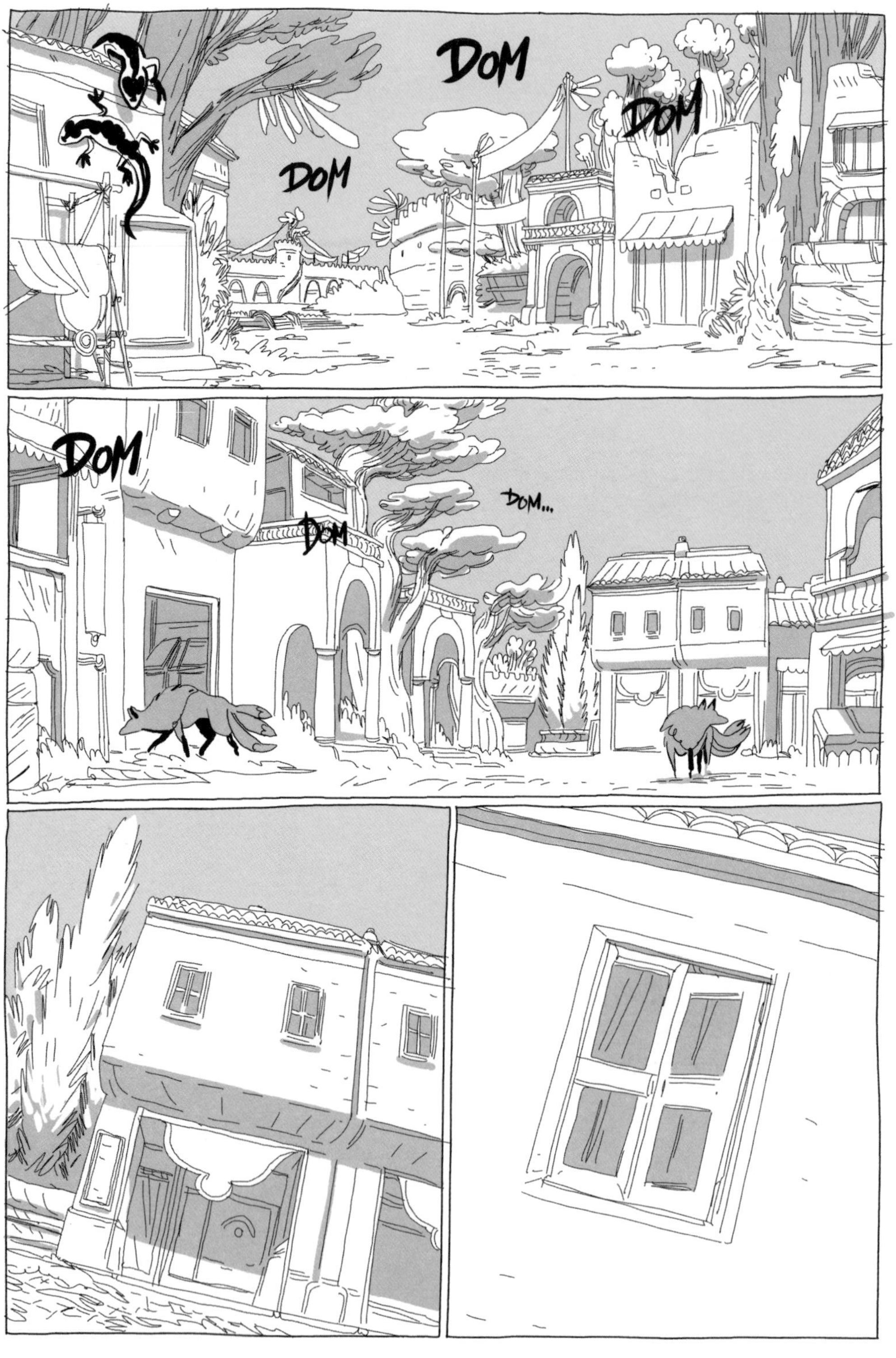
DOM
DOM
DOM
DOM
DOM
DOM...

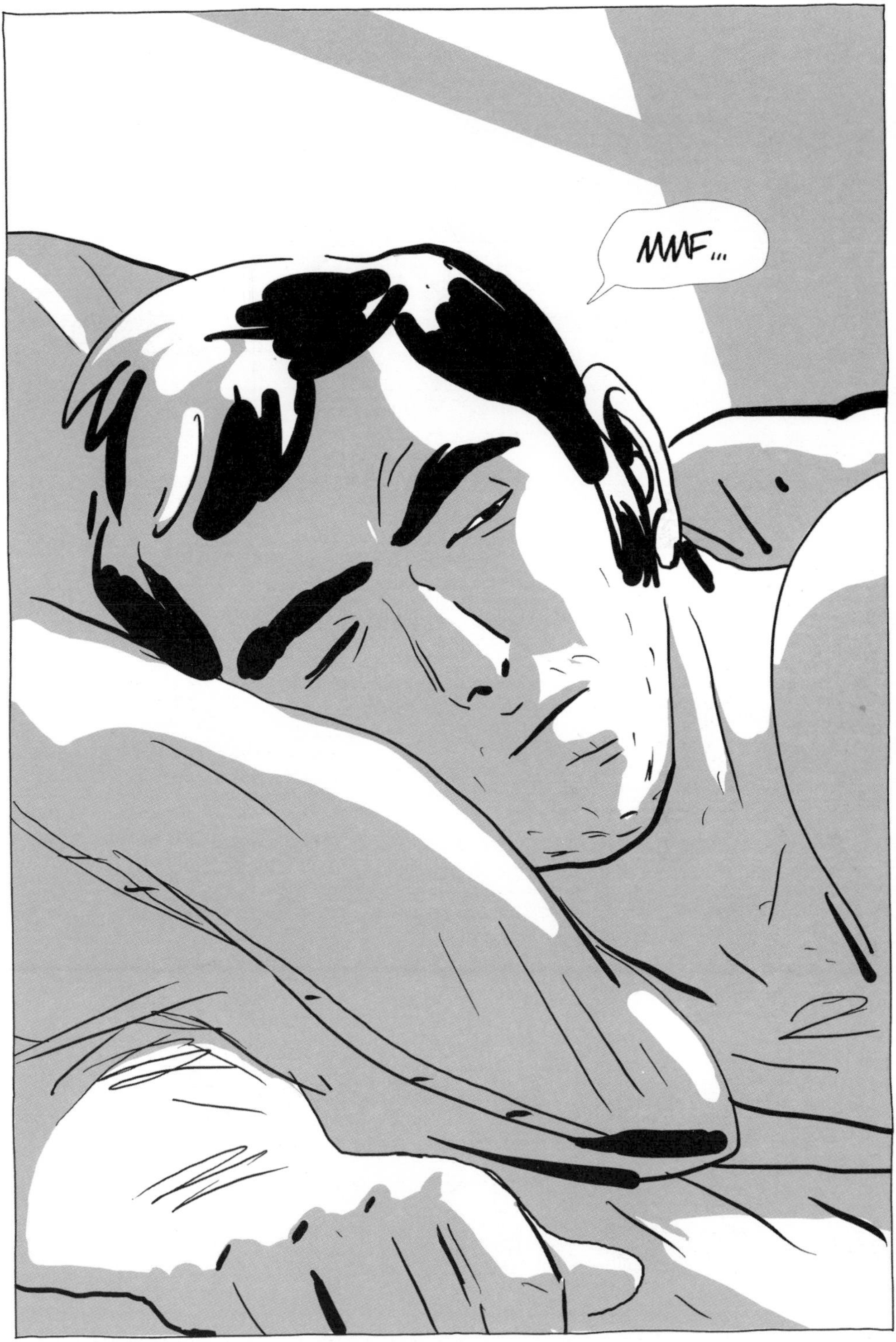
MMF...

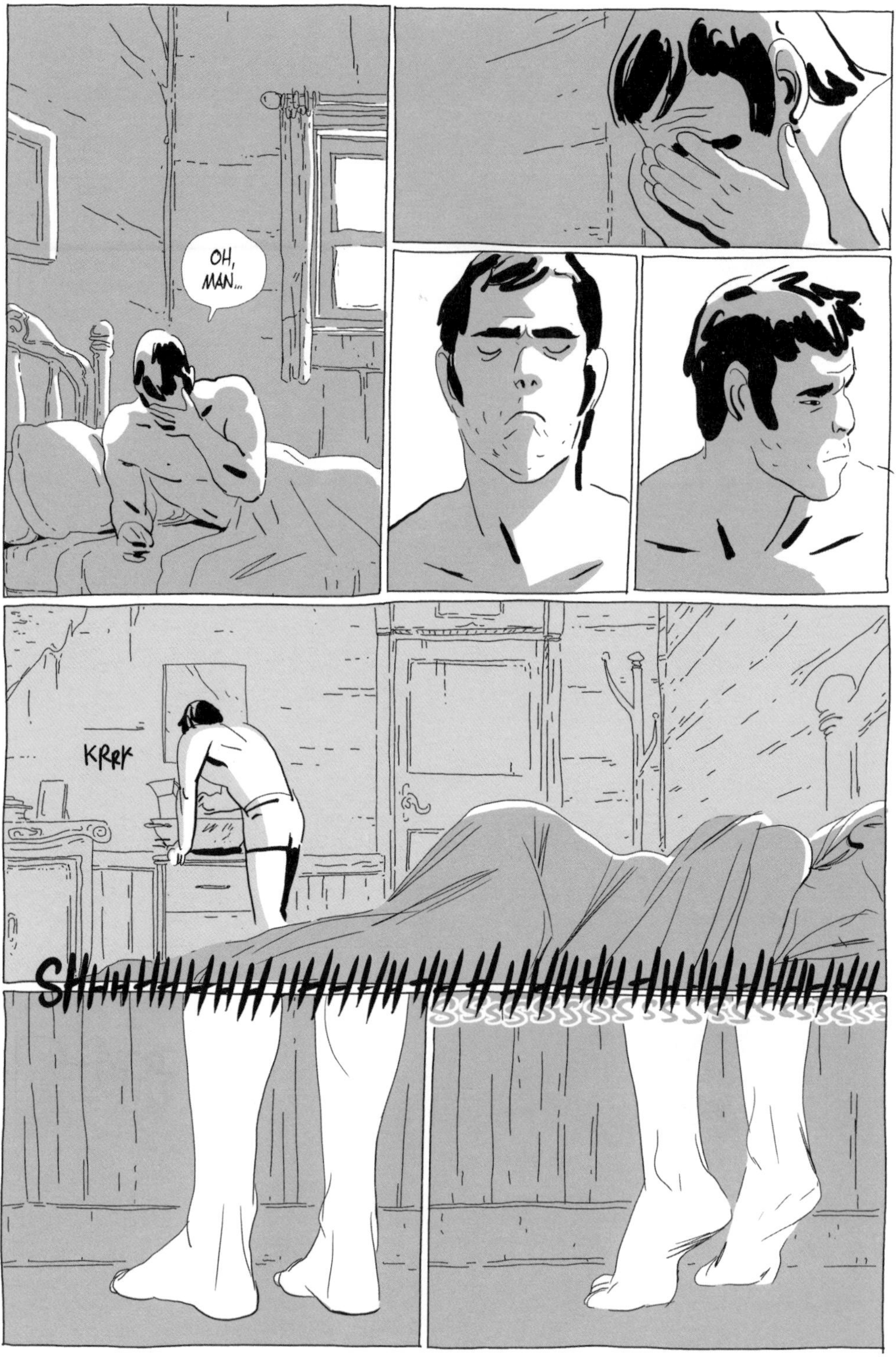
OH, MAN...
KRRK
SHHHHHHHHHHHHHHHHHHHHHHHHHHHHHHHHHHHHHHH

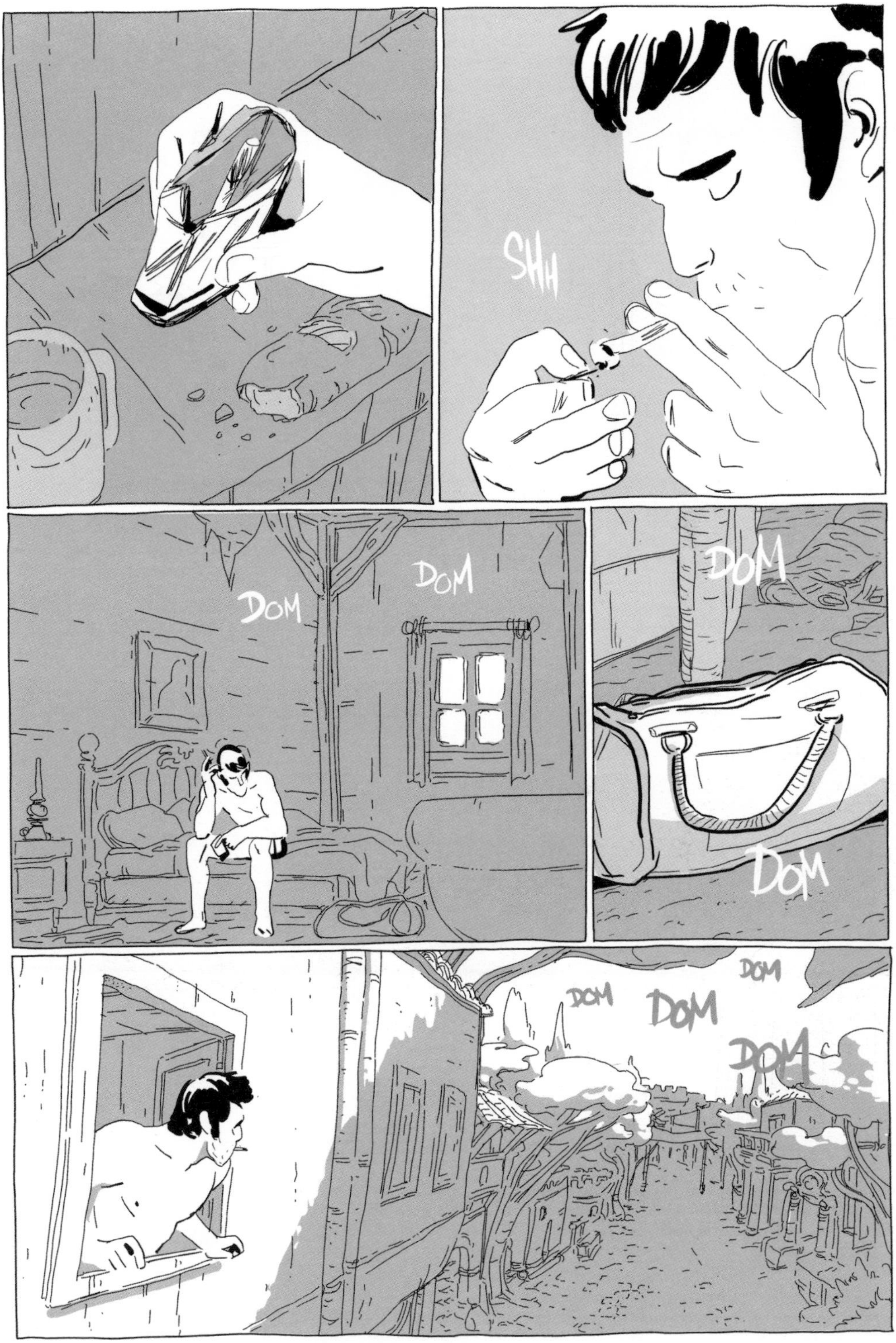
SHH
DOM
DOM
DOM
DOM
DOM
DOM
DOM
DOM

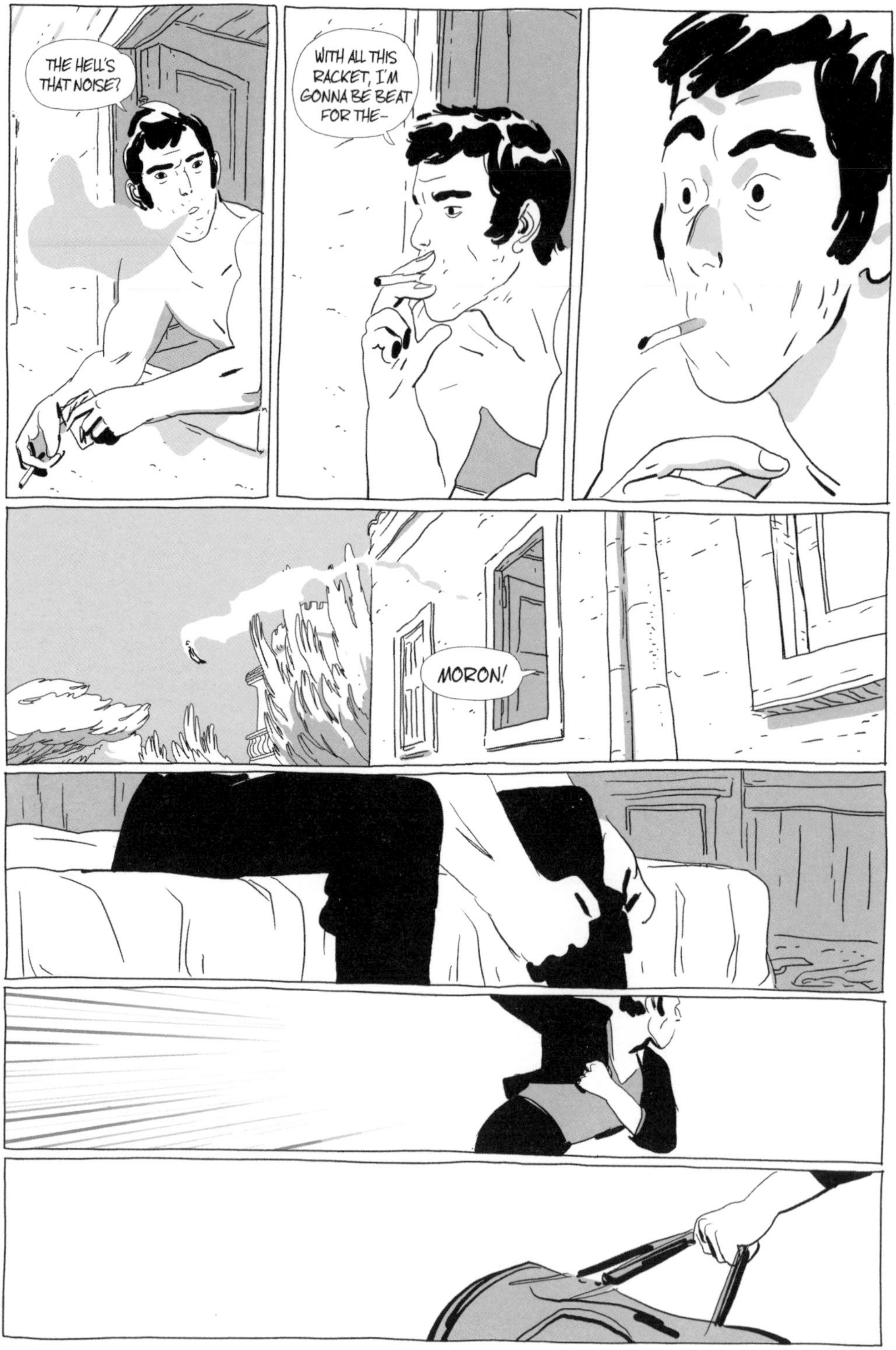
THE HELL'S THAT NOISE?
WITH ALL THIS RACKET, I'M GONNA BE BEAT FOR THE--
MORON!

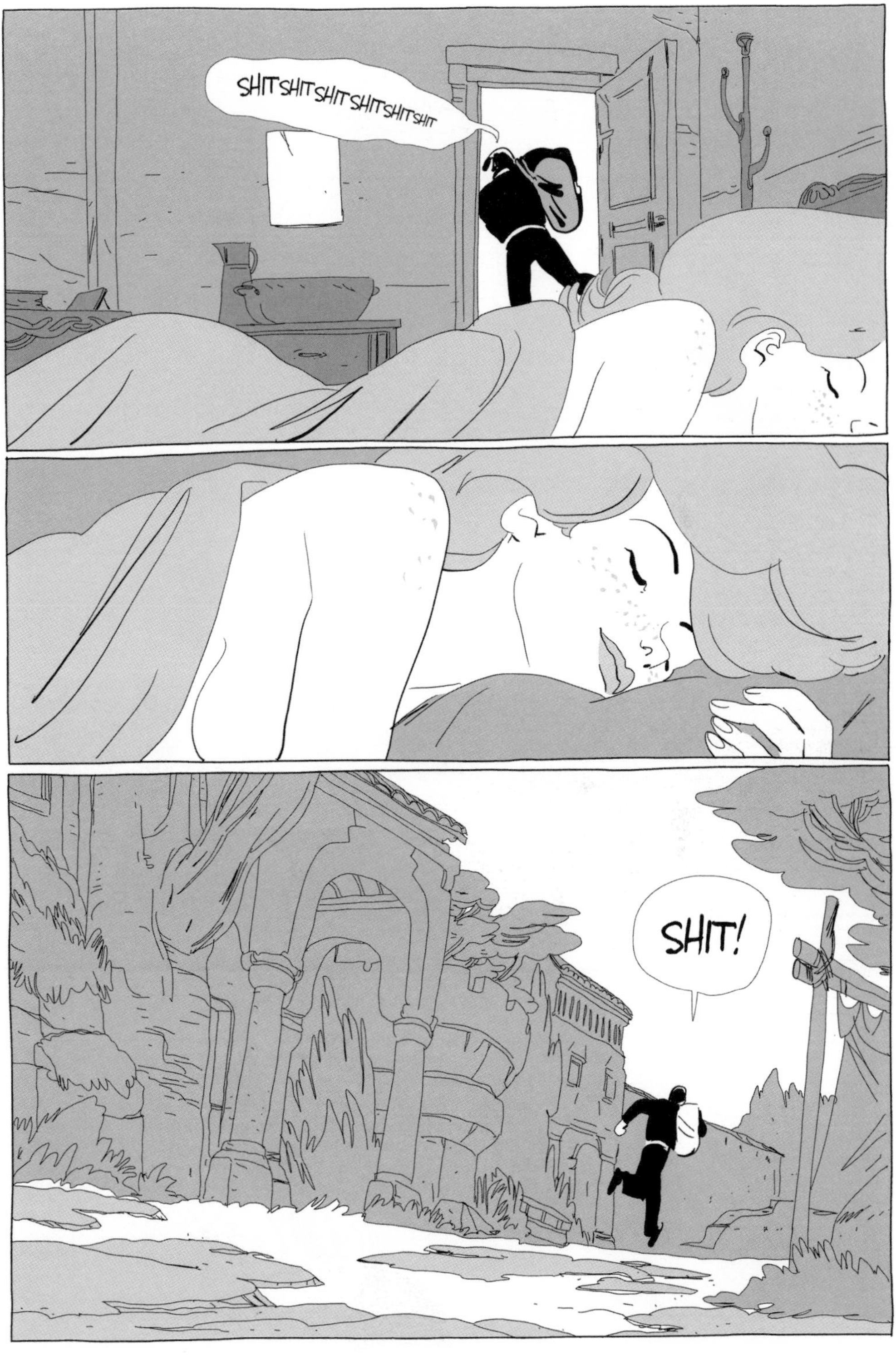
SHITSHITSHITSHITSHITSHIT
SHIT!

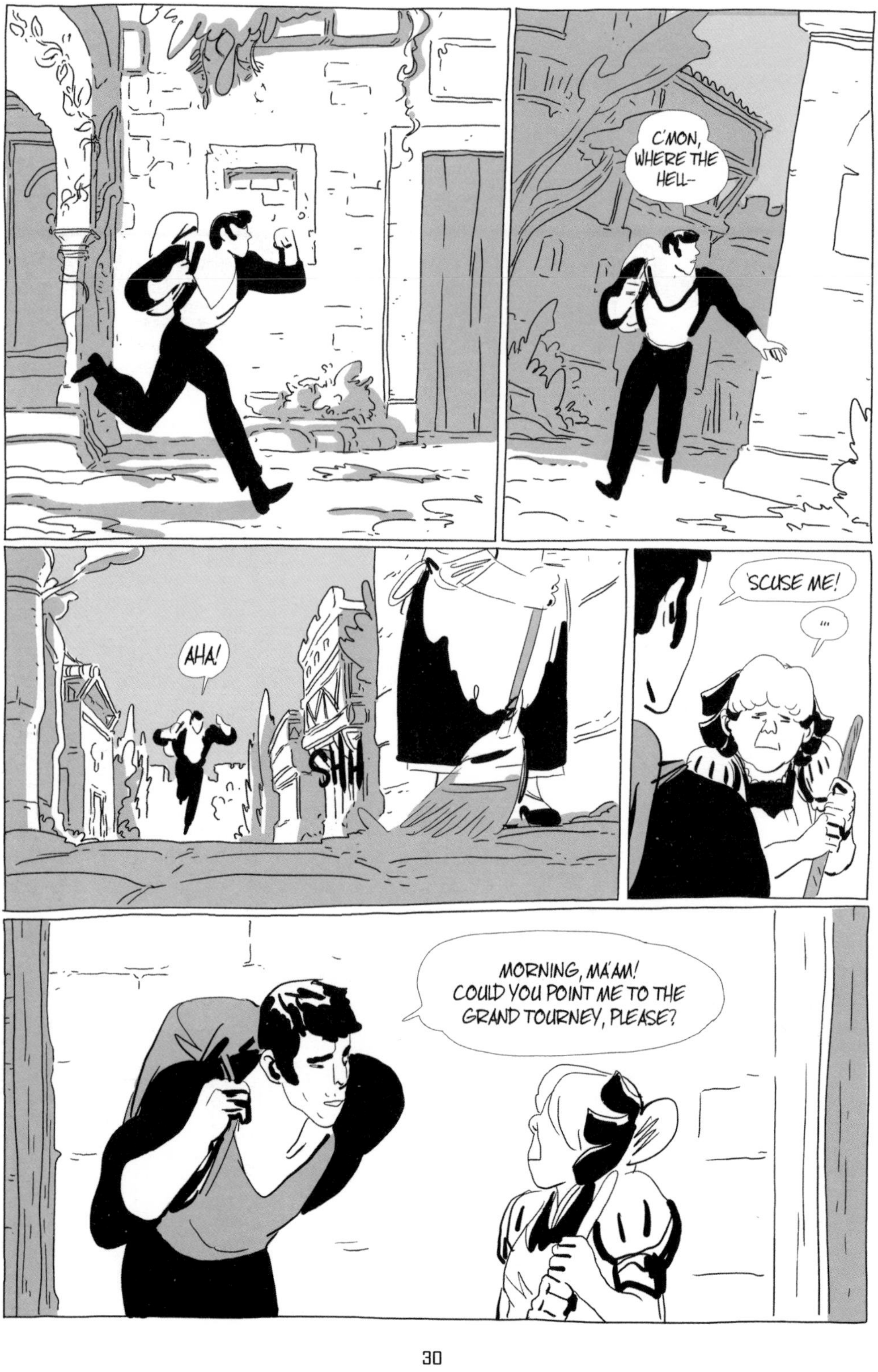
C'MON, WHERE THE HELL-
AHA!
SHH
'SCUSE ME!
...
MORNING, MA'AM! COULD YOU POINT ME TO THE GRAND TOURNEY, PLEASE?

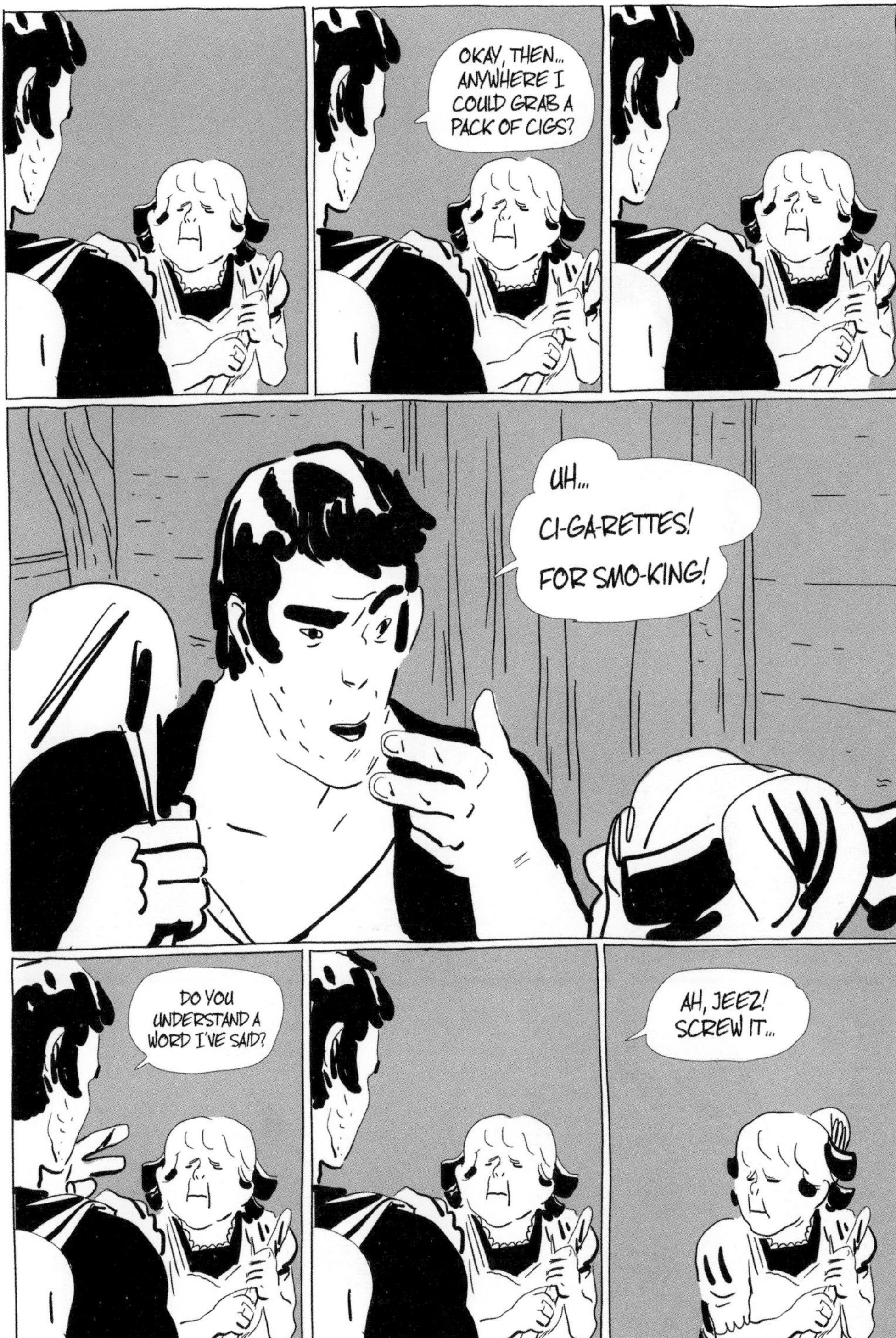
OKAY, THEN... ANYWHERE I COULD GRAB A PACK OF CIGS?
UH... CI-GA-RETTES! FOR SMO-KING!
DO YOU UNDERSTAND A WORD I'VE SAID?
AH, JEEZ! SCREW IT...

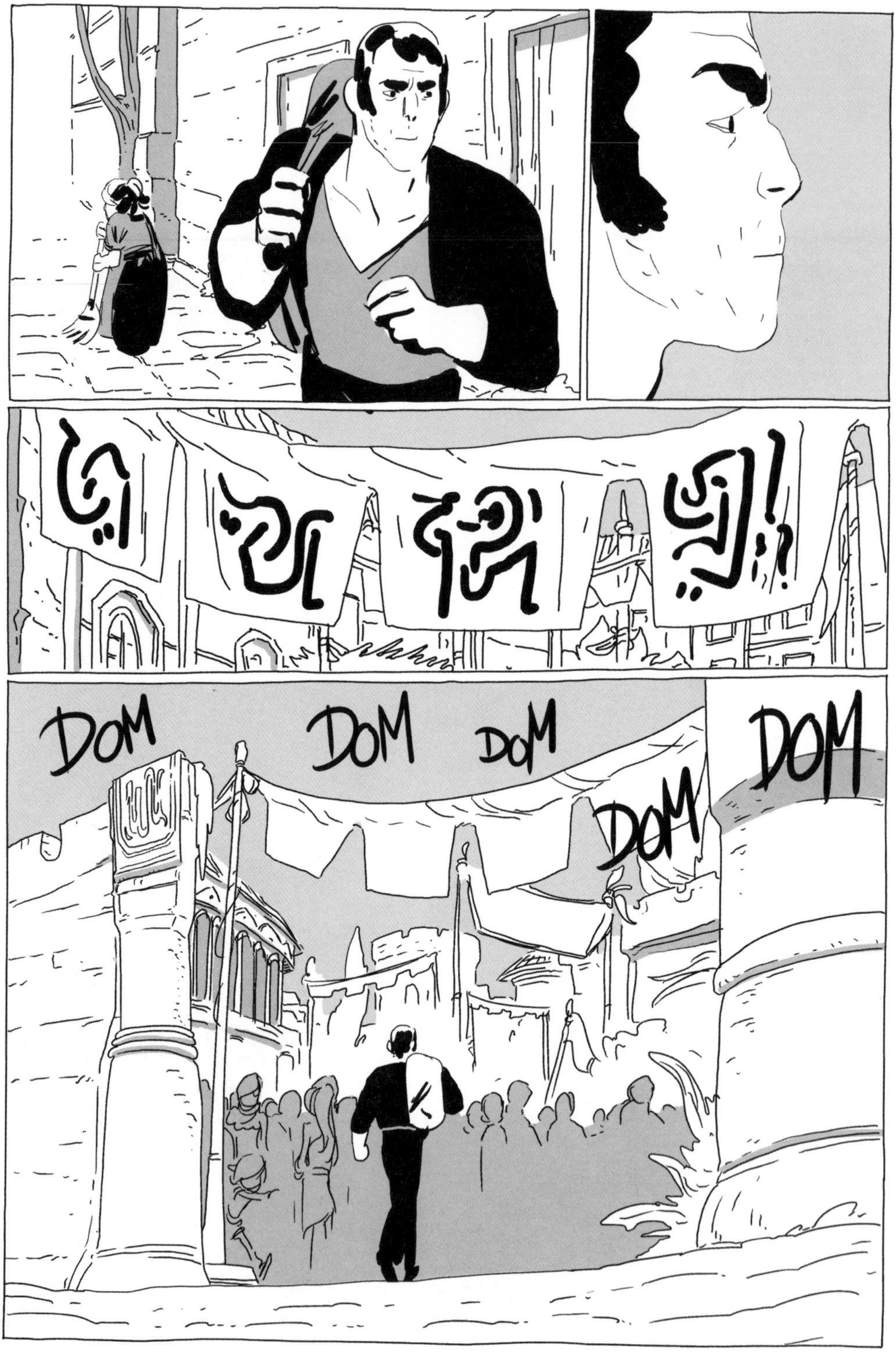
DOM
DOM
DOM
DOM
DOM

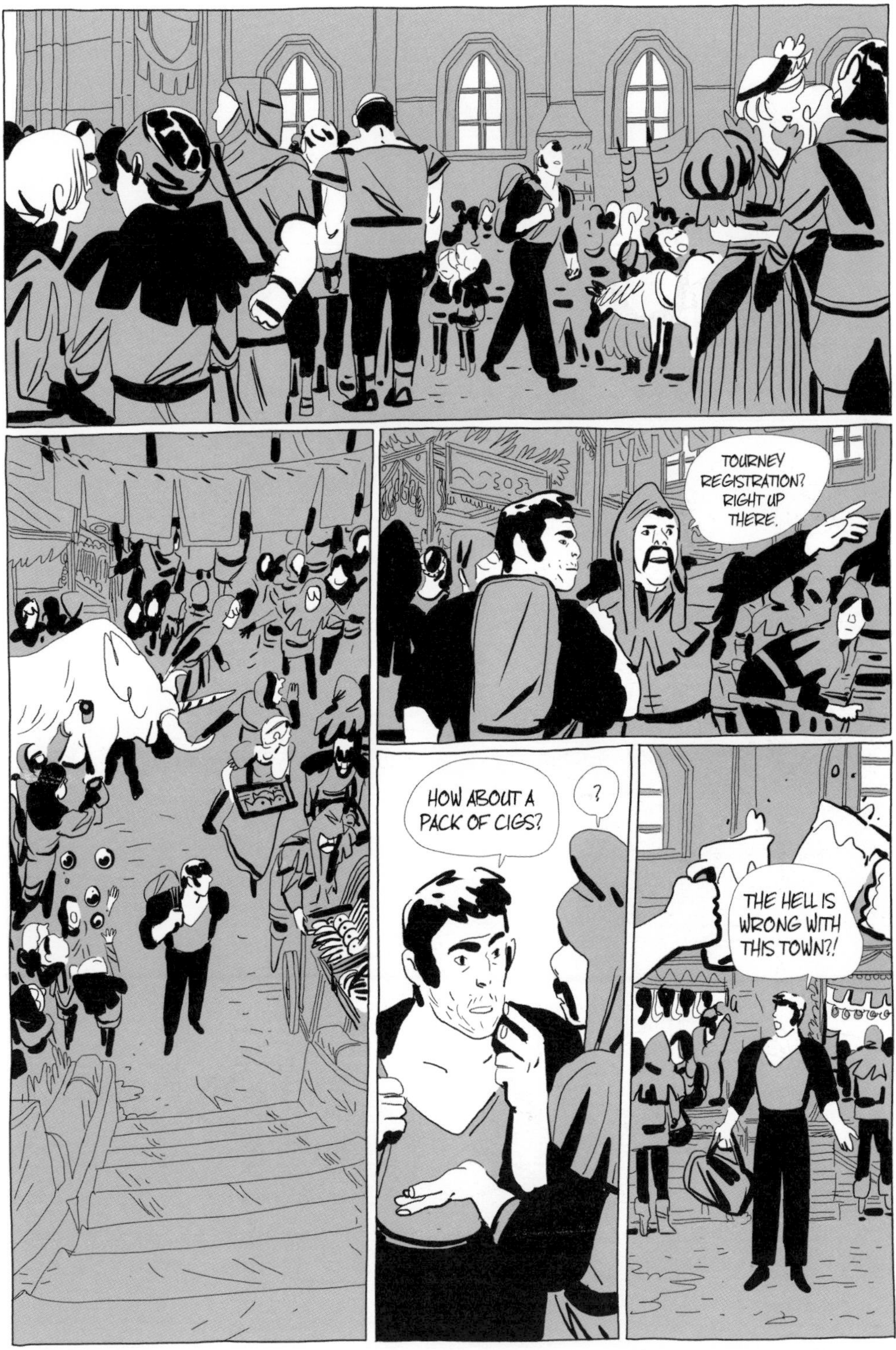
TOURNEY REGISTRATION? RIGHT UP THERE.
HOW ABOUT A PACK OF CIGS?
?
THE HELL IS WRONG WITH THIS TOWN?!

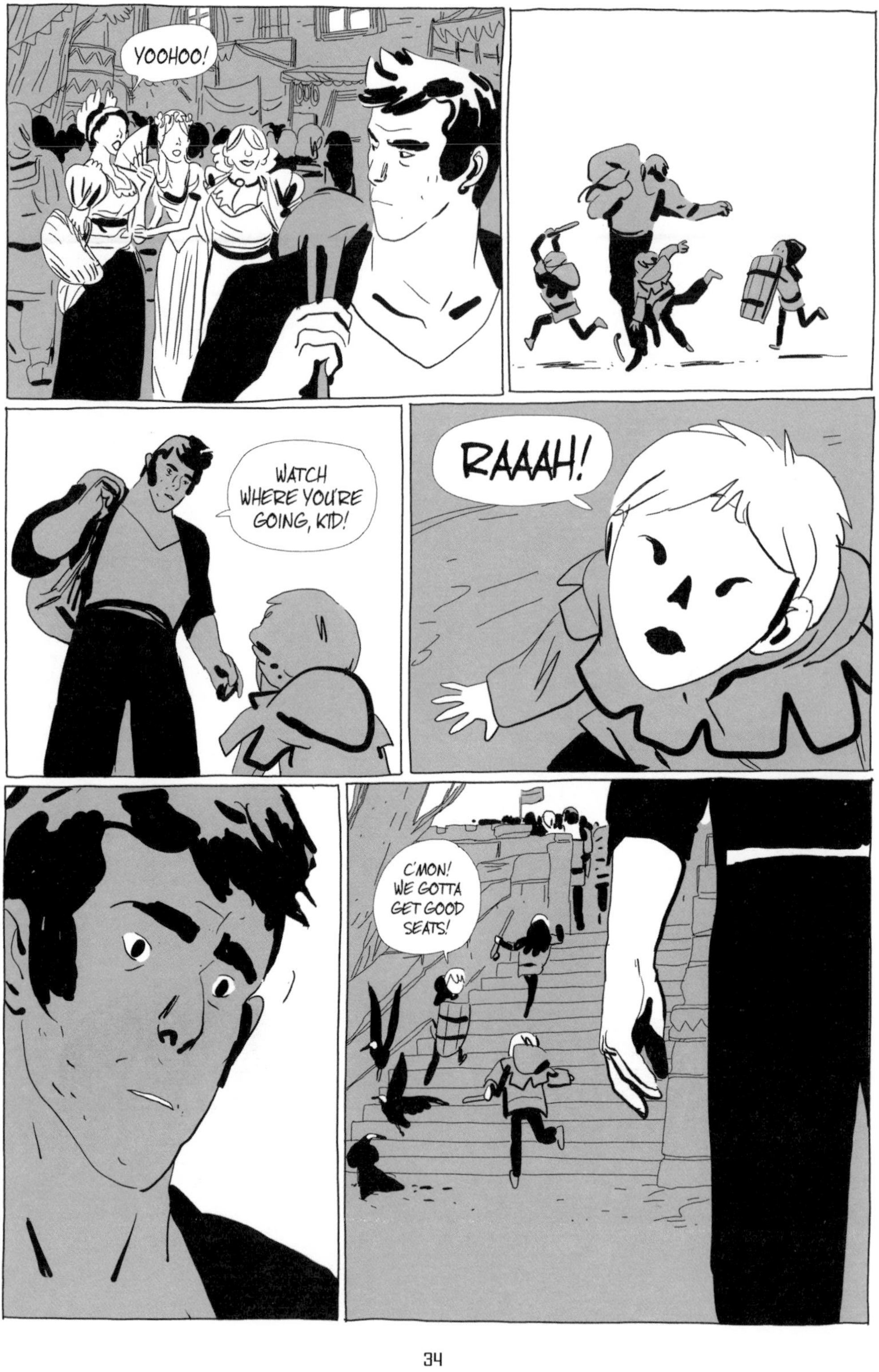
YOOHOO!
WATCH WHERE YOU'RE GOING, KID!
RAAAH!
C'MON! WE GOTTA GET GOOD SEATS!

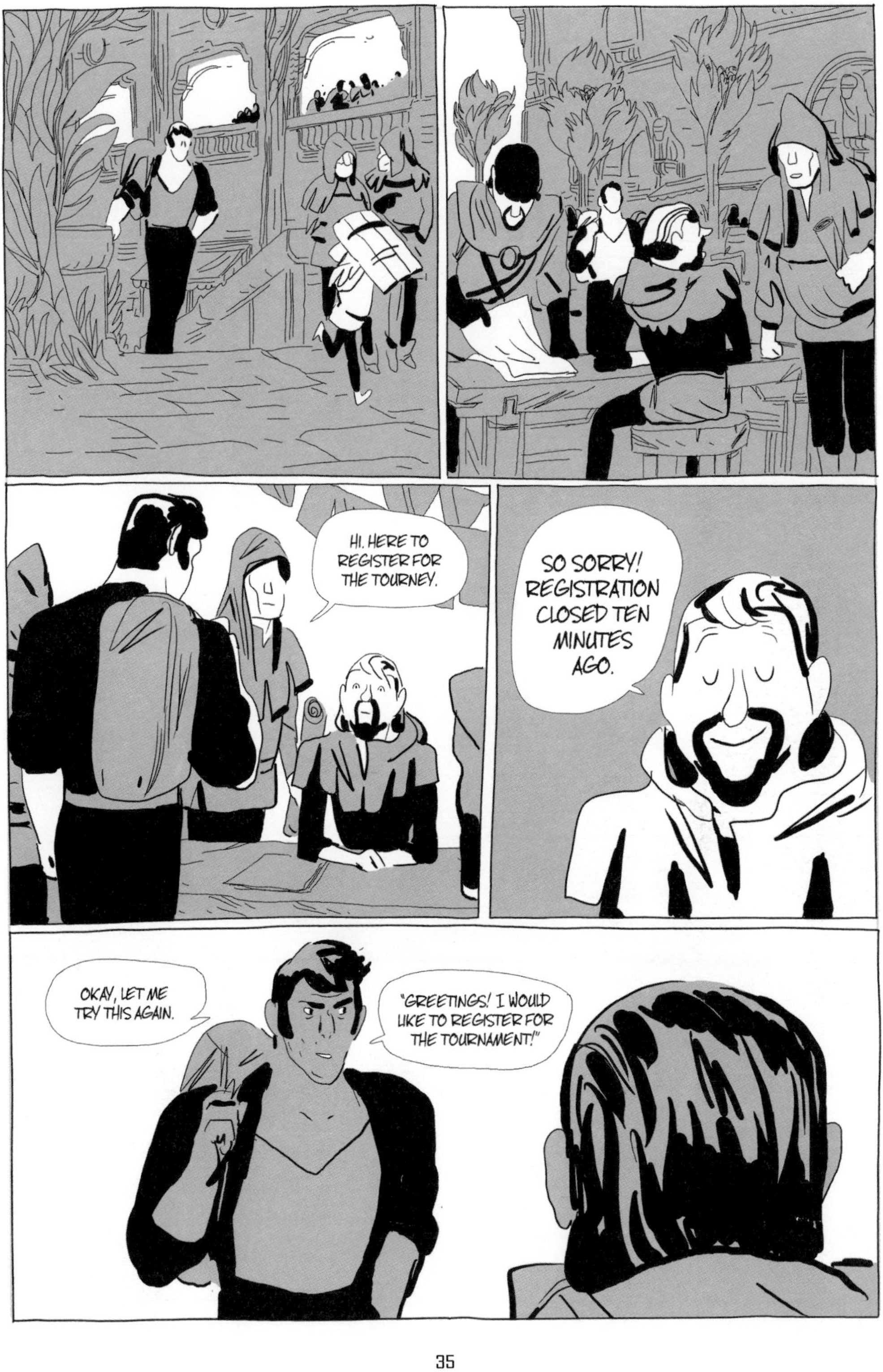
HI. HERE TO REGISTER FOR THE TOURNEY.
SO SORRY! REGISTRATION CLOSED TEN MINUTES AGO.
OKAY, LET ME TRY THIS AGAIN.
"GREETINGS! I WOULD LIKE TO REGISTER FOR THE TOURNAMENT!"

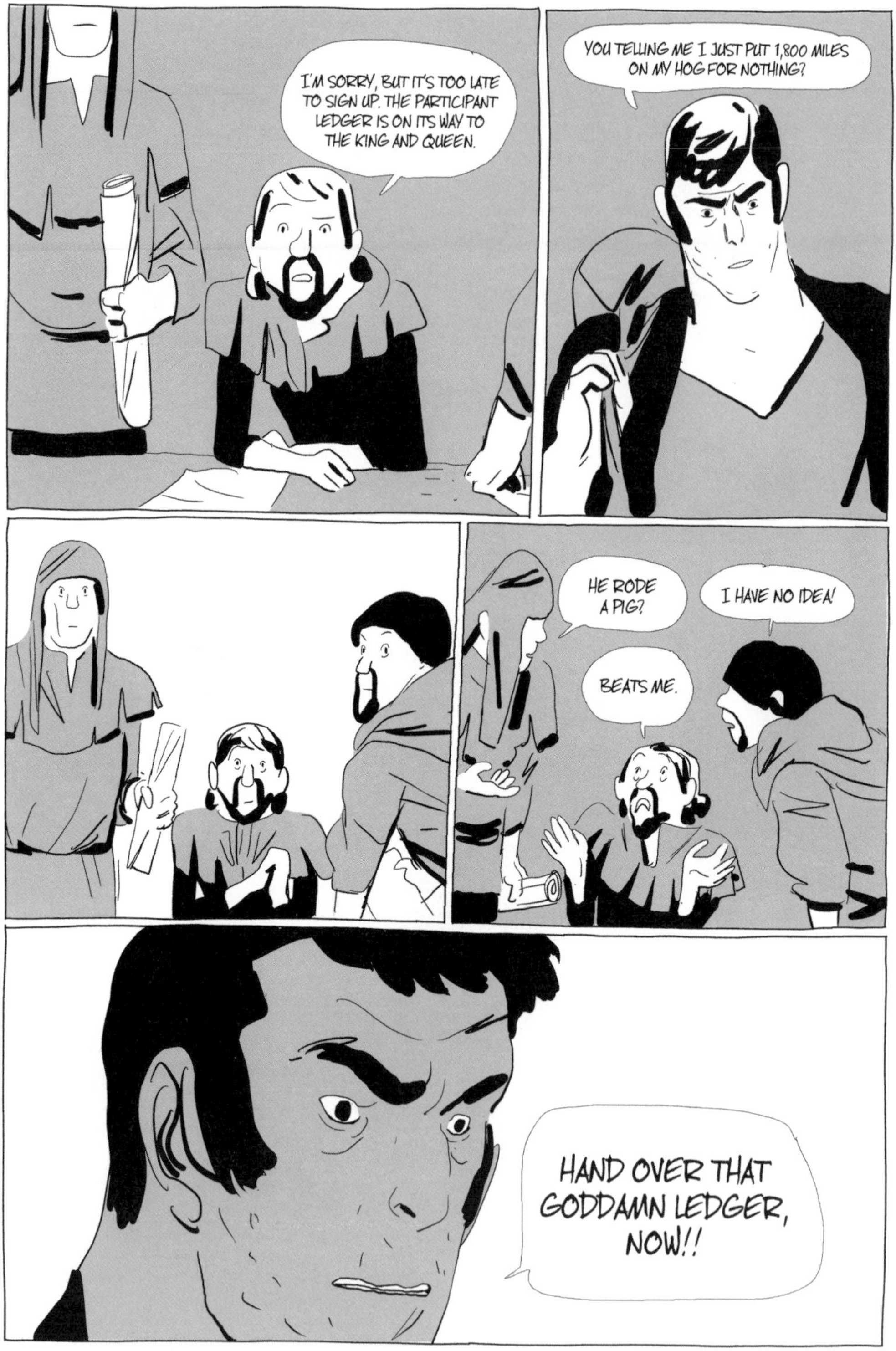
I'M SORRY, BUT IT'S TOO LATE TO SIGN UP. THE PARTICIPANT LEDGER IS ON ITS WAY TO THE KING AND QUEEN.
YOU TELLING ME I JUST PUT 1,800 MILES ON MY HOG FOR NOTHING?
HE RODE A PIG?
I HAVE NO IDEA!
BEATS ME.
HAND OVER THAT GODDAMN LEDGER, NOW!!

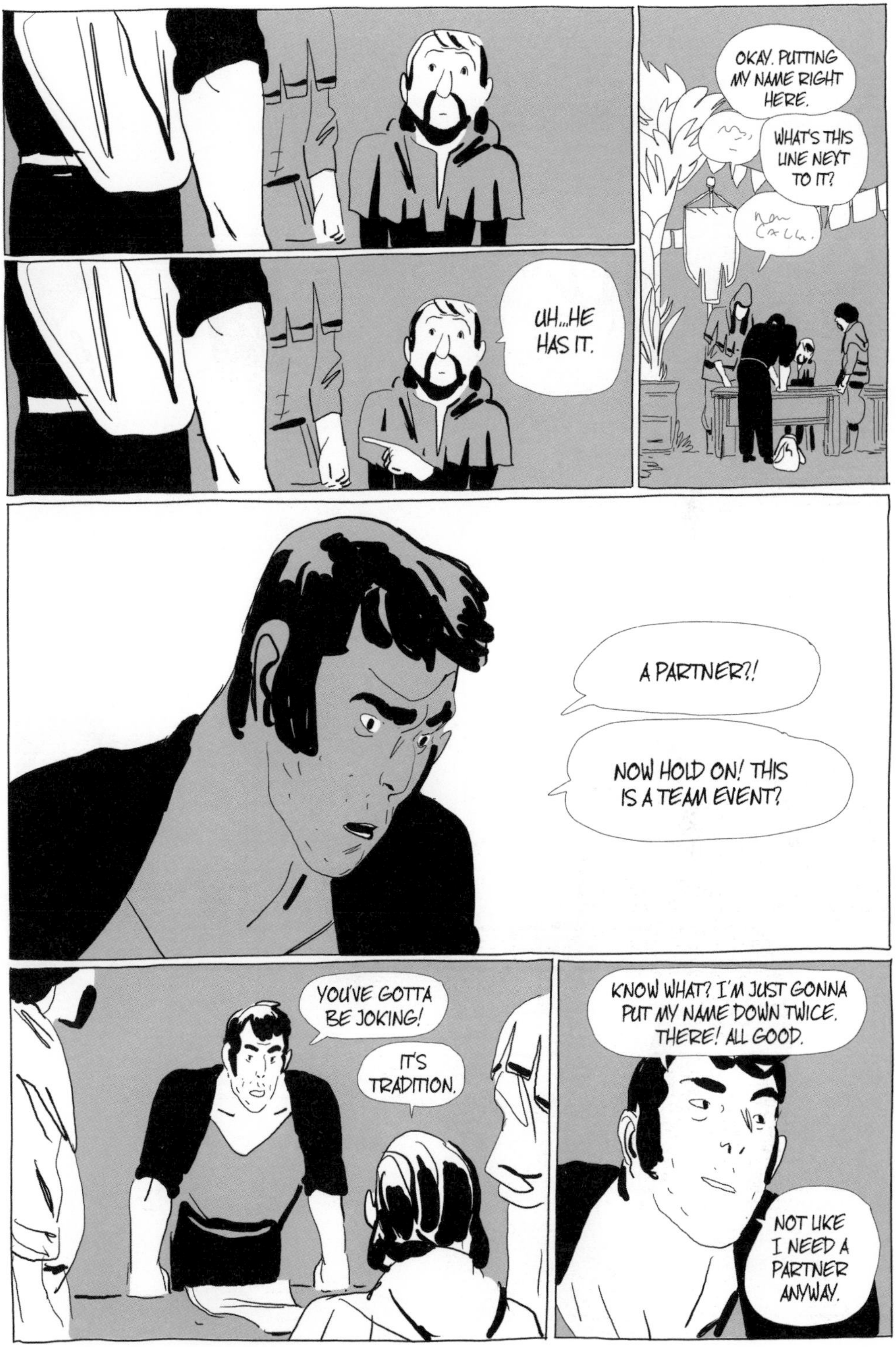
OKAY. PUTTING MY NAME RIGHT HERE.
WHAT'S THIS LINE NEXT TO IT?
UH...HE HAS IT.
A PARTNER?!
NOW HOLD ON! THIS IS A TEAM EVENT?
YOU'VE GOTTA BE JOKING!
IT'S TRADITION.
KNOW WHAT? I'M JUST GONNA PUT MY NAME DOWN TWICE. THERE! ALL GOOD.
NOT LIKE I NEED A PARTNER ANYWAY.

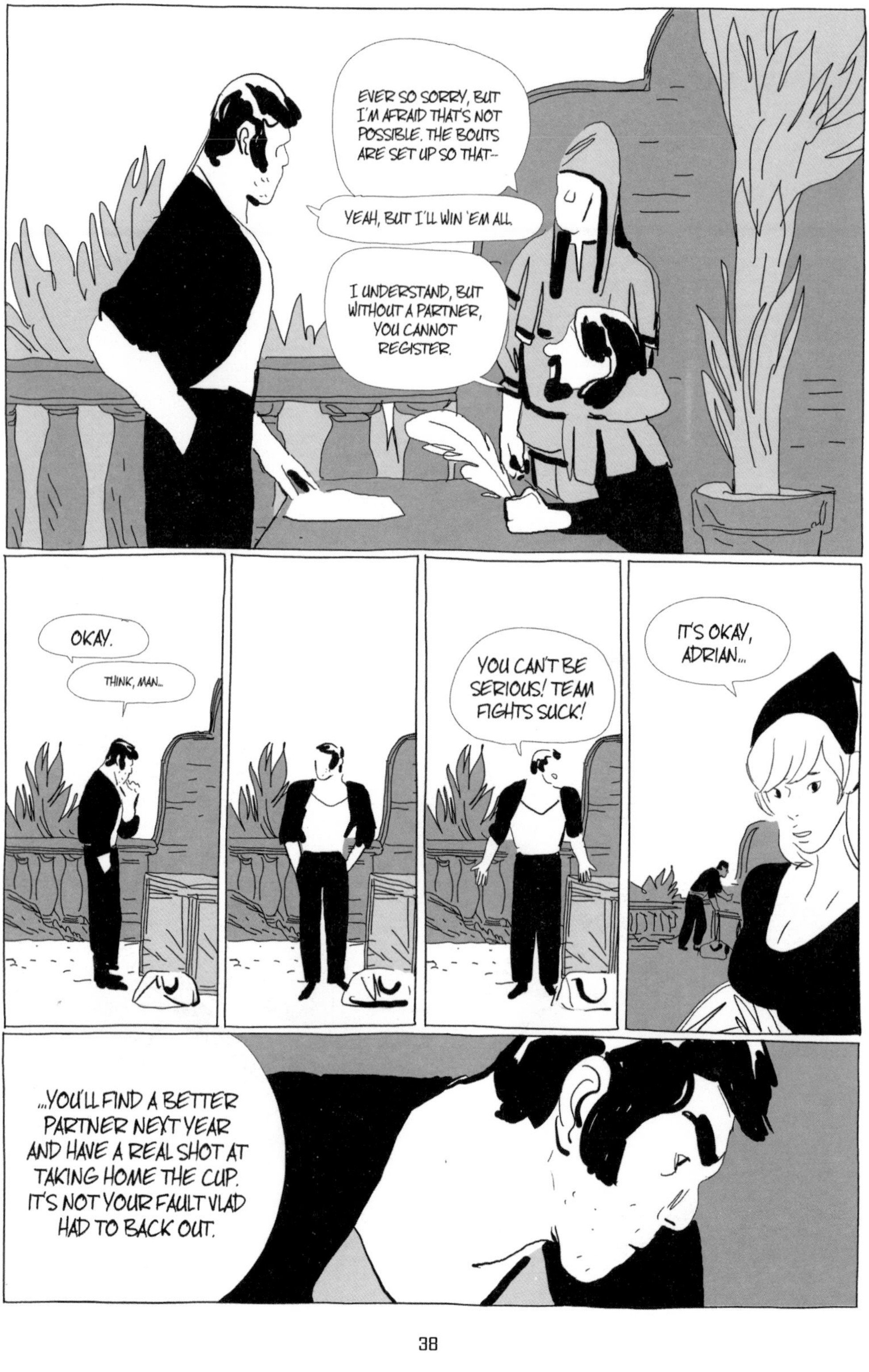
EVER SO SORRY, BUT I'M AFRAID THAT'S NOT POSSIBLE. THE BOUTS ARE SET UP SO THAT--
YEAH, BUT I'LL WIN 'EM ALL.
I UNDERSTAND, BUT WITHOUT A PARTNER, YOU CANNOT REGISTER.
OKAY.
THINK, MAN...
YOU CAN'T BE SERIOUS! TEAM FIGHTS SUCK!
IT'S OKAY, ADRIAN...
...YOU'LL FIND A BETTER PARTNER NEXT YEAR AND HAVE A REAL SHOT AT TAKING HOME THE CUP. IT'S NOT YOUR FAULT VLAD HAD TO BACK OUT.

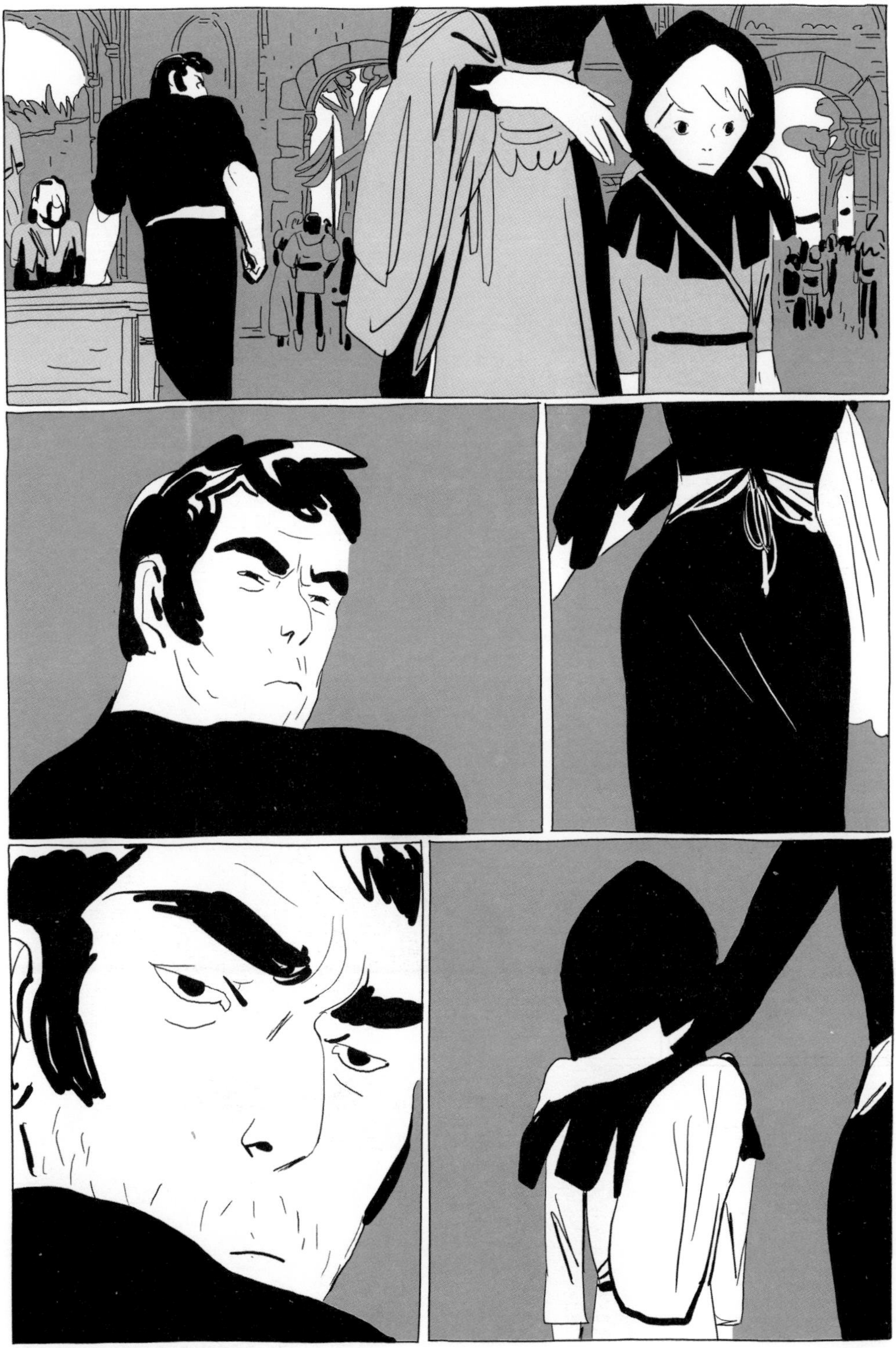

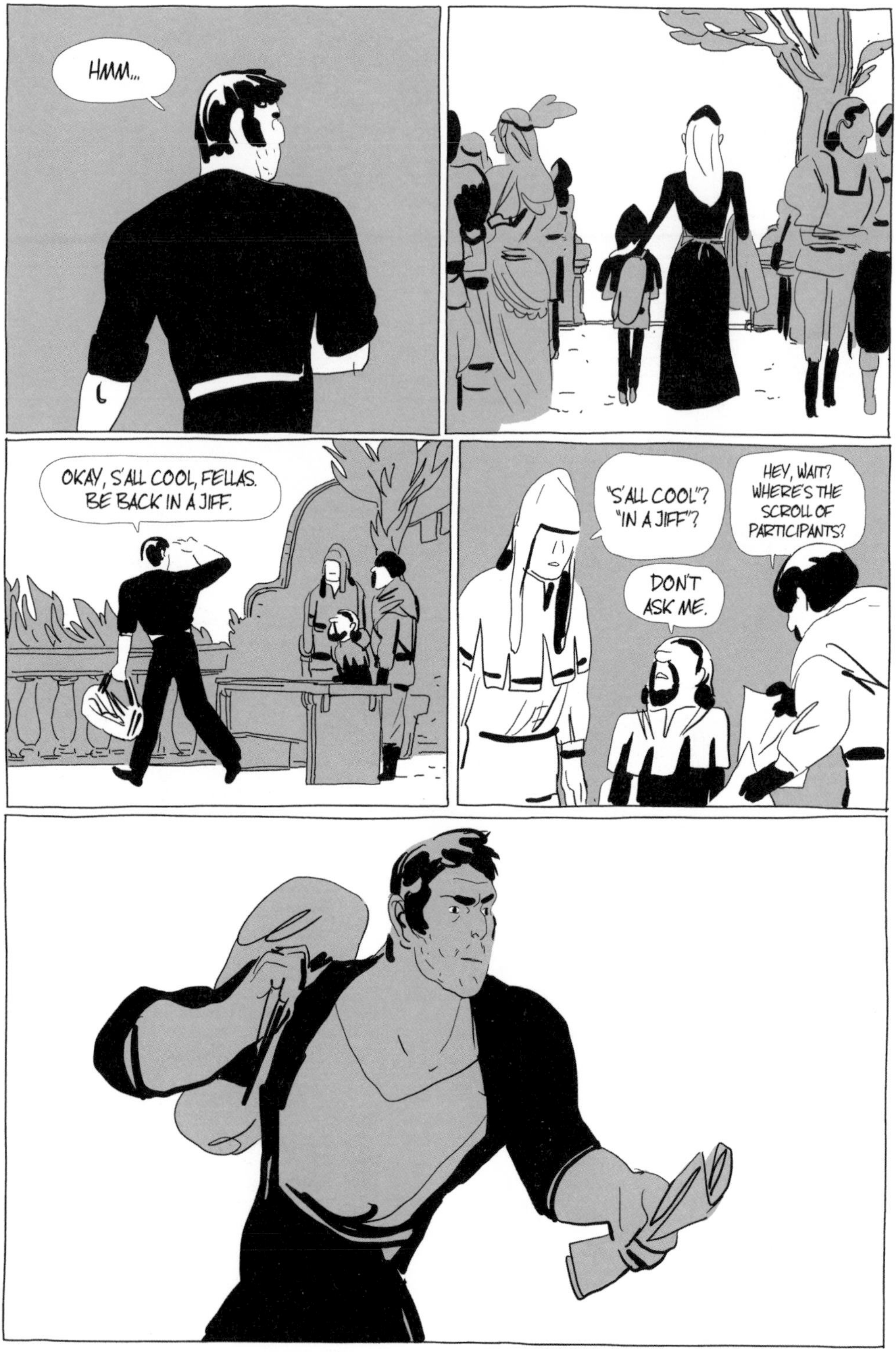
HMM...
OKAY, S'ALL COOL, FELLAS. BE BACK IN A JIFF.
"S'ALL COOL"? "IN A JIFF"?
HEY, WAIT? WHERE'S THE SCROLL OF PARTICIPANTS?
DON'T ASK ME.

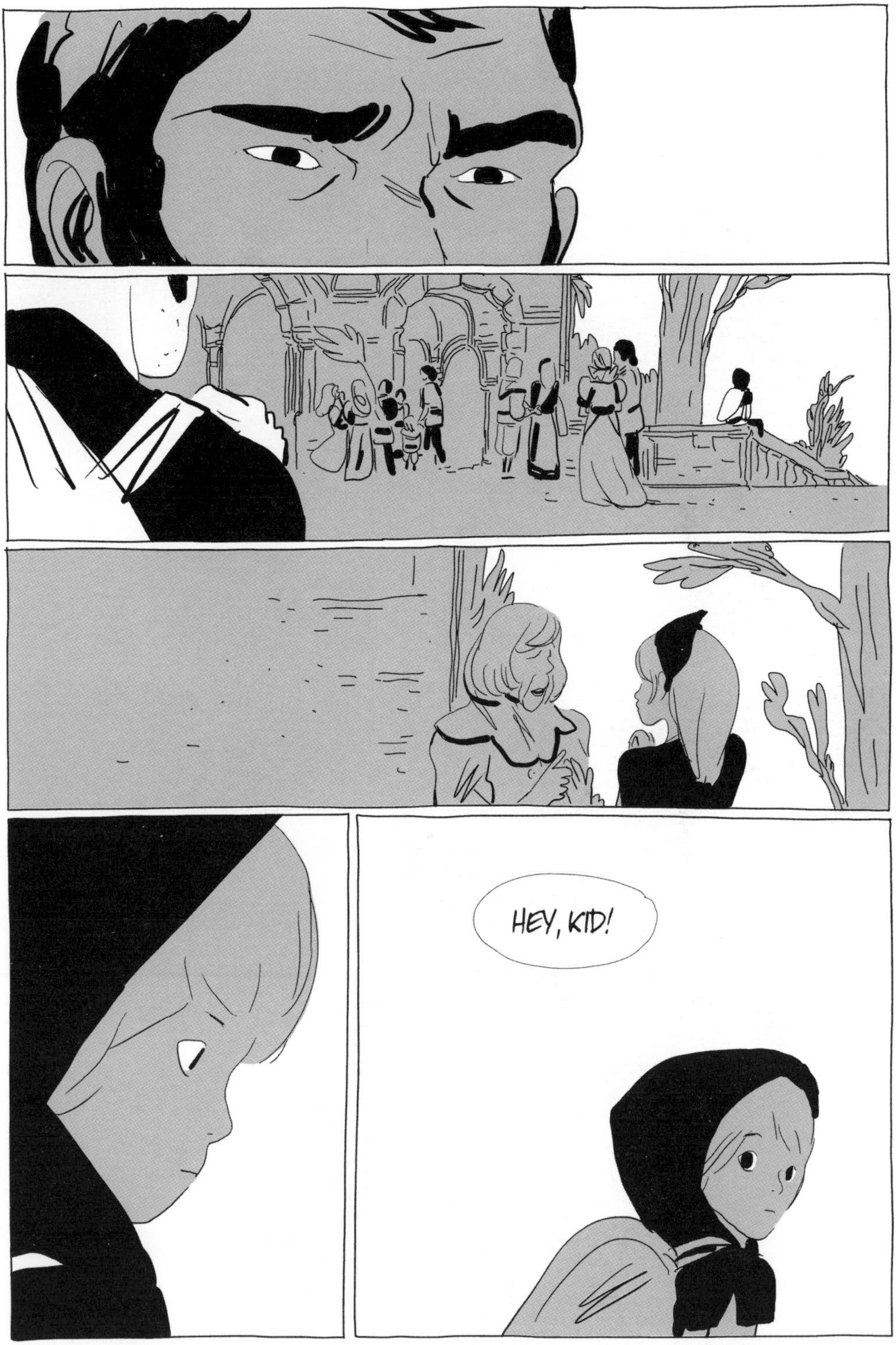
HEY, KID!

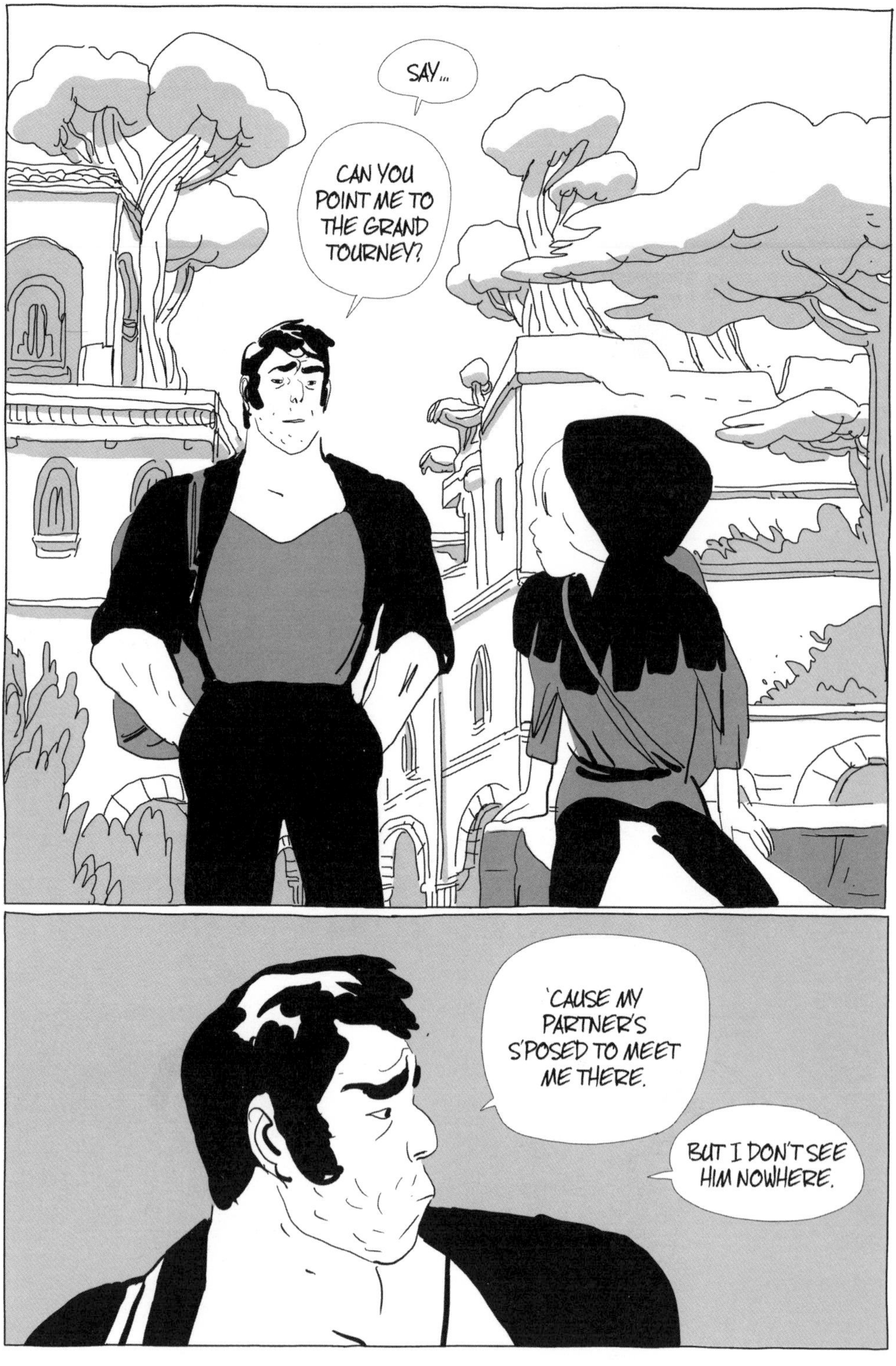
SAY...
CAN YOU POINT ME TO THE GRAND TOURNEY?
'CAUSE MY PARTNER'S S'POSED TO MEET ME THERE.
BUT I DON'T SEE HIM NOWHERE.

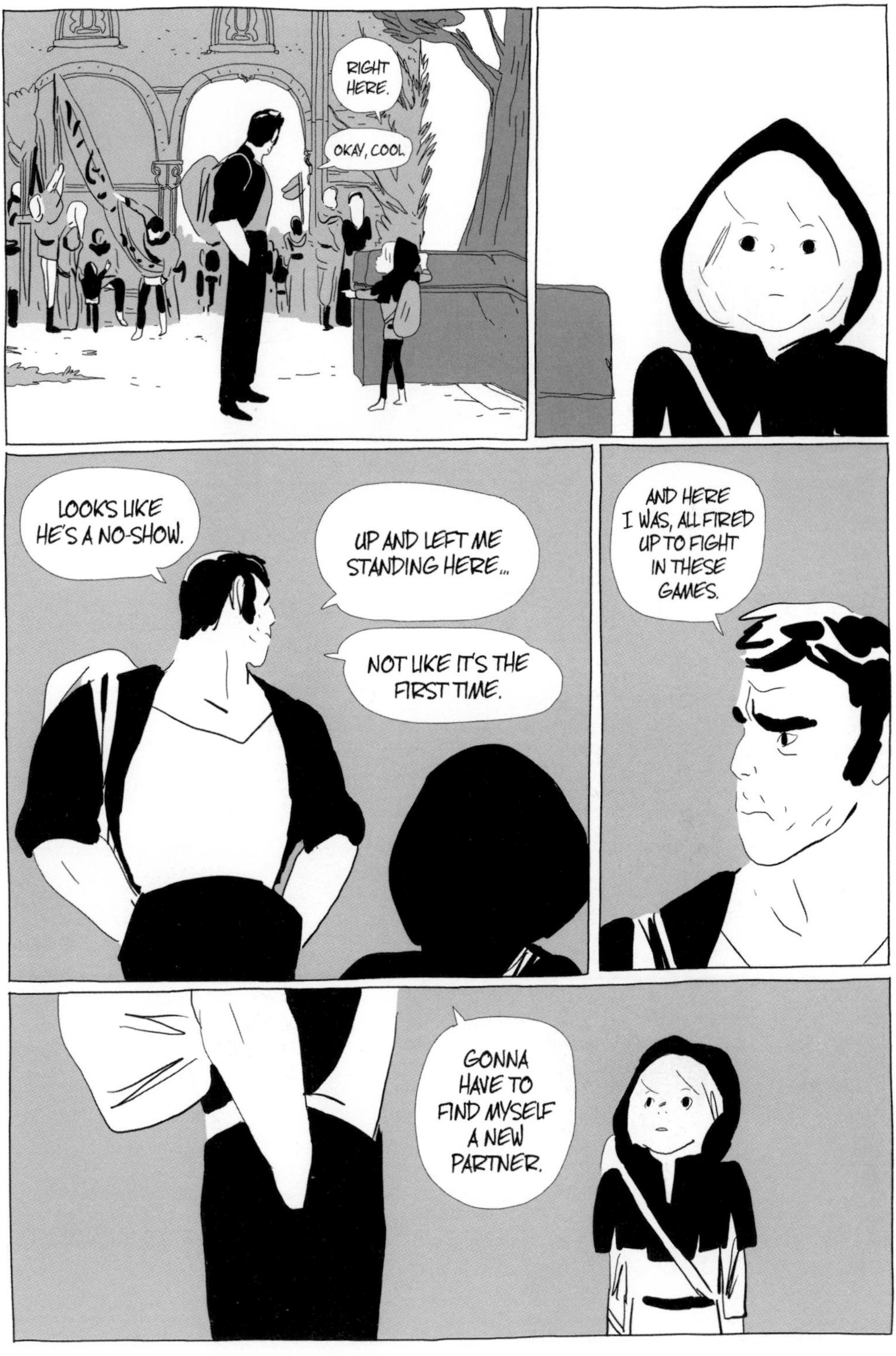
RIGHT HERE.
OKAY, COOL.
LOOKS LIKE HE'S A NO-SHOW.
UP AND LEFT ME STANDING HERE...
NOT LIKE IT'S THE FIRST TIME.
AND HERE I WAS, ALL FIRED UP TO FIGHT IN THESE GAMES.
GONNA HAVE TO FIND MYSELF A NEW PARTNER.

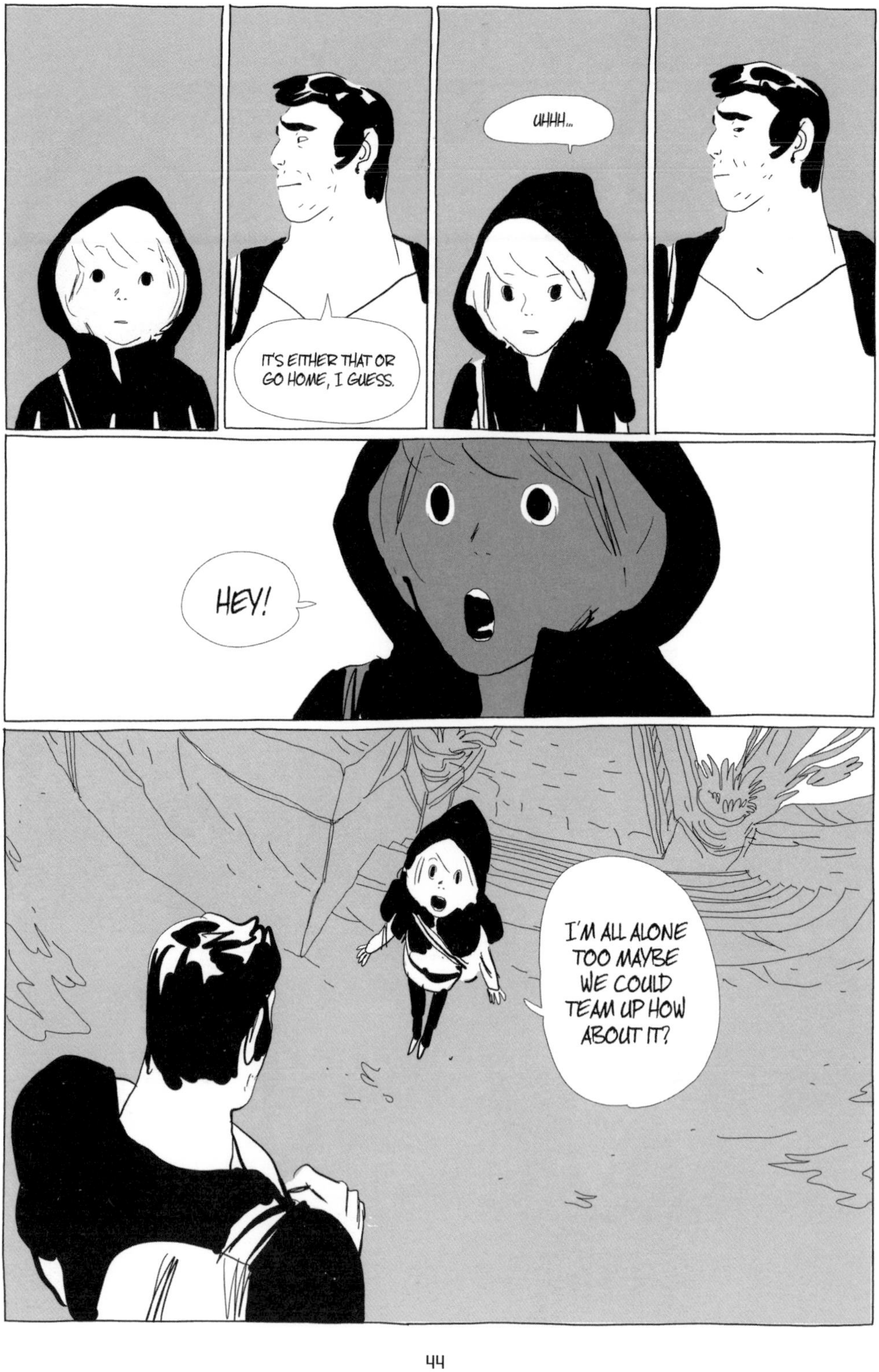
IT'S EITHER THAT OR GO HOME, I GUESS.
UHHH...
HEY!
I'M ALL ALONE TOO MAYBE WE COULD TEAM UP HOW ABOUT IT?

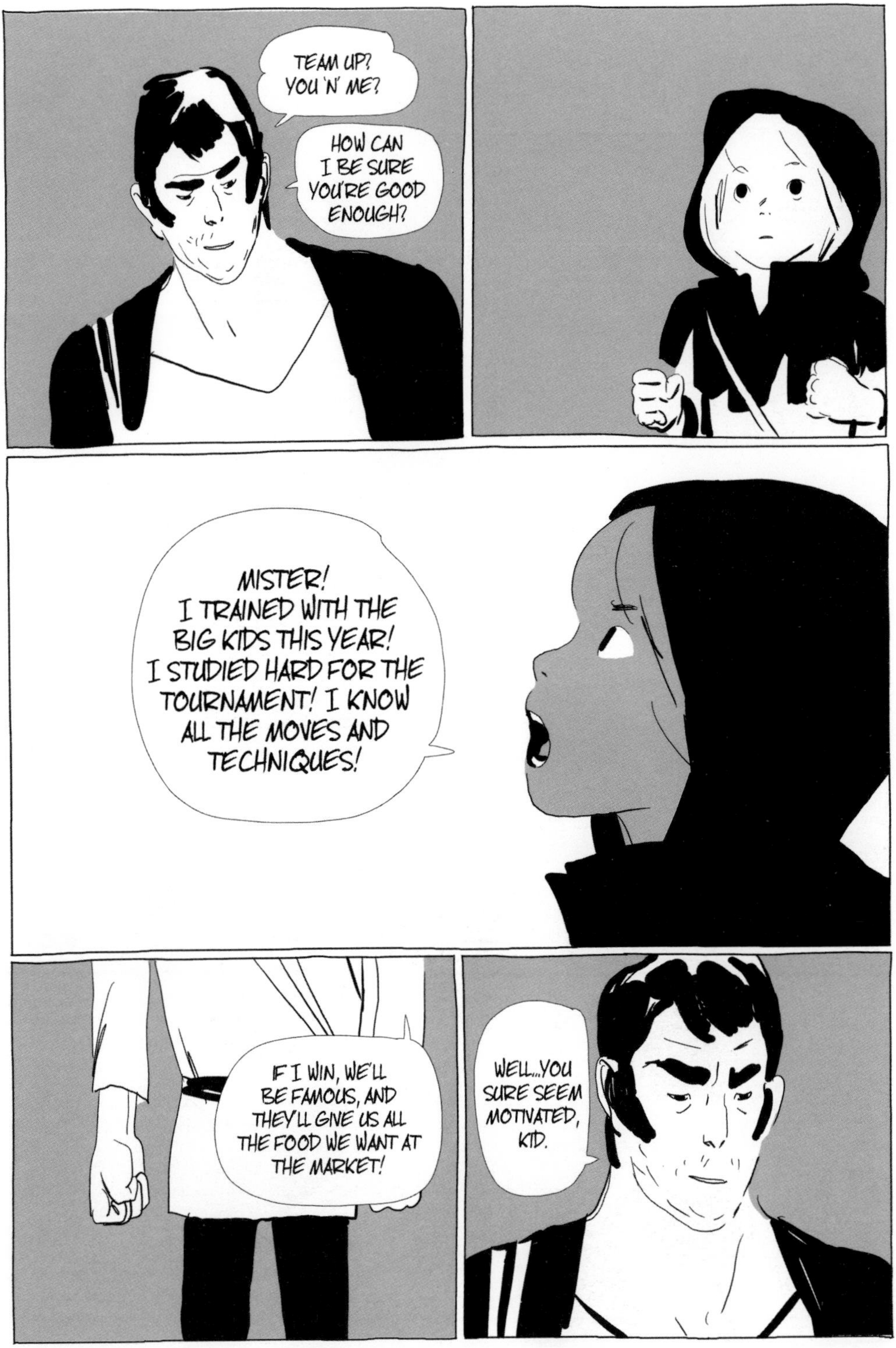
TEAM UP? YOU 'N' ME?
HOW CAN I BE SURE YOU'RE GOOD ENOUGH?
MISTER! I TRAINED WITH THE BIG KIDS THIS YEAR! I STUDIED HARD FOR THE TOURNAMENT! I KNOW ALL THE MOVES AND TECHNIQUES!
IF I WIN, WE'LL BE FAMOUS, AND THEY'LL GIVE US ALL THE FOOD WE WANT AT THE MARKET!
WELL...YOU SURE SEEM MOTIVATED, KID.

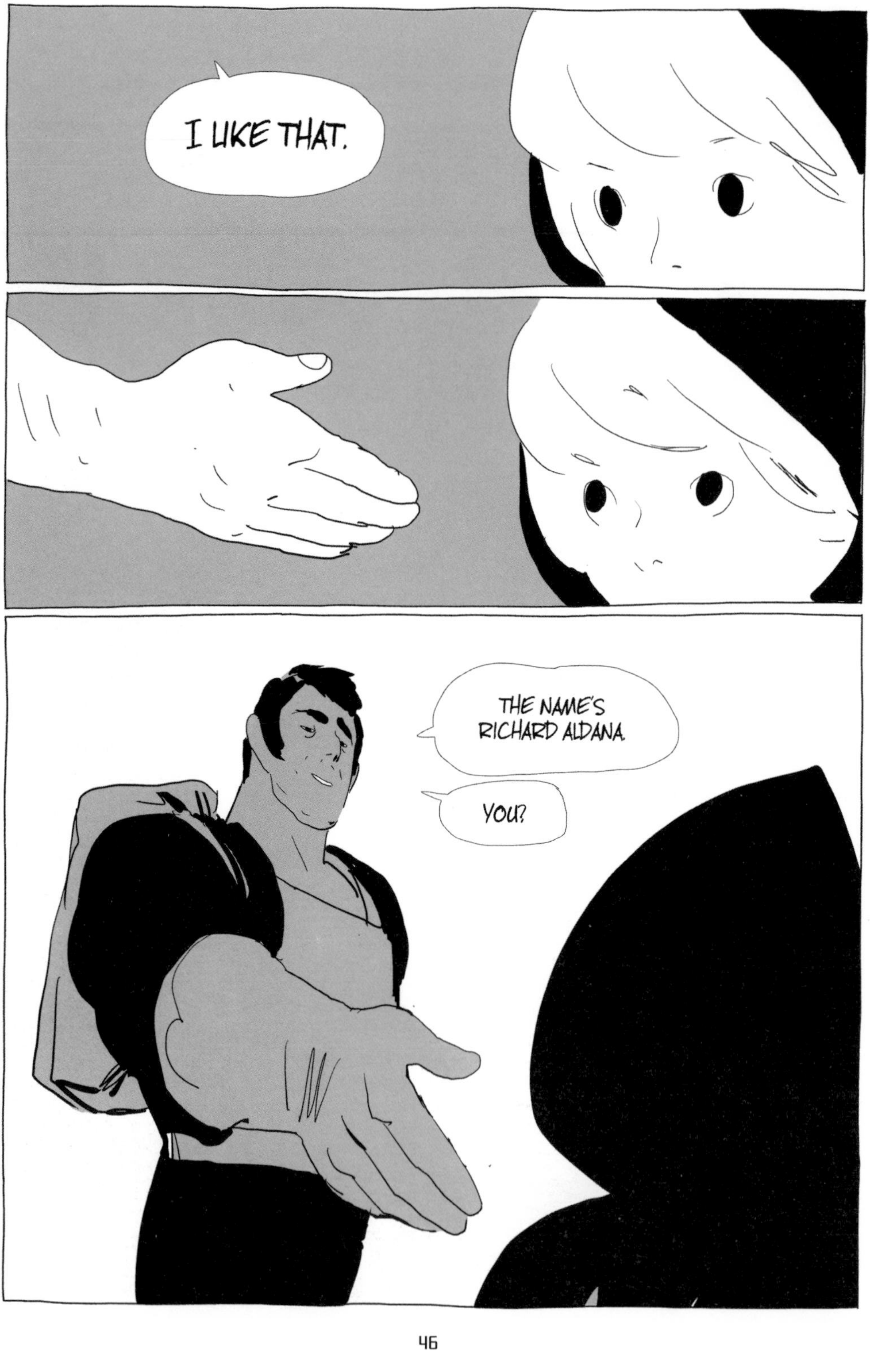
I LIKE THAT.
THE NAME'S RICHARD ALDANA.
YOU?

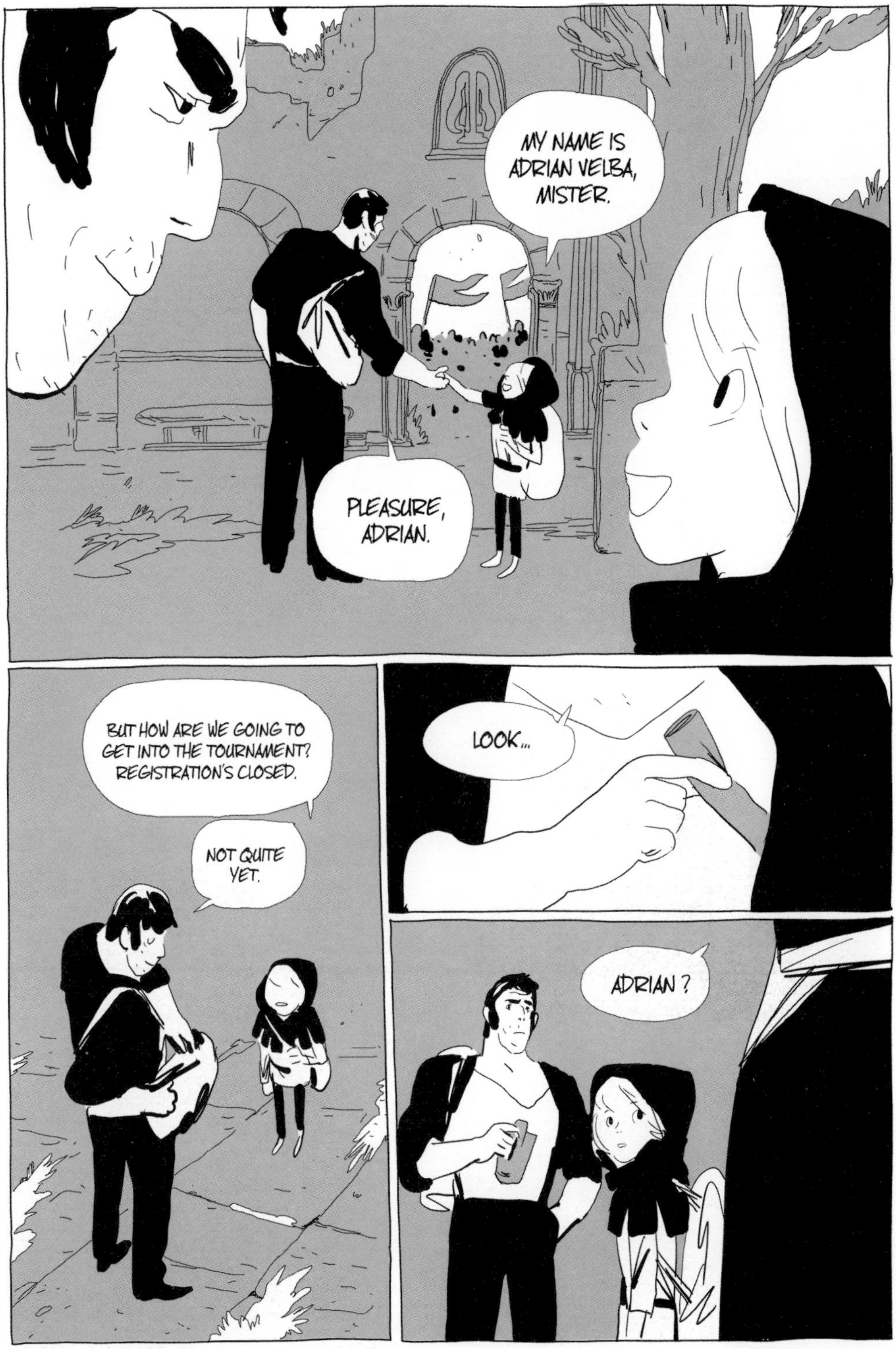
MY NAME IS ADRIAN VELBA, MISTER.
PLEASURE, ADRIAN.
BUT HOW ARE WE GOING TO GET INTO THE TOURNAMENT? REGISTRATION'S CLOSED.
NOT QUITE YET.
LOOK...
ADRIAN ?

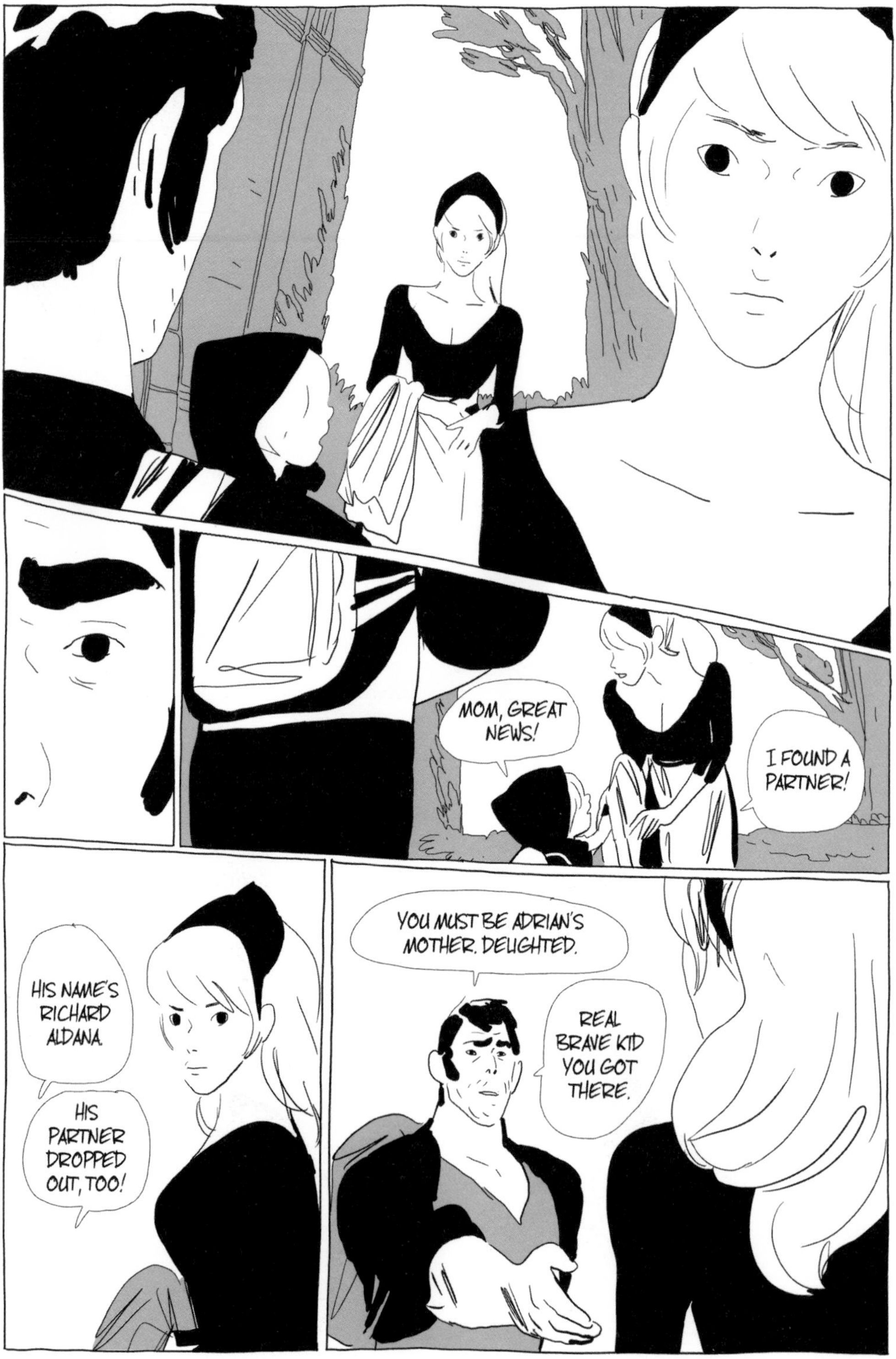
MOM, GREAT NEWS!
I FOUND A PARTNER!
HIS NAME'S RICHARD ALDANA.
HIS PARTNER DROPPED OUT, TOO!
YOU MUST BE ADRIAN'S MOTHER. DELIGHTED.
REAL BRAVE KID YOU GOT THERE.

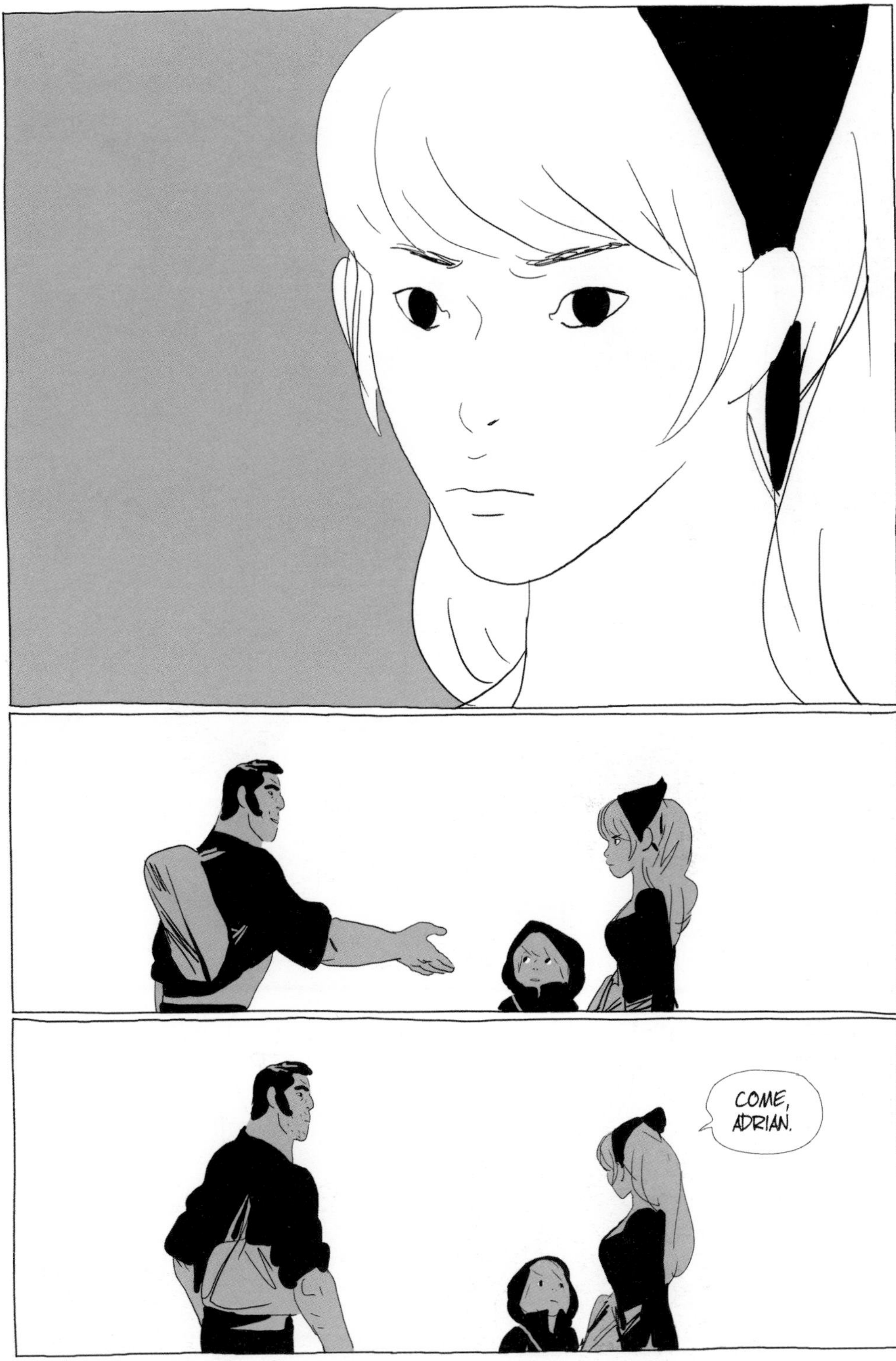
COME, ADRIAN.

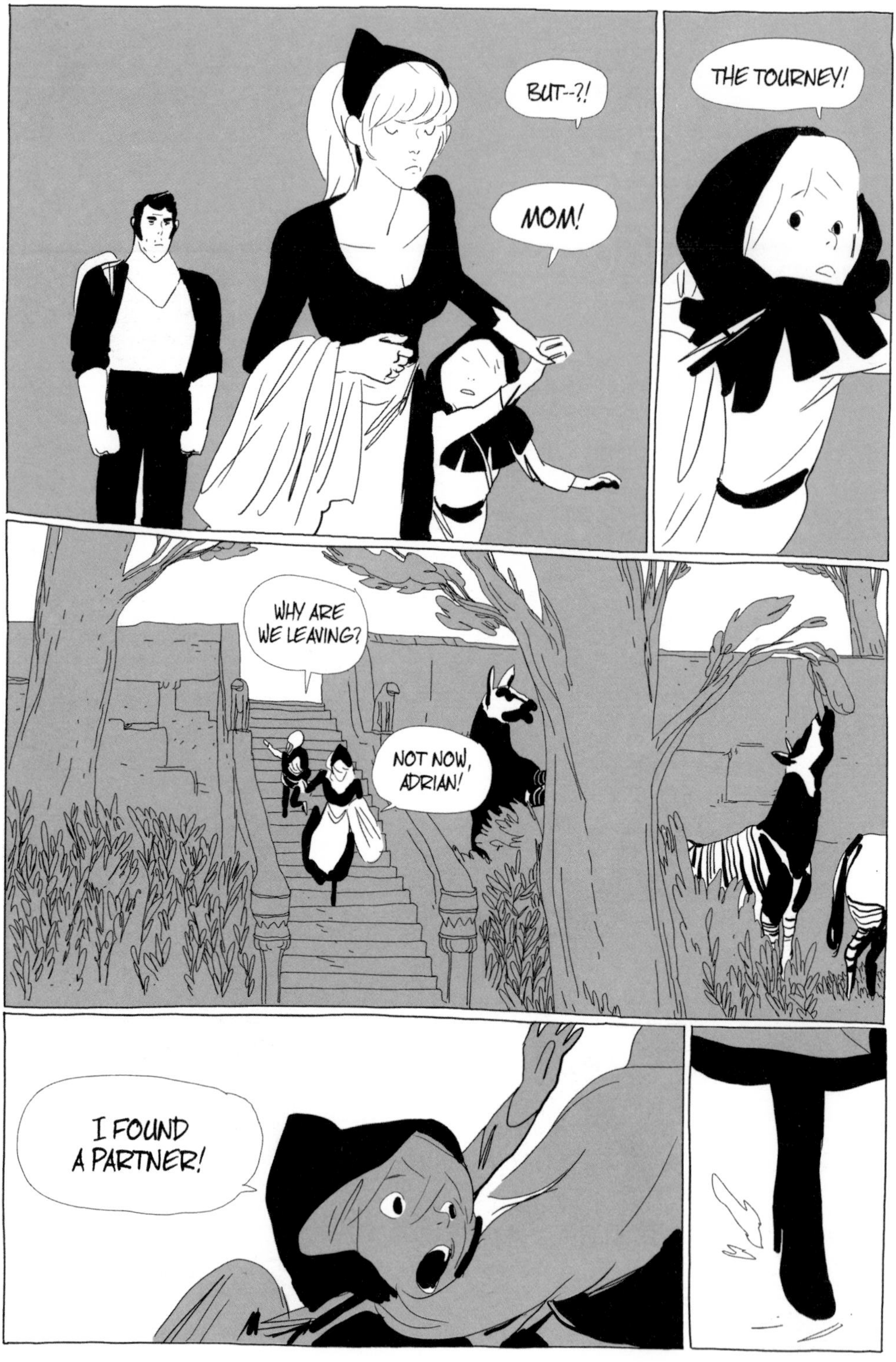
BUT--?!
MOM!
THE TOURNEY!
WHY ARE WE LEAVING?
NOT NOW, ADRIAN!
I FOUND A PARTNER!

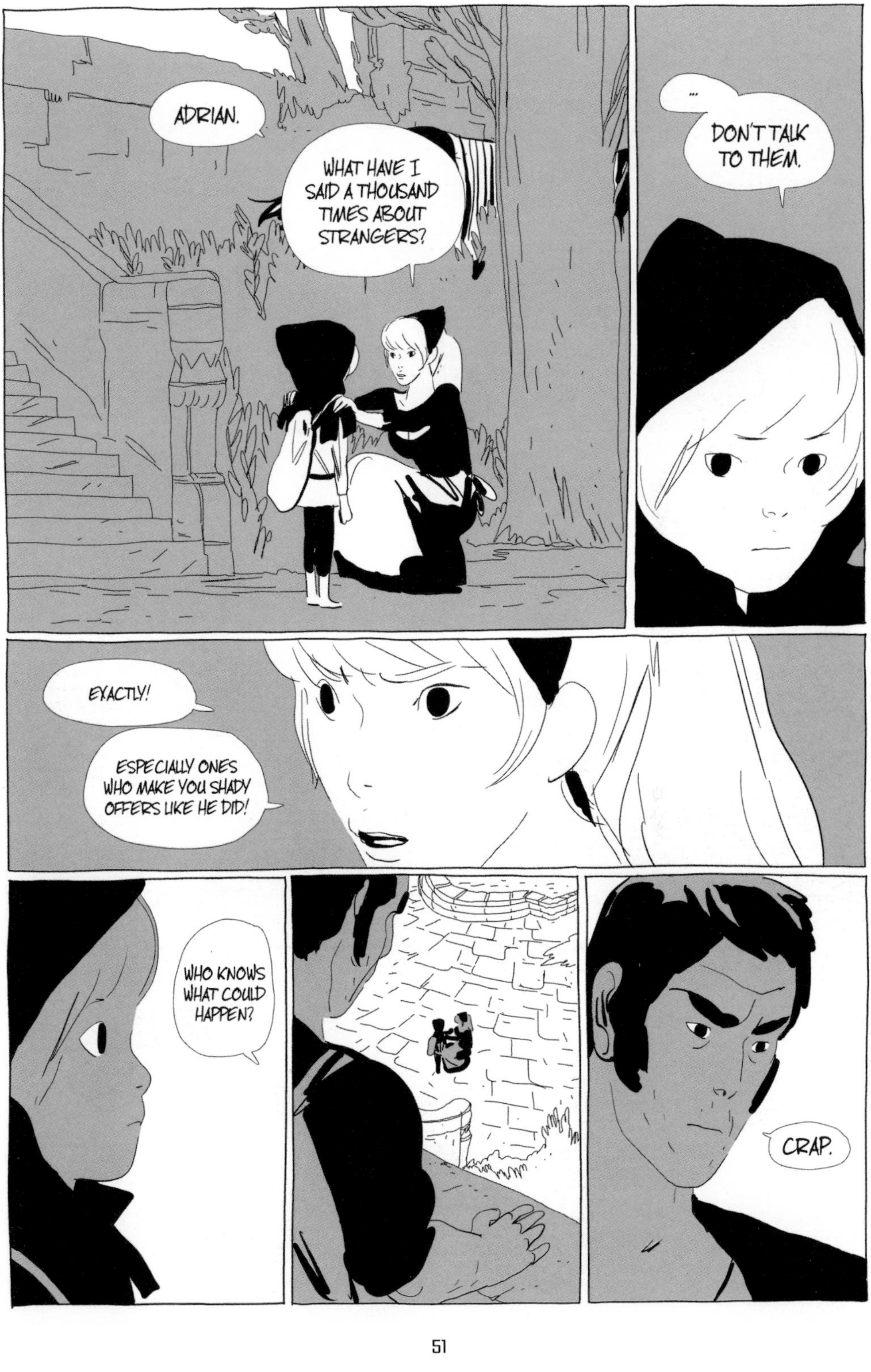
ADRIAN.
WHAT HAVE I SAID A THOUSAND TIMES ABOUT STRANGERS?
...
DON'T TALK TO THEM.
EXACTLY!
ESPECIALLY ONES WHO MAKE YOU SHADY OFFERS LIKE HE DID!
WHO KNOWS WHAT COULD HAPPEN?
CRAP.

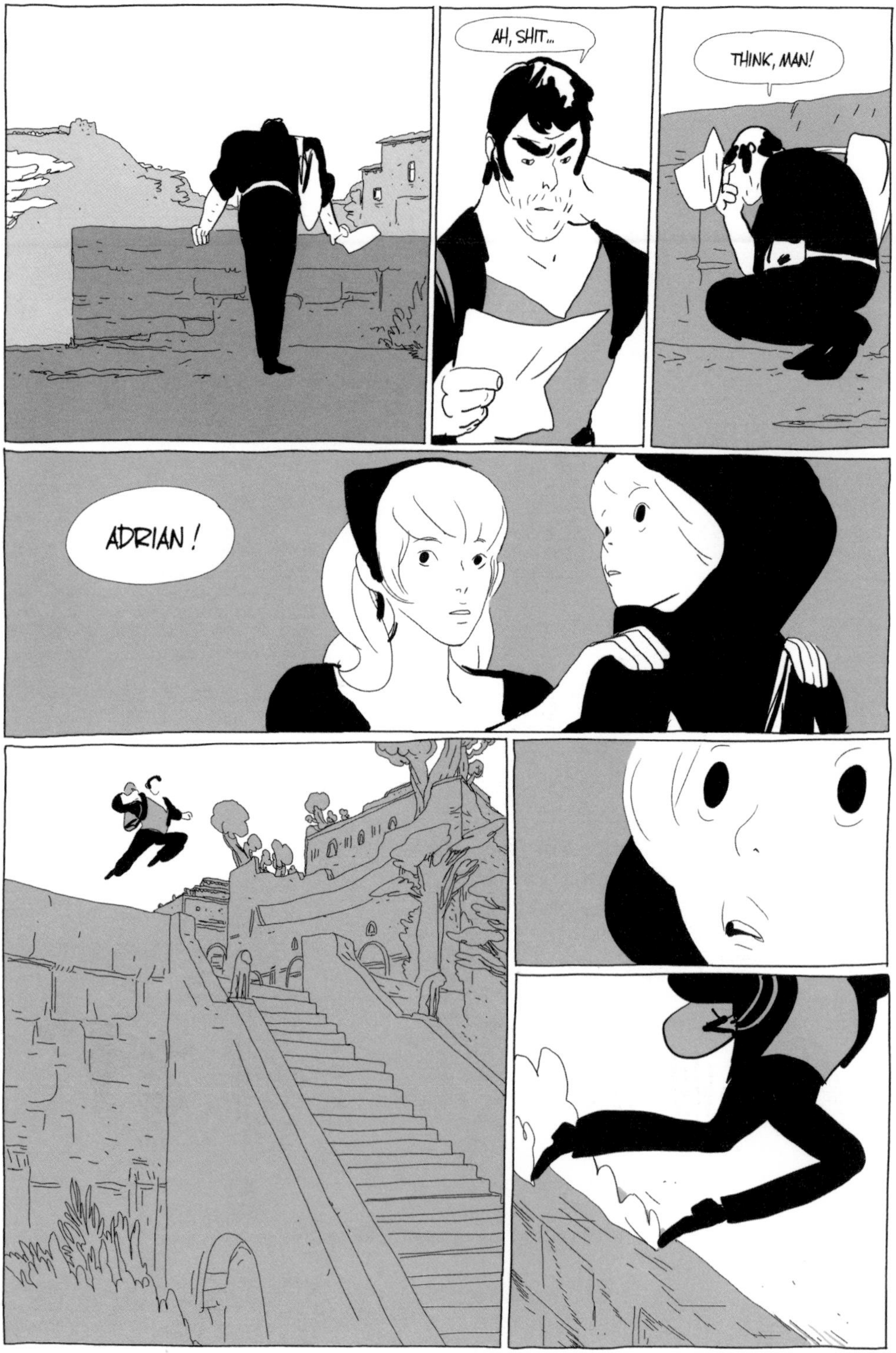
AH, SHIT...
THINK, MAN!
ADRIAN!

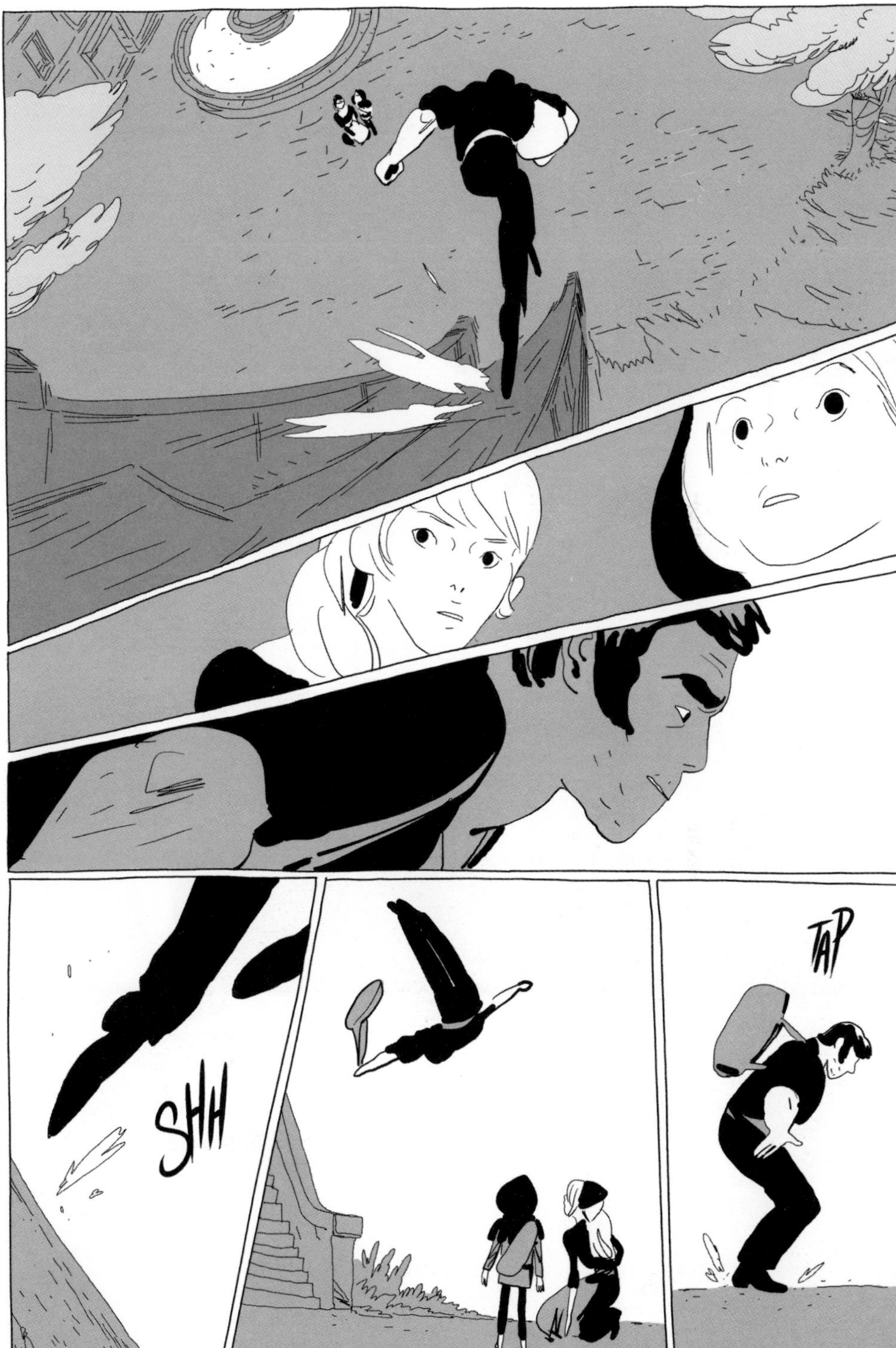
SHH
TAP

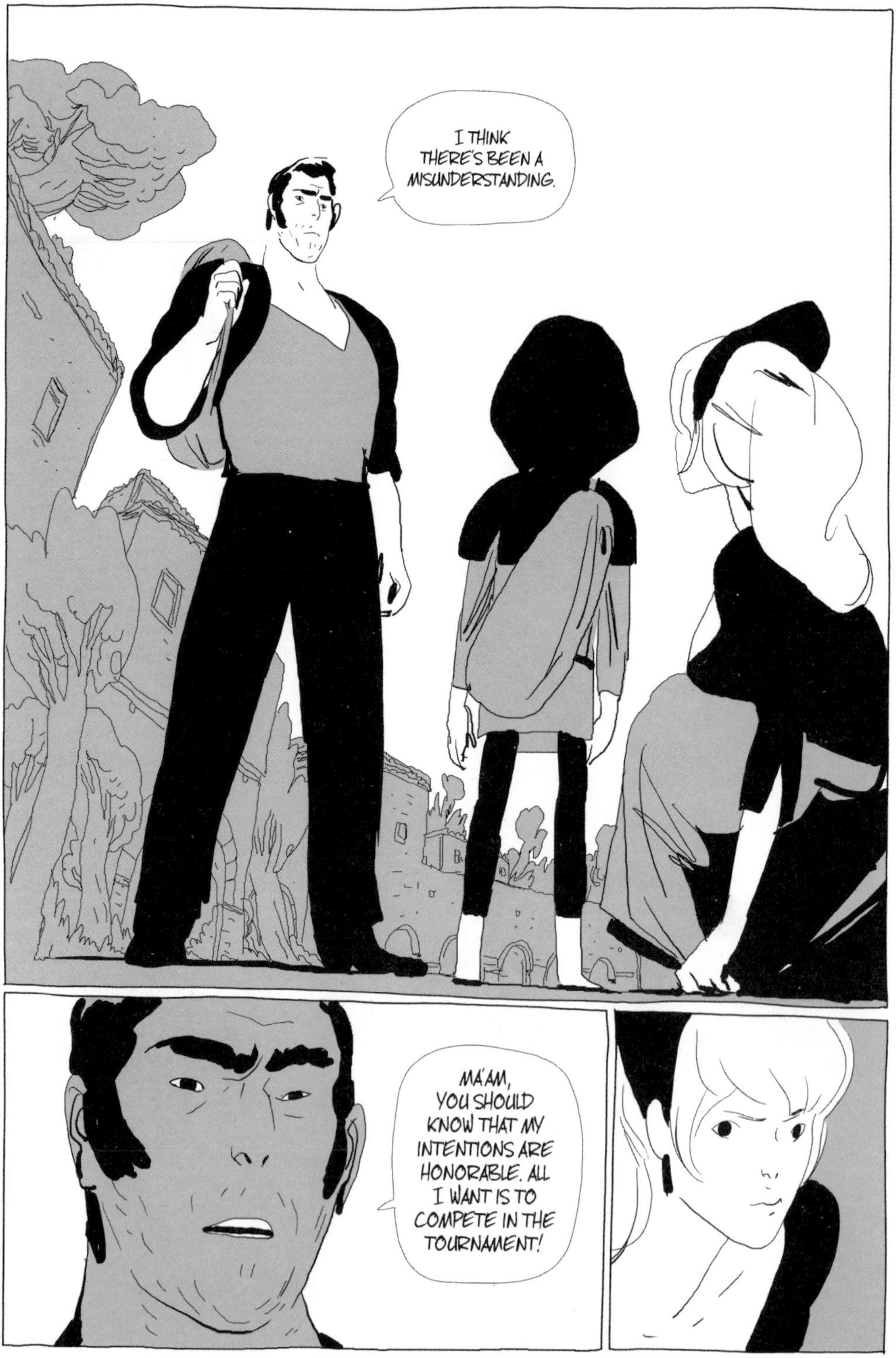
I THINK THERE'S BEEN A MISUNDERSTANDING.
MA'AM, YOU SHOULD KNOW THAT MY INTENTIONS ARE HONORABLE. ALL I WANT IS TO COMPETE IN THE TOURNAMENT!

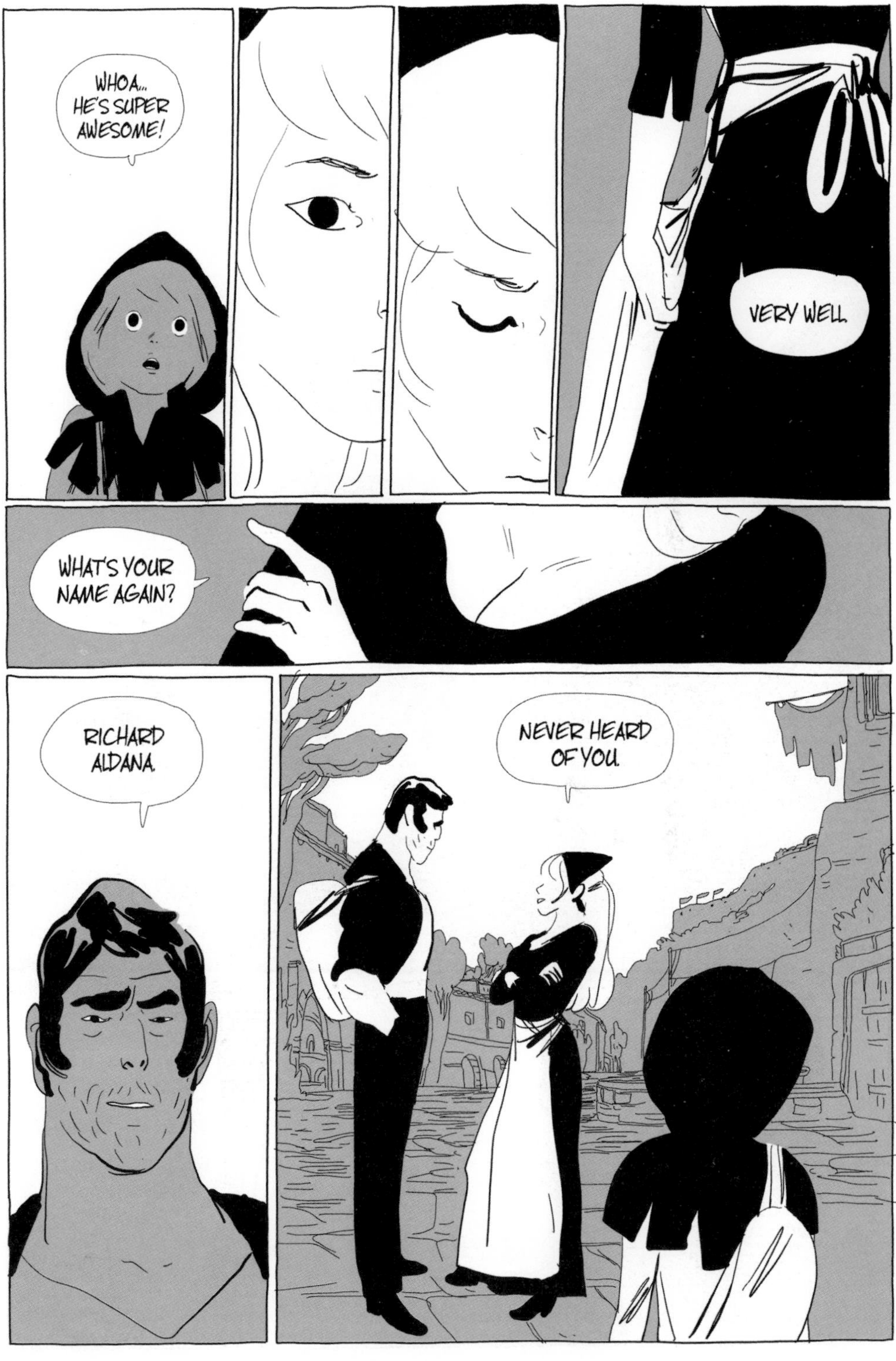
WHOA... HE'S SUPER AWESOME!
VERY WELL.
WHAT'S YOUR NAME AGAIN?
RICHARD ALDANA.
NEVER HEARD OF YOU.

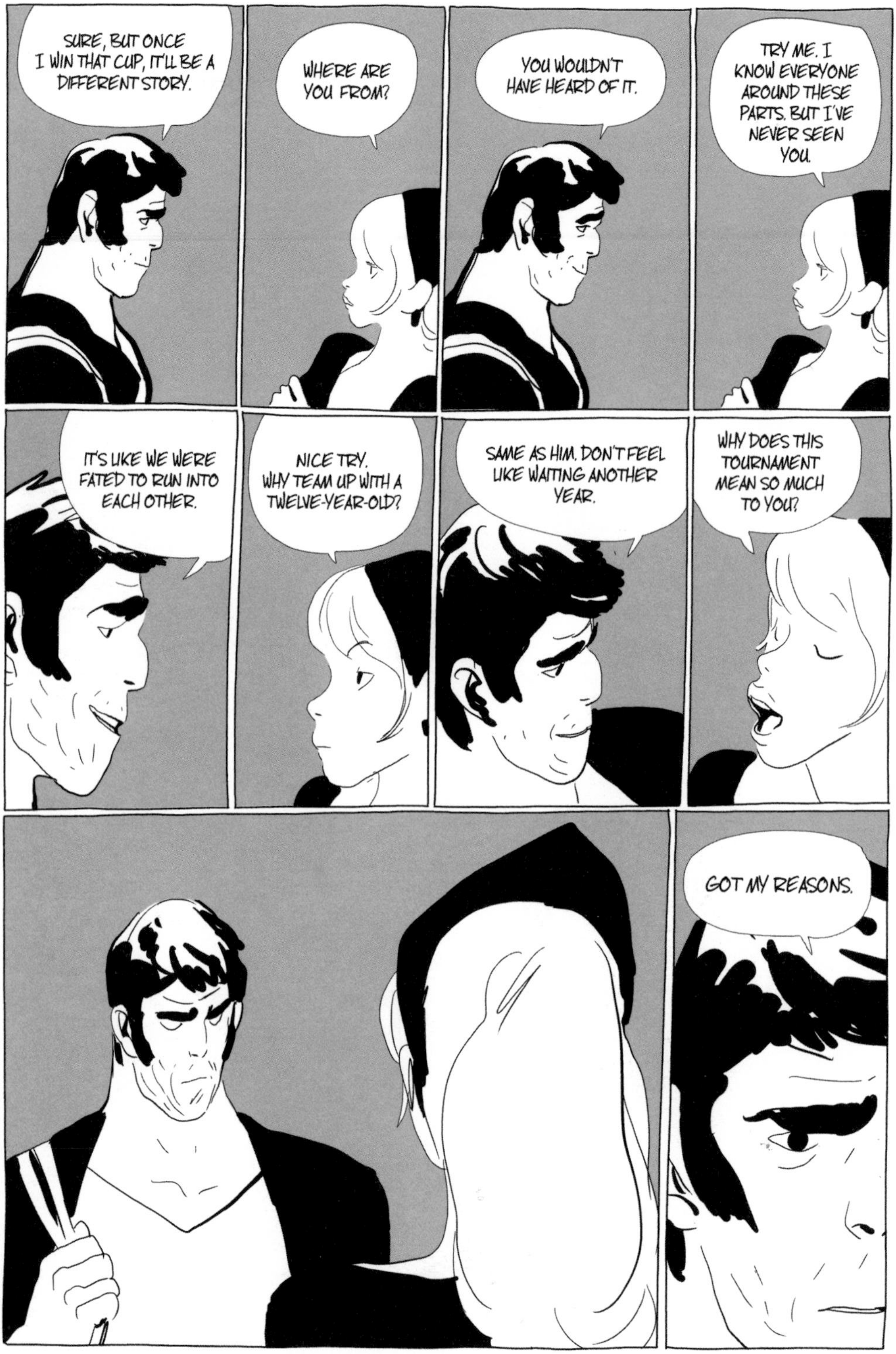
SURE, BUT ONCE I WIN THAT CUP, IT'LL BE A DIFFERENT STORY.
WHERE ARE YOU FROM?
YOU WOULDN'T HAVE HEARD OF IT.
TRY ME. I KNOW EVERYONE AROUND THESE PARTS. BUT I'VE NEVER SEEN YOU.
IT'S LIKE WE WERE FATED TO RUN INTO EACH OTHER.
NICE TRY. WHY TEAM UP WITH A TWELVE-YEAR-OLD?
SAME AS HIM. DON'T FEEL LIKE WAITING ANOTHER YEAR.
WHY DOES THIS TOURNAMENT MEAN SO MUCH TO YOU?
GOT MY REASONS.

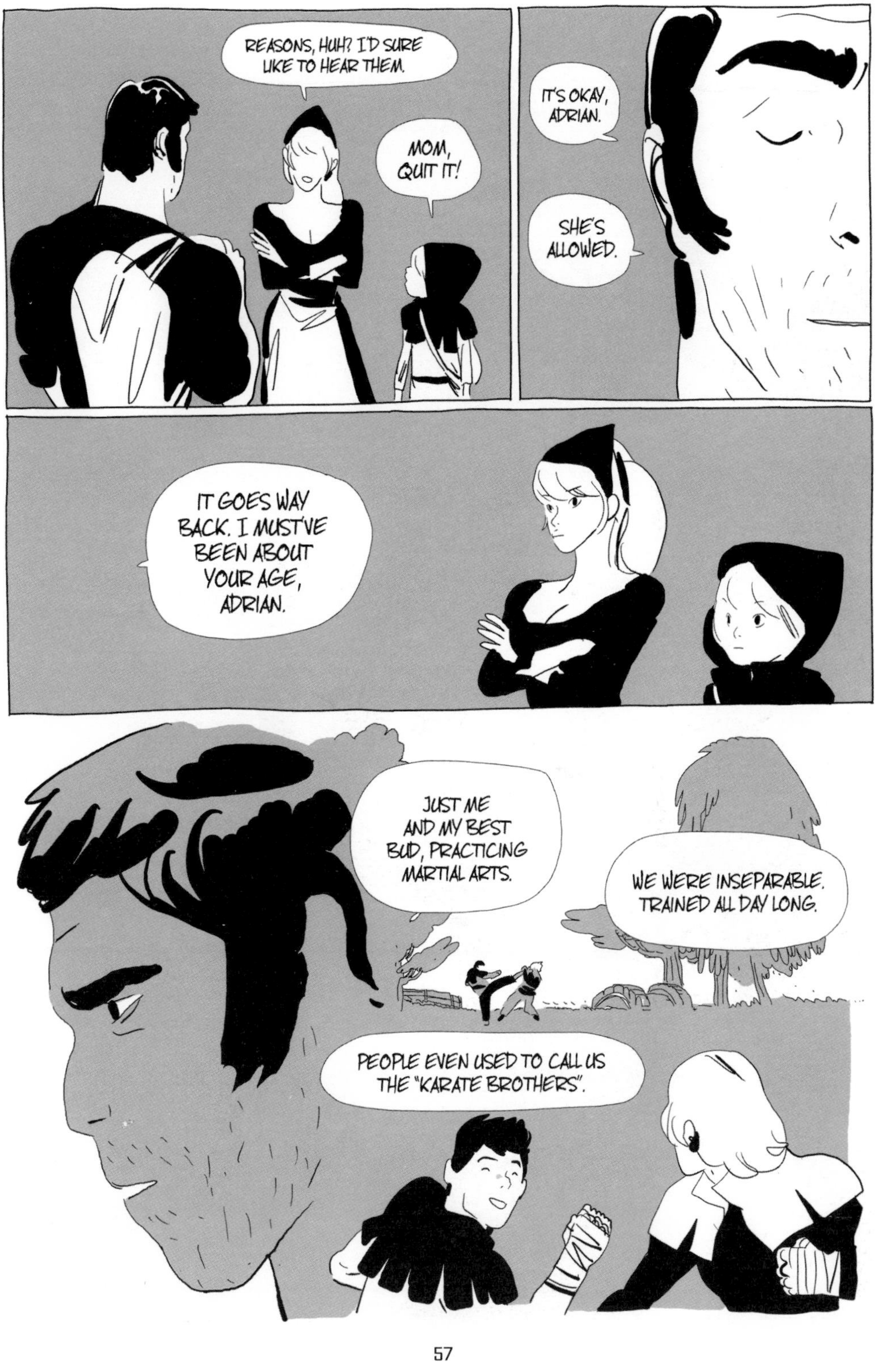
REASONS, HUH? I'D SURE LIKE TO HEAR THEM.
MOM, QUIT IT!
IT'S OKAY, ADRIAN.
SHE'S ALLOWED.
IT GOES WAY BACK. I MUST'VE BEEN ABOUT YOUR AGE, ADRIAN.
JUST ME AND MY BEST BUD, PRACTICING MARTIAL ARTS.
WE WERE INSEPARABLE. TRAINED ALL DAY LONG.
PEOPLE EVEN USED TO CALL US THE "KARATE BROTHERS".

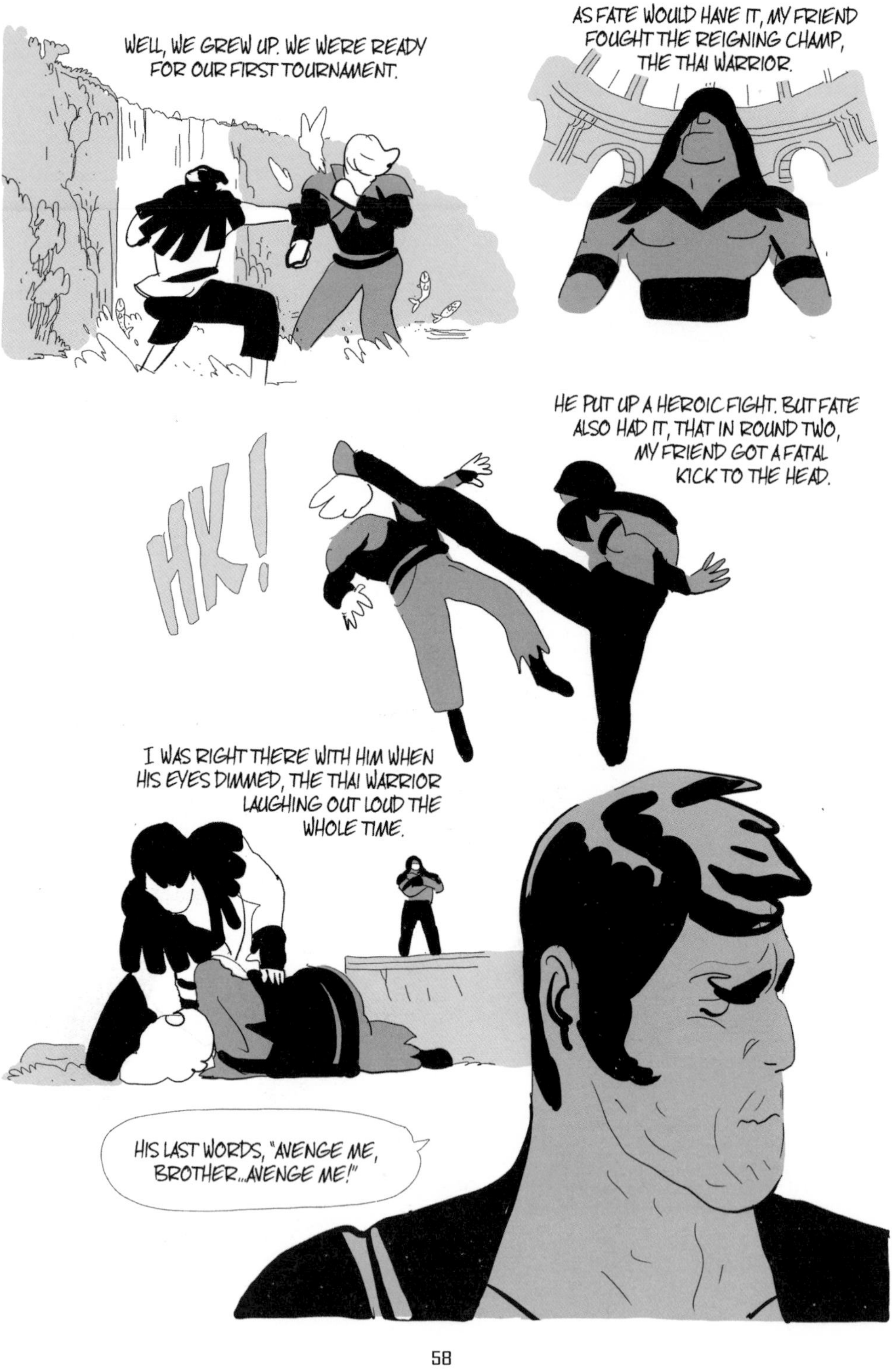
WELL, WE GREW UP. WE WERE READY FOR OUR FIRST TOURNAMENT.
AS FATE WOULD HAVE IT, MY FRIEND FOUGHT THE REIGNING CHAMP, THE THAI WARRIOR.
HK!
HE PUT UP A HEROIC FIGHT. BUT FATE ALSO HAD IT, THAT IN ROUND TWO, MY FRIEND GOT A FATAL KICK TO THE HEAD.
I WAS RIGHT THERE WITH HIM WHEN HIS EYES DIMMED, THE THAI WARRIOR LAUGHING OUT LOUD THE WHOLE TIME.
HIS LAST WORDS, "AVENGE ME, BROTHER...AVENGE ME!"

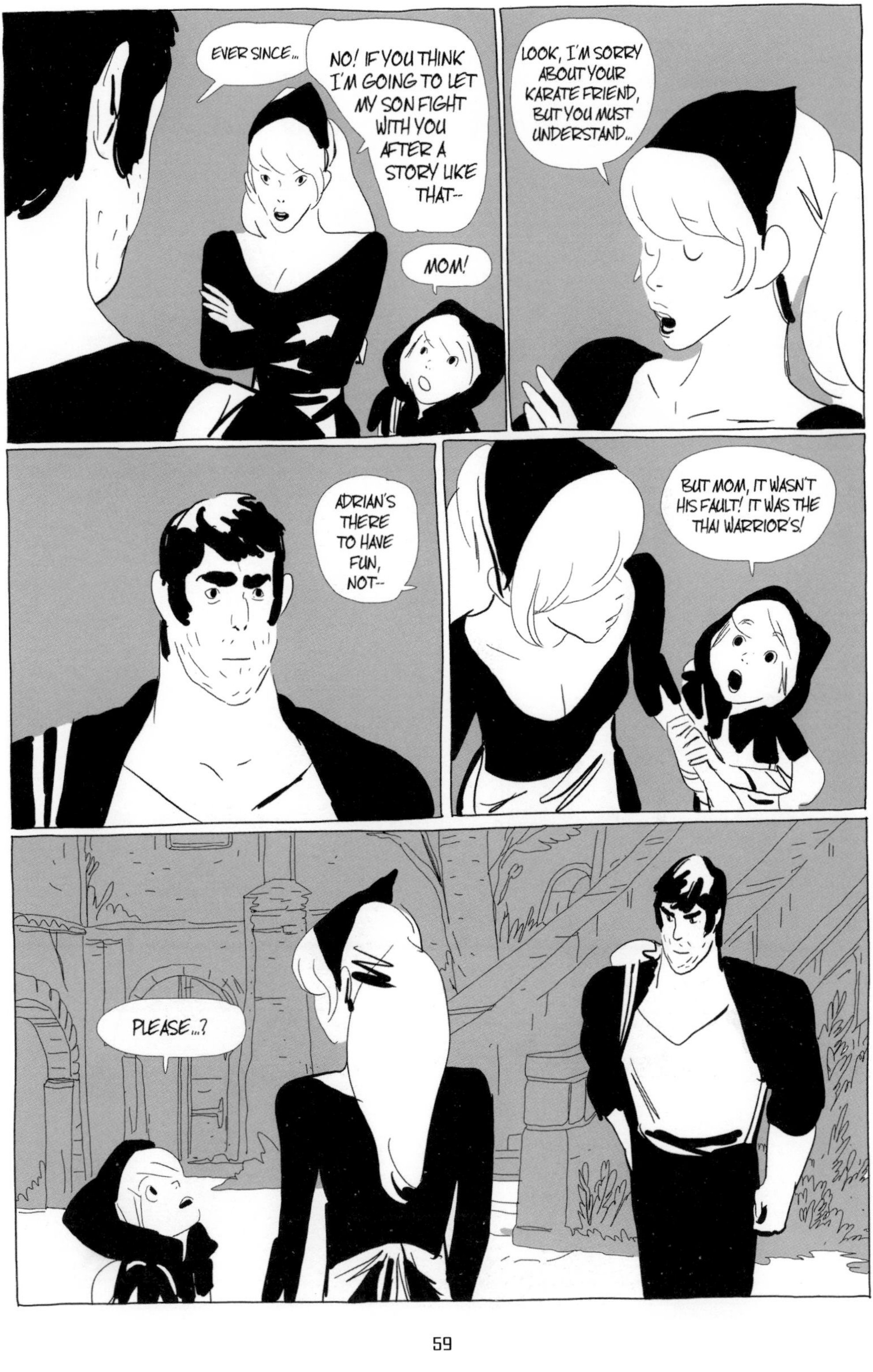
EVER SINCE...
NO! IF YOU THINK I'M GOING TO LET MY SON FIGHT WITH YOU AFTER A STORY LIKE THAT--
MOM!
LOOK, I'M SORRY ABOUT YOUR KARATE FRIEND, BUT YOU MUST UNDERSTAND...
ADRIAN'S THERE TO HAVE FUN, NOT--
BUT MOM, IT WASN'T HIS FAULT! IT WAS THE THAI WARRIOR'S!
PLEASE...?

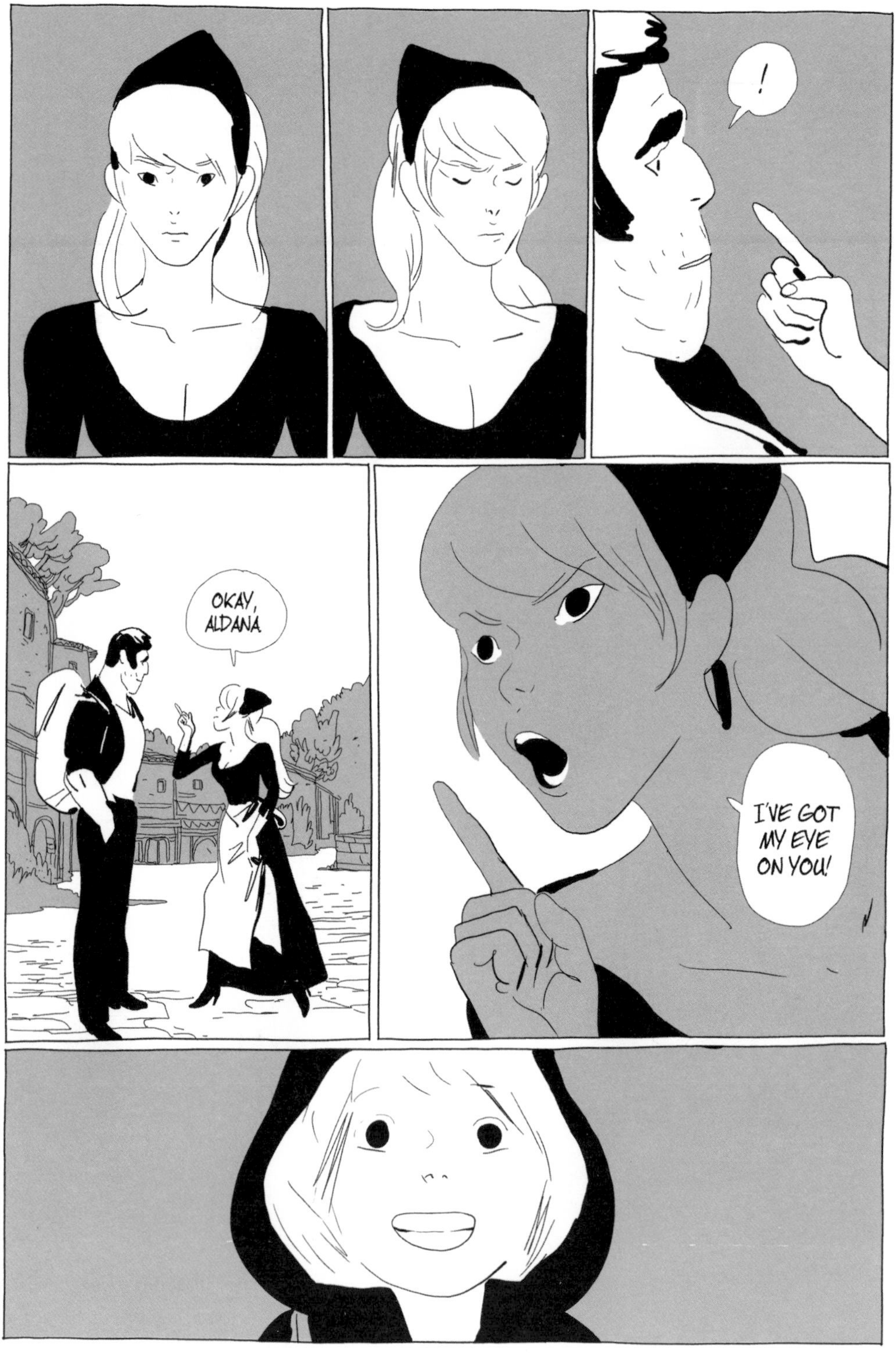
!
OKAY, ALDANA
I'VE GOT MY EYE ON YOU!

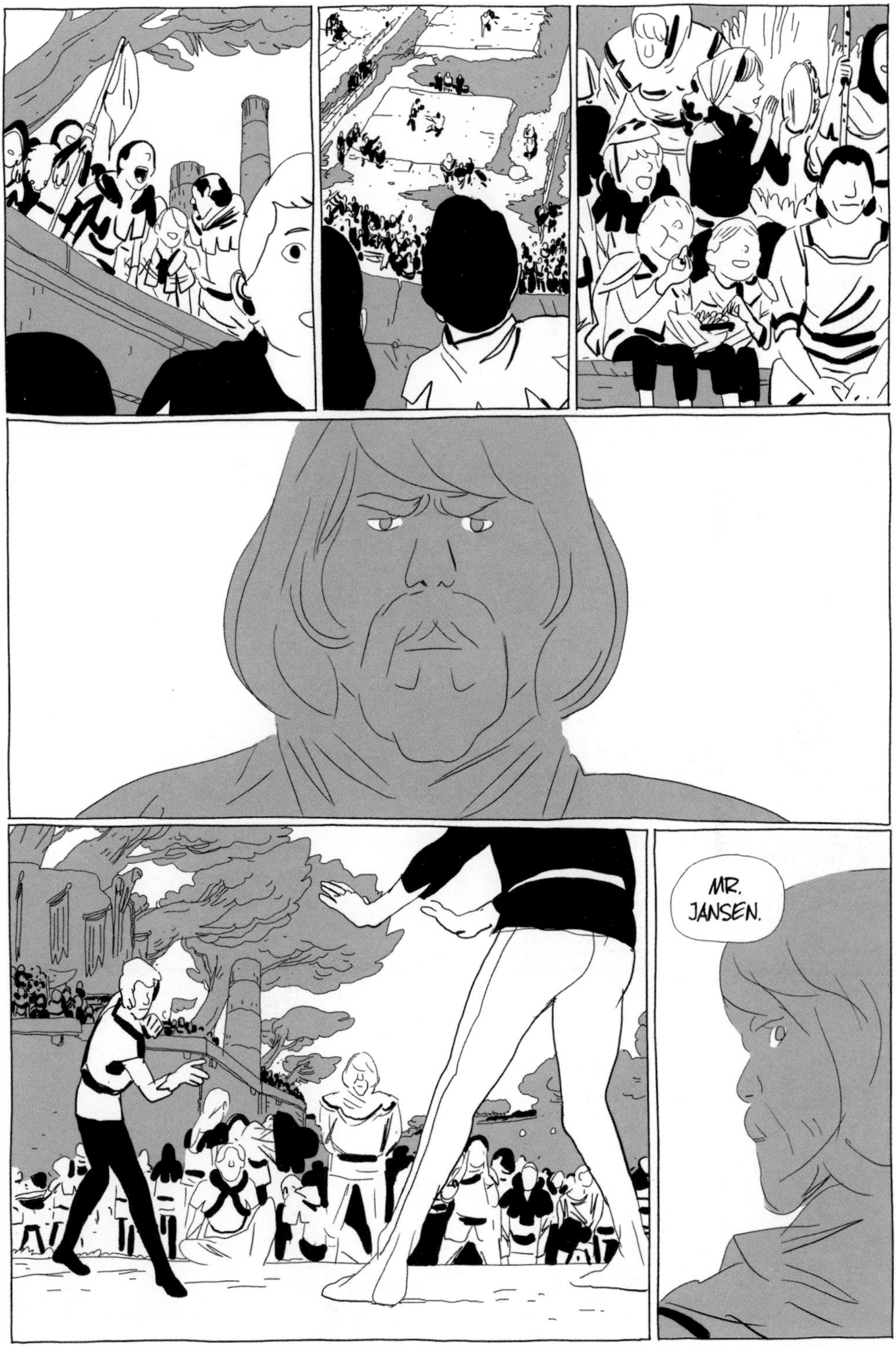
MR. JANSEN.

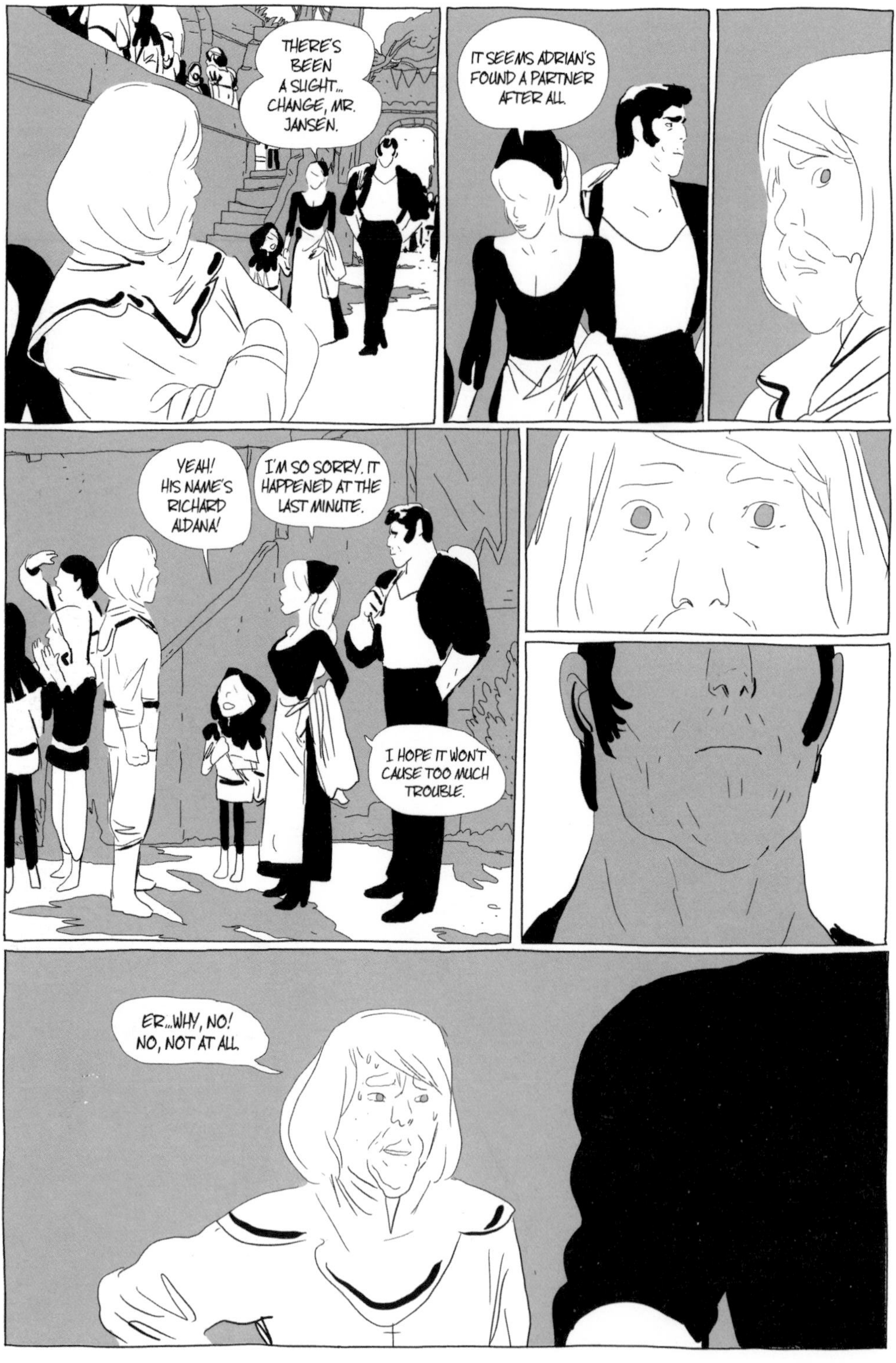
THERE'S BEEN A SLIGHT... CHANGE, MR. JANSEN.
IT SEEMS ADRIAN'S FOUND A PARTNER AFTER ALL.
YEAH! HIS NAME'S RICHARD ALDANA!
I'M SO SORRY. IT HAPPENED AT THE LAST MINUTE.
I HOPE IT WON'T CAUSE TOO MUCH TROUBLE.
ER...WHY, NO! NO, NOT AT ALL.

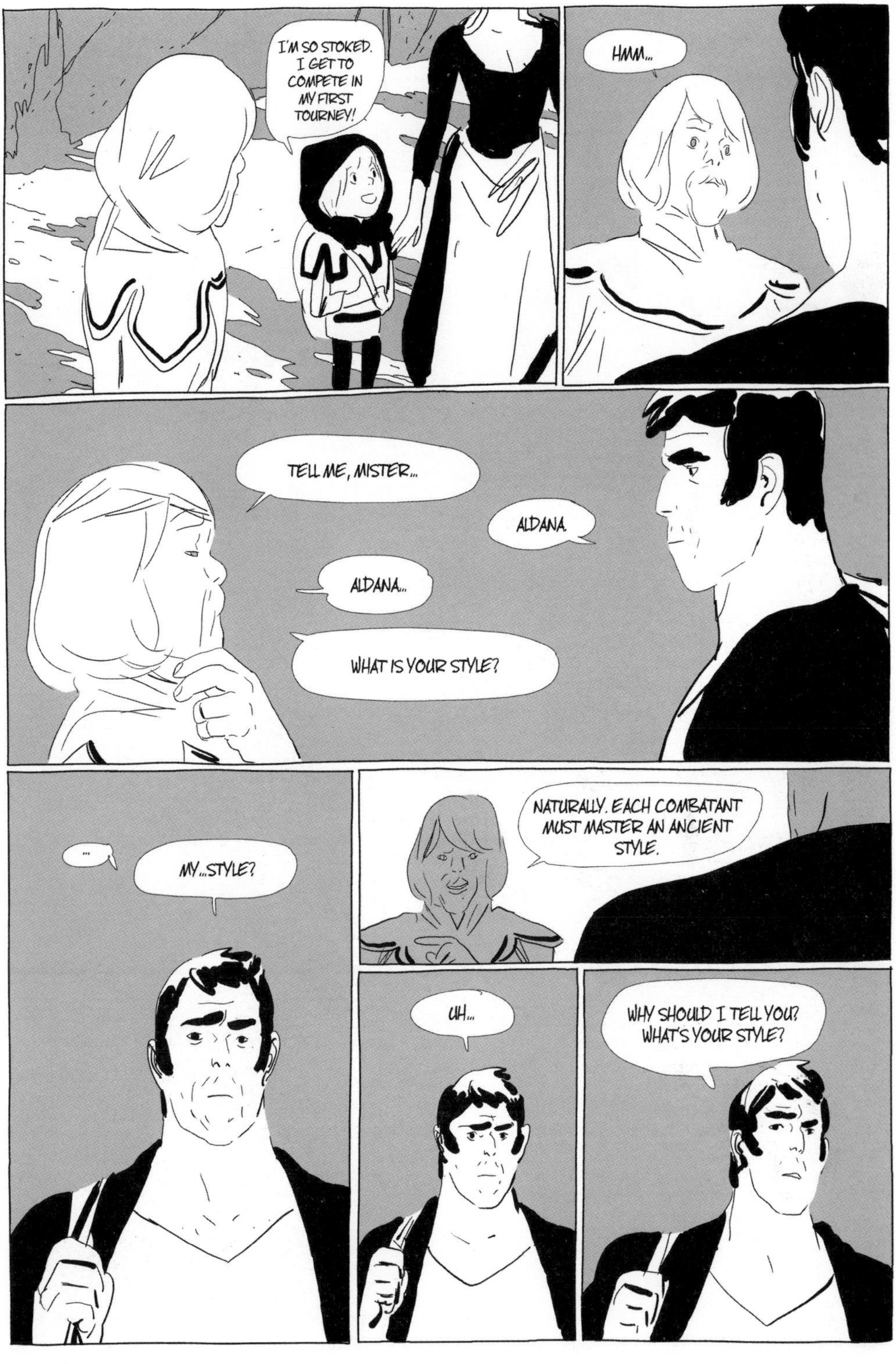
I'M SO STOKED. I GET TO COMPETE IN MY FIRST TOURNEY!
HMM...
TELL ME, MISTER...
ALDANA.
ALDANA...
WHAT IS YOUR STYLE?
...
MY...STYLE?
NATURALLY. EACH COMBATANT MUST MASTER AN ANCIENT STYLE.
UH...
WHY SHOULD I TELL YOU? WHAT'S YOUR STYLE?

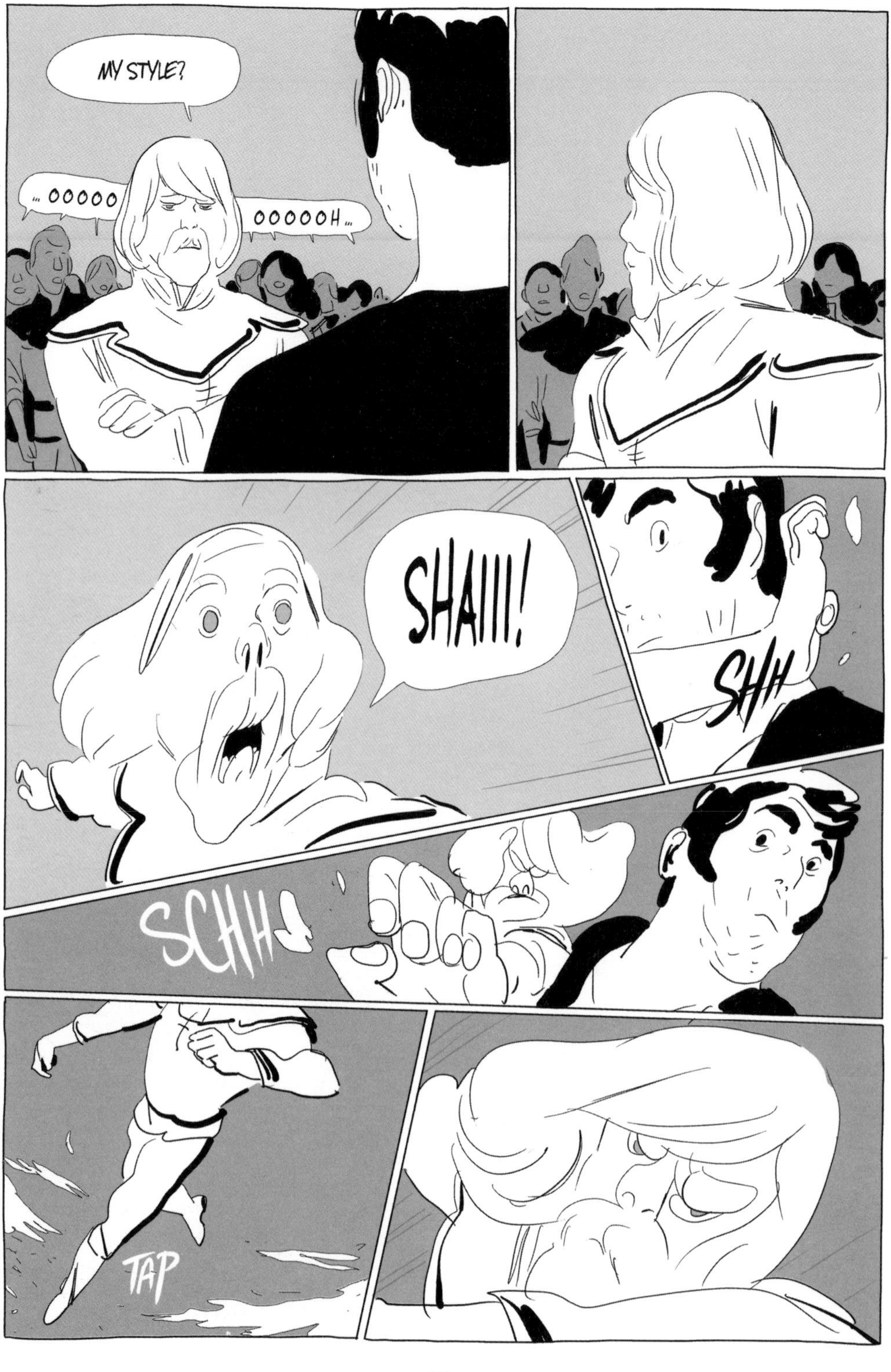
MY STYLE?
...OOOOO
OOOOOH...
SHAIII!
SHH
SCHH
TAP

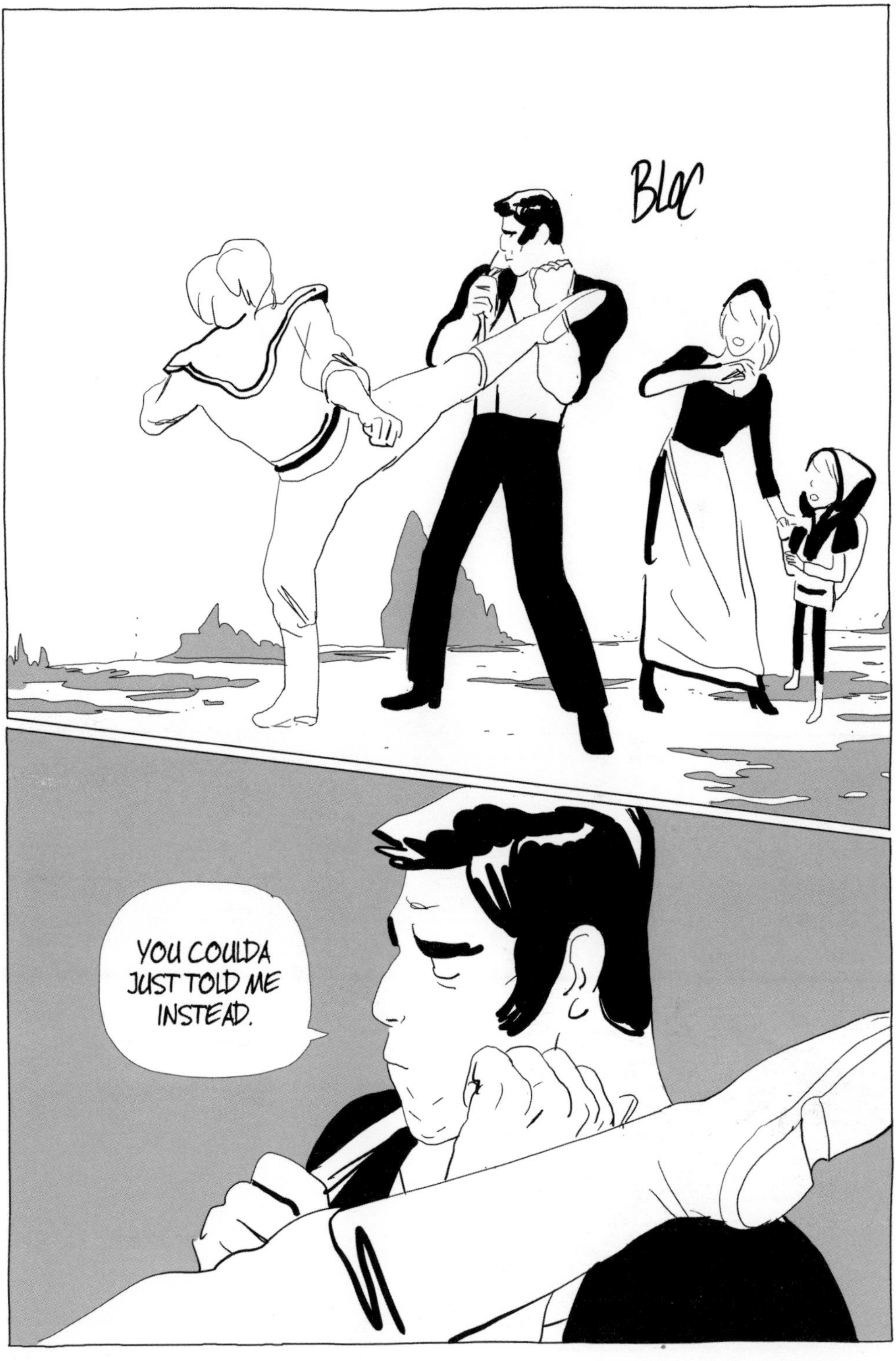
BLOC
YOU COULDA JUST TOLD ME INSTEAD.

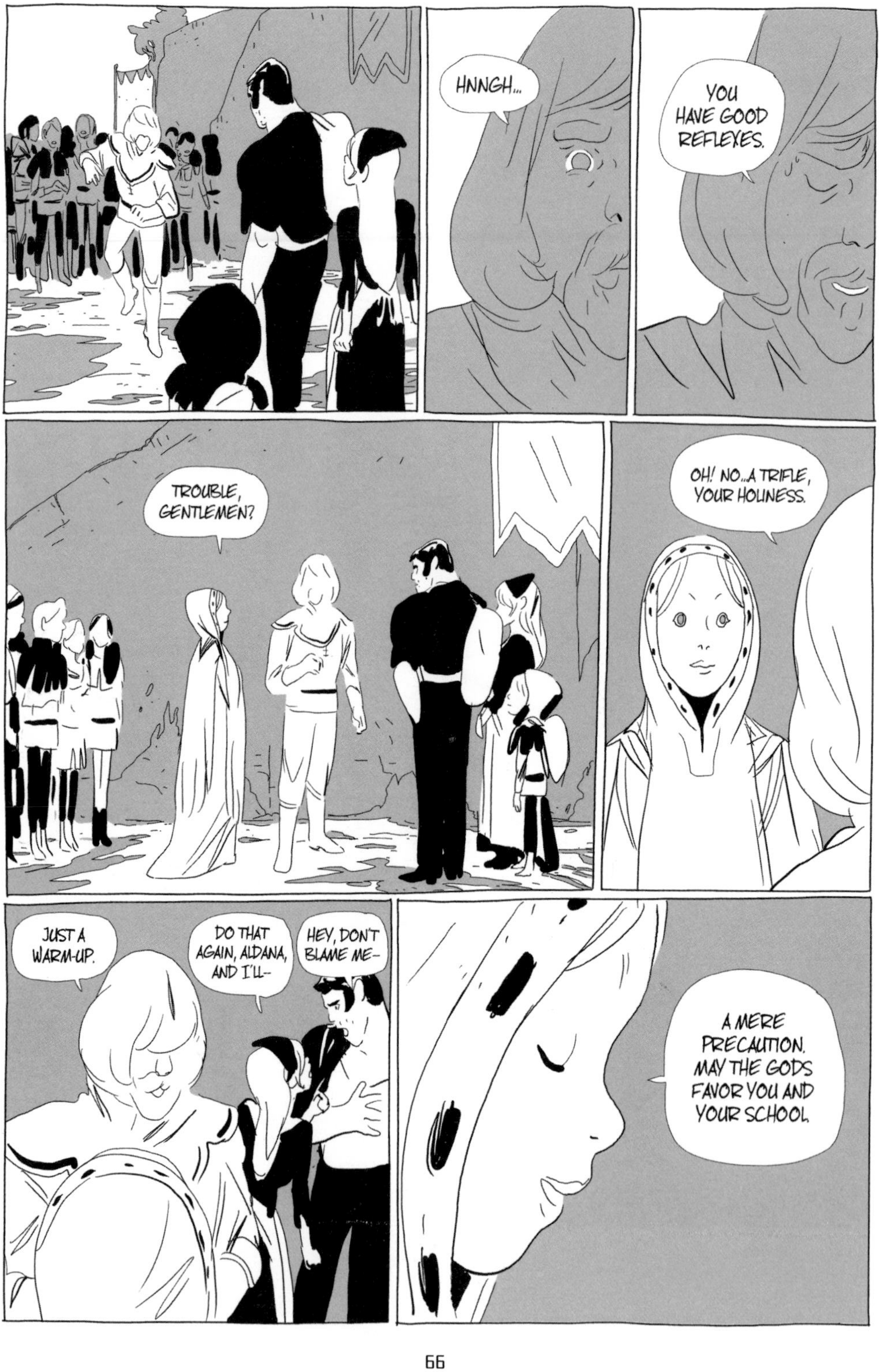
HNNGH...
YOU HAVE GOOD REFLEXES.
TROUBLE, GENTLEMEN?
OH! NO...A TRIFLE, YOUR HOLINESS.
JUST A WARM-UP.
DO THAT AGAIN, ALDANA, AND I'LL--
HEY, DON'T BLAME ME--
A MERE PRECAUTION. MAY THE GODS FAVOR YOU AND YOUR SCHOOL.

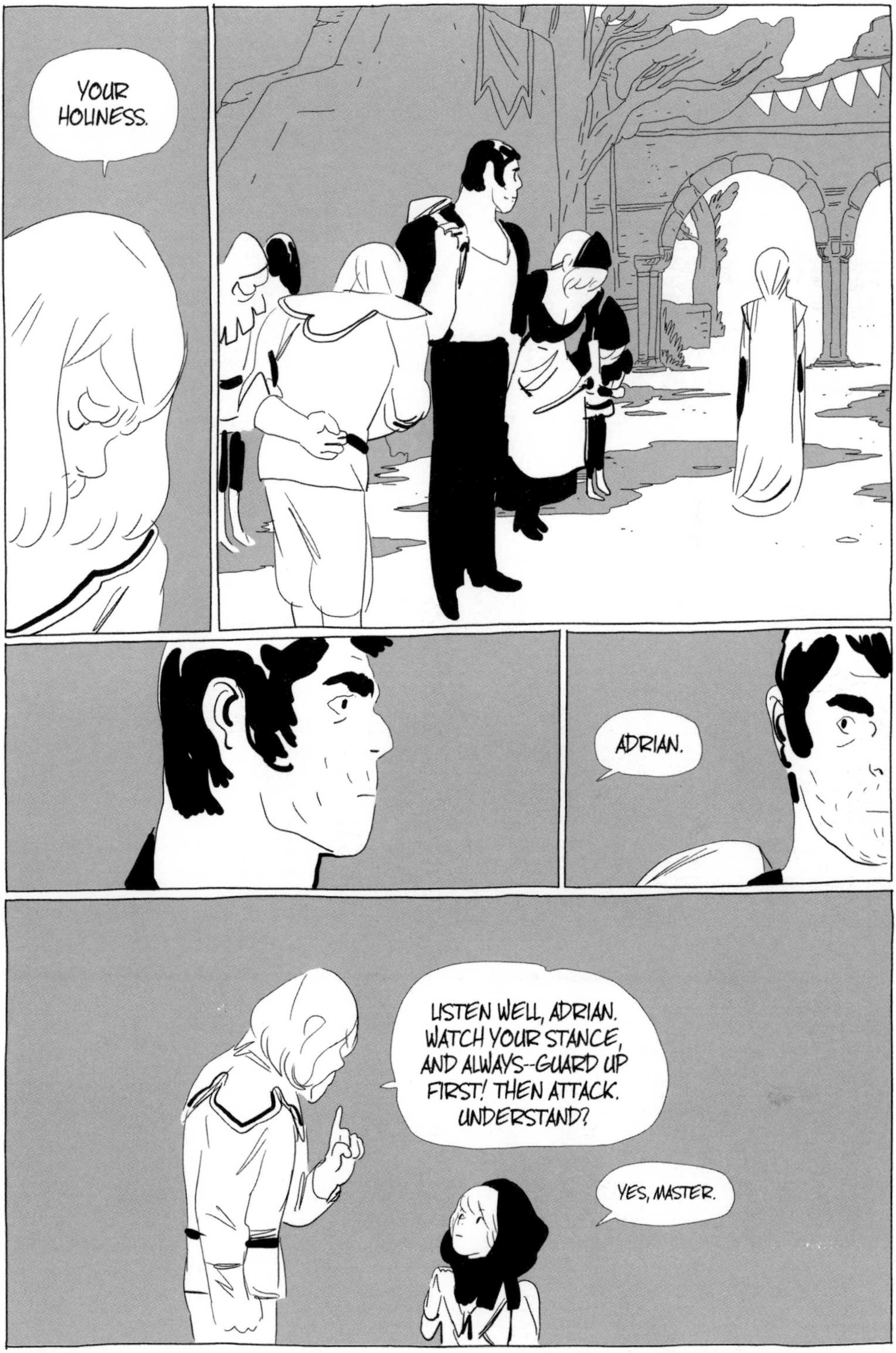
YOUR HOLINESS.
ADRIAN.
LISTEN WELL, ADRIAN. WATCH YOUR STANCE, AND ALWAYS--GUARD UP FIRST! THEN ATTACK. UNDERSTAND?
YES, MASTER.

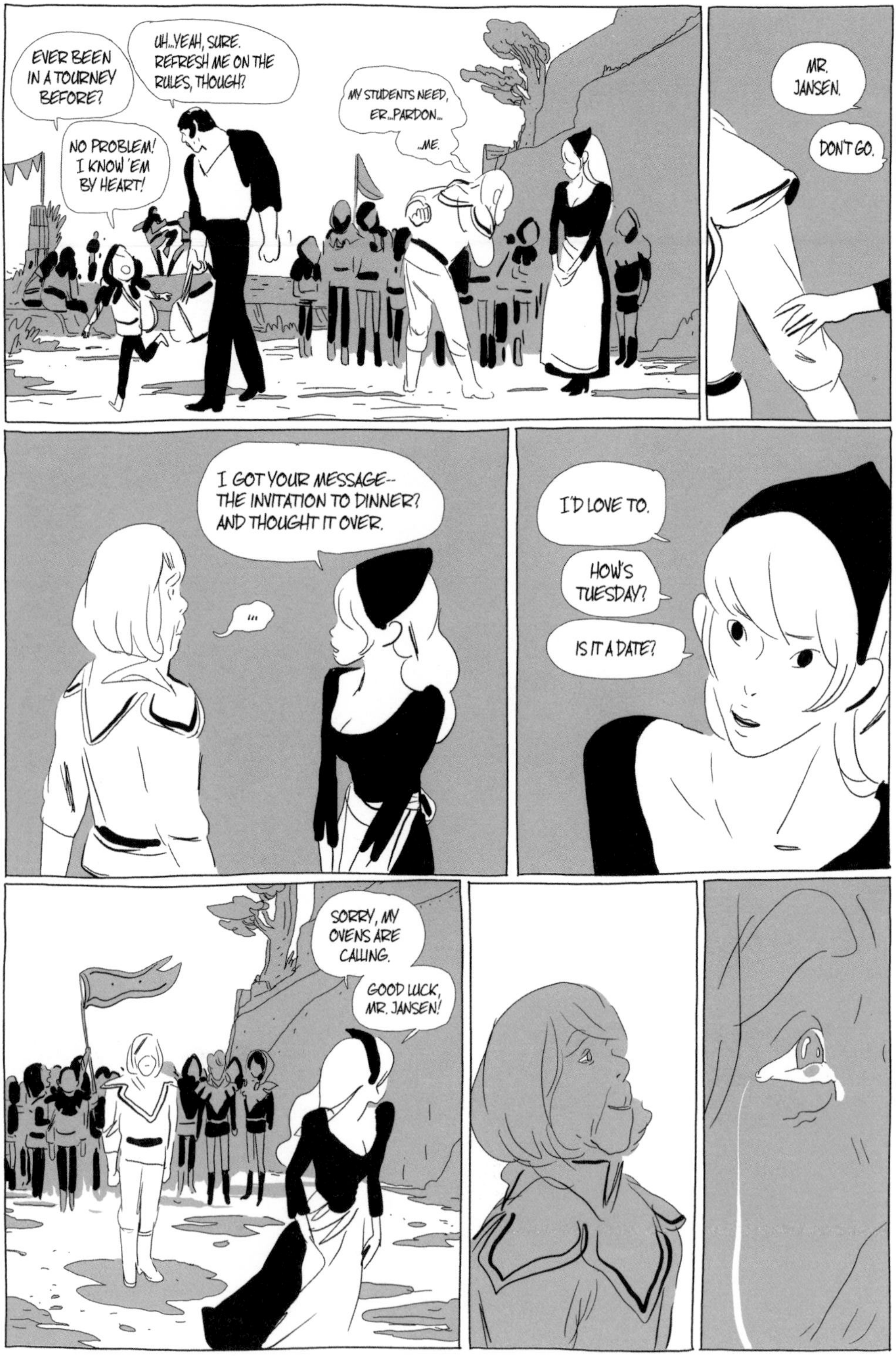
EVER BEEN IN A TOURNEY BEFORE?
UH...YEAH, SURE. REFRESH ME ON THE RULES, THOUGH?
NO PROBLEM! I KNOW 'EM BY HEART!
MY STUDENTS NEED, ER...PARDON...
...ME.
MR. JANSEN.
DON'T GO.
I GOT YOUR MESSAGE-- THE INVITATION TO DINNER? AND THOUGHT IT OVER.
...
I'D LOVE TO.
HOW'S TUESDAY?
IS IT A DATE?
SORRY, MY OVENS ARE CALLING.
GOOD LUCK, MR. JANSEN!

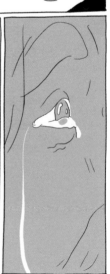

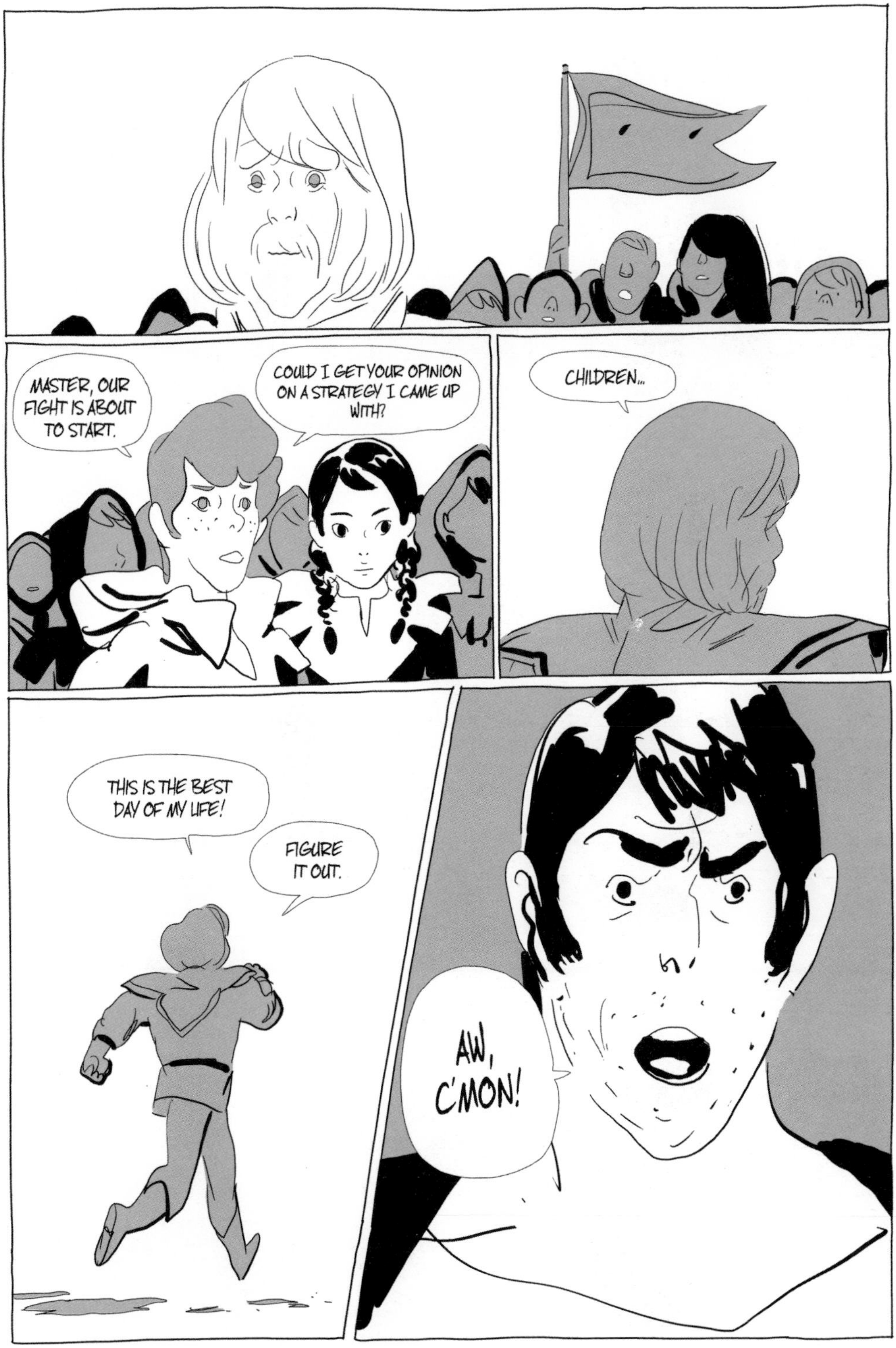
MASTER, OUR FIGHT IS ABOUT TO START.
COULD I GET YOUR OPINION ON A STRATEGY I CAME UP WITH?
CHILDREN...
THIS IS THE BEST DAY OF MY LIFE!
FIGURE IT OUT.
AW, C'MON!

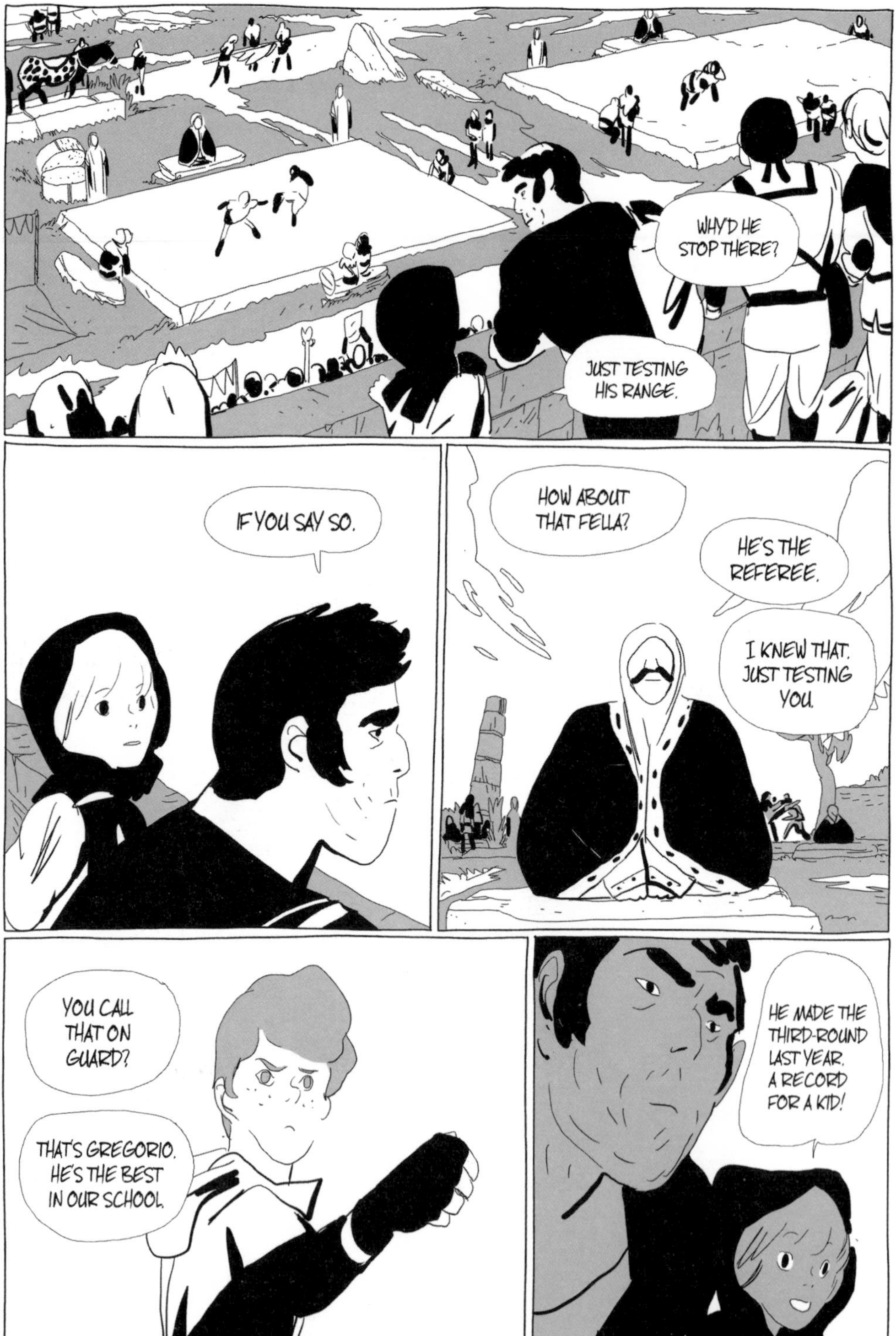
WHY'D HE STOP THERE?
JUST TESTING HIS RANGE.
IF YOU SAY SO.
HOW ABOUT THAT FELLA?
HE'S THE REFEREE.
I KNEW THAT. JUST TESTING YOU.
YOU CALL THAT ON GUARD?
THAT'S GREGORIO. HE'S THE BEST IN OUR SCHOOL.
HE MADE THE THIRD-ROUND LAST YEAR. A RECORD FOR A KID!

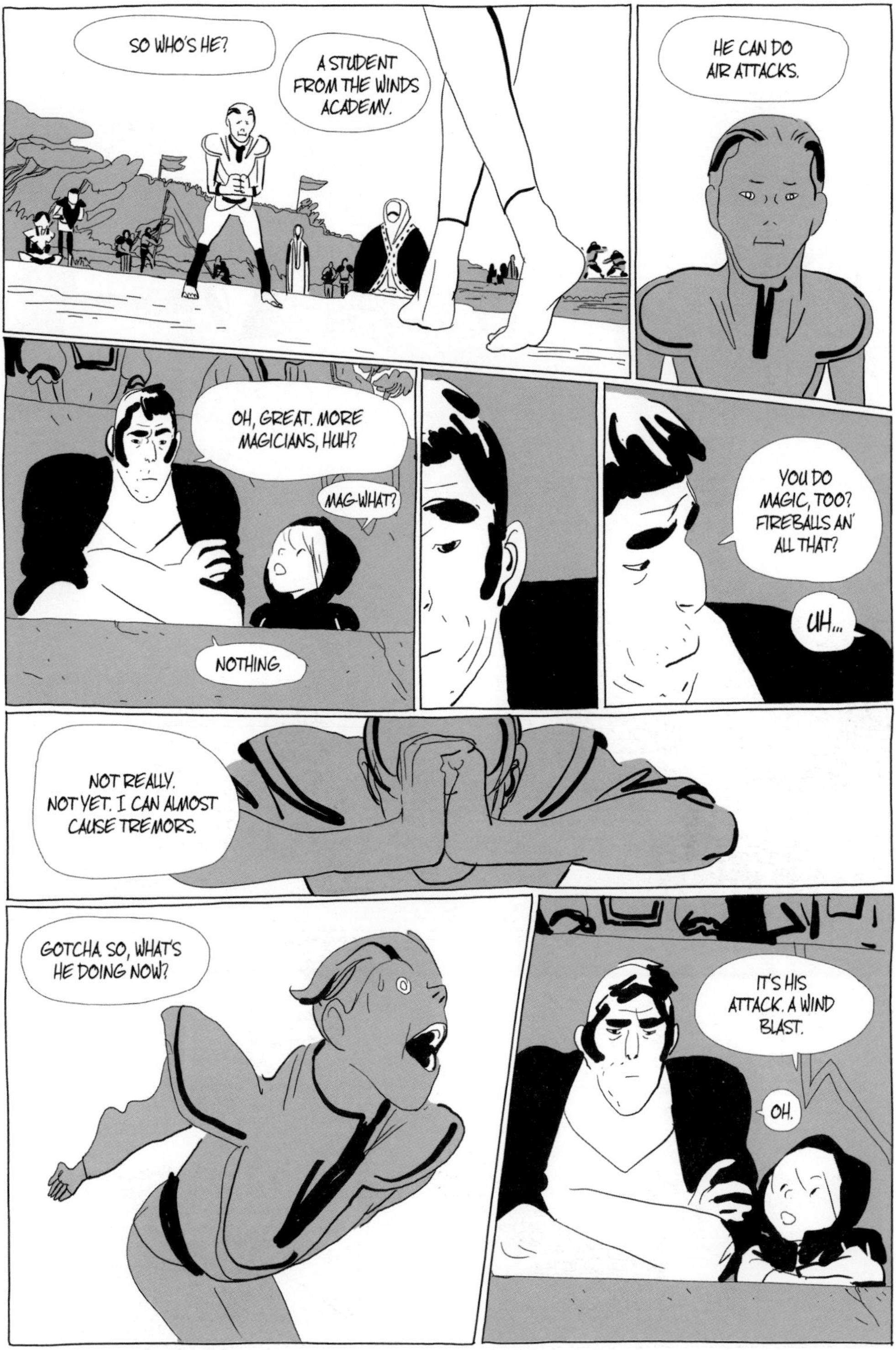
SO WHO'S HE?
A STUDENT FROM THE WINDS ACADEMY.
HE CAN DO AIR ATTACKS.
OH, GREAT. MORE MAGICIANS, HUH?
MAG-WHAT?
NOTHING.
YOU DO MAGIC, TOO? FIREBALLS AN' ALL THAT?
UH...
NOT REALLY. NOT YET. I CAN ALMOST CAUSE TREMORS.
GOTCHA. SO, WHAT'S HE DOING NOW?
IT'S HIS ATTACK. A WIND BLAST.
OH.

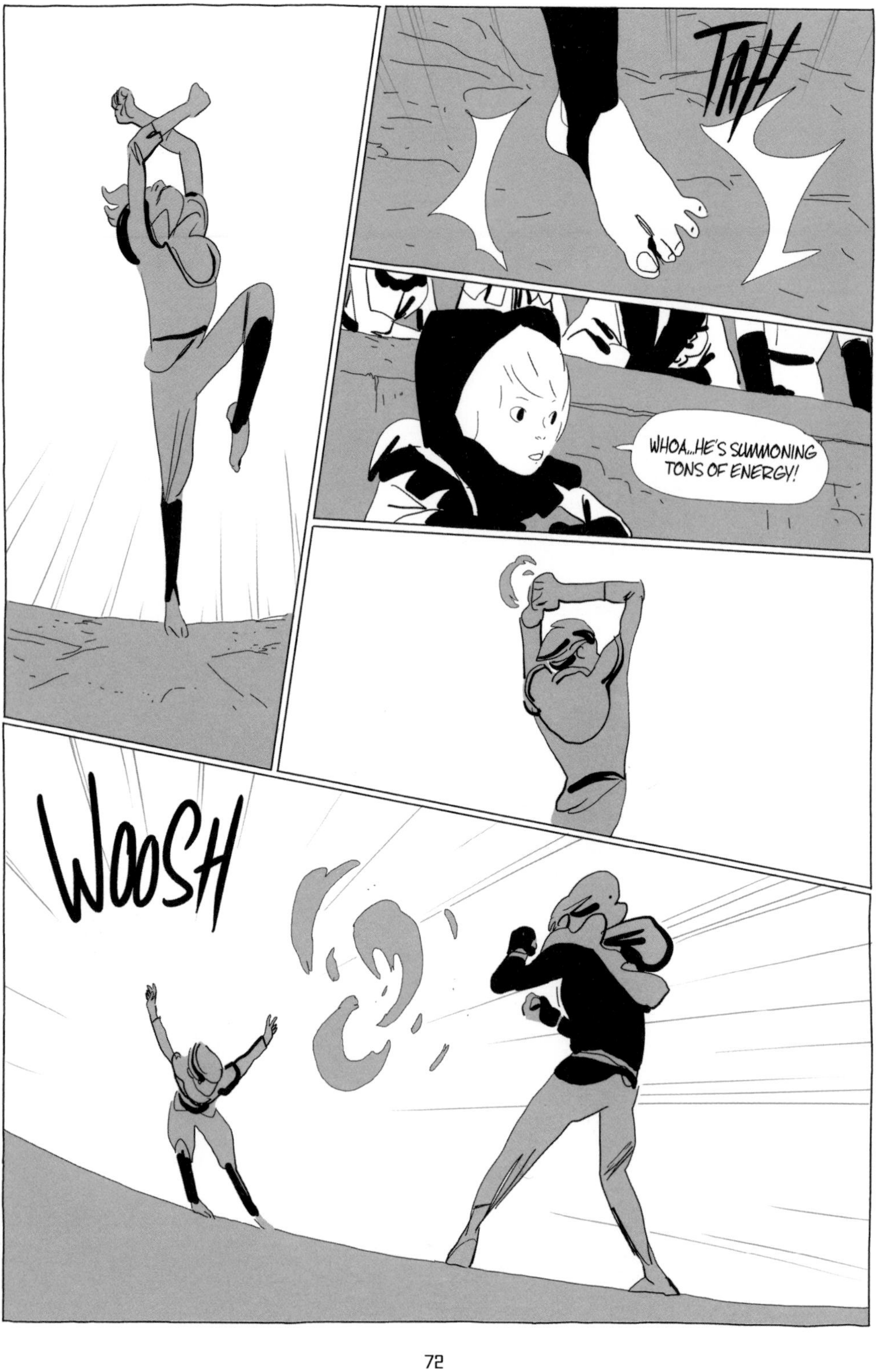
TAH
WHOA...HE'S SUMMONING TONS OF ENERGY!
WOOSH

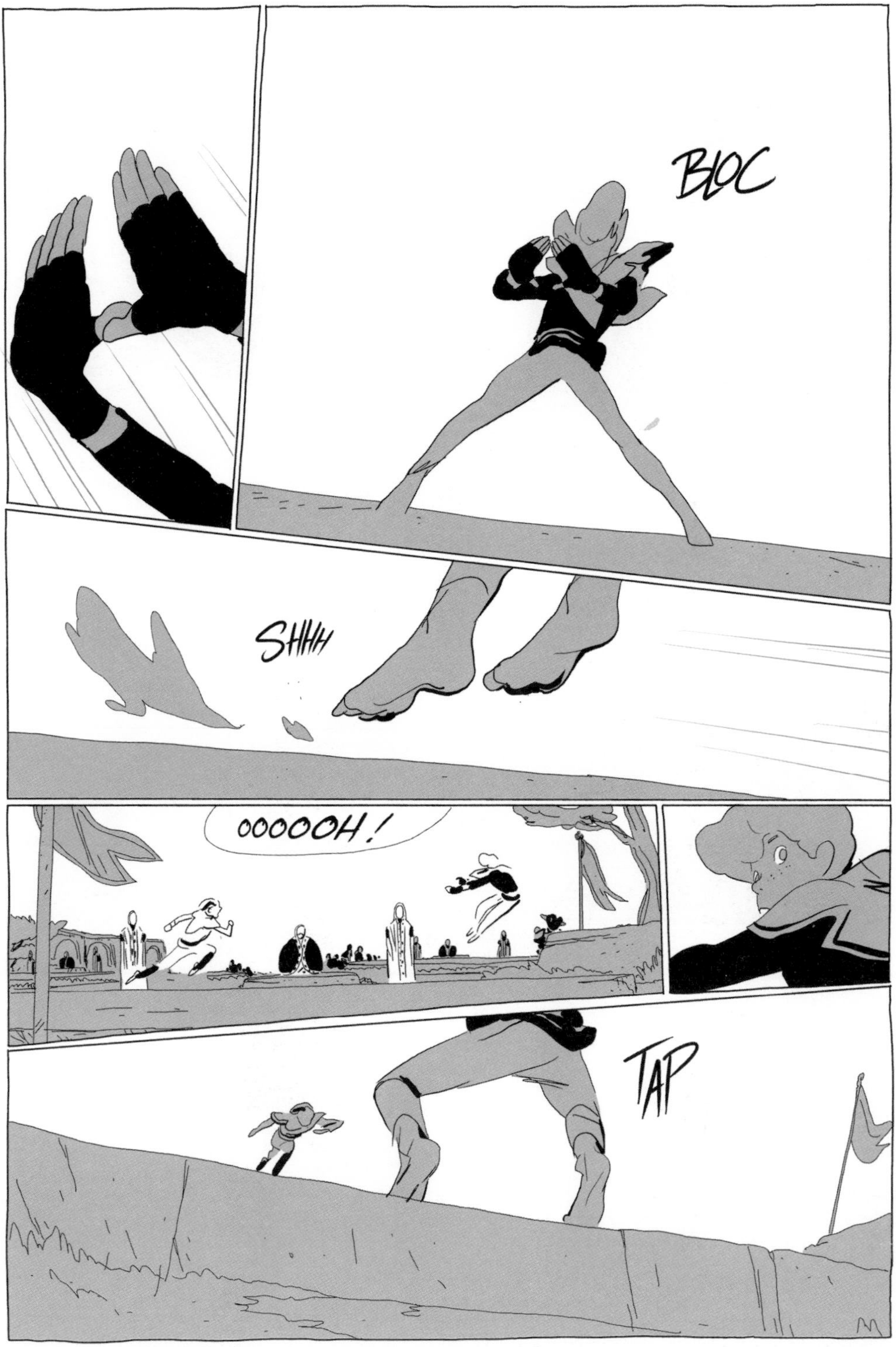
BLOC
SHHH
OOOOOH!
TAP

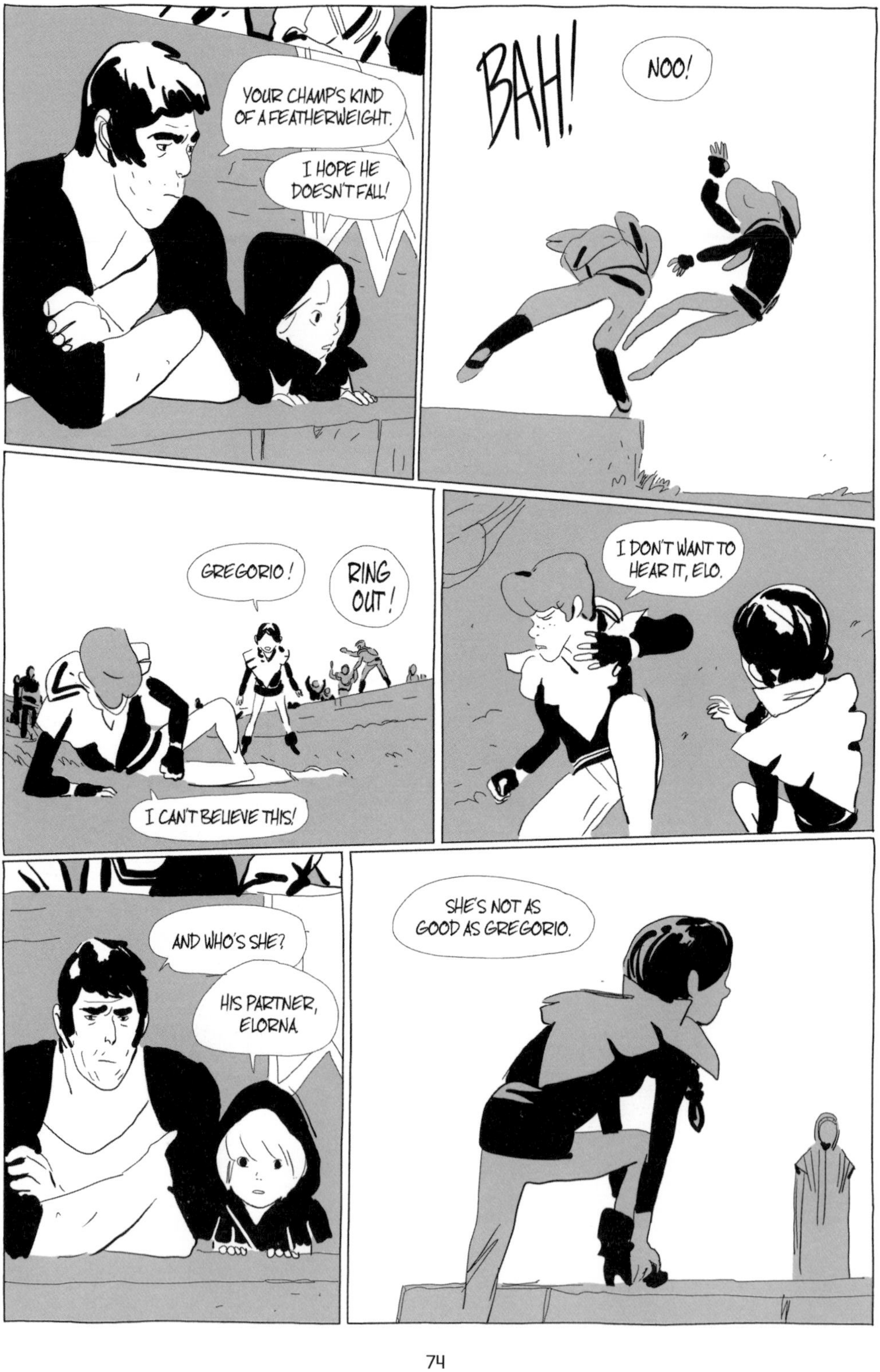
YOUR CHAMP'S KIND OF A FEATHERWEIGHT.
I HOPE HE DOESN'T FALL!
BAH!
NOO!
GREGORIO!
RING OUT!
I CAN'T BELIEVE THIS!
I DON'T WANT TO HEAR IT, ELO.
AND WHO'S SHE?
HIS PARTNER, ELORNA.
SHE'S NOT AS GOOD AS GREGORIO.

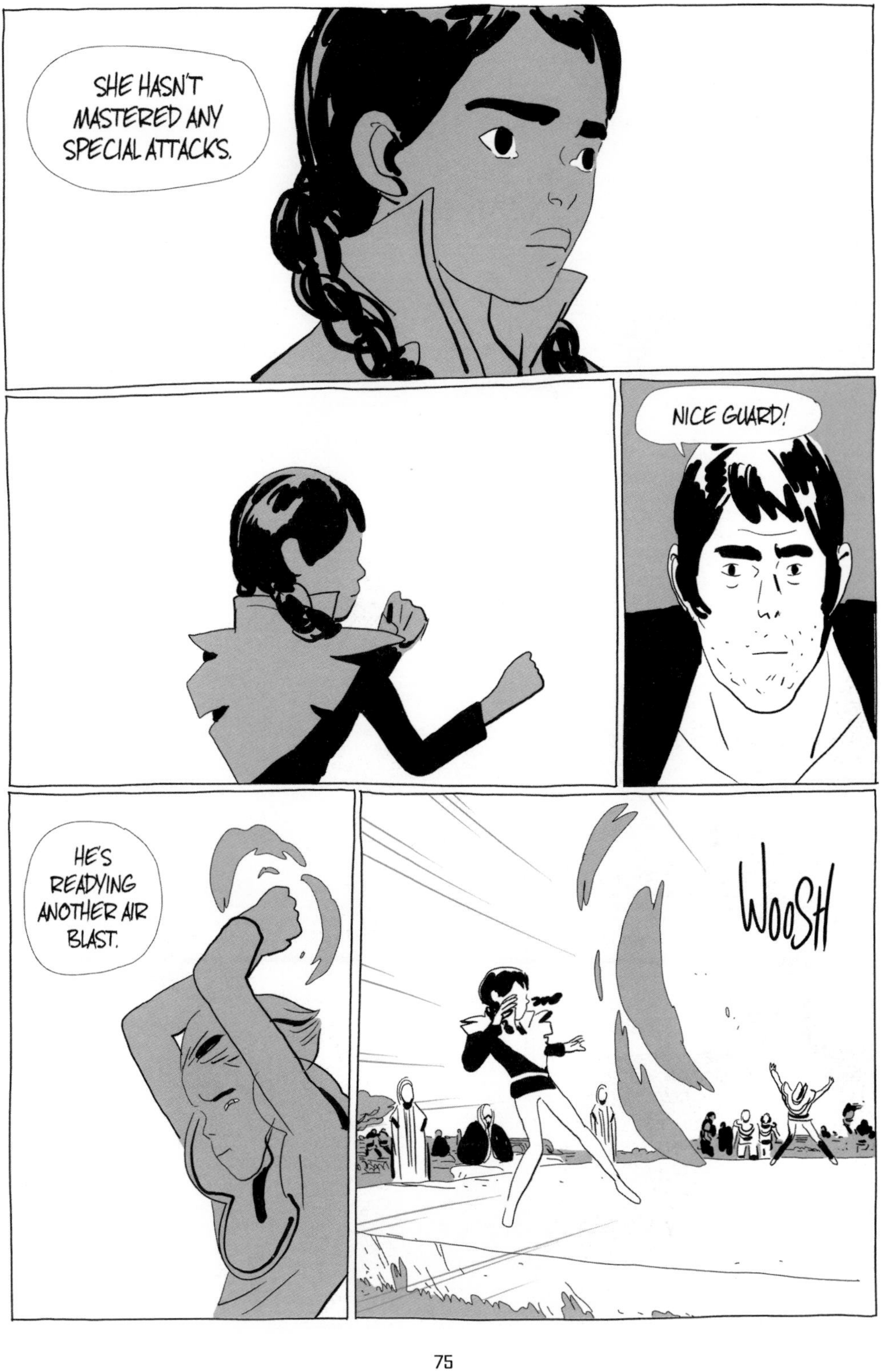
SHE HASN'T MASTERED ANY SPECIAL ATTACKS.
NICE GUARD!
HE'S READYING ANOTHER AIR BLAST.
WOOSH

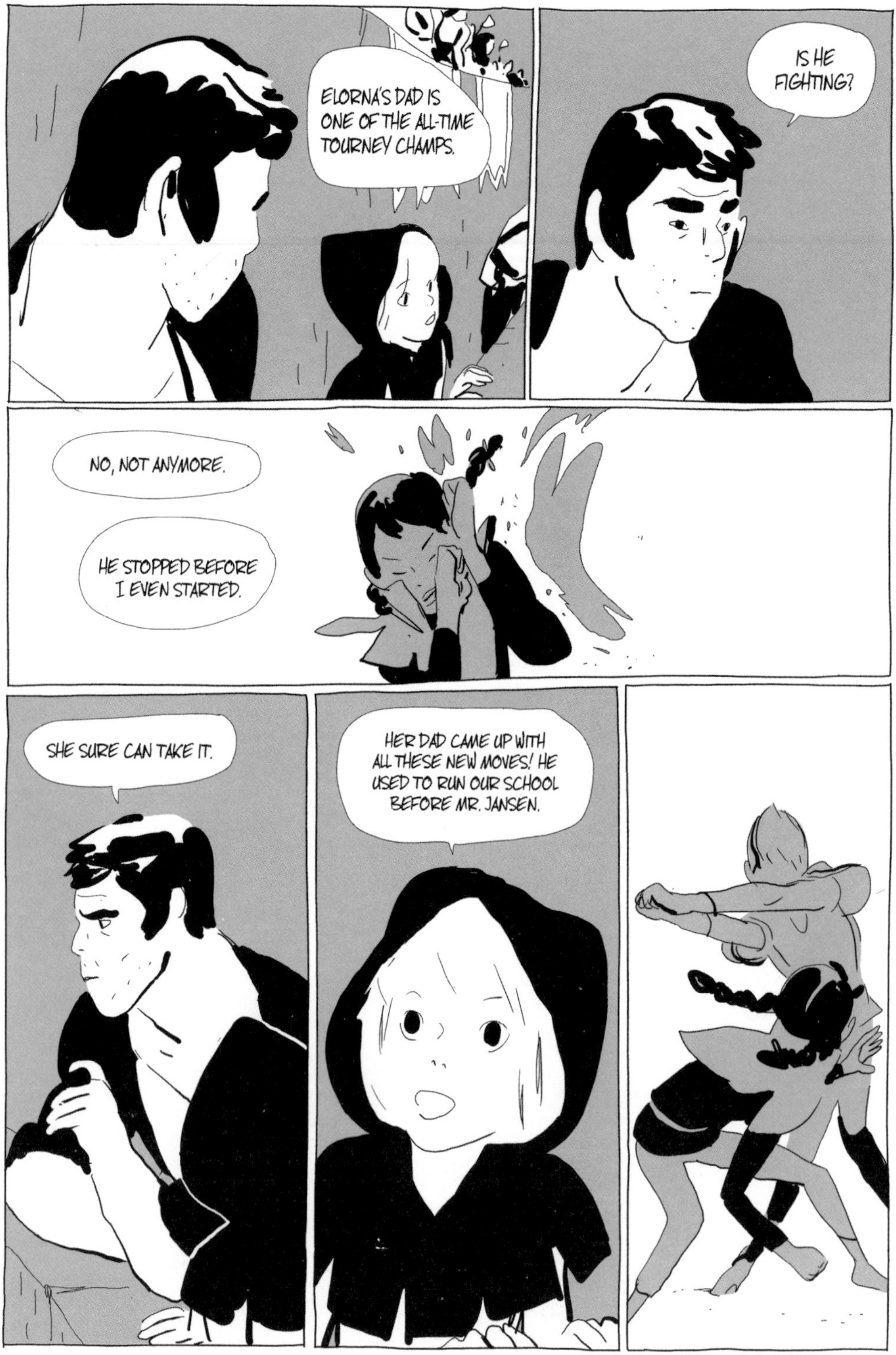
ELORNA'S DAD IS ONE OF THE ALL-TIME TOURNEY CHAMPS.
IS HE FIGHTING?
NO, NOT ANYMORE.
HE STOPPED BEFORE I EVEN STARTED.
SHE SURE CAN TAKE IT.
HER DAD CAME UP WITH ALL THESE NEW MOVES! HE USED TO RUN OUR SCHOOL BEFORE MR. JANSEN.

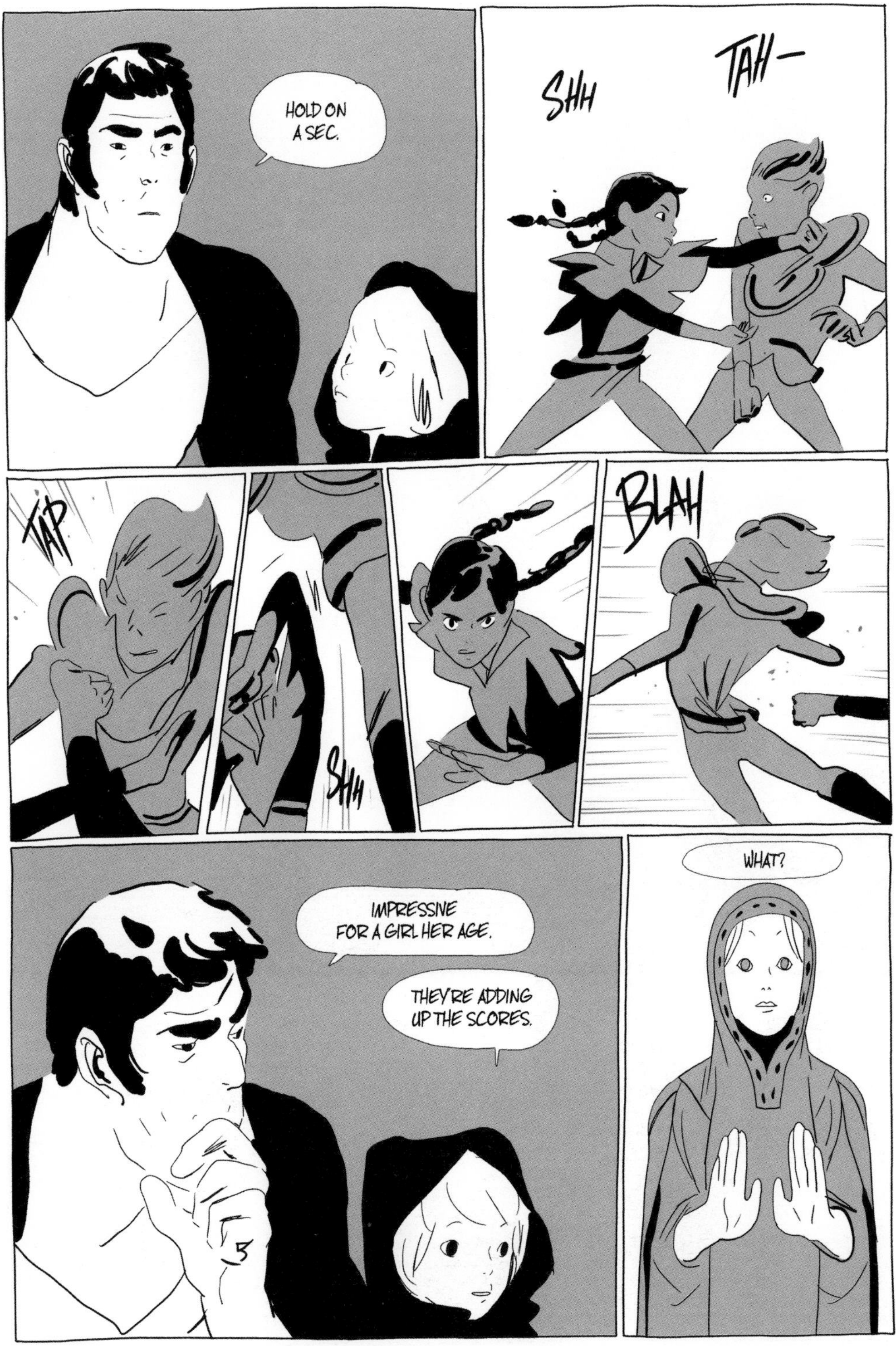
HOLD ON A SEC.
SHH
TAH–
TAP
SHH
BLAH
IMPRESSIVE FOR A GIRL HER AGE.
THEY'RE ADDING UP THE SCORES.
WHAT?

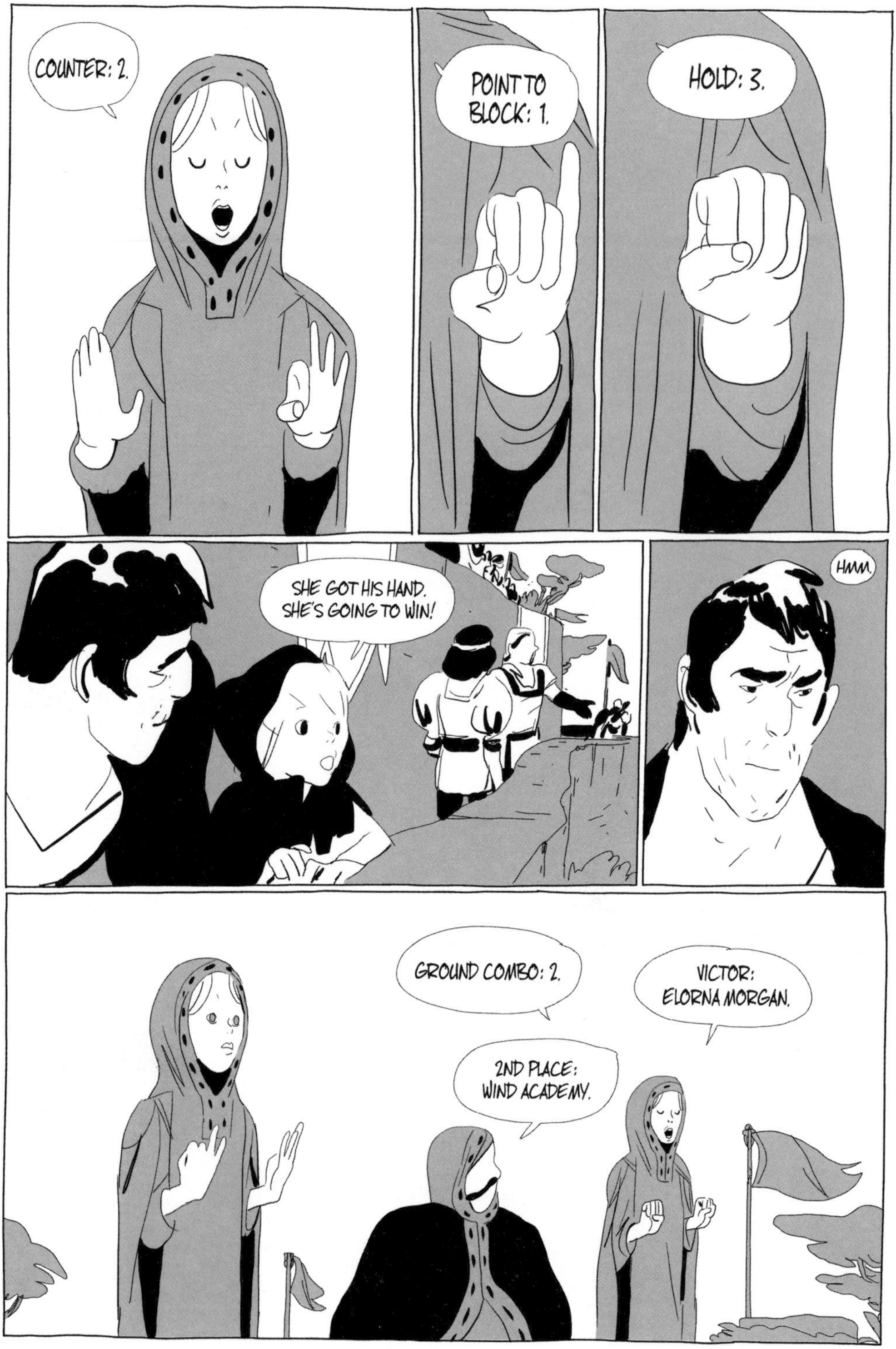
COUNTER: 2.
POINT TO BLOCK: 1.
HOLD: 3.
SHE GOT HIS HAND. SHE'S GOING TO WIN!
HMM.
GROUND COMBO: 2.
VICTOR: ELORNA MORGAN.
2ND PLACE: WIND ACADEMY.

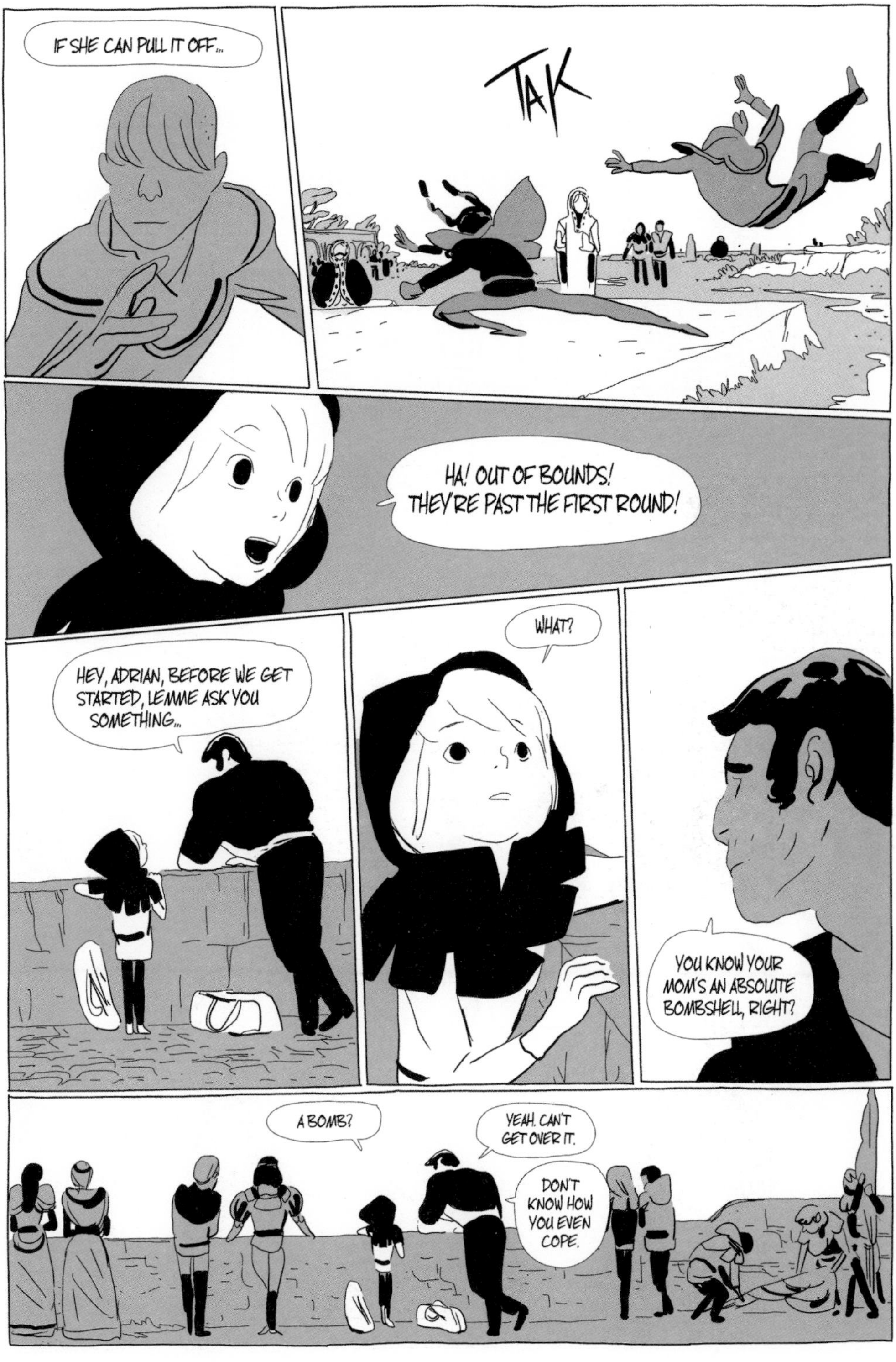
IF SHE CAN PULL IT OFF...
TAK
HA! OUT OF BOUNDS!
THEY'RE PAST THE FIRST ROUND!
HEY, ADRIAN, BEFORE WE GET STARTED, LEMME ASK YOU SOMETHING...
WHAT?
YOU KNOW YOUR MOM'S AN ABSOLUTE BOMBSHELL, RIGHT?
A BOMB?
YEAH. CAN'T GET OVER IT.
DON'T KNOW HOW YOU EVEN COPE.

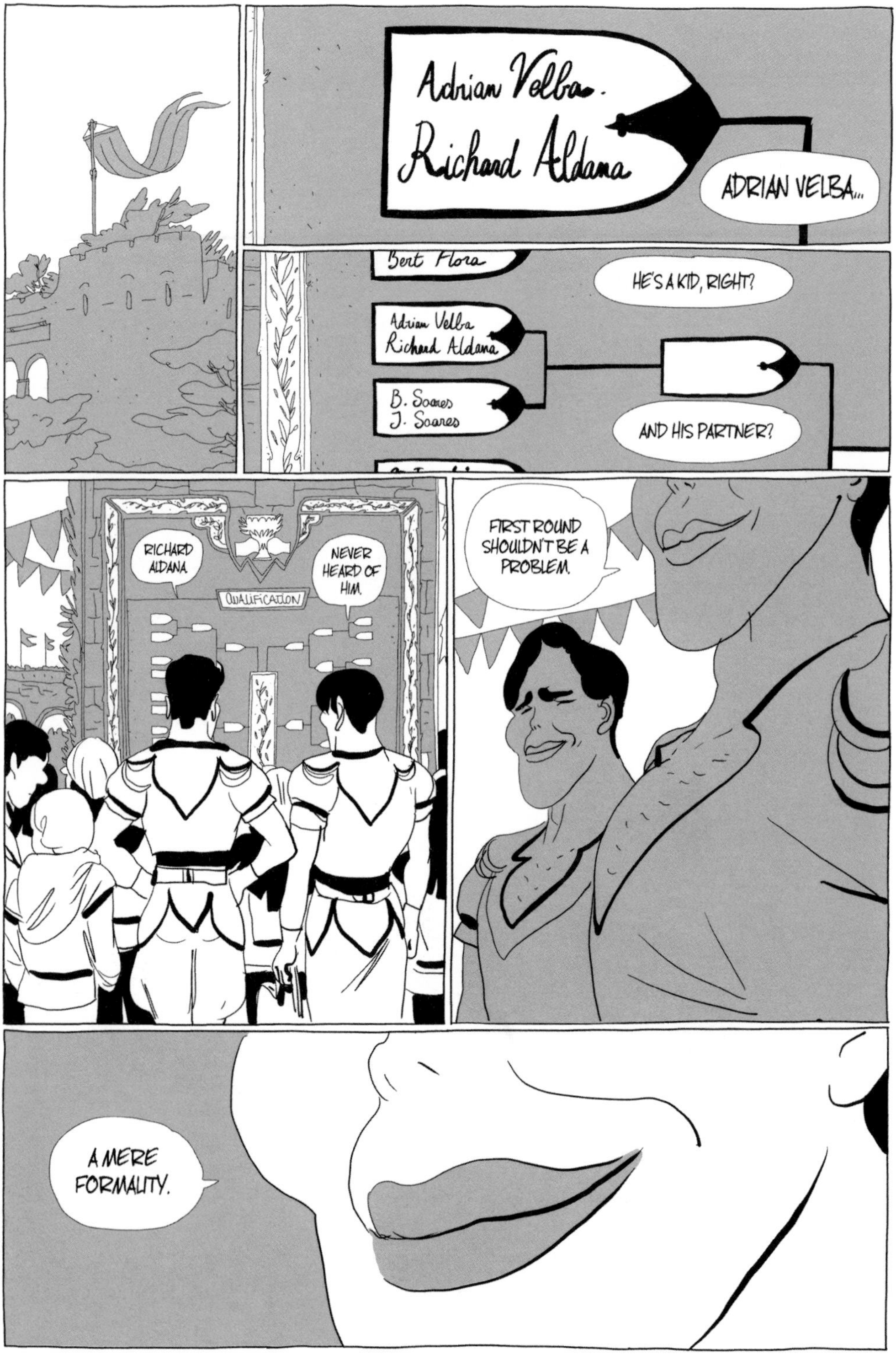
Adrian Velba
Richard Aldana
ADRIAN VELBA...
Bert Flora
HE'S A KID, RIGHT?
Adrian Velba
Richard Aldana
B. Soares
J. Soares
AND HIS PARTNER?
RICHARD ALDANA.
NEVER HEARD OF HIM.
QUALIFICATION
FIRST ROUND SHOULDN'T BE A PROBLEM.
A MERE FORMALITY.

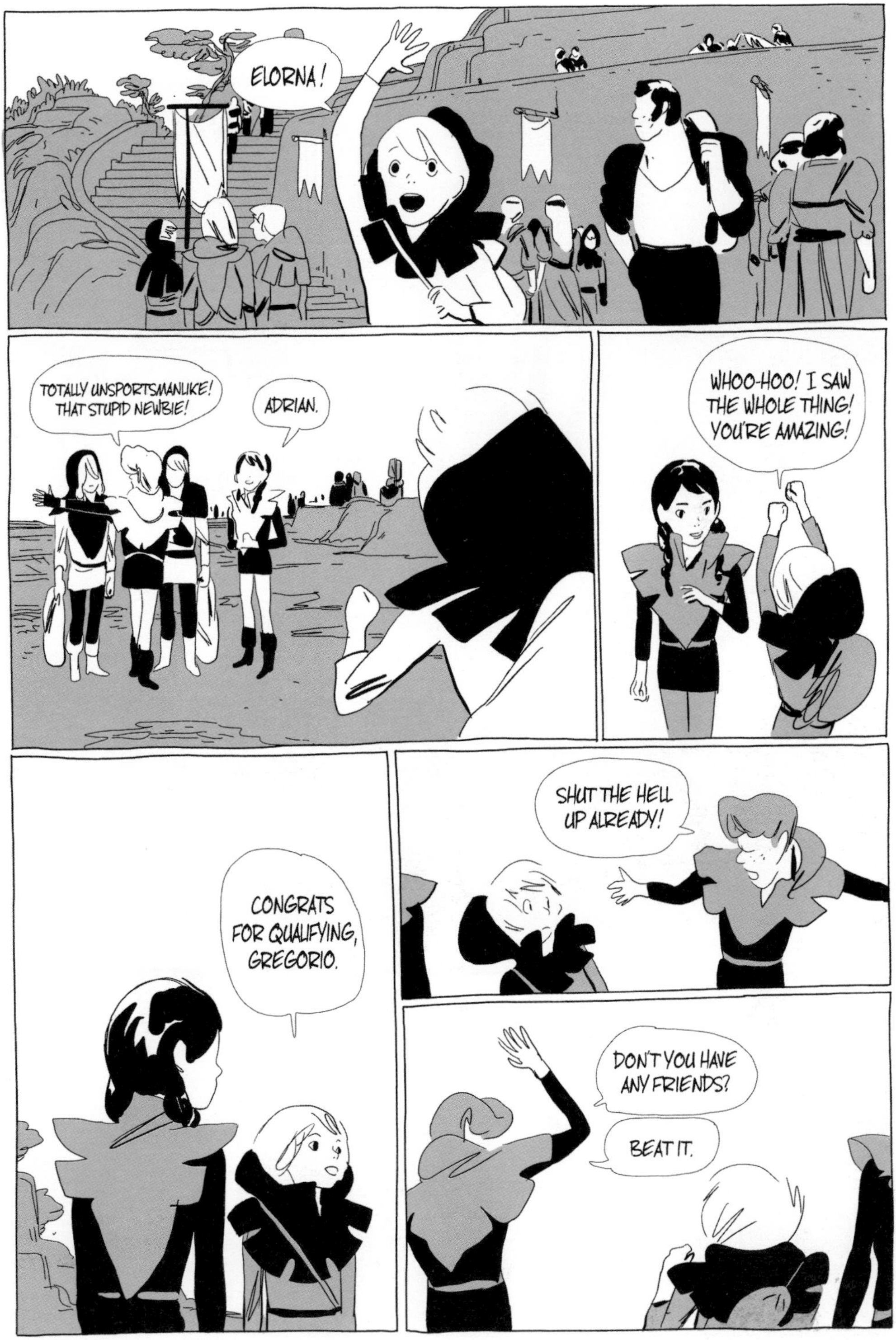
ELORNA!
TOTALLY UNSPORTSMANLIKE! THAT STUPID NEWBIE!
ADRIAN.
WHOO-HOO! I SAW THE WHOLE THING! YOU'RE AMAZING!
CONGRATS FOR QUALIFYING, GREGORIO.
SHUT THE HELL UP ALREADY!
DON'T YOU HAVE ANY FRIENDS?
BEAT IT.

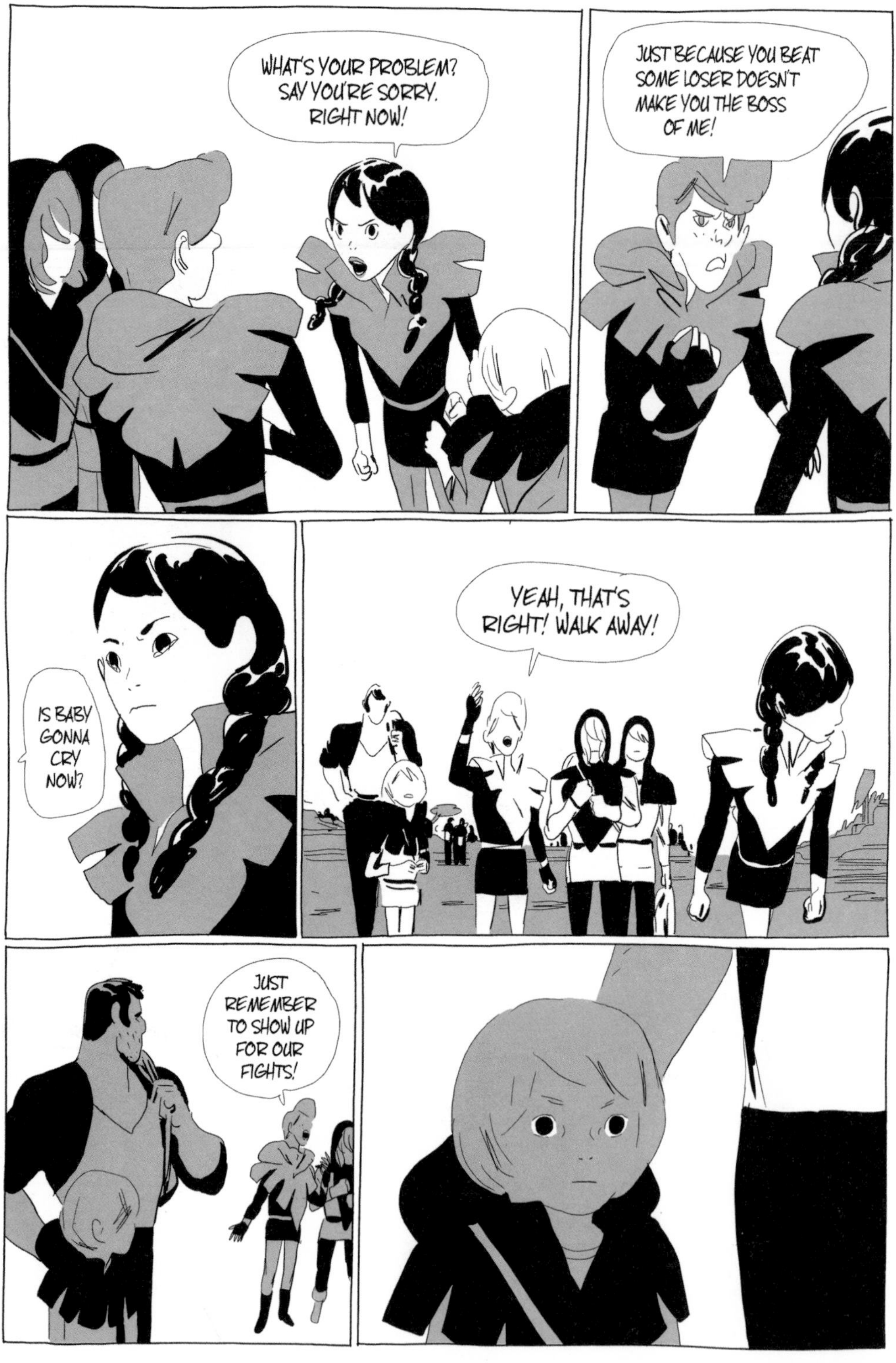
WHAT'S YOUR PROBLEM? SAY YOU'RE SORRY. RIGHT NOW!
JUST BECAUSE YOU BEAT SOME LOSER DOESN'T MAKE YOU THE BOSS OF ME!
IS BABY GONNA CRY NOW?
YEAH, THAT'S RIGHT! WALK AWAY!
JUST REMEMBER TO SHOW UP FOR OUR FIGHTS!

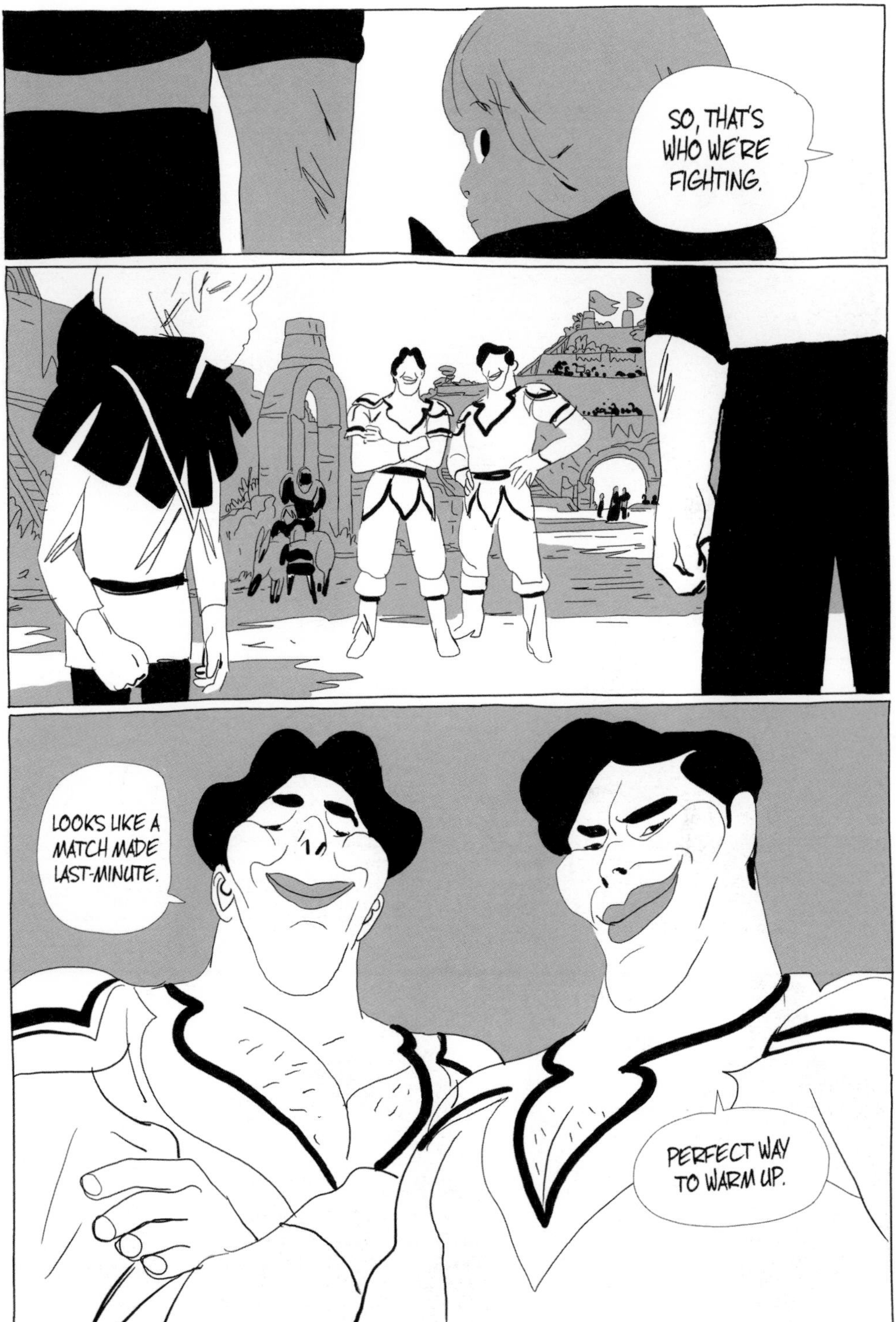
SO, THAT'S WHO WE'RE FIGHTING.
LOOKS LIKE A MATCH MADE LAST-MINUTE.
PERFECT WAY TO WARM UP.

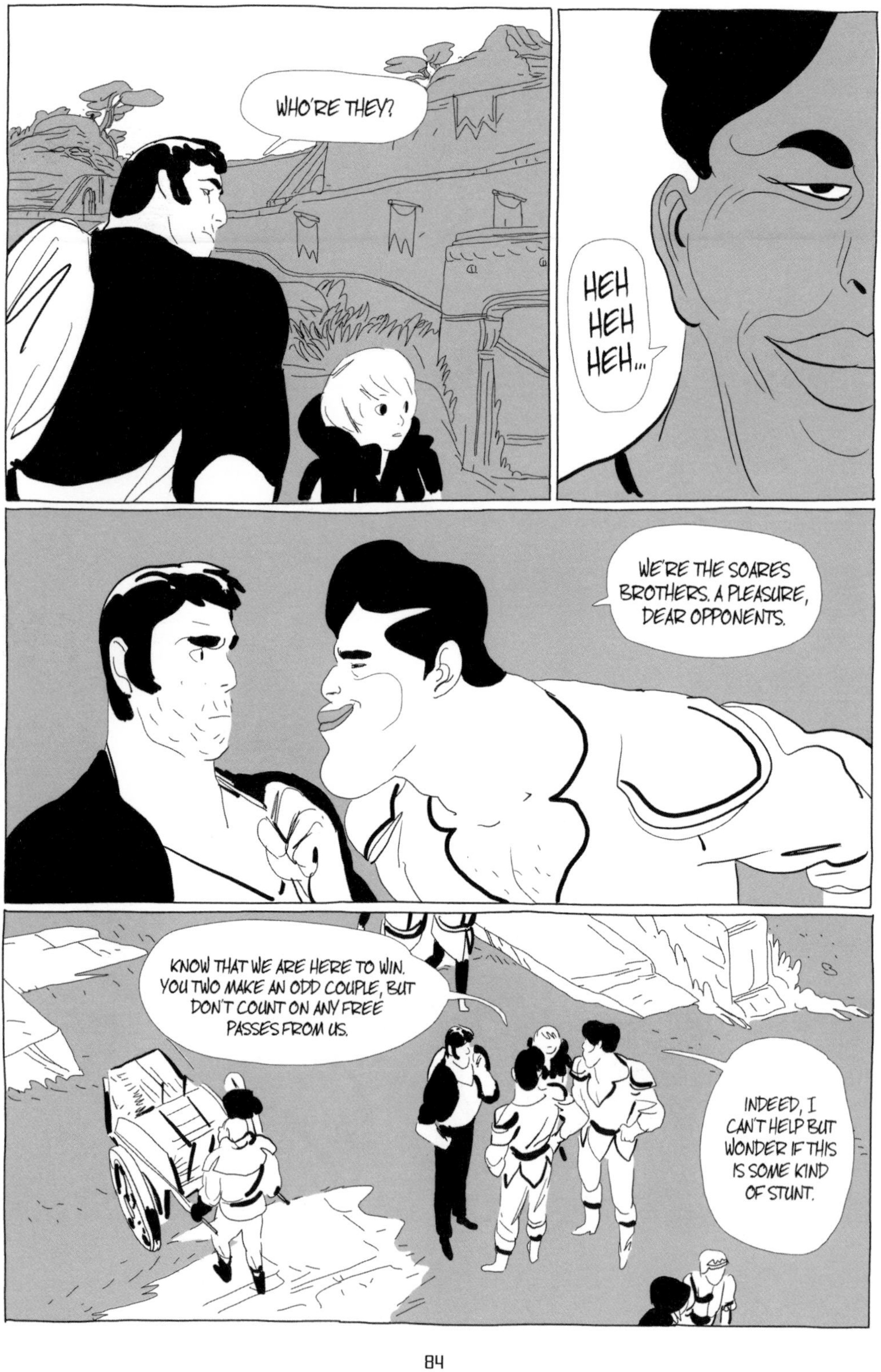
WHO'RE THEY?
HEH HEH HEH...
WE'RE THE SOARES BROTHERS. A PLEASURE, DEAR OPPONENTS.
KNOW THAT WE ARE HERE TO WIN. YOU TWO MAKE AN ODD COUPLE, BUT DON'T COUNT ON ANY FREE PASSES FROM US.
INDEED, I CAN'T HELP BUT WONDER IF THIS IS SOME KIND OF STUNT.

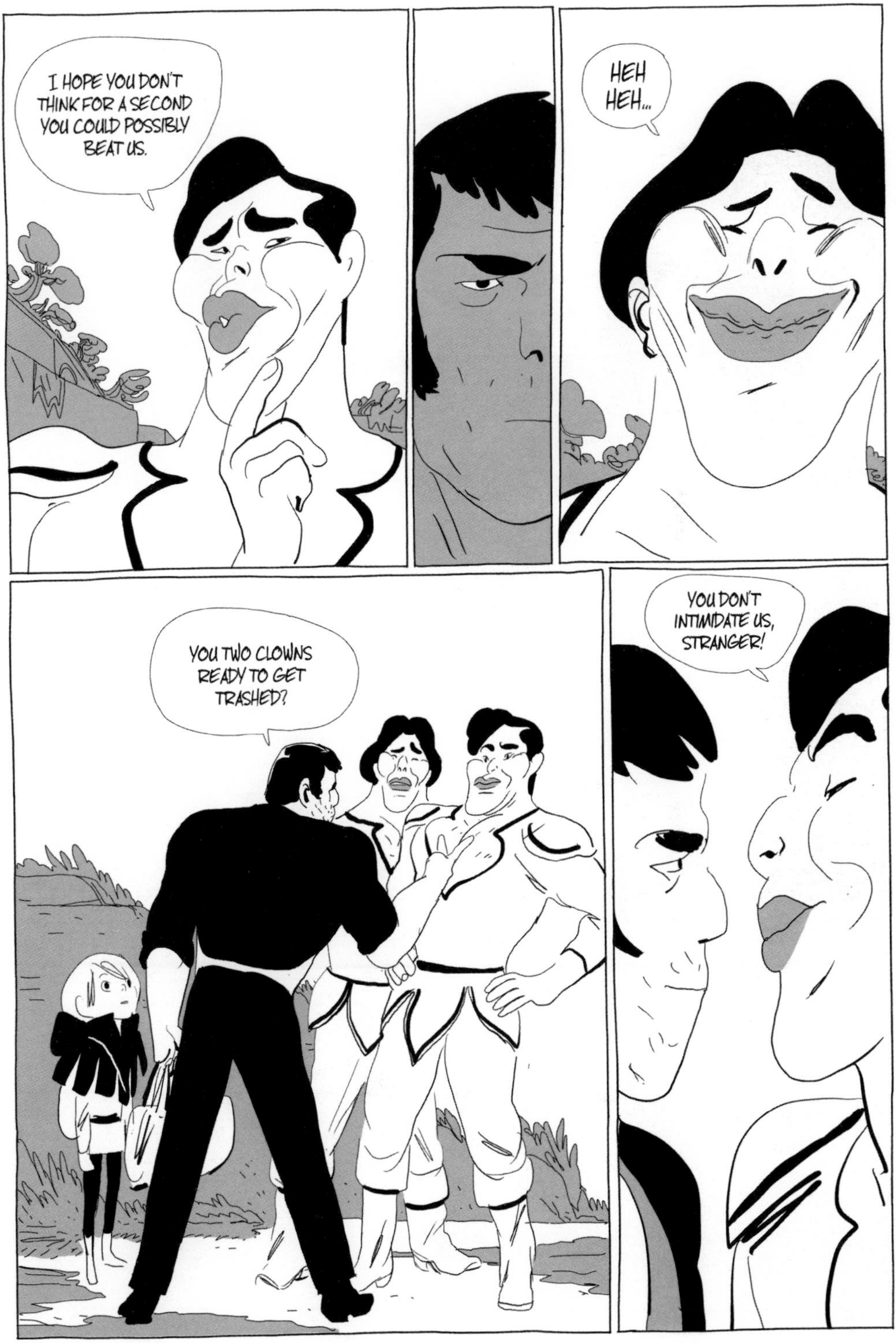
I HOPE YOU DON'T THINK FOR A SECOND YOU COULD POSSIBLY BEAT US.
HEH HEH...
YOU TWO CLOWNS READY TO GET TRASHED?
YOU DON'T INTIMIDATE US, STRANGER!

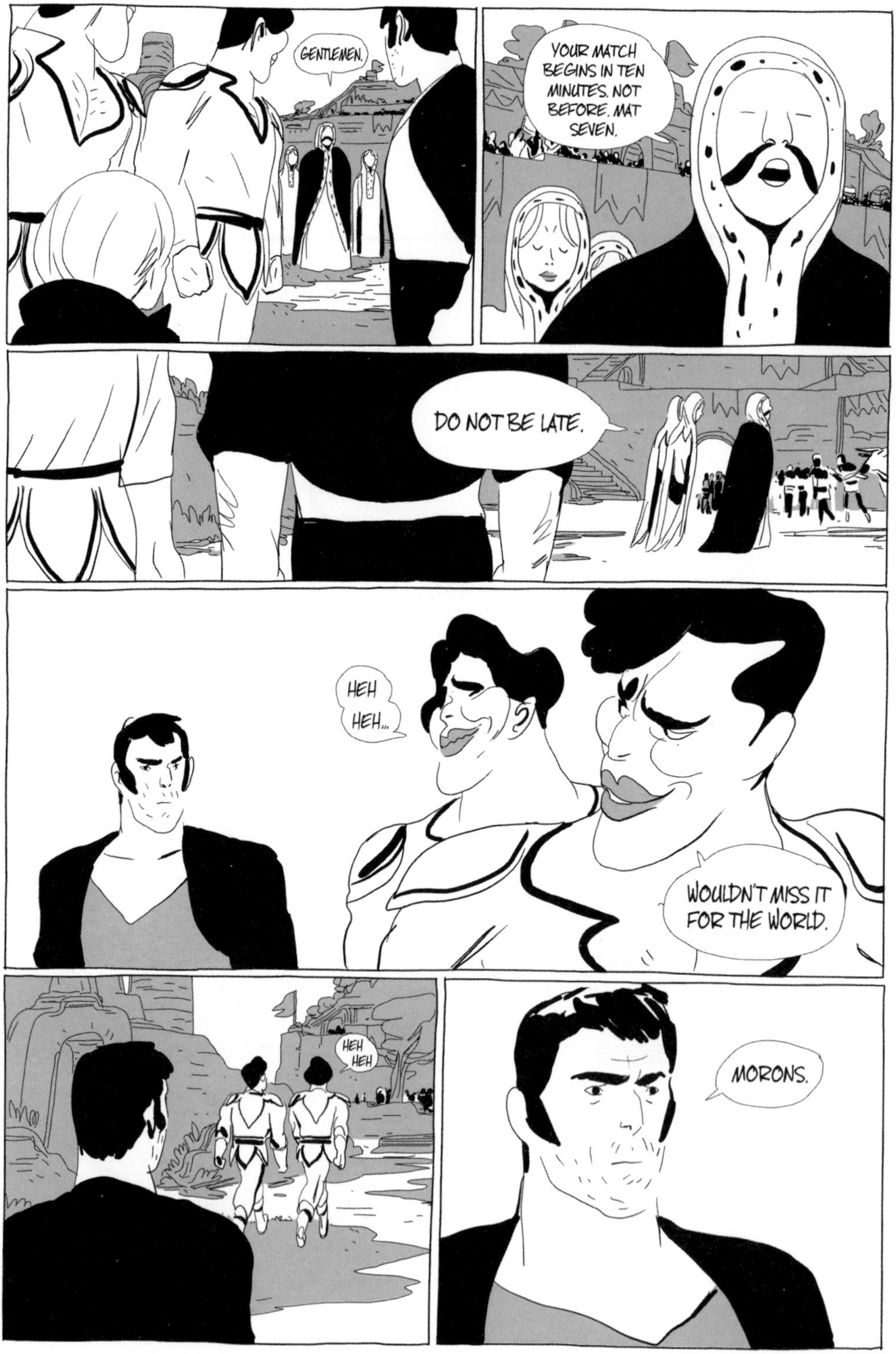
GENTLEMEN.
YOUR MATCH BEGINS IN TEN MINUTES. NOT BEFORE. MAT SEVEN.
DO NOT BE LATE.
HEH HEH...
WOULDN'T MISS IT FOR THE WORLD.
HEH HEH
MORONS.

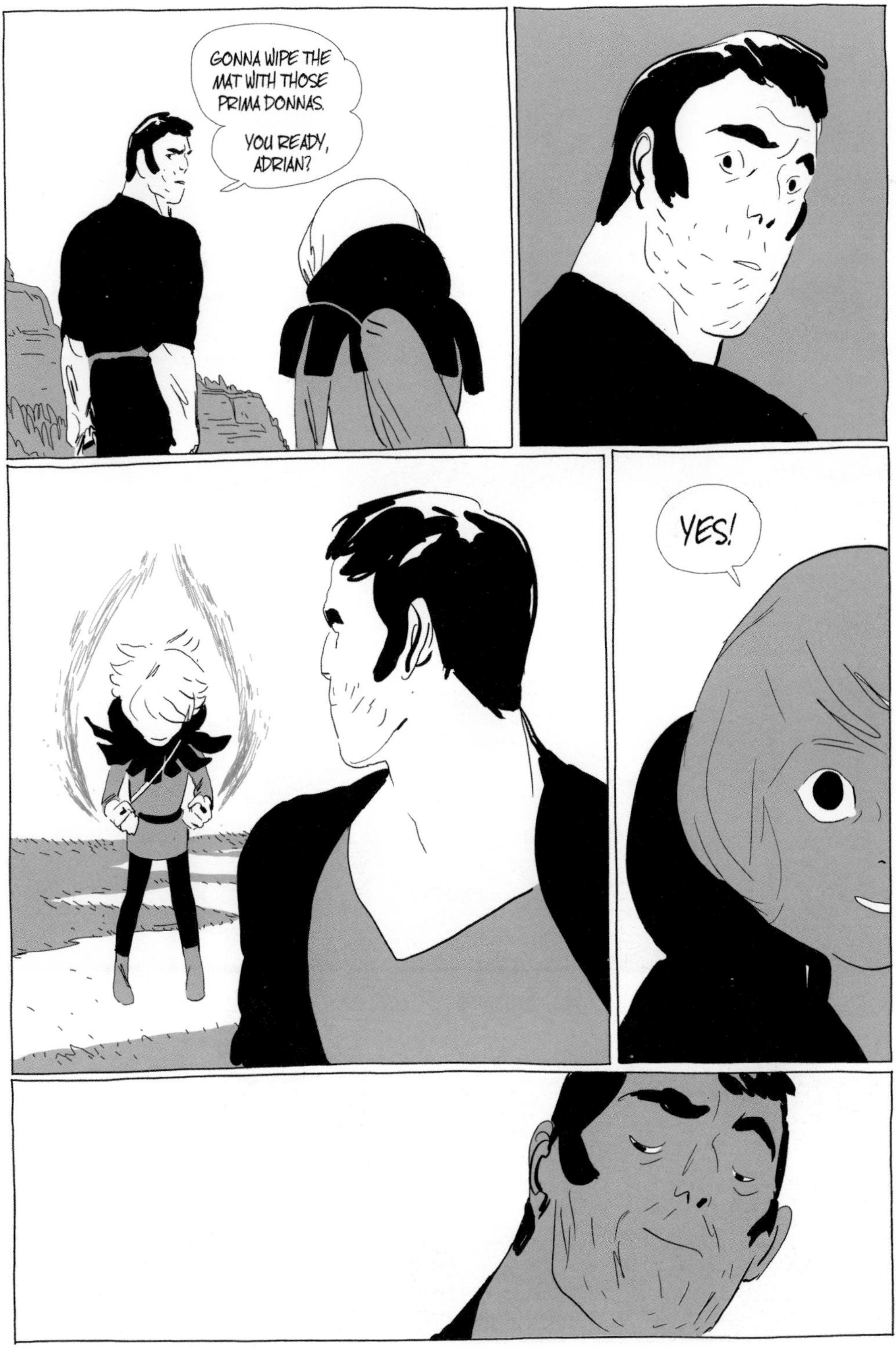
GONNA WIPE THE MAT WITH THOSE PRIMA DONNAS.
YOU READY, ADRIAN?
YES!

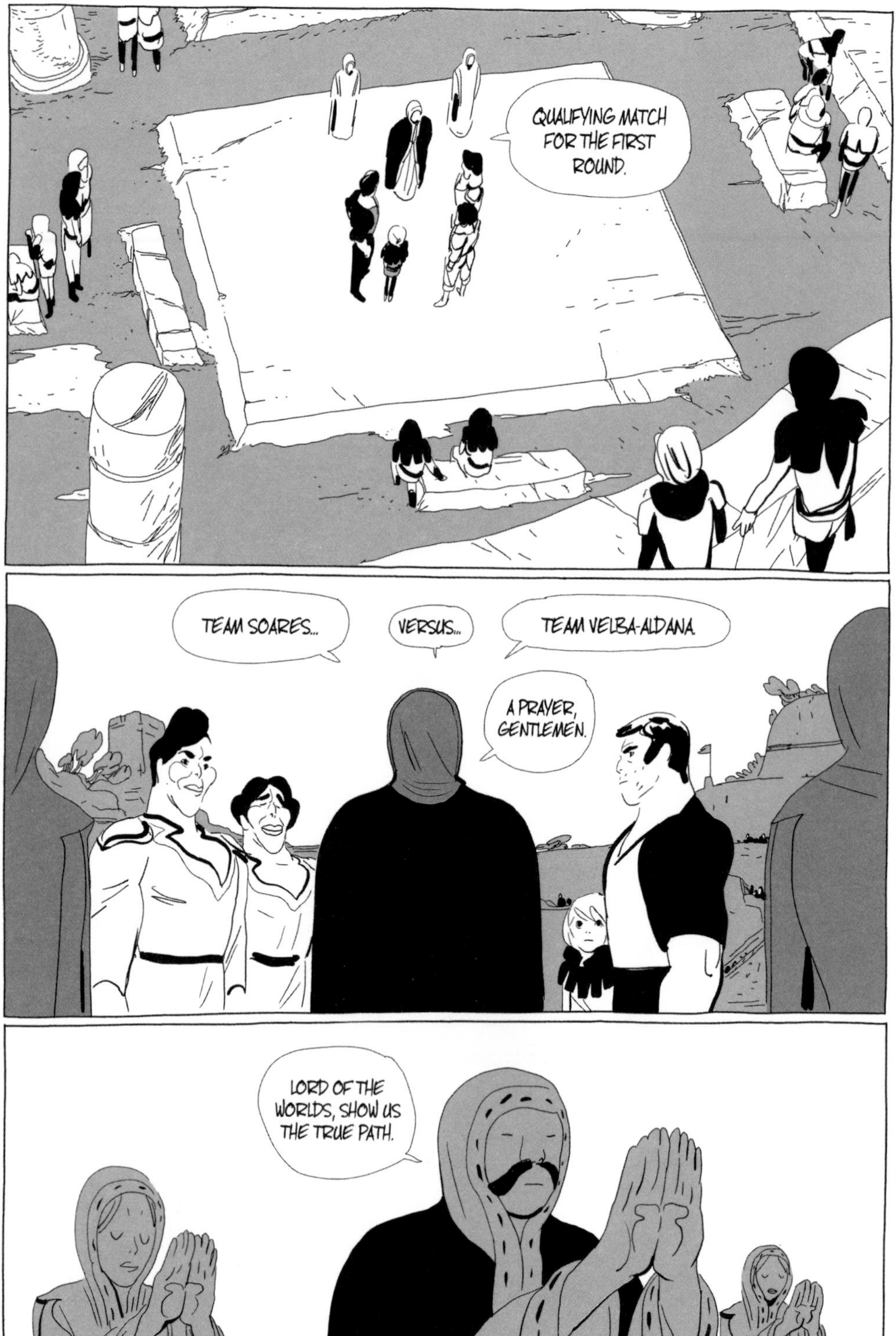
QUALIFYING MATCH FOR THE FIRST ROUND.
TEAM SOARES...
VERSUS...
TEAM VELBA-ALDANA.
A PRAYER, GENTLEMEN.
LORD OF THE WORLDS, SHOW US THE TRUE PATH.

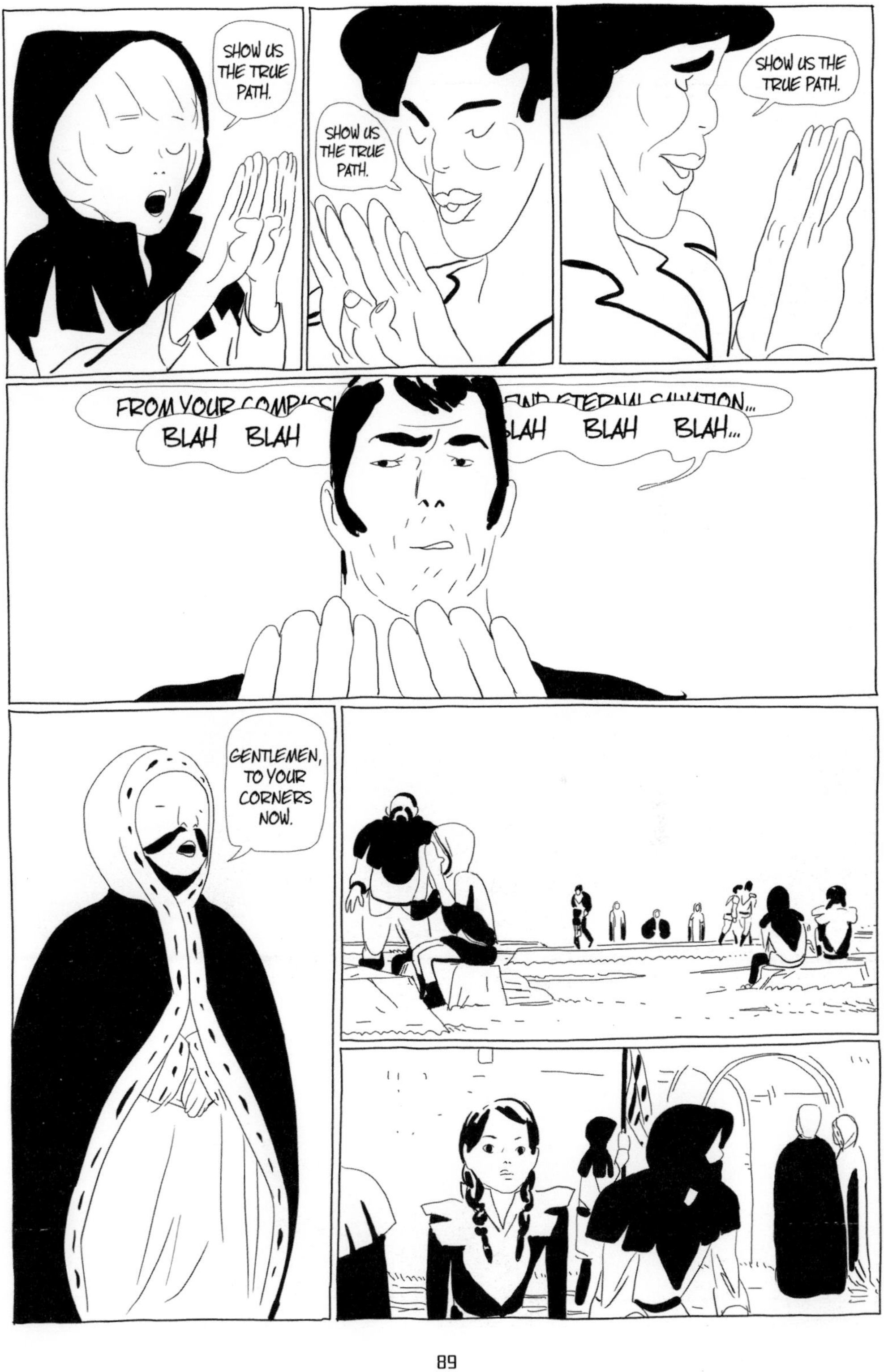
SHOW US THE TRUE PATH.
SHOW US THE TRUE PATH.
SHOW US THE TRUE PATH.
BLAH BLAH
BLAH BLAH BLAH...
GENTLEMEN, TO YOUR CORNERS NOW.

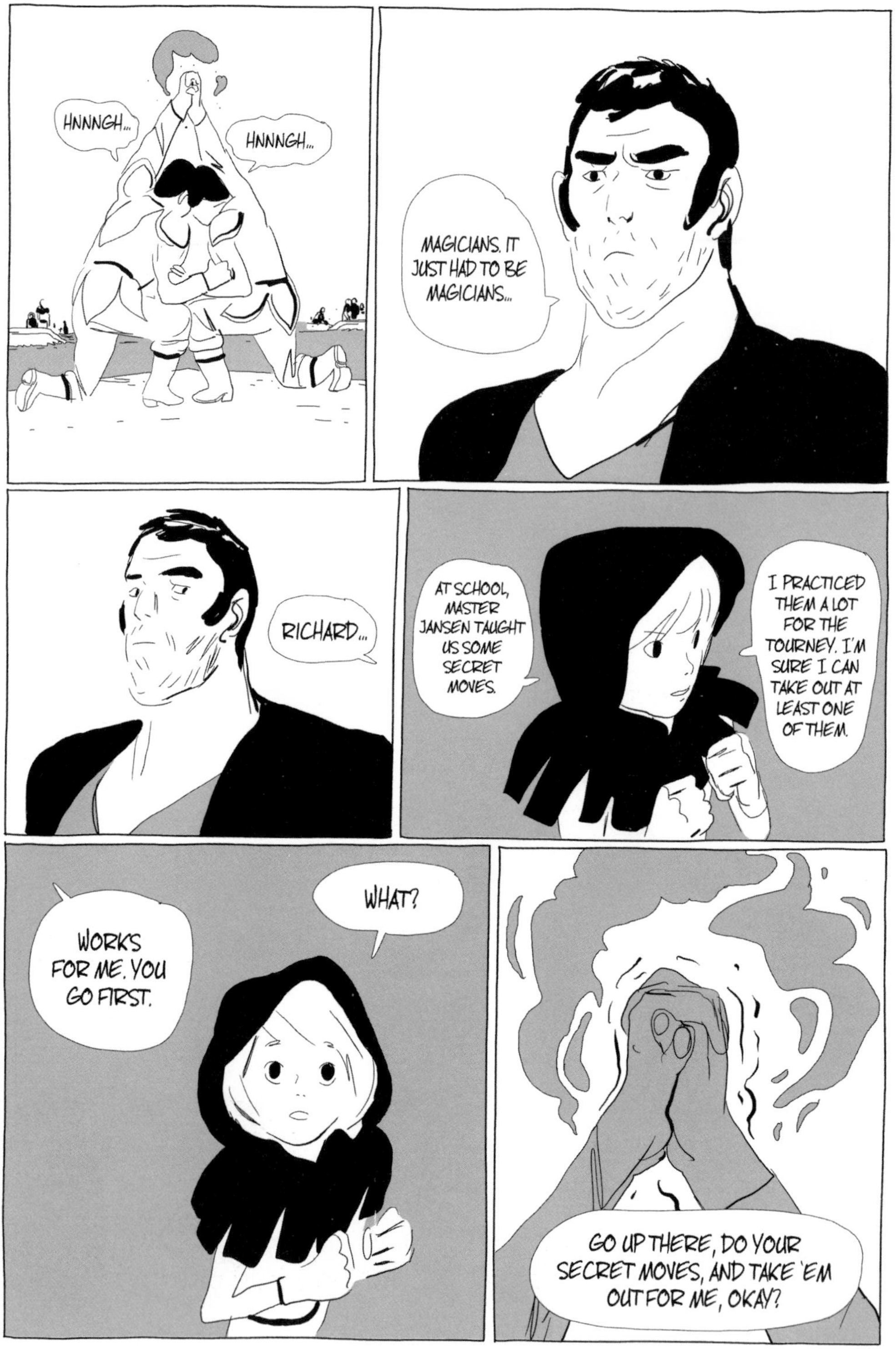
HNNNGH...
HNNNGH...
MAGICIANS. IT JUST HAD TO BE MAGICIANS...
RICHARD...
AT SCHOOL, MASTER JANSEN TAUGHT US SOME SECRET MOVES.
I PRACTICED THEM A LOT FOR THE TOURNEY. I'M SURE I CAN TAKE OUT AT LEAST ONE OF THEM.
WORKS FOR ME. YOU GO FIRST.
WHAT?
GO UP THERE, DO YOUR SECRET MOVES, AND TAKE 'EM OUT FOR ME, OKAY?

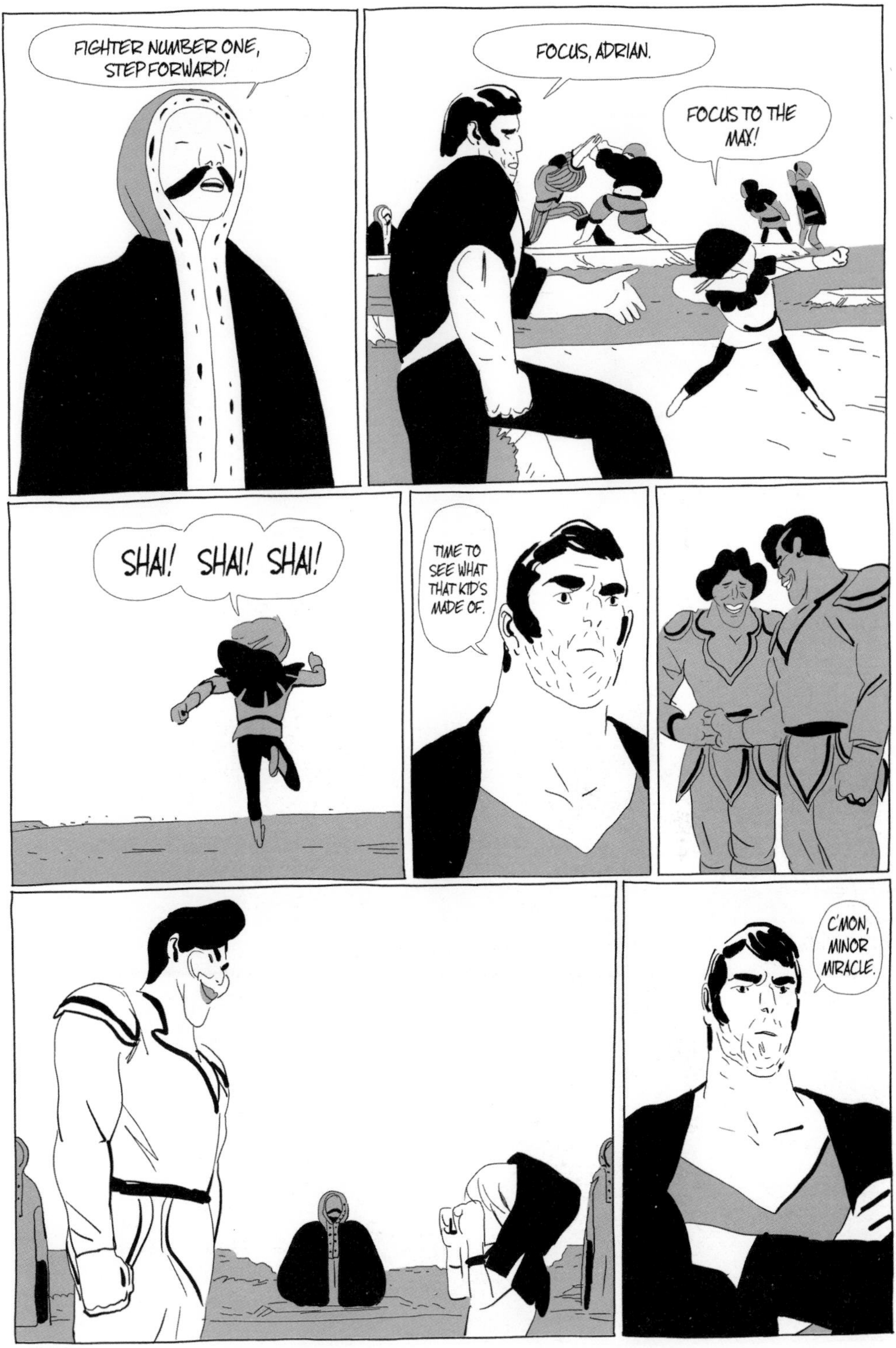
FIGHTER NUMBER ONE, STEP FORWARD!
FOCUS, ADRIAN.
FOCUS TO THE MAX!
SHAI! SHAI! SHAI!
TIME TO SEE WHAT THAT KID'S MADE OF.
C'MON, MINOR MIRACLE.

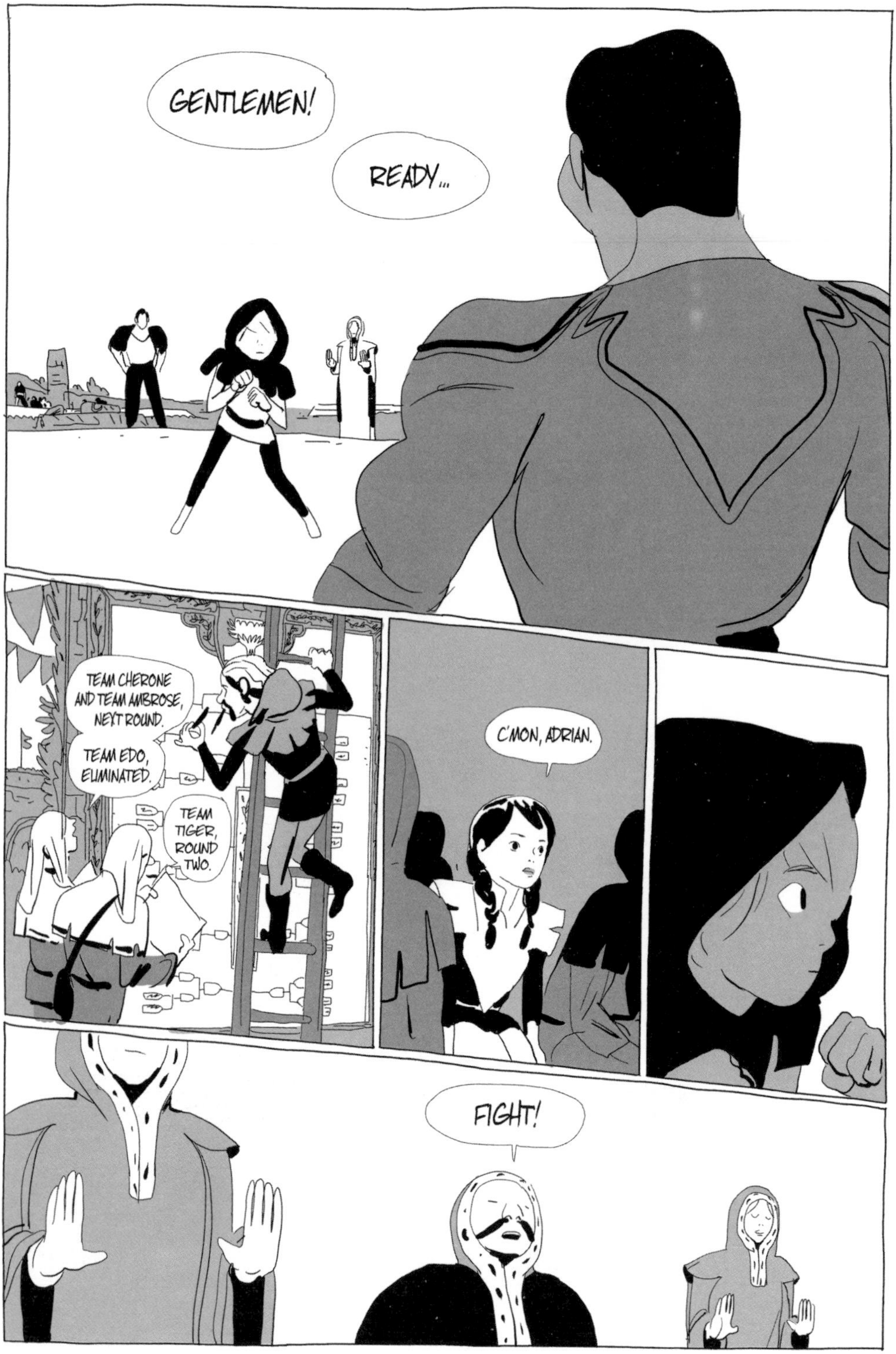
GENTLEMEN!
READY...
TEAM CHERONE AND TEAM AMBROSE, NEXT ROUND.
TEAM EDO, ELIMINATED.
TEAM TIGER, ROUND TWO.
C'MON, ADRIAN.
FIGHT!

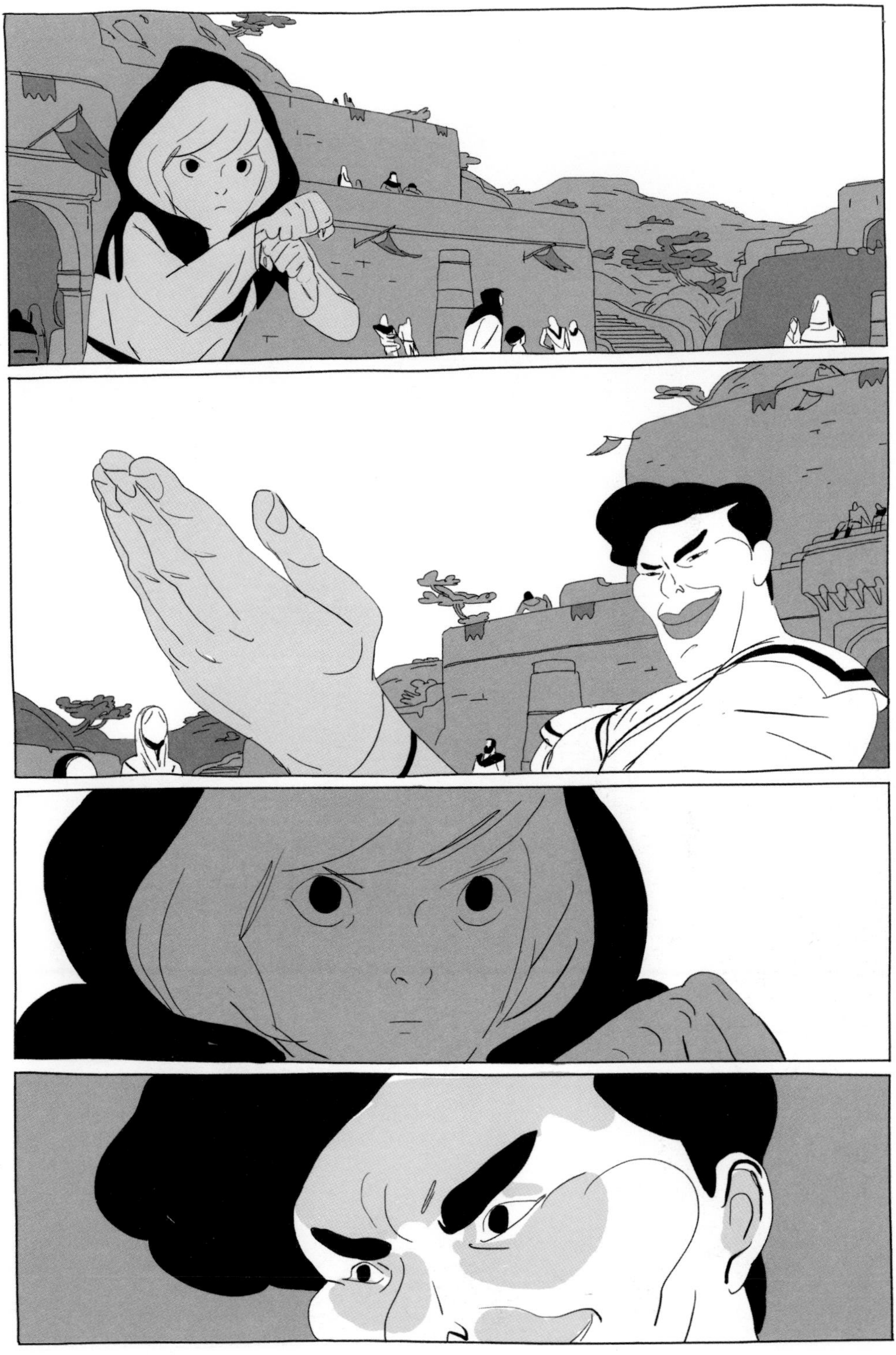

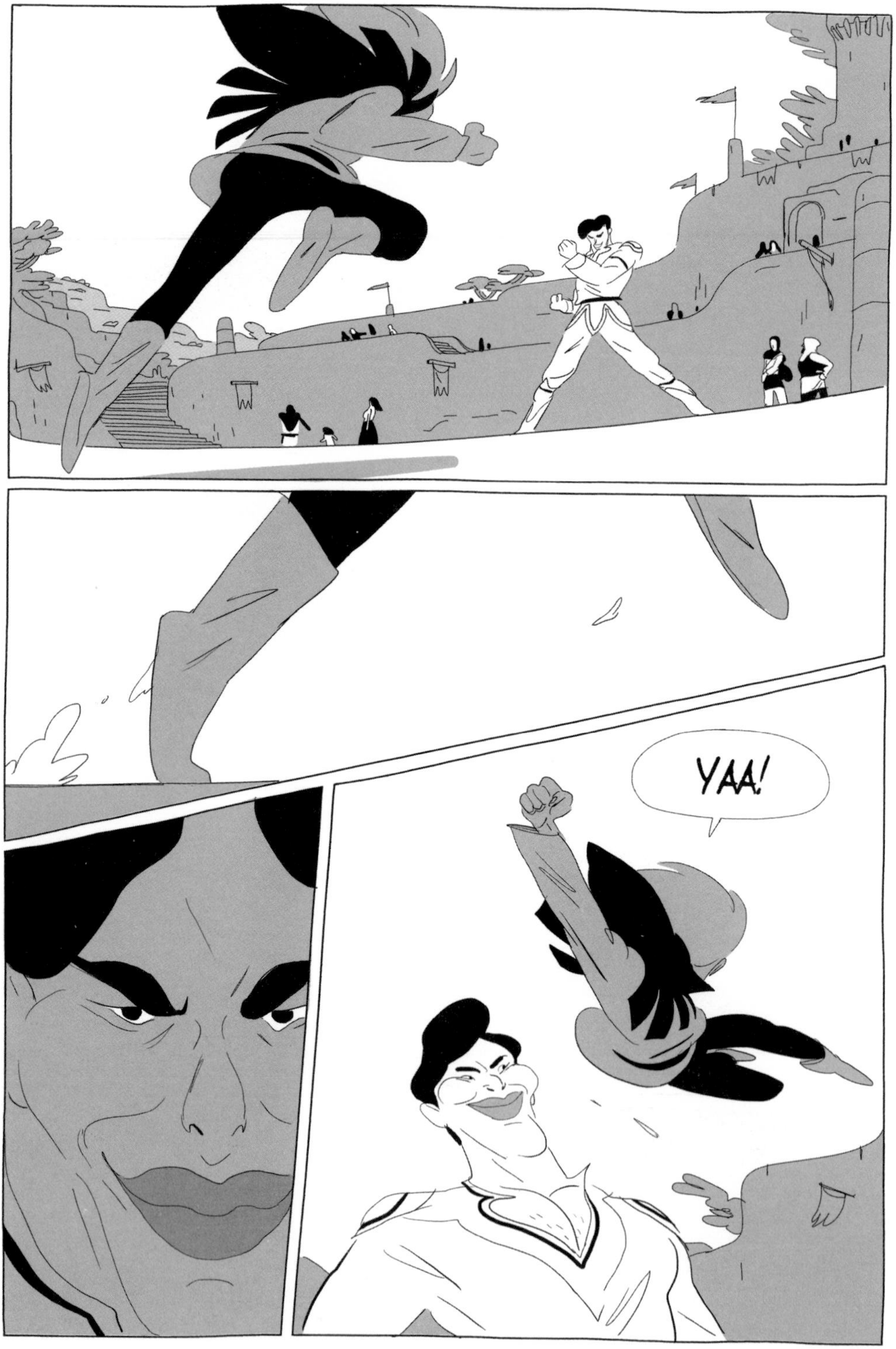
YAA!

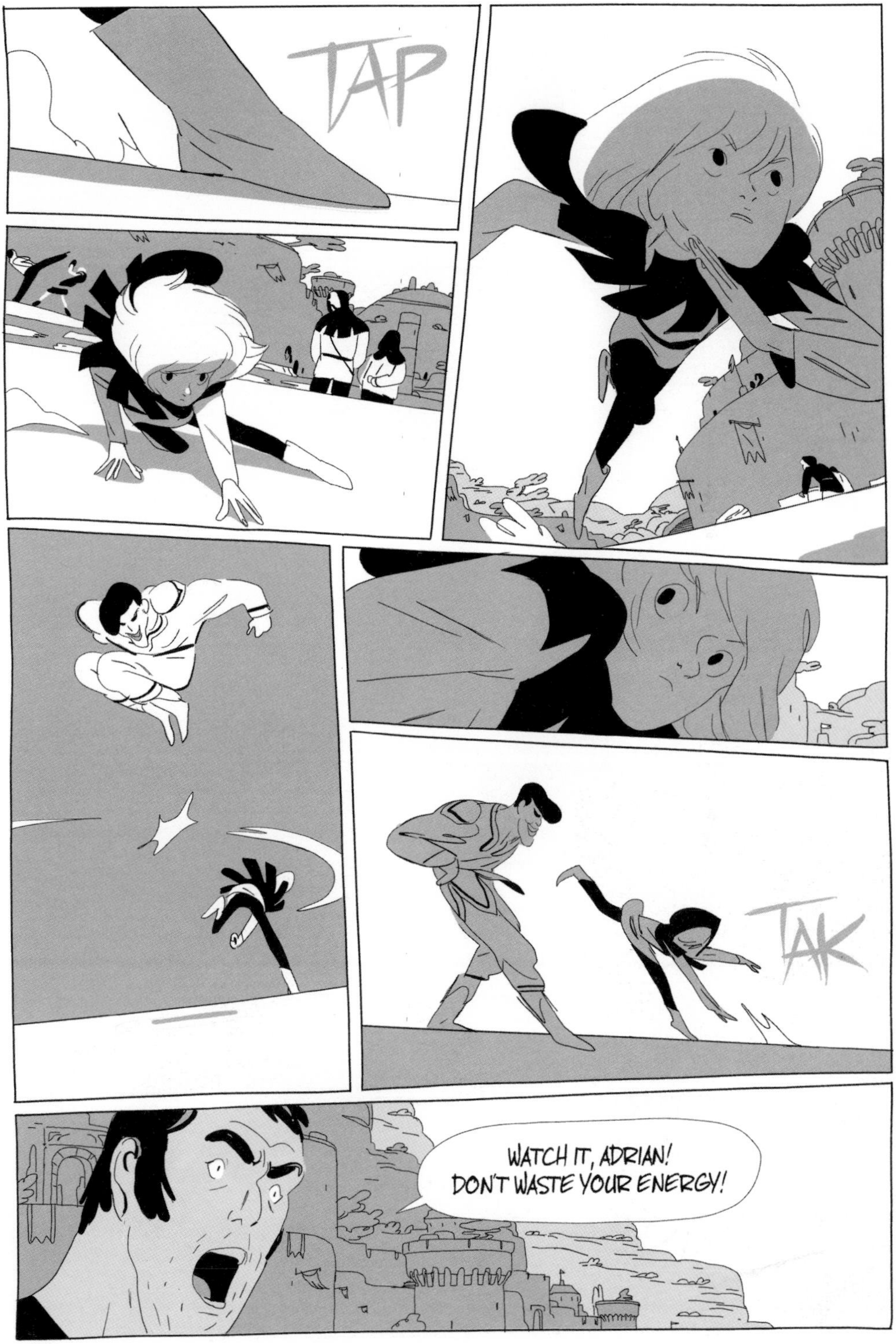
TAP
TAK
WATCH IT, ADRIAN!
DON'T WASTE YOUR ENERGY!

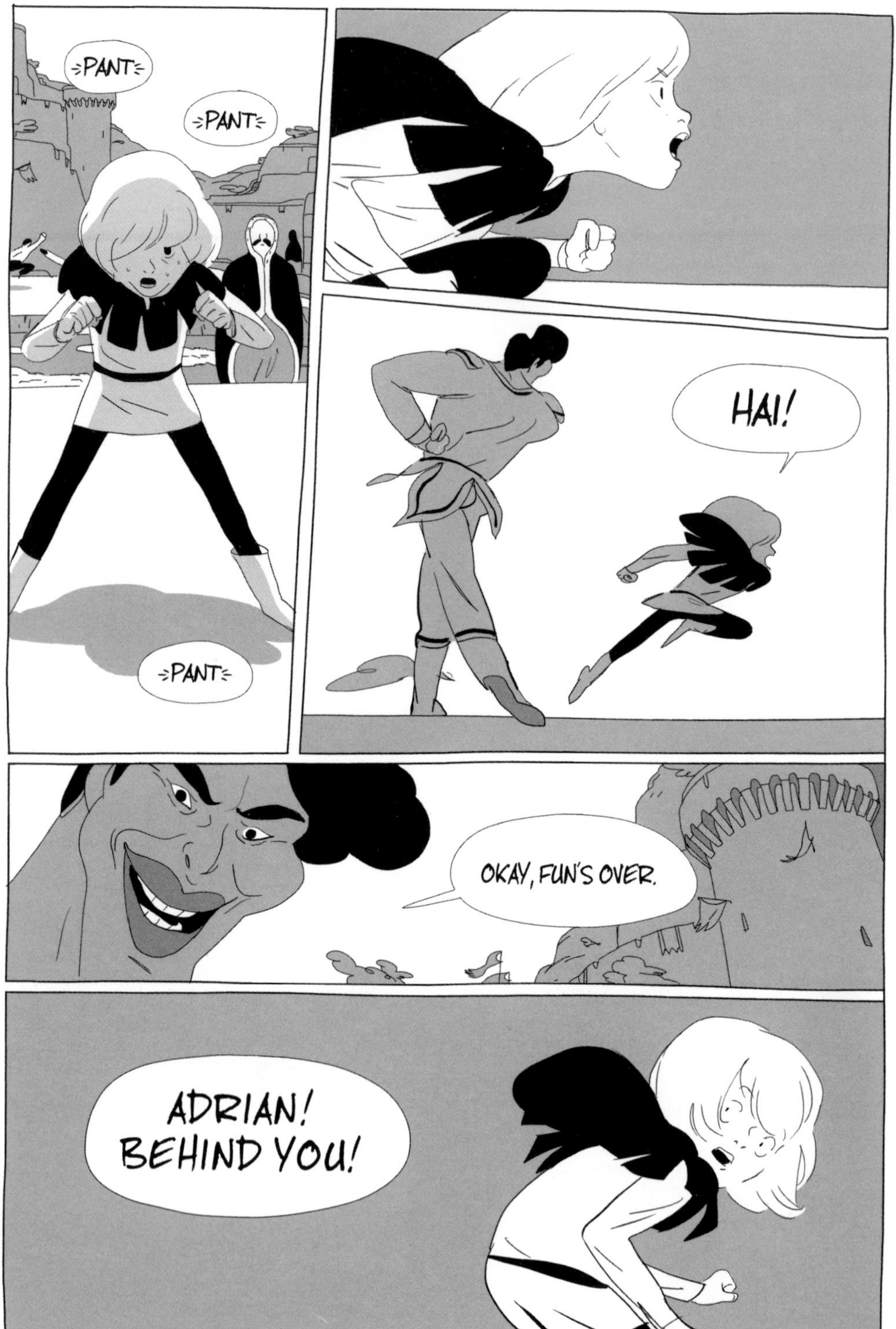
PANT
PANT
PANT
HAI!
OKAY, FUN'S OVER.
ADRIAN!
BEHIND YOU!

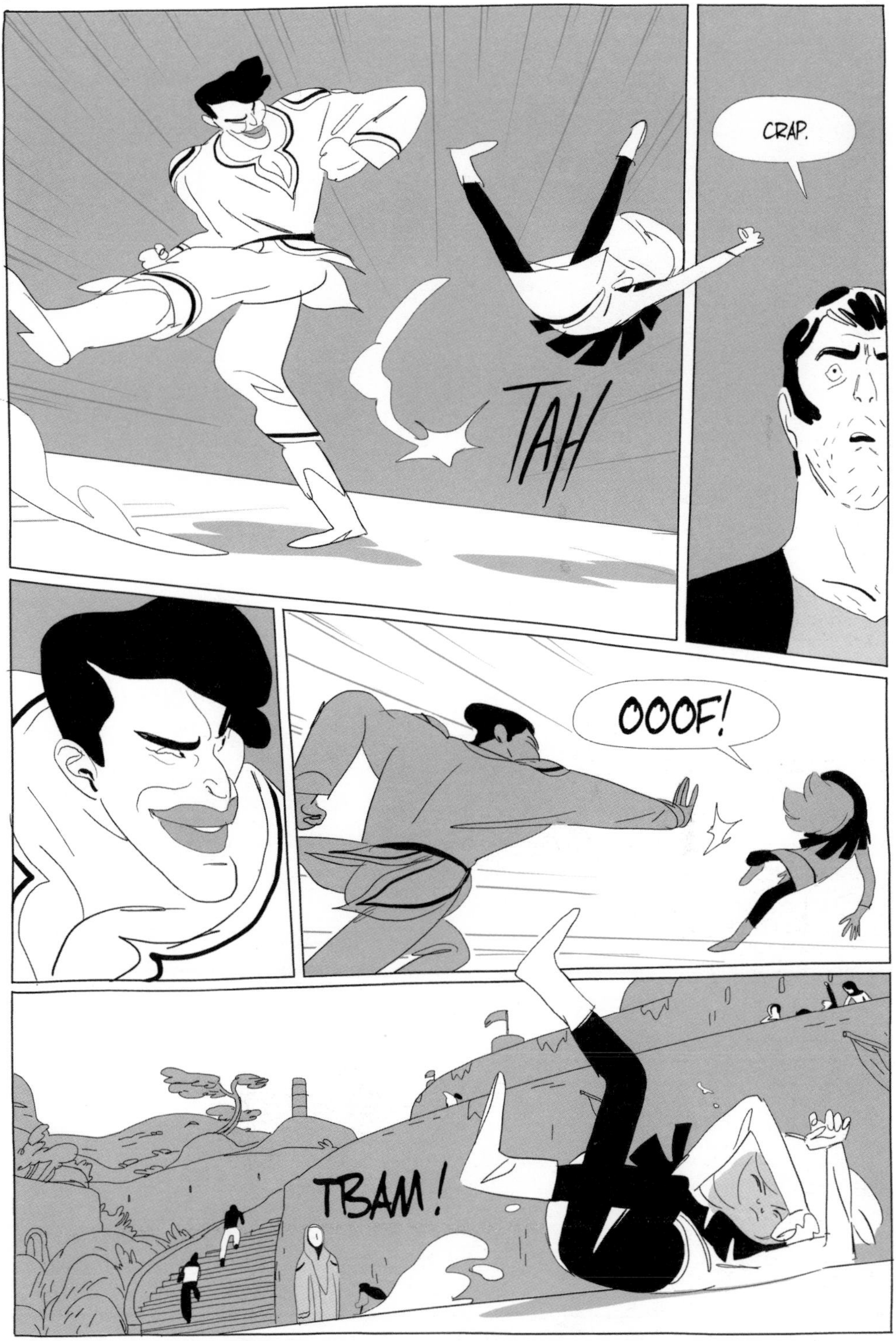
TAH
CRAP.
OOOF!
TBAM!

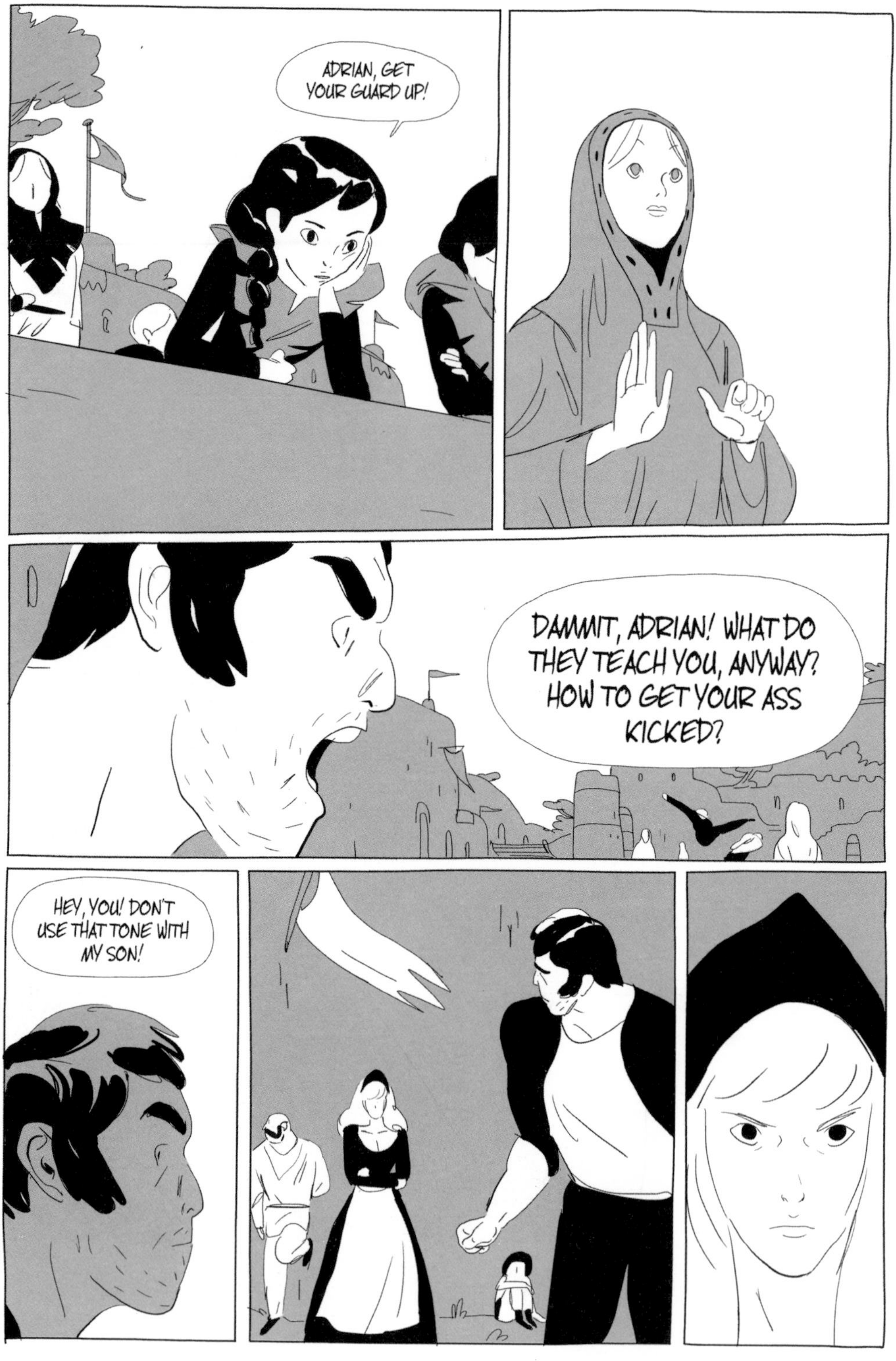
ADRIAN, GET YOUR GUARD UP!
DAMMIT, ADRIAN! WHAT DO THEY TEACH YOU, ANYWAY? HOW TO GET YOUR ASS KICKED?
HEY, YOU! DON'T USE THAT TONE WITH MY SON!

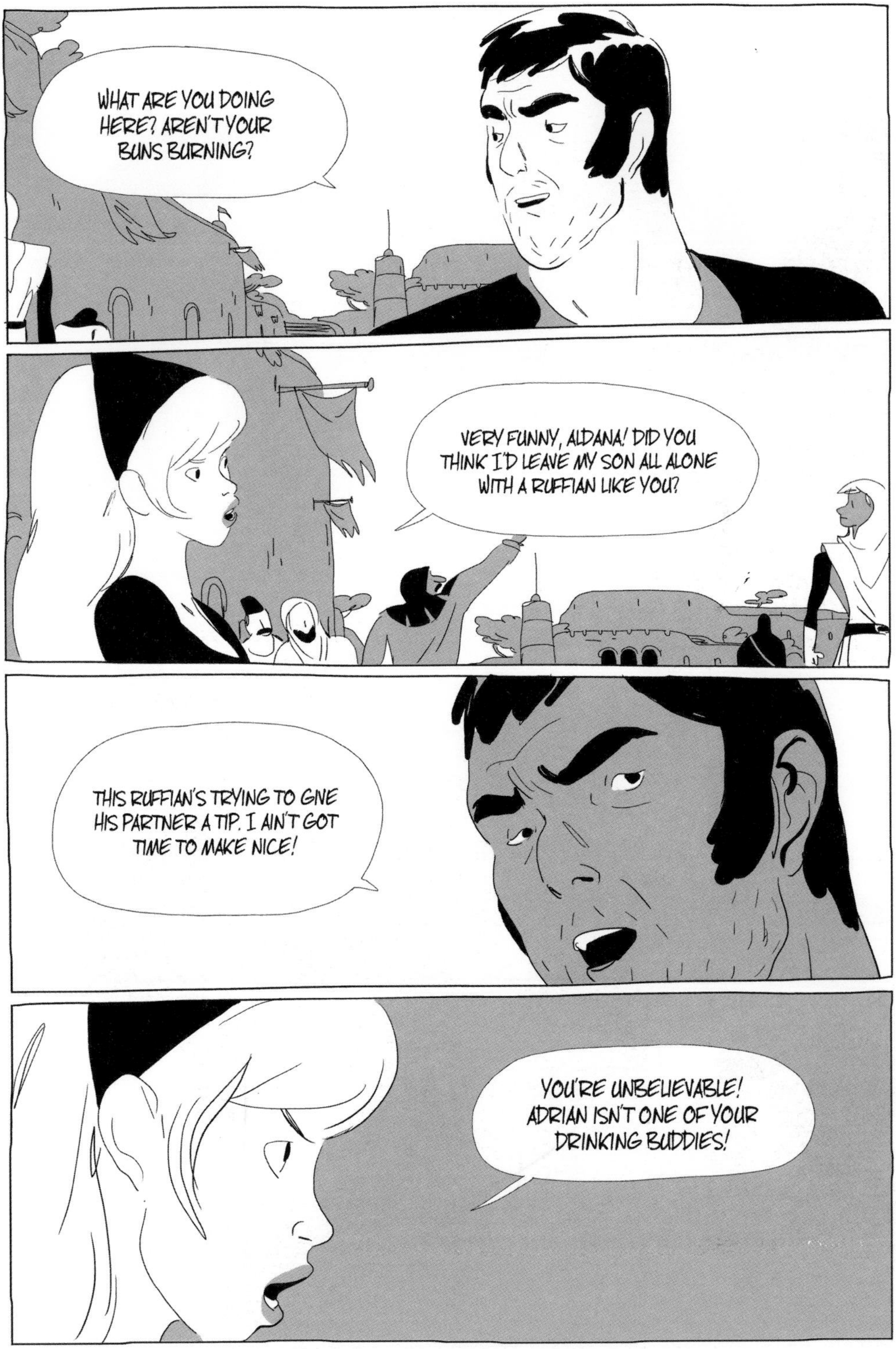
WHAT ARE YOU DOING HERE? AREN'T YOUR BUNS BURNING?
VERY FUNNY, ALDANA! DID YOU THINK I'D LEAVE MY SON ALL ALONE WITH A RUFFIAN LIKE YOU?
THIS RUFFIAN'S TRYING TO GIVE HIS PARTNER A TIP. I AIN'T GOT TIME TO MAKE NICE!
YOU'RE UNBELIEVABLE! ADRIAN ISN'T ONE OF YOUR DRINKING BUDDIES!

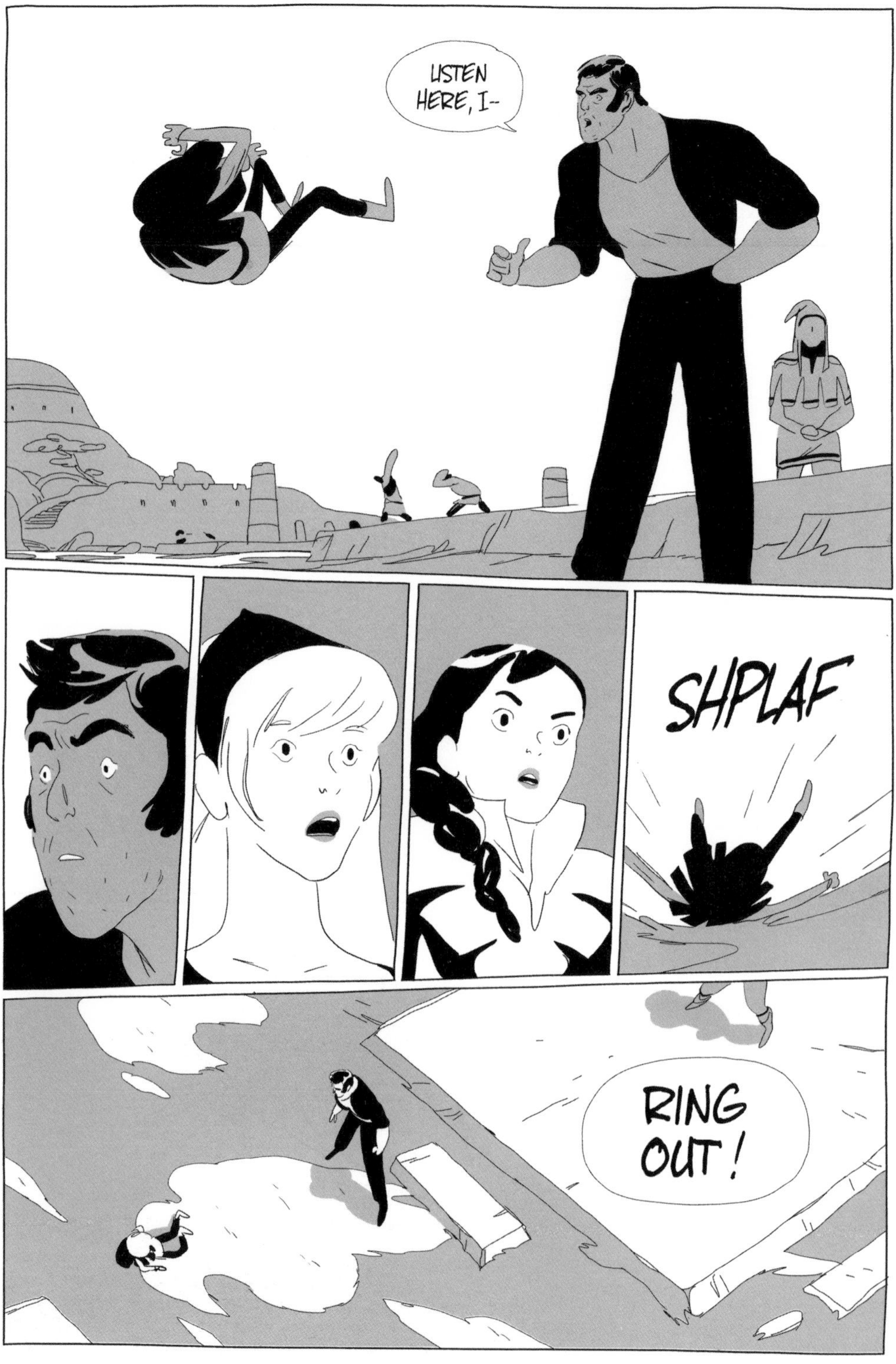
LISTEN HERE, I--
SHPLAF
RING OUT!

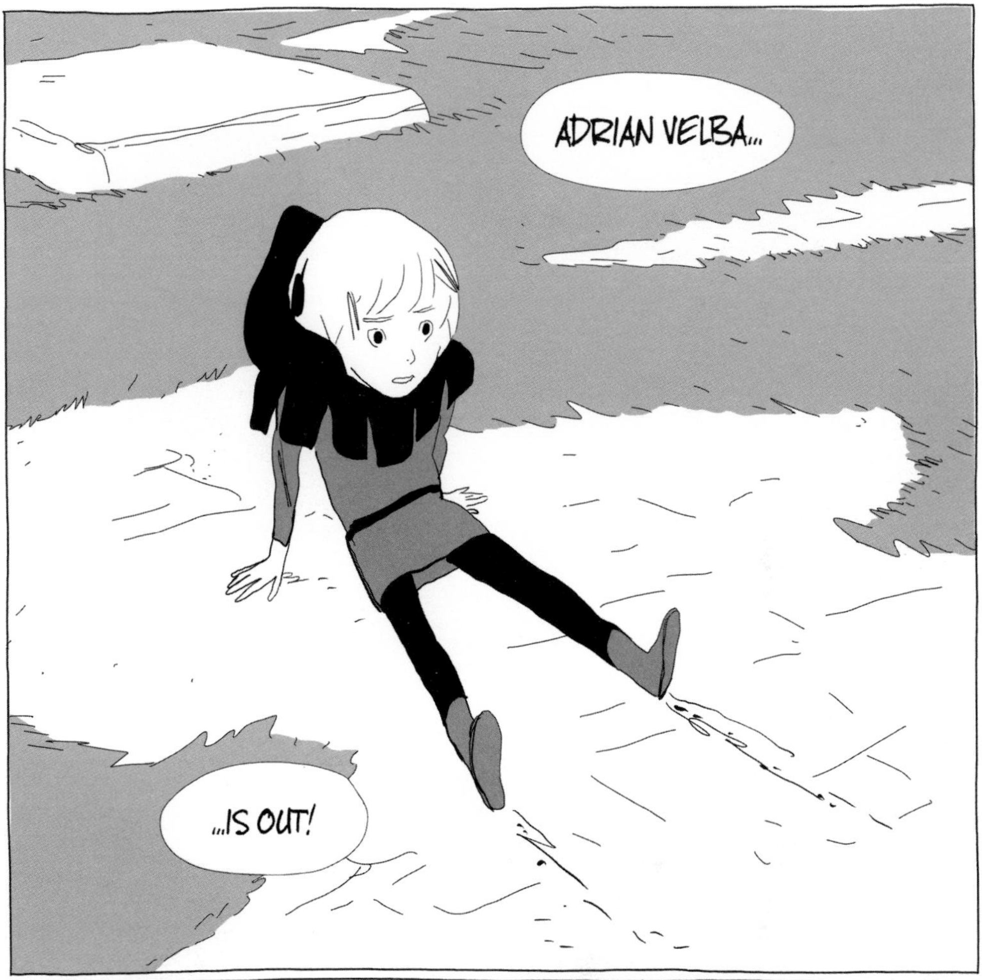
ADRIAN VELBA...
...IS OUT!

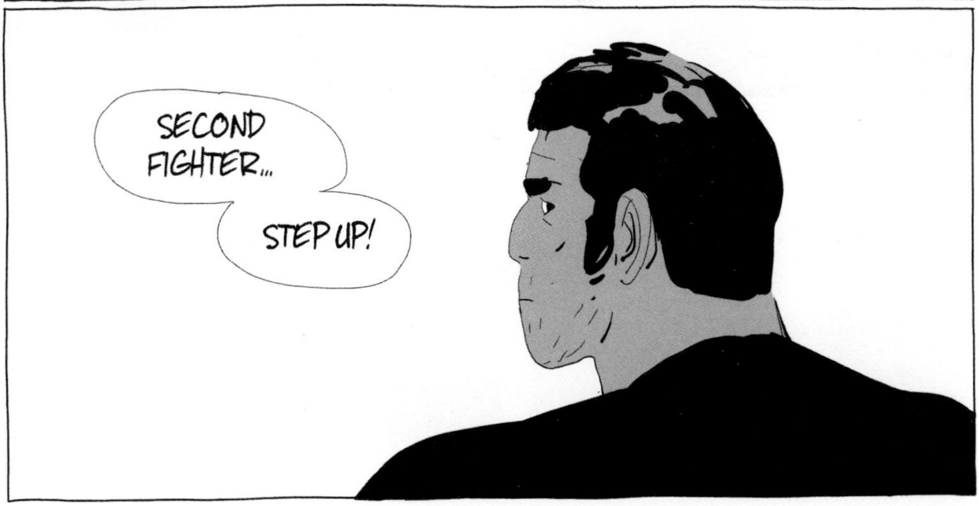
SECOND FIGHTER...
STEP UP!

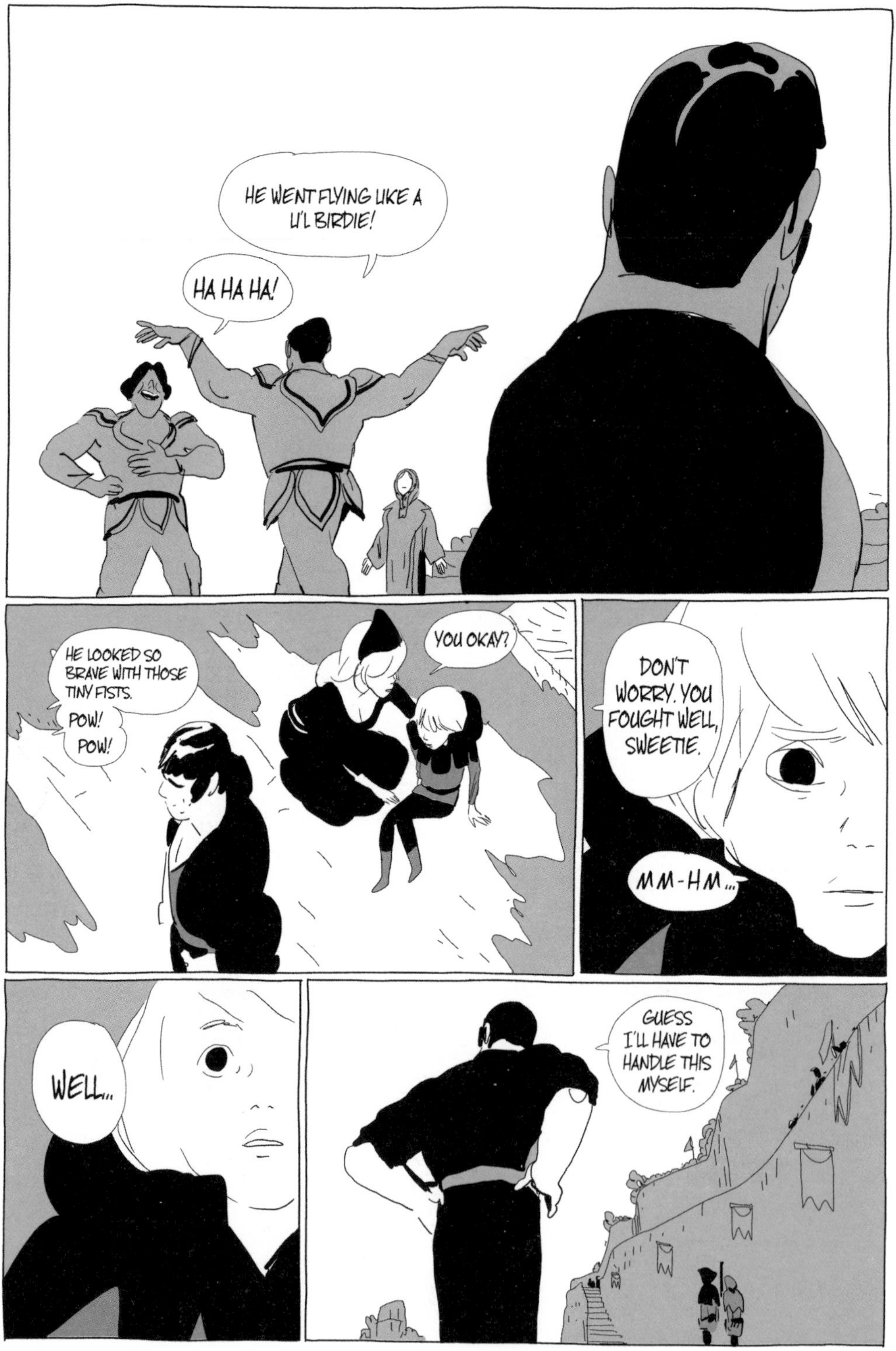
HE WENT FLYING LIKE A LI'L BIRDIE!
HA HA HA!
HE LOOKED SO BRAVE WITH THOSE TINY FISTS.
POW!
POW!
YOU OKAY?
DON'T WORRY. YOU FOUGHT WELL, SWEETIE.
MM-HM...
WELL...
GUESS I'LL HAVE TO HANDLE THIS MYSELF.

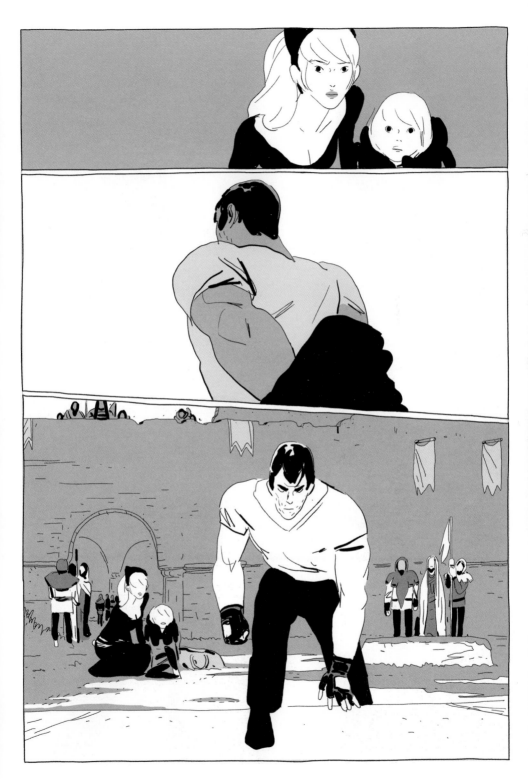

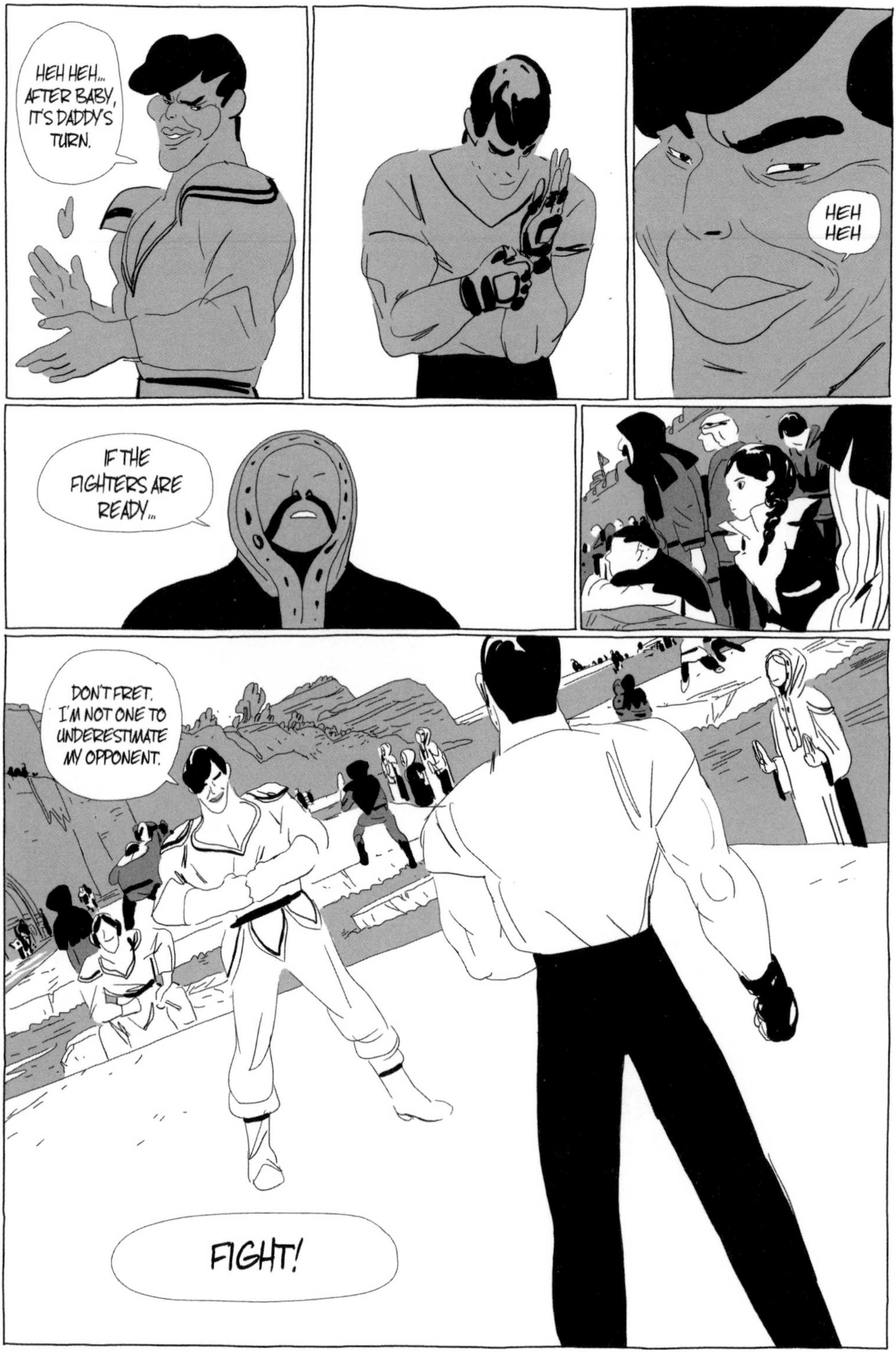
HEH HEH... AFTER BABY, IT'S DADDY'S TURN.
HEH HEH
IF THE FIGHTERS ARE READY...
DON'T FRET. I'M NOT ONE TO UNDERESTIMATE MY OPPONENT.
FIGHT!

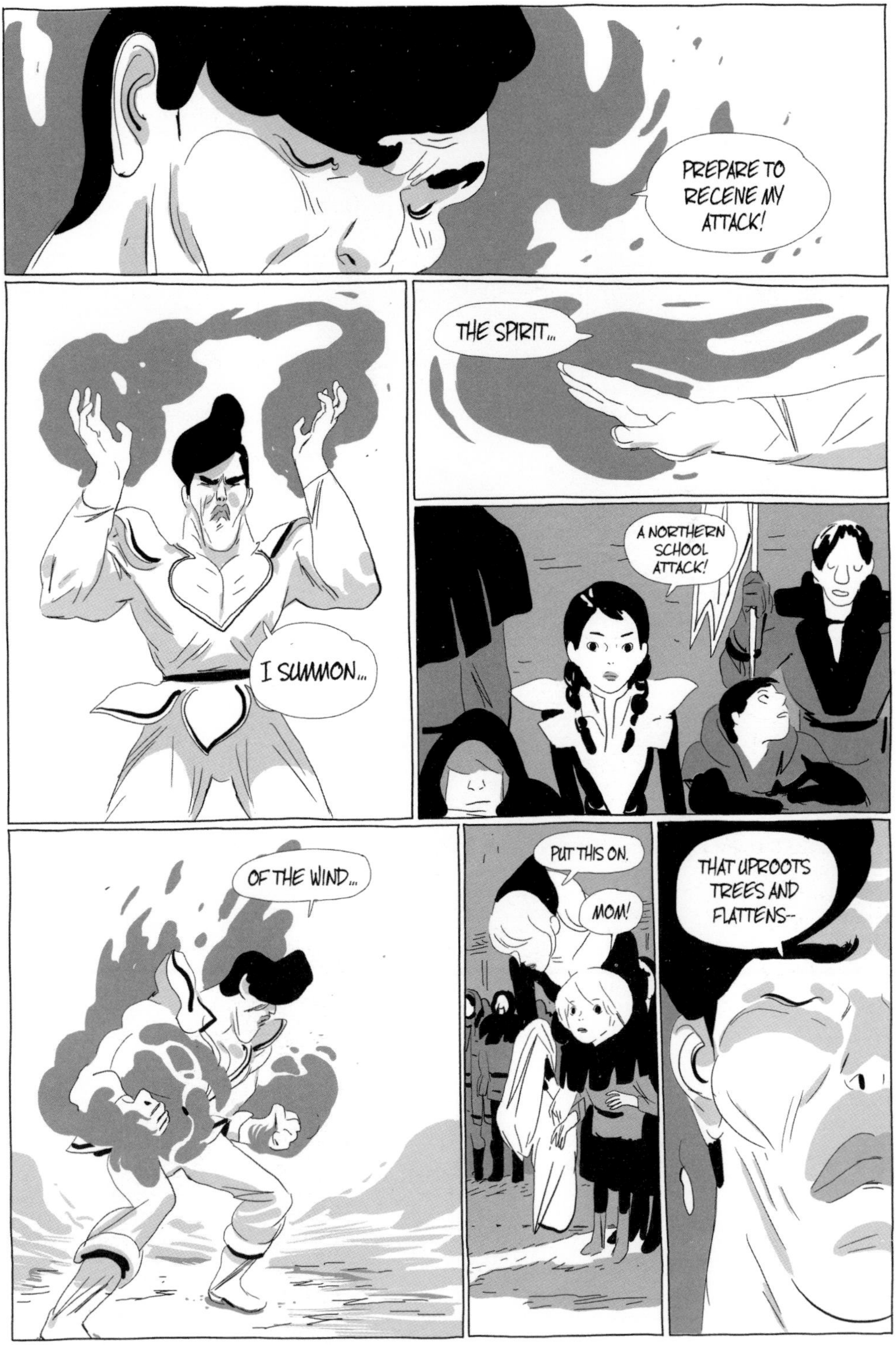
PREPARE TO RECEIVE MY ATTACK!
I SUMMON...
THE SPIRIT...
A NORTHERN SCHOOL ATTACK!
OF THE WIND...
PUT THIS ON.
MOM!
THAT UPROOTS TREES AND FLATTENS--

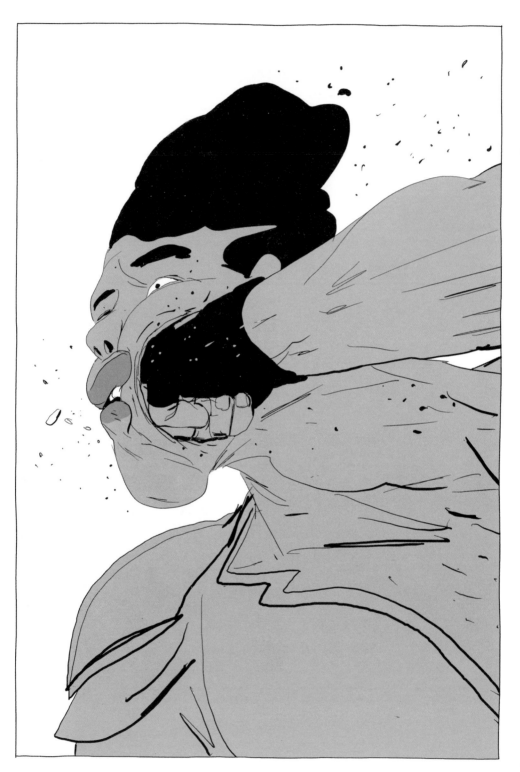

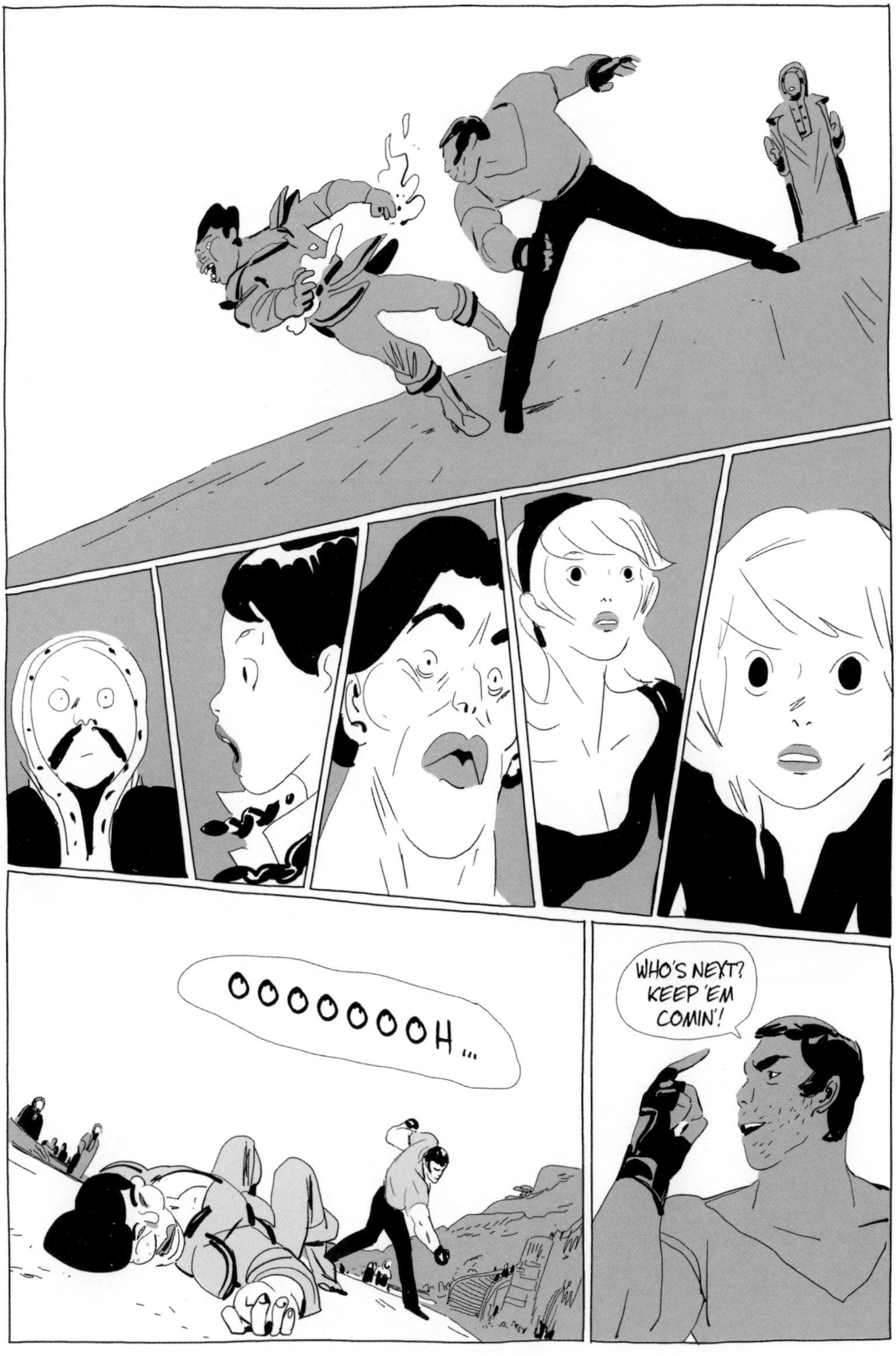
OOOOOOOH...
WHO'S NEXT? KEEP 'EM COMIN'!

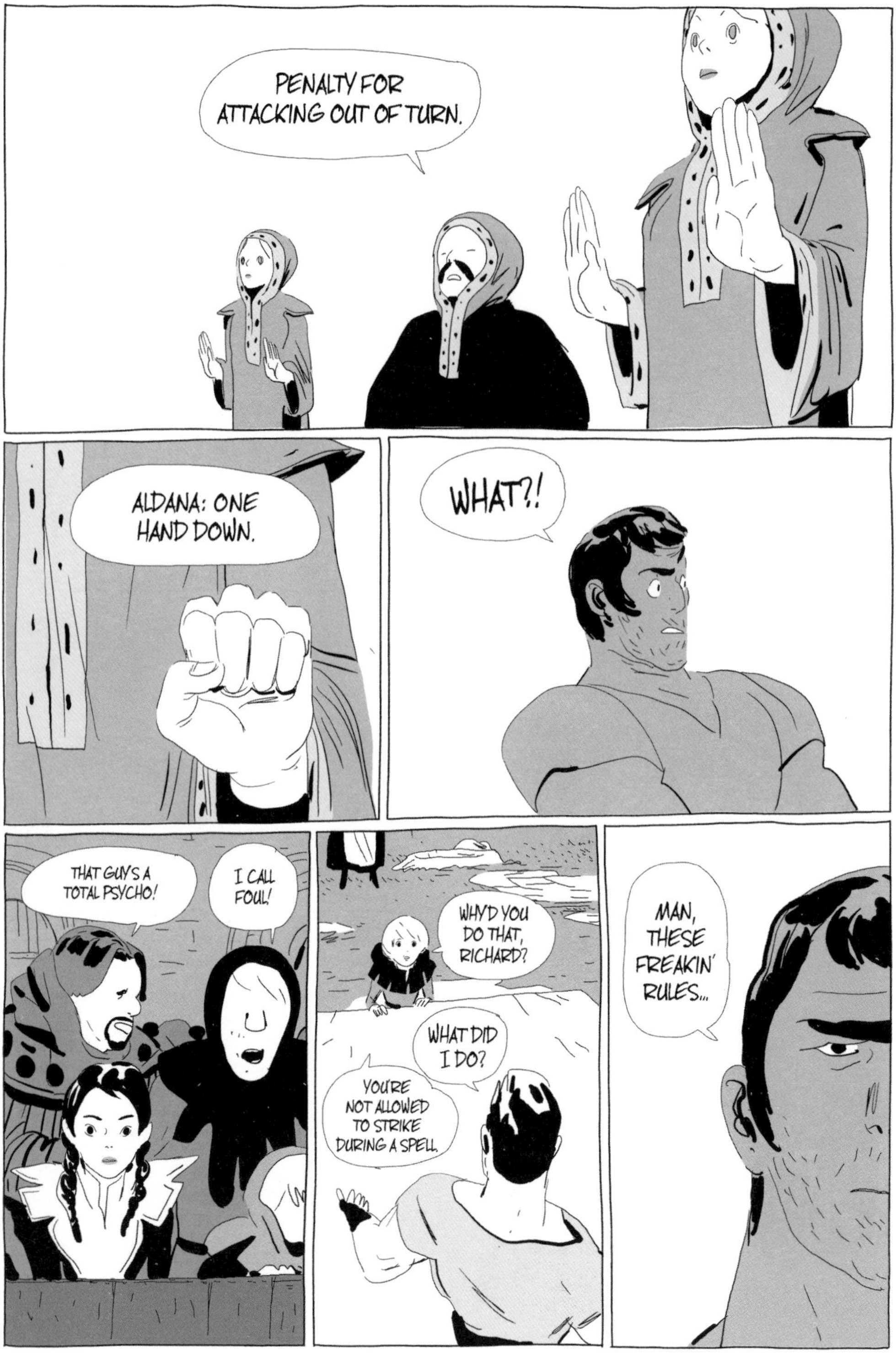
PENALTY FOR ATTACKING OUT OF TURN.
ALDANA: ONE HAND DOWN.
WHAT?!
THAT GUY'S A TOTAL PSYCHO!
I CALL FOUL!
WHY'D YOU DO THAT, RICHARD?
WHAT DID I DO?
YOU'RE NOT ALLOWED TO STRIKE DURING A SPELL.
MAN, THESE FREAKIN' RULES...

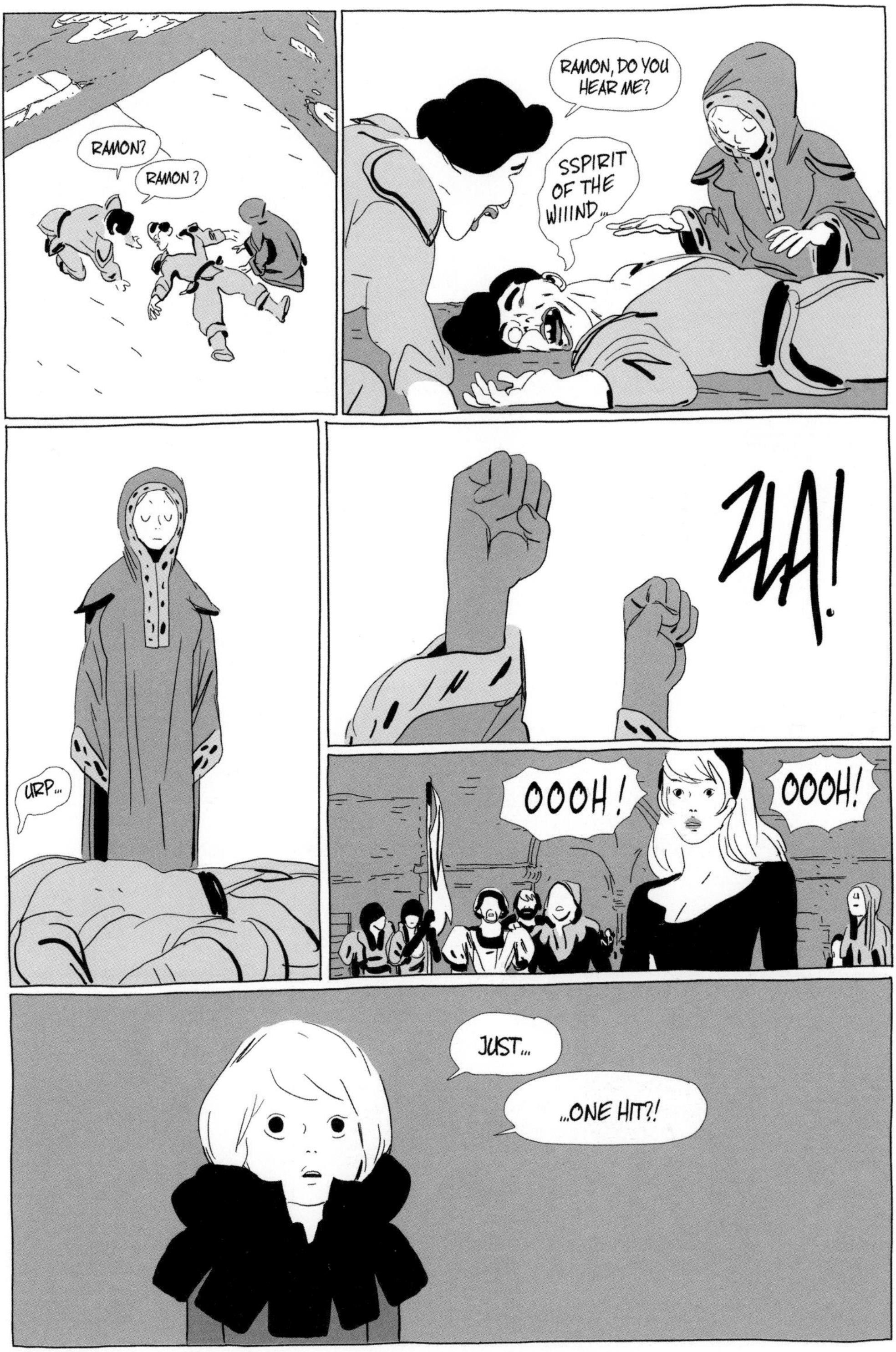
RAMON?
RAMON ?
RAMON, DO YOU HEAR ME?
SSPIRIT OF THE WIIIND...
URP...
ZLA!
OOOH!
OOOH!
JUST...
...ONE HIT?!

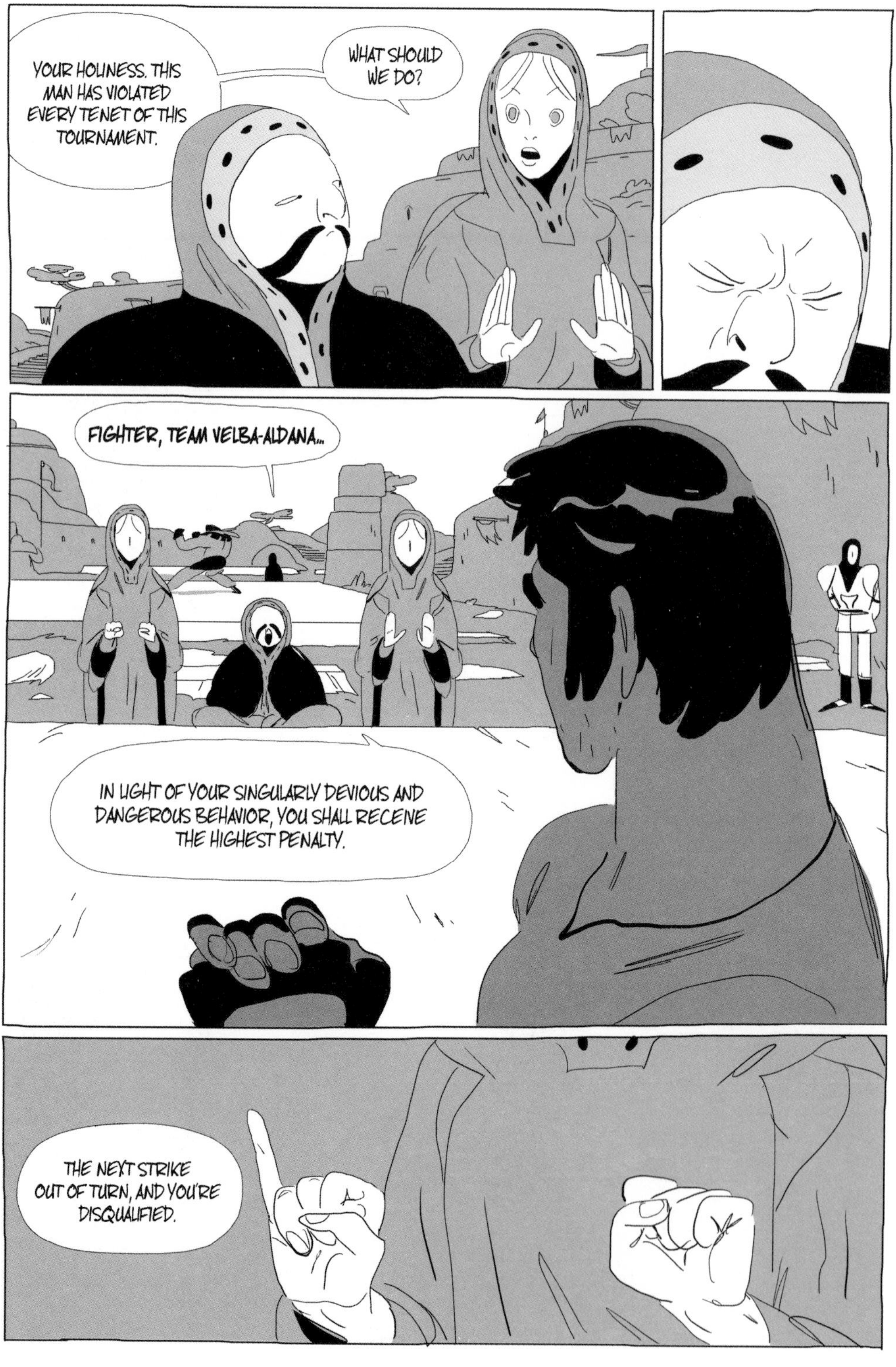
YOUR HOLINESS. THIS MAN HAS VIOLATED EVERY TENET OF THIS TOURNAMENT.
WHAT SHOULD WE DO?
FIGHTER, TEAM VELBA-ALDANA...
IN LIGHT OF YOUR SINGULARLY DEVIOUS AND DANGEROUS BEHAVIOR, YOU SHALL RECEIVE THE HIGHEST PENALTY.
THE NEXT STRIKE OUT OF TURN, AND YOU'RE DISQUALIFIED.

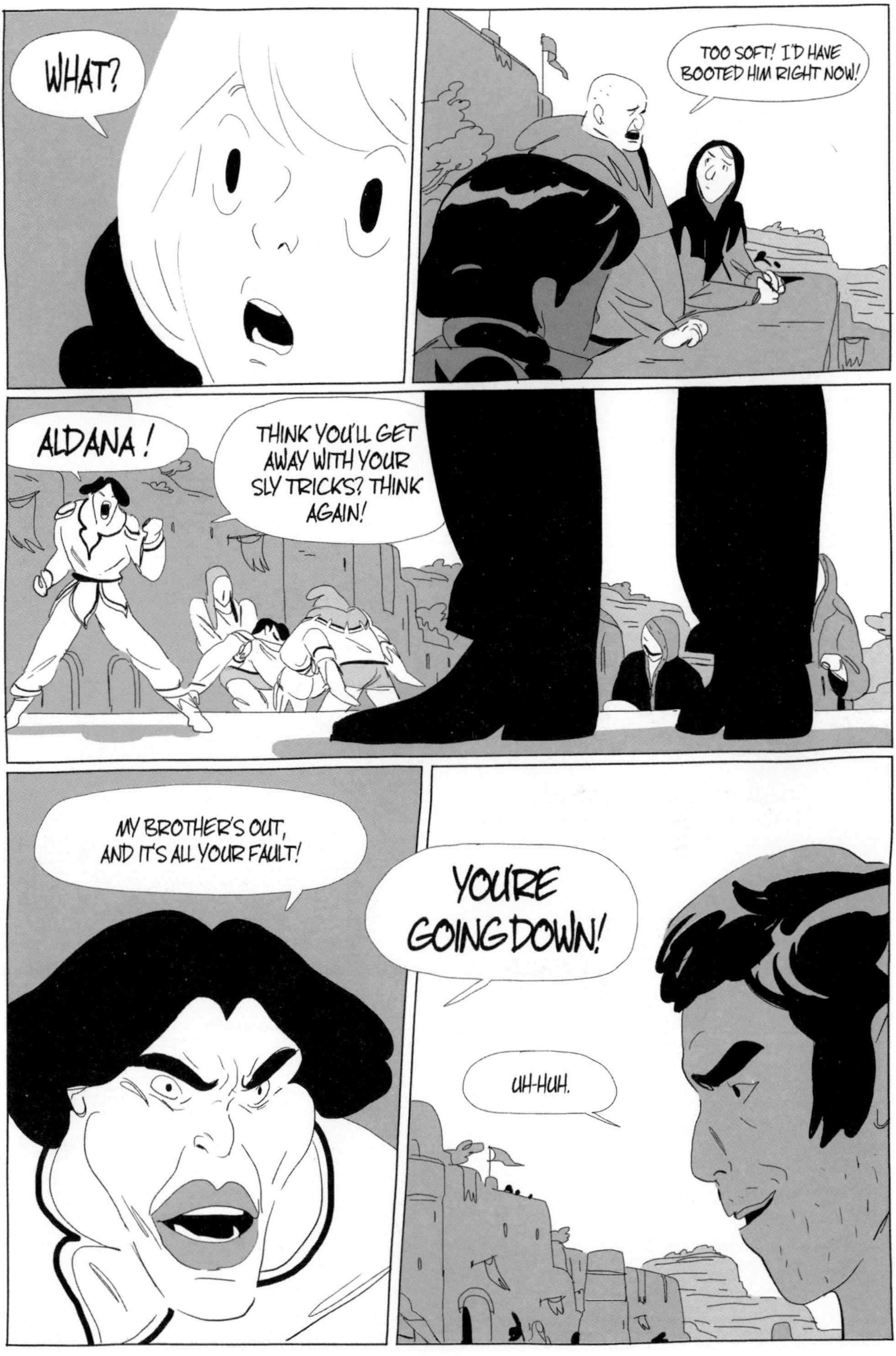
WHAT?
TOO SOFT! I'D HAVE BOOTED HIM RIGHT NOW!
ALDANA!
THINK YOU'LL GET AWAY WITH YOUR SLY TRICKS? THINK AGAIN!
MY BROTHER'S OUT, AND IT'S ALL YOUR FAULT!
YOU'RE GOING DOWN!
UH-HUH.

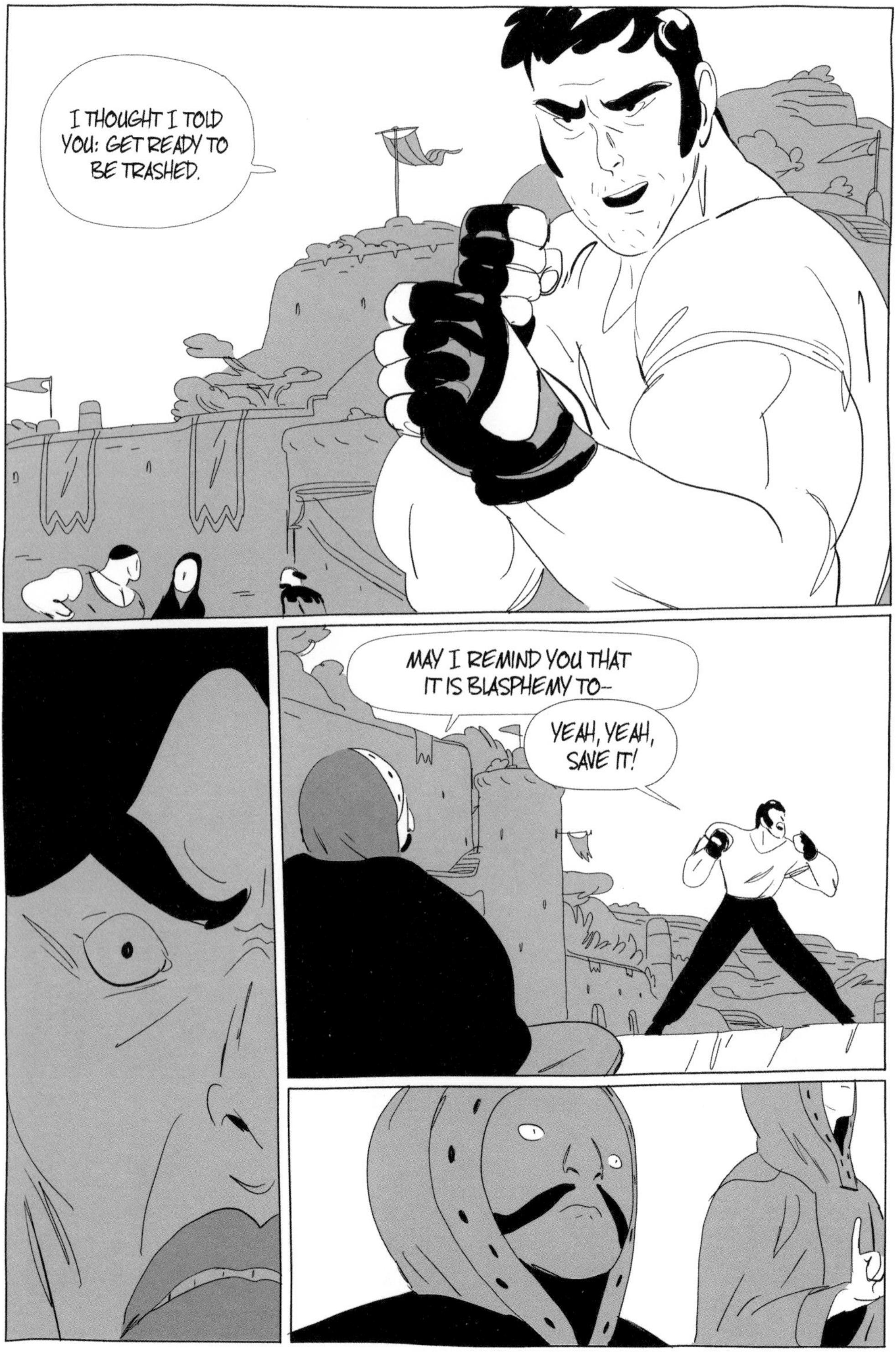
I THOUGHT I TOLD YOU: GET READY TO BE TRASHED.
MAY I REMIND YOU THAT IT IS BLASPHEMY TO--
YEAH, YEAH, SAVE IT!

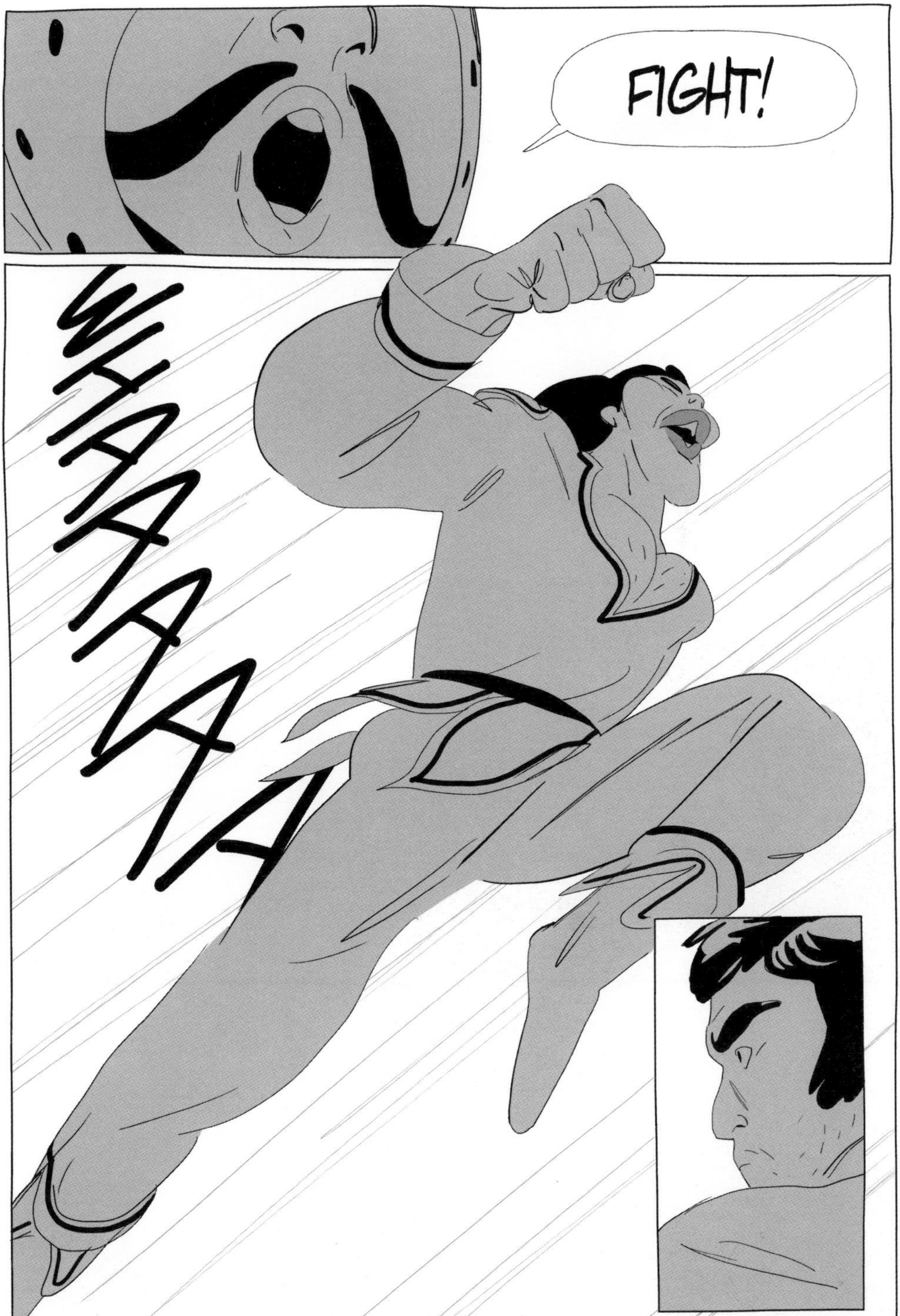
FIGHT!
WHAAAAA

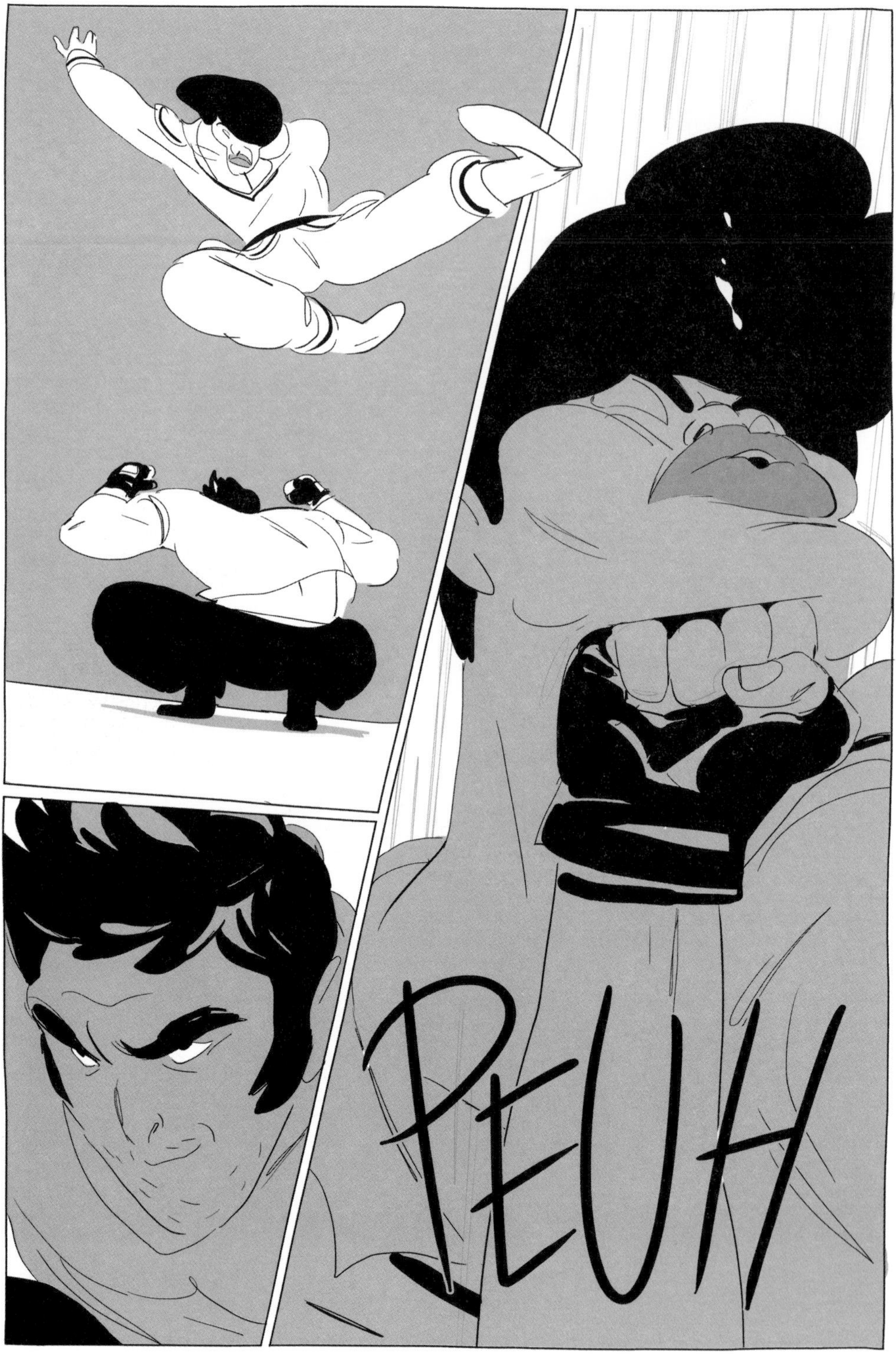
PEUH

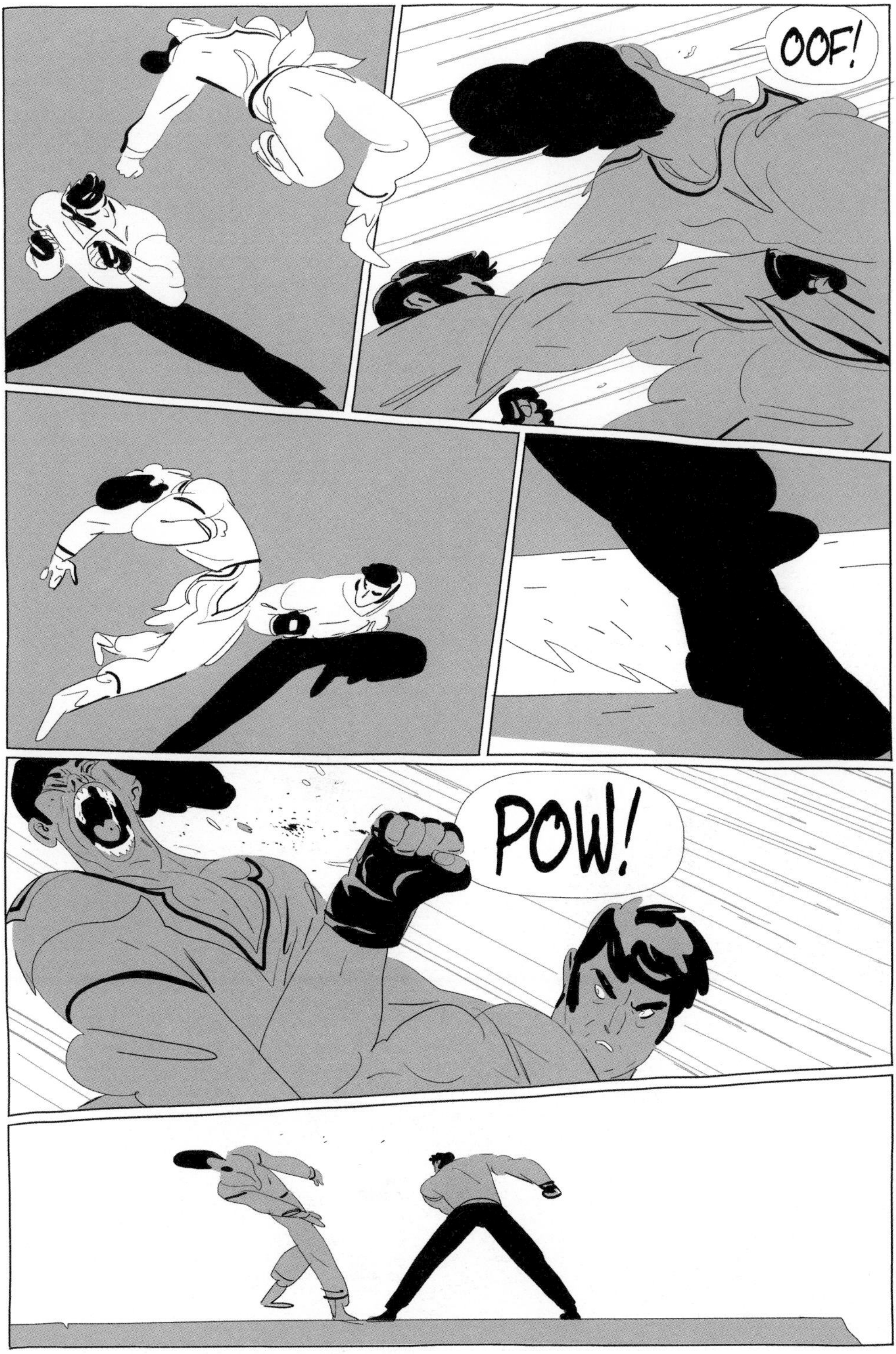
OOF!
POW!

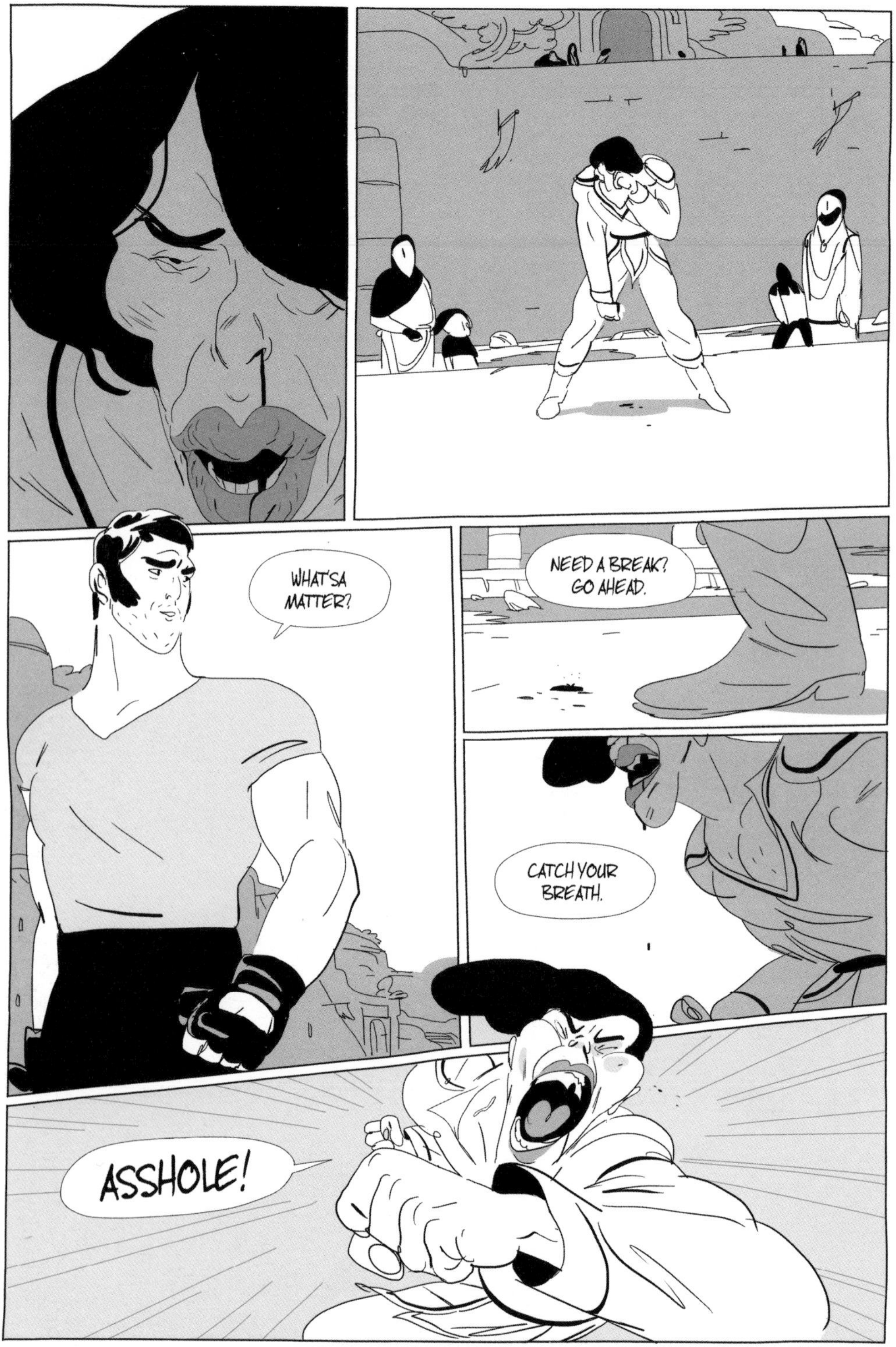
WHAT'SA MATTER?
NEED A BREAK? GO AHEAD.
CATCH YOUR BREATH.
ASSHOLE!

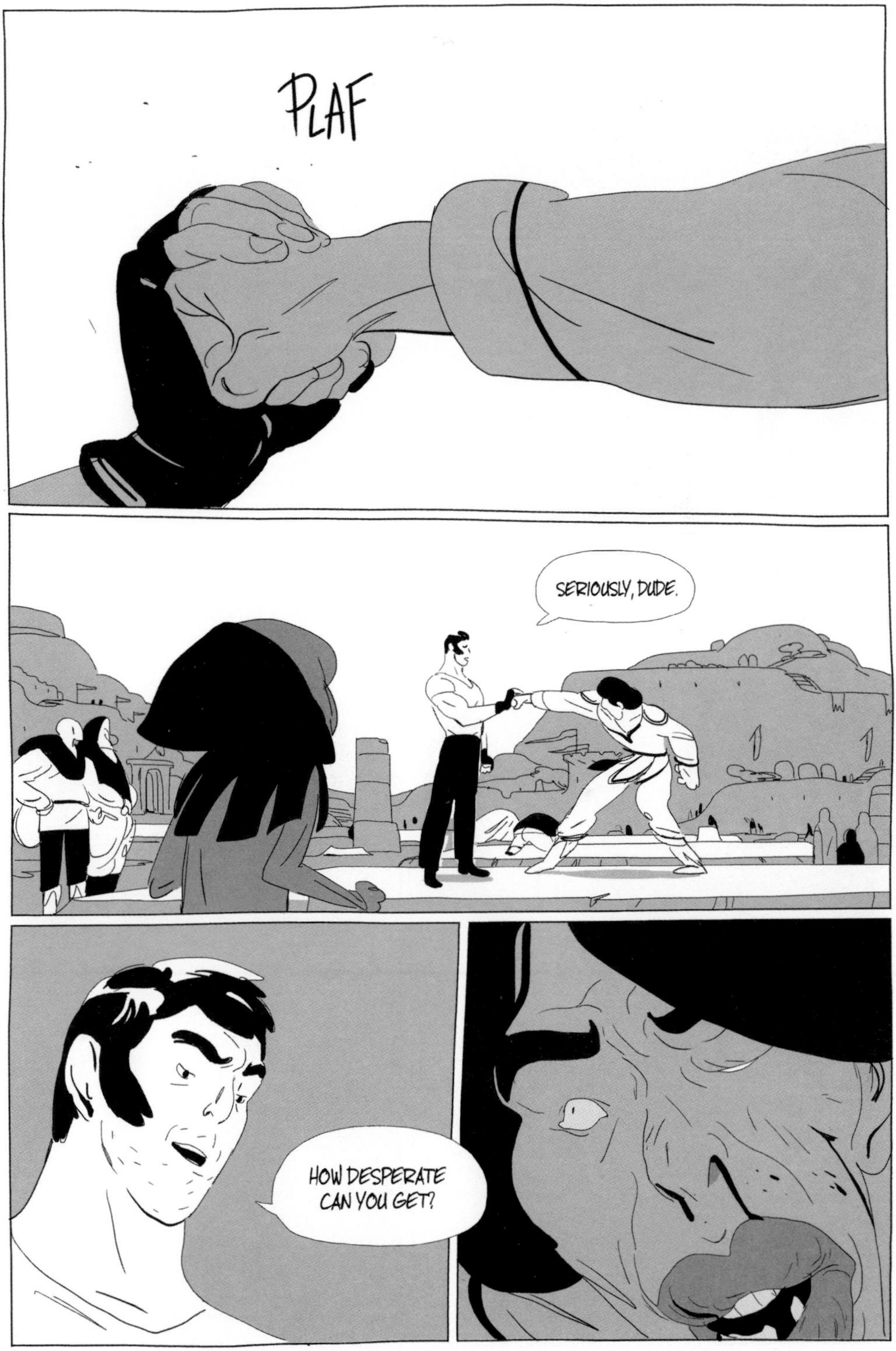
PLAF
SERIOUSLY, DUDE.
HOW DESPERATE CAN YOU GET?

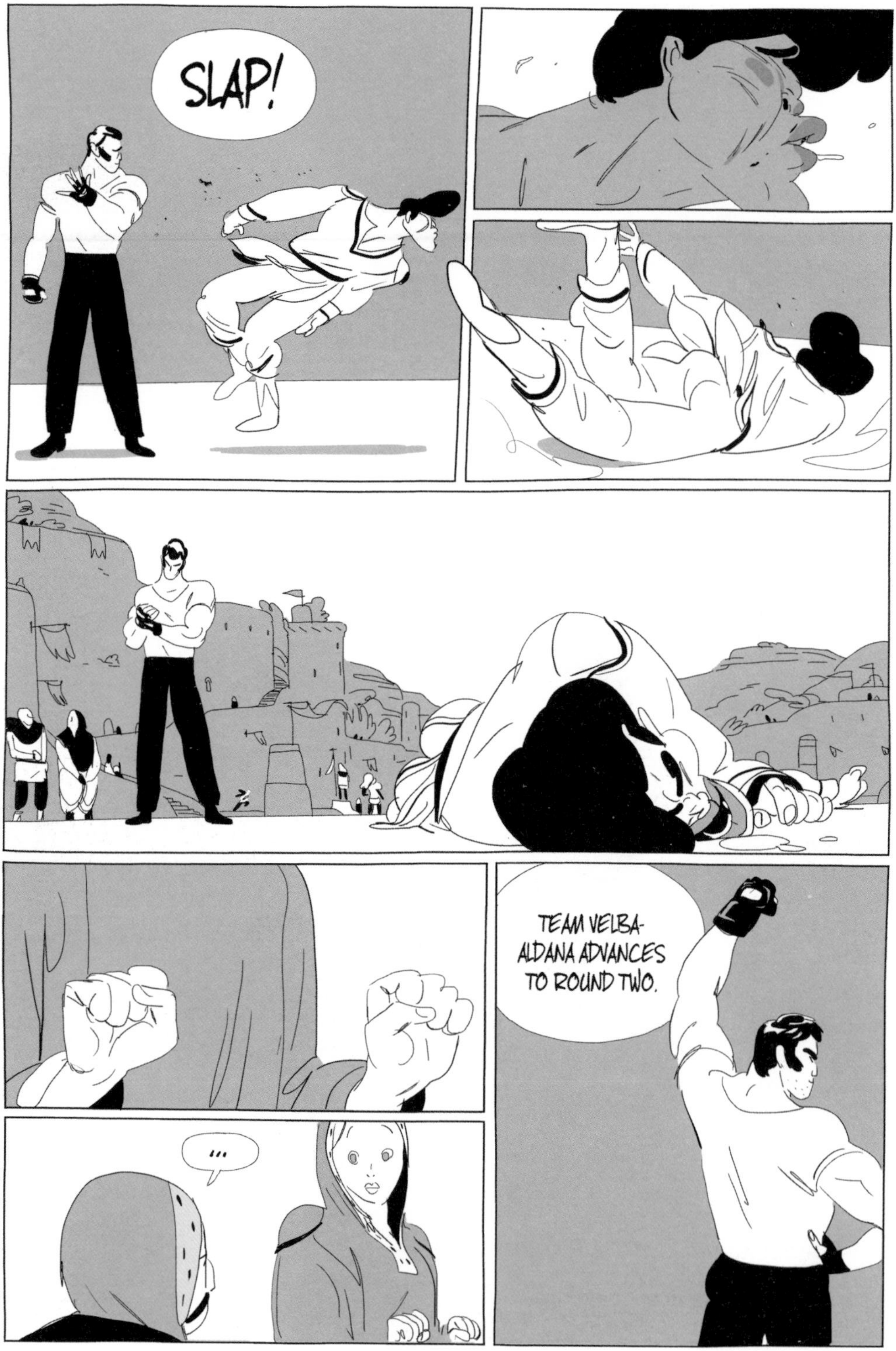
SLAP!
...
TEAM VELBA-ALDANA ADVANCES TO ROUND TWO.

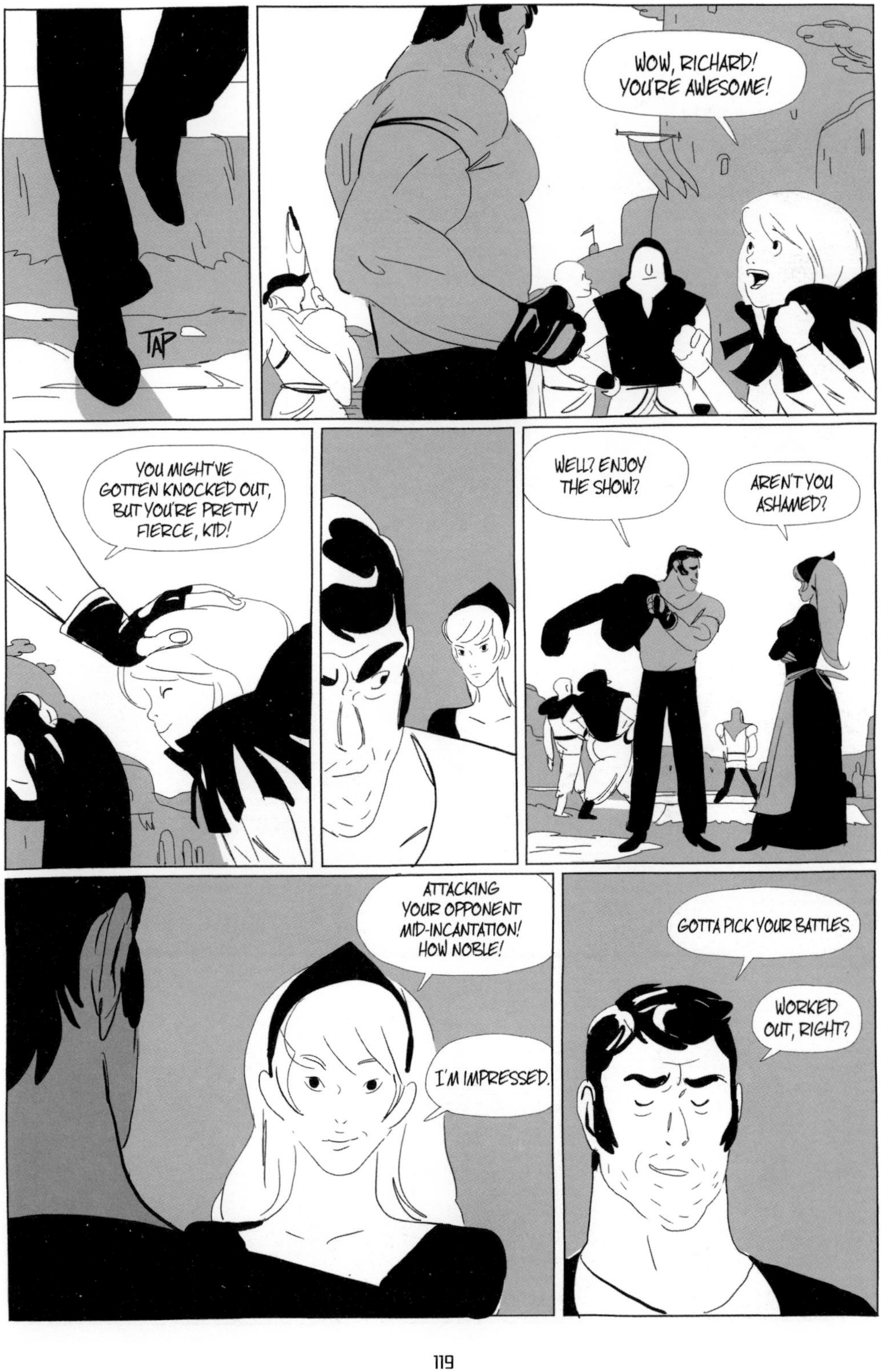
TAP
WOW, RICHARD! YOU'RE AWESOME!
YOU MIGHT'VE GOTTEN KNOCKED OUT, BUT YOU'RE PRETTY FIERCE, KID!
WELL? ENJOY THE SHOW?
AREN'T YOU ASHAMED?
ATTACKING YOUR OPPONENT MID-INCANTATION! HOW NOBLE!
I'M IMPRESSED.
GOTTA PICK YOUR BATTLES.
WORKED OUT, RIGHT?

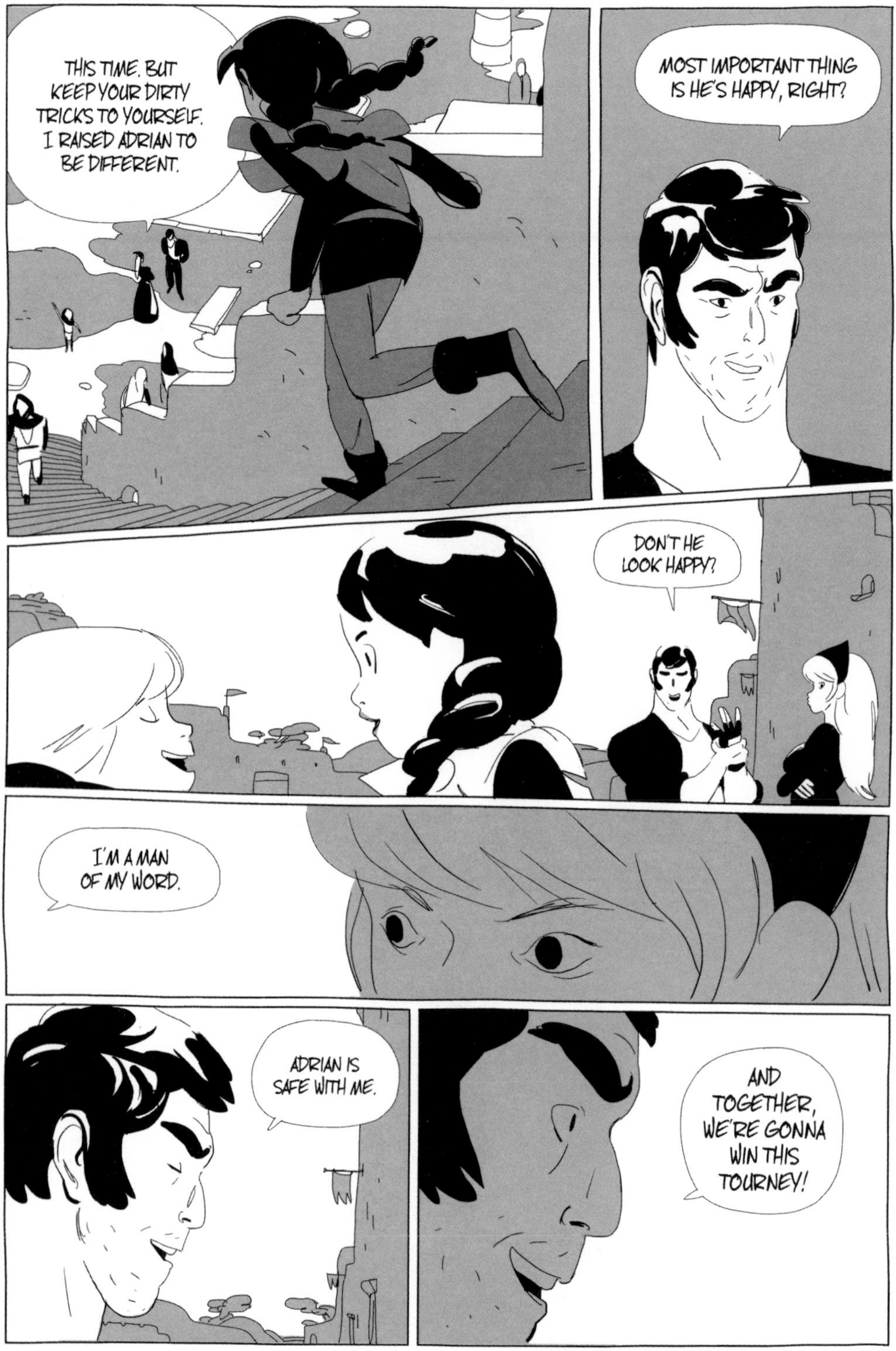
THIS TIME. BUT KEEP YOUR DIRTY TRICKS TO YOURSELF. I RAISED ADRIAN TO BE DIFFERENT.
MOST IMPORTANT THING IS HE'S HAPPY, RIGHT?
DON'T HE LOOK HAPPY?
I'M A MAN OF MY WORD.
ADRIAN IS SAFE WITH ME.
AND TOGETHER, WE'RE GONNA WIN THIS TOURNEY!

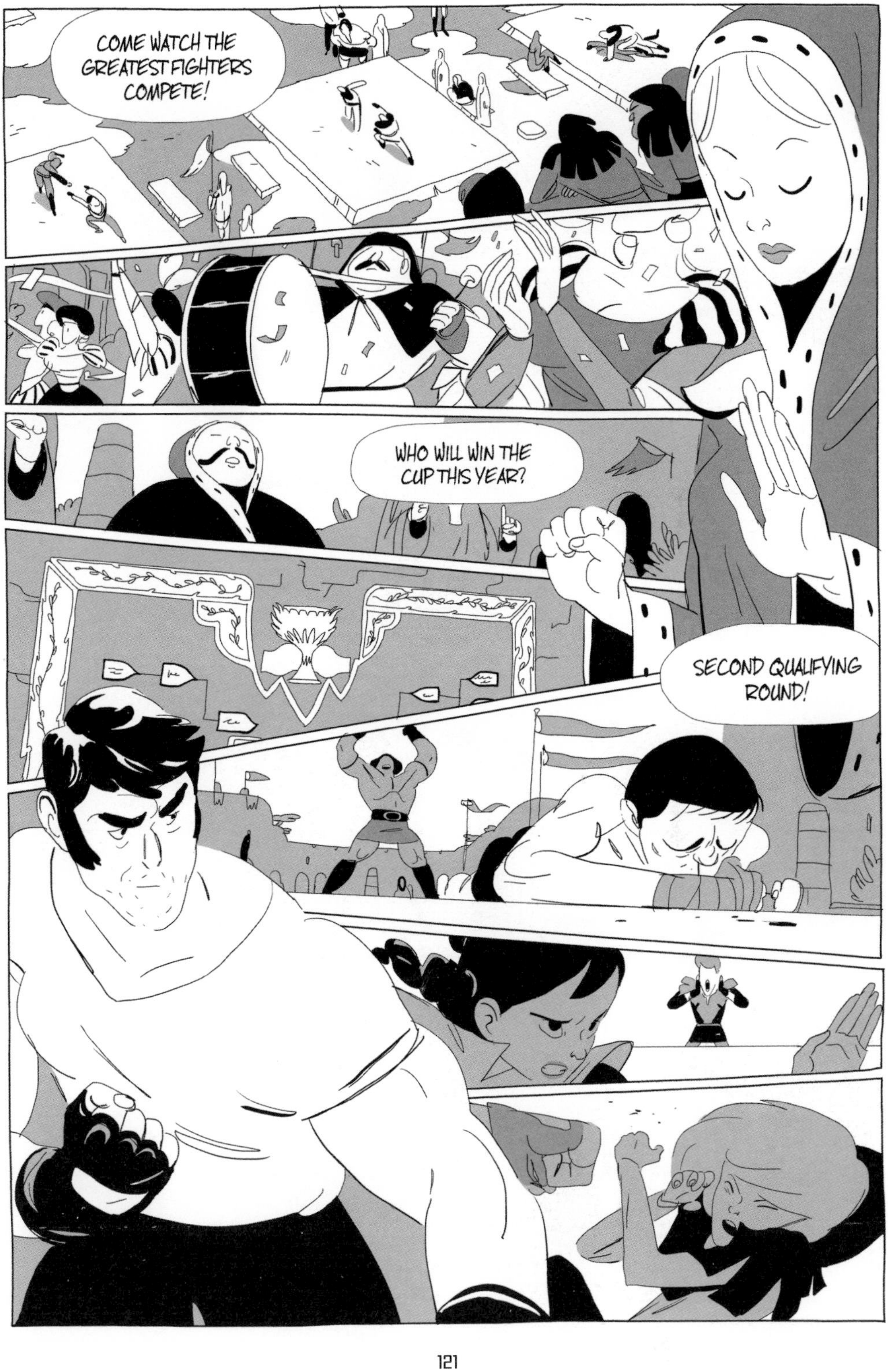
COME WATCH THE GREATEST FIGHTERS COMPETE!
WHO WILL WIN THE CUP THIS YEAR?
SECOND QUALIFYING ROUND!

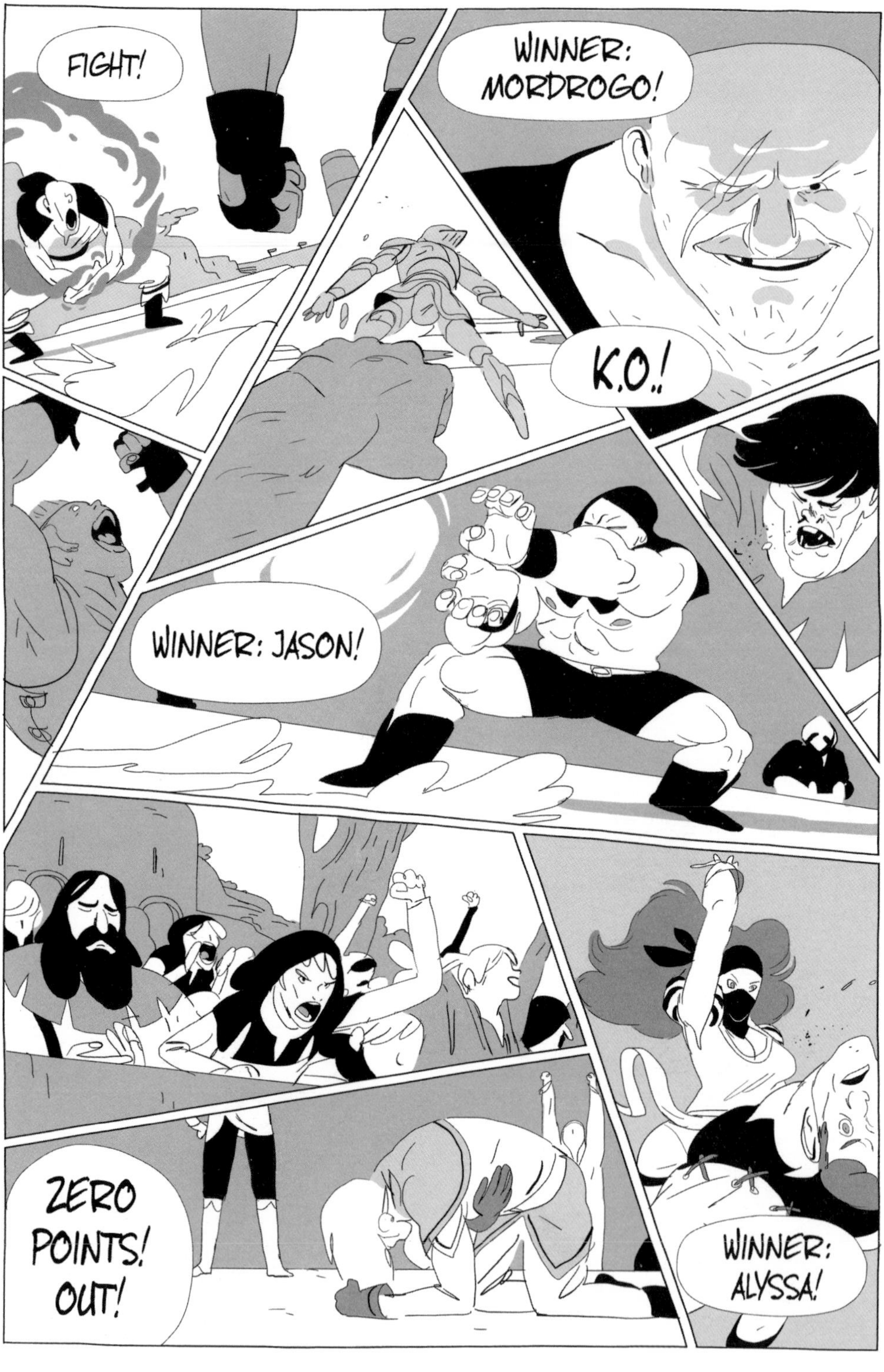
FIGHT!
WINNER: MORDROGO!
K.O.!
WINNER: JASON!
ZERO POINTS! OUT!
WINNER: ALYSSA!

WINNER: ELORNA!

WINNER: ALDANA!

WINNER: GREGORIO!

OUT!

HEY, MARIANNE! HEARD YOUR KID'S STILL IN THE RUNNING!

TAKE THE DAY OFF IF YOU WANT.

I'M OKAY, BOSS! ADRIAN'S A BIG BOY.

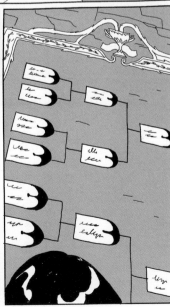

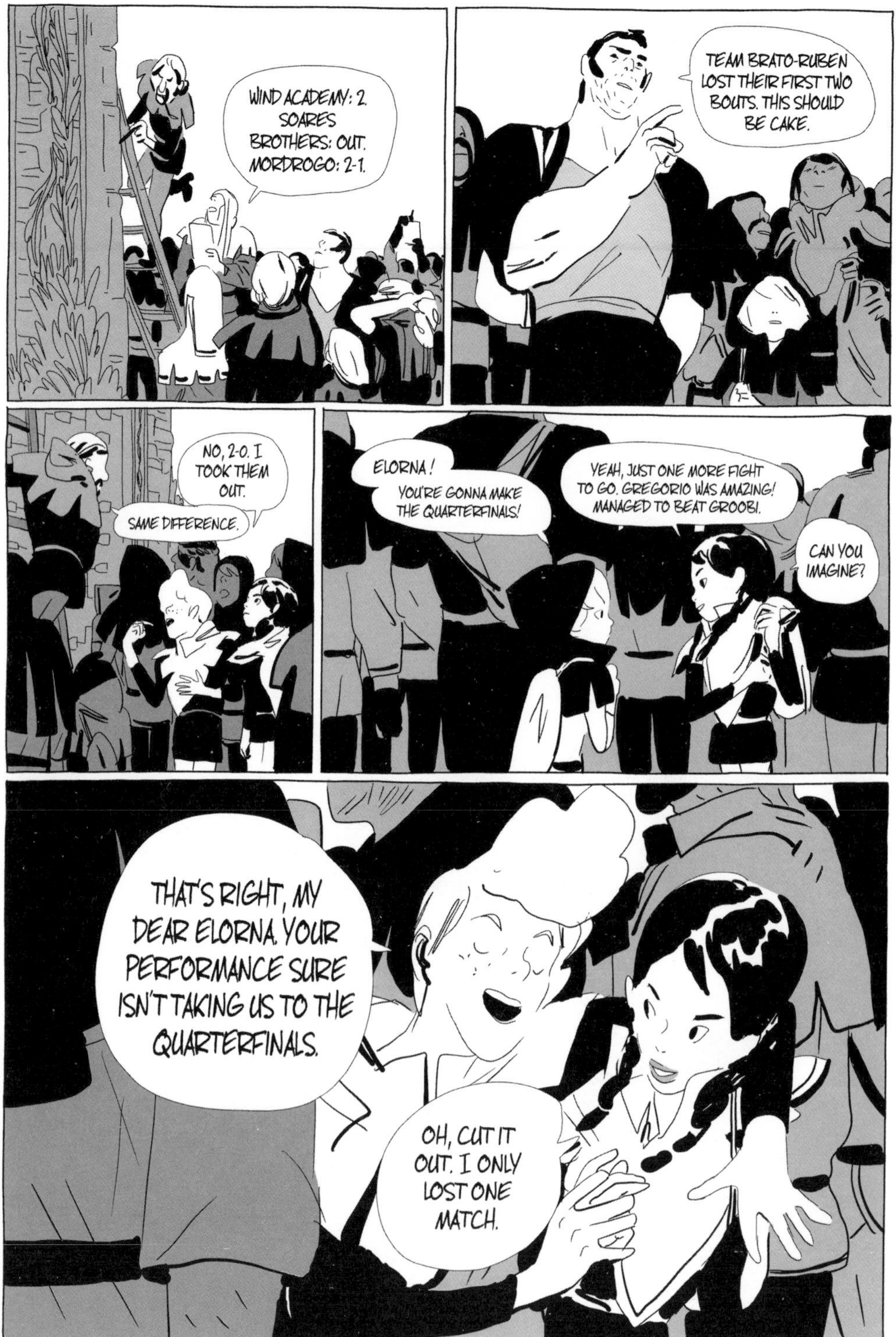
WIND ACADEMY: 2. SOARES BROTHERS: OUT. MORDROGO: 2-1.
TEAM BRATO-RUBEN LOST THEIR FIRST TWO BOUTS. THIS SHOULD BE CAKE.
NO, 2-0. I TOOK THEM OUT.
SAME DIFFERENCE.
ELORNA!
YOU'RE GONNA MAKE THE QUARTERFINALS!
YEAH, JUST ONE MORE FIGHT TO GO. GREGORIO WAS AMAZING! MANAGED TO BEAT GROOBI.
CAN YOU IMAGINE?
THAT'S RIGHT, MY DEAR ELORNA. YOUR PERFORMANCE SURE ISN'T TAKING US TO THE QUARTERFINALS.
OH, CUT IT OUT. I ONLY LOST ONE MATCH.

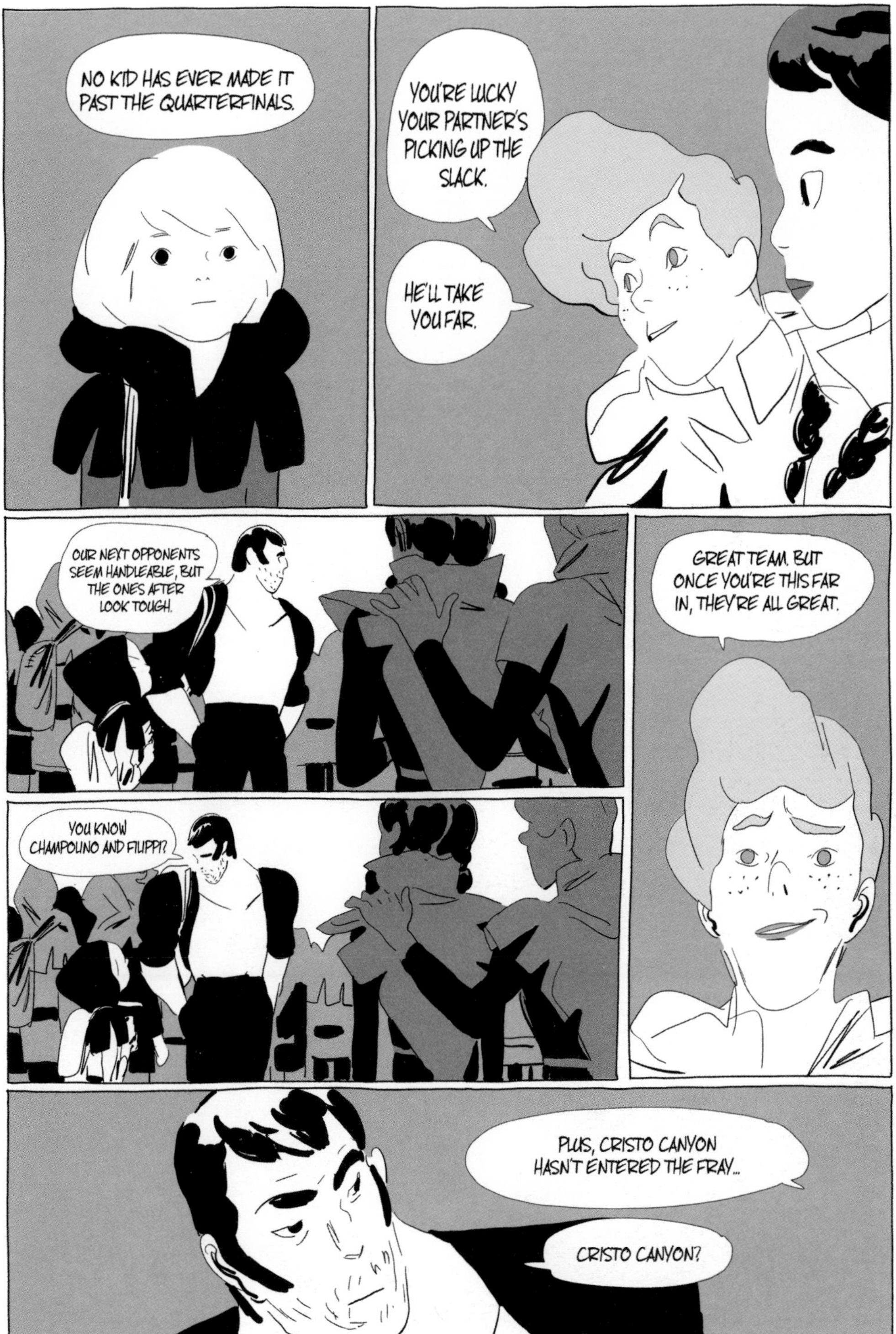
NO KID HAS EVER MADE IT PAST THE QUARTERFINALS.
YOU'RE LUCKY YOUR PARTNER'S PICKING UP THE SLACK.
HE'LL TAKE YOU FAR.
OUR NEXT OPPONENTS SEEM HANDLEABLE, BUT THE ONES AFTER LOOK TOUGH.
GREAT TEAM. BUT ONCE YOU'RE THIS FAR IN, THEY'RE ALL GREAT.
YOU KNOW CHAMPOLINO AND FILIPPI?
PLUS, CRISTO CANYON HASN'T ENTERED THE FRAY...
CRISTO CANYON?

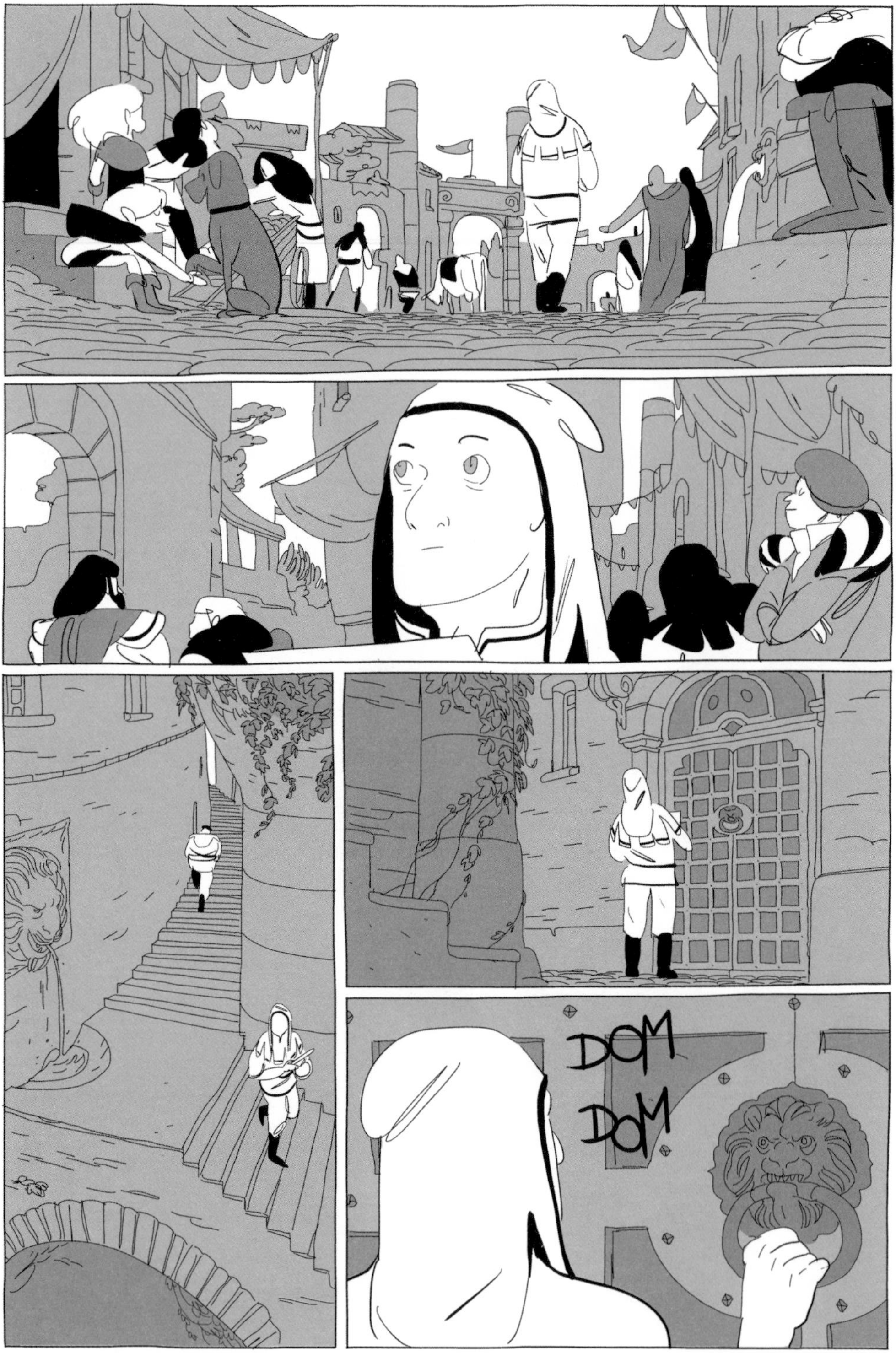

DOM
DOM

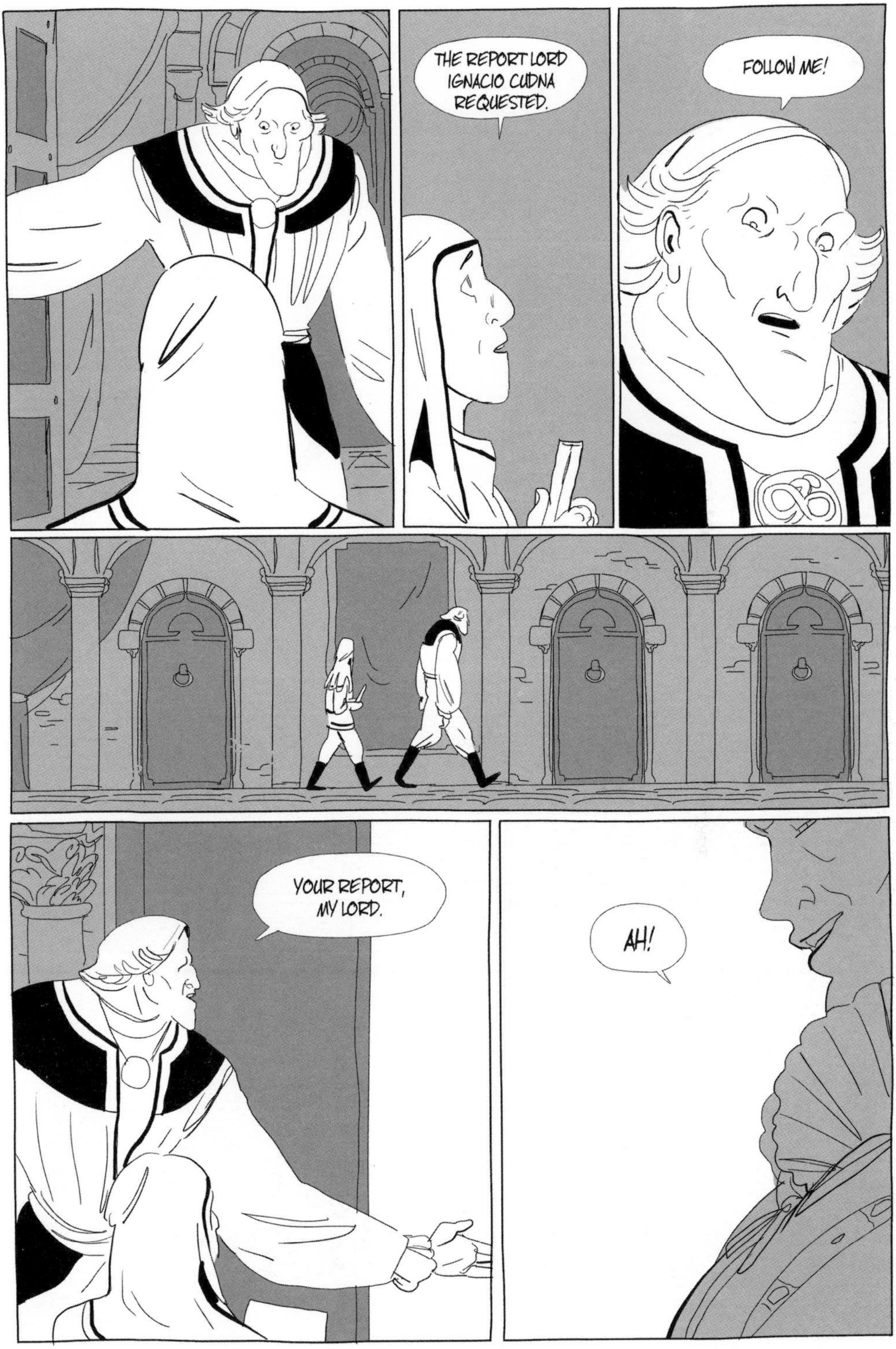
THE REPORT LORD IGNACIO CUDNA REQUESTED.
FOLLOW ME!
YOUR REPORT, MY LORD.
AH!

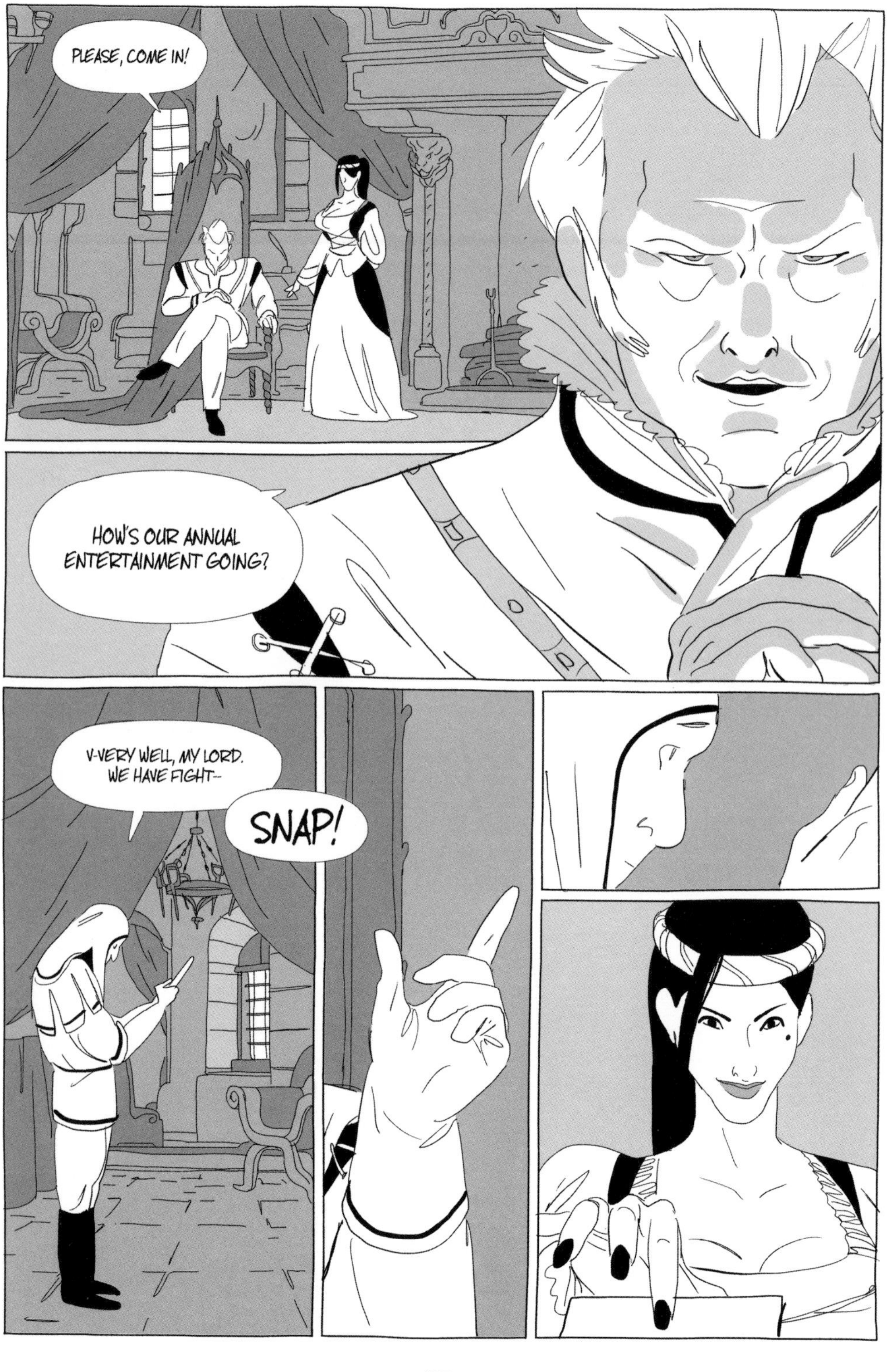
PLEASE, COME IN!
HOW'S OUR ANNUAL ENTERTAINMENT GOING?
V-VERY WELL, MY LORD. WE HAVE FIGHT--
SNAP!

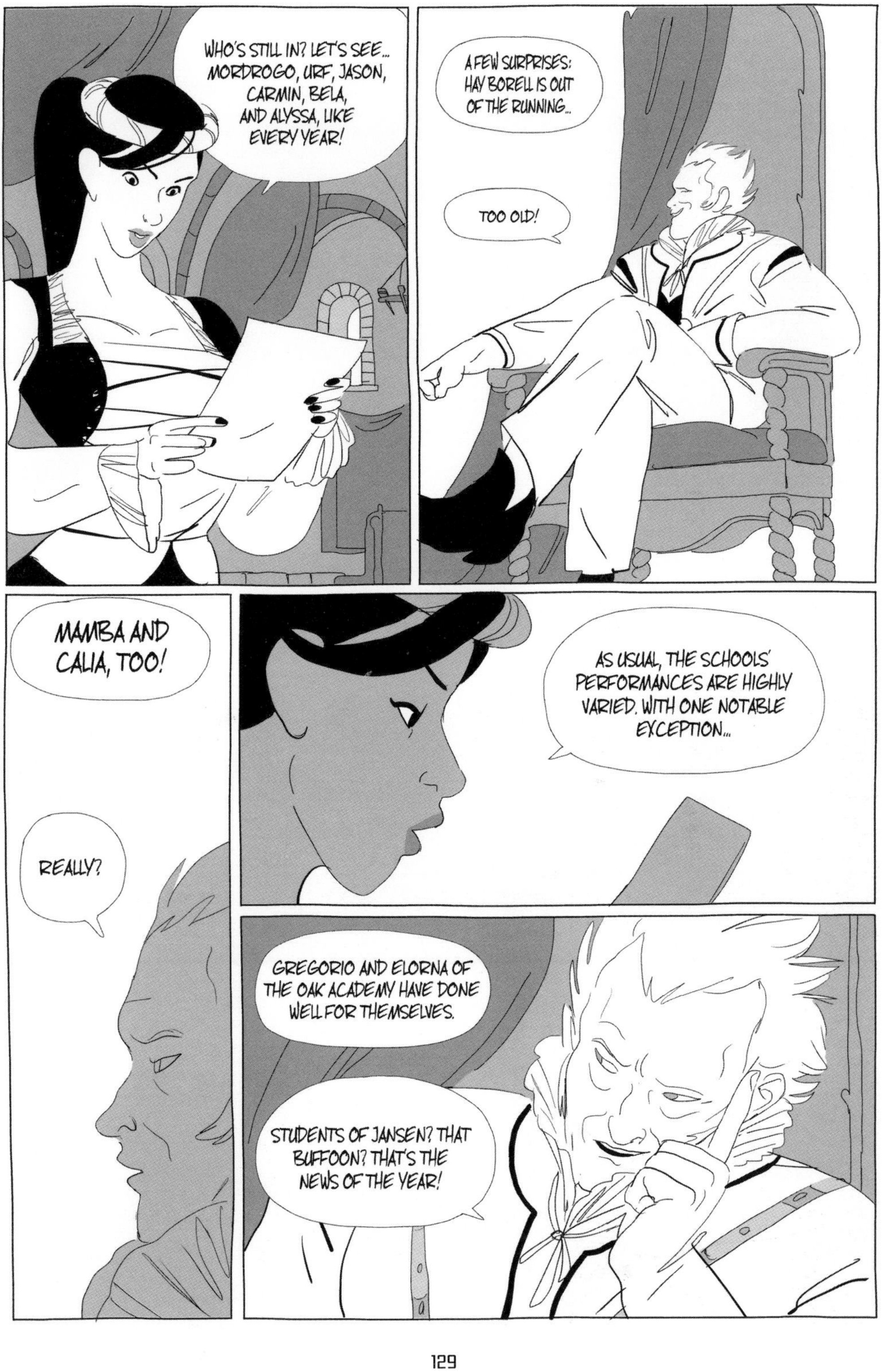
WHO'S STILL IN? LET'S SEE... MORDROGO, URF, JASON, CARMIN, BELA, AND ALYSSA, LIKE EVERY YEAR!
A FEW SURPRISES: HAY BORELL IS OUT OF THE RUNNING...
TOO OLD!
MAMBA AND CALIA, TOO!
AS USUAL, THE SCHOOLS' PERFORMANCES ARE HIGHLY VARIED. WITH ONE NOTABLE EXCEPTION...
REALLY?
GREGORIO AND ELORNA OF THE OAK ACADEMY HAVE DONE WELL FOR THEMSELVES.
STUDENTS OF JANSEN? THAT BUFFOON? THAT'S THE NEWS OF THE YEAR!

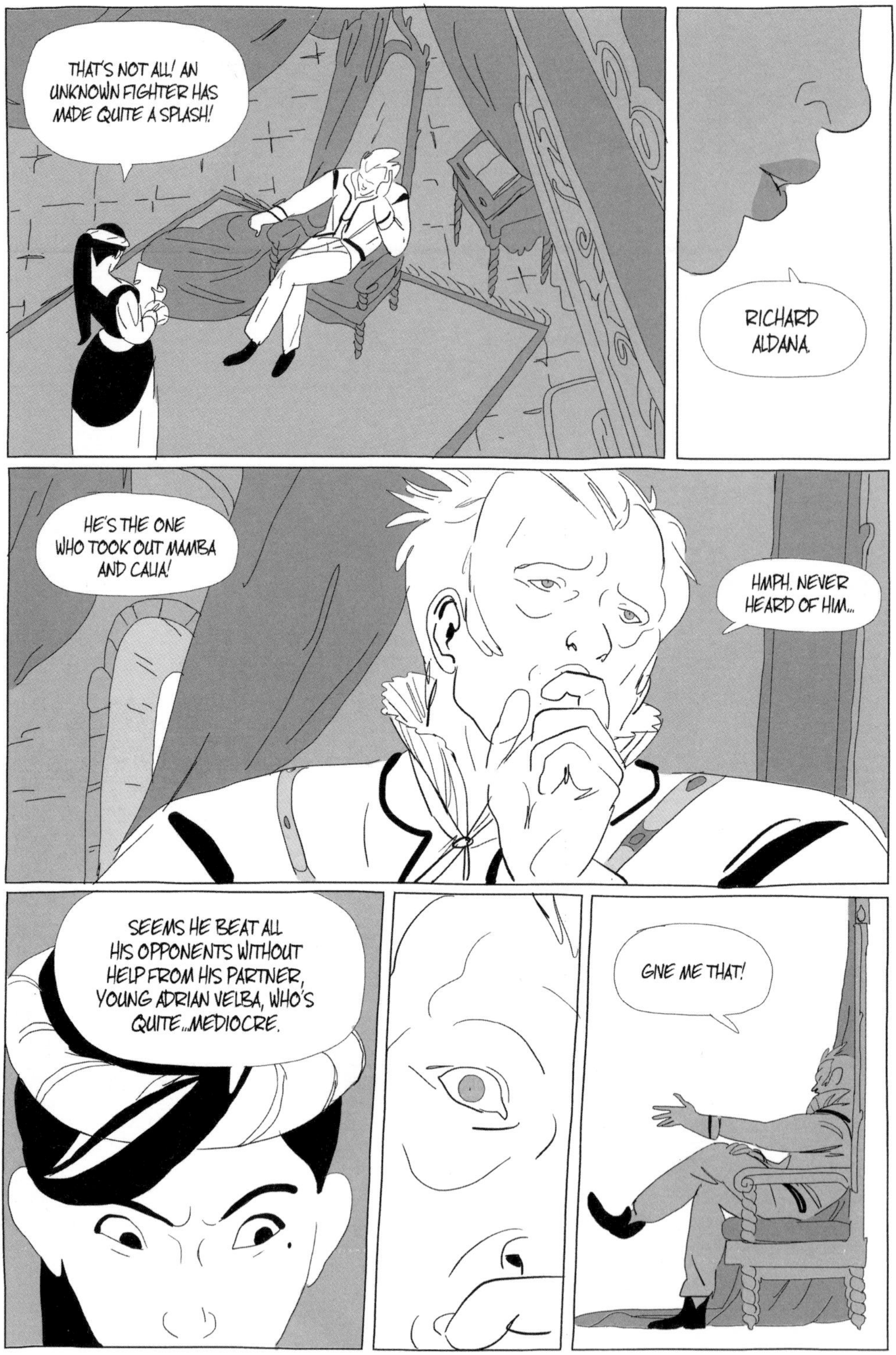
THAT'S NOT ALL! AN UNKNOWN FIGHTER HAS MADE QUITE A SPLASH!
RICHARD ALDANA.
HE'S THE ONE WHO TOOK OUT MAMBA AND CALIA!
HMPH. NEVER HEARD OF HIM...
SEEMS HE BEAT ALL HIS OPPONENTS WITHOUT HELP FROM HIS PARTNER, YOUNG ADRIAN VELBA, WHO'S QUITE...MEDIOCRE.
GIVE ME THAT!

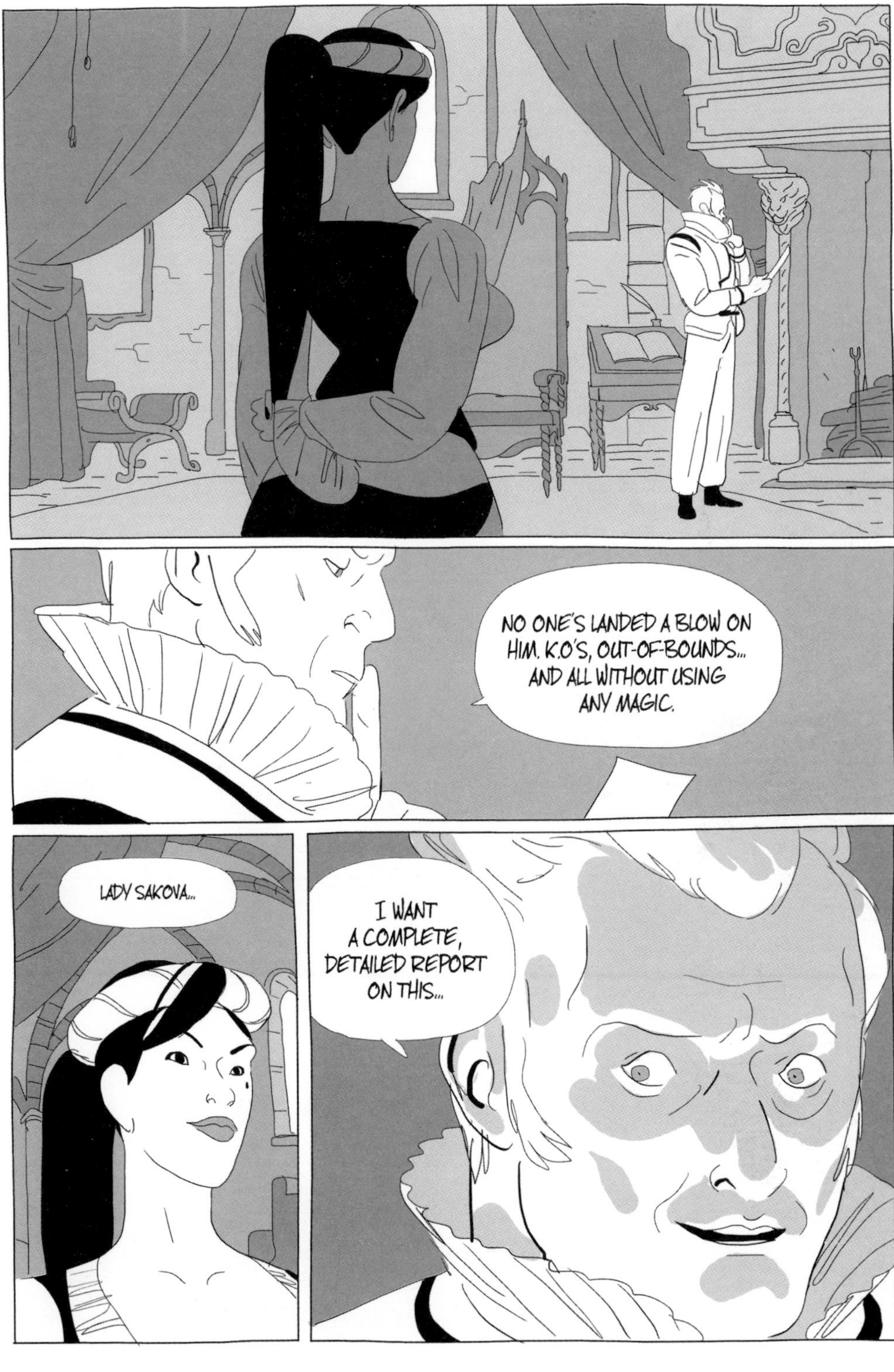
NO ONE'S LANDED A BLOW ON HIM. K.O'S, OUT-OF-BOUNDS... AND ALL WITHOUT USING ANY MAGIC.
LADY SAKOVA...
I WANT A COMPLETE, DETAILED REPORT ON THIS...

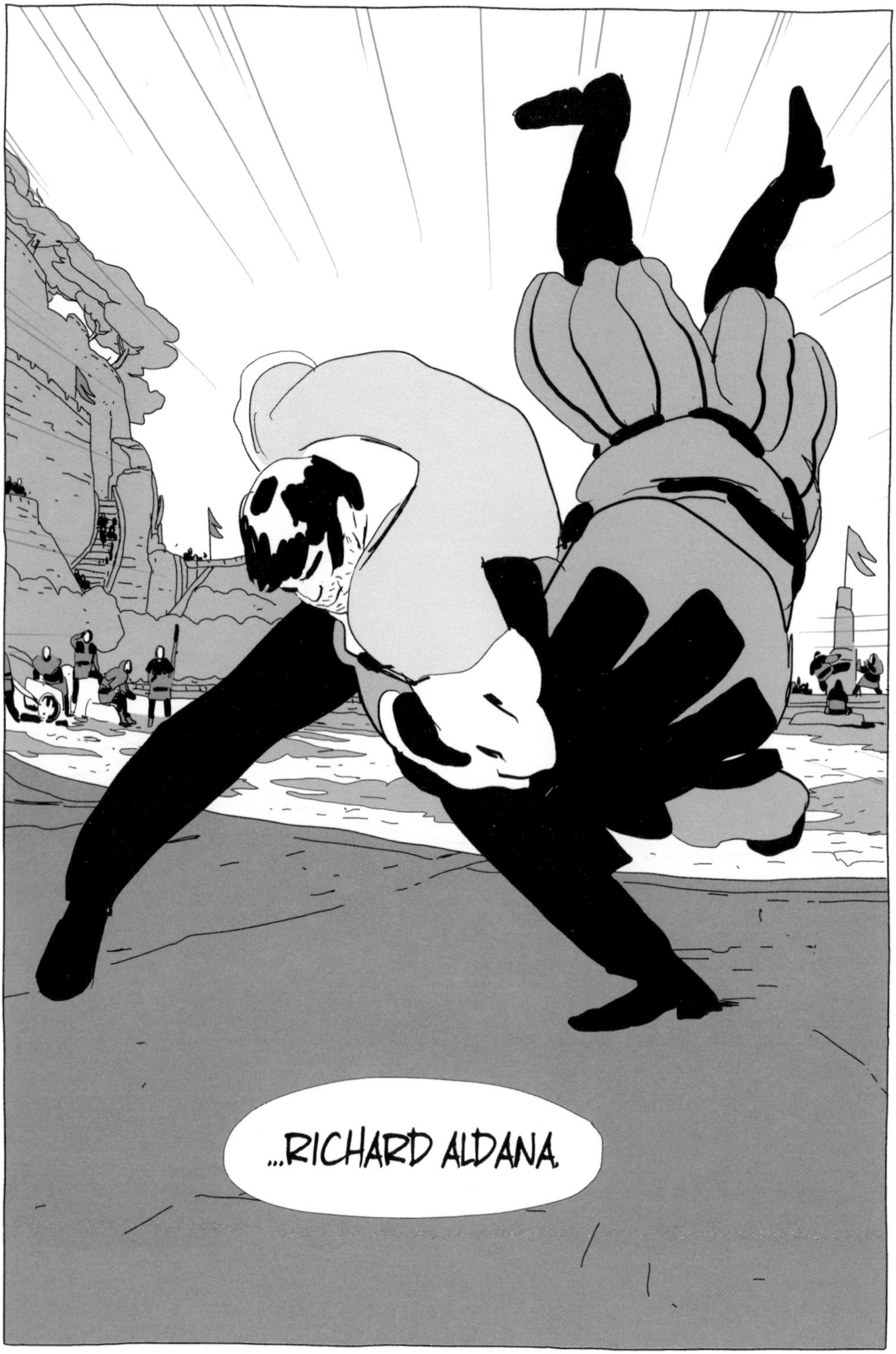
...RICHARD ALDANA.

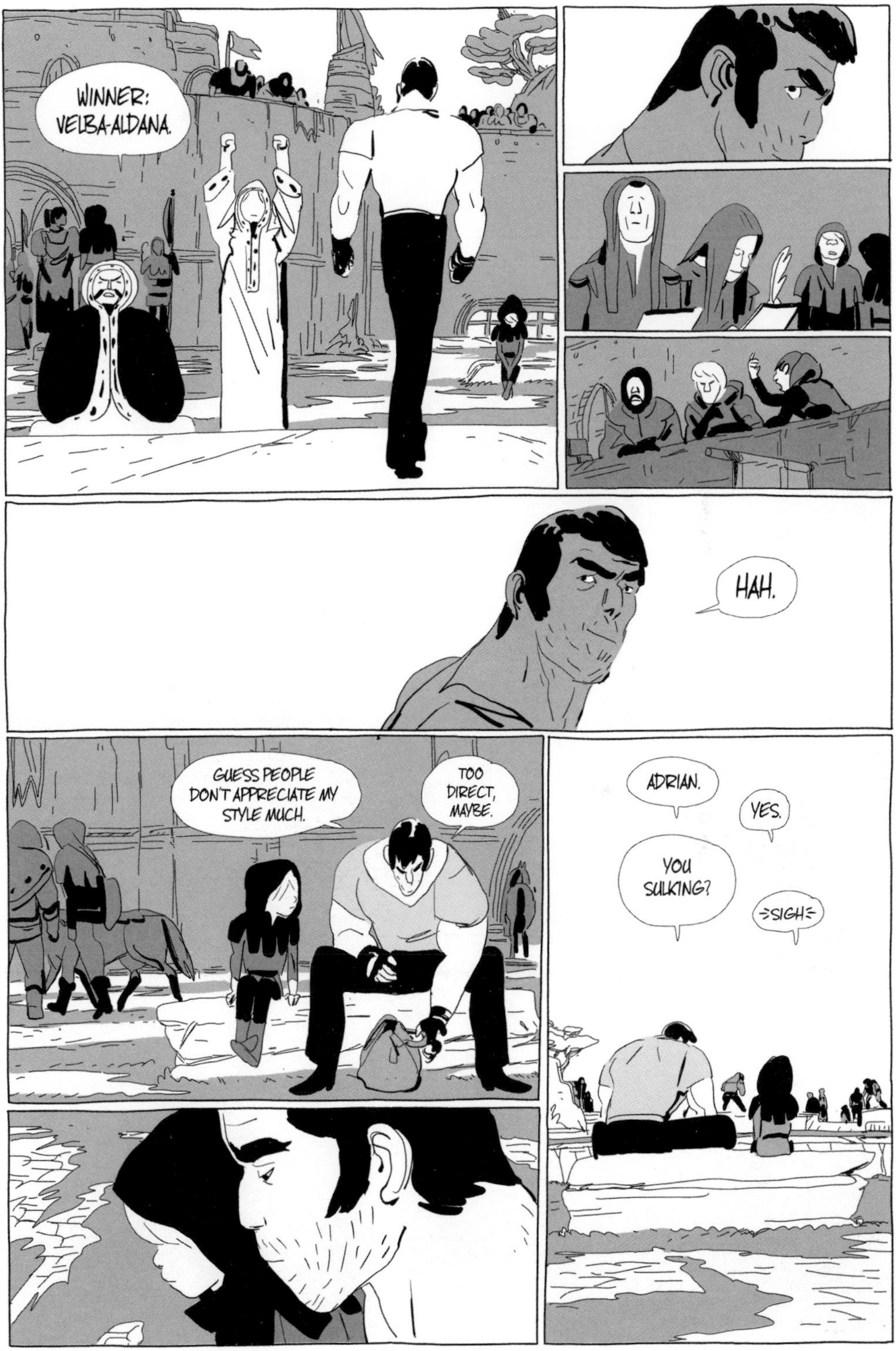
WINNER: VELBA-ALDANA.
HAH.
GUESS PEOPLE DON'T APPRECIATE MY STYLE MUCH.
TOO DIRECT, MAYBE.
ADRIAN.
YES.
YOU SULKING?
=SIGH=

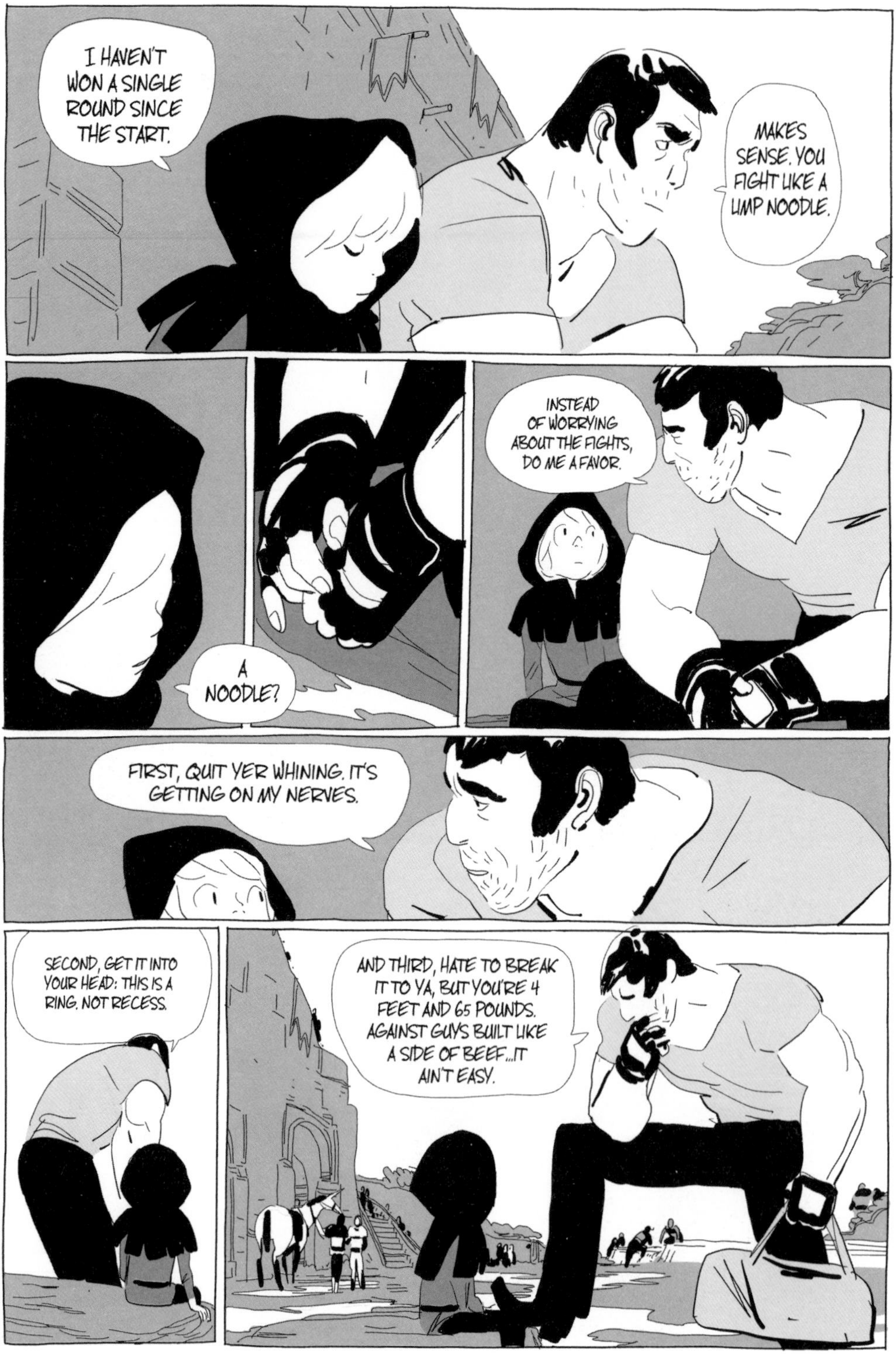
I HAVEN'T WON A SINGLE ROUND SINCE THE START.
MAKES SENSE. YOU FIGHT LIKE A LIMP NOODLE.
A NOODLE?
INSTEAD OF WORRYING ABOUT THE FIGHTS, DO ME A FAVOR.
FIRST, QUIT YER WHINING. IT'S GETTING ON MY NERVES.
SECOND, GET IT INTO YOUR HEAD: THIS IS A RING. NOT RECESS.
AND THIRD, HATE TO BREAK IT TO YA, BUT YOU'RE 4 FEET AND 65 POUNDS. AGAINST GUYS BUILT LIKE A SIDE OF BEEF...IT AIN'T EASY.

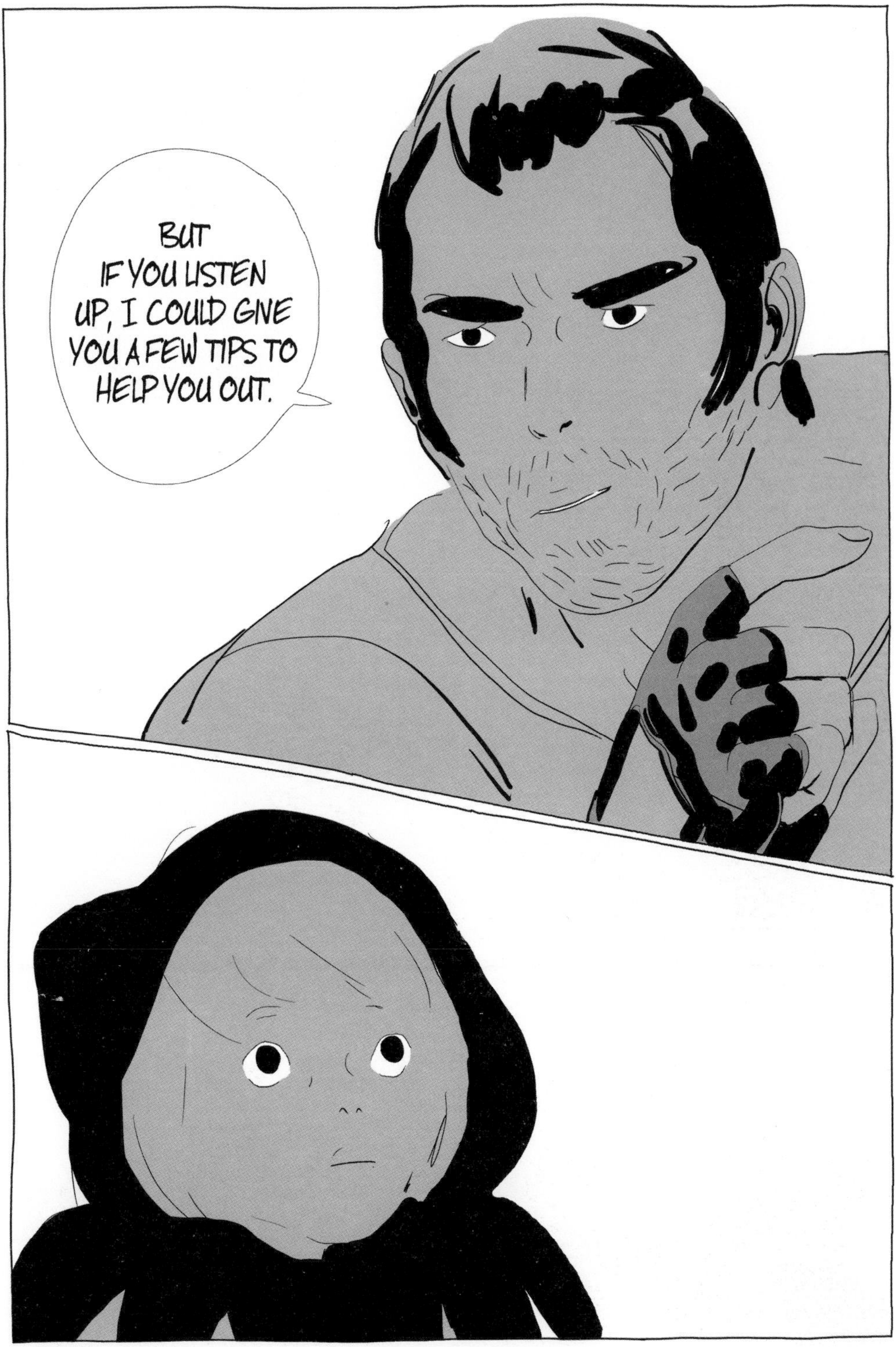
BUT IF YOU LISTEN UP, I COULD GIVE YOU A FEW TIPS TO HELP YOU OUT.

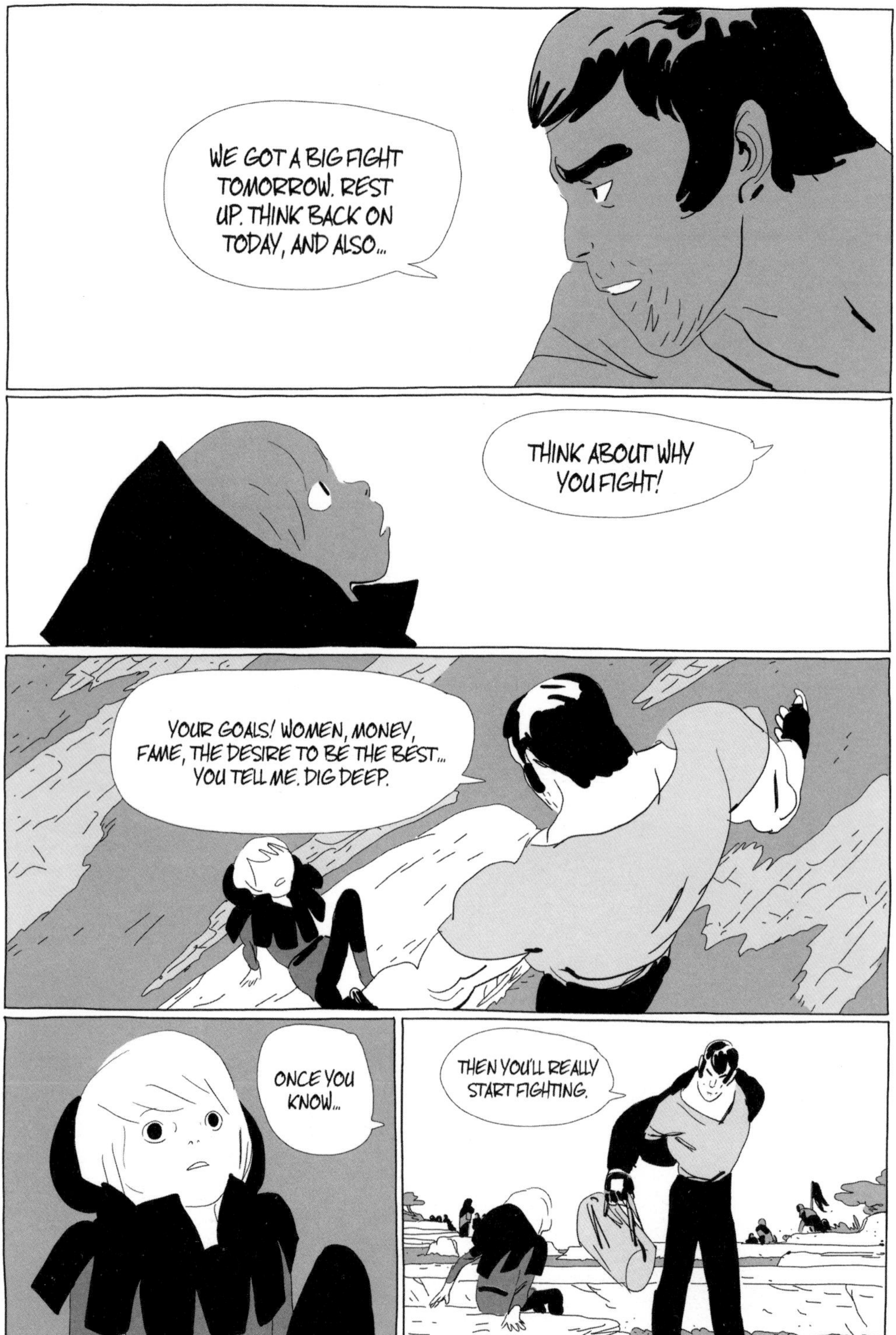
WE GOT A BIG FIGHT TOMORROW. REST UP. THINK BACK ON TODAY, AND ALSO...
THINK ABOUT WHY YOU FIGHT!
YOUR GOALS! WOMEN, MONEY, FAME, THE DESIRE TO BE THE BEST... YOU TELL ME. DIG DEEP.
ONCE YOU KNOW...
THEN YOU'LL REALLY START FIGHTING.

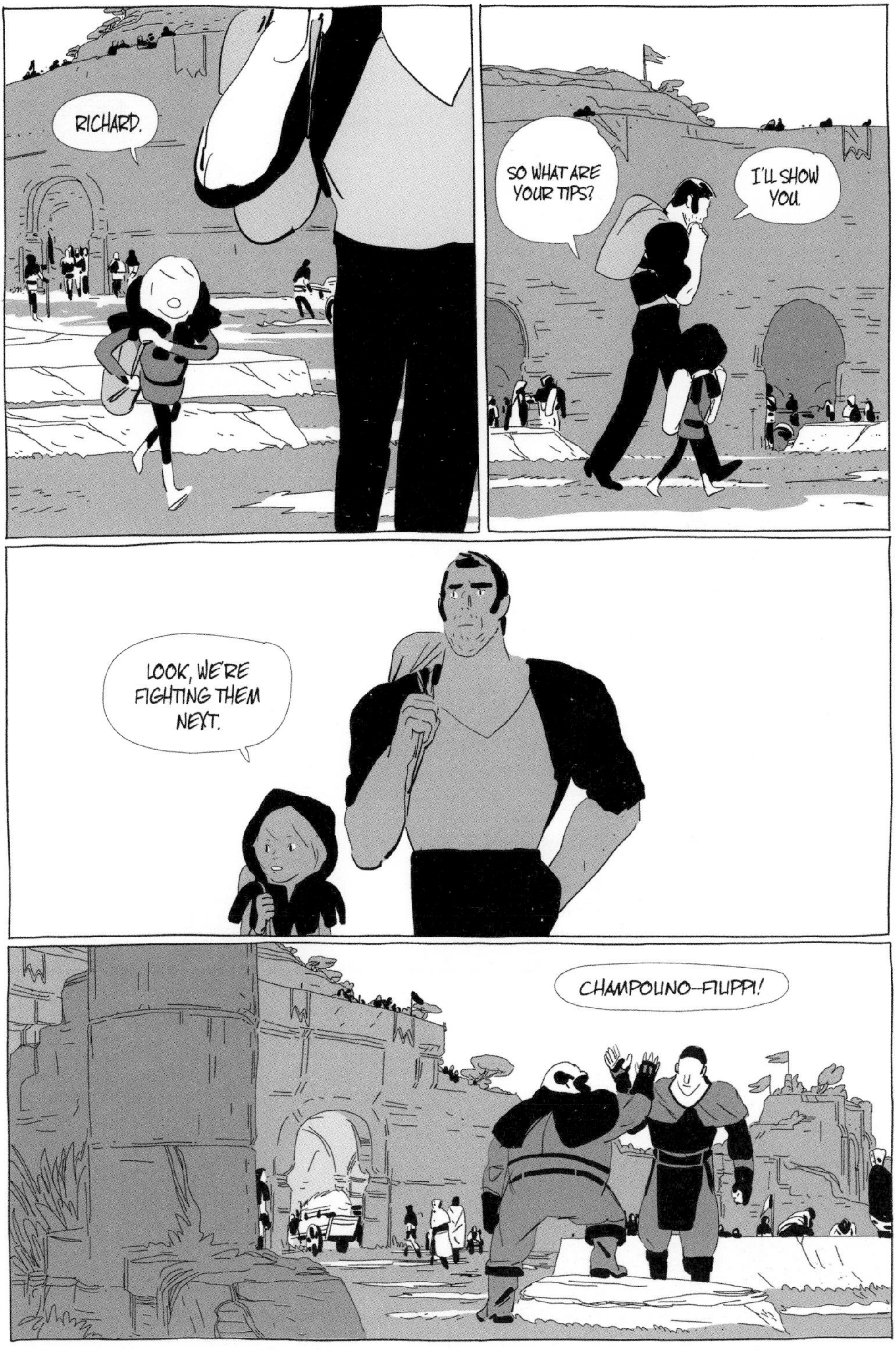

RICHARD.
SO WHAT ARE YOUR TIPS?
I'LL SHOW YOU.
LOOK, WE'RE FIGHTING THEM NEXT.
CHAMPOLINO-FILIPPI!

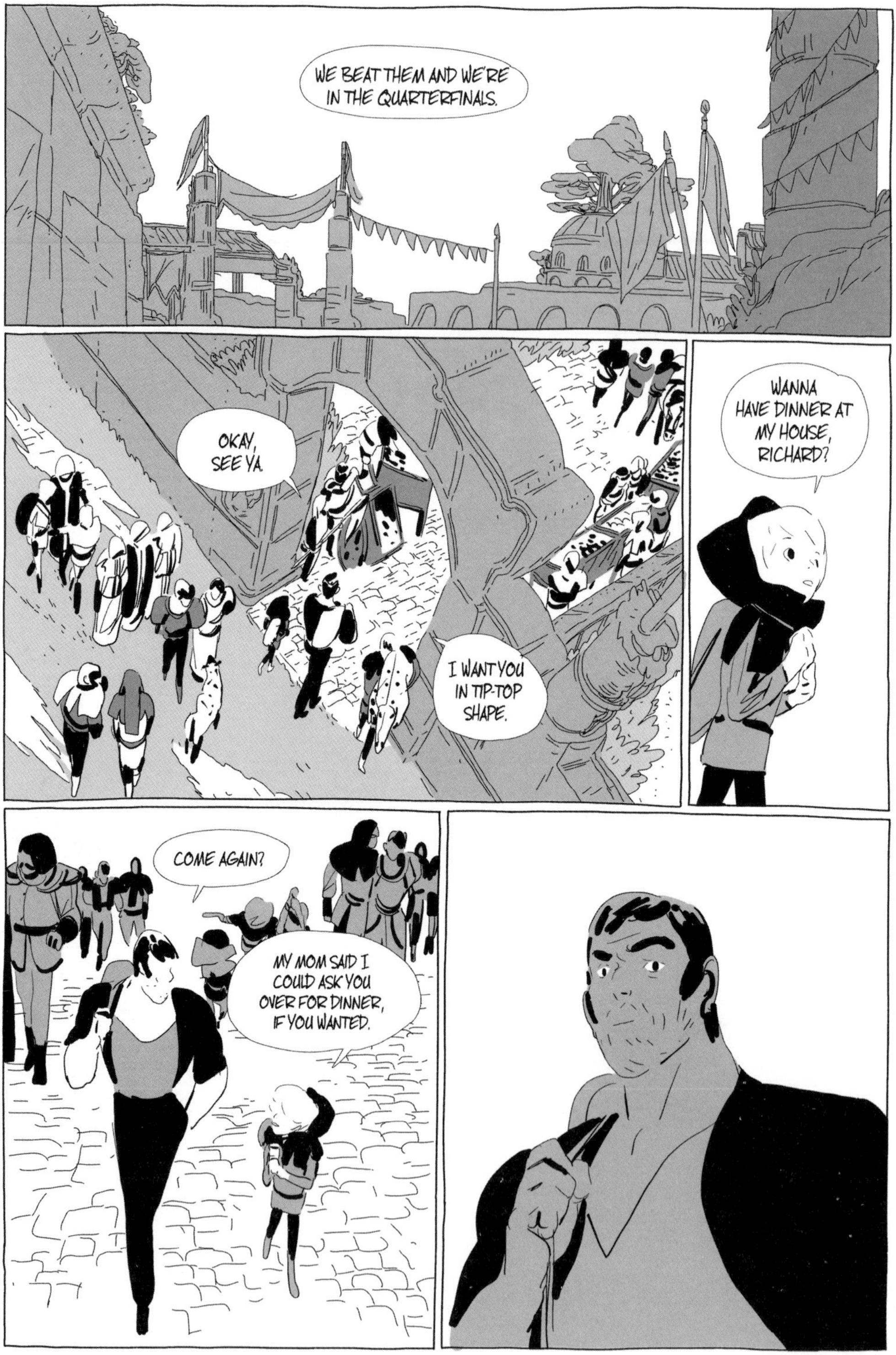
WE BEAT THEM AND WE'RE IN THE QUARTERFINALS.
OKAY, SEE YA.
I WANT YOU IN TIP-TOP SHAPE.
WANNA HAVE DINNER AT MY HOUSE, RICHARD?
COME AGAIN?
MY MOM SAID I COULD ASK YOU OVER FOR DINNER, IF YOU WANTED.

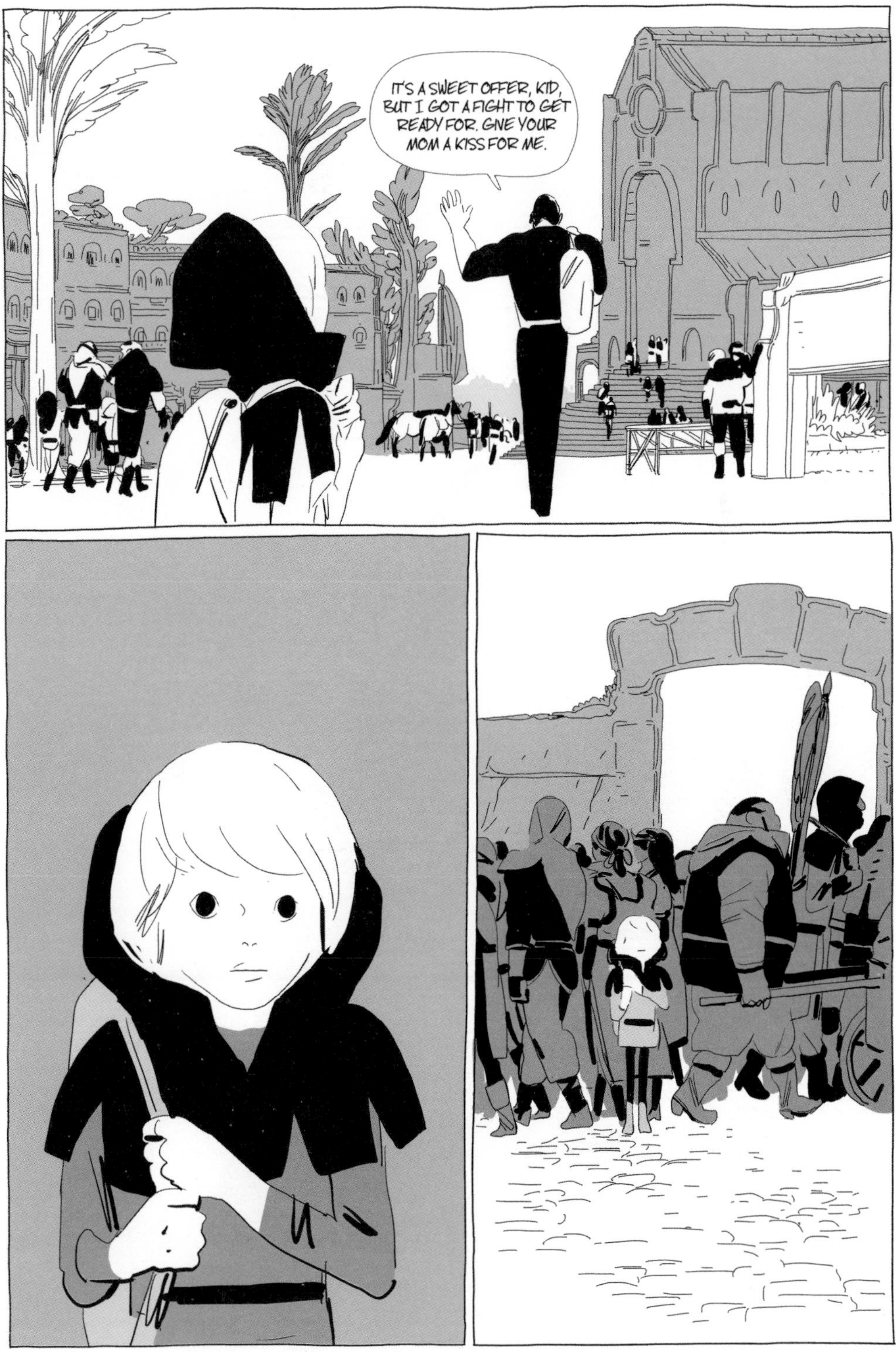
IT'S A SWEET OFFER, KID, BUT I GOT A FIGHT TO GET READY FOR. GIVE YOUR MOM A KISS FOR ME.

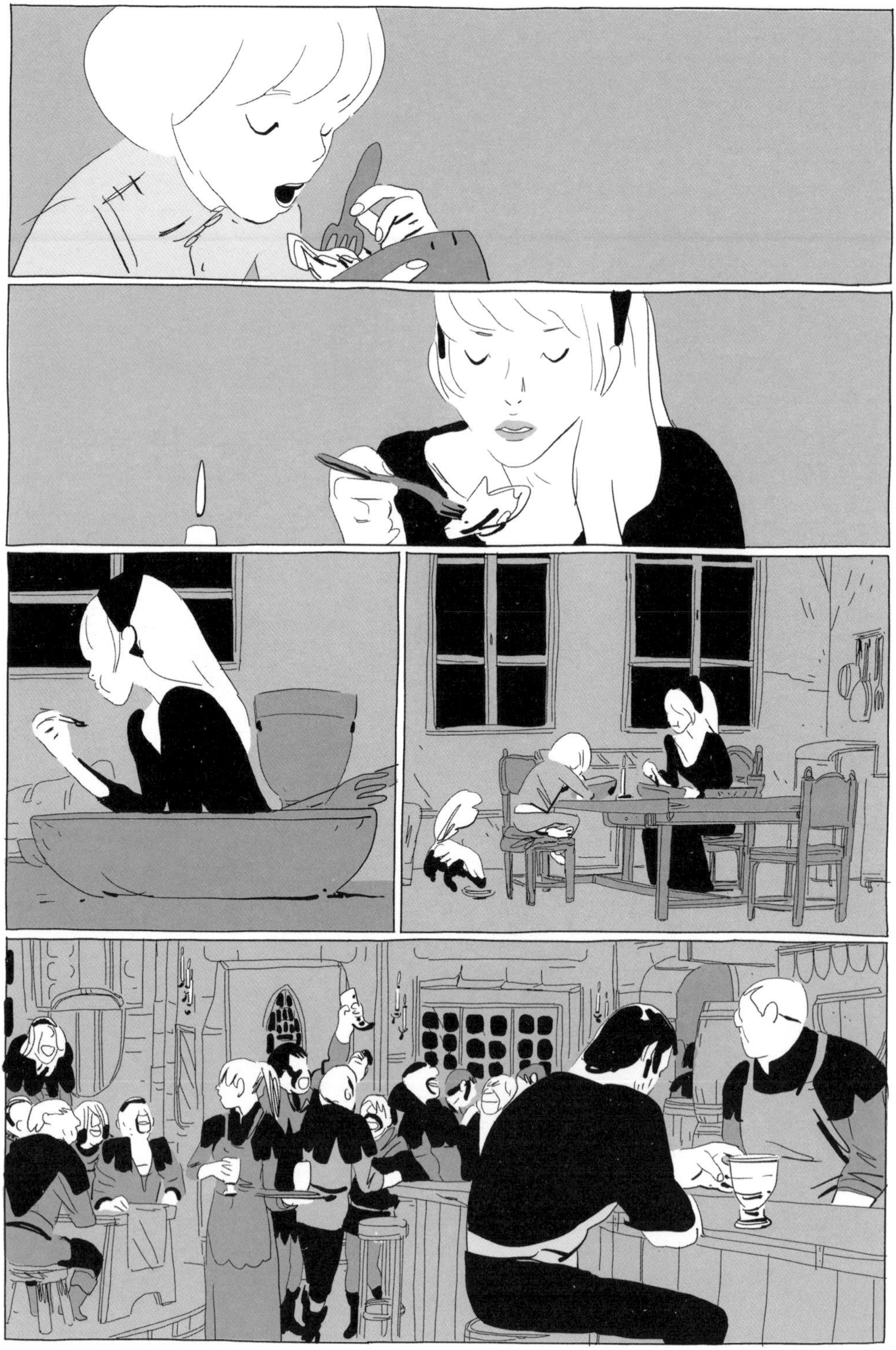

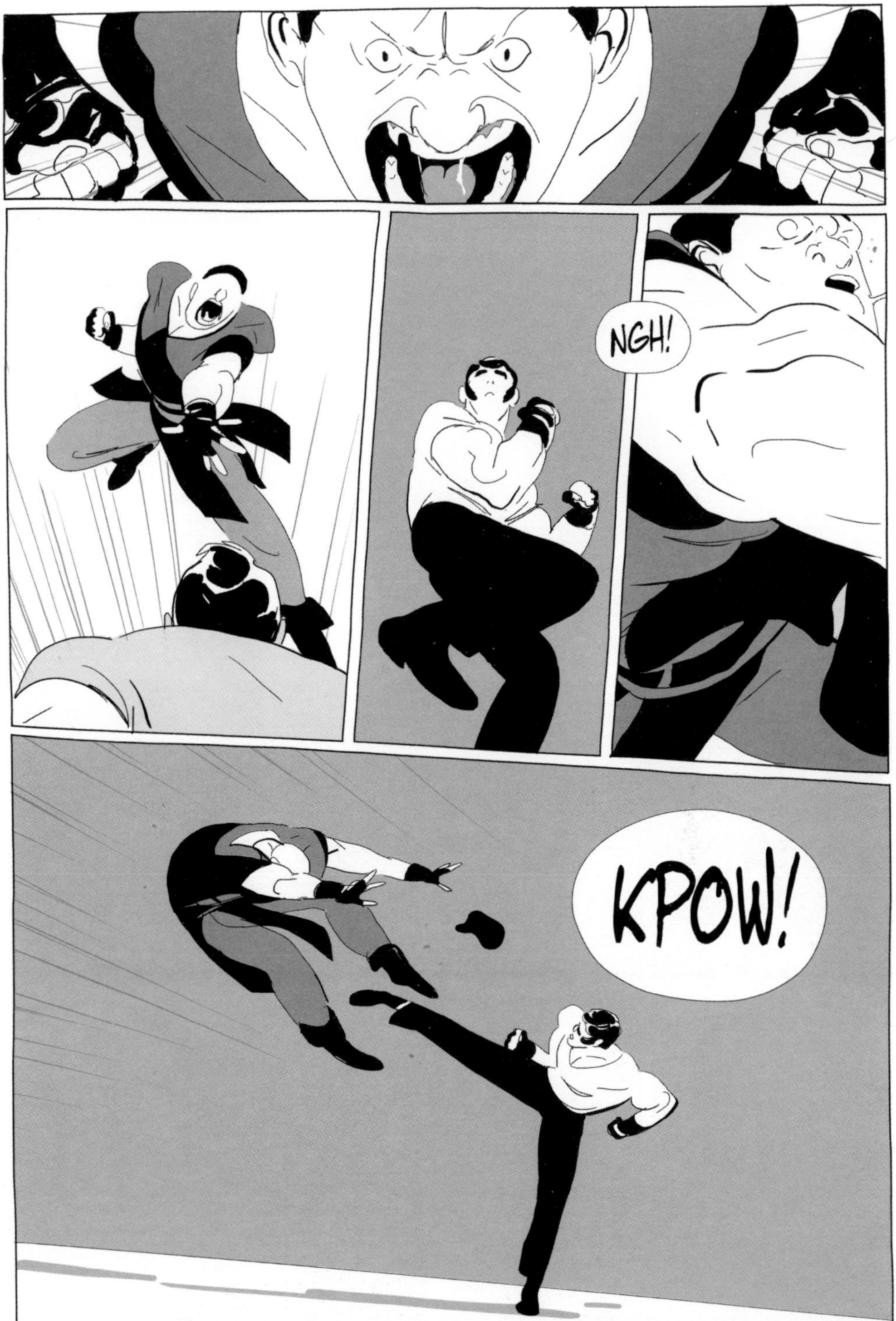
NGH!
KPOW!

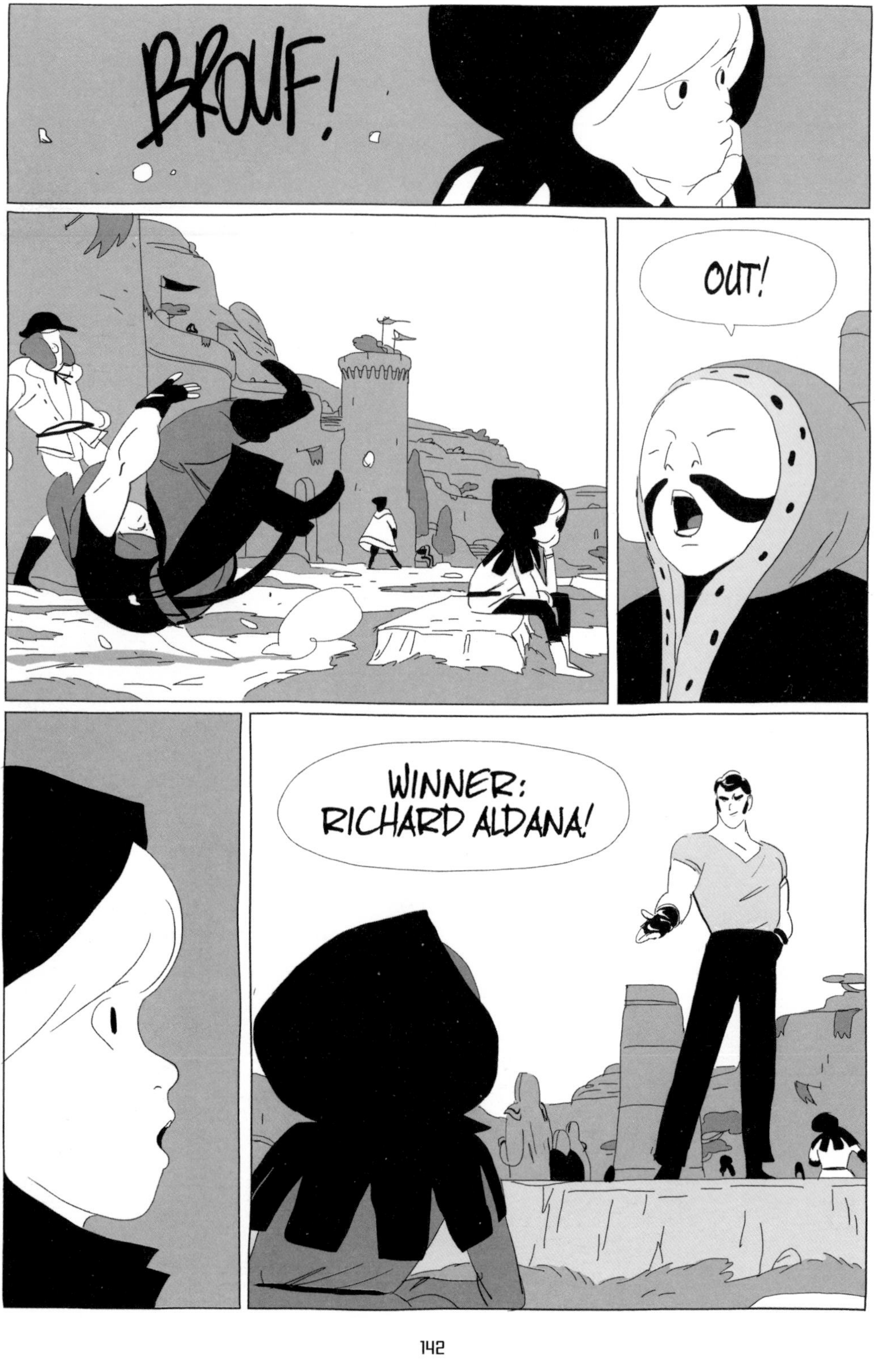
BROUF!
OUT!
WINNER: RICHARD ALDANA!

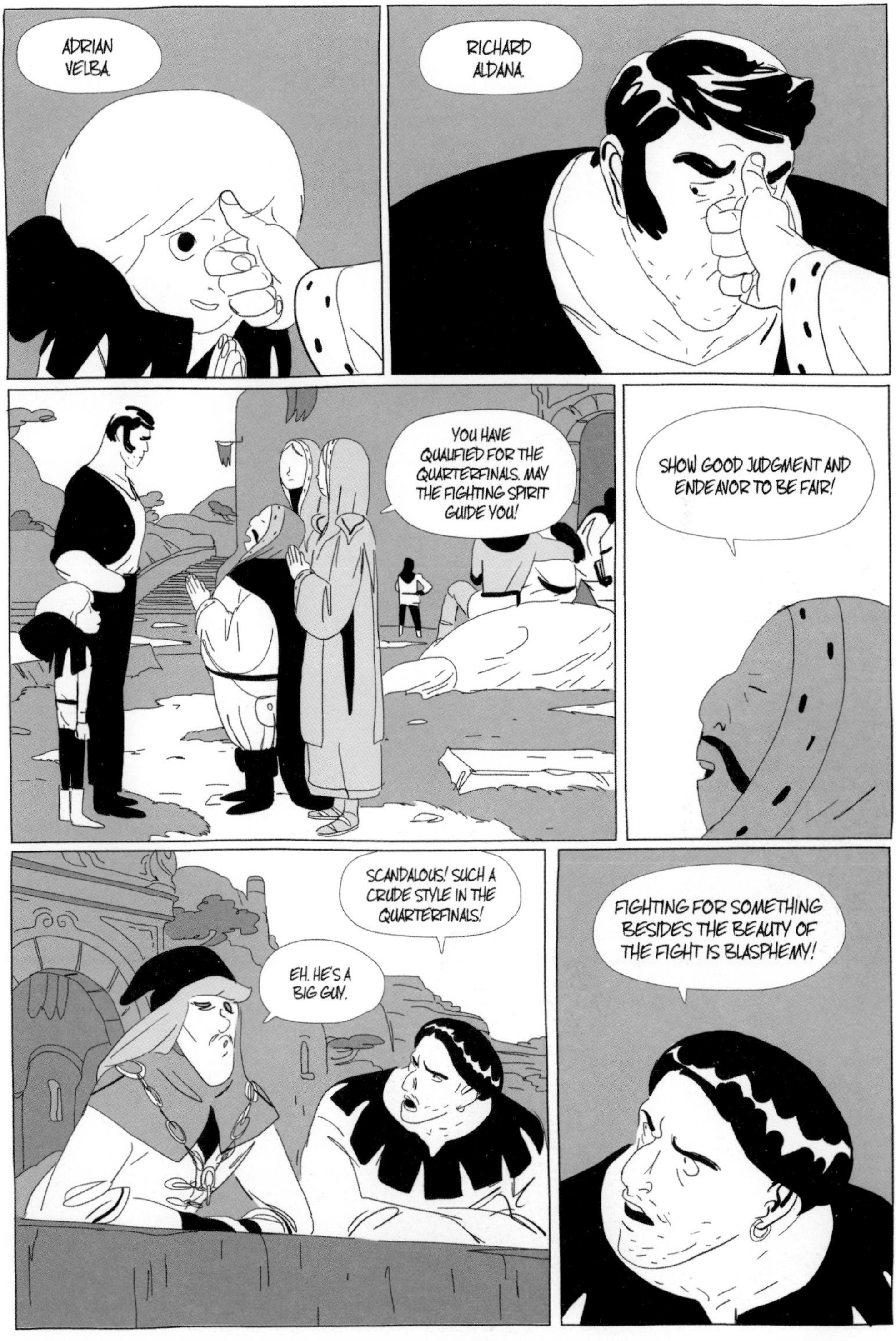
ADRIAN VELBA.
RICHARD ALDANA.
YOU HAVE QUALIFIED FOR THE QUARTERFINALS. MAY THE FIGHTING SPIRIT GUIDE YOU!
SHOW GOOD JUDGMENT AND ENDEAVOR TO BE FAIR!
SCANDALOUS! SUCH A CRUDE STYLE IN THE QUARTERFINALS!
EH. HE'S A BIG GUY.
FIGHTING FOR SOMETHING BESIDES THE BEAUTY OF THE FIGHT IS BLASPHEMY!

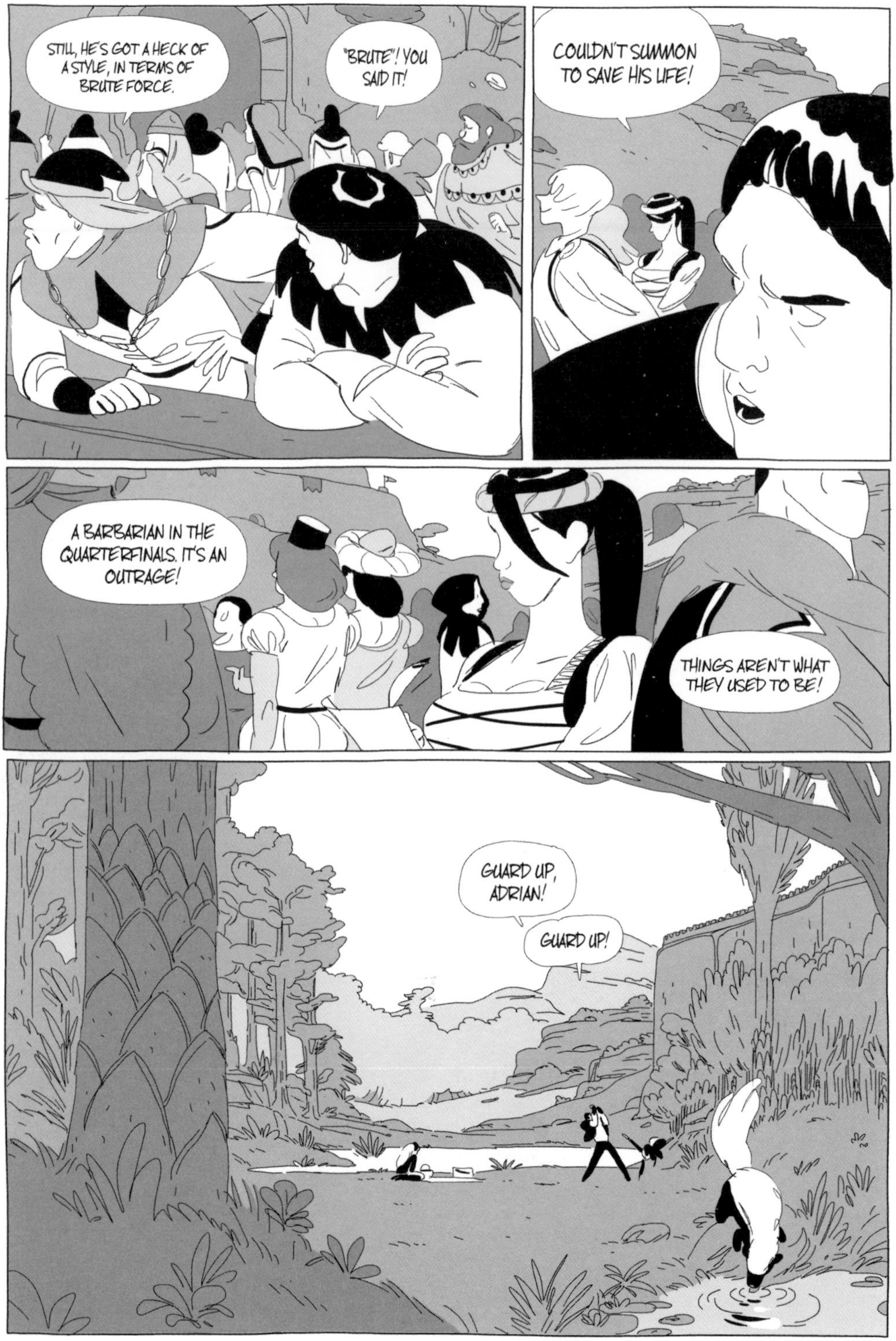
STILL, HE'S GOT A HECK OF A STYLE, IN TERMS OF BRUTE FORCE.
"BRUTE"! YOU SAID IT!
COULDN'T SUMMON TO SAVE HIS LIFE!
A BARBARIAN IN THE QUARTERFINALS. IT'S AN OUTRAGE!
THINGS AREN'T WHAT THEY USED TO BE!
GUARD UP, ADRIAN!
GUARD UP!

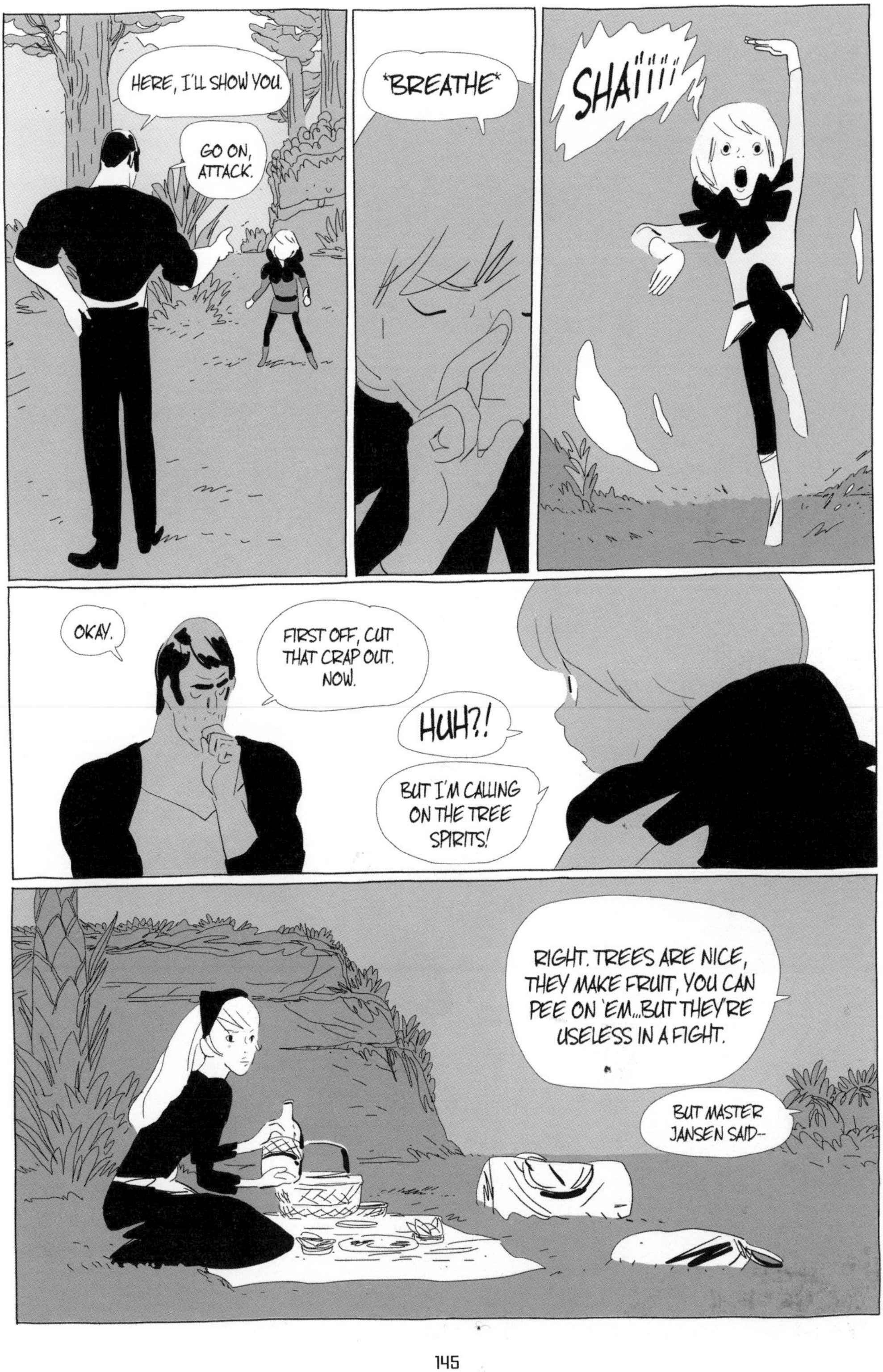
HERE, I'LL SHOW YOU.
GO ON, ATTACK.
BREATHE
SHAÏÏÏÏÏ
OKAY.
FIRST OFF, CUT THAT CRAP OUT. NOW.
HUH?!
BUT I'M CALLING ON THE TREE SPIRITS!
RIGHT. TREES ARE NICE, THEY MAKE FRUIT, YOU CAN PEE ON 'EM...BUT THEY'RE USELESS IN A FIGHT.
BUT MASTER JANSEN SAID--

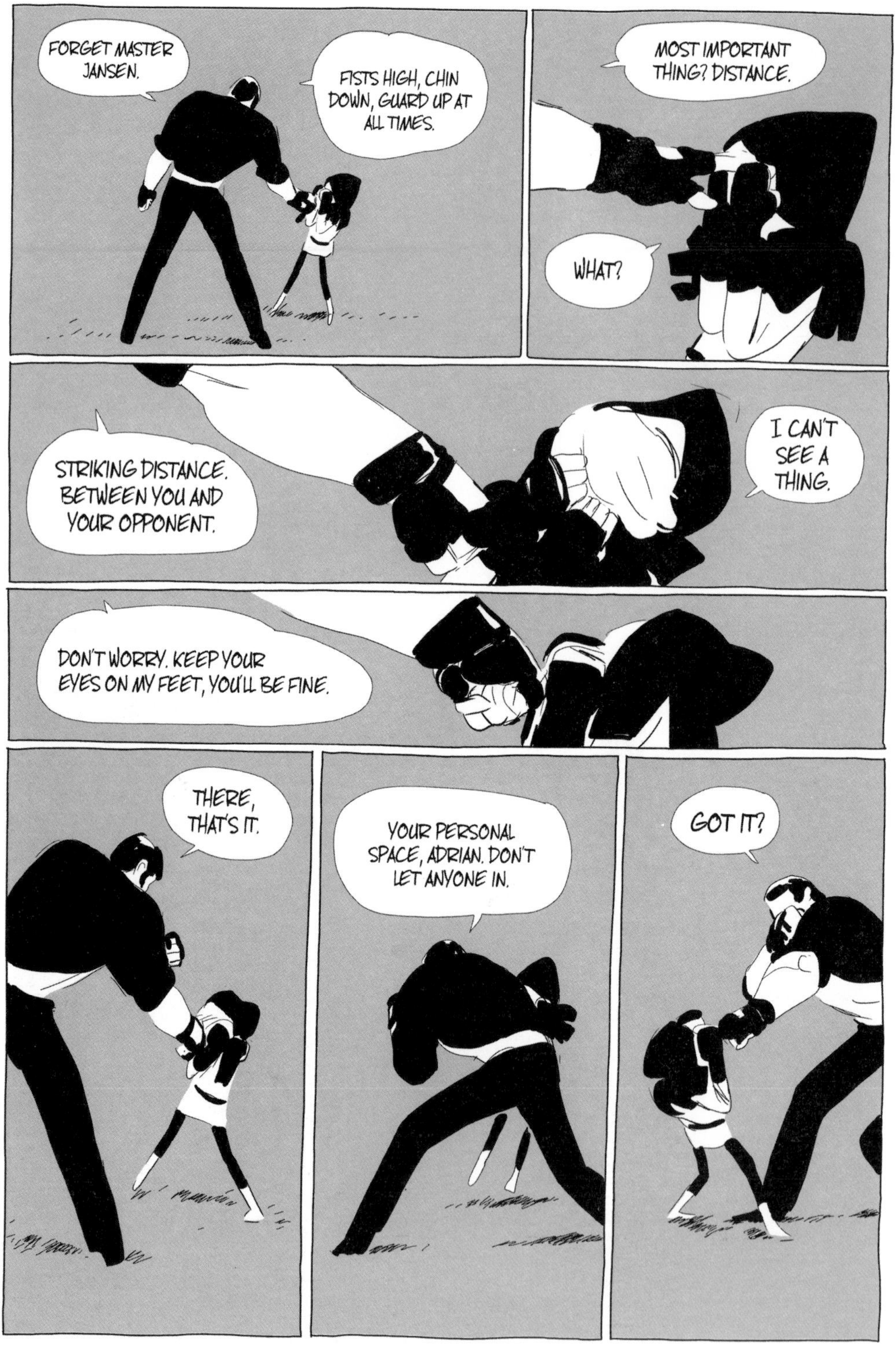
FORGET MASTER JANSEN.
FISTS HIGH, CHIN DOWN, GUARD UP AT ALL TIMES.
MOST IMPORTANT THING? DISTANCE.
WHAT?
STRIKING DISTANCE. BETWEEN YOU AND YOUR OPPONENT.
I CAN'T SEE A THING.
DON'T WORRY. KEEP YOUR EYES ON MY FEET, YOU'LL BE FINE.
THERE, THAT'S IT.
YOUR PERSONAL SPACE, ADRIAN. DON'T LET ANYONE IN.
GOT IT?

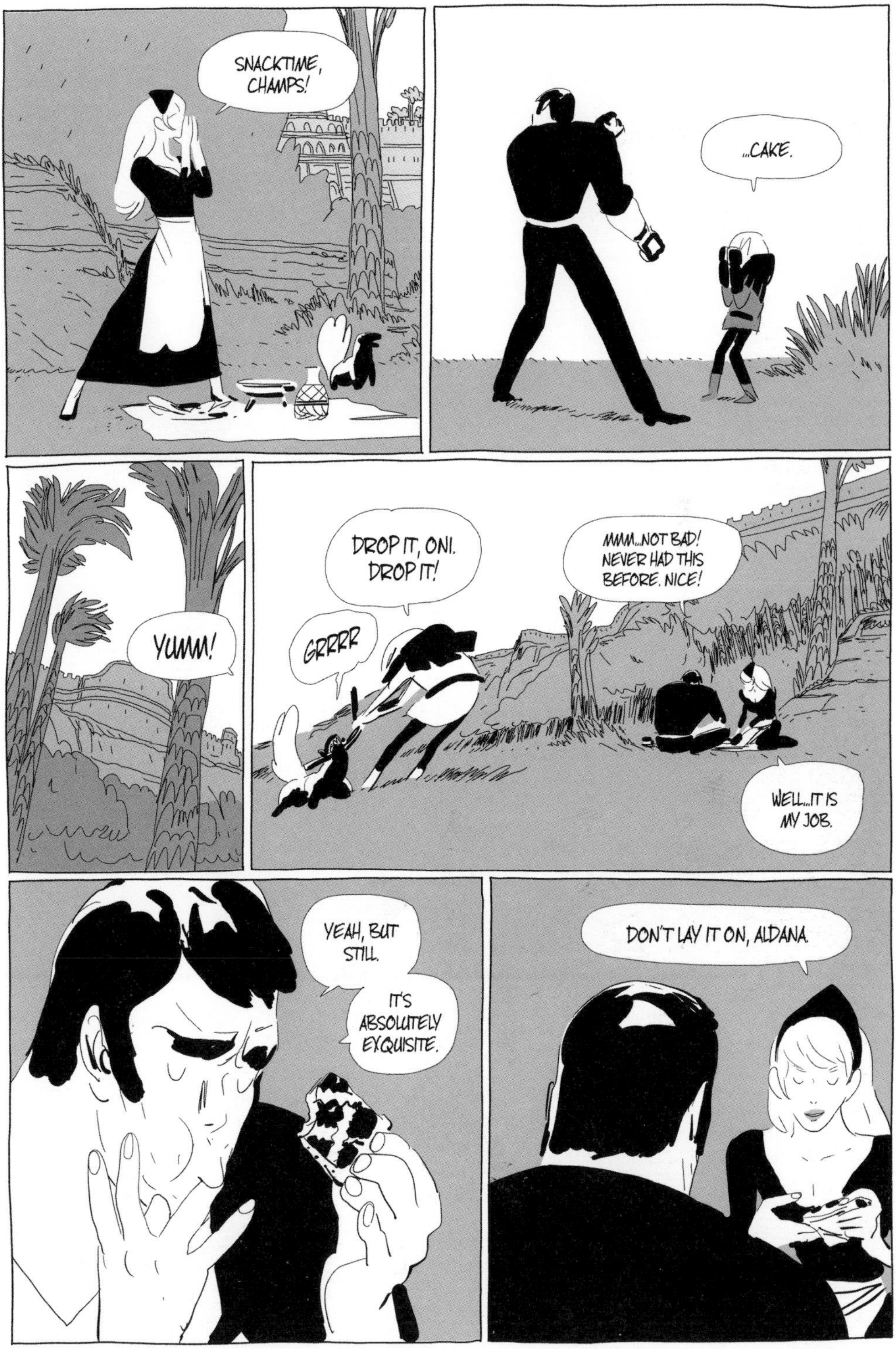
SNACKTIME, CHAMPS!
...CAKE.
YUMM!
DROP IT, ONI. DROP IT!
GRRRR
MMM...NOT BAD! NEVER HAD THIS BEFORE. NICE!
WELL...IT IS MY JOB.
YEAH, BUT STILL.
IT'S ABSOLUTELY EXQUISITE.
DON'T LAY IT ON, ALDANA.

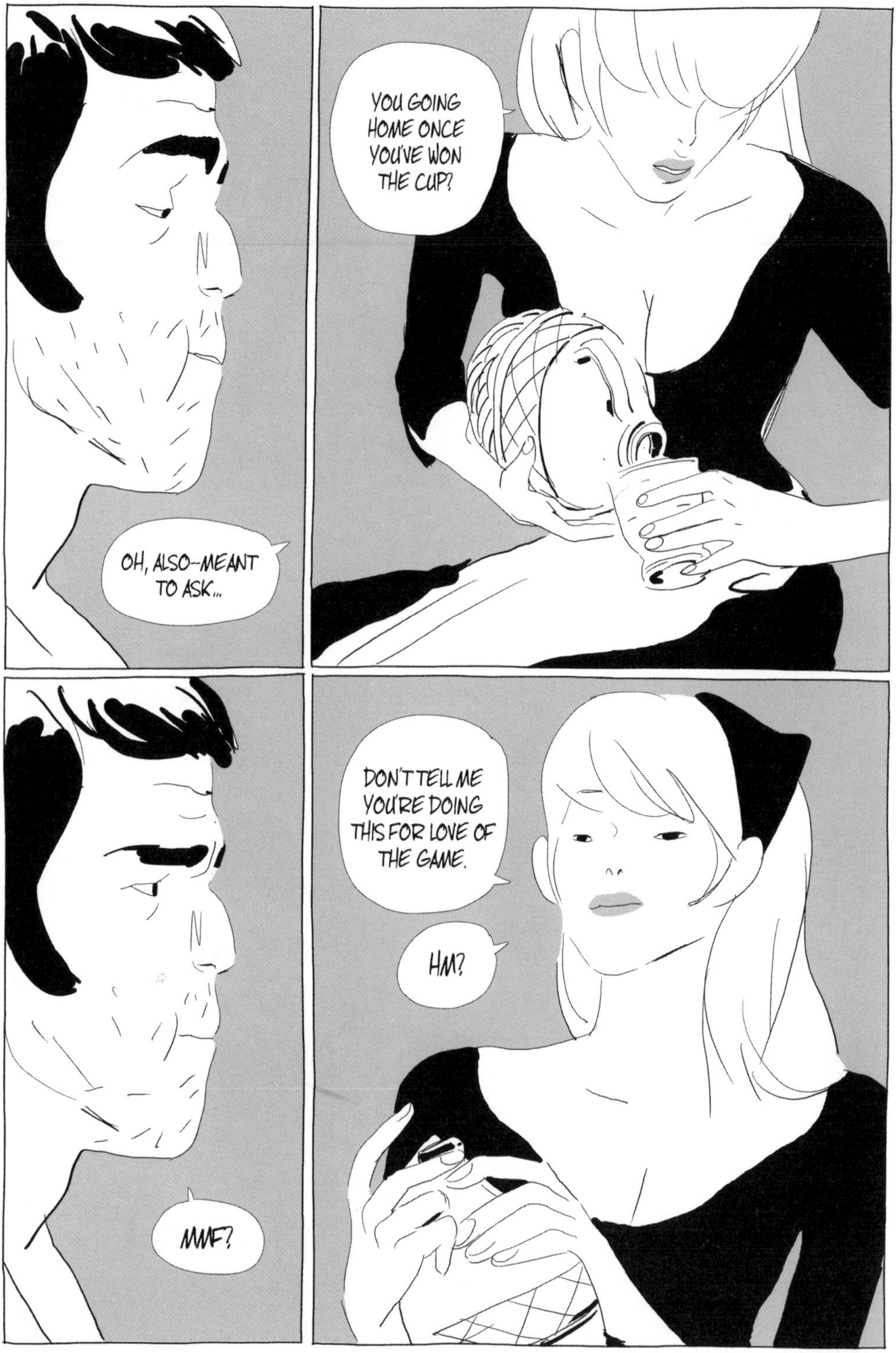
YOU GOING HOME ONCE YOU'VE WON THE CUP?
OH, ALSO--MEANT TO ASK...
DON'T TELL ME YOU'RE DOING THIS FOR LOVE OF THE GAME.
HM?
MMF?

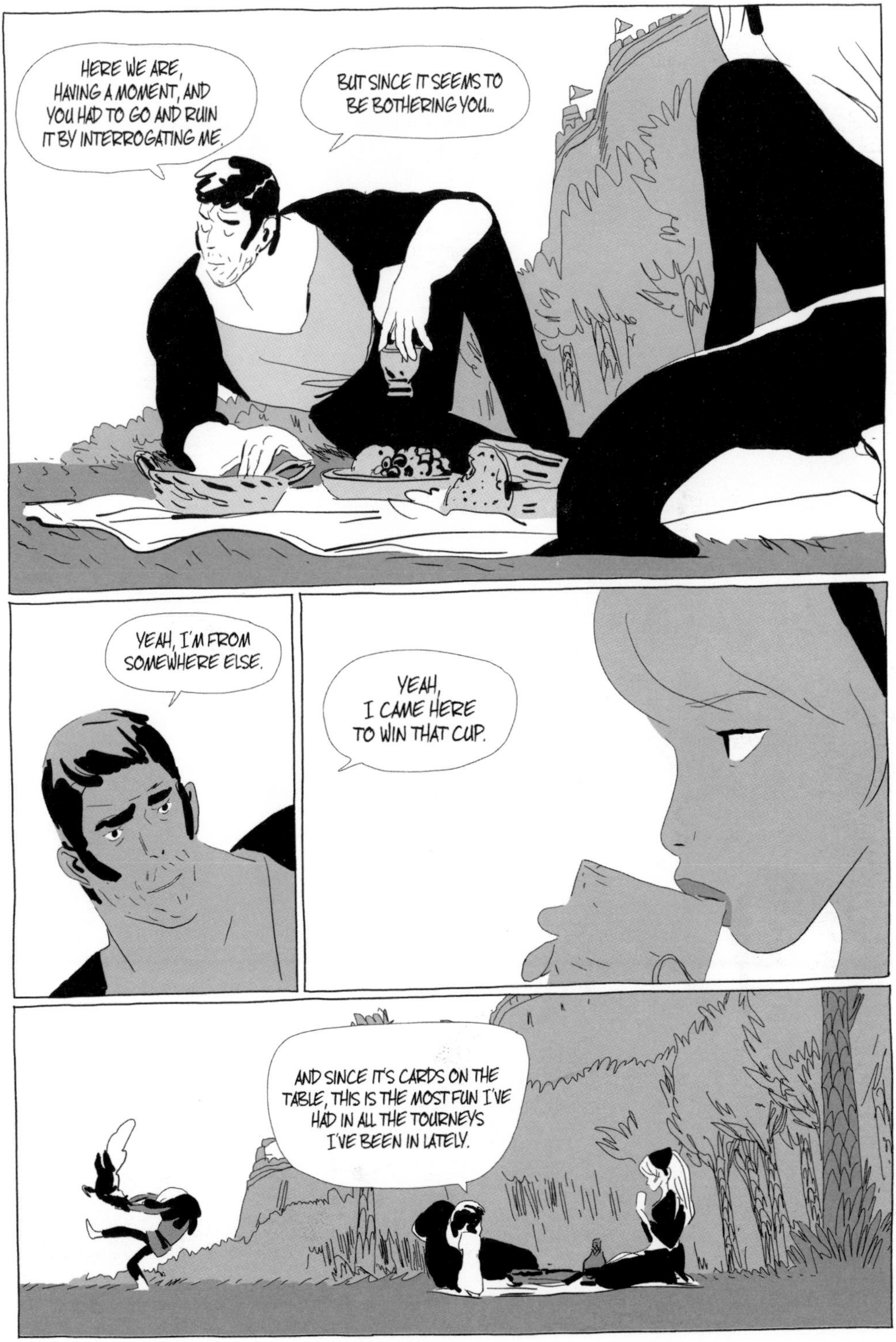
HERE WE ARE, HAVING A MOMENT, AND YOU HAD TO GO AND RUIN IT BY INTERROGATING ME.
BUT SINCE IT SEEMS TO BE BOTHERING YOU...
YEAH, I'M FROM SOMEWHERE ELSE.
YEAH, I CAME HERE TO WIN THAT CUP.
AND SINCE IT'S CARDS ON THE TABLE, THIS IS THE MOST FUN I'VE HAD IN ALL THE TOURNEYS I'VE BEEN IN LATELY.

MIND WATCHING OVER OUR THINGS? I'M GOING TO DIP MY FEET IN.

NO PROB.

YOU BRING A BATHING SUIT?

JUST KEEP AN EYE ON THE FOOD, ALDANA

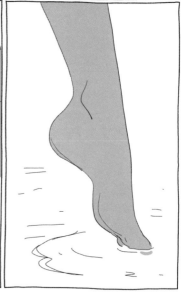

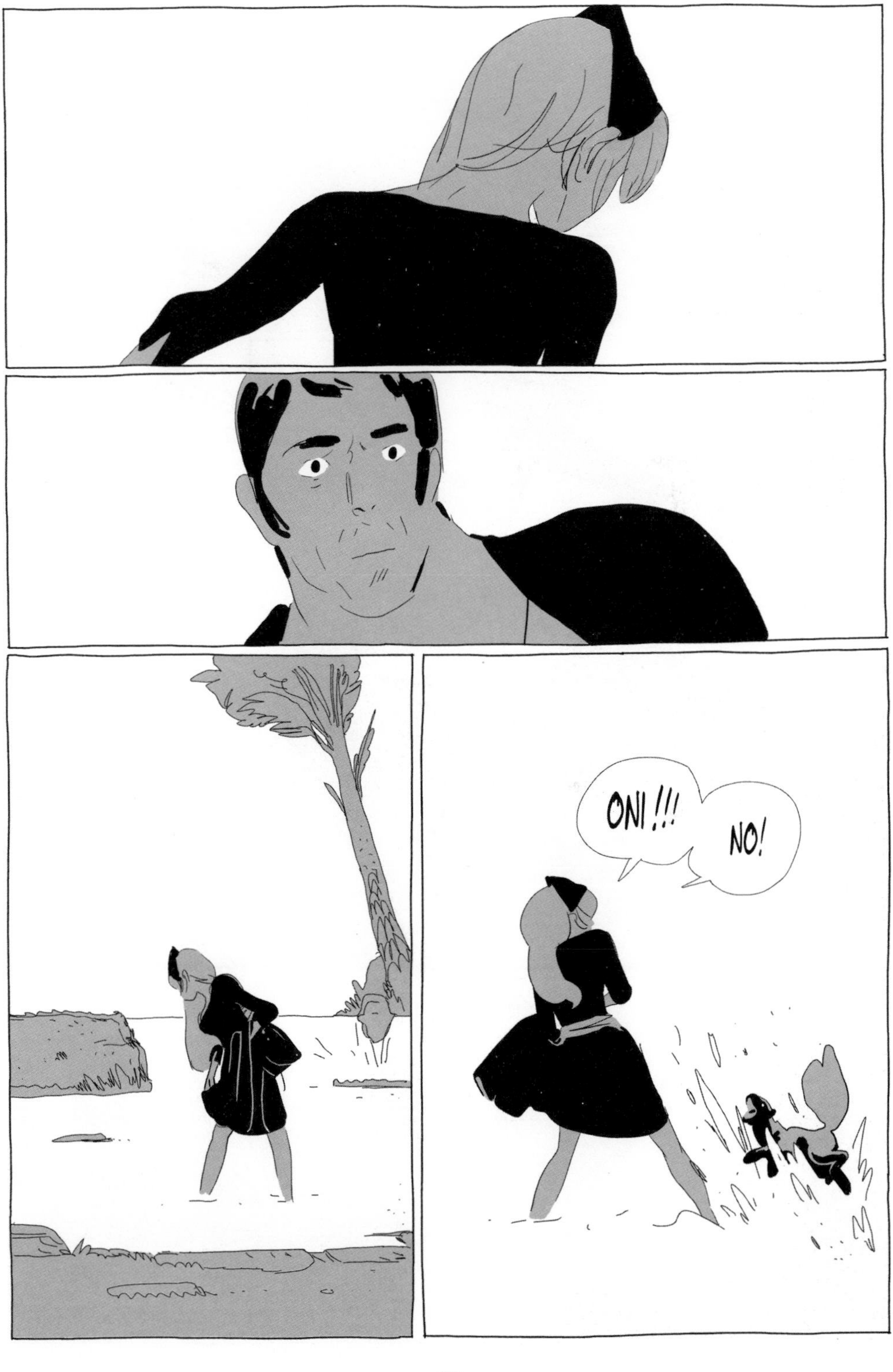
ONI!!!
NO!

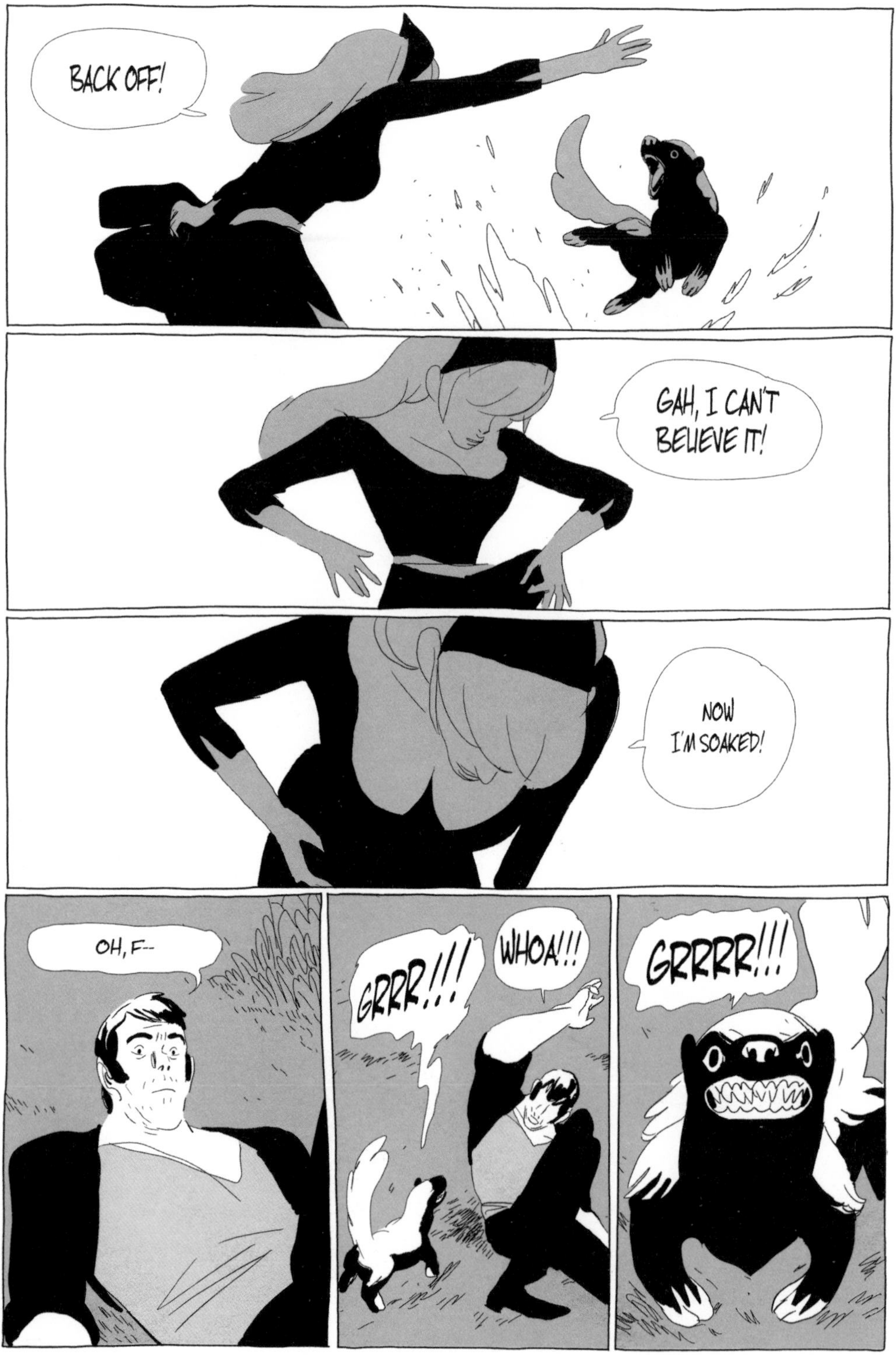
BACK OFF!
GAH, I CAN'T BELIEVE IT!
NOW I'M SOAKED!
OH, F--
GRRR!!!
WHOA!!!
GRRRR!!!

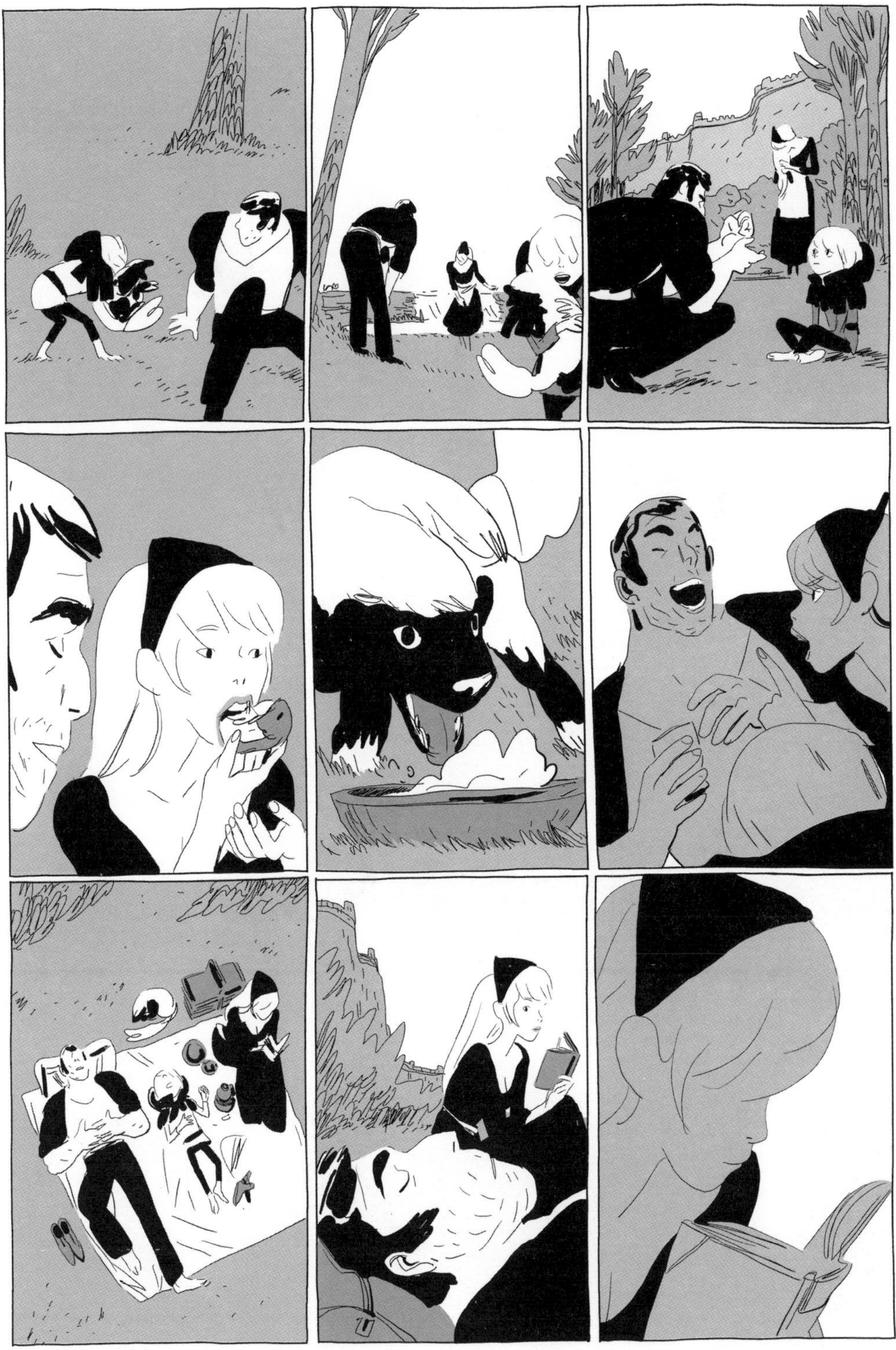

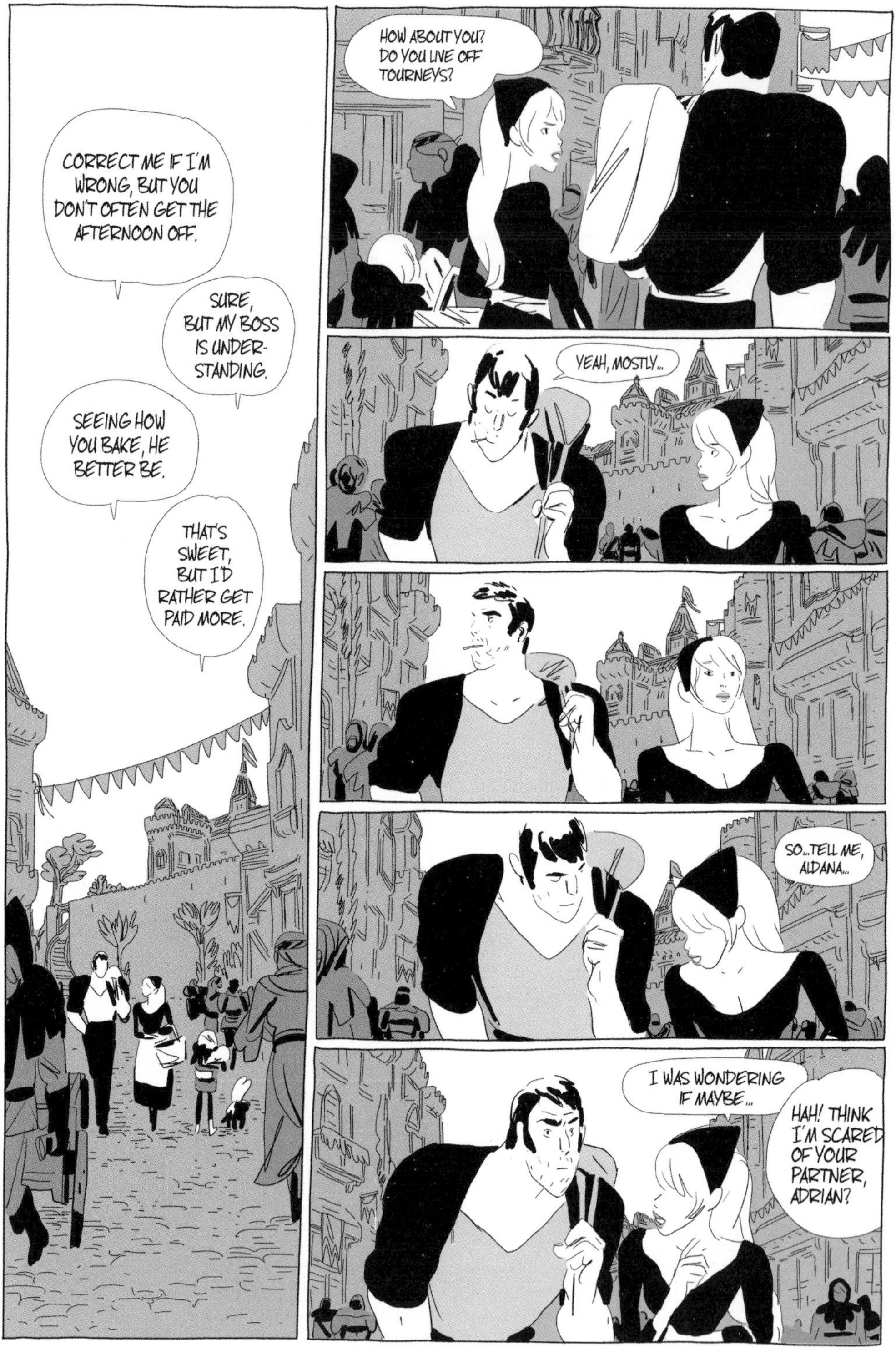
CORRECT ME IF I'M WRONG, BUT YOU DON'T OFTEN GET THE AFTERNOON OFF.
SURE, BUT MY BOSS IS UNDER-STANDING.
SEEING HOW YOU BAKE, HE BETTER BE.
THAT'S SWEET, BUT I'D RATHER GET PAID MORE.
HOW ABOUT YOU? DO YOU LIVE OFF TOURNEYS?
YEAH, MOSTLY...
SO...TELL ME, ALDANA...
I WAS WONDERING IF MAYBE...
HAH! THINK I'M SCARED OF YOUR PARTNER, ADRIAN?

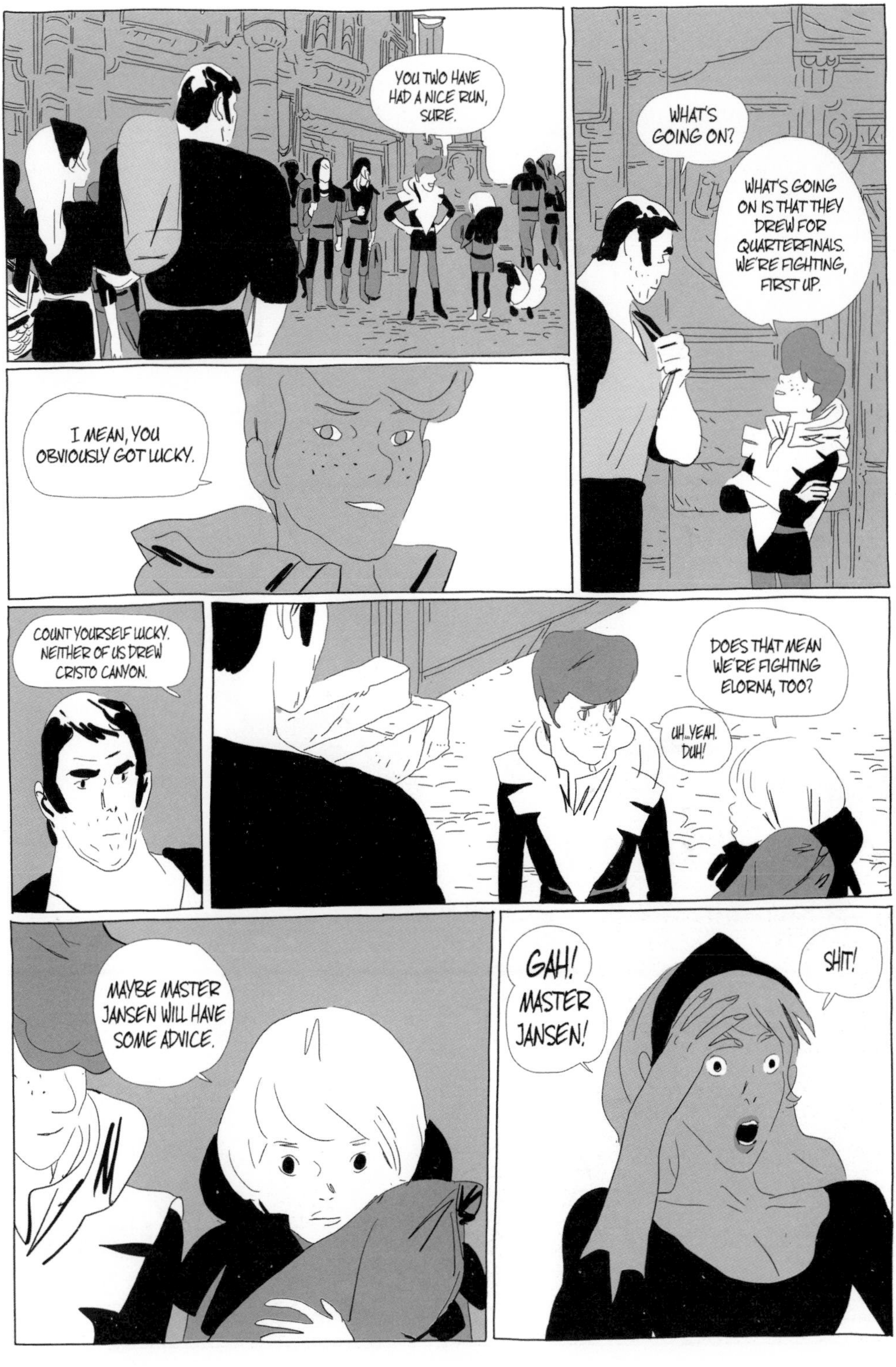
YOU TWO HAVE HAD A NICE RUN, SURE.
WHAT'S GOING ON?
WHAT'S GOING ON IS THAT THEY DREW FOR QUARTERFINALS. WE'RE FIGHTING, FIRST UP.
I MEAN, YOU OBVIOUSLY GOT LUCKY.
COUNT YOURSELF LUCKY. NEITHER OF US DREW CRISTO CANYON.
DOES THAT MEAN WE'RE FIGHTING ELORNA, TOO?
UH...YEAH. DUH!
MAYBE MASTER JANSEN WILL HAVE SOME ADVICE.
GAH! MASTER JANSEN!
SHIT!

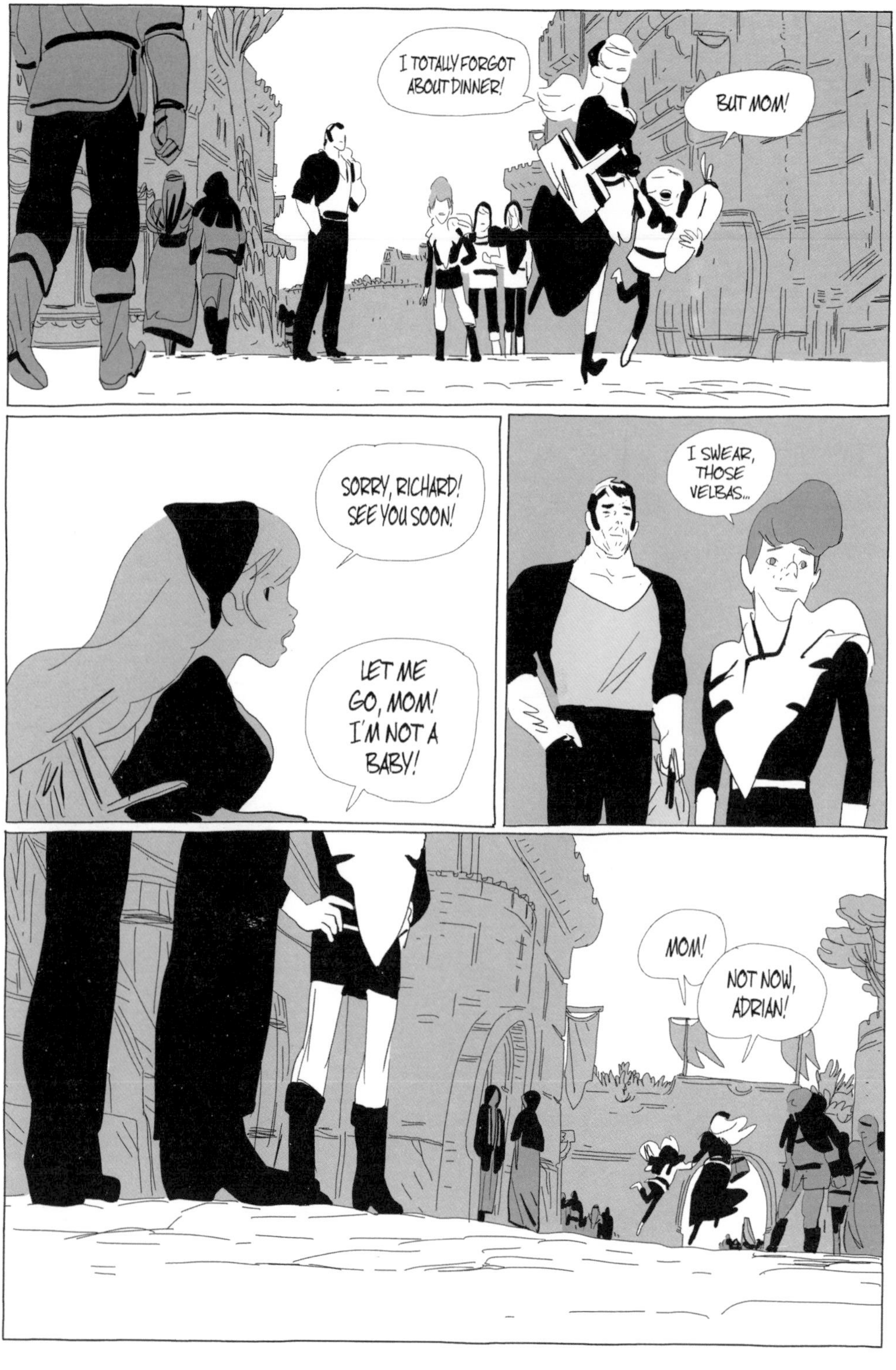
I TOTALLY FORGOT ABOUT DINNER!
BUT MOM!
SORRY, RICHARD! SEE YOU SOON!
LET ME GO, MOM! I'M NOT A BABY!
I SWEAR, THOSE VELBAS...
MOM!
NOT NOW, ADRIAN!

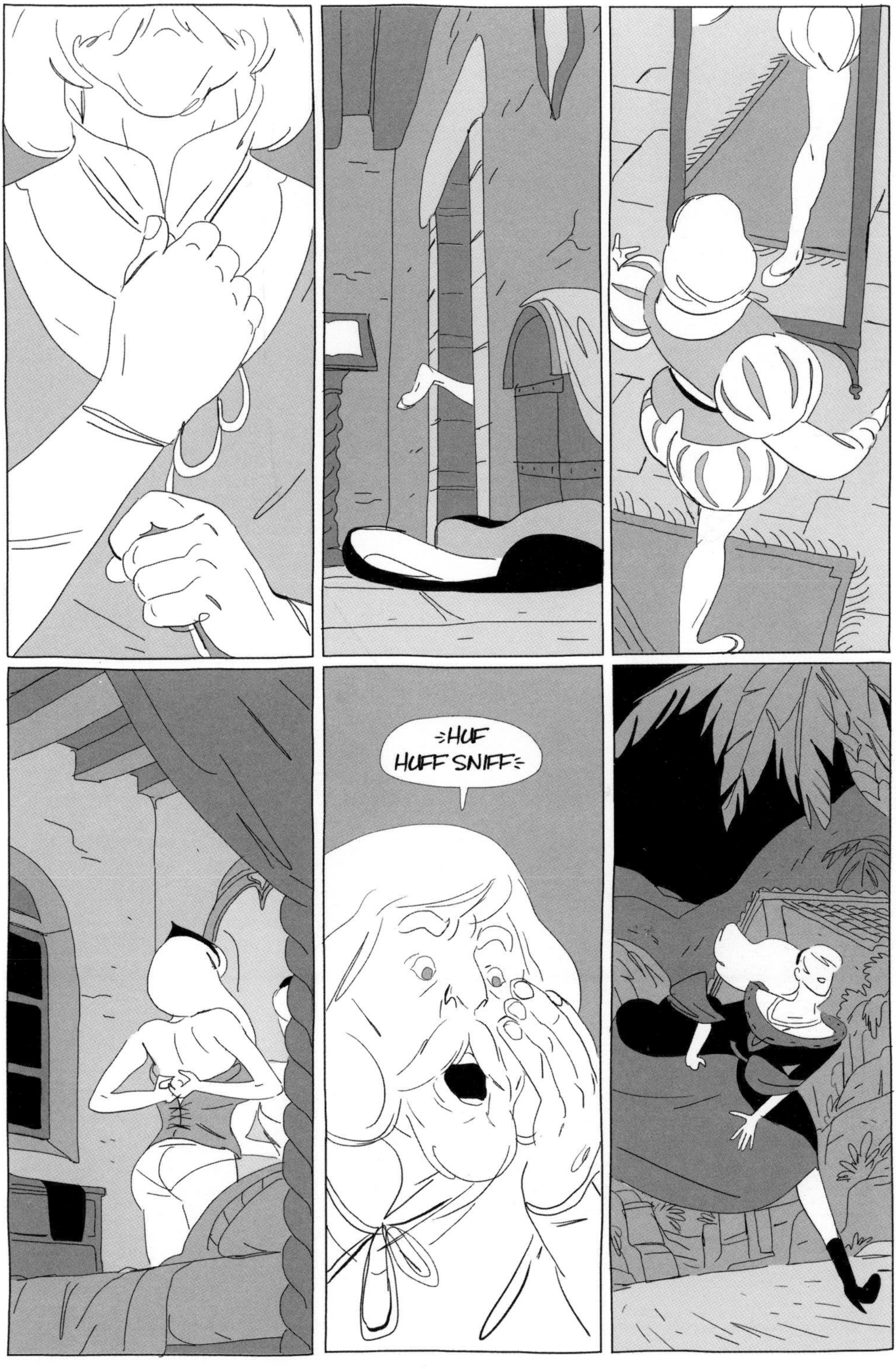
HUF
HUFF SNIFF

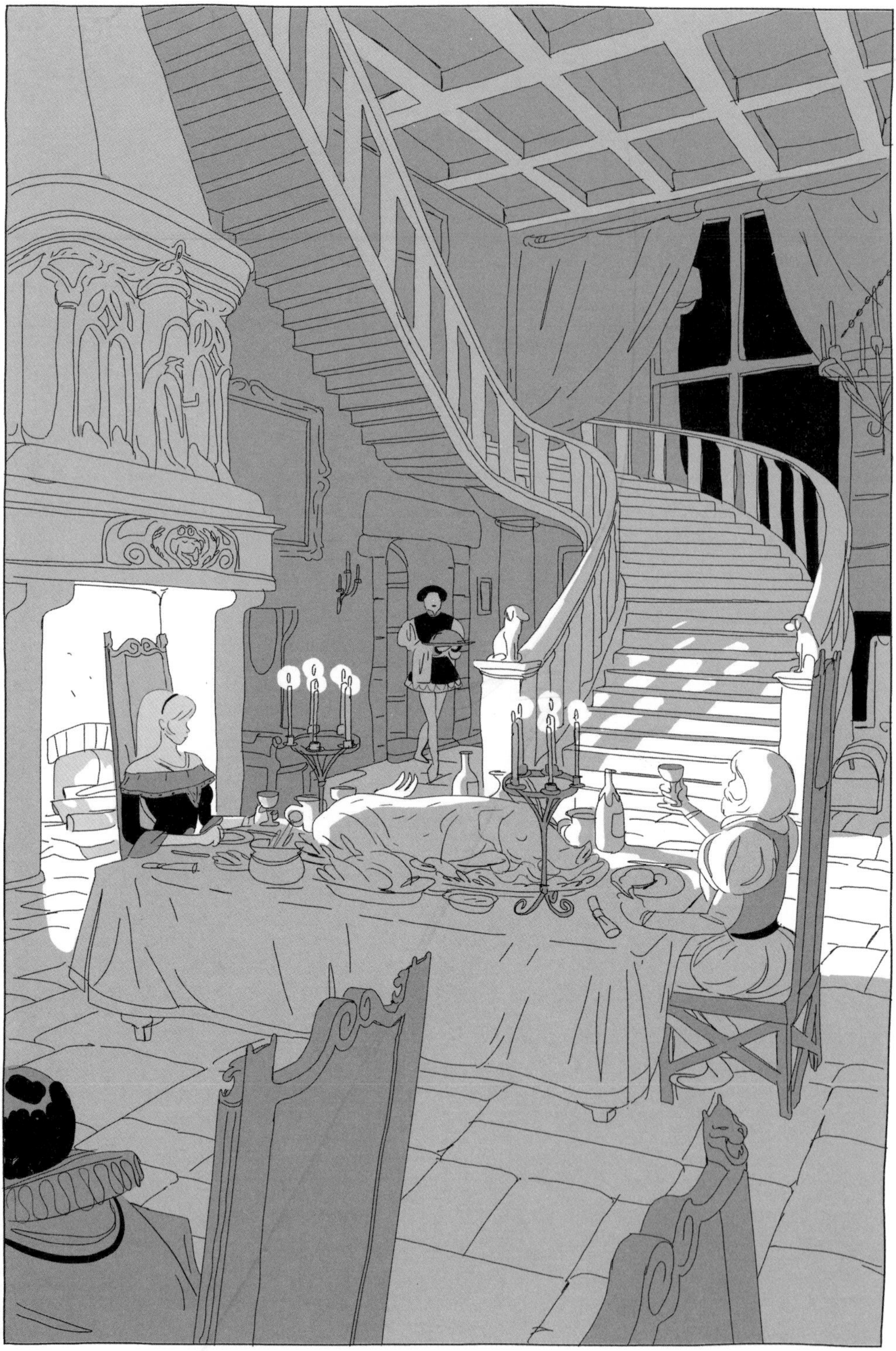

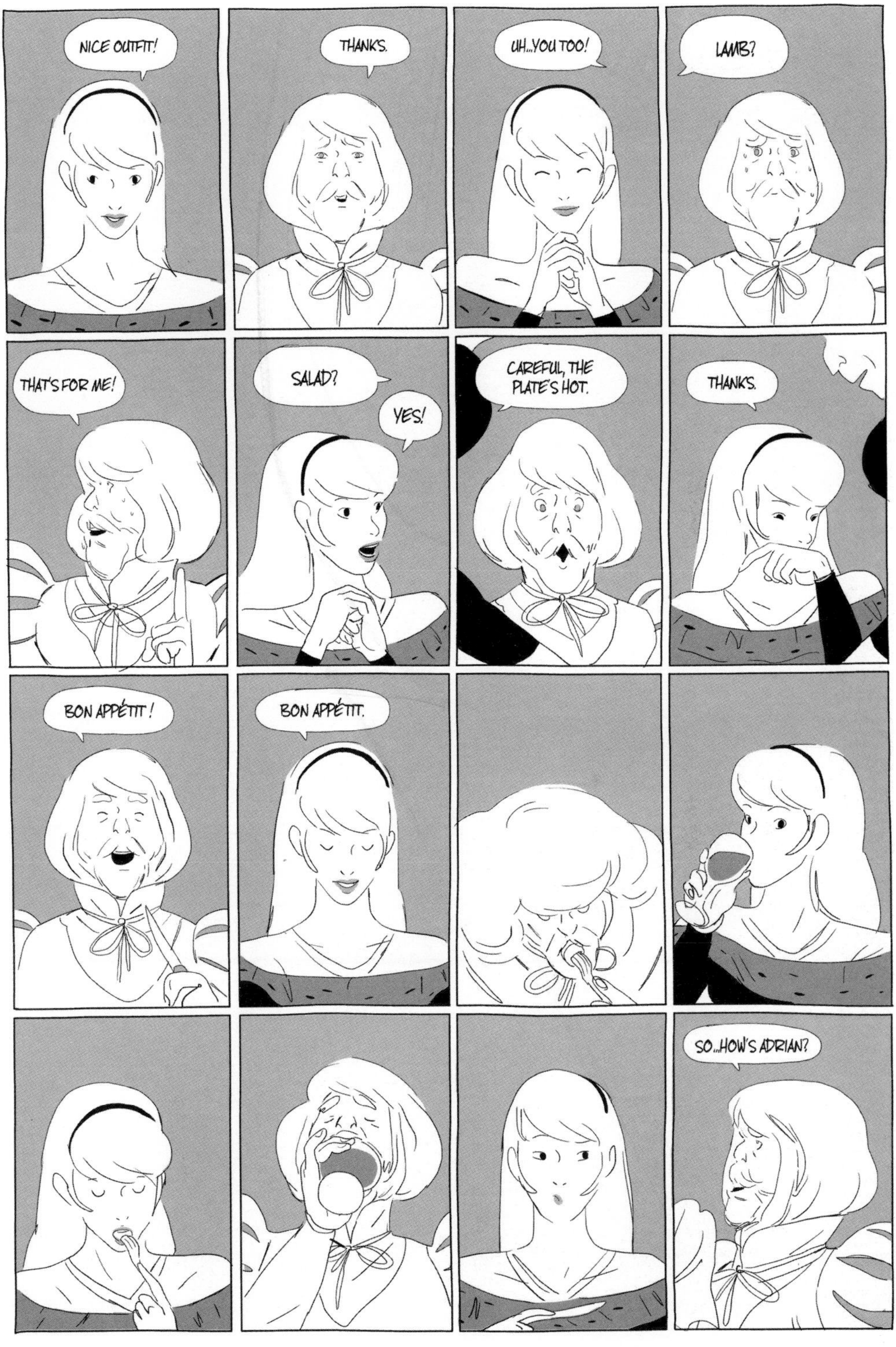
NICE OUTFIT!
THANKS.
UH...YOU TOO!
LAMB?
THAT'S FOR ME!
SALAD?
YES!
CAREFUL, THE PLATE'S HOT.
THANKS.
BON APPÉTIT!
BON APPÉTIT.
SO...HOW'S ADRIAN?

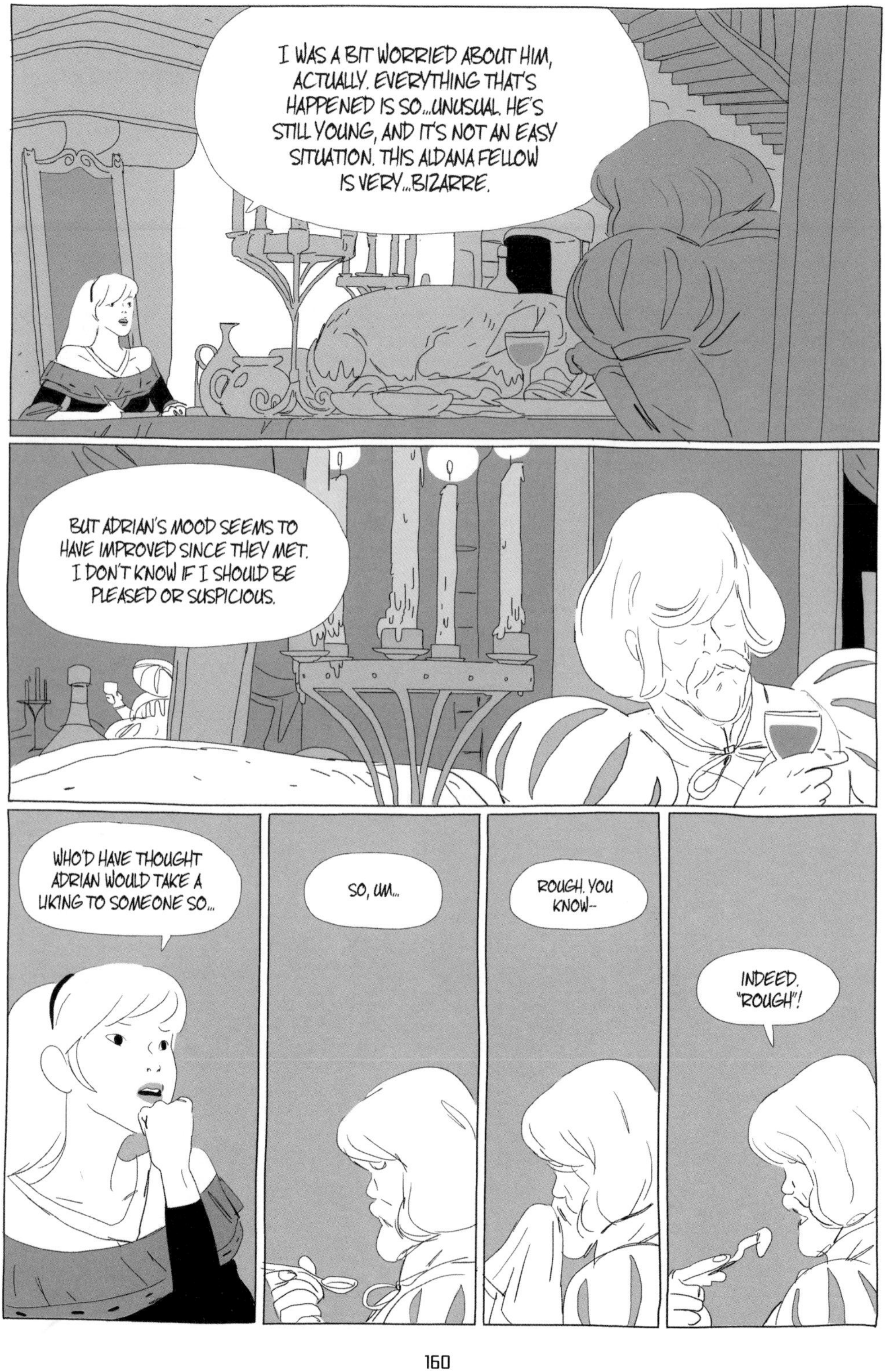
I WAS A BIT WORRIED ABOUT HIM, ACTUALLY. EVERYTHING THAT'S HAPPENED IS SO...UNUSUAL. HE'S STILL YOUNG, AND IT'S NOT AN EASY SITUATION. THIS ALDANA FELLOW IS VERY...BIZARRE.
BUT ADRIAN'S MOOD SEEMS TO HAVE IMPROVED SINCE THEY MET. I DON'T KNOW IF I SHOULD BE PLEASED OR SUSPICIOUS.
WHO'D HAVE THOUGHT ADRIAN WOULD TAKE A LIKING TO SOMEONE SO...
SO, UM...
ROUGH. YOU KNOW--
INDEED. "ROUGH"!

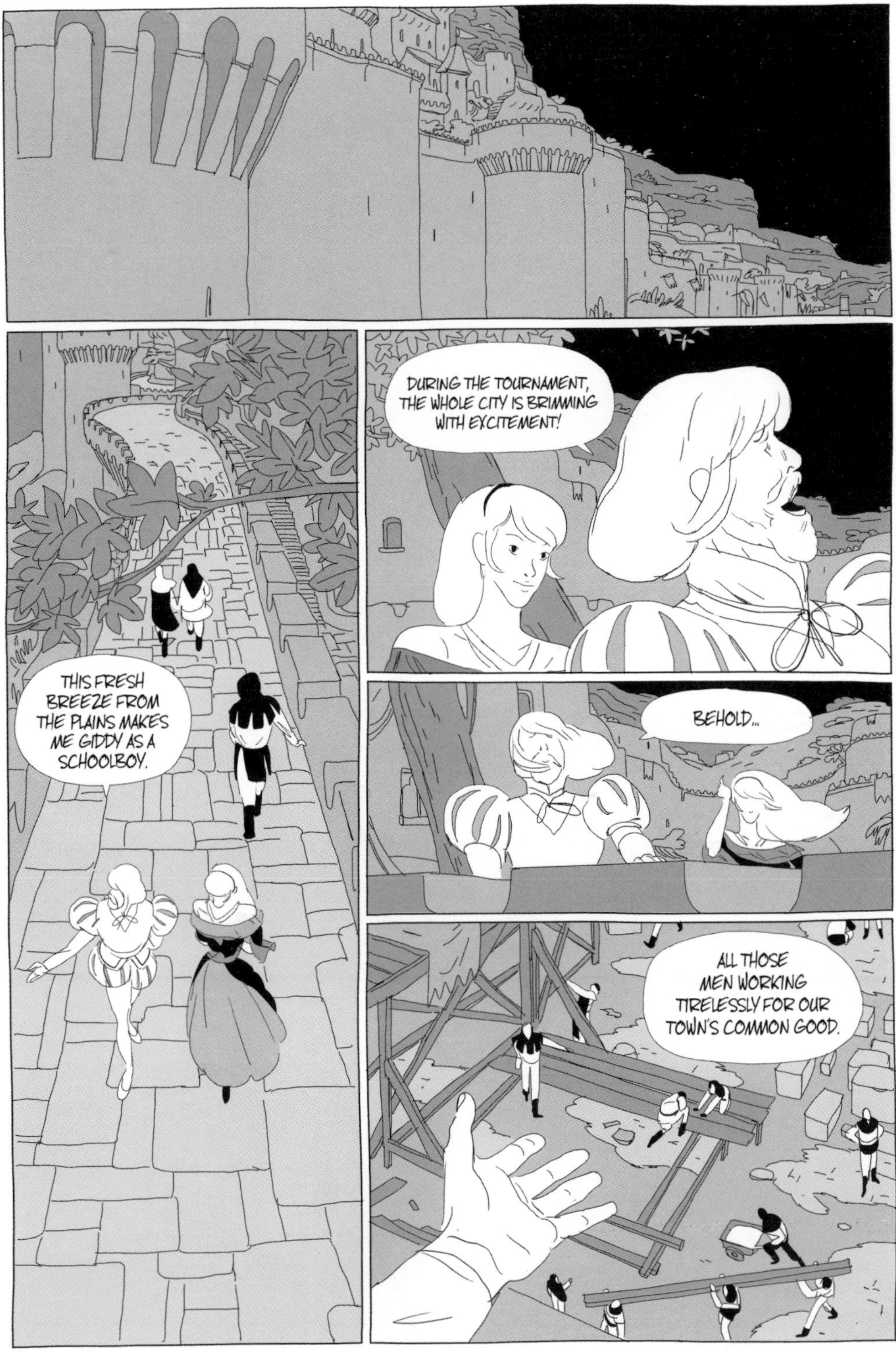
THIS FRESH BREEZE FROM THE PLAINS MAKES ME GIDDY AS A SCHOOLBOY.
DURING THE TOURNAMENT, THE WHOLE CITY IS BRIMMING WITH EXCITEMENT!
BEHOLD...
ALL THOSE MEN WORKING TIRELESSLY FOR OUR TOWN'S COMMON GOOD.

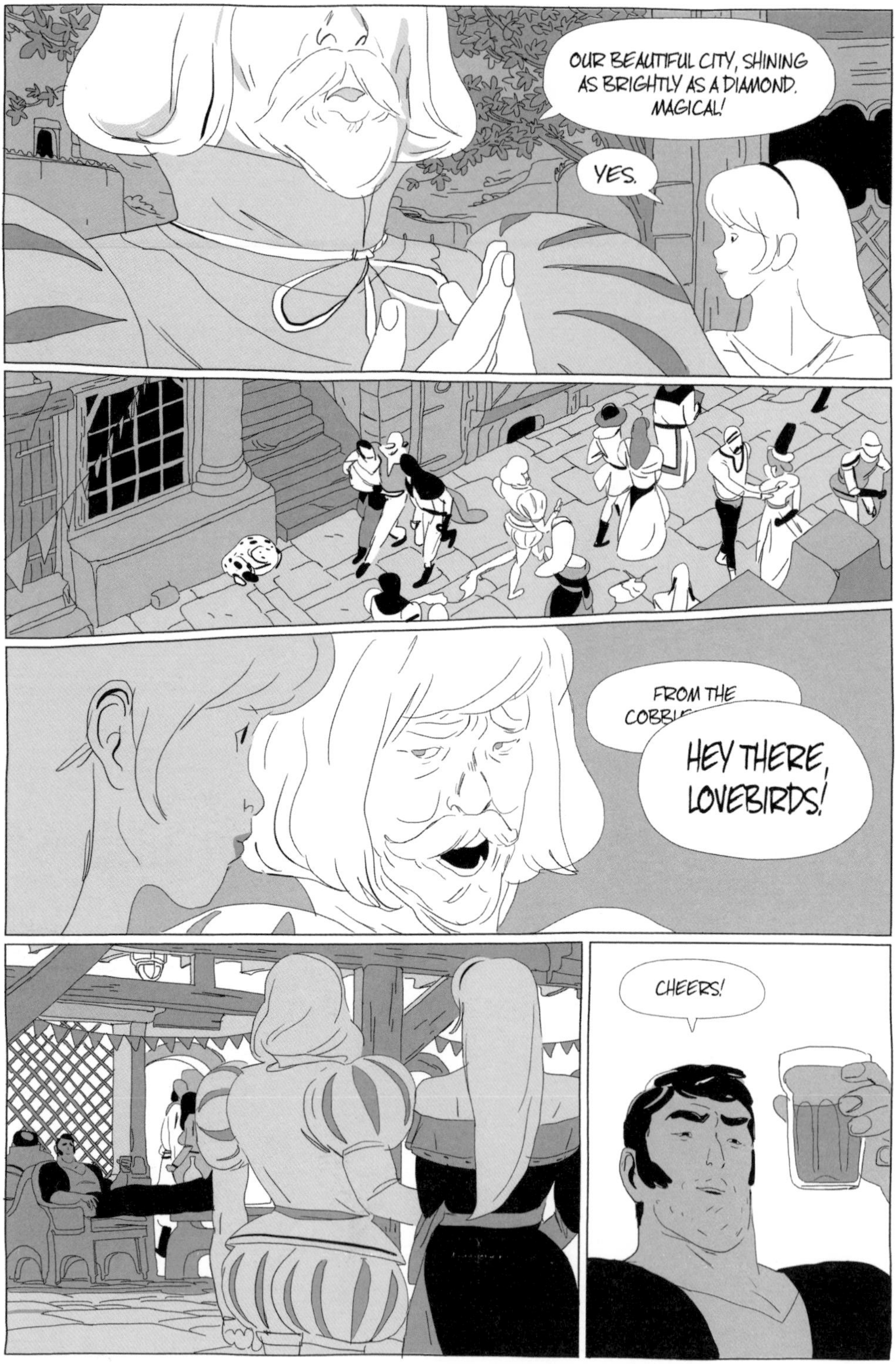
OUR BEAUTIFUL CITY, SHINING AS BRIGHTLY AS A DIAMOND. MAGICAL!
YES.
FROM THE COBBL
HEY THERE, LOVEBIRDS!
CHEERS!

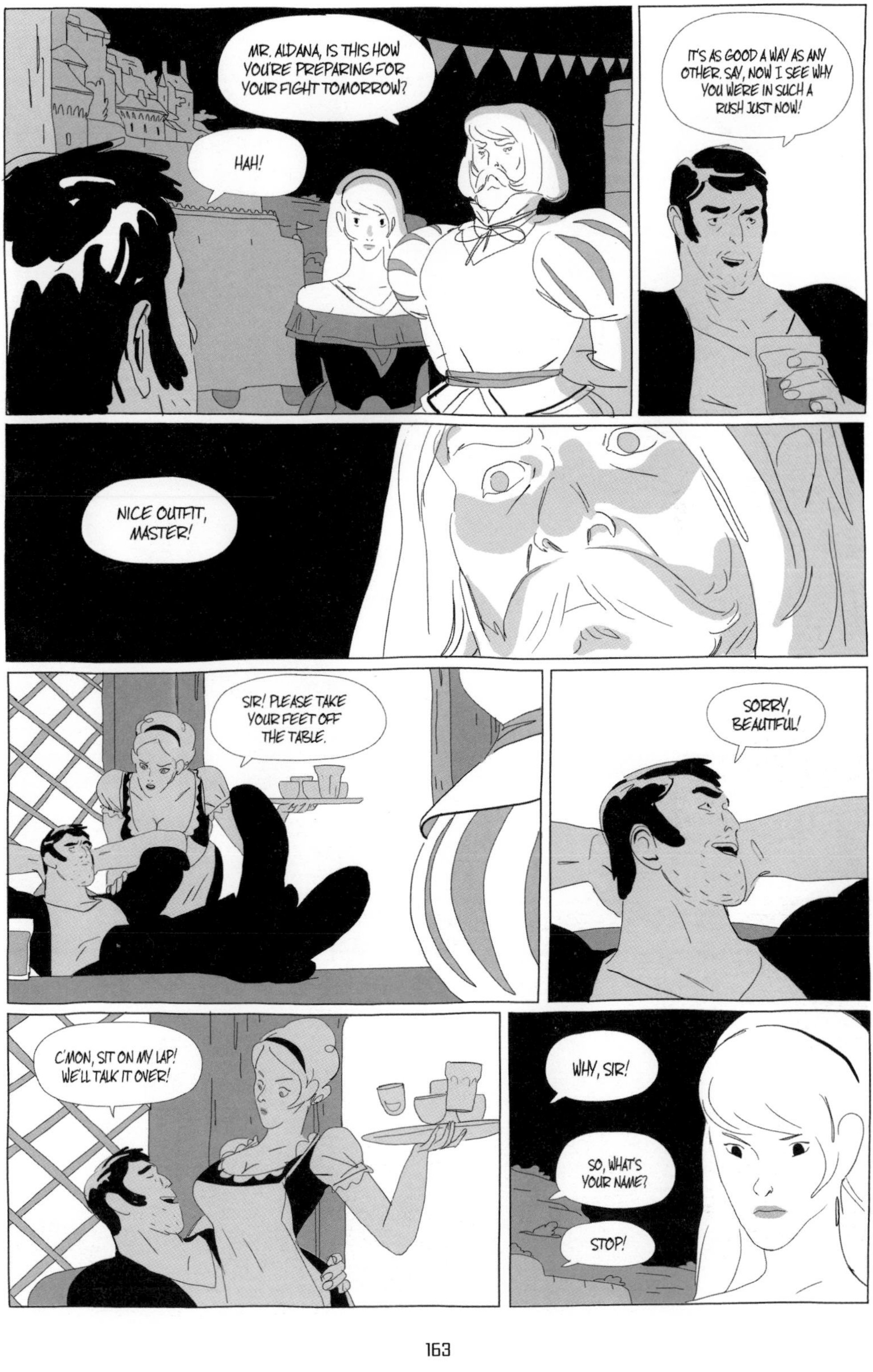
MR. ALDANA, IS THIS HOW YOU'RE PREPARING FOR YOUR FIGHT TOMORROW?
HAH!
IT'S AS GOOD A WAY AS ANY OTHER. SAY, NOW I SEE WHY YOU WERE IN SUCH A RUSH JUST NOW!
NICE OUTFIT, MASTER!
SIR! PLEASE TAKE YOUR FEET OFF THE TABLE.
SORRY, BEAUTIFUL!
C'MON, SIT ON MY LAP! WE'LL TALK IT OVER!
WHY, SIR!
SO, WHAT'S YOUR NAME?
STOP!

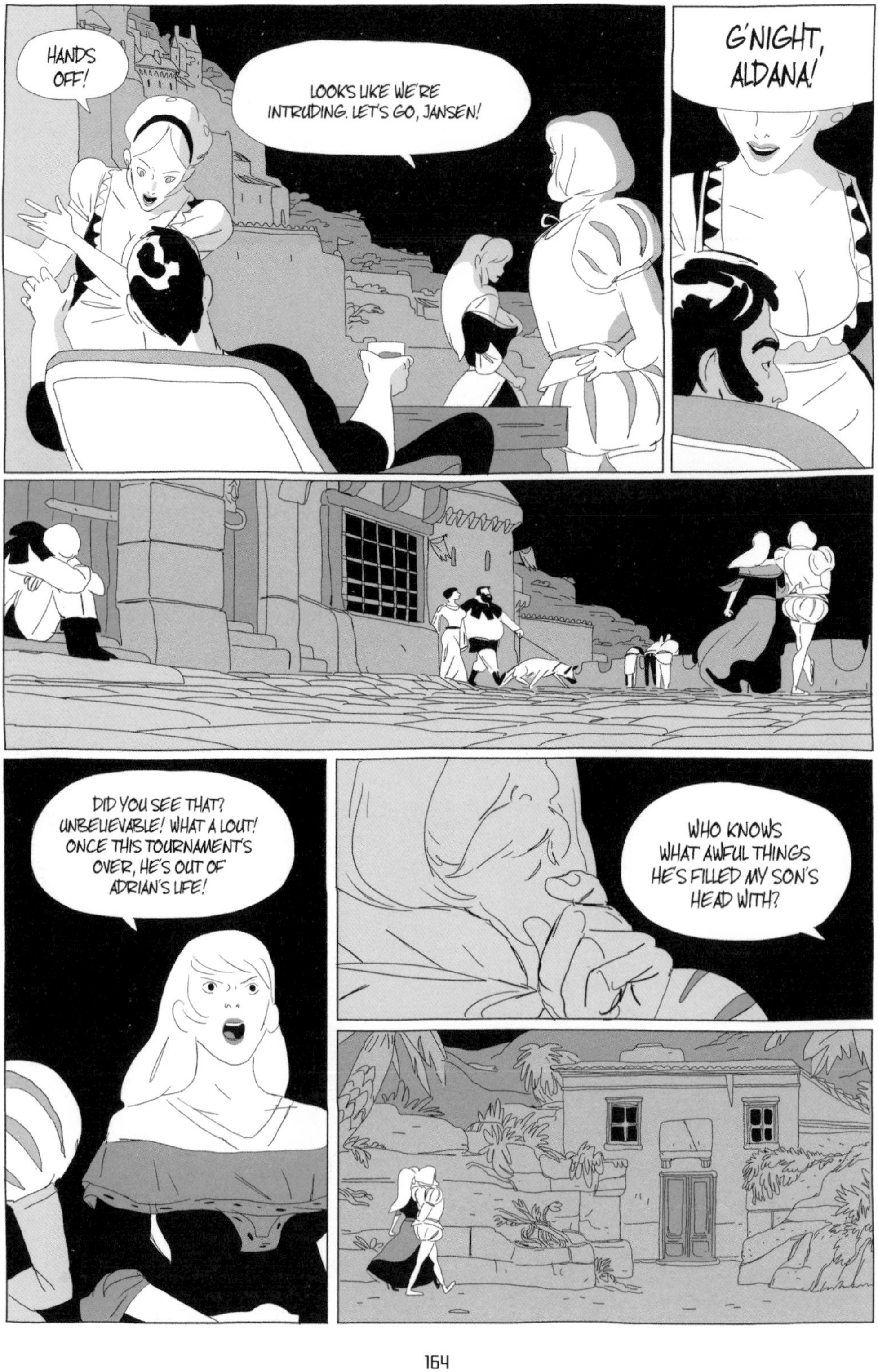
HANDS OFF!
LOOKS LIKE WE'RE INTRUDING. LET'S GO, JANSEN!
G'NIGHT, ALDANA!
DID YOU SEE THAT? UNBELIEVABLE! WHAT A LOUT! ONCE THIS TOURNAMENT'S OVER, HE'S OUT OF ADRIAN'S LIFE!
WHO KNOWS WHAT AWFUL THINGS HE'S FILLED MY SON'S HEAD WITH?

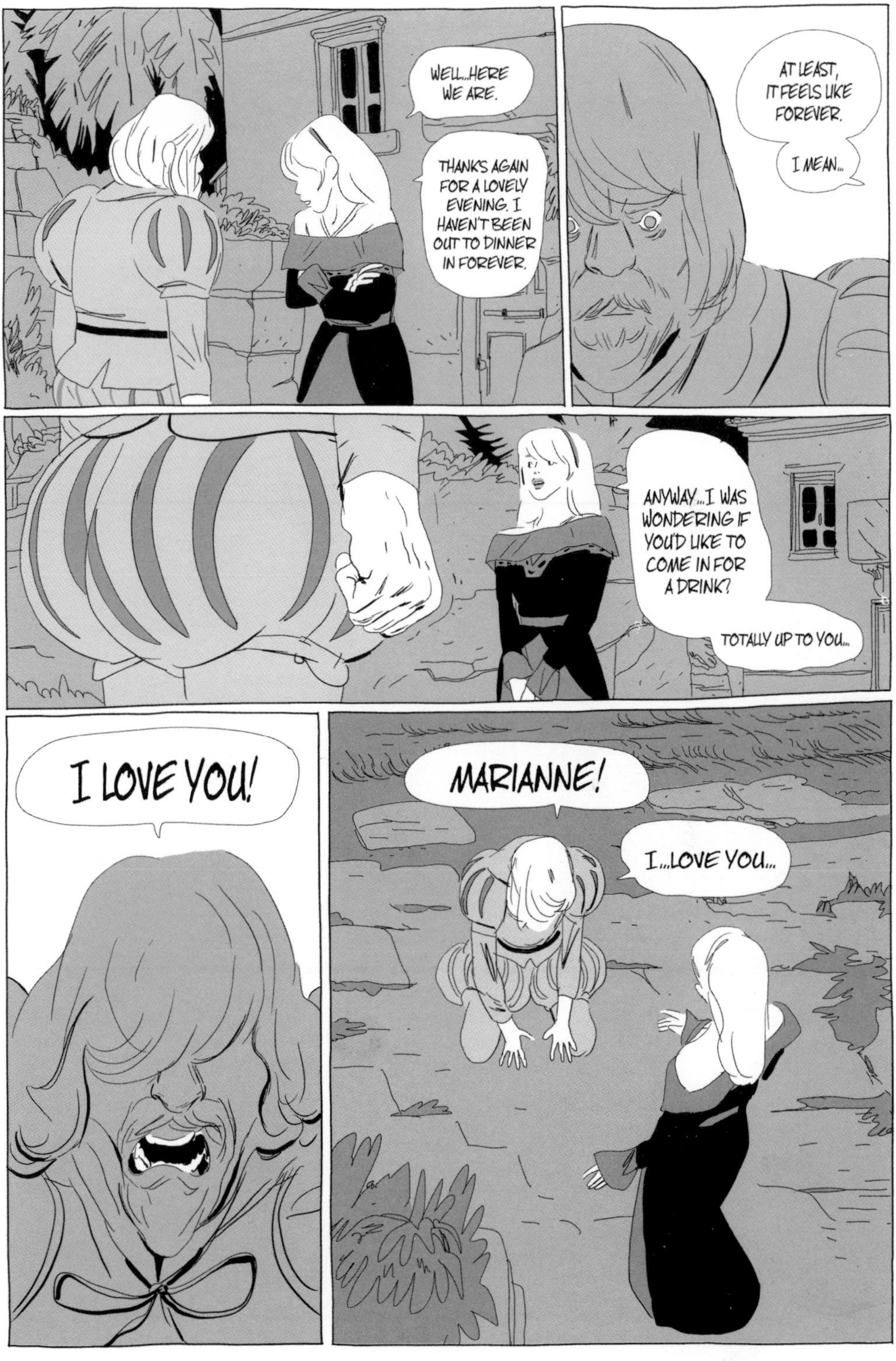
WELL...HERE WE ARE.
THANKS AGAIN FOR A LOVELY EVENING. I HAVEN'T BEEN OUT TO DINNER IN FOREVER.
AT LEAST, IT FEELS LIKE FOREVER.
I MEAN...
ANYWAY...I WAS WONDERING IF YOU'D LIKE TO COME IN FOR A DRINK?
TOTALLY UP TO YOU...
I LOVE YOU!
MARIANNE!
I...LOVE YOU...

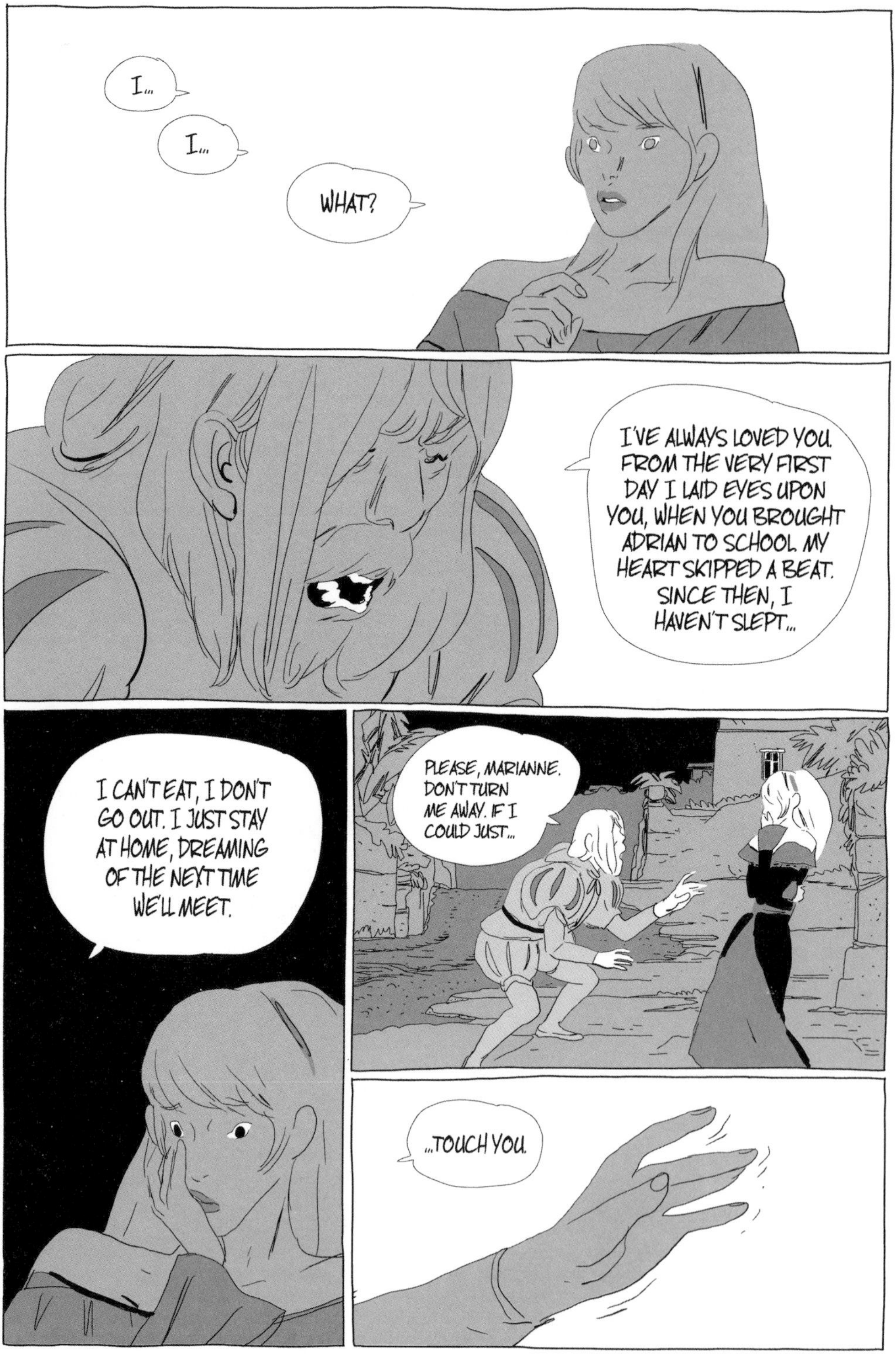
I...
I...
WHAT?
I'VE ALWAYS LOVED YOU. FROM THE VERY FIRST DAY I LAID EYES UPON YOU, WHEN YOU BROUGHT ADRIAN TO SCHOOL. MY HEART SKIPPED A BEAT. SINCE THEN, I HAVEN'T SLEPT...
I CAN'T EAT, I DON'T GO OUT. I JUST STAY AT HOME, DREAMING OF THE NEXT TIME WE'LL MEET.
PLEASE, MARIANNE. DON'T TURN ME AWAY. IF I COULD JUST...
...TOUCH YOU.

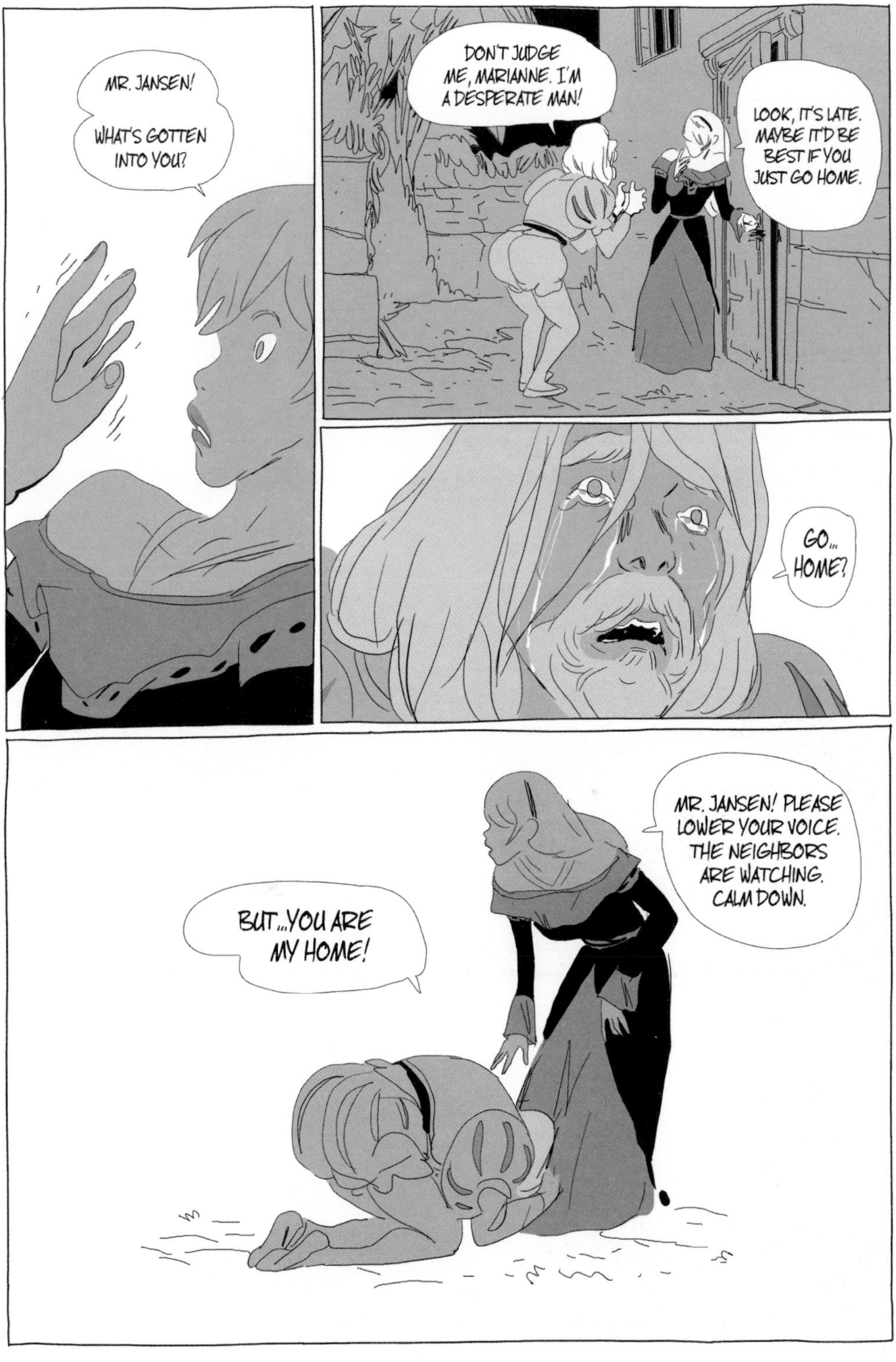
MR. JANSEN!
WHAT'S GOTTEN INTO YOU?
DON'T JUDGE ME, MARIANNE. I'M A DESPERATE MAN!
LOOK, IT'S LATE. MAYBE IT'D BE BEST IF YOU JUST GO HOME.
GO... HOME?
MR. JANSEN! PLEASE LOWER YOUR VOICE. THE NEIGHBORS ARE WATCHING. CALM DOWN.
BUT...YOU ARE MY HOME!

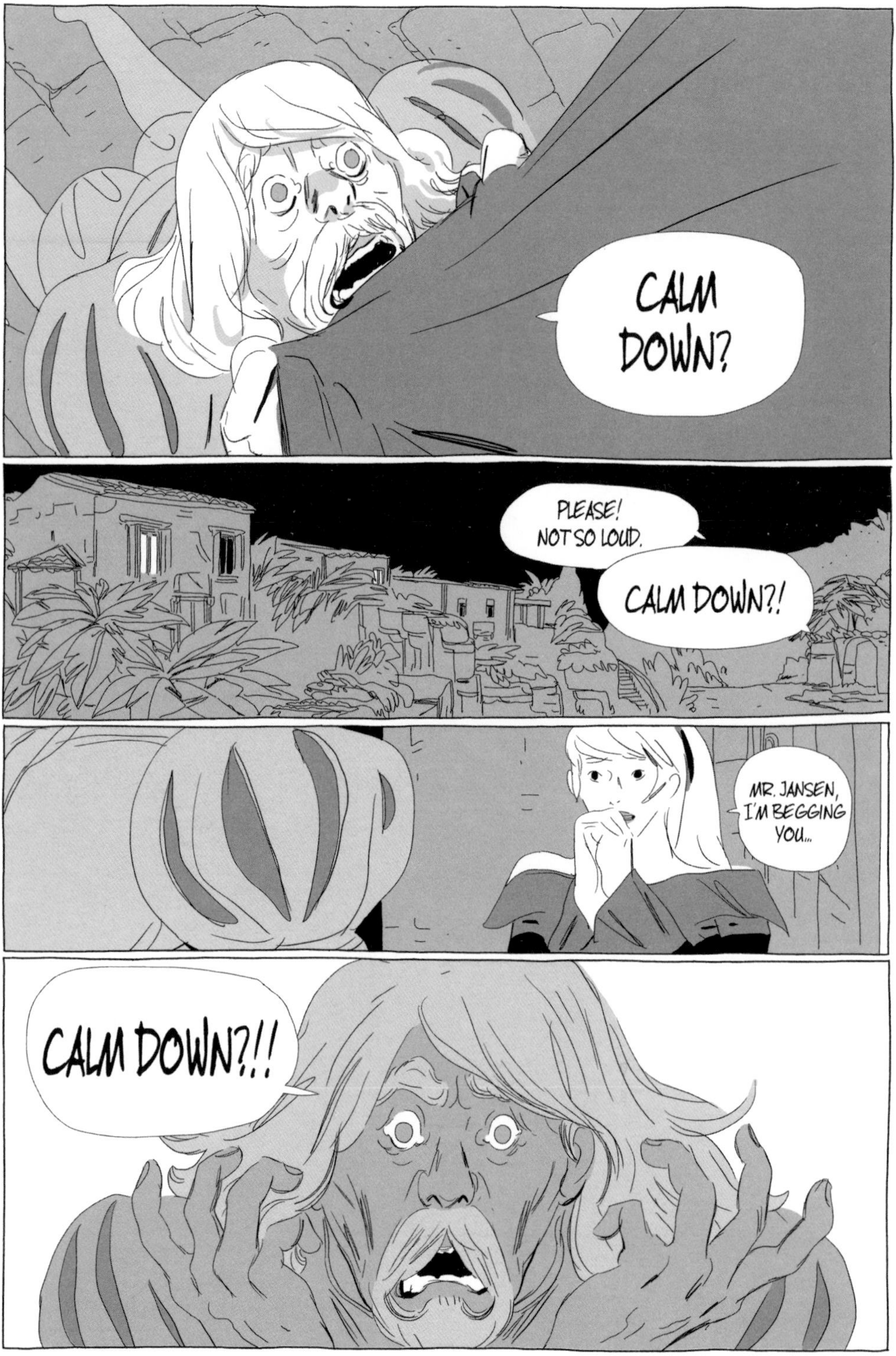
CALM DOWN?
PLEASE! NOT SO LOUD.
CALM DOWN?!
MR. JANSEN, I'M BEGGING YOU...
CALM DOWN?!!

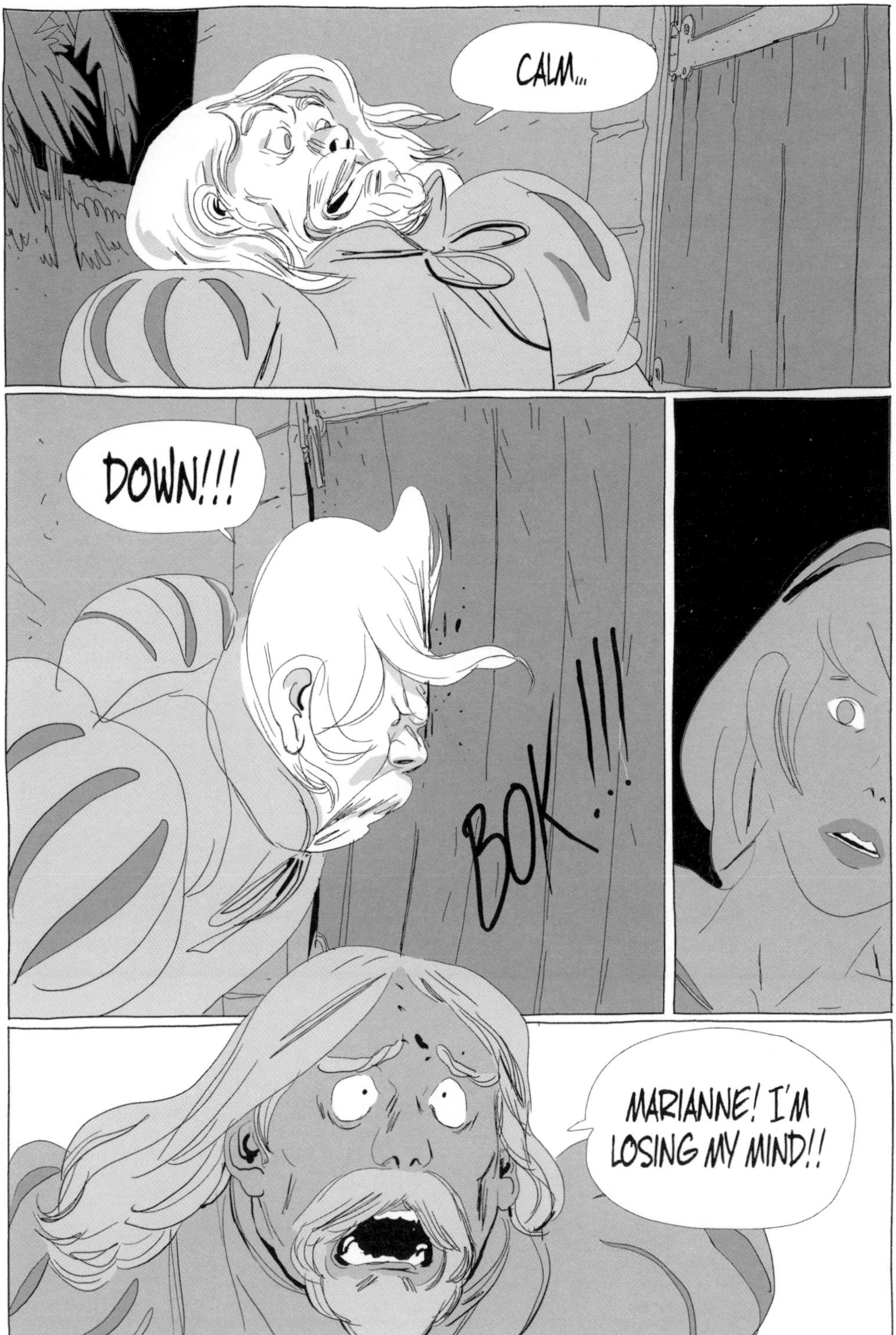
CALM...
DOWN!!!
BOK!!!
MARIANNE! I'M LOSING MY MIND!!

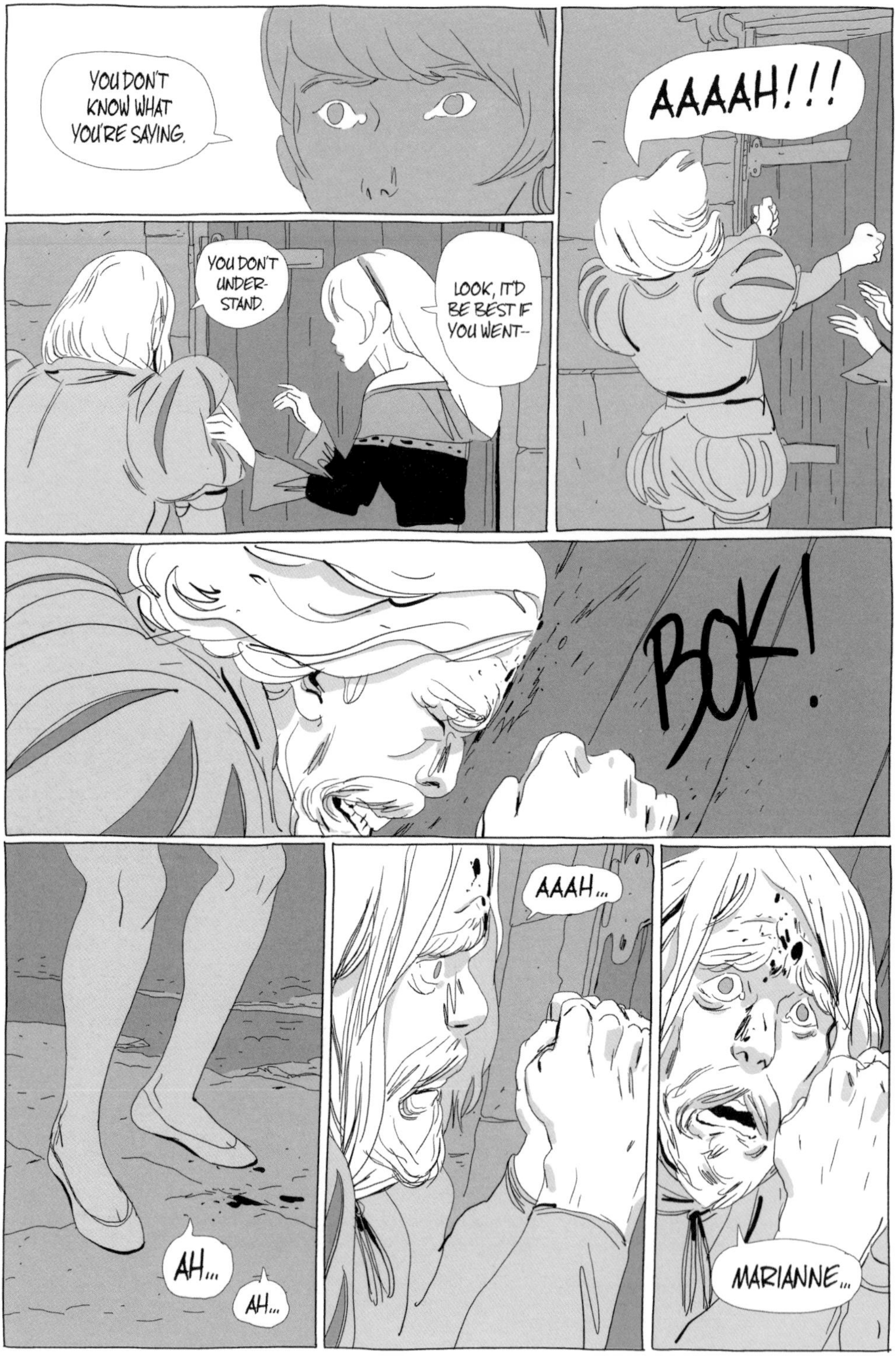
YOU DON'T KNOW WHAT YOU'RE SAYING.
AAAAH!!!
YOU DON'T UNDER-STAND.
LOOK, IT'D BE BEST IF YOU WENT--
BOK!
AH...
AH...
AAAH...
MARIANNE...

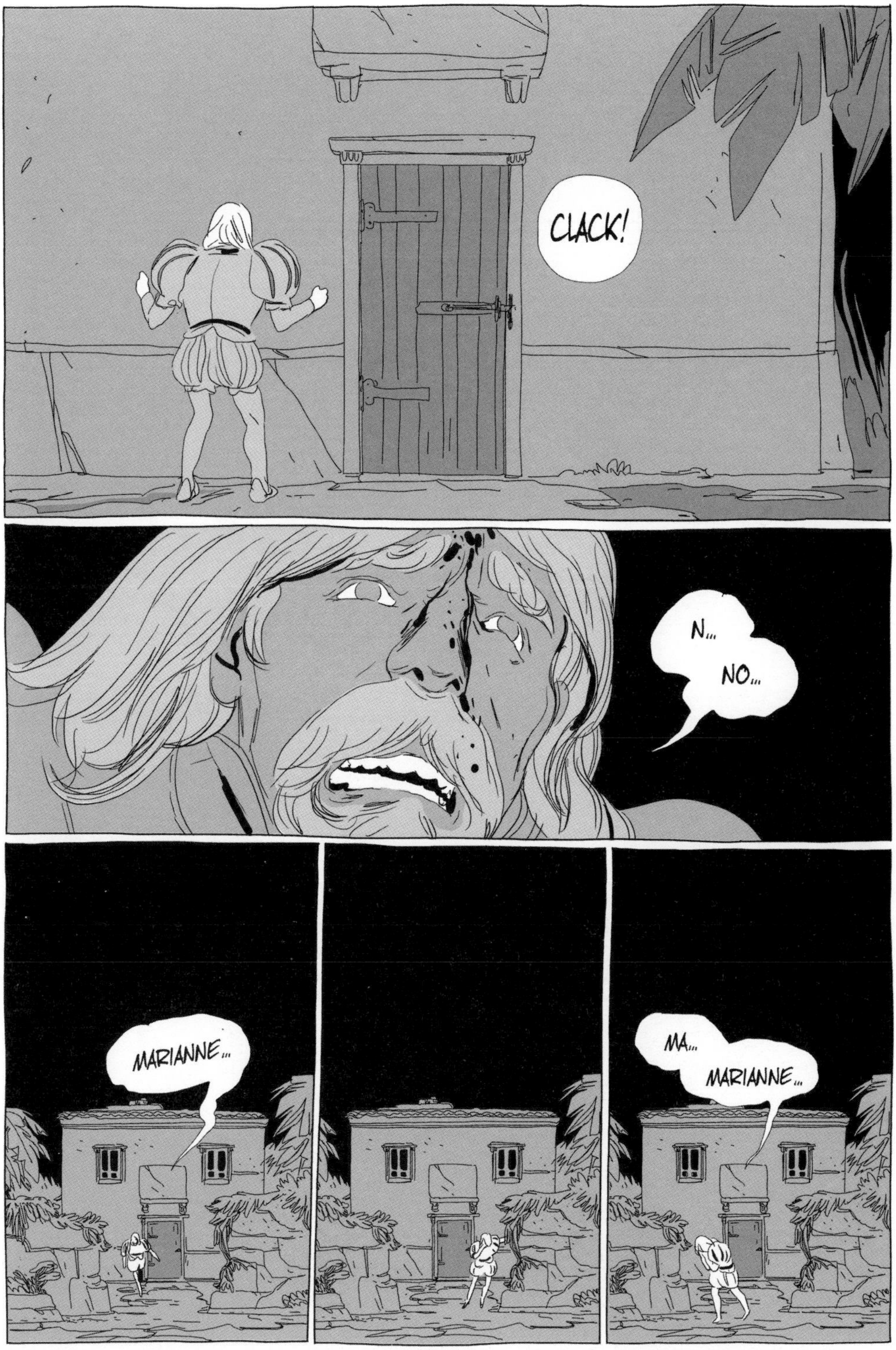
CLACK!
N...
NO...
MARIANNE...
MA...
MARIANNE...

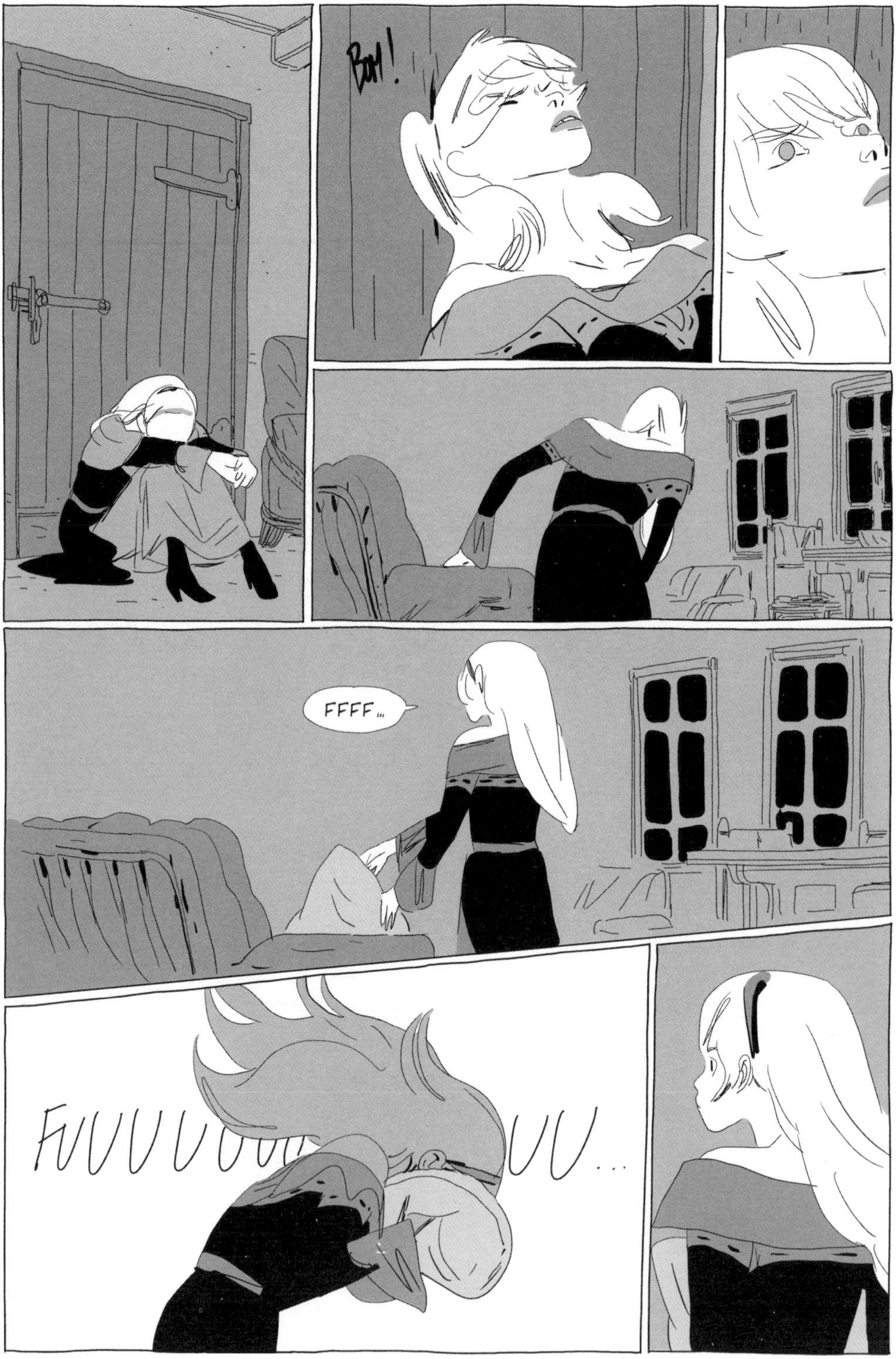
BOM!
FFFF...
FUUUUUUUUU...

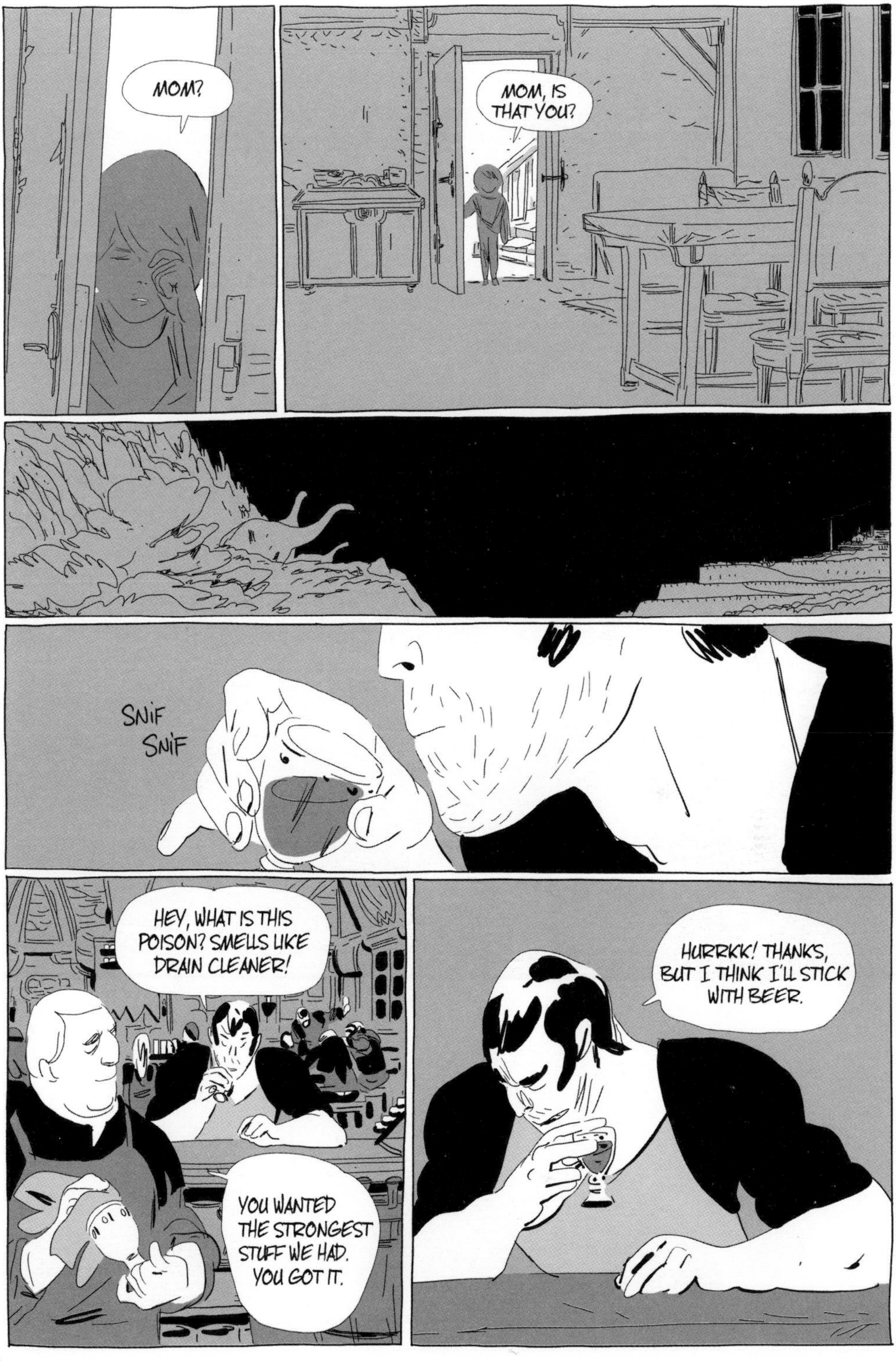
MOM?
MOM, IS THAT YOU?
SNIF SNIF
HEY, WHAT IS THIS POISON? SMELLS LIKE DRAIN CLEANER!
YOU WANTED THE STRONGEST STUFF WE HAD. YOU GOT IT.
HURRKK! THANKS, BUT I THINK I'LL STICK WITH BEER.

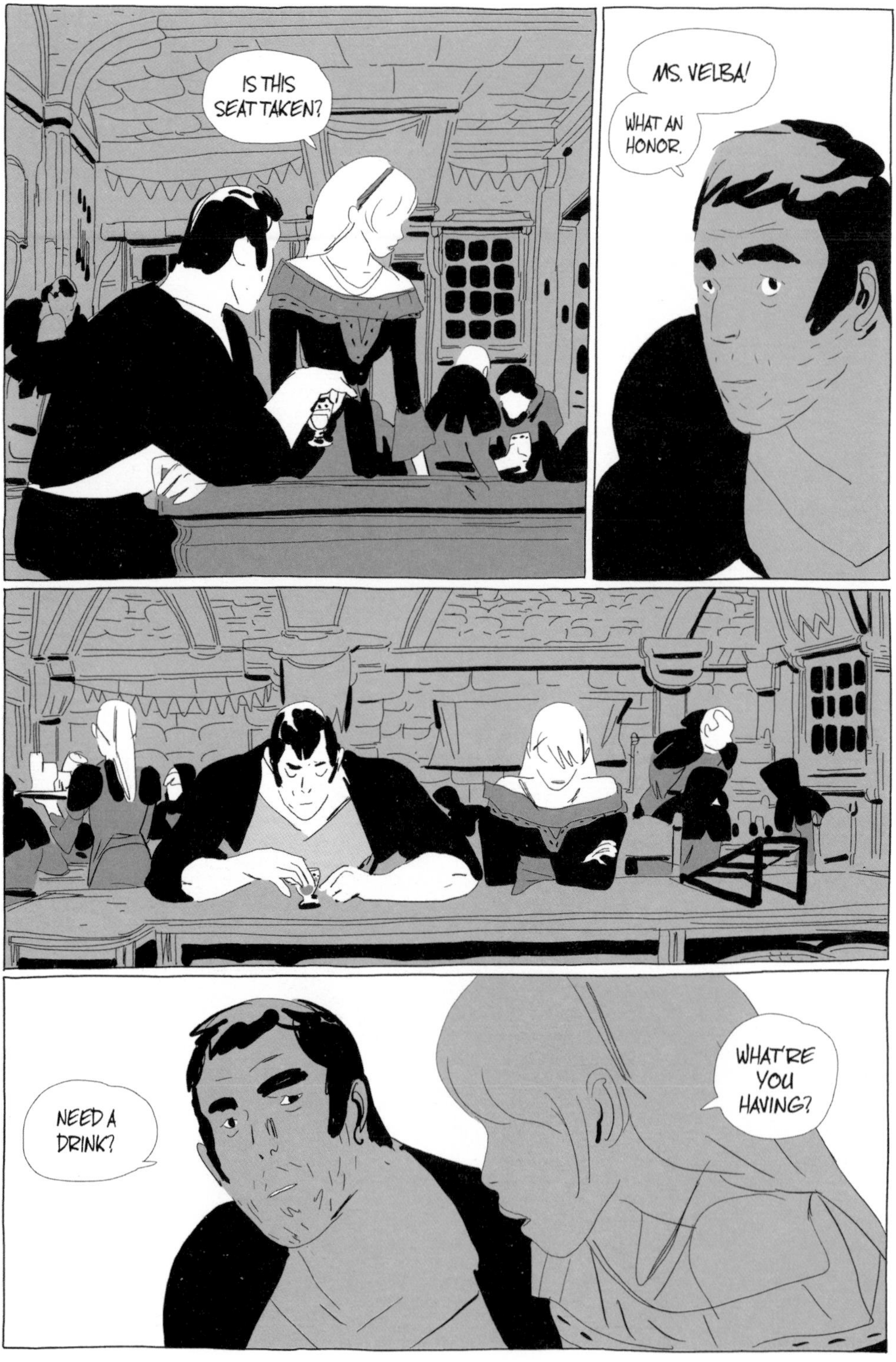
IS THIS SEAT TAKEN?
MS. VELBA!
WHAT AN HONOR.
NEED A DRINK?
WHAT'RE YOU HAVING?

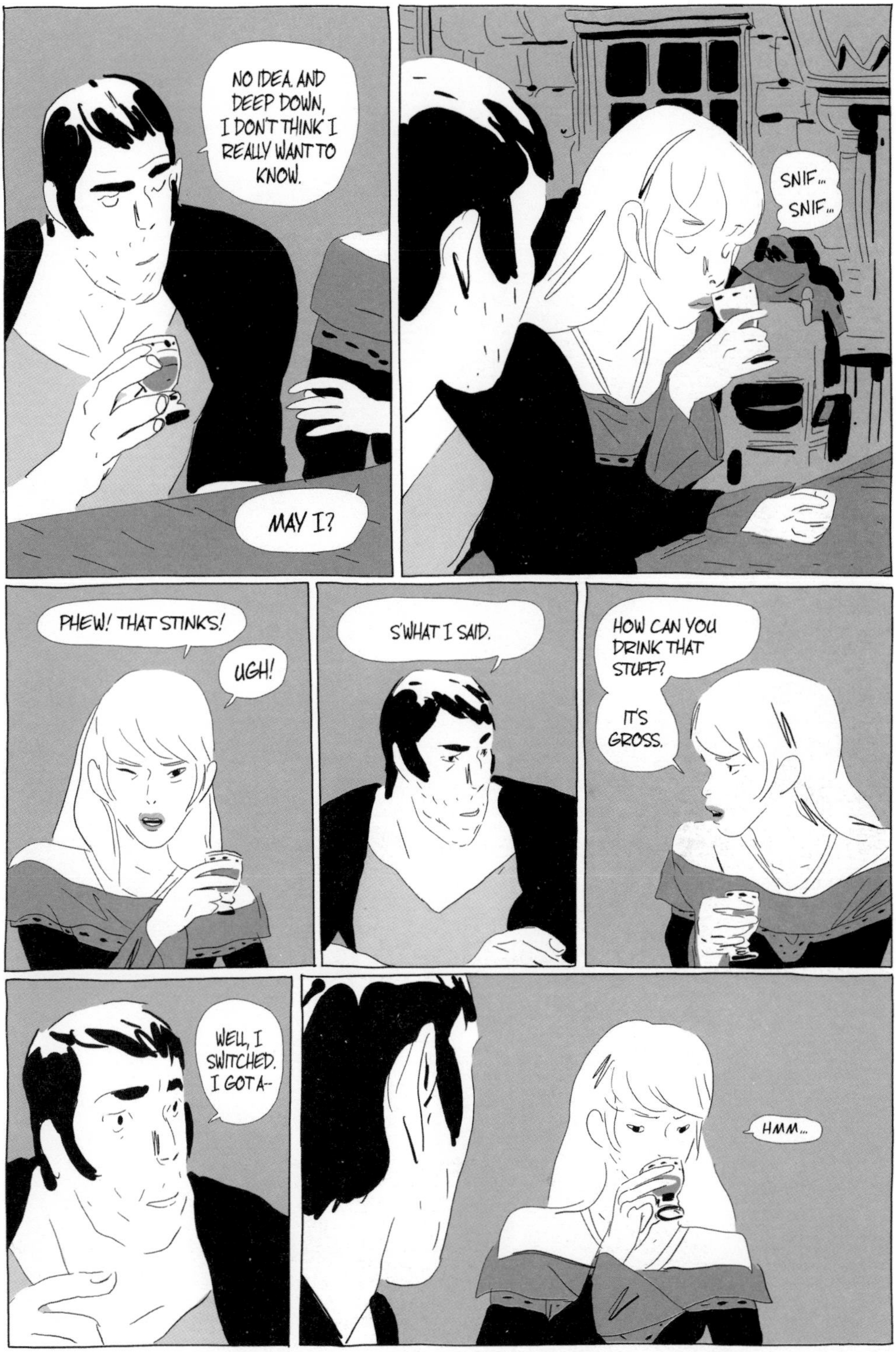
NO IDEA. AND DEEP DOWN, I DON'T THINK I REALLY WANT TO KNOW.
MAY I?
SNIF... SNIF...
PHEW! THAT STINKS!
UGH!
S'WHAT I SAID.
HOW CAN YOU DRINK THAT STUFF?
IT'S GROSS.
WELL, I SWITCHED. I GOT A--
HMM...

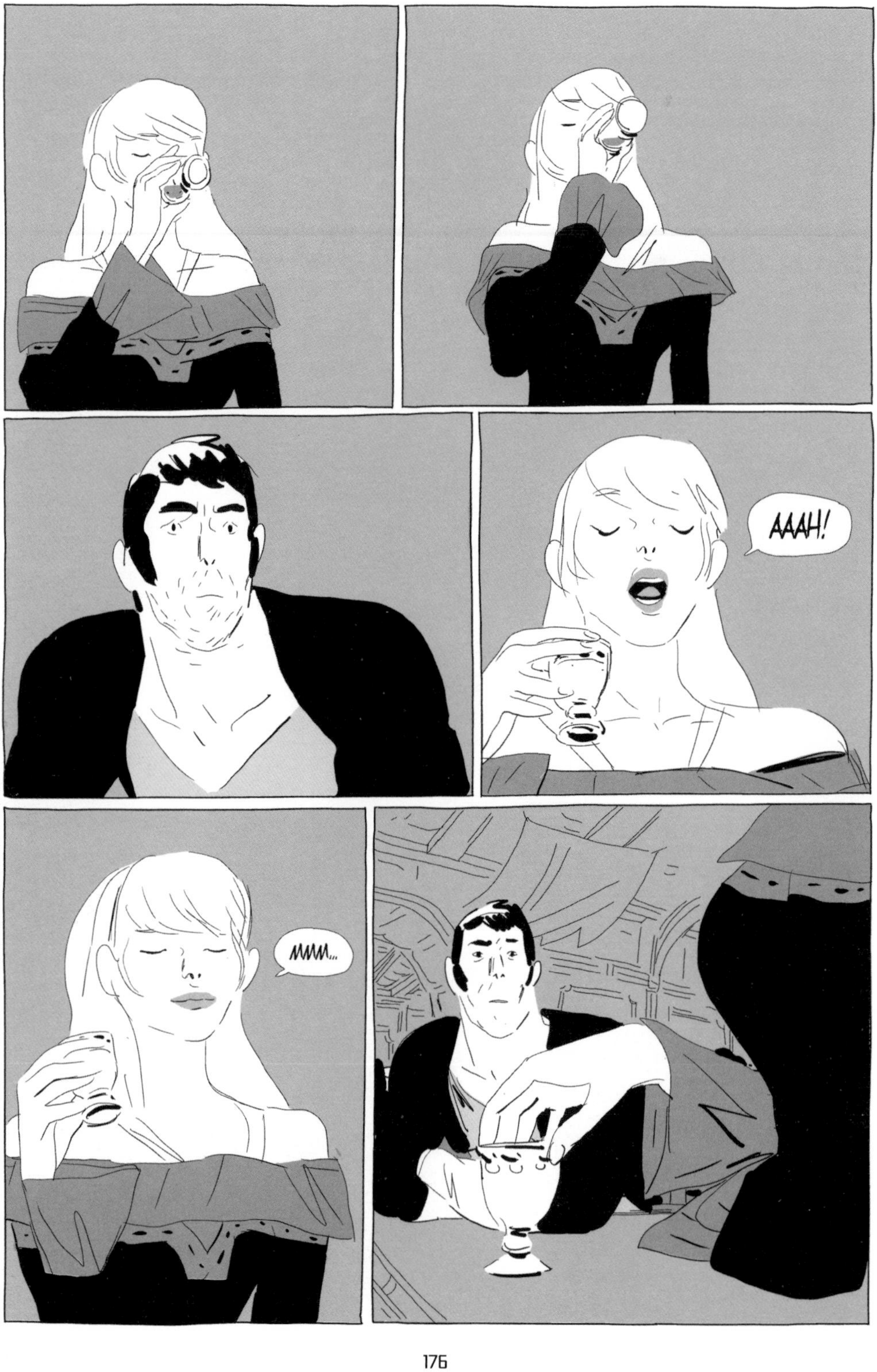
AAAH!
MMM...

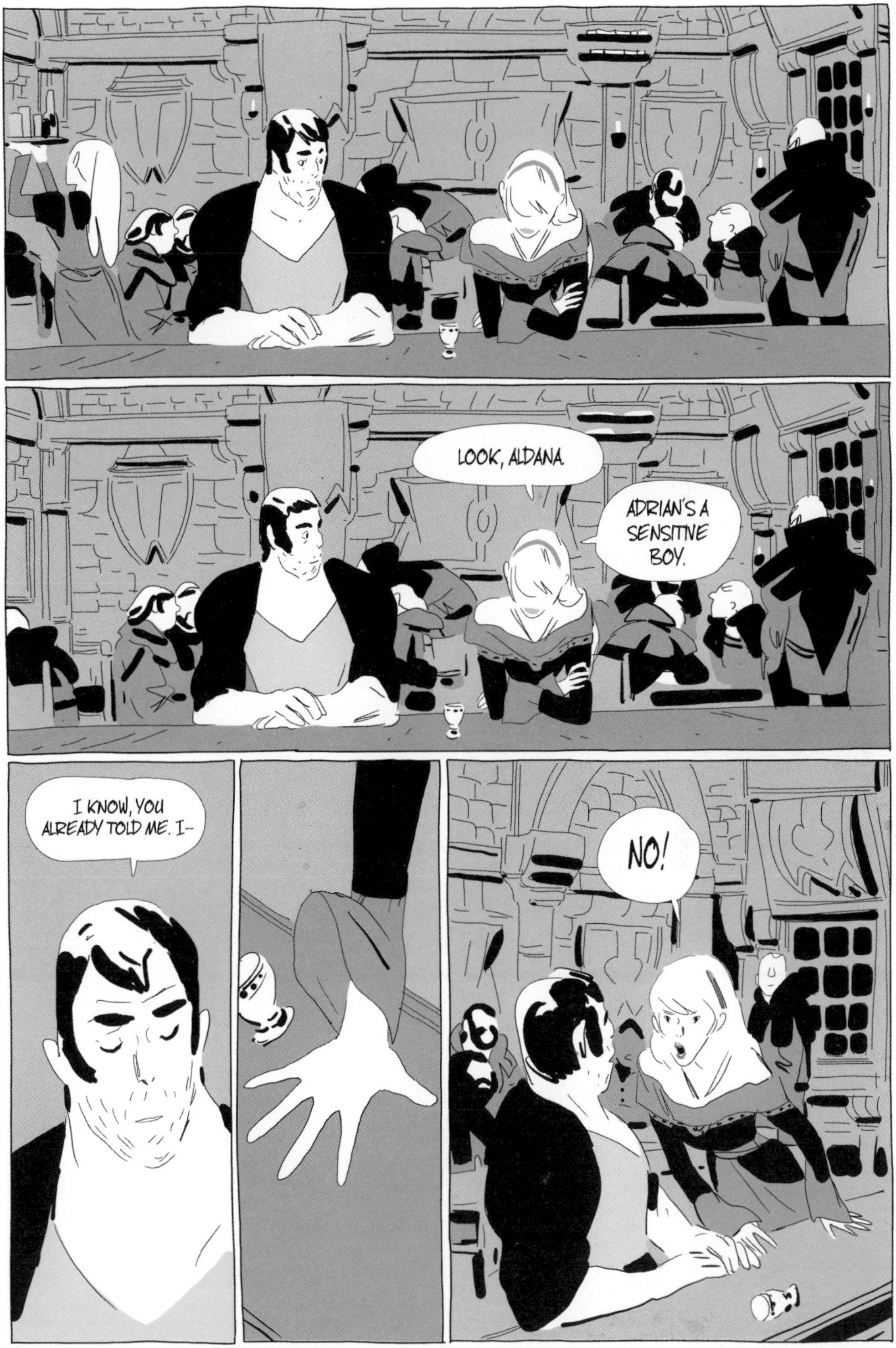
LOOK, ALDANA.
ADRIAN'S A SENSITIVE BOY.
I KNOW, YOU ALREADY TOLD ME. I--
NO!

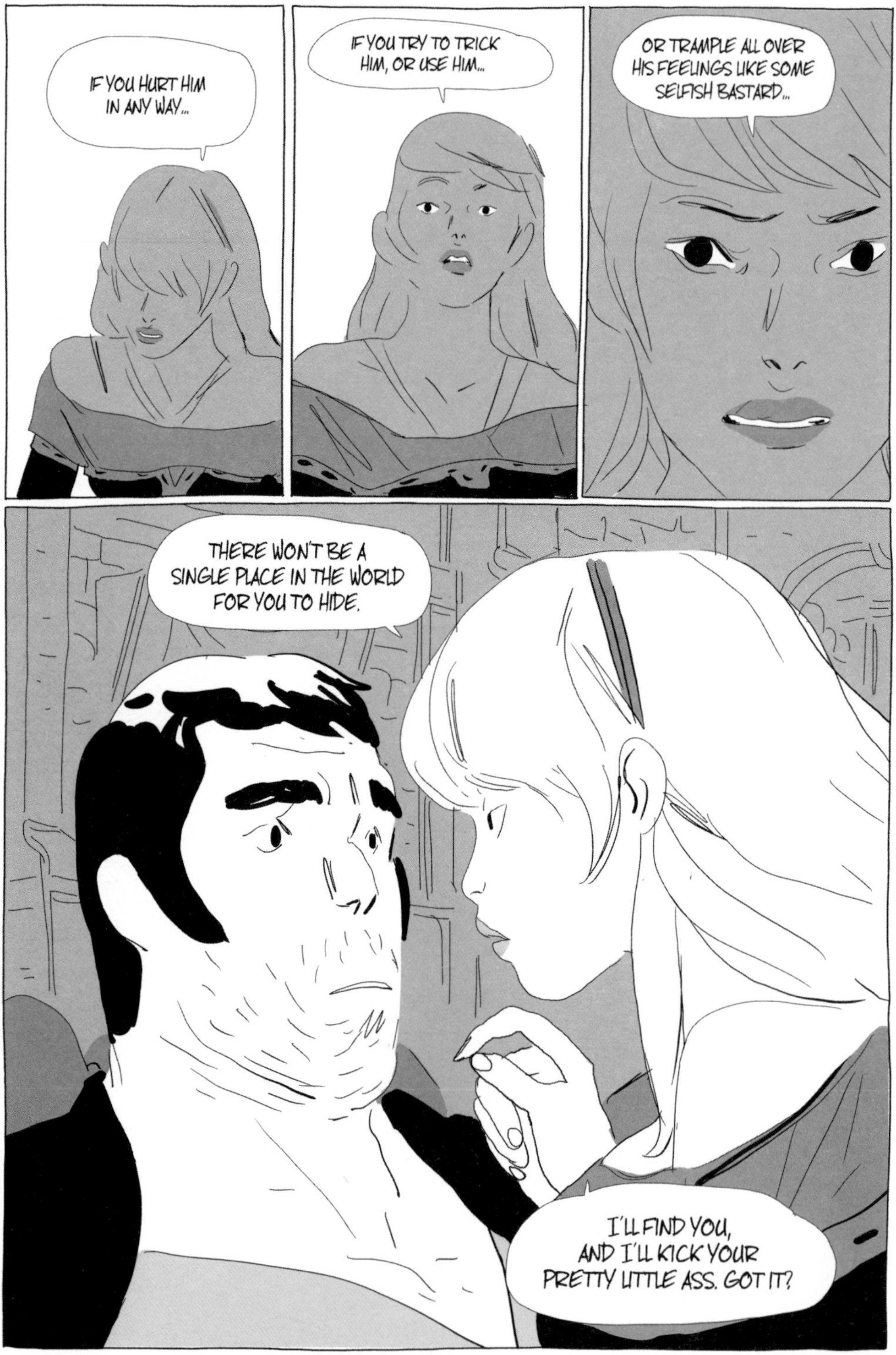
IF YOU HURT HIM IN ANY WAY...
IF YOU TRY TO TRICK HIM, OR USE HIM...
OR TRAMPLE ALL OVER HIS FEELINGS LIKE SOME SELFISH BASTARD...
THERE WON'T BE A SINGLE PLACE IN THE WORLD FOR YOU TO HIDE.
I'LL FIND YOU, AND I'LL KICK YOUR PRETTY LITTLE ASS. GOT IT?

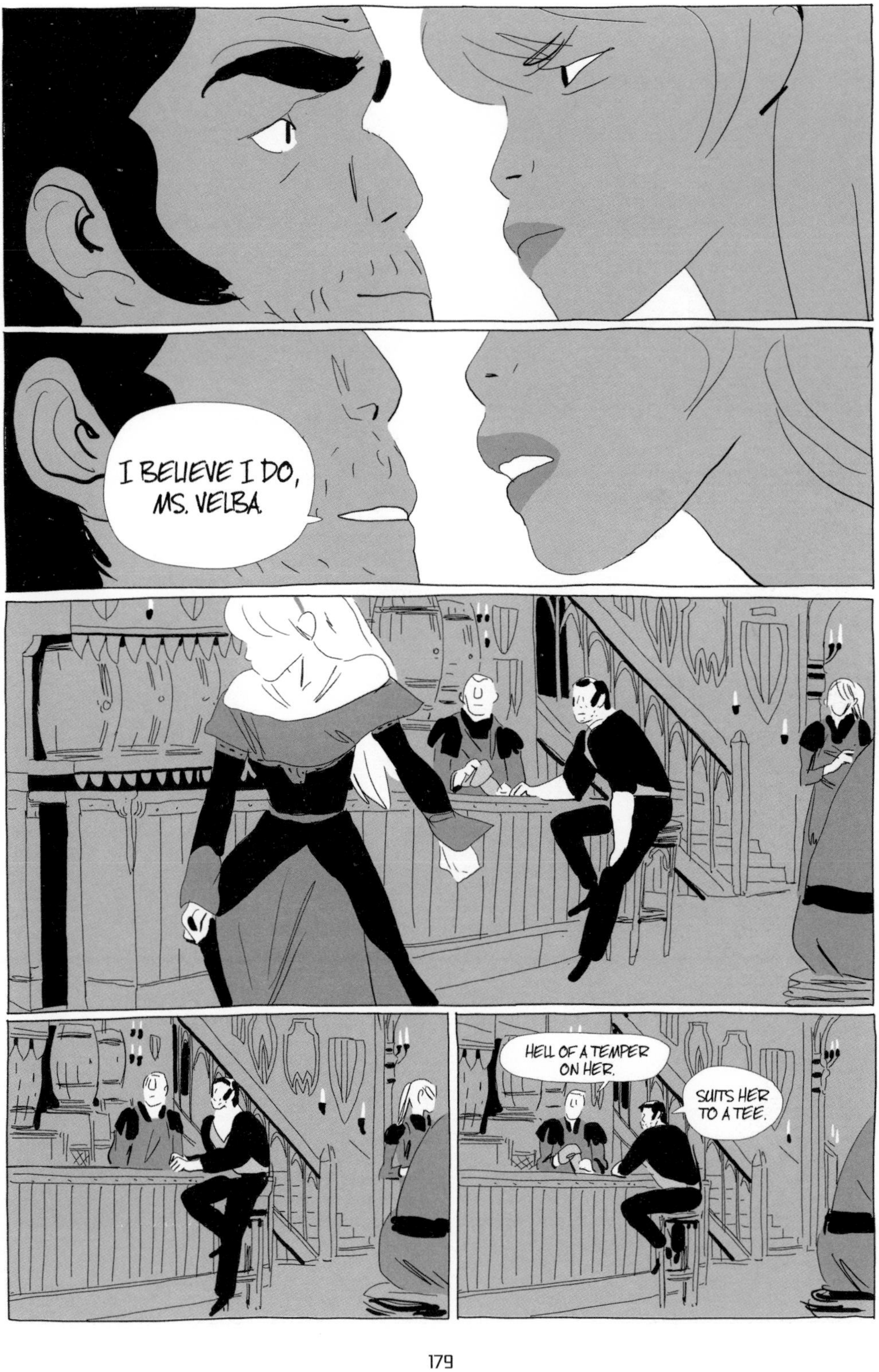
I BELIEVE I DO, MS. VELBA.
HELL OF A TEMPER ON HER.
SUITS HER TO A TEE.

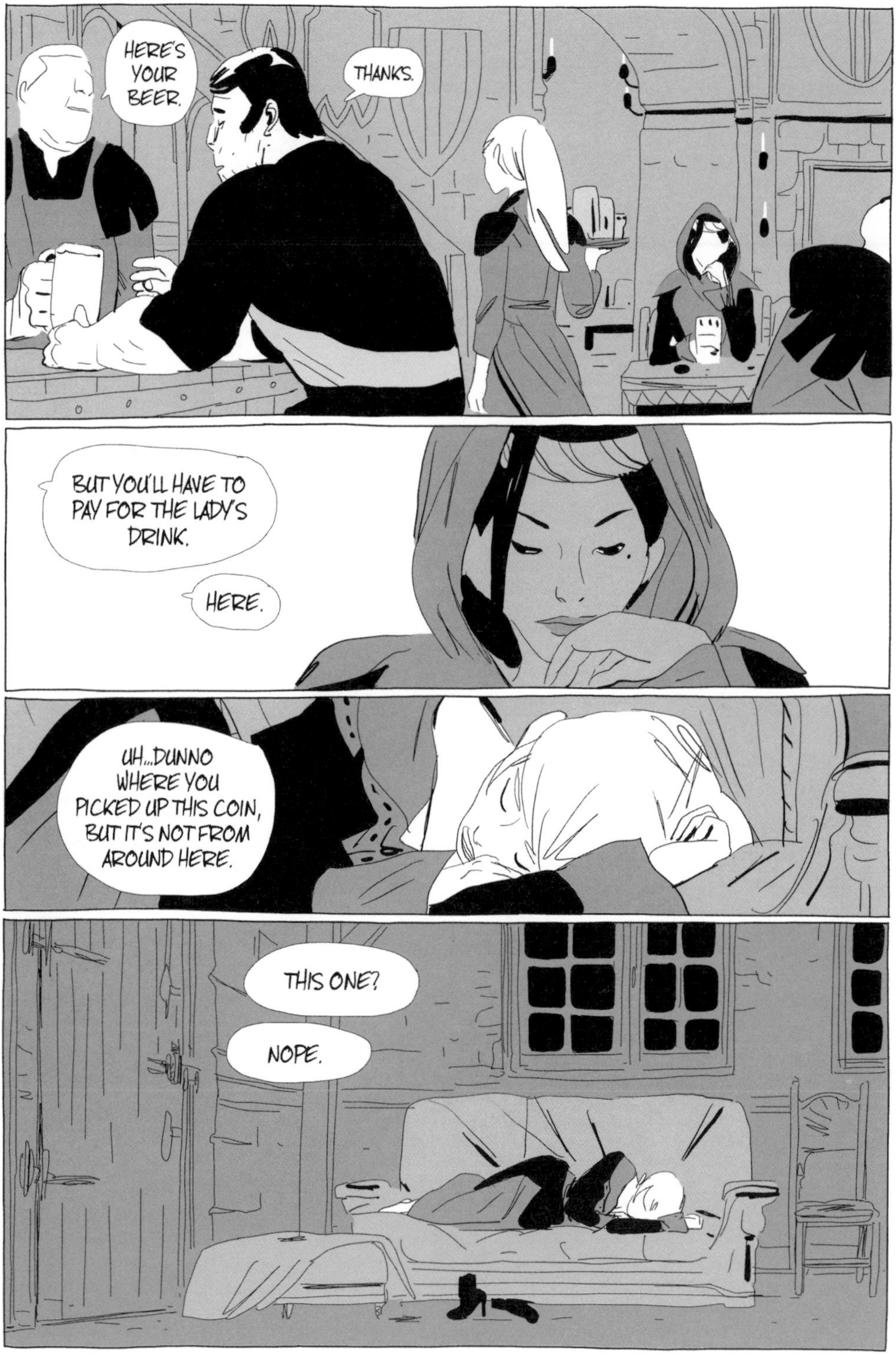
HERE'S YOUR BEER.
THANKS.
BUT YOU'LL HAVE TO PAY FOR THE LADY'S DRINK.
HERE.
UH...DUNNO WHERE YOU PICKED UP THIS COIN, BUT IT'S NOT FROM AROUND HERE.
THIS ONE?
NOPE.

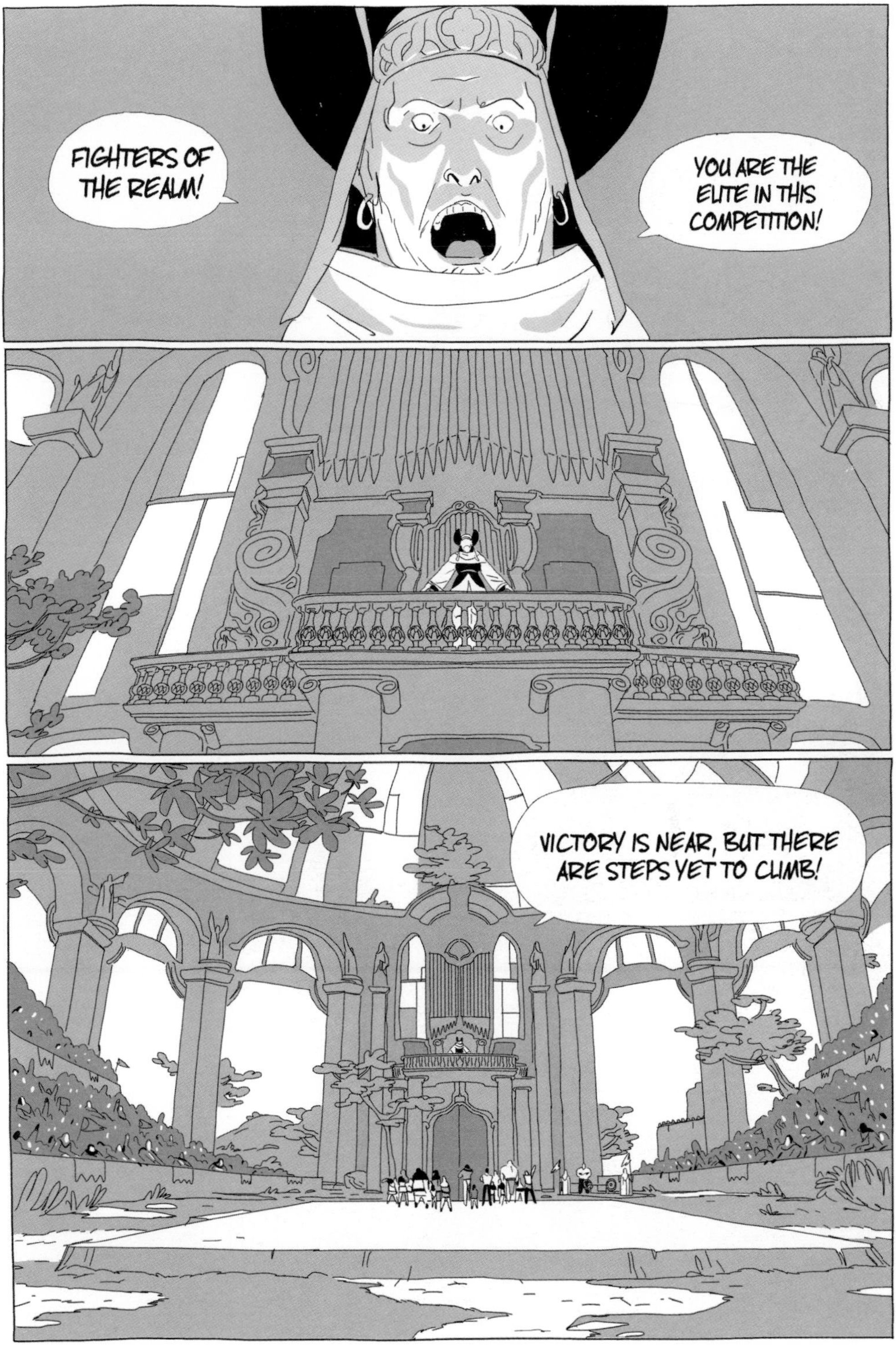
FIGHTERS OF THE REALM!
YOU ARE THE ELITE IN THIS COMPETITION!
VICTORY IS NEAR, BUT THERE ARE STEPS YET TO CLIMB!

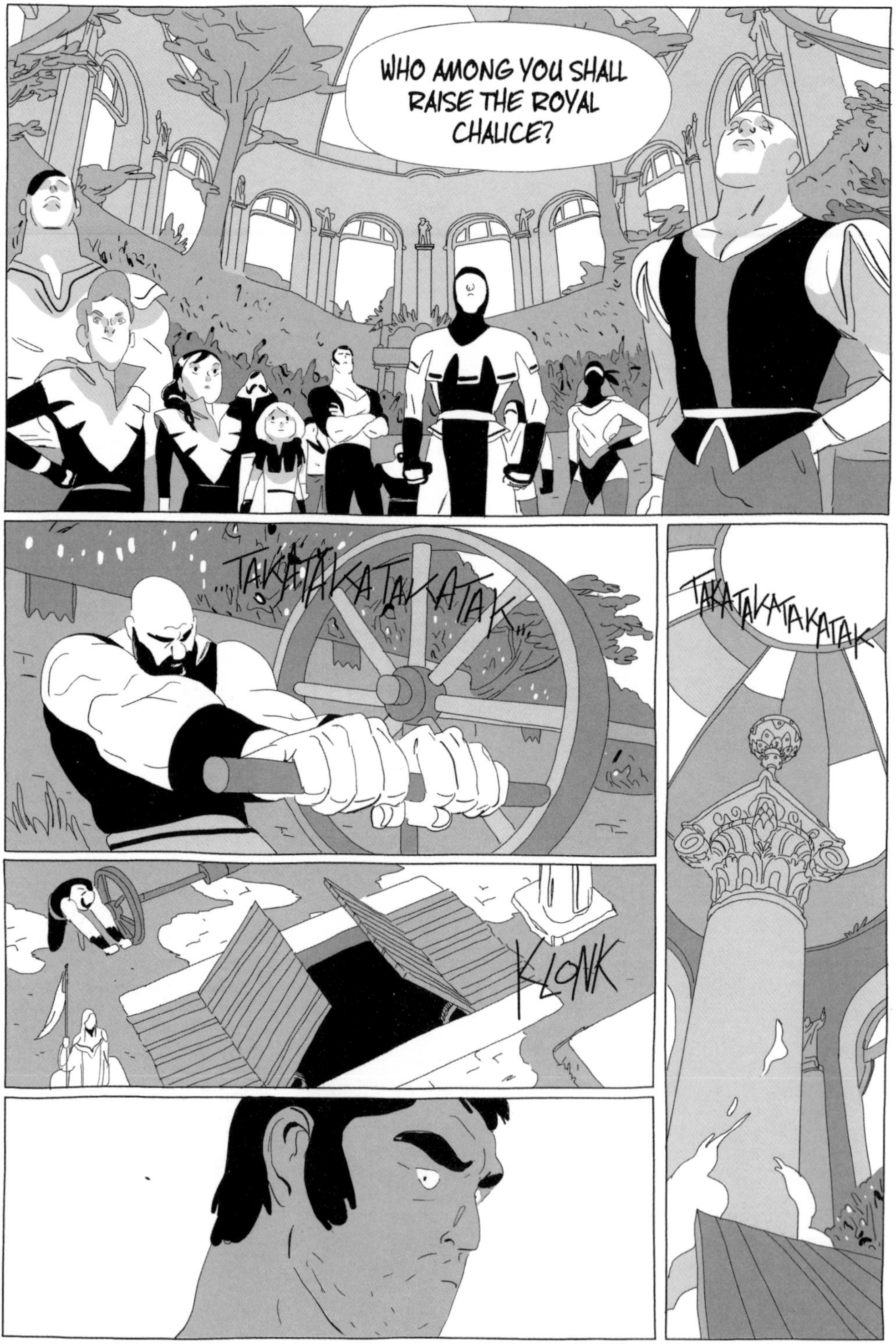
WHO AMONG YOU SHALL RAISE THE ROYAL CHALICE?
...TAKATAKATAKATAK...
TAKATAKATAKATAK
KLONK

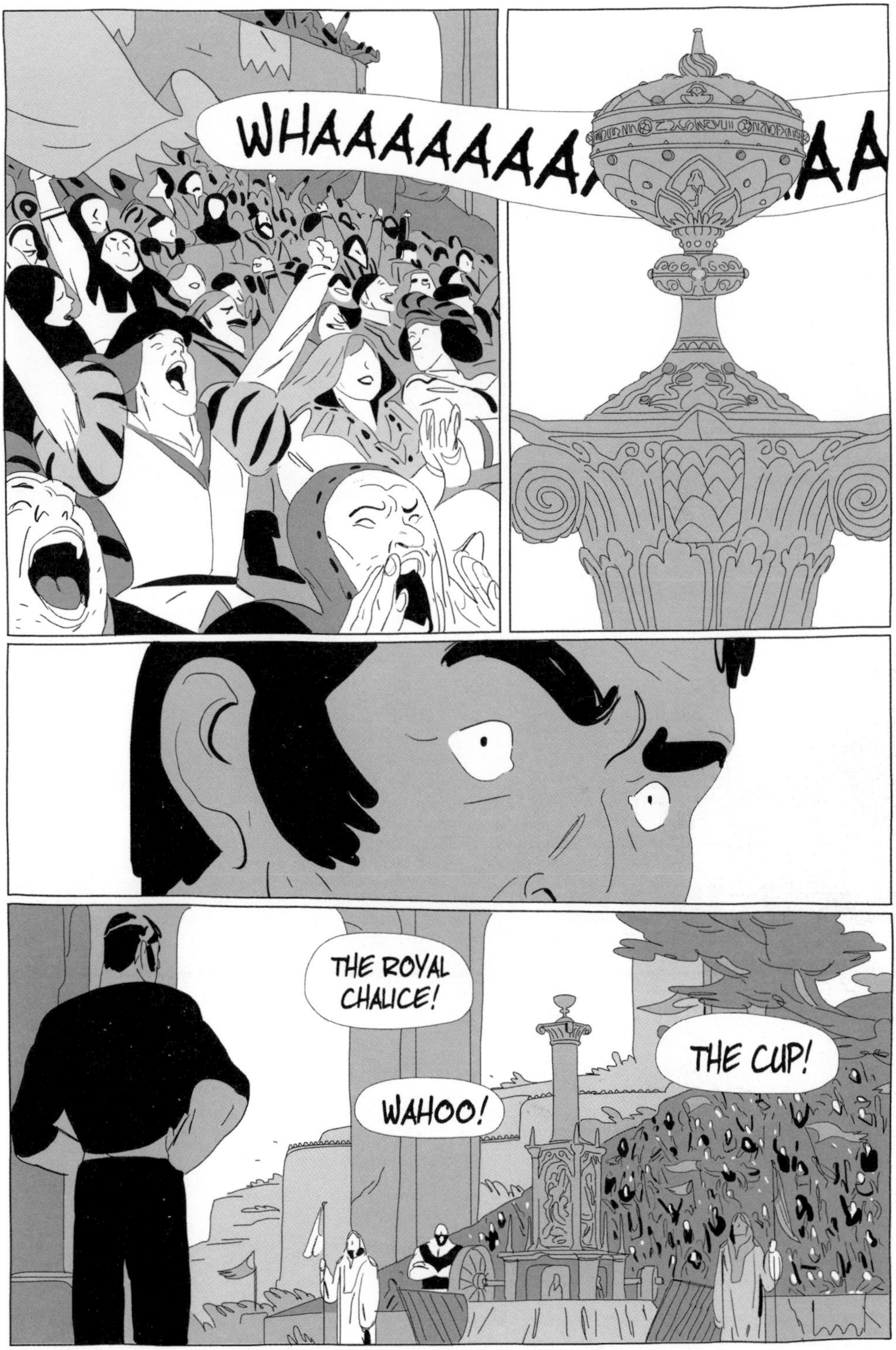
WHAAAAAAAAAAAA
THE ROYAL CHALICE!
WAHOO!
THE CUP!

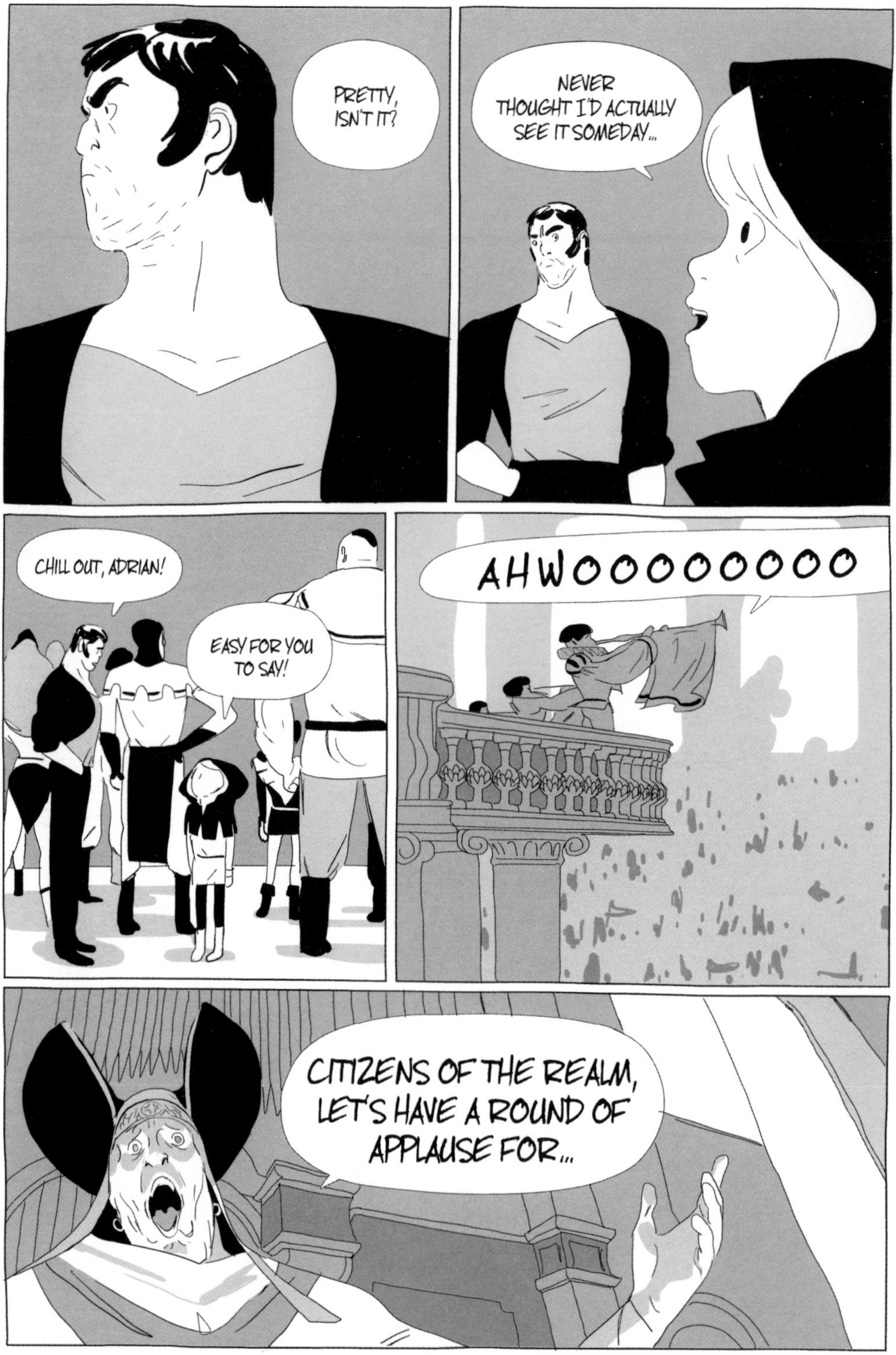
PRETTY, ISN'T IT?
NEVER THOUGHT I'D ACTUALLY SEE IT SOMEDAY...
CHILL OUT, ADRIAN!
EASY FOR YOU TO SAY!
AHWOOOOOOOOO
CITIZENS OF THE REALM, LET'S HAVE A ROUND OF APPLAUSE FOR...

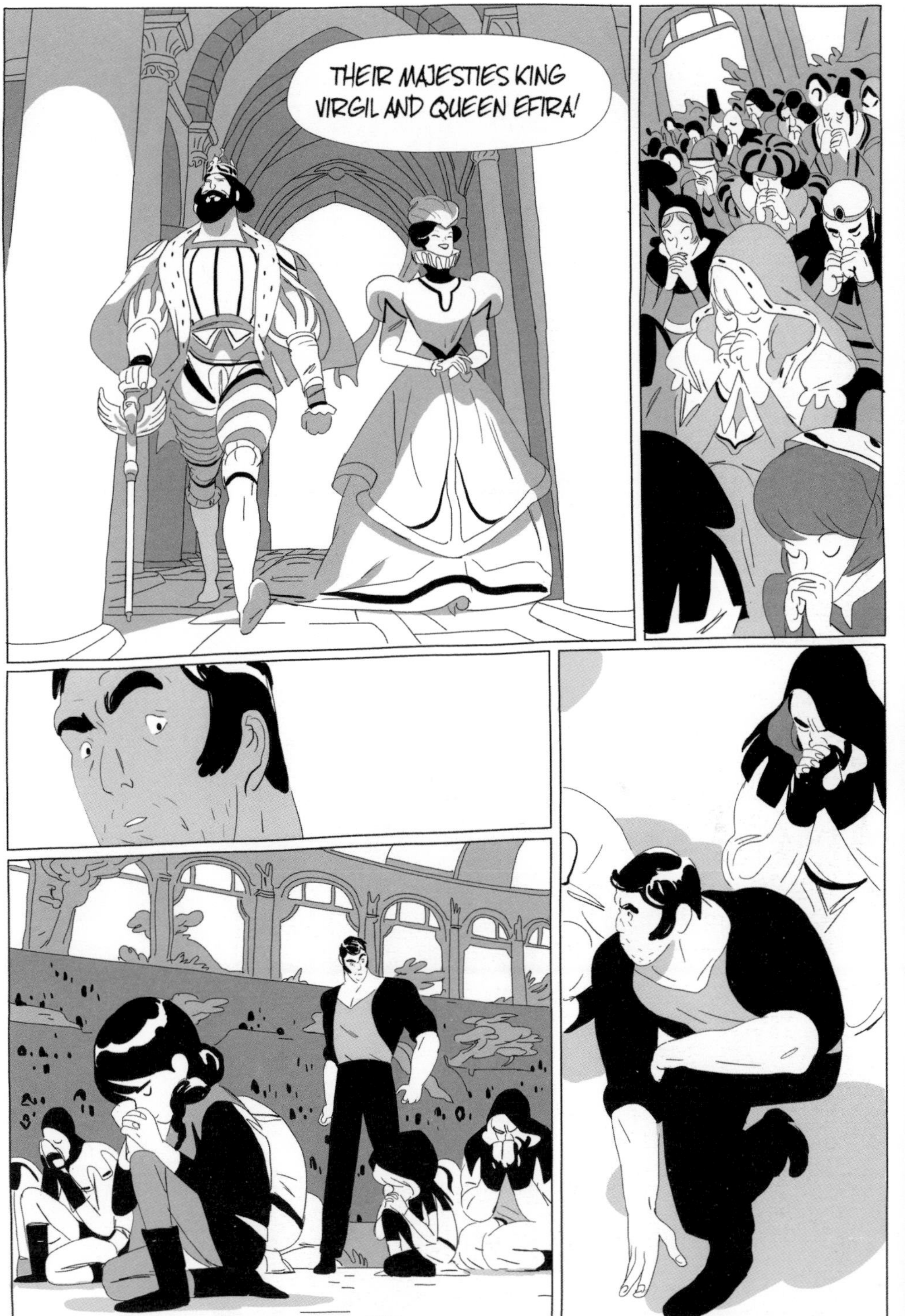
THEIR MAJESTIES KING VIRGIL AND QUEEN EFIRA!

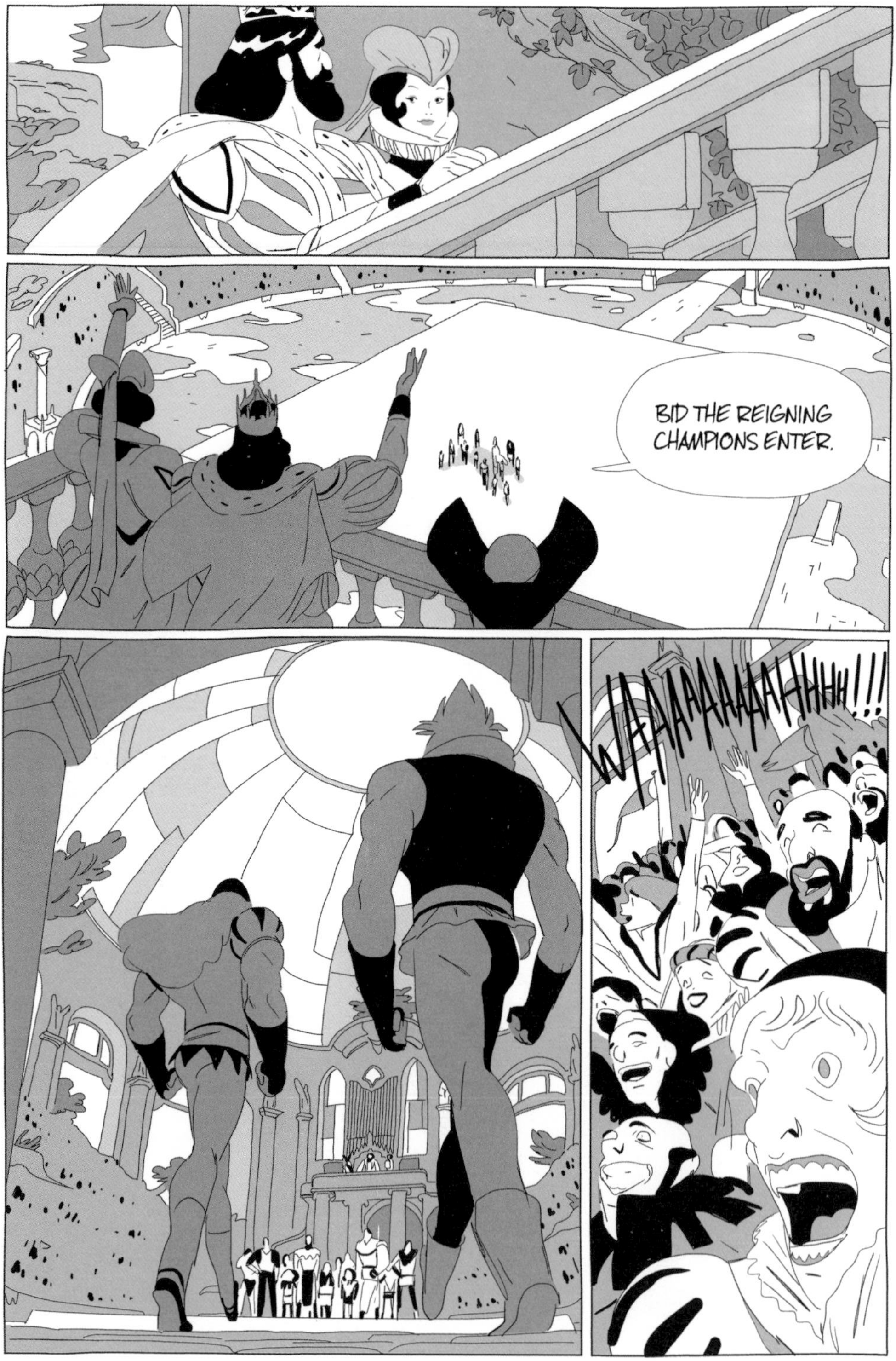
BID THE REIGNING CHAMPIONS ENTER.
WAAAAAAAAAHHHH!!!

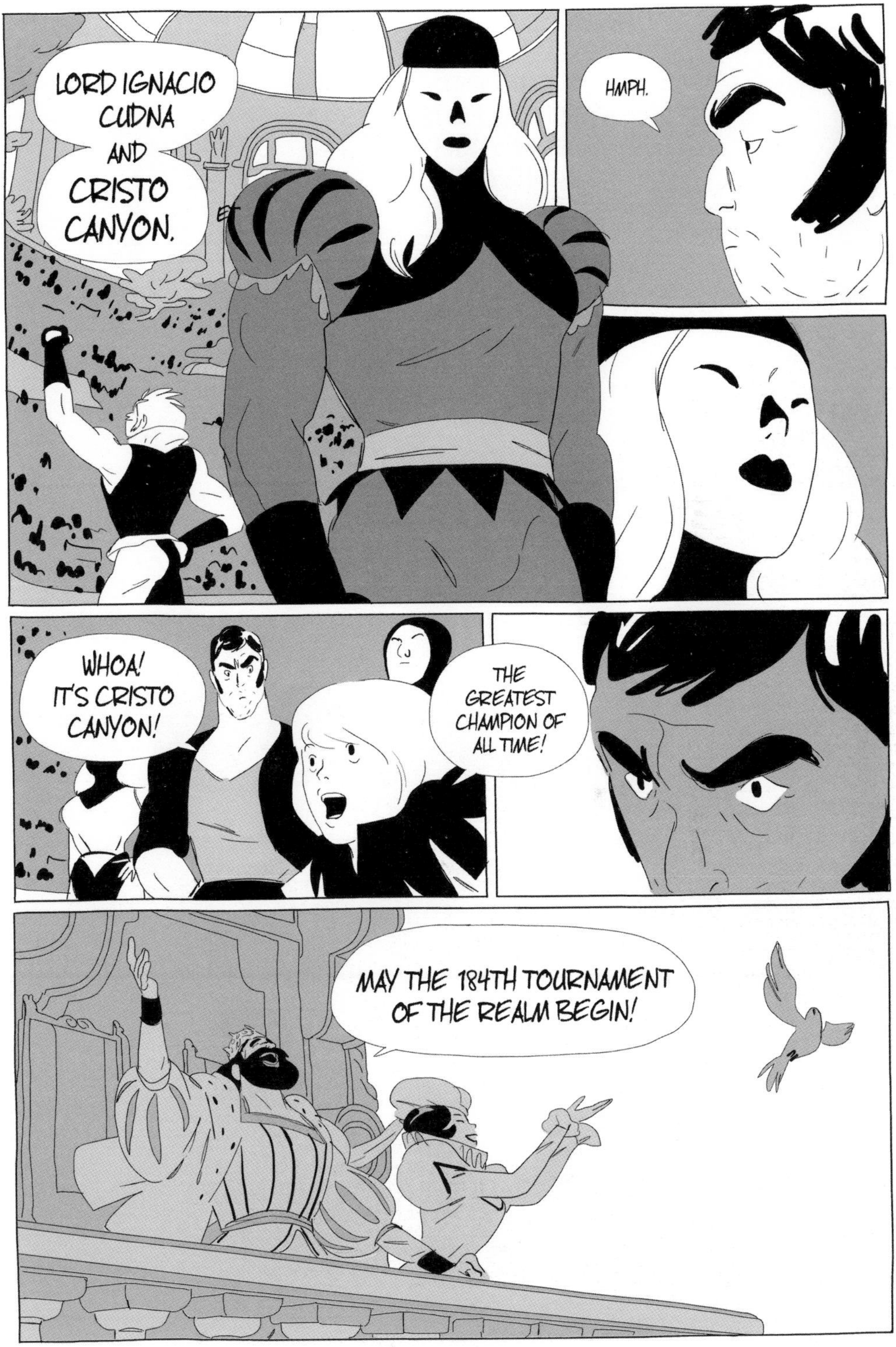
LORD IGNACIO CUDNA AND CRISTO CANYON.
HMPH.
WHOA! IT'S CRISTO CANYON!
THE GREATEST CHAMPION OF ALL TIME!
MAY THE 184TH TOURNAMENT OF THE REALM BEGIN!

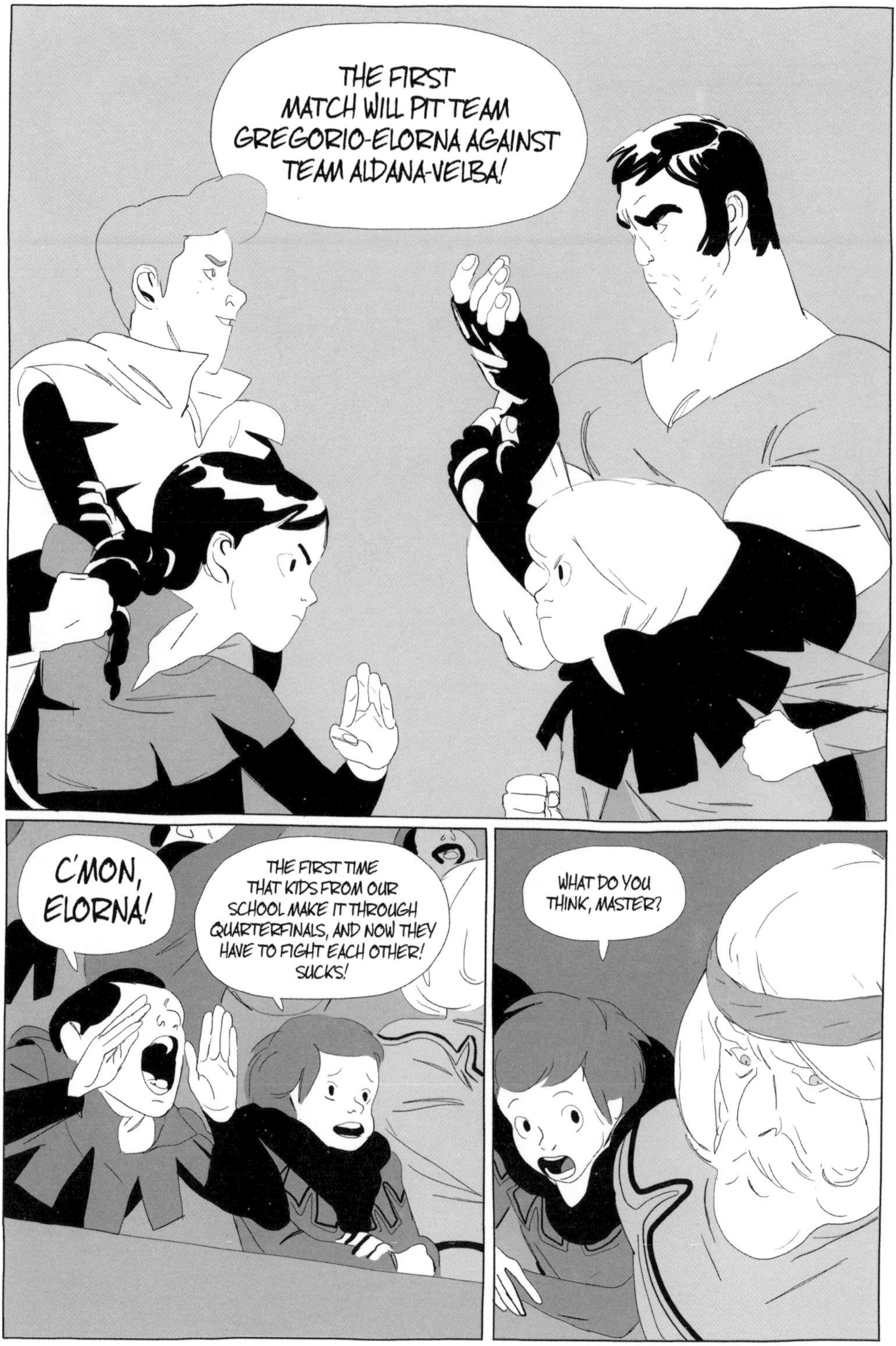
THE FIRST MATCH WILL PIT TEAM GREGORIO-ELORNA AGAINST TEAM ALDANA-VELBA!
C'MON, ELORNA!
THE FIRST TIME THAT KIDS FROM OUR SCHOOL MAKE IT THROUGH QUARTERFINALS, AND NOW THEY HAVE TO FIGHT EACH OTHER! SUCKS!
WHAT DO YOU THINK, MASTER?

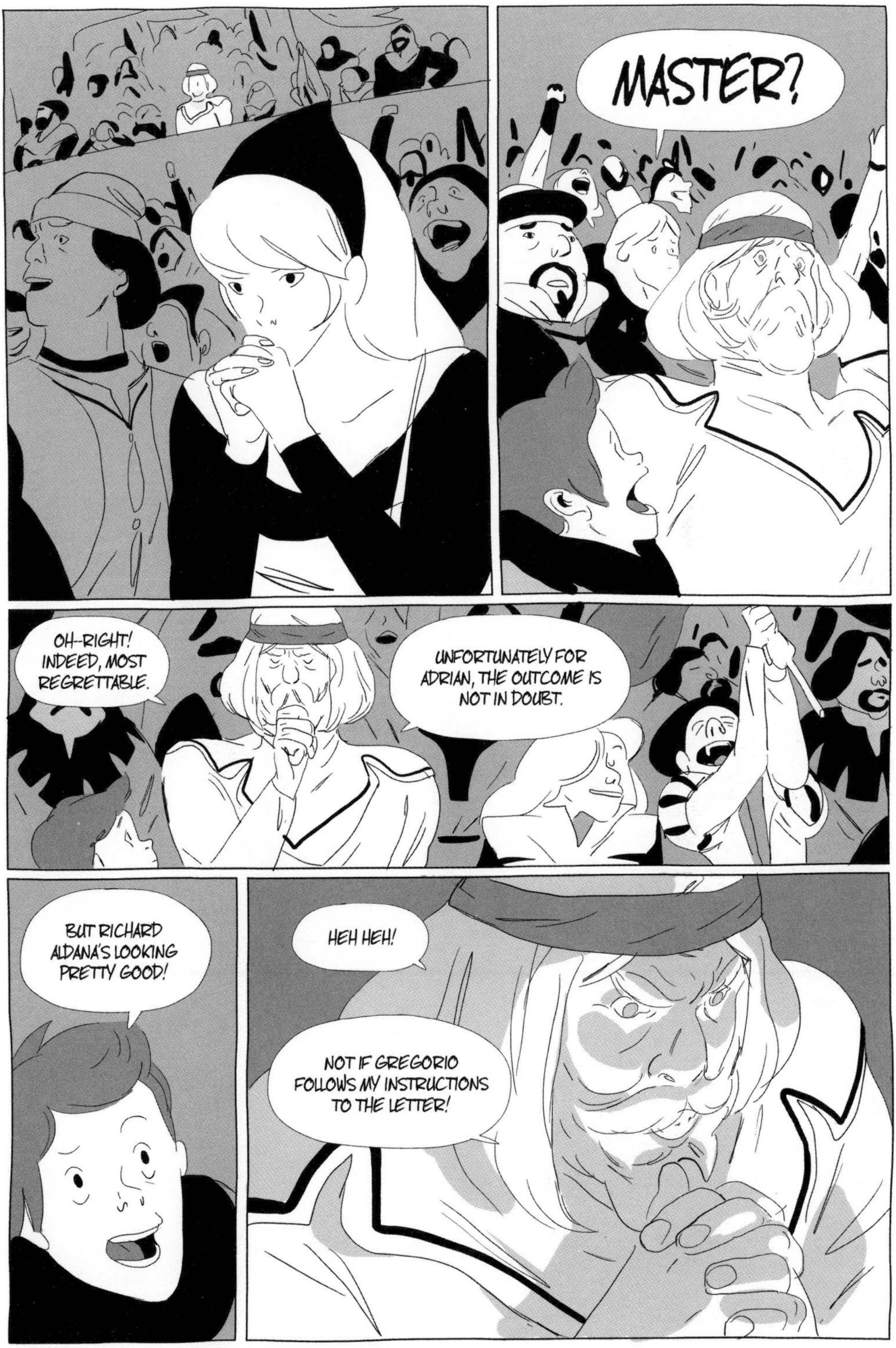
MASTER?
OH--RIGHT! INDEED, MOST REGRETTABLE.
UNFORTUNATELY FOR ADRIAN, THE OUTCOME IS NOT IN DOUBT.
BUT RICHARD ALDANA'S LOOKING PRETTY GOOD!
HEH HEH!
NOT IF GREGORIO FOLLOWS MY INSTRUCTIONS TO THE LETTER!

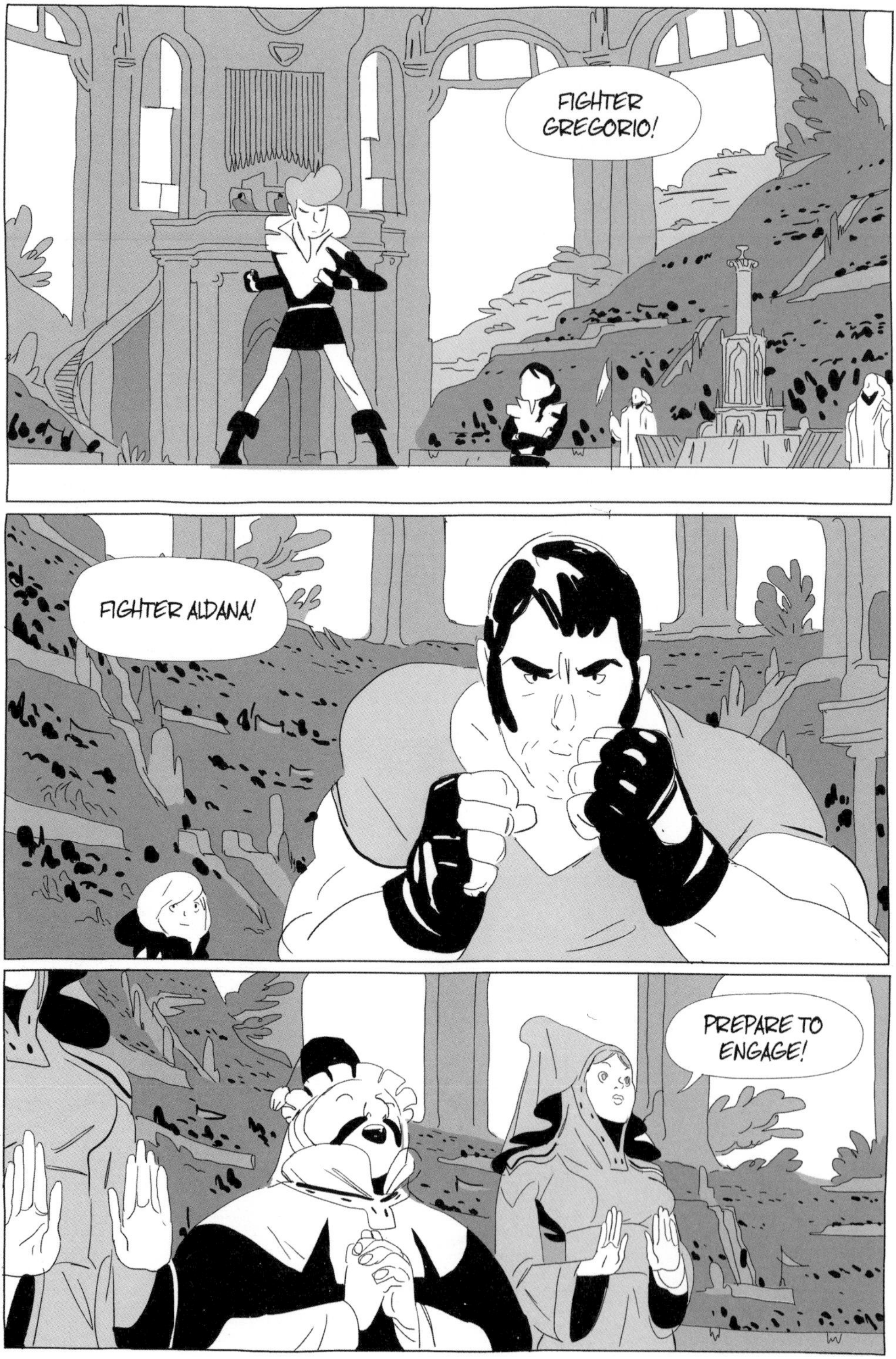
FIGHTER GREGORIO!
FIGHTER ALDANA!
PREPARE TO ENGAGE!

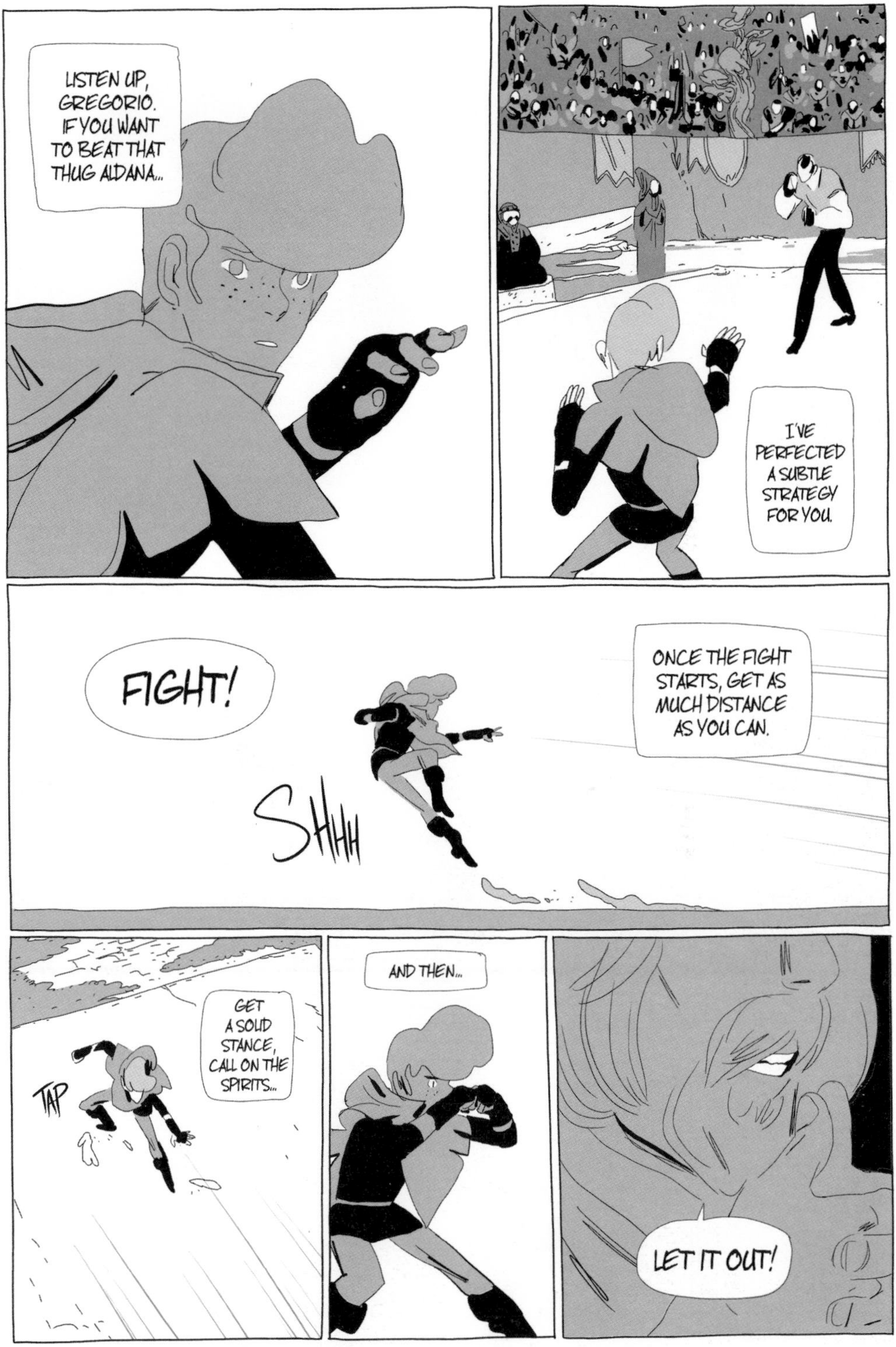
LISTEN UP, GREGORIO. IF YOU WANT TO BEAT THAT THUG ALDANA...
I'VE PERFECTED A SUBTLE STRATEGY FOR YOU.
FIGHT!
ONCE THE FIGHT STARTS, GET AS MUCH DISTANCE AS YOU CAN.
SHHH
TAP
GET A SOLID STANCE, CALL ON THE SPIRITS...
AND THEN...
LET IT OUT!

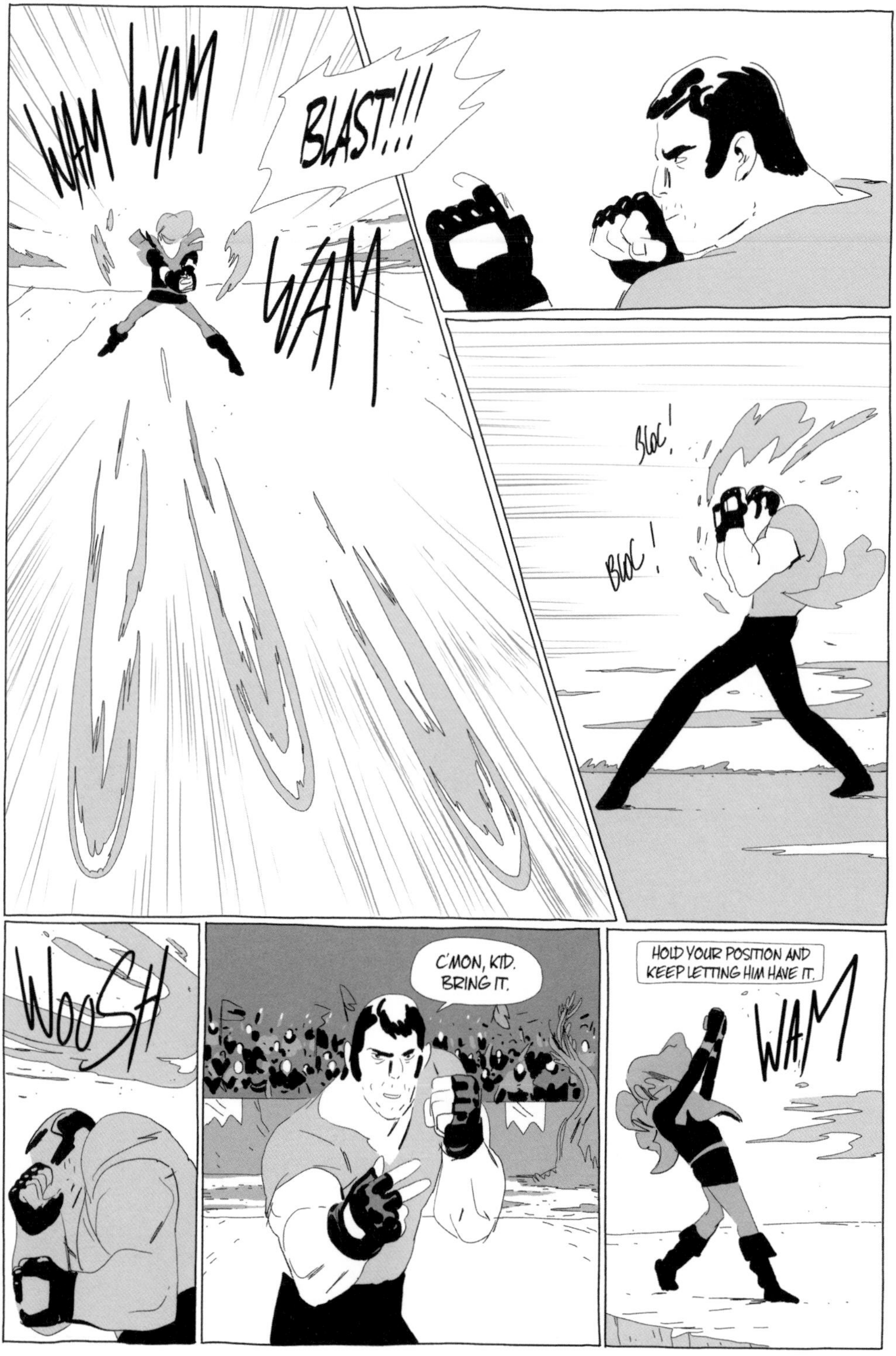
WAM WAM
BLAST!!!
WAM
BLOC!
BLOC!
WOOSH
C'MON, KID. BRING IT.
HOLD YOUR POSITION AND KEEP LETTING HIM HAVE IT.
WAM

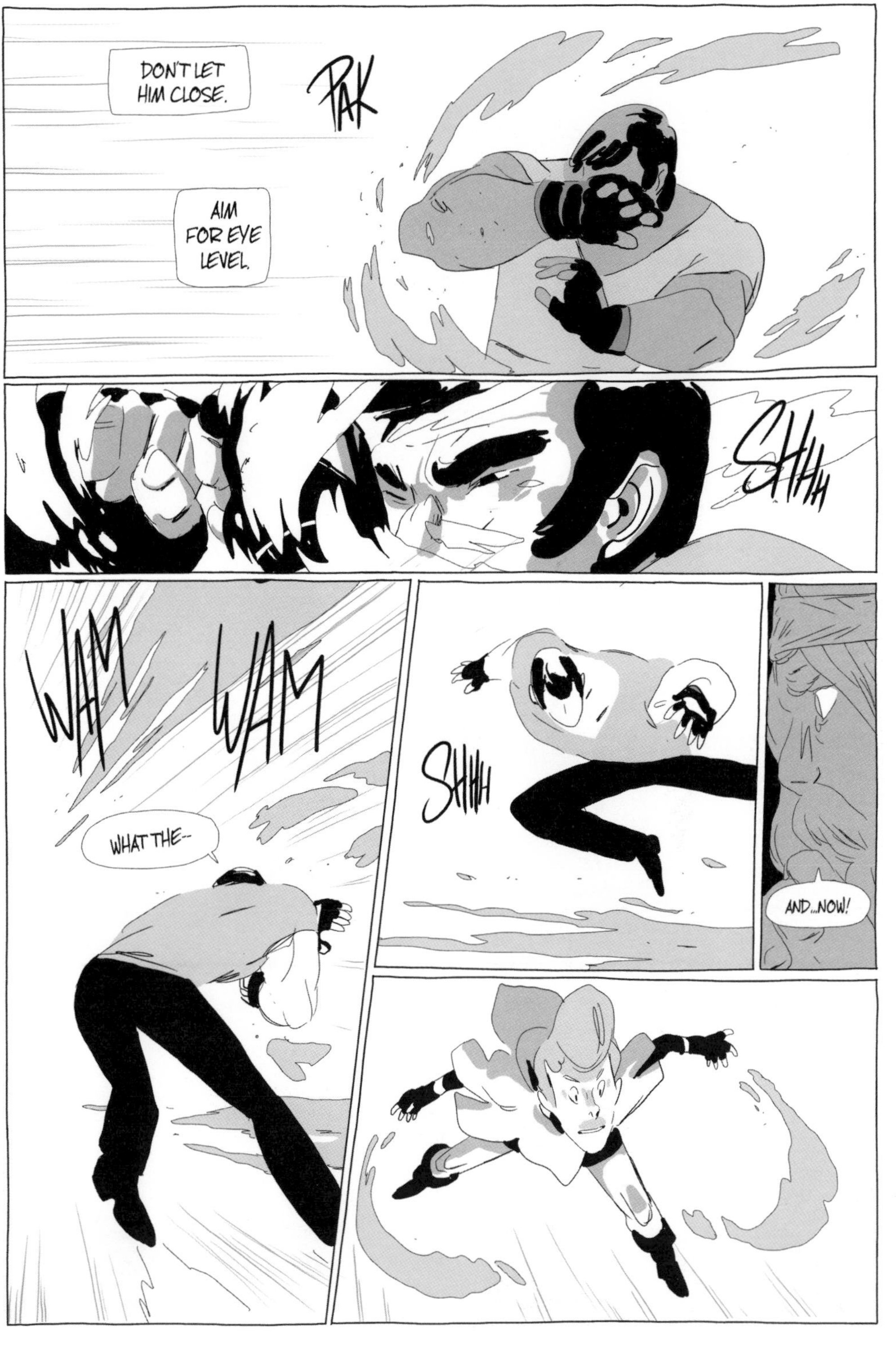
DON'T LET HIM CLOSE.
PAK
AIM FOR EYE LEVEL.
SHHH
WAM WAM
WHAT THE--
SHHH
AND...NOW!

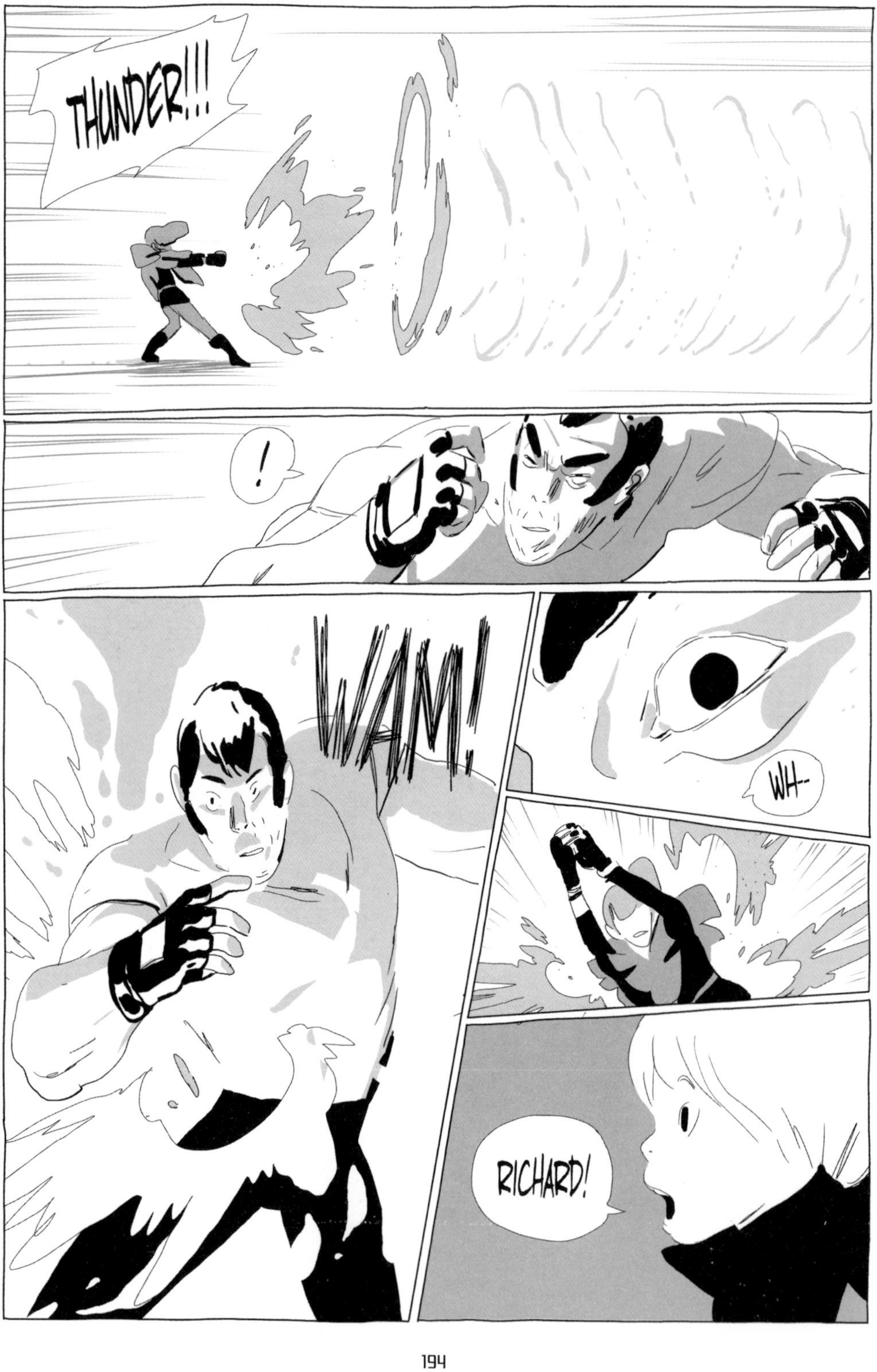
THUNDER!!!
!
WAM!
WH-
RICHARD!

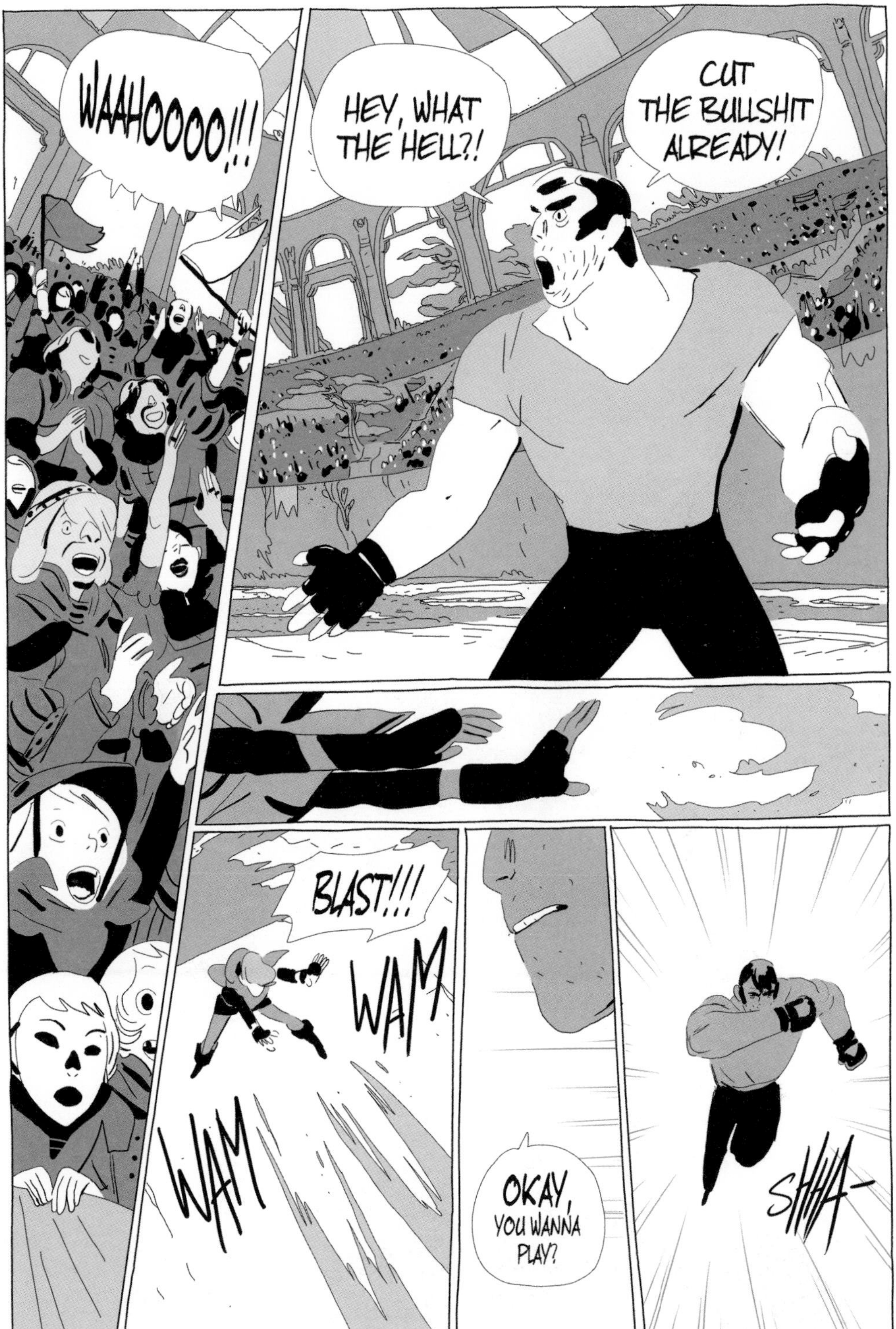
WAAHOOOO!!!
HEY, WHAT THE HELL?!
CUT THE BULLSHIT ALREADY!
BLAST!!!
WAM
WAM
OKAY, YOU WANNA PLAY?
SHHA-

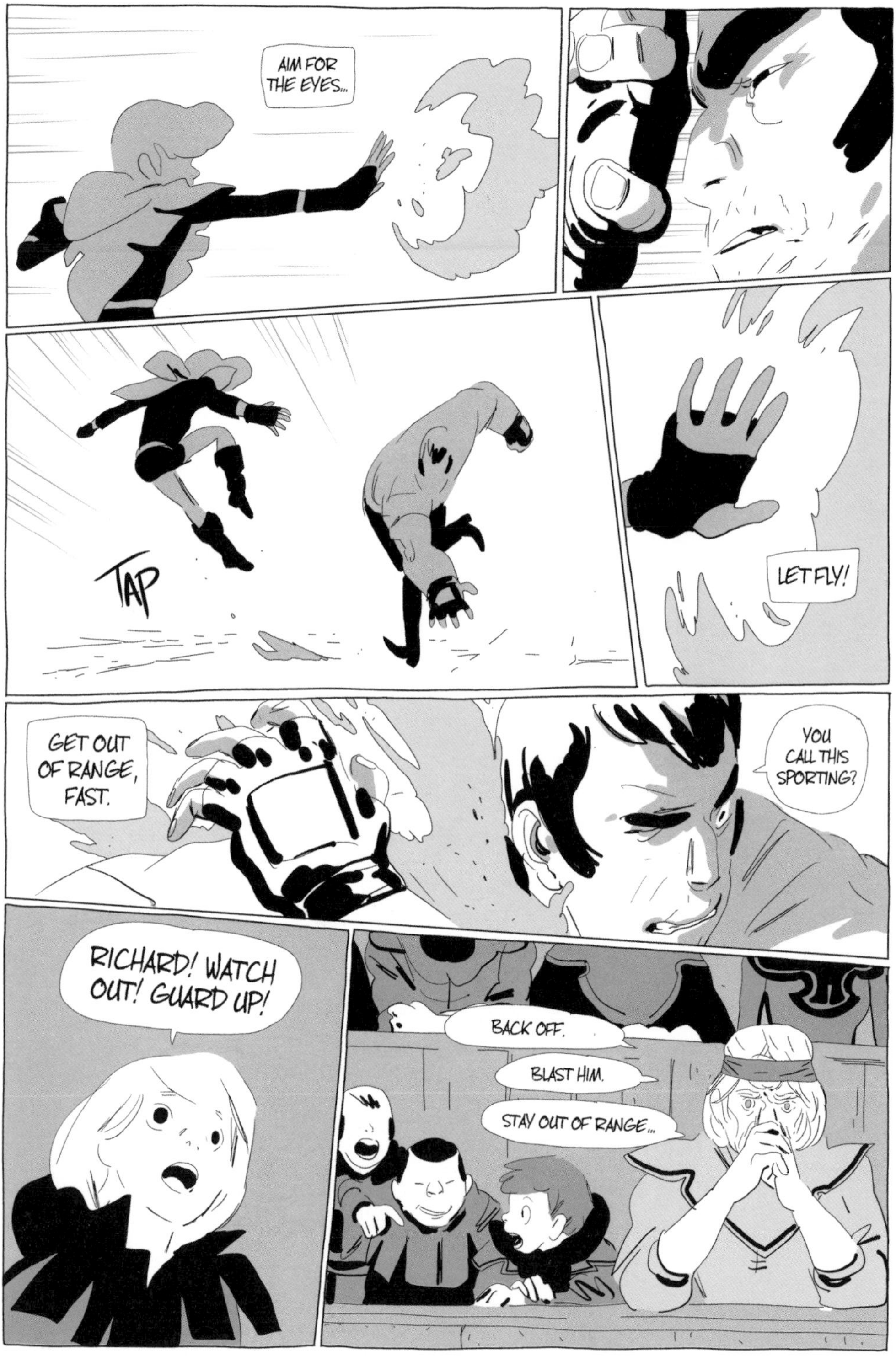
AIM FOR THE EYES...
TAP
LET FLY!
GET OUT OF RANGE, FAST.
YOU CALL THIS SPORTING?
RICHARD! WATCH OUT! GUARD UP!
BACK OFF.
BLAST HIM.
STAY OUT OF RANGE...

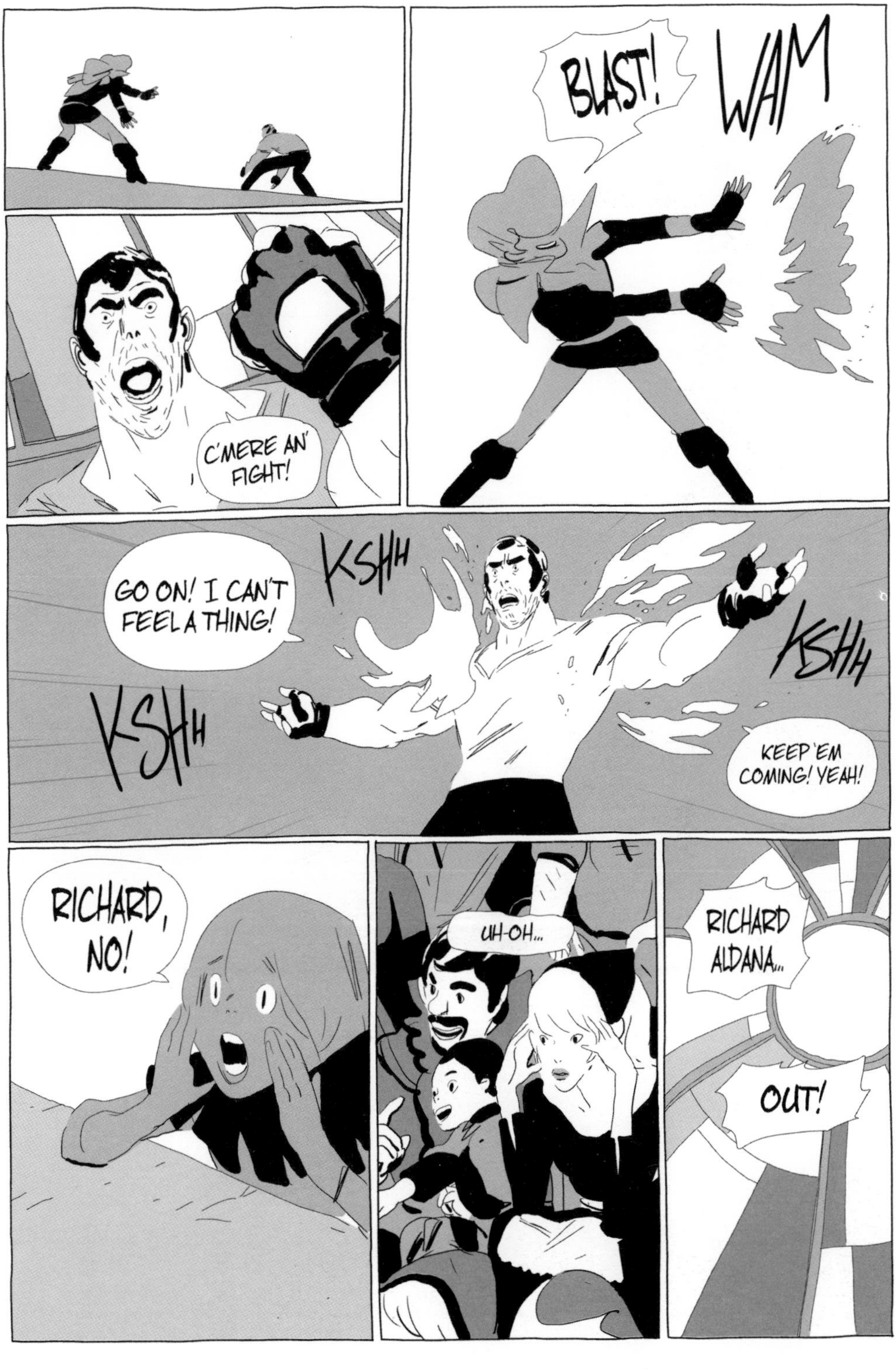
BLAST!
WAM
C'MERE AN'
FIGHT!
GO ON! I CAN'T
FEEL A THING!
KSHH
KSHH
KSHH
KEEP 'EM
COMING! YEAH!
RICHARD,
NO!
UH-OH...
RICHARD
ALDANA...
OUT!

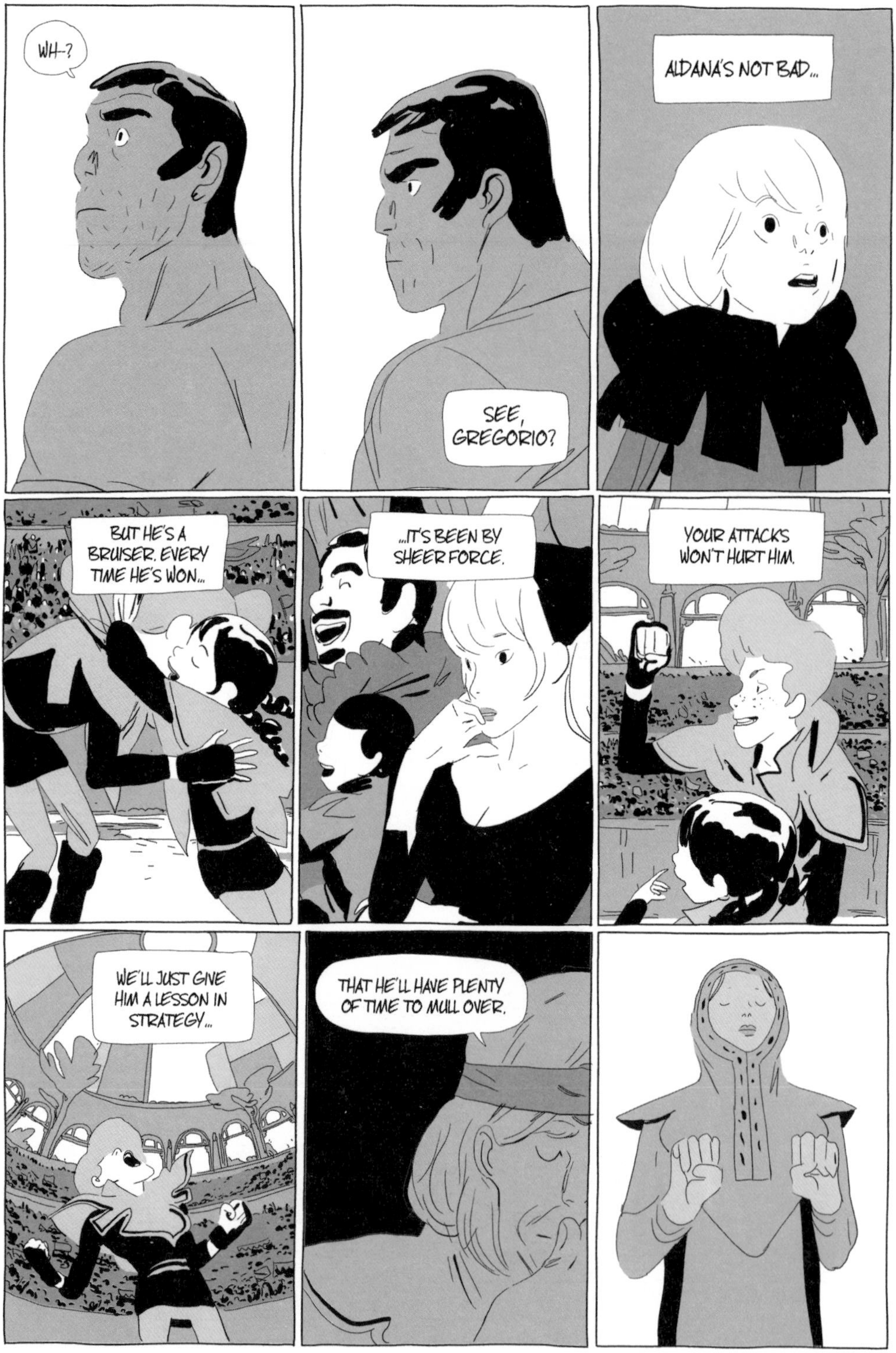
WH-?
SEE, GREGORIO?
ALDANA'S NOT BAD...
BUT HE'S A BRUISER. EVERY TIME HE'S WON...
...IT'S BEEN BY SHEER FORCE.
YOUR ATTACKS WON'T HURT HIM.
WE'LL JUST GIVE HIM A LESSON IN STRATEGY...
THAT HE'LL HAVE PLENTY OF TIME TO MULL OVER.

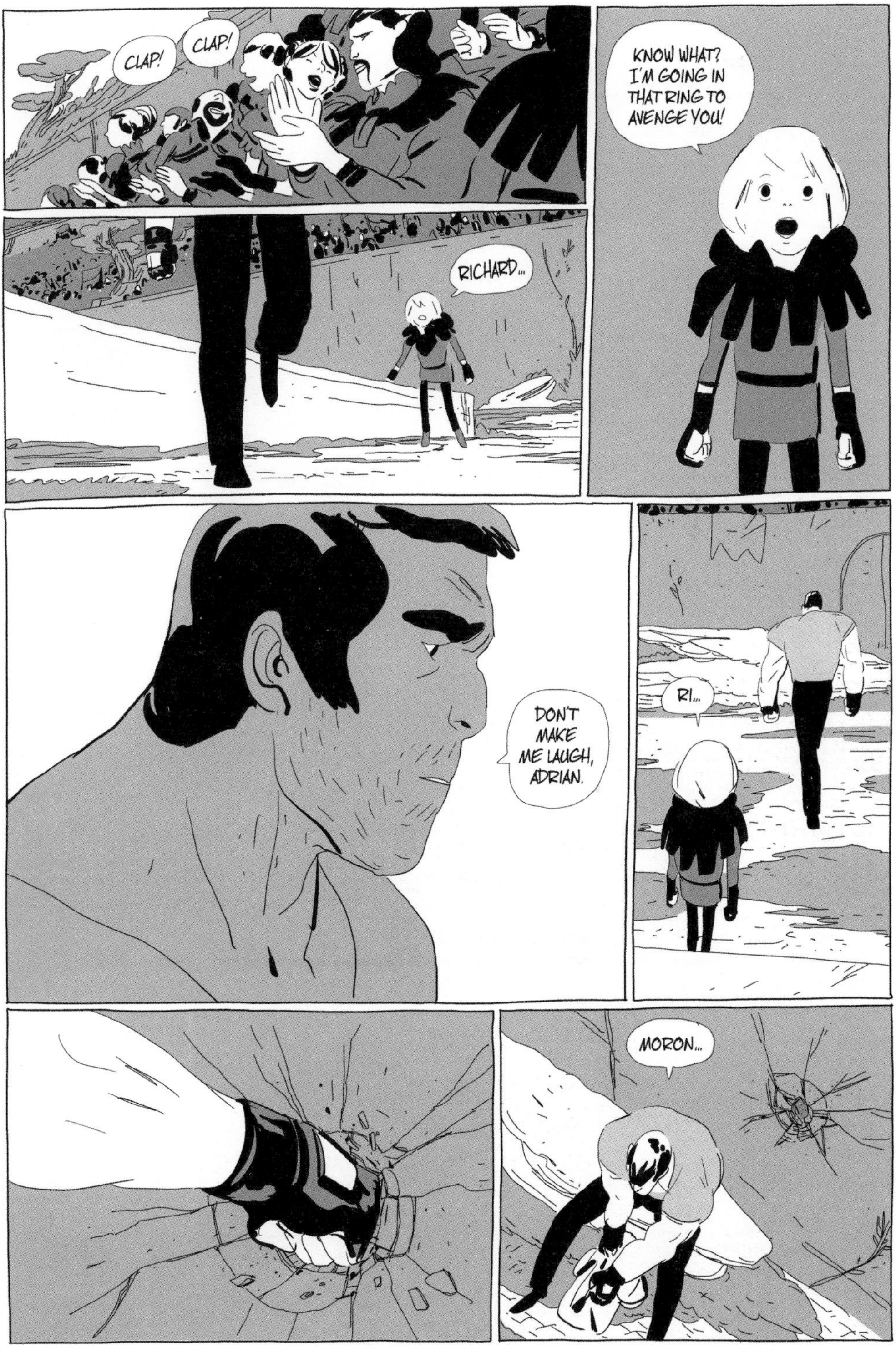
CLAP!
CLAP!
KNOW WHAT? I'M GOING IN THAT RING TO AVENGE YOU!
RICHARD...
DON'T MAKE ME LAUGH, ADRIAN.
RI...
MORON...

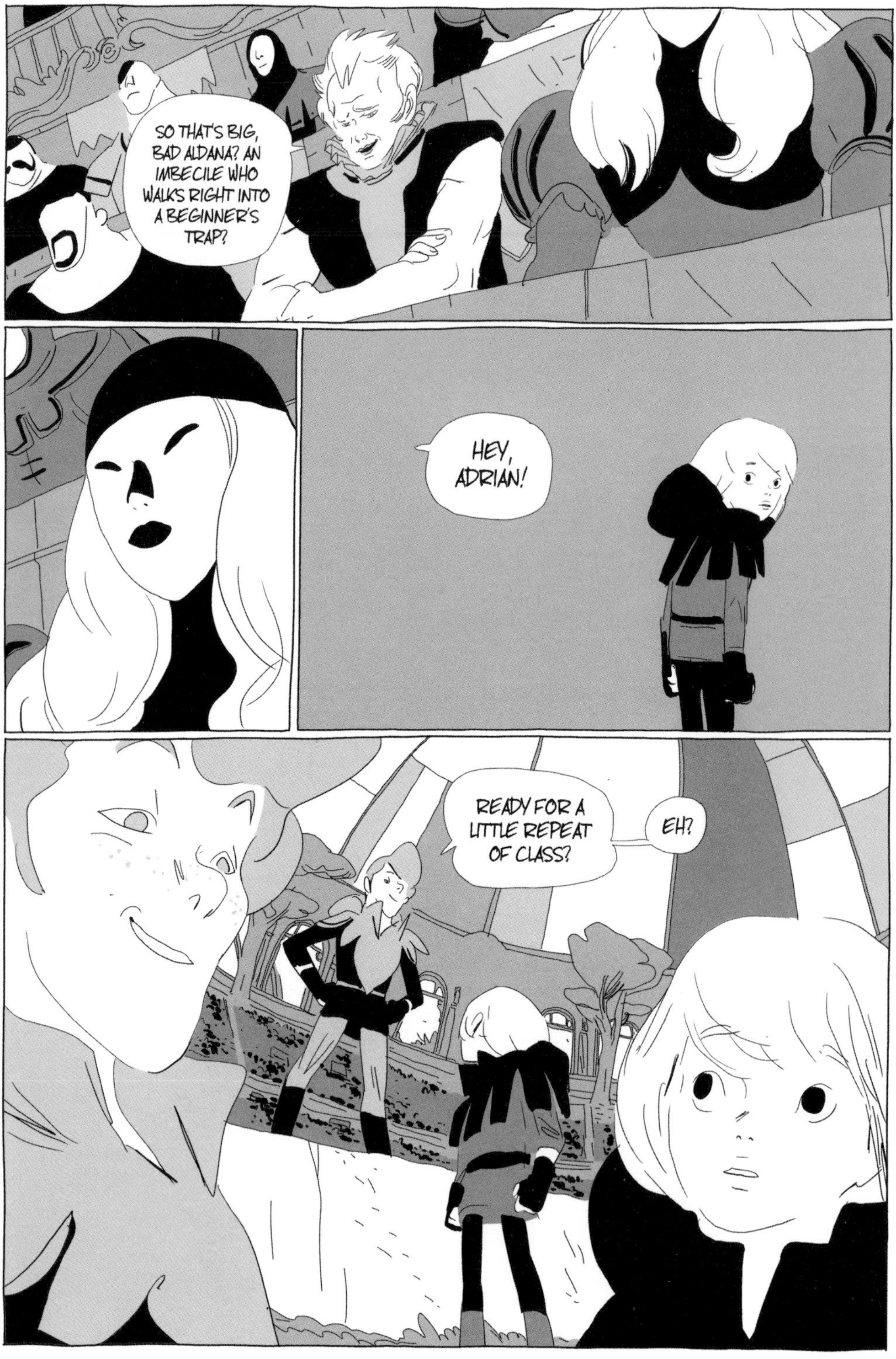
SO THAT'S BIG, BAD ALDANA? AN IMBECILE WHO WALKS RIGHT INTO A BEGINNER'S TRAP?
HEY, ADRIAN!
READY FOR A LITTLE REPEAT OF CLASS?
EH?

CHAPTER
TWO

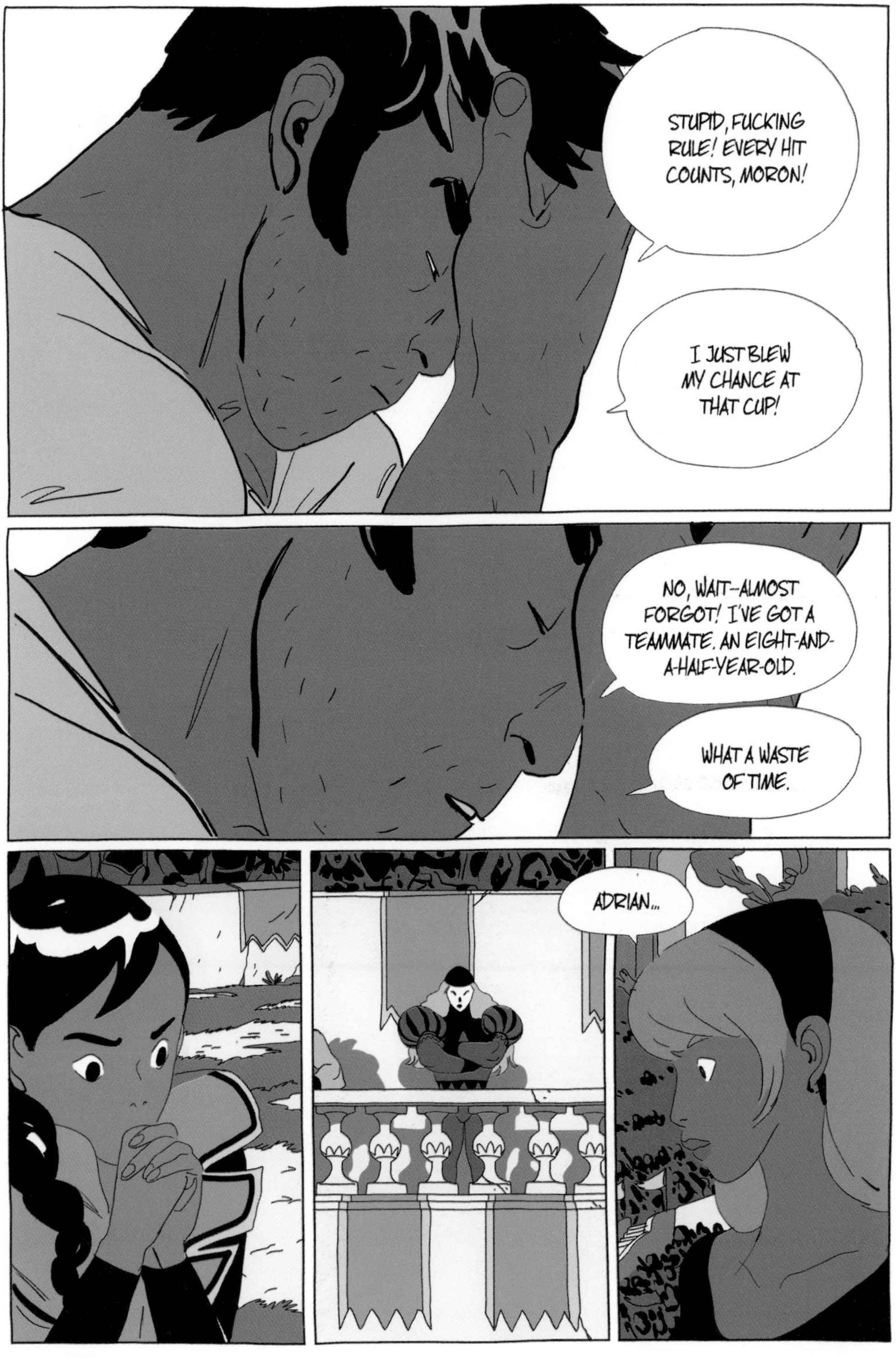
STUPID, FUCKING RULE! EVERY HIT COUNTS, MORON!
I JUST BLEW MY CHANCE AT THAT CUP!
NO, WAIT--ALMOST FORGOT! I'VE GOT A TEAMMATE. AN EIGHT-AND-A-HALF-YEAR-OLD.
WHAT A WASTE OF TIME.
ADRIAN...

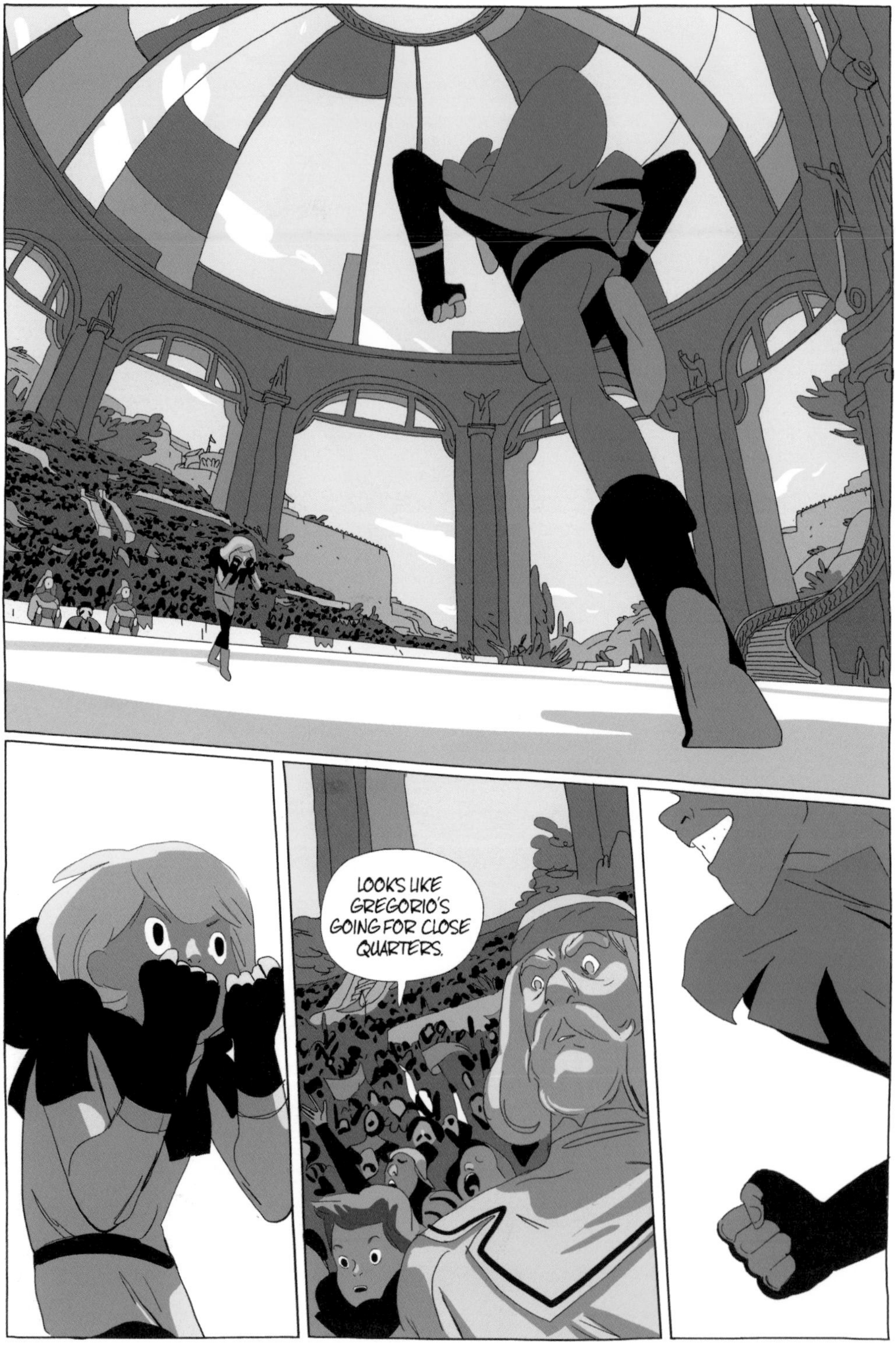
LOOKS LIKE GREGORIO'S GOING FOR CLOSE QUARTERS.

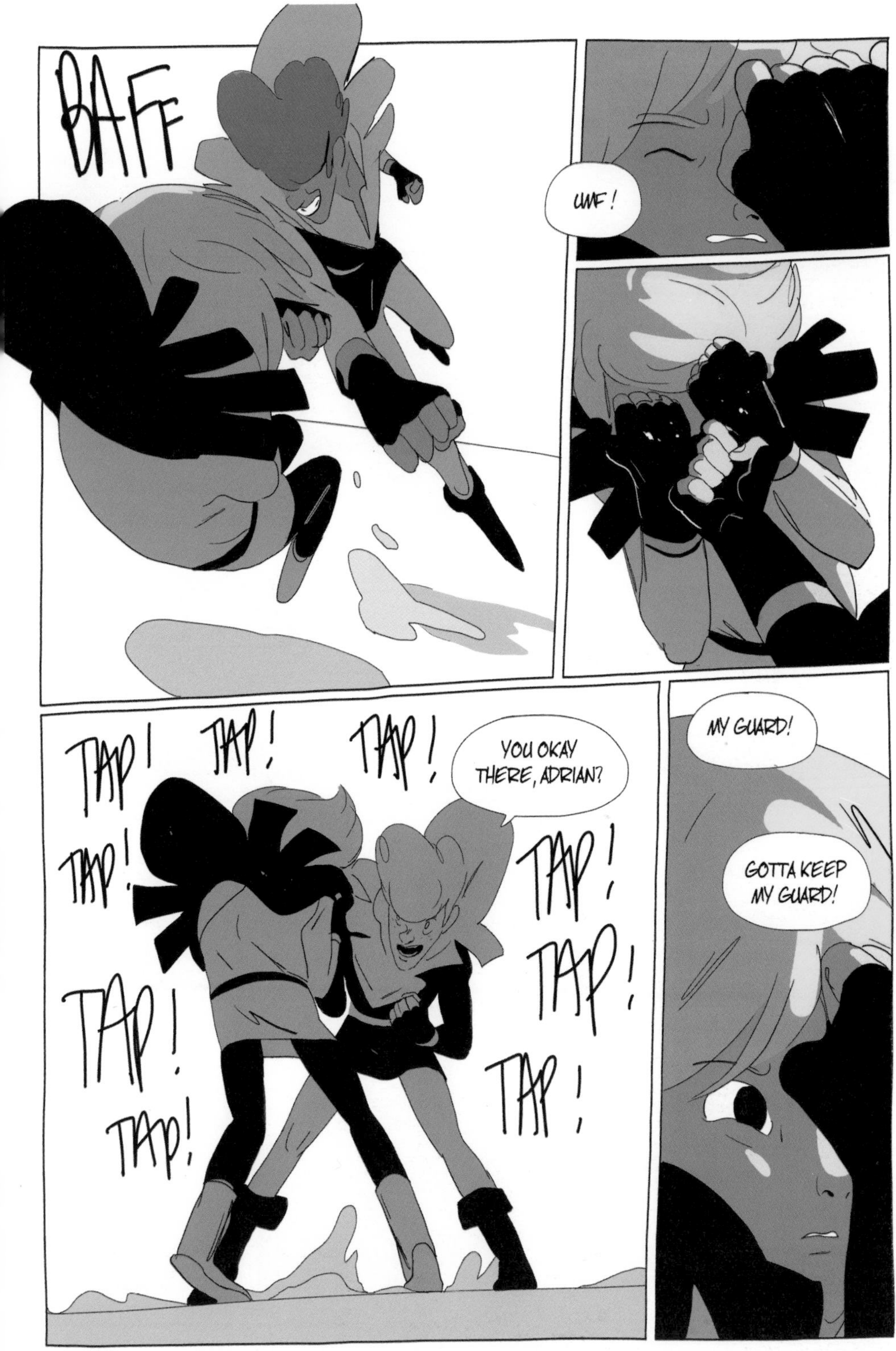
BAFF
UMF!
TAP! TAP! TAP!
YOU OKAY THERE, ADRIAN?
TAP!
TAP!
TAP!
TAP!
TAP!
TAP!
MY GUARD!
GOTTA KEEP MY GUARD!

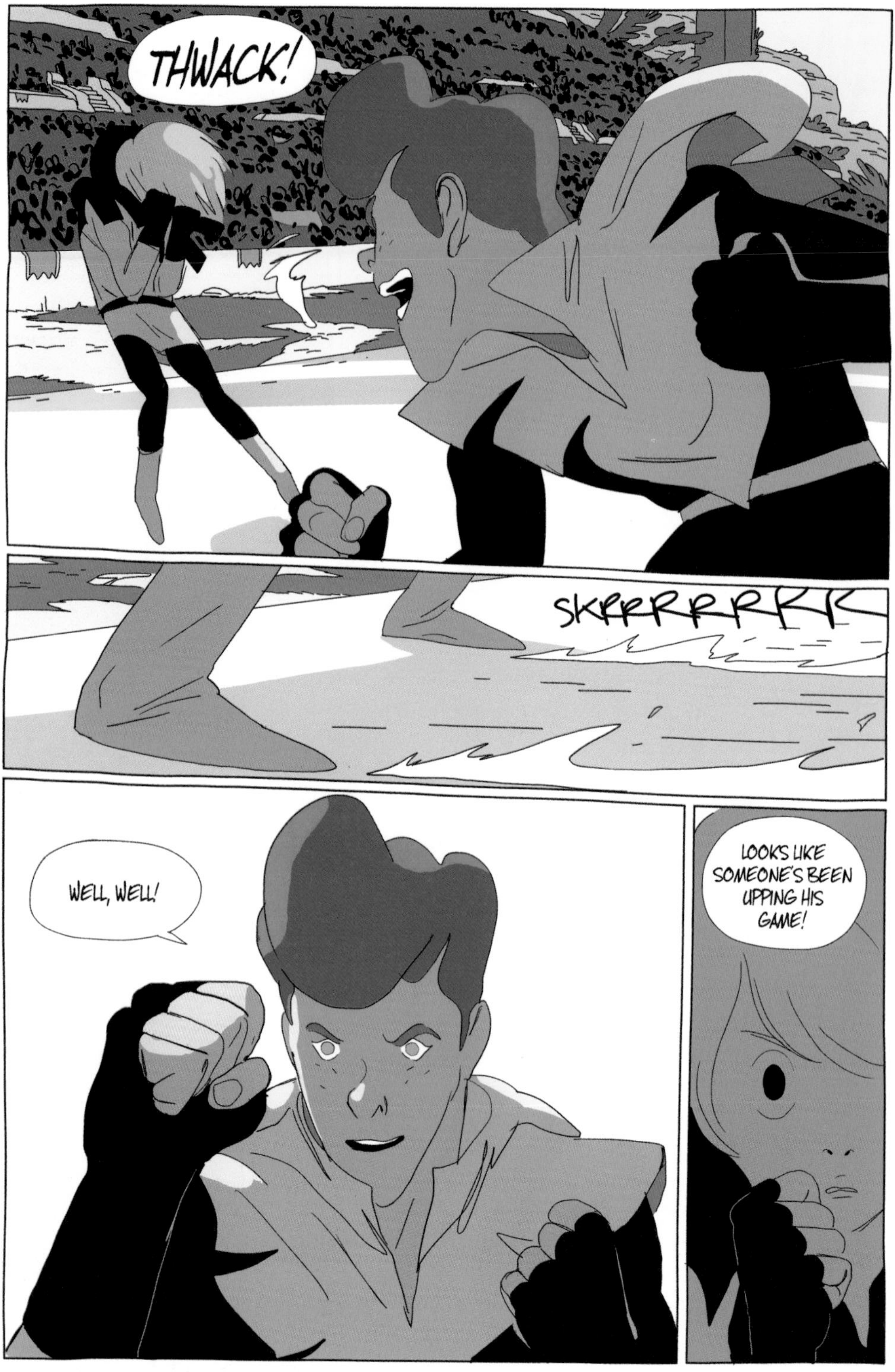
THWACK!
SKRRRRRKK
WELL, WELL!
LOOKS LIKE SOMEONE'S BEEN UPPING HIS GAME!

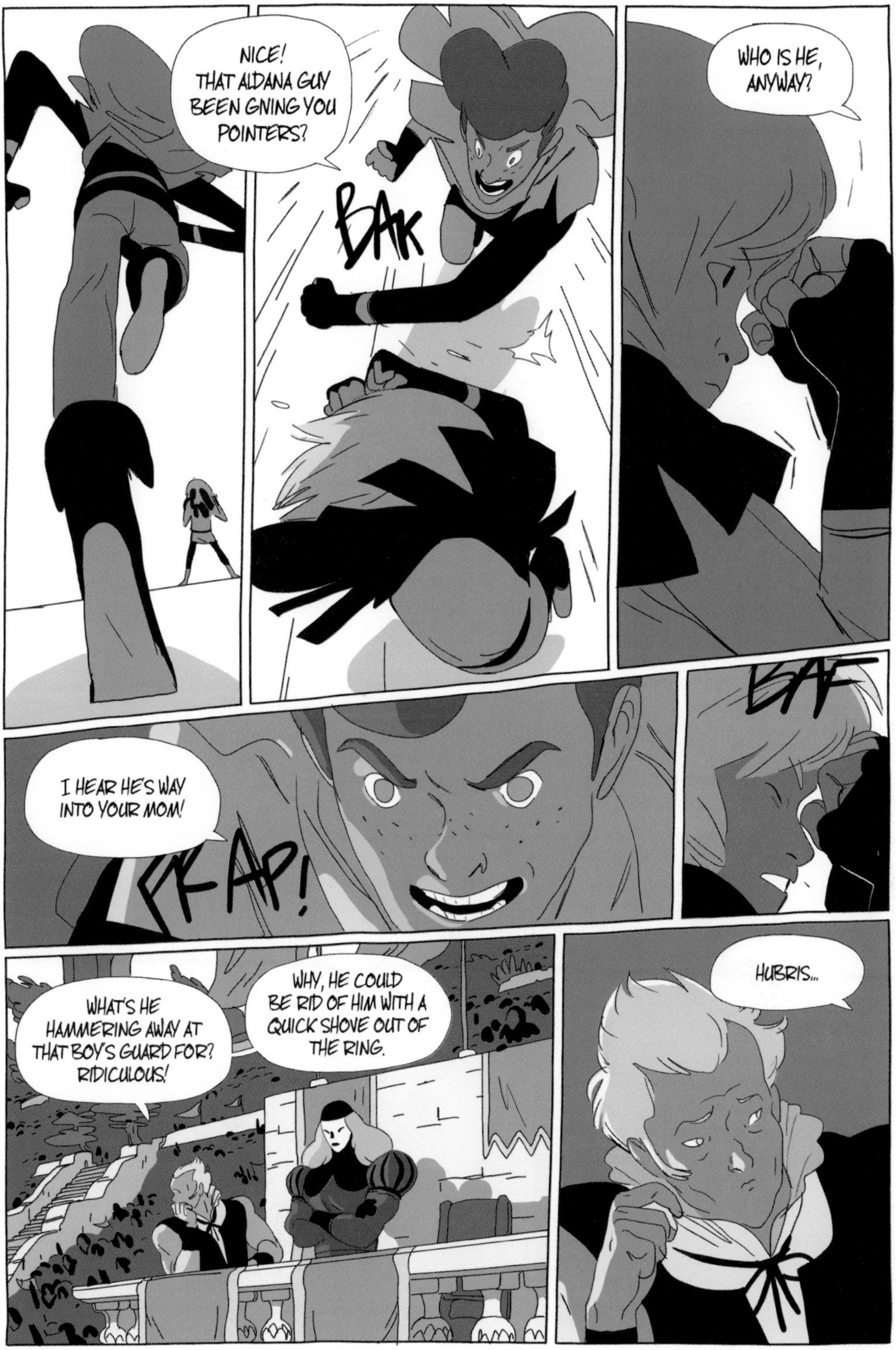
NICE! THAT ALDANA GUY BEEN GIVING YOU POINTERS?
BAK
WHO IS HE, ANYWAY?
I HEAR HE'S WAY INTO YOUR MOM!
KRAP!
BAF
WHAT'S HE HAMMERING AWAY AT THAT BOY'S GUARD FOR? RIDICULOUS!
WHY, HE COULD BE RID OF HIM WITH A QUICK SHOVE OUT OF THE RING.
HUBRIS...

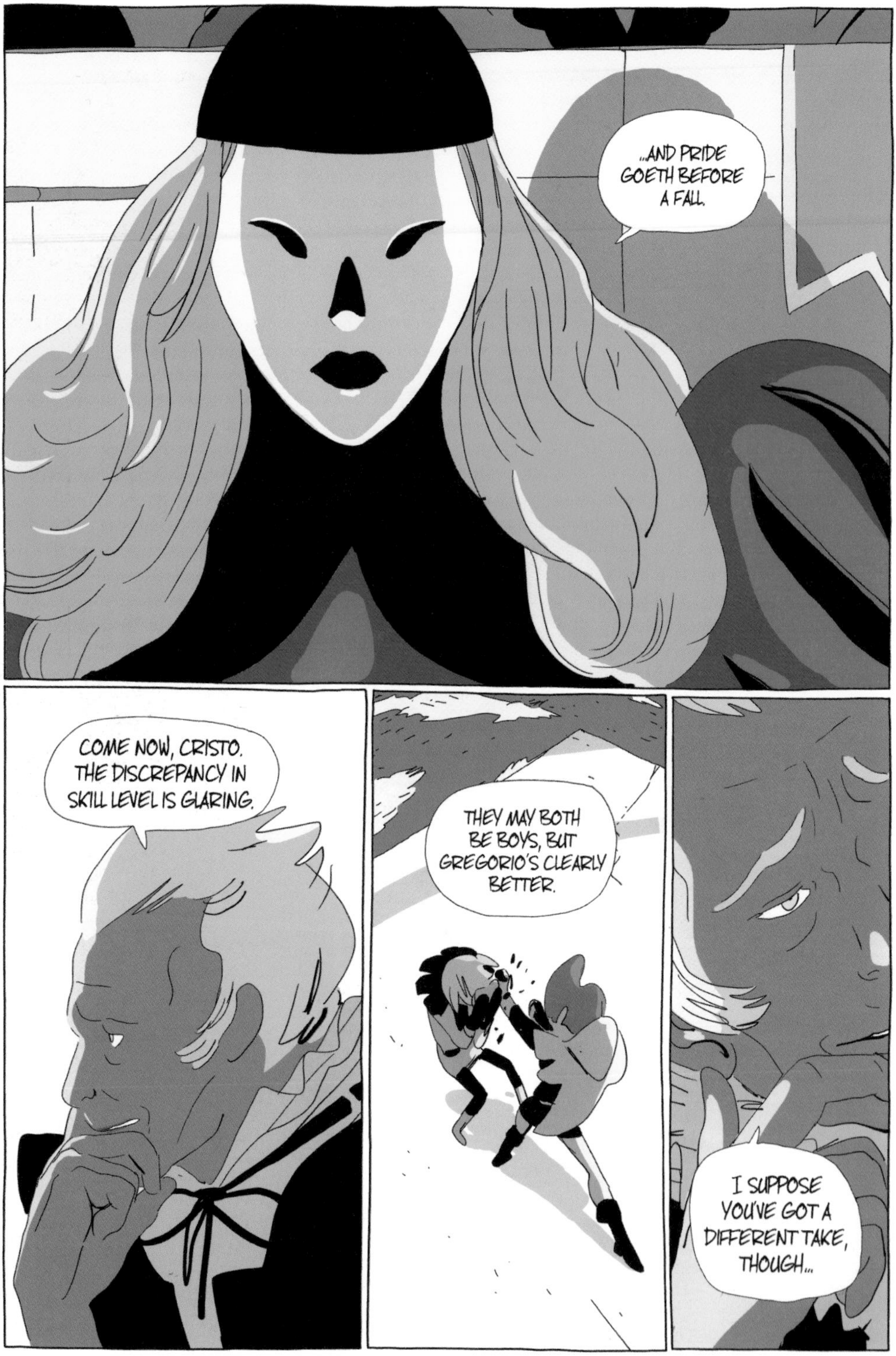
...AND PRIDE GOETH BEFORE A FALL.
COME NOW, CRISTO. THE DISCREPANCY IN SKILL LEVEL IS GLARING.
THEY MAY BOTH BE BOYS, BUT GREGORIO'S CLEARLY BETTER.
I SUPPOSE YOU'VE GOT A DIFFERENT TAKE, THOUGH...

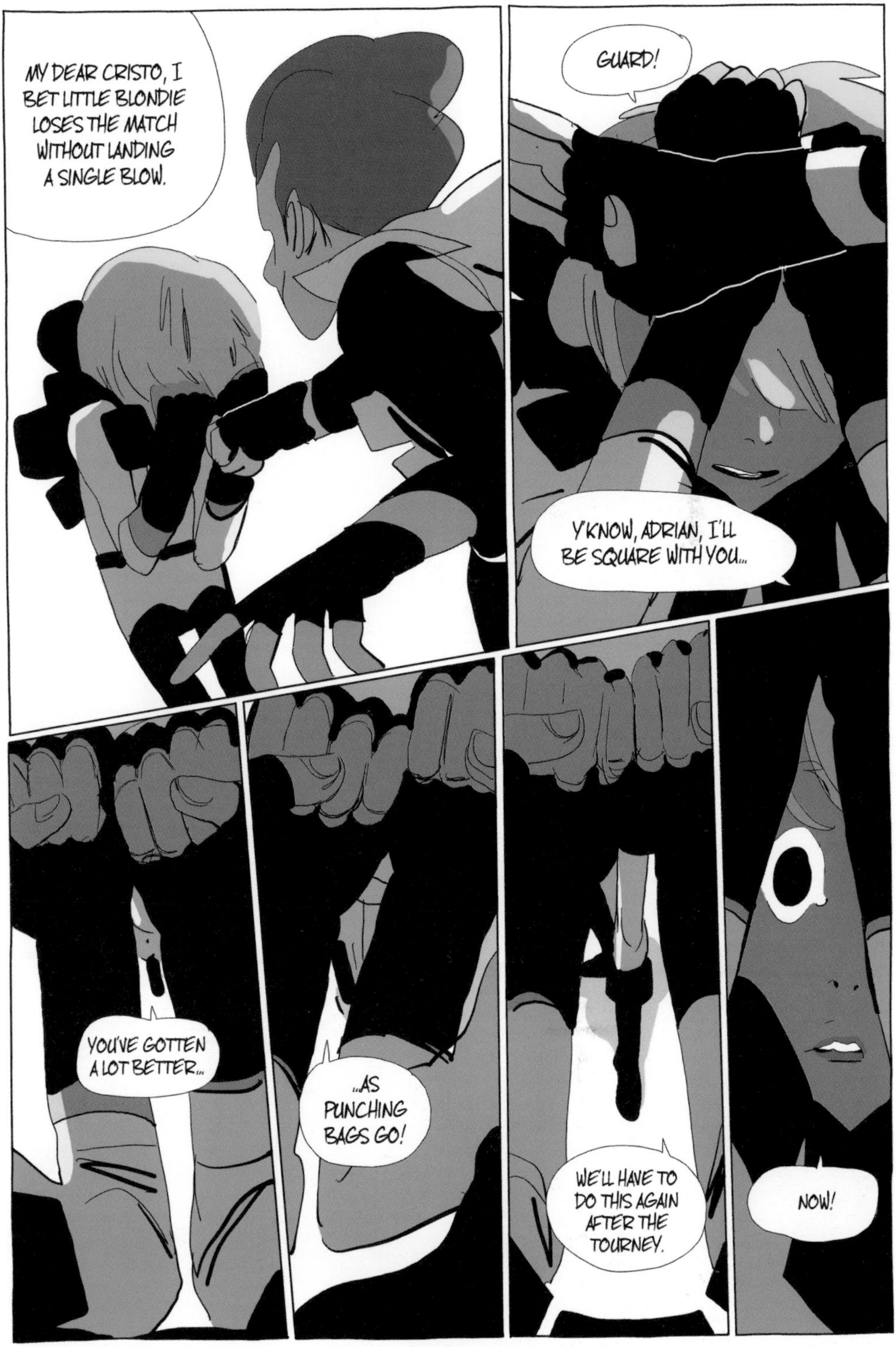
MY DEAR CRISTO, I BET LITTLE BLONDIE LOSES THE MATCH WITHOUT LANDING A SINGLE BLOW.
GUARD!
Y'KNOW, ADRIAN, I'LL BE SQUARE WITH YOU...
YOU'VE GOTTEN A LOT BETTER...
...AS PUNCHING BAGS GO!
WE'LL HAVE TO DO THIS AGAIN AFTER THE TOURNEY.
NOW!

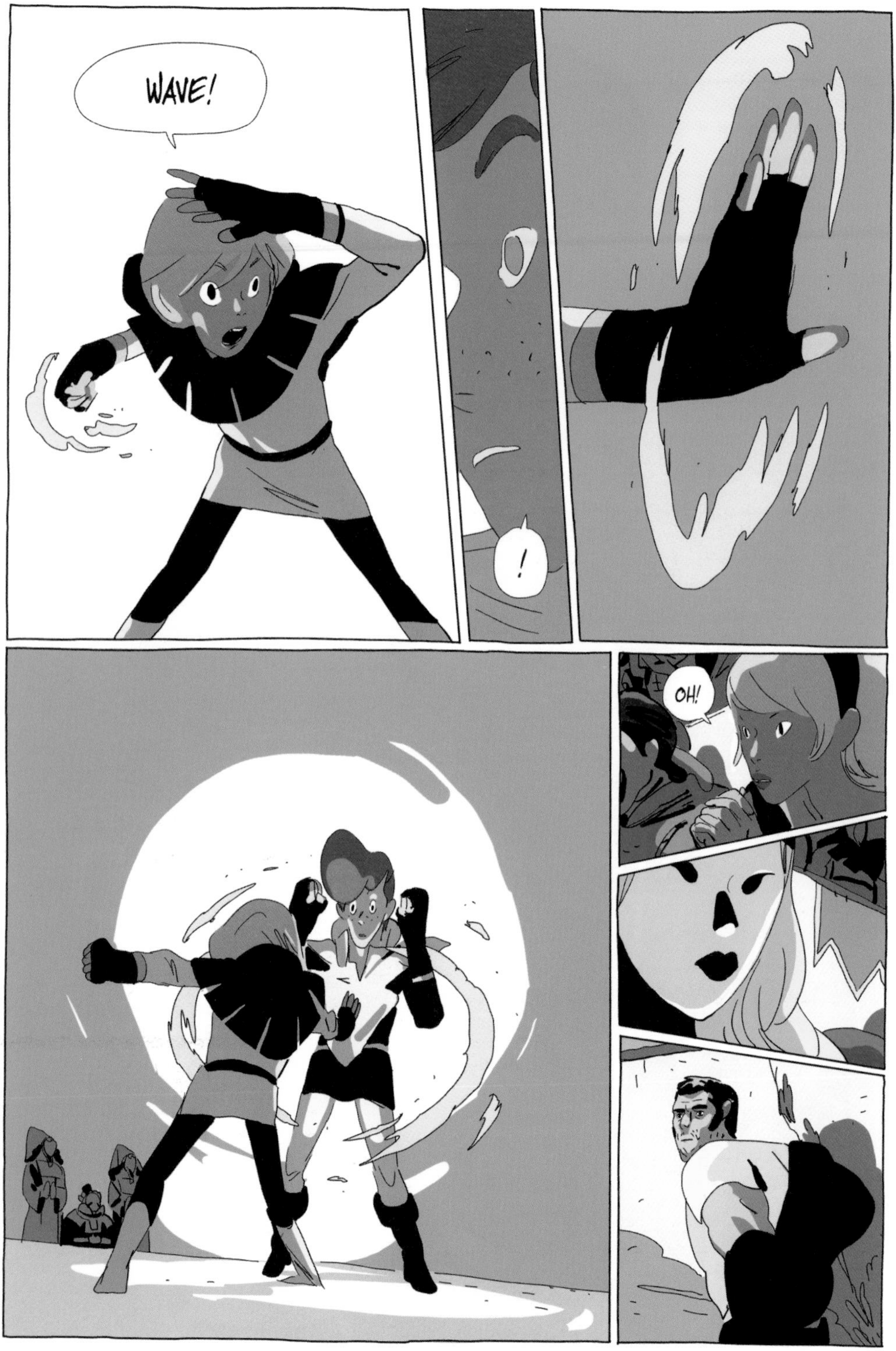
WAVE!
!
OH!

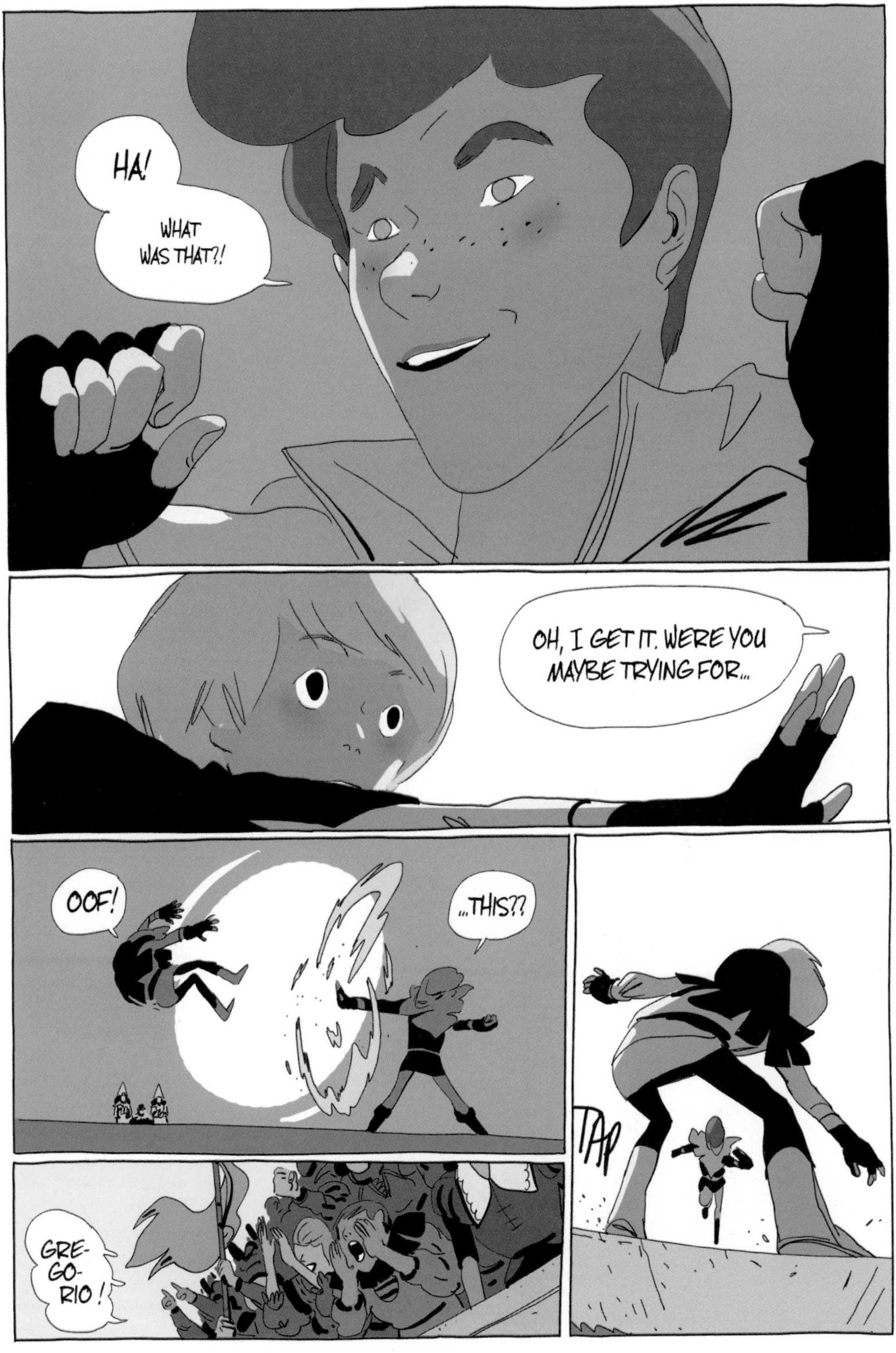
HA!
WHAT WAS THAT?!
OH, I GET IT. WERE YOU MAYBE TRYING FOR...
OOF!
...THIS??
TAP
GRE-GO-RIO!

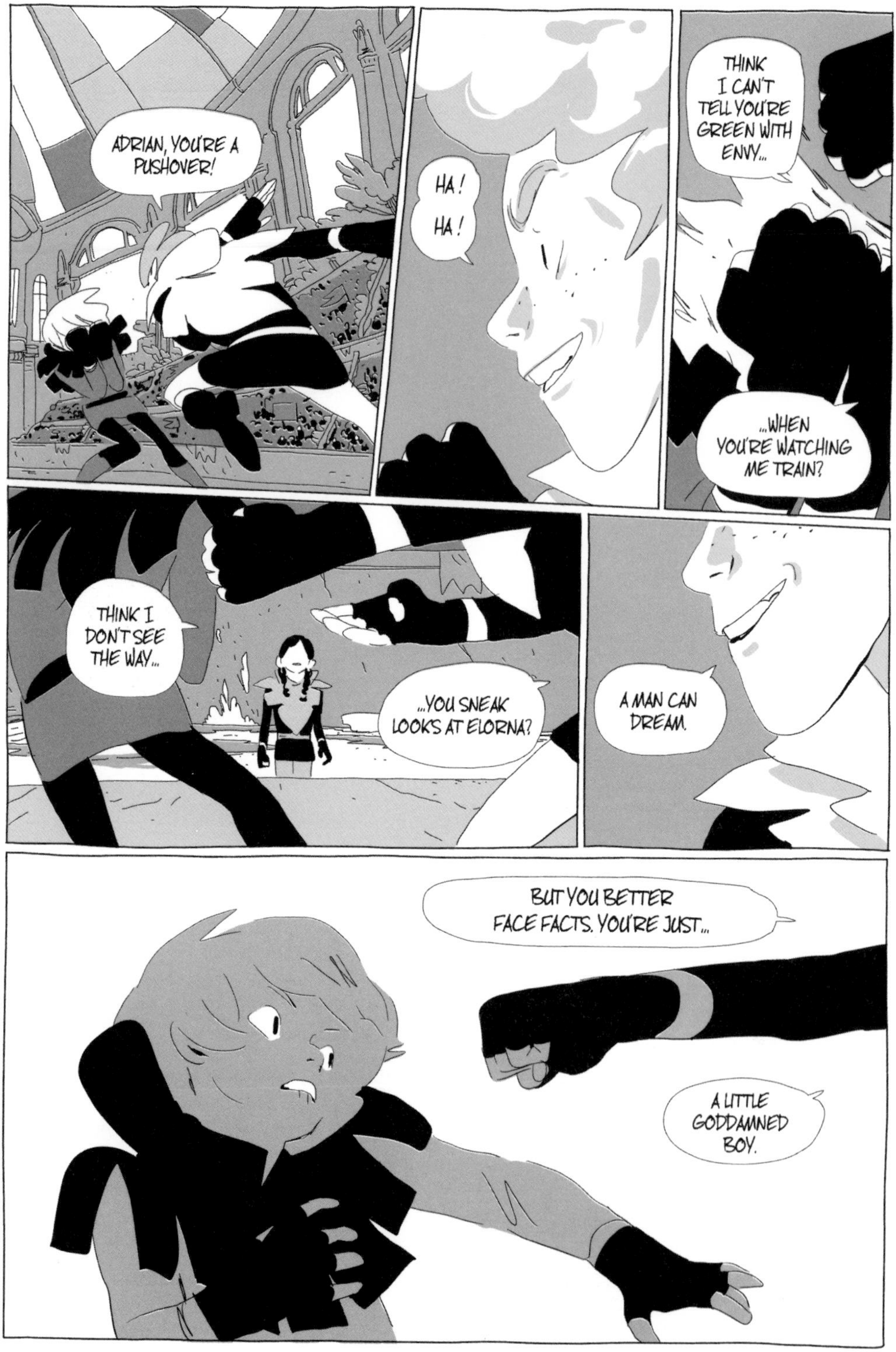
ADRIAN, YOU'RE A PUSHOVER!
HA! HA!
THINK I CAN'T TELL YOU'RE GREEN WITH ENVY...
...WHEN YOU'RE WATCHING ME TRAIN?
THINK I DON'T SEE THE WAY...
...YOU SNEAK LOOKS AT ELORNA?
A MAN CAN DREAM.
BUT YOU BETTER FACE FACTS. YOU'RE JUST...
A LITTLE GODDAMNED BOY.

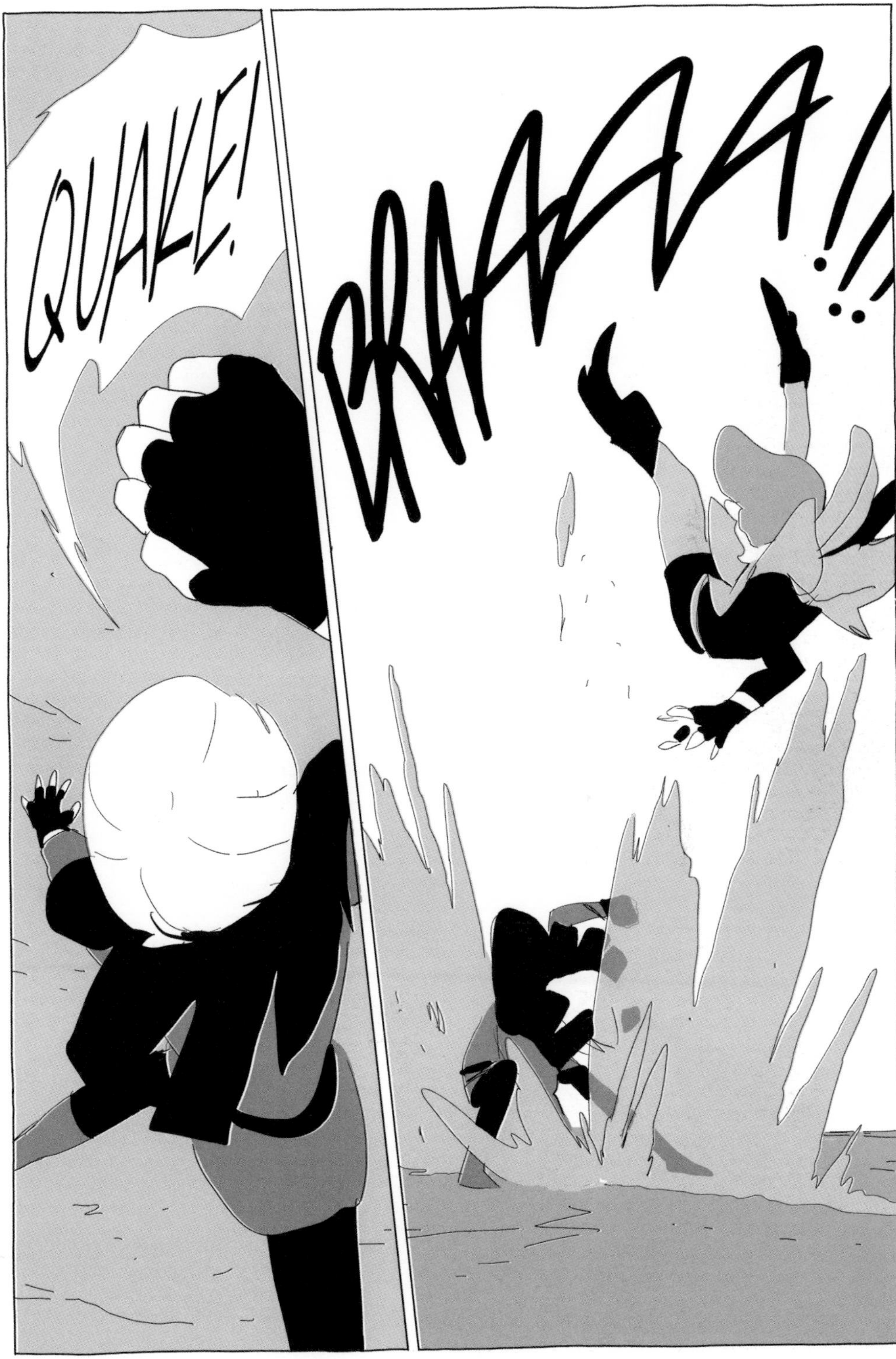
QUAKE!
BRAAAAA!!!

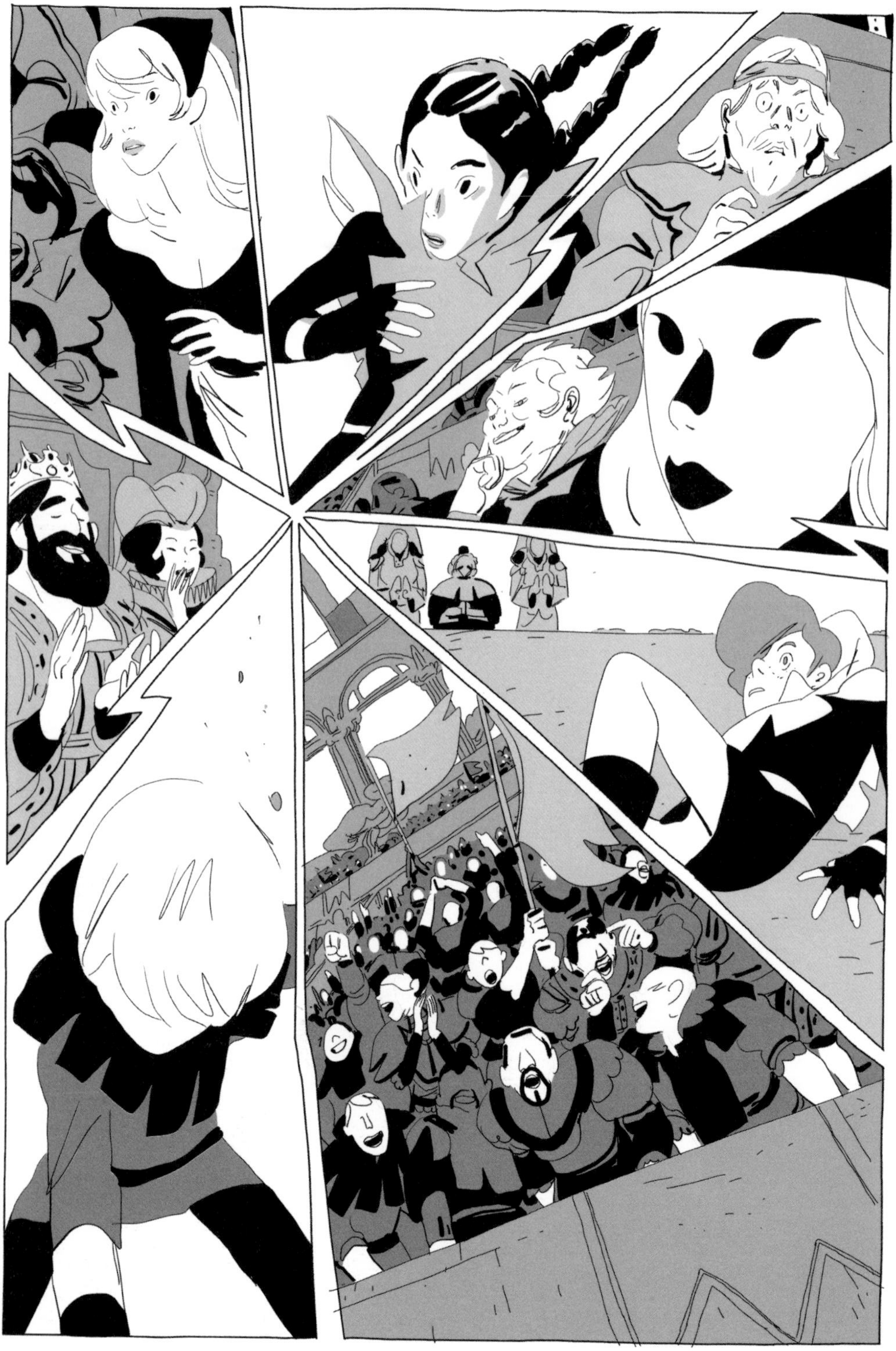

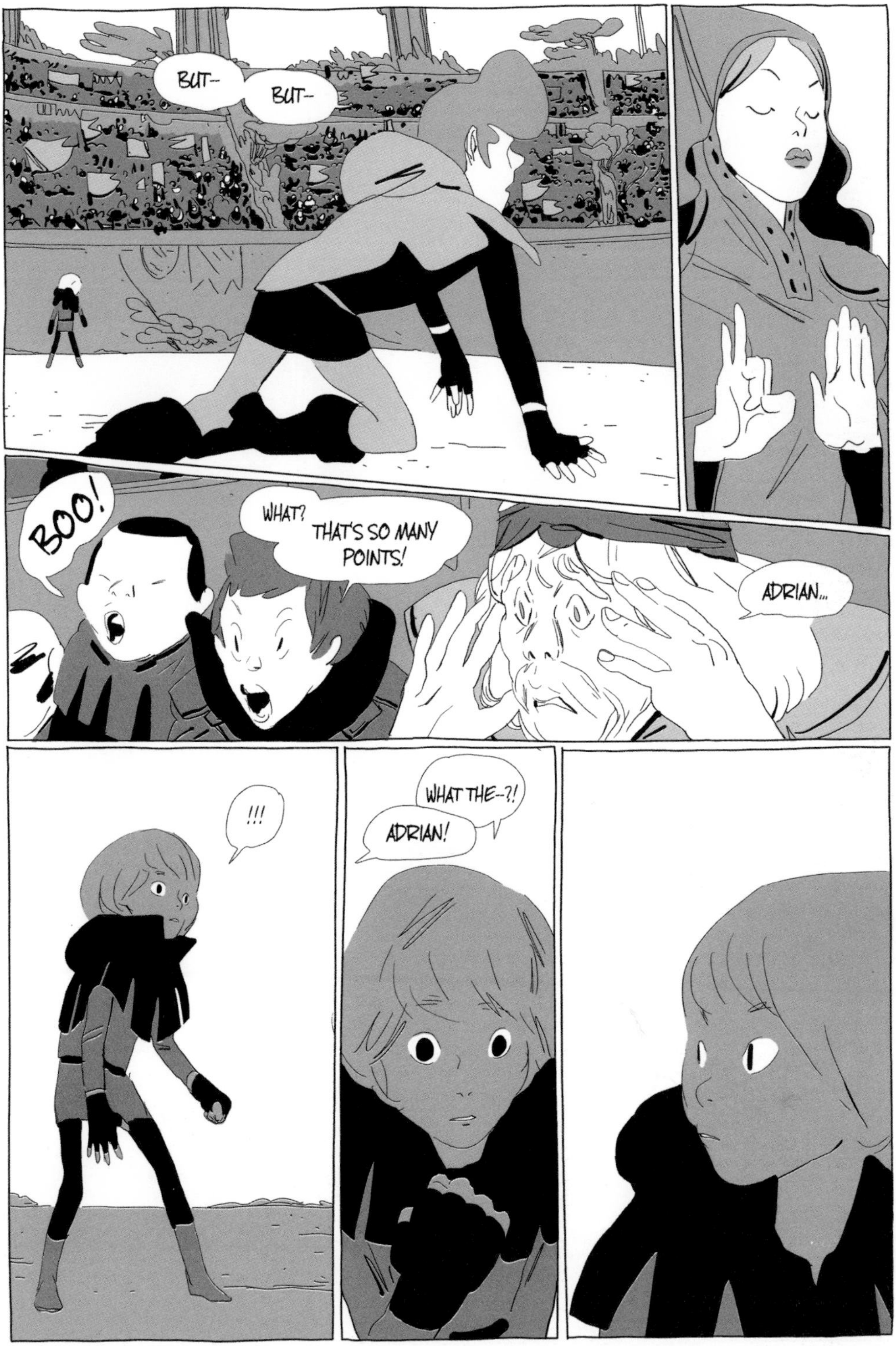
BUT--
BUT--
BOO!
WHAT?
THAT'S SO MANY POINTS!
ADRIAN...
!!!
WHAT THE--?!
ADRIAN!

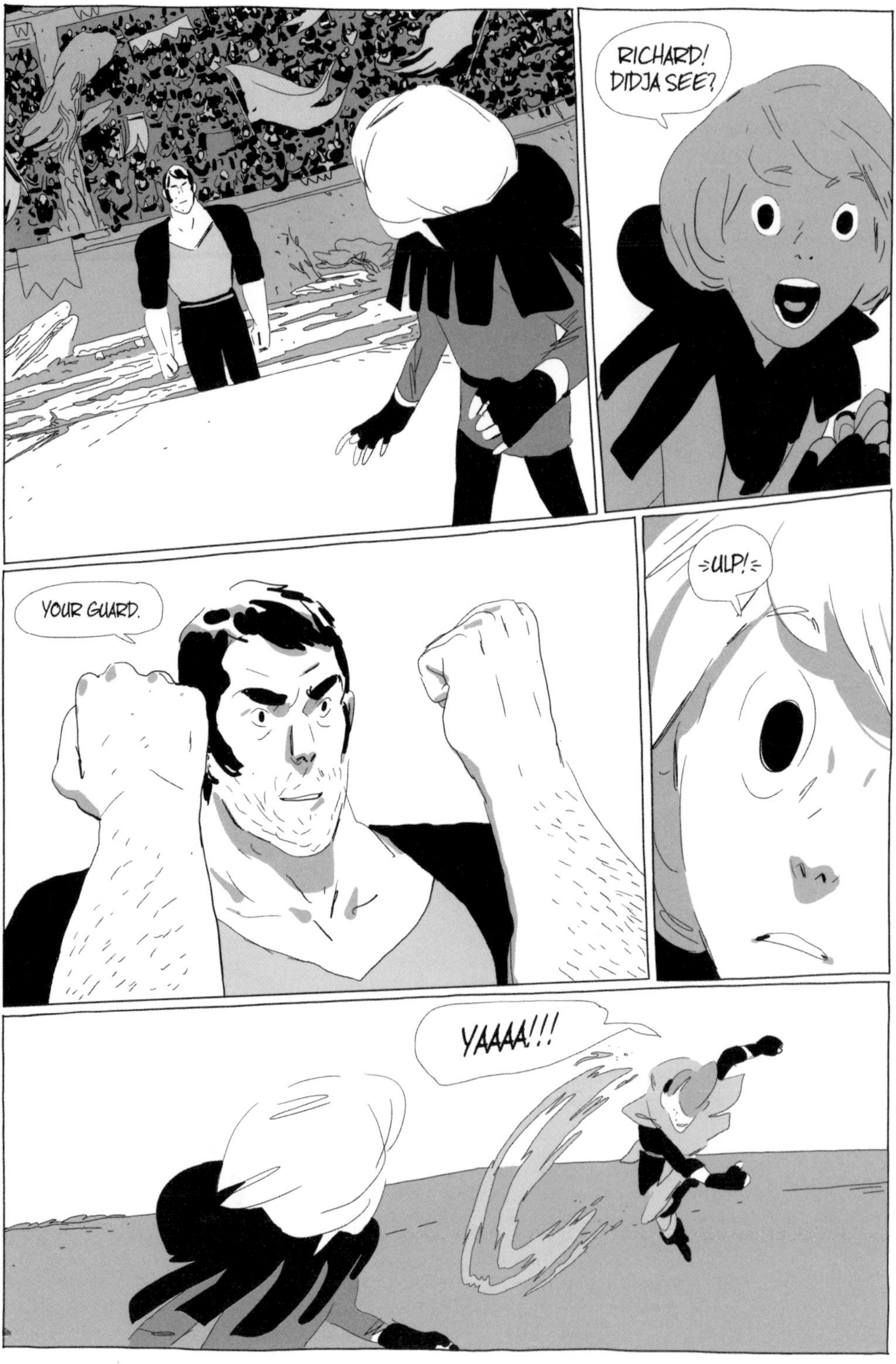
RICHARD! DIDJA SEE?
YOUR GUARD.
ULP!
YAAAA!!!

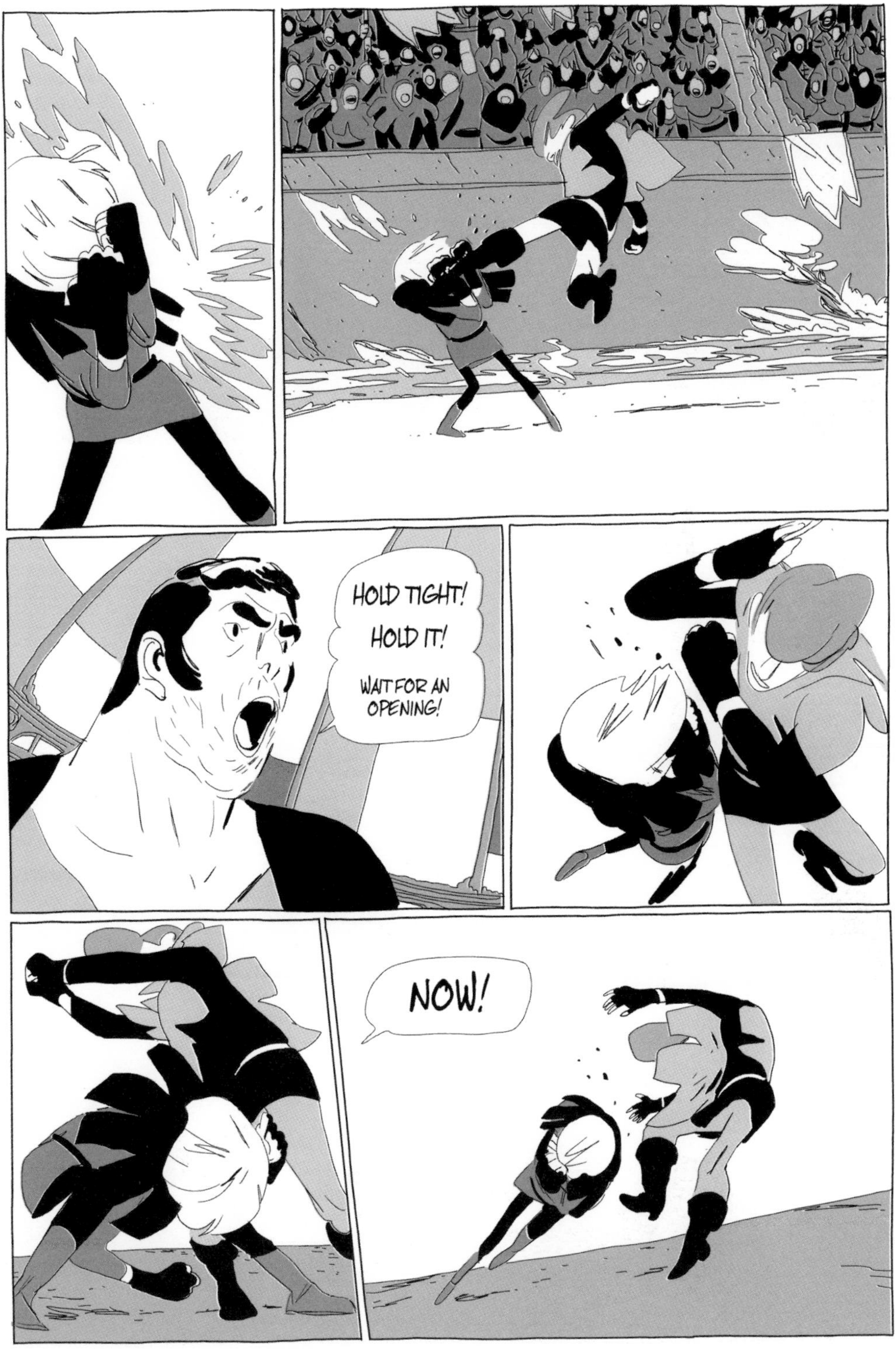
HOLD TIGHT!
HOLD IT!
WAIT FOR AN OPENING!
NOW!

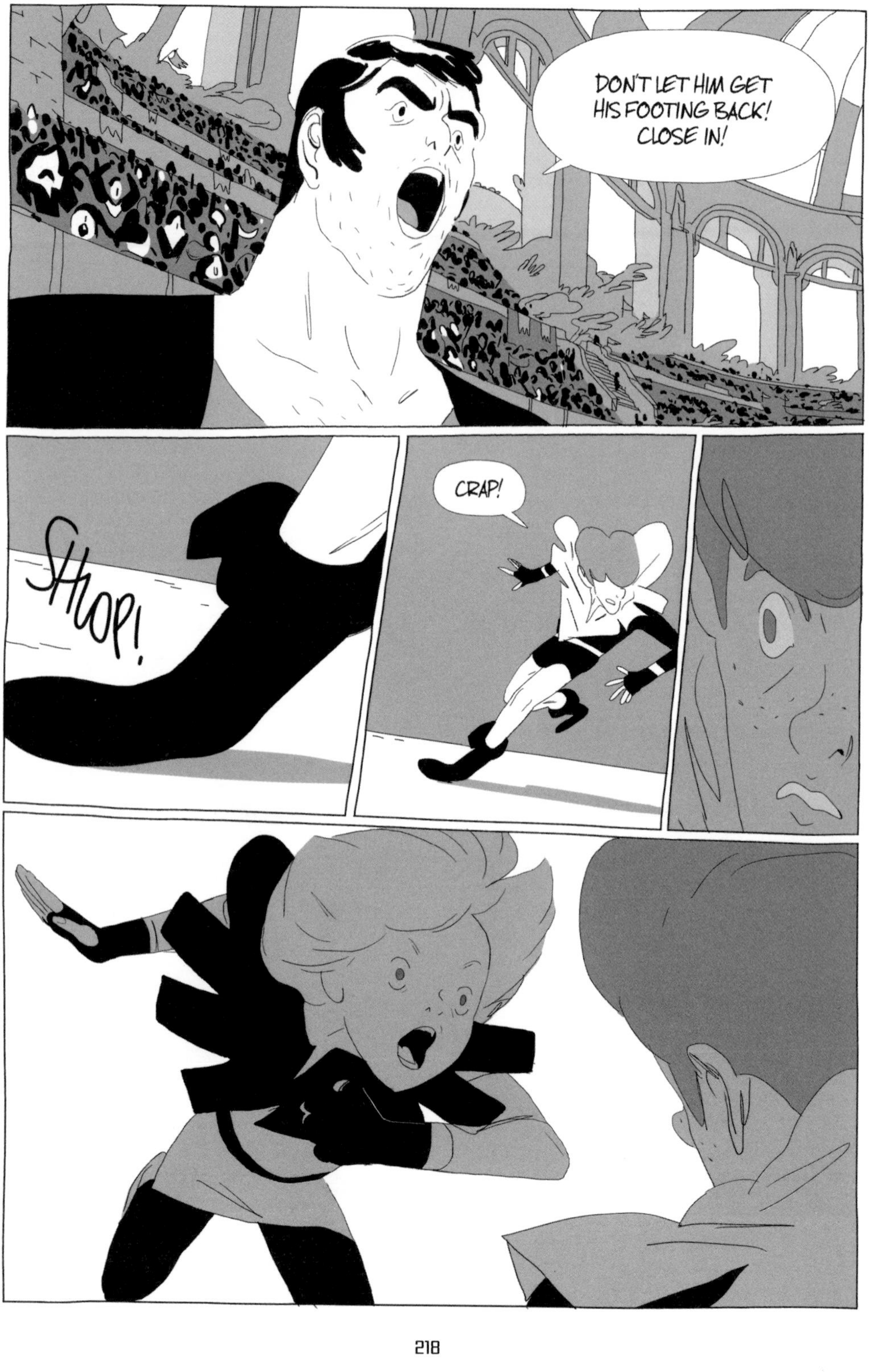
DON'T LET HIM GET HIS FOOTING BACK! CLOSE IN!
SHLOP!
CRAP!

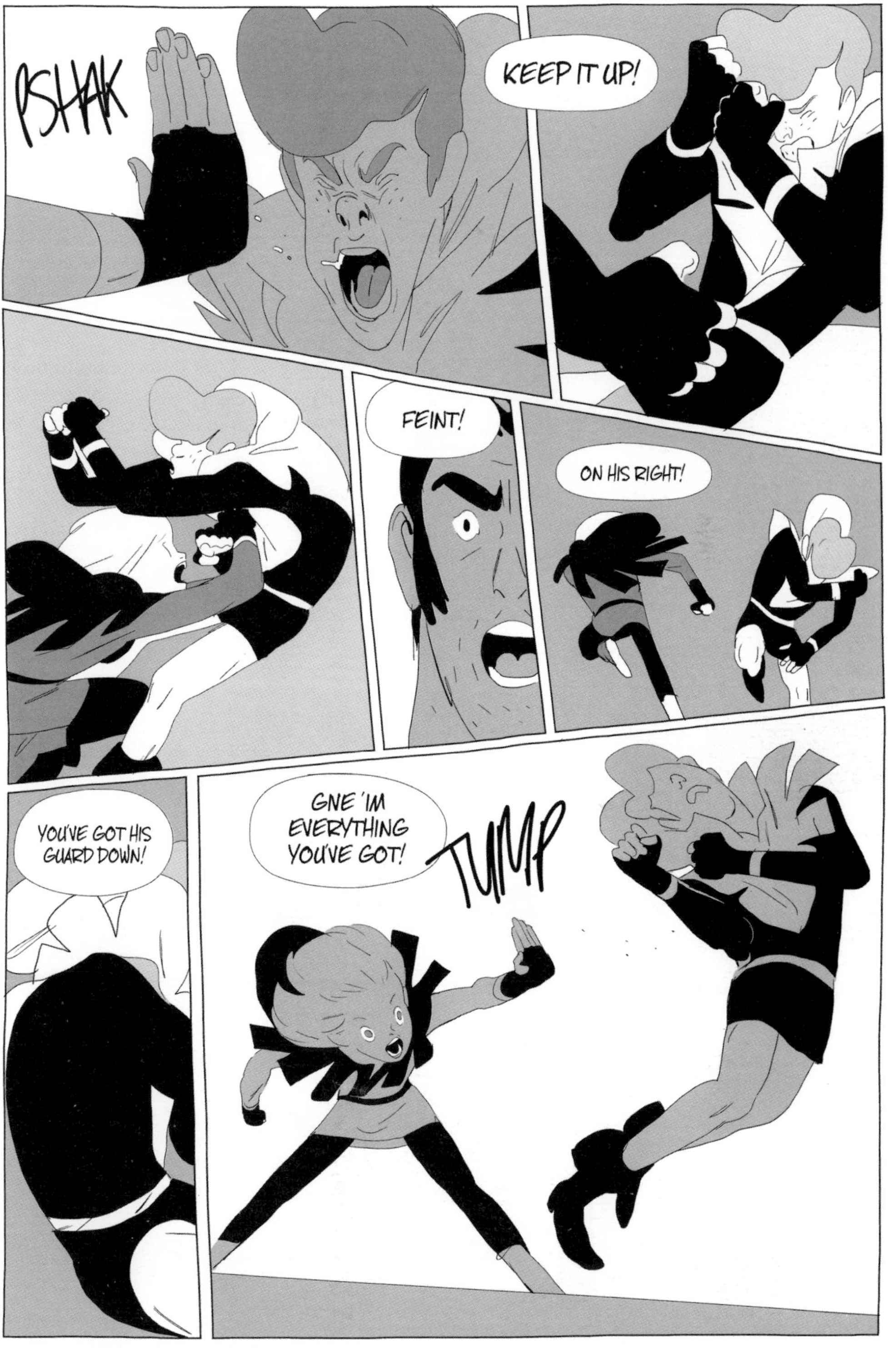
PSHAK
KEEP IT UP!
FEINT!
ON HIS RIGHT!
YOU'VE GOT HIS GUARD DOWN!
GNE 'IM EVERYTHING YOU'VE GOT!
TUMP

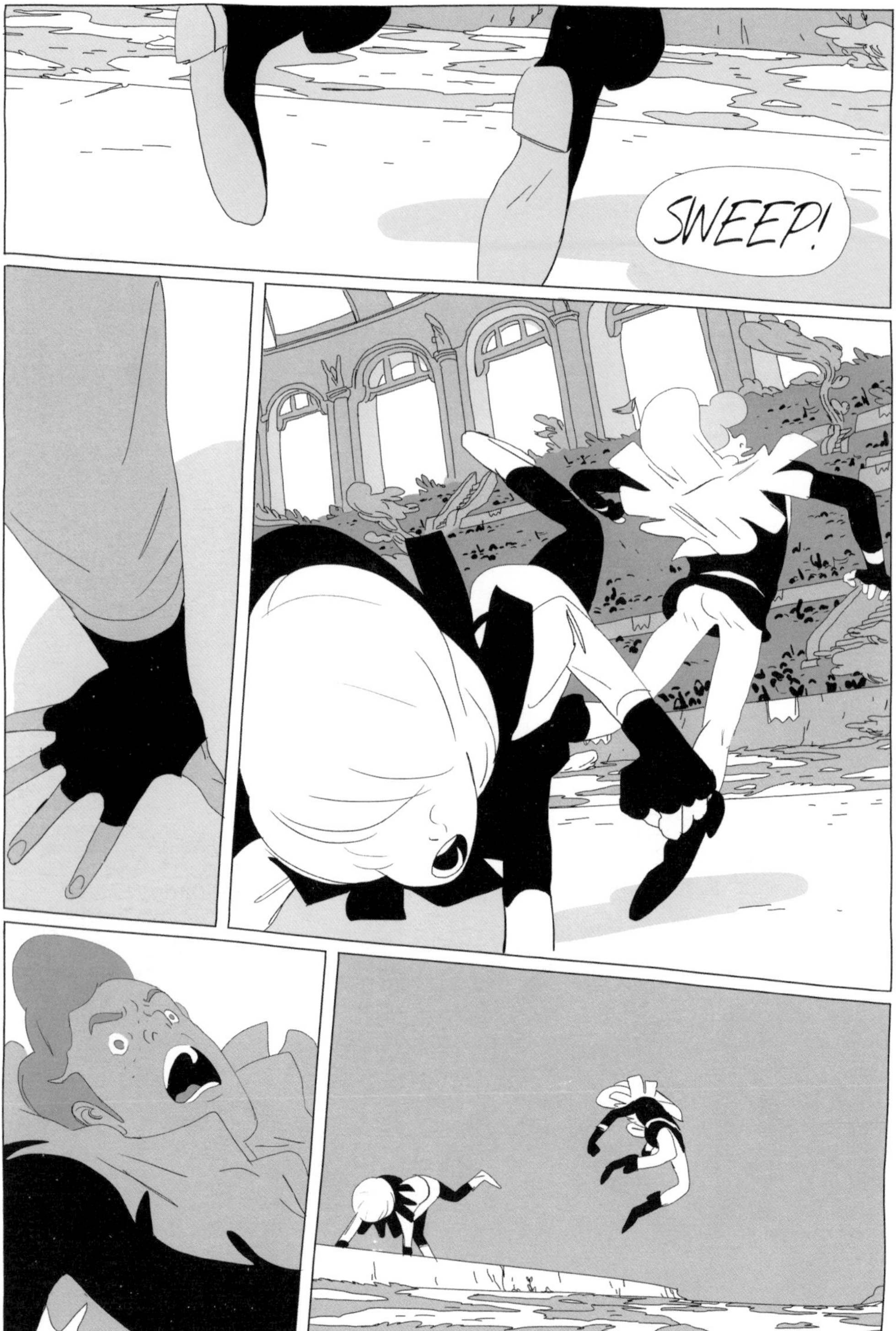
SWEEP!

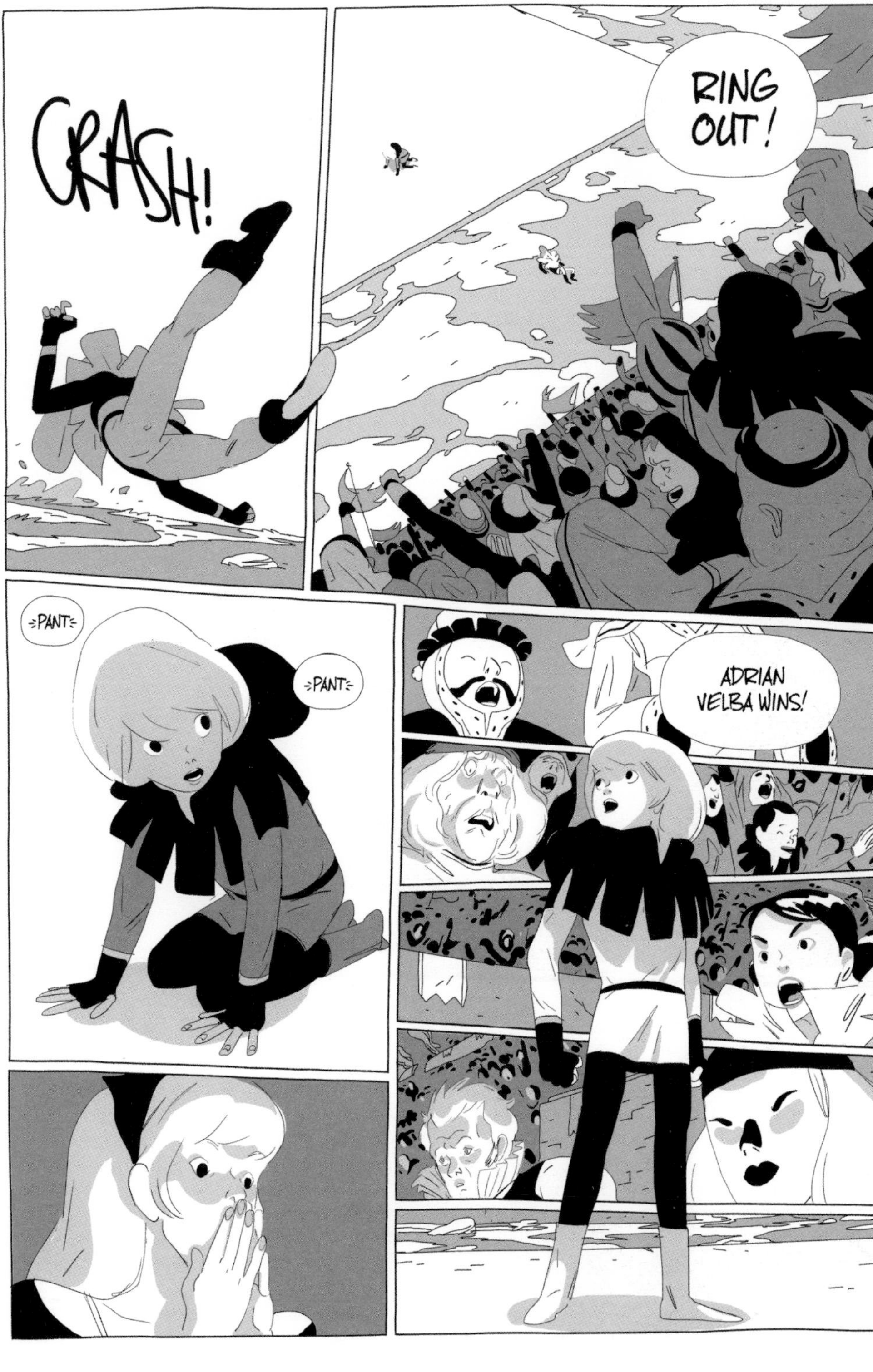
CRASH!
RING OUT!
PANT
PANT
ADRIAN VELBA WINS!

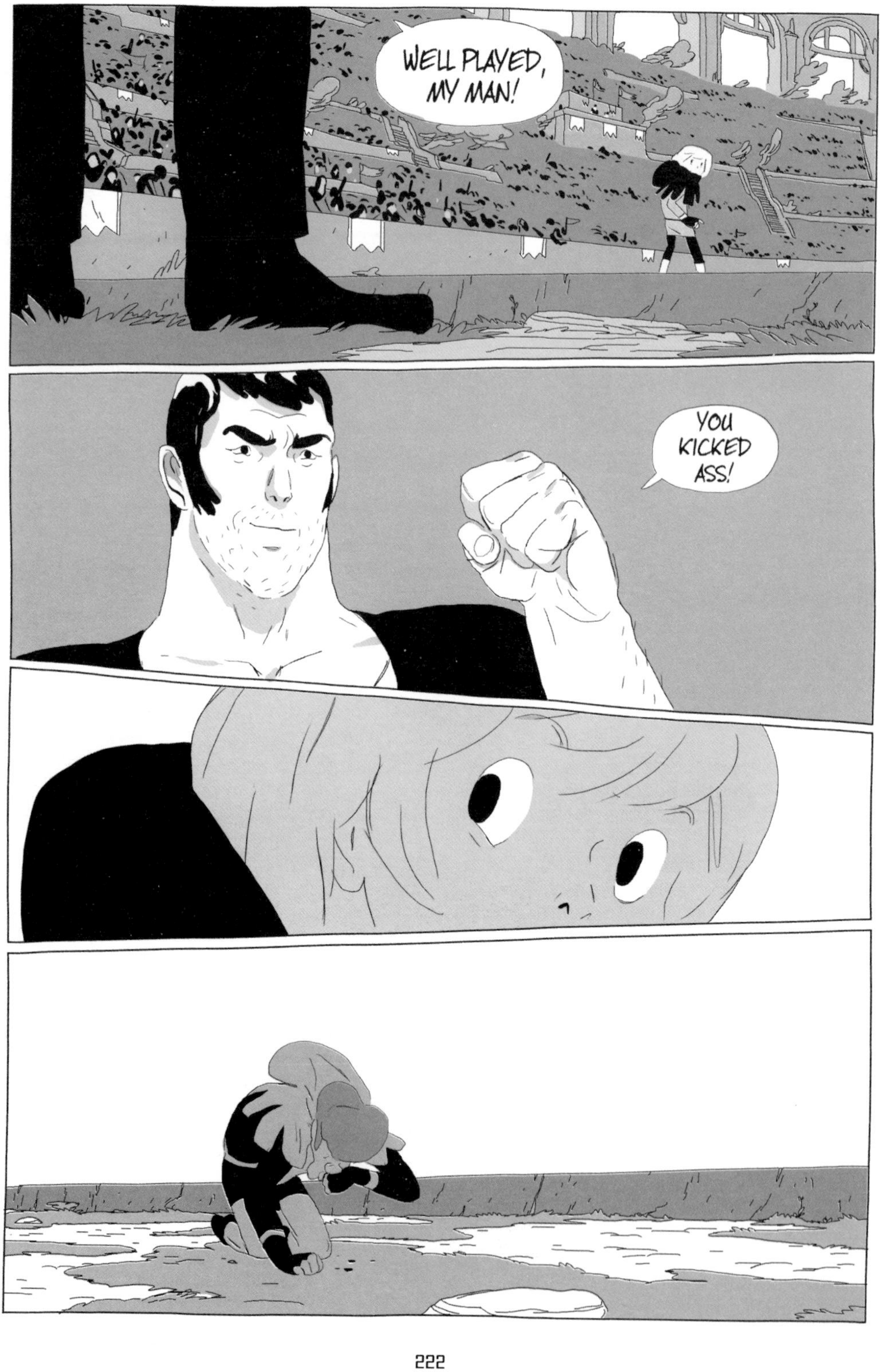
WELL PLAYED, MY MAN!
YOU KICKED ASS!

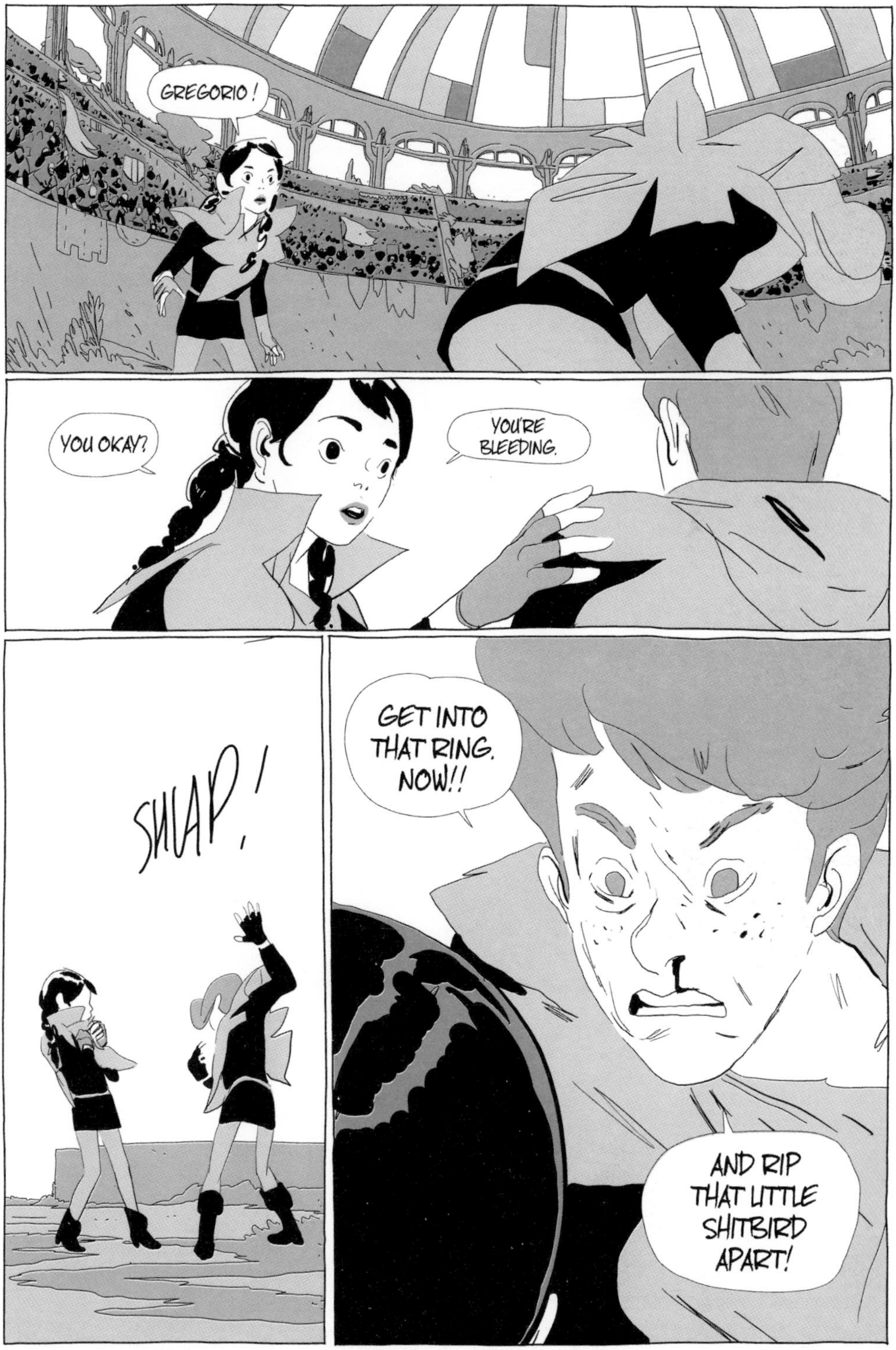
GREGORIO!
YOU OKAY?
YOU'RE BLEEDING.
SHLAP!
GET INTO THAT RING. NOW!!
AND RIP THAT LITTLE SHITBIRD APART!

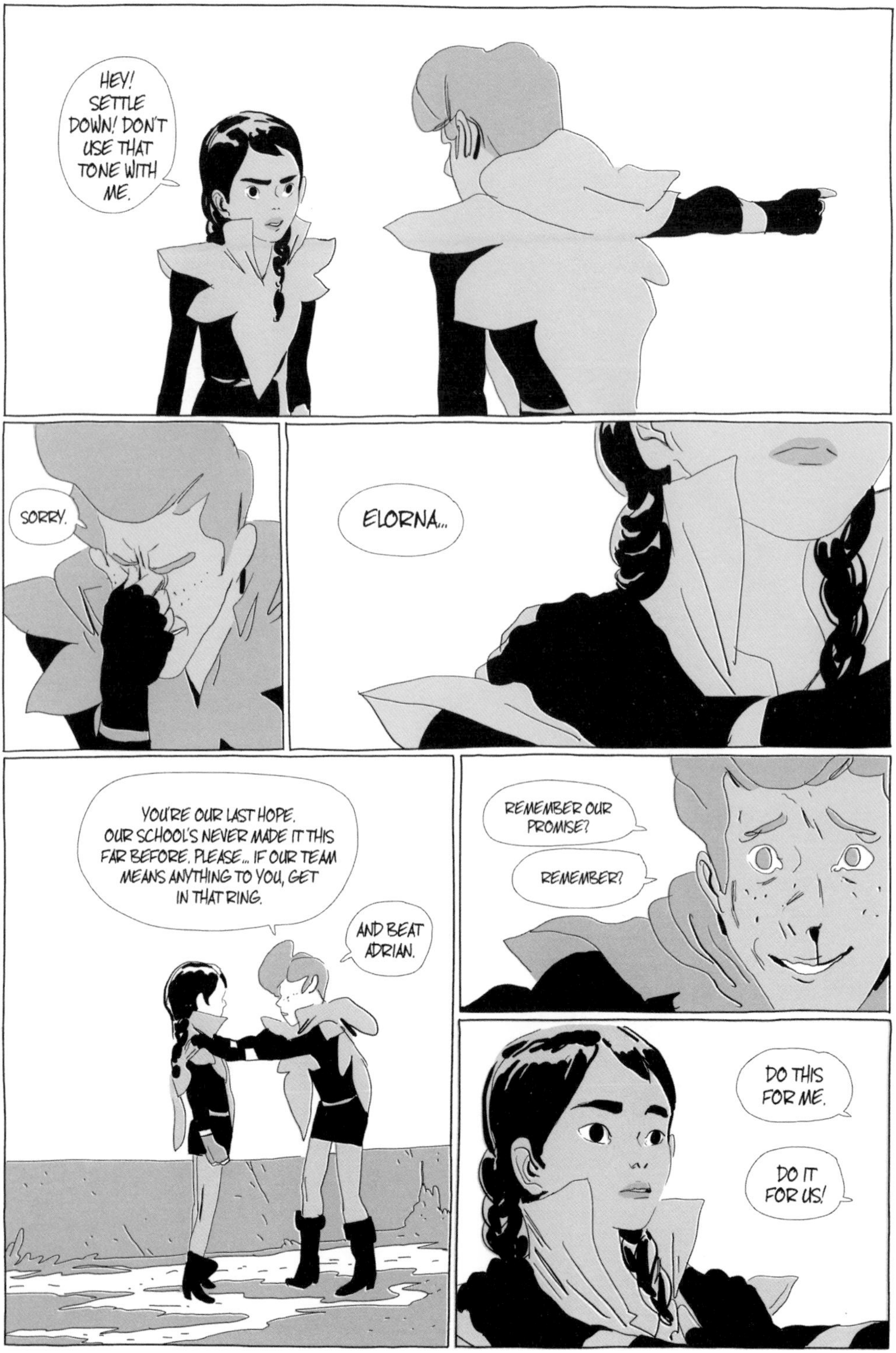
HEY! SETTLE DOWN! DON'T USE THAT TONE WITH ME.
SORRY.
ELORNA...
YOU'RE OUR LAST HOPE. OUR SCHOOL'S NEVER MADE IT THIS FAR BEFORE. PLEASE... IF OUR TEAM MEANS ANYTHING TO YOU, GET IN THAT RING.
AND BEAT ADRIAN.
REMEMBER OUR PROMISE?
REMEMBER?
DO THIS FOR ME.
DO IT FOR US!

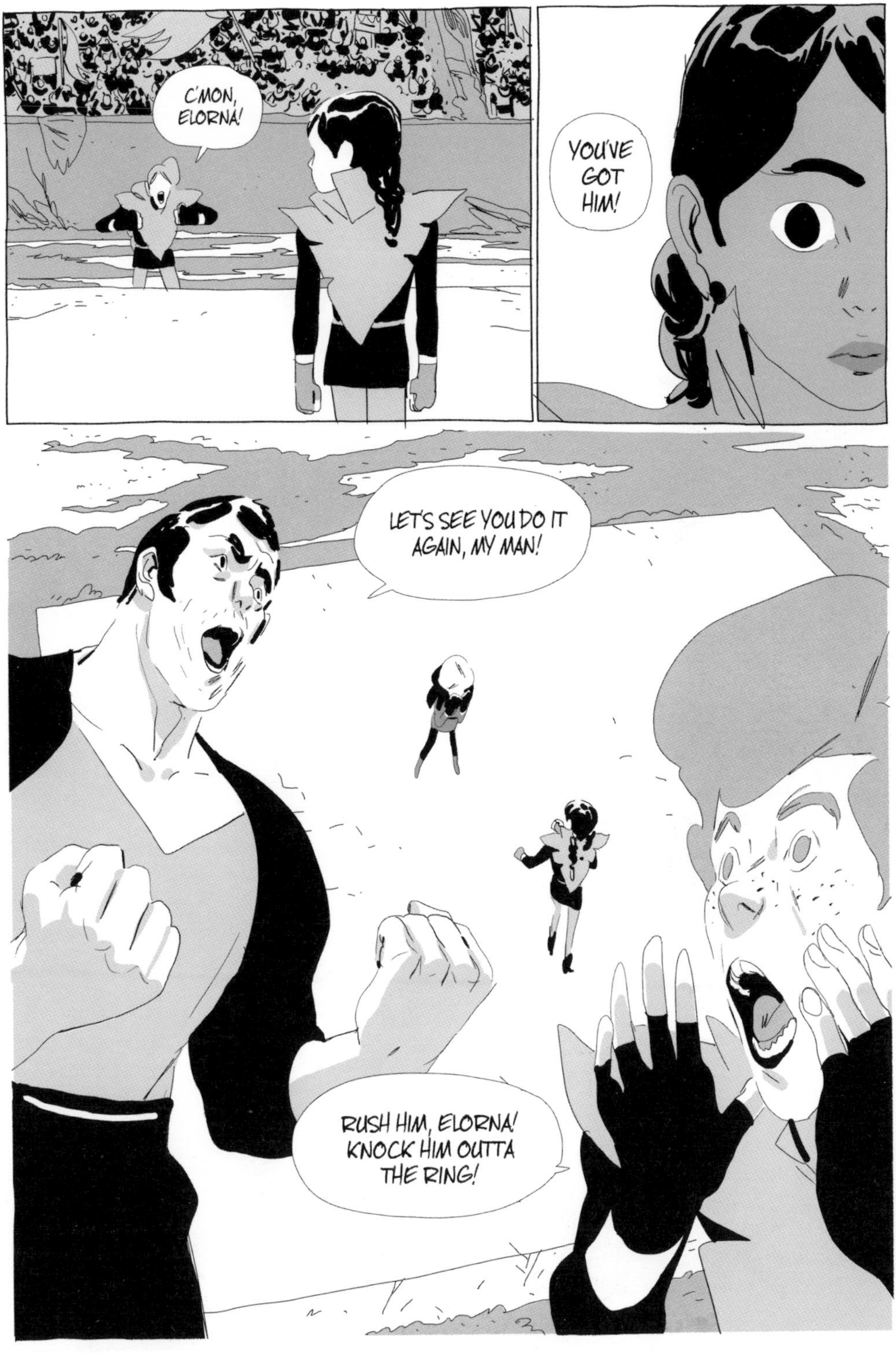
C'MON, ELORNA!
YOU'VE GOT HIM!
LET'S SEE YOU DO IT AGAIN, MY MAN!
RUSH HIM, ELORNA! KNOCK HIM OUTTA THE RING!

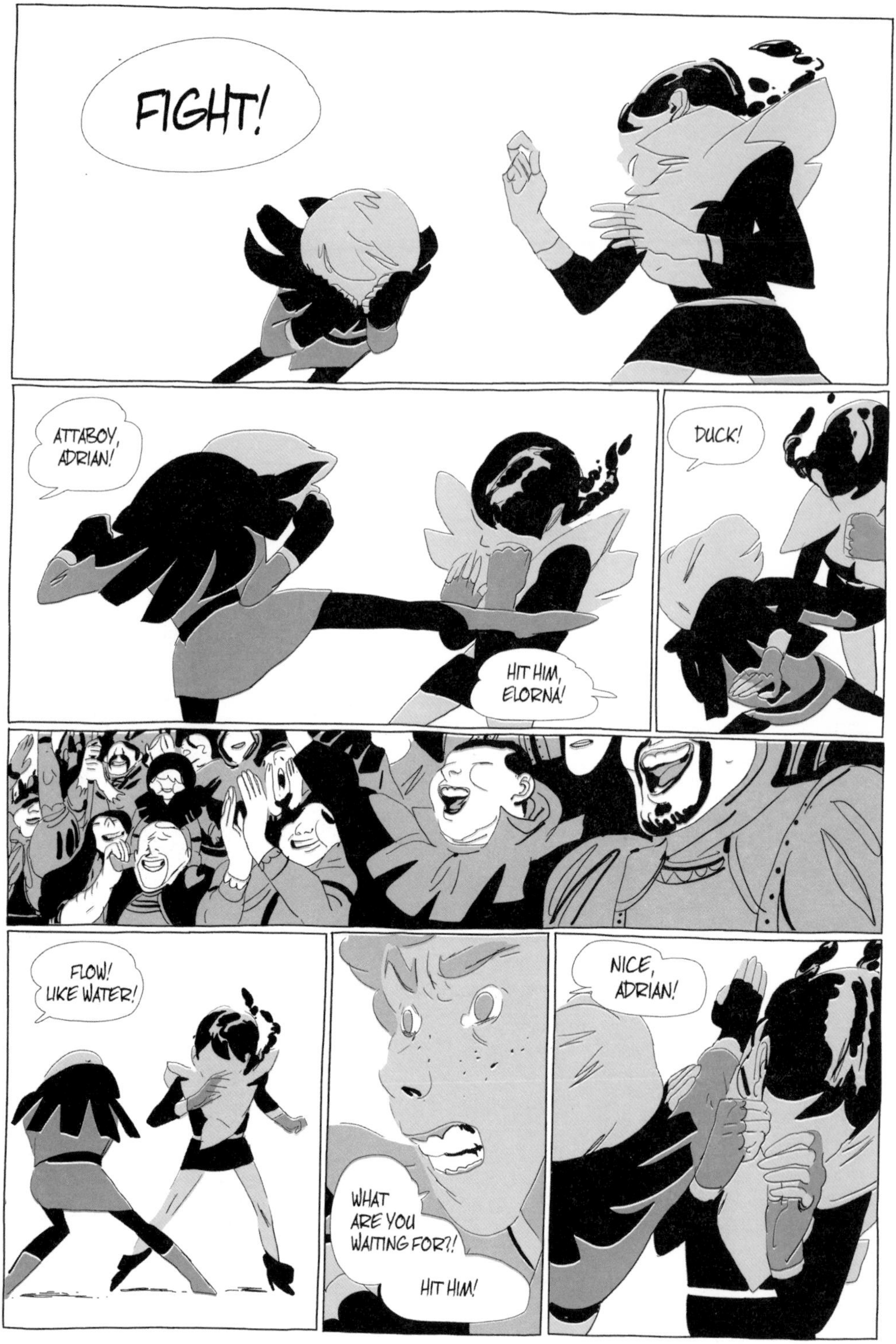
FIGHT!
ATTABOY, ADRIAN!
HIT HIM, ELORNA!
DUCK!
FLOW! LIKE WATER!
WHAT ARE YOU WAITING FOR?!
HIT HIM!
NICE, ADRIAN!

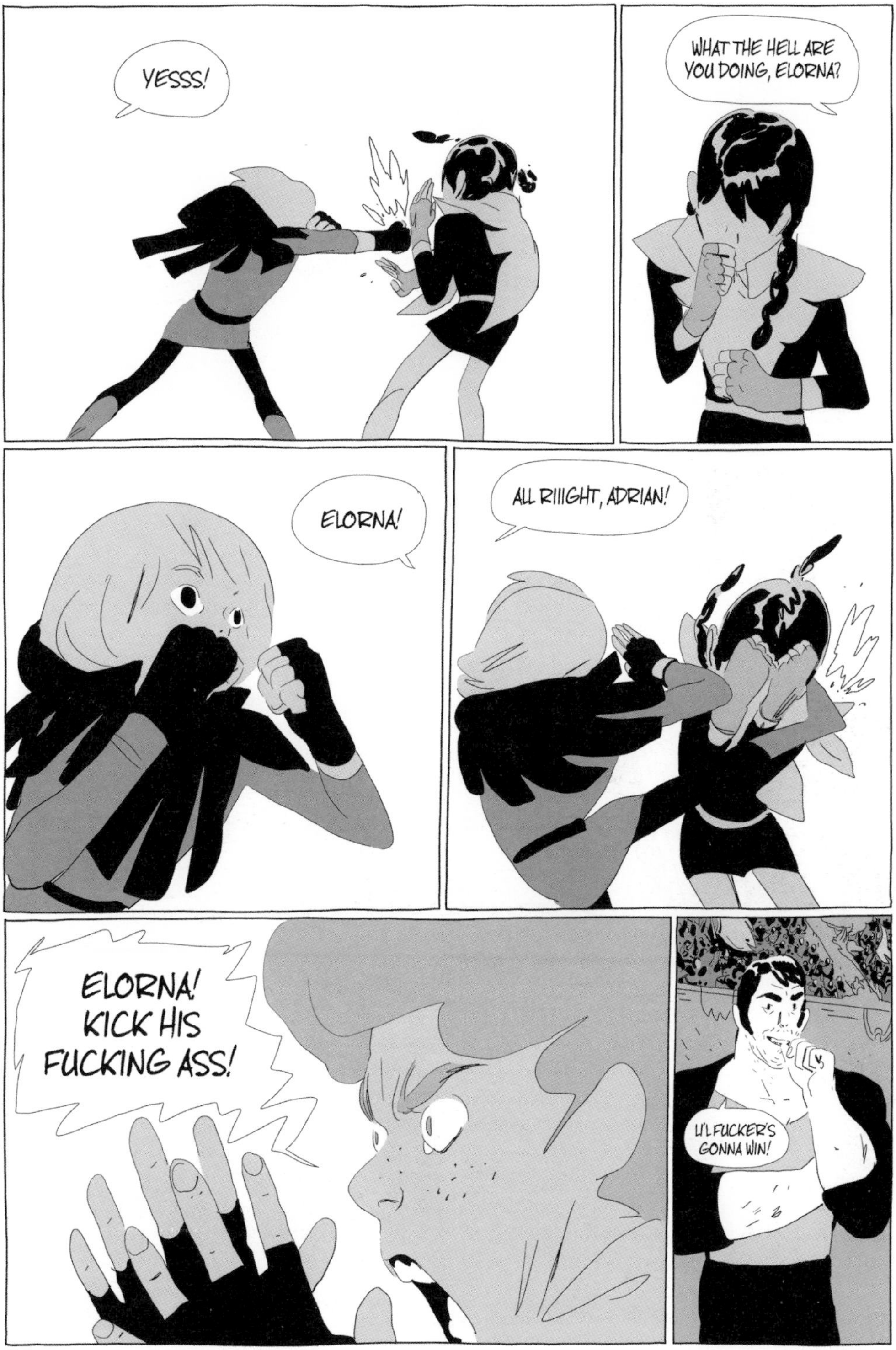
YESSS!
WHAT THE HELL ARE YOU DOING, ELORNA?
ELORNA!
ALL RIIIGHT, ADRIAN!
ELORNA! KICK HIS FUCKING ASS!
LI'L FUCKER'S GONNA WIN!

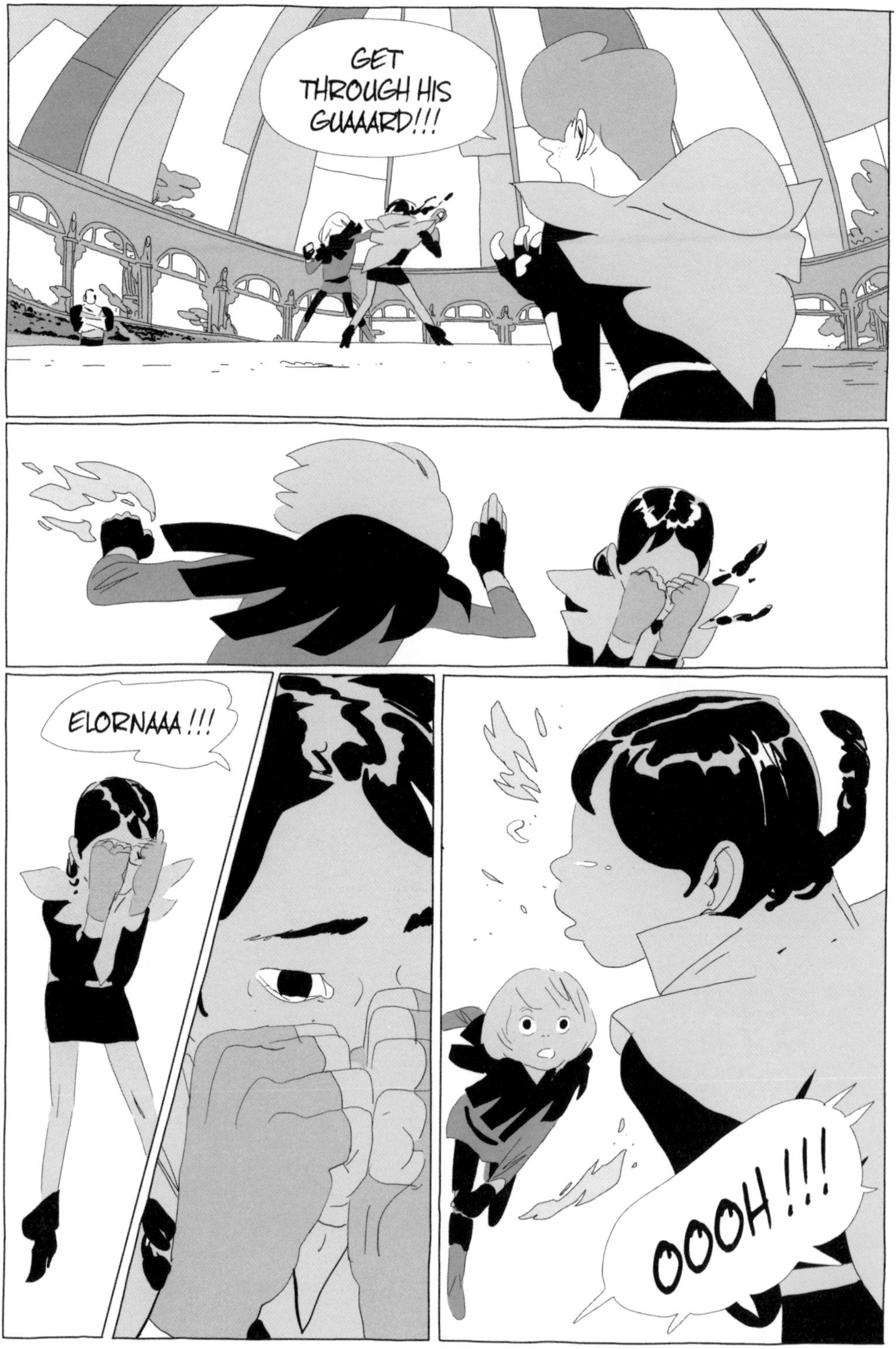
GET THROUGH HIS GUAAARD!!!
ELORNAAA!!!
OOOH!!!

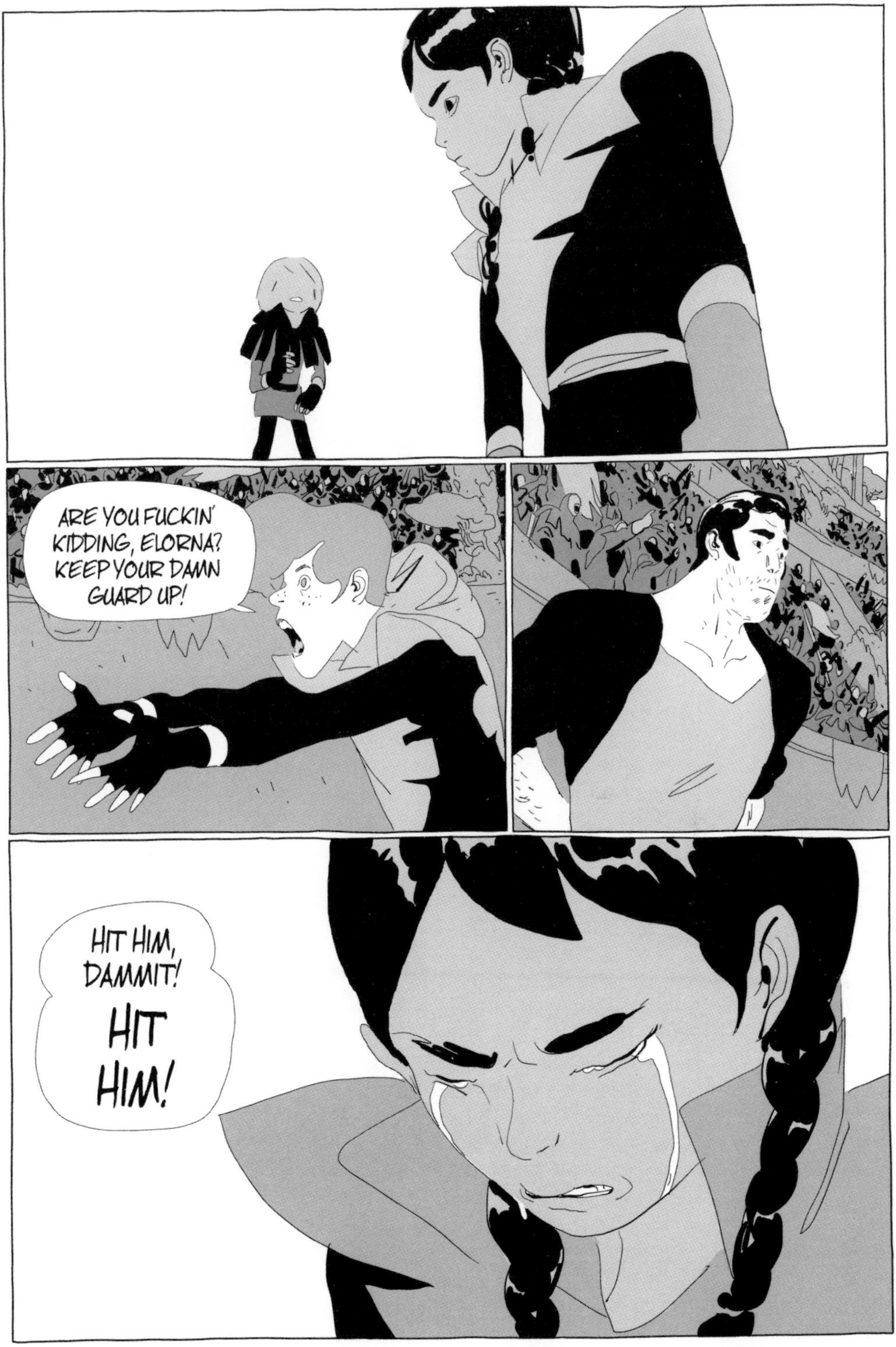
ARE YOU FUCKIN' KIDDING, ELORNA? KEEP YOUR DAMN GUARD UP!
HIT HIM, DAMMIT! HIT HIM!

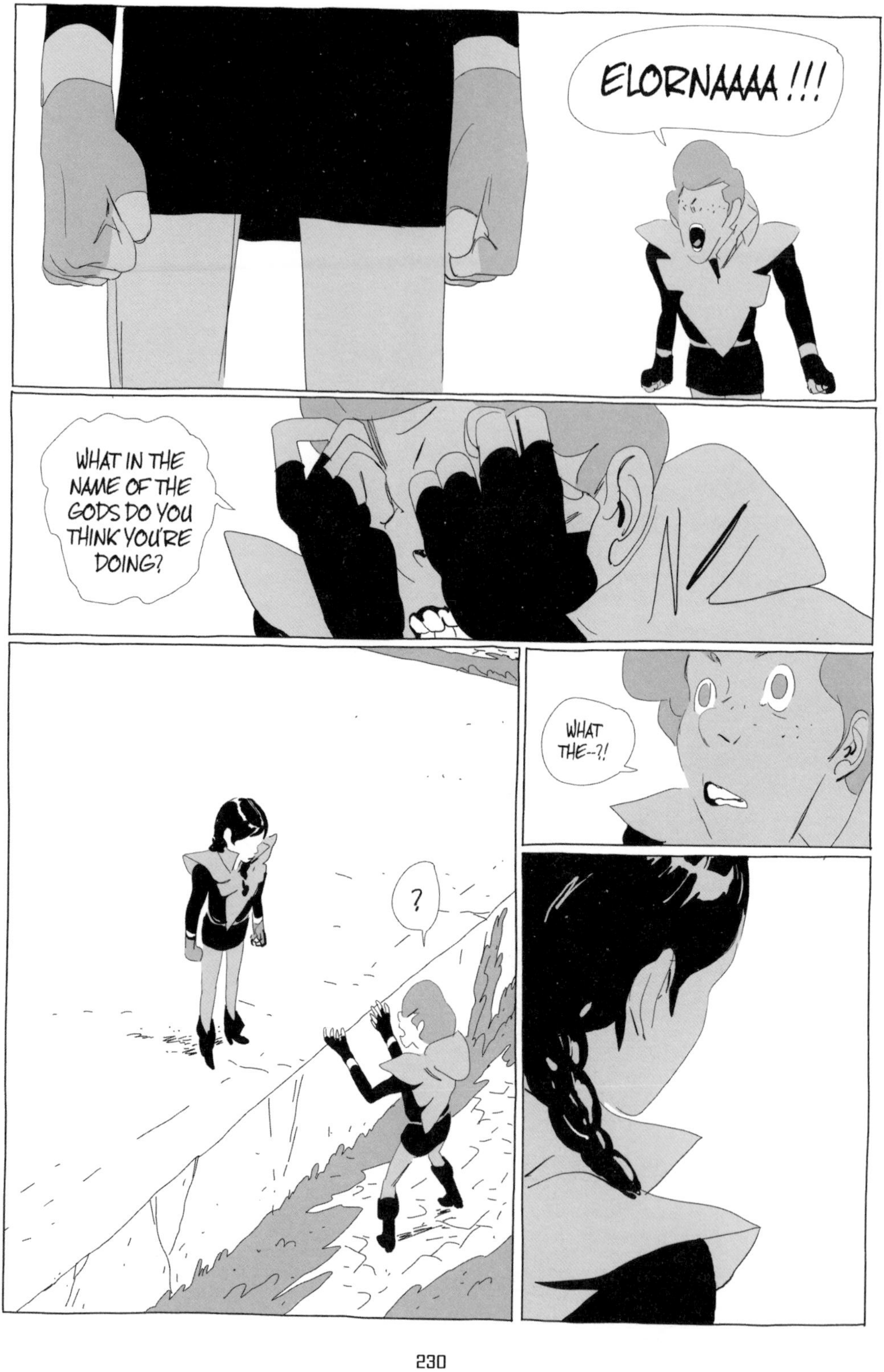
ELORNAAAA!!!
WHAT IN THE NAME OF THE GODS DO YOU THINK YOU'RE DOING?
WHAT THE--?!
?

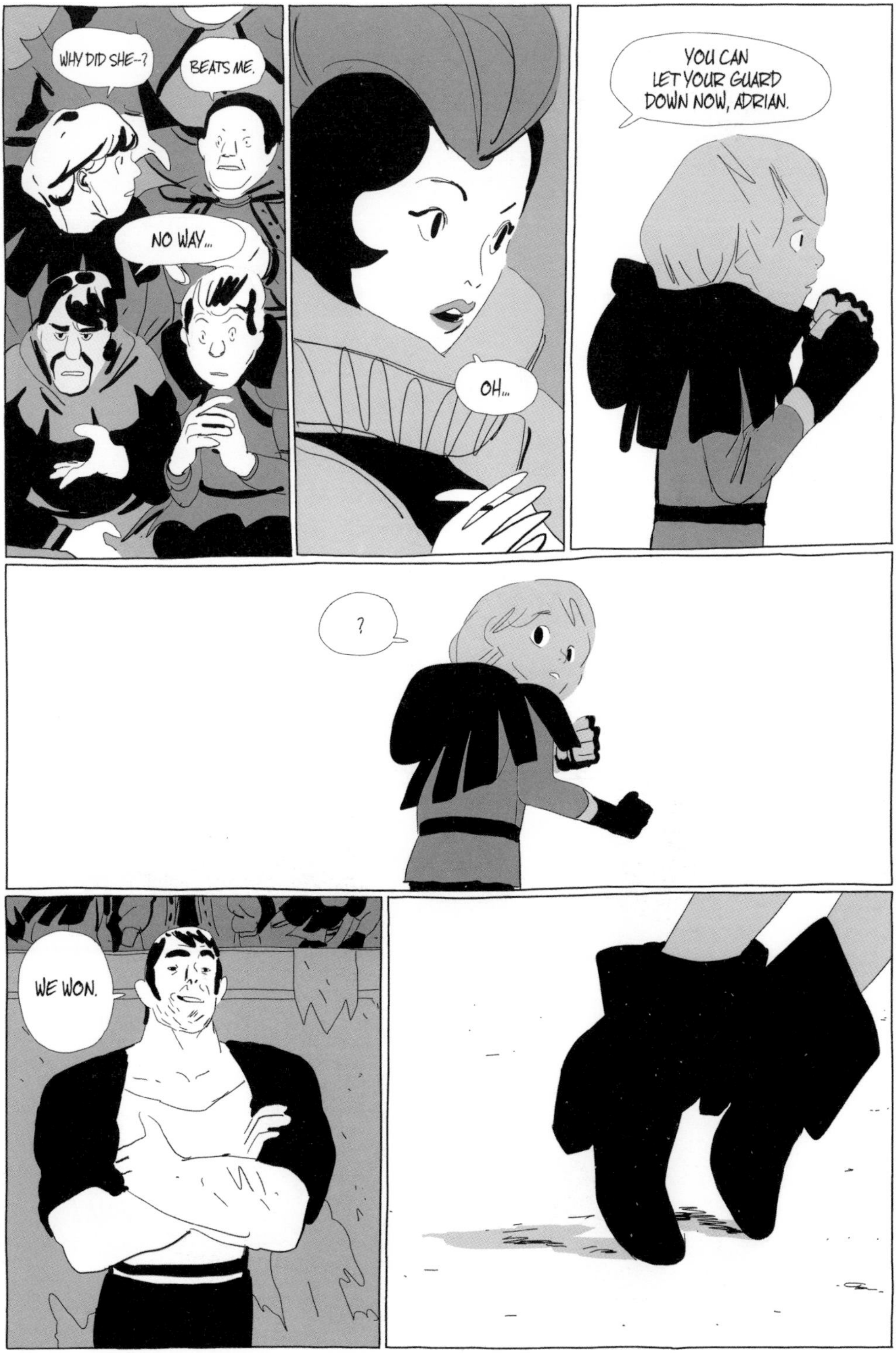
WHY DID SHE--?
BEATS ME.
NO WAY...
OH...
YOU CAN LET YOUR GUARD DOWN NOW, ADRIAN.
?
WE WON.

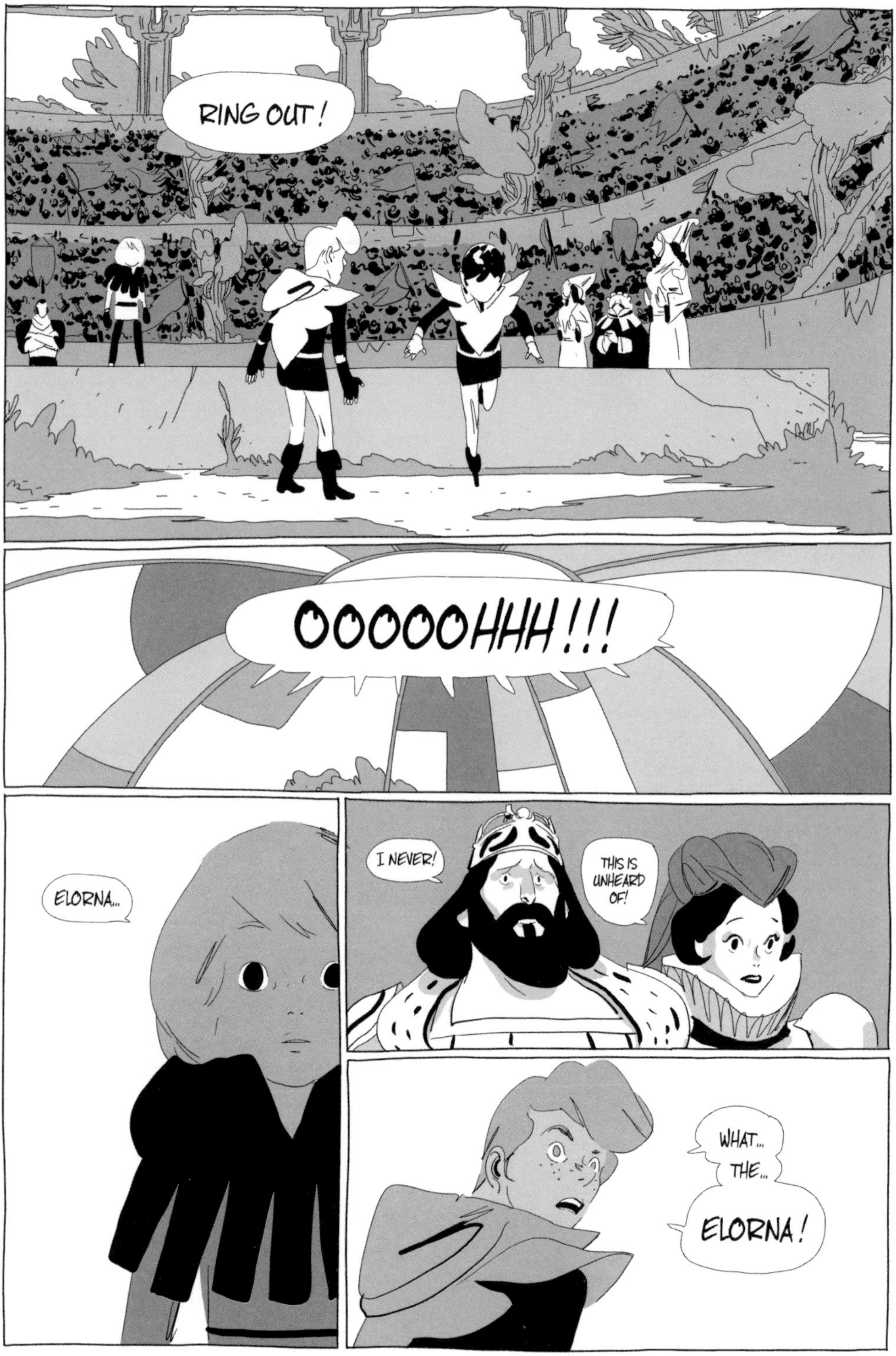
RING OUT!
OOOOOHHH!!!
ELORNA...
I NEVER!
THIS IS UNHEARD OF!
WHAT... THE...
ELORNA!

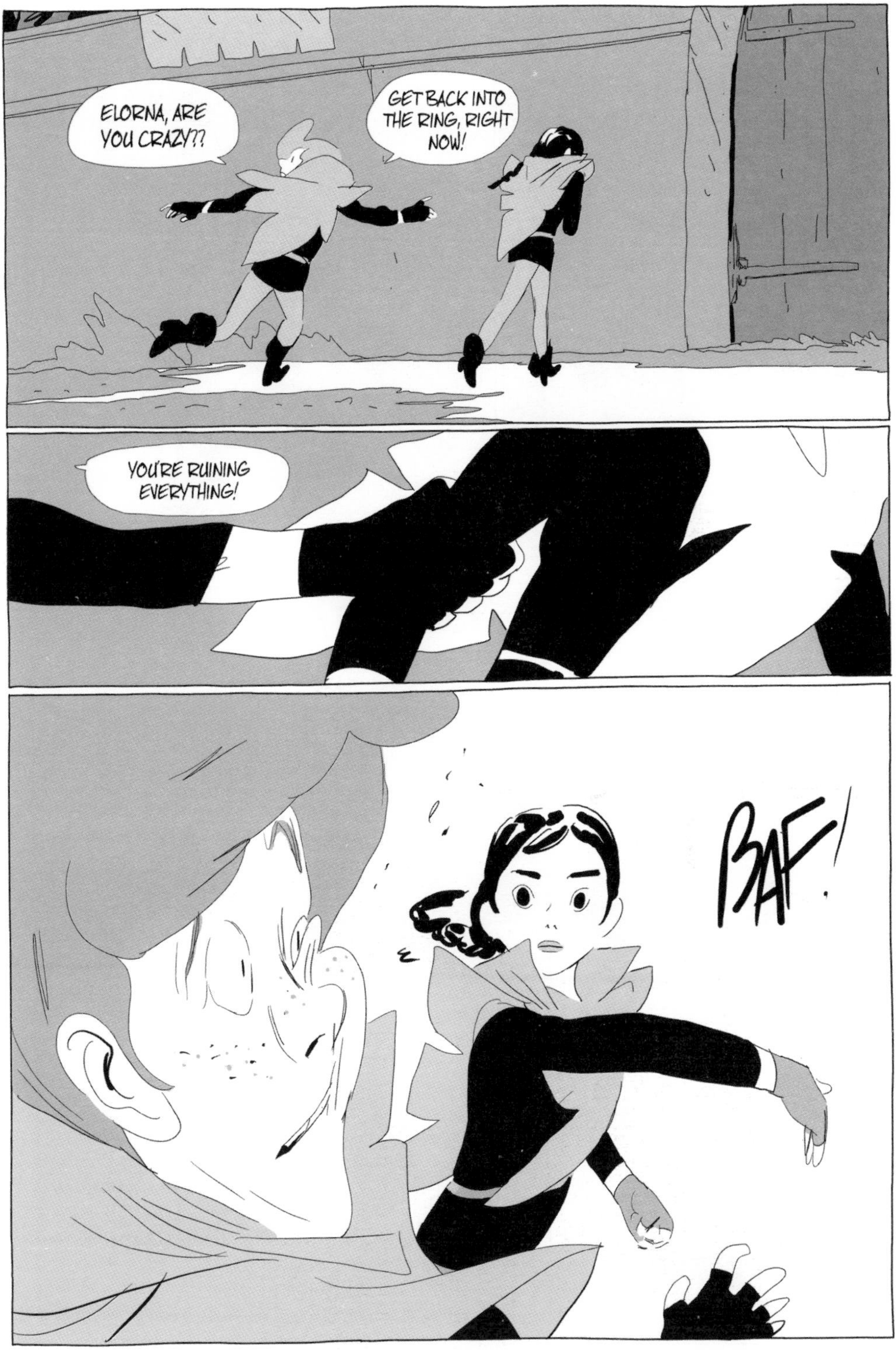
ELORNA, ARE YOU CRAZY??
GET BACK INTO THE RING, RIGHT NOW!
YOU'RE RUINING EVERYTHING!
BAF!

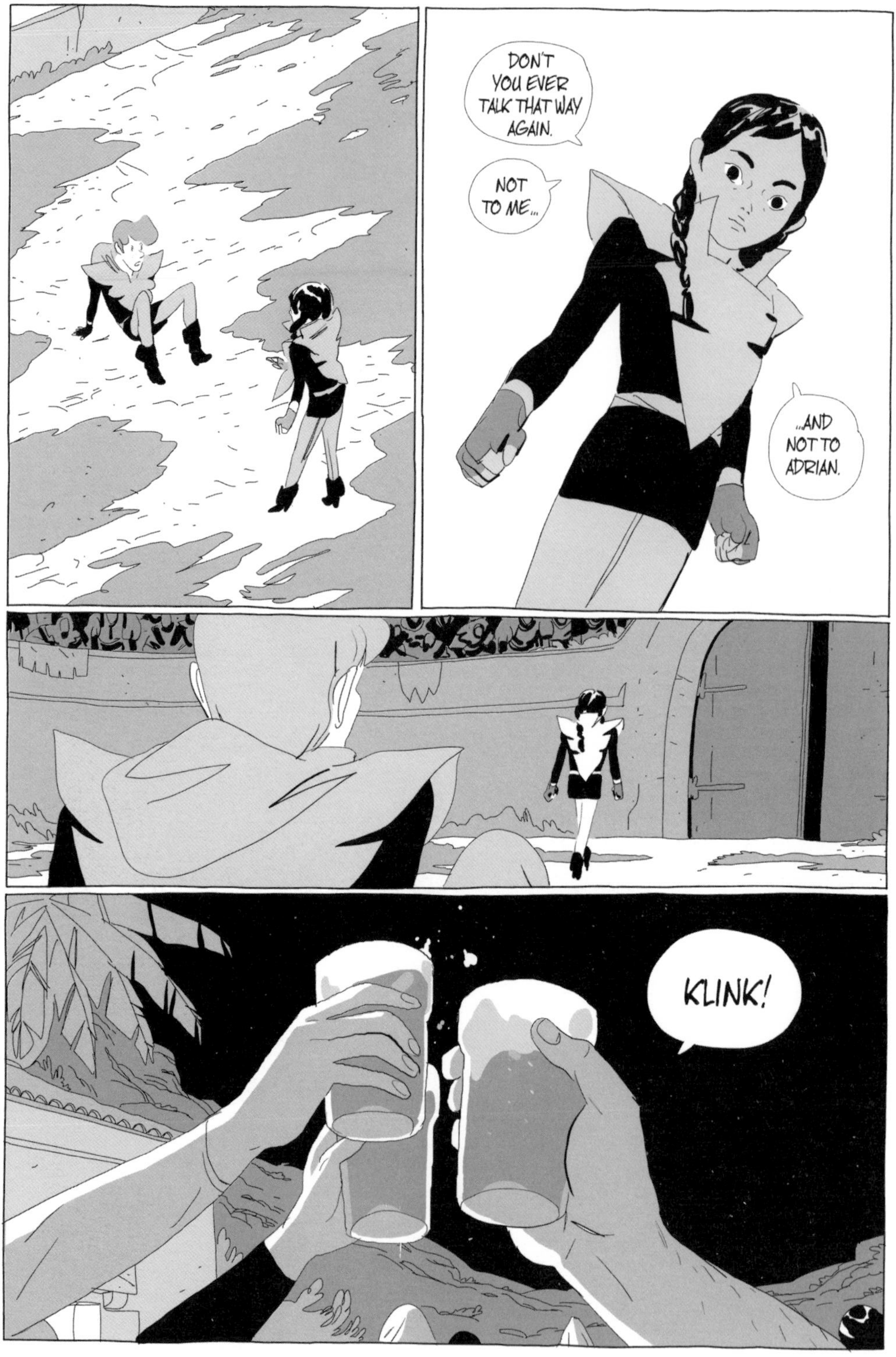
DON'T YOU EVER TALK THAT WAY AGAIN.
NOT TO ME...
...AND NOT TO ADRIAN.
KLINK!

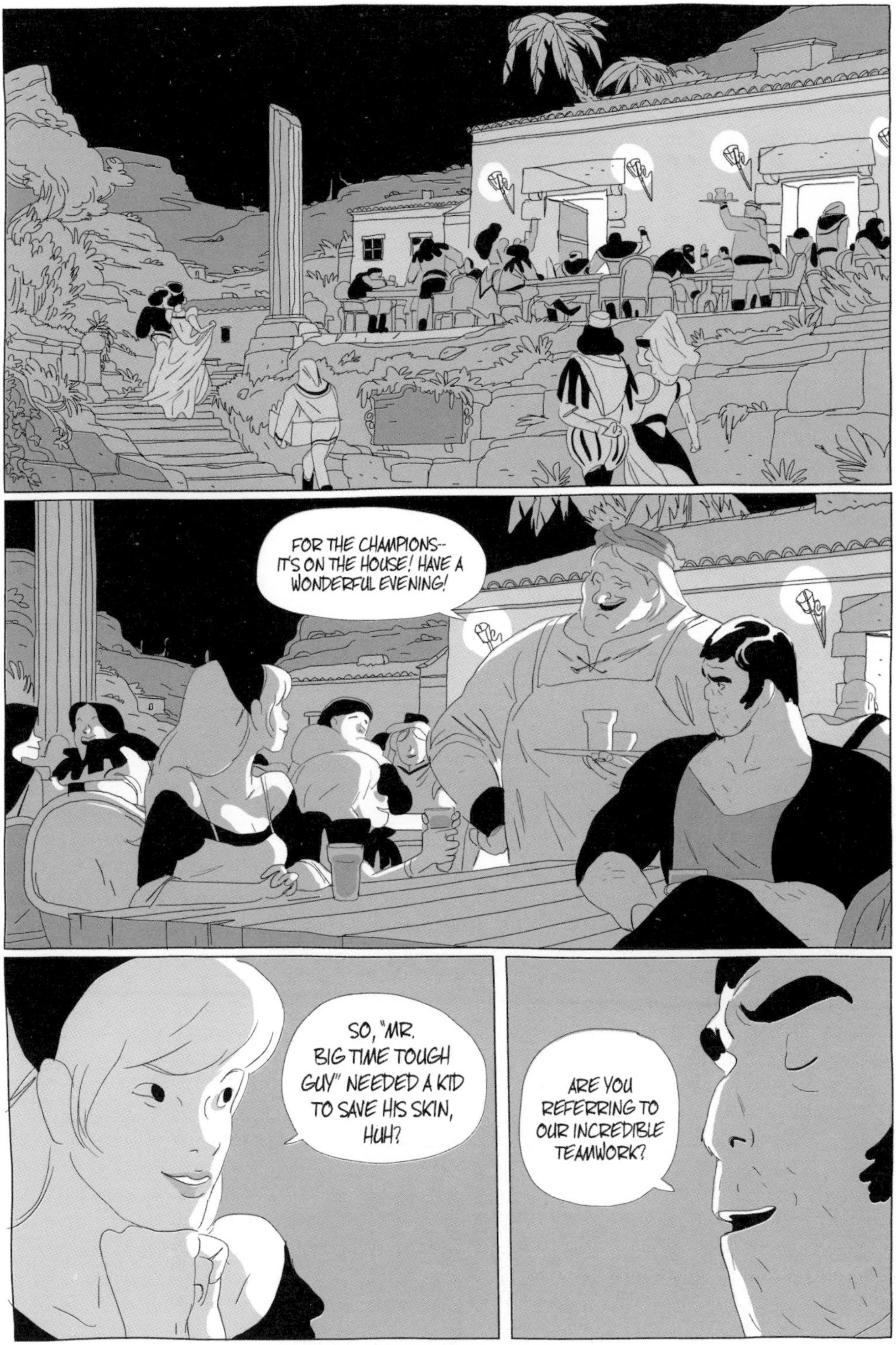
FOR THE CHAMPIONS-- IT'S ON THE HOUSE! HAVE A WONDERFUL EVENING!
SO, "MR. BIG TIME TOUGH GUY" NEEDED A KID TO SAVE HIS SKIN, HUH?
ARE YOU REFERRING TO OUR INCREDIBLE TEAMWORK?

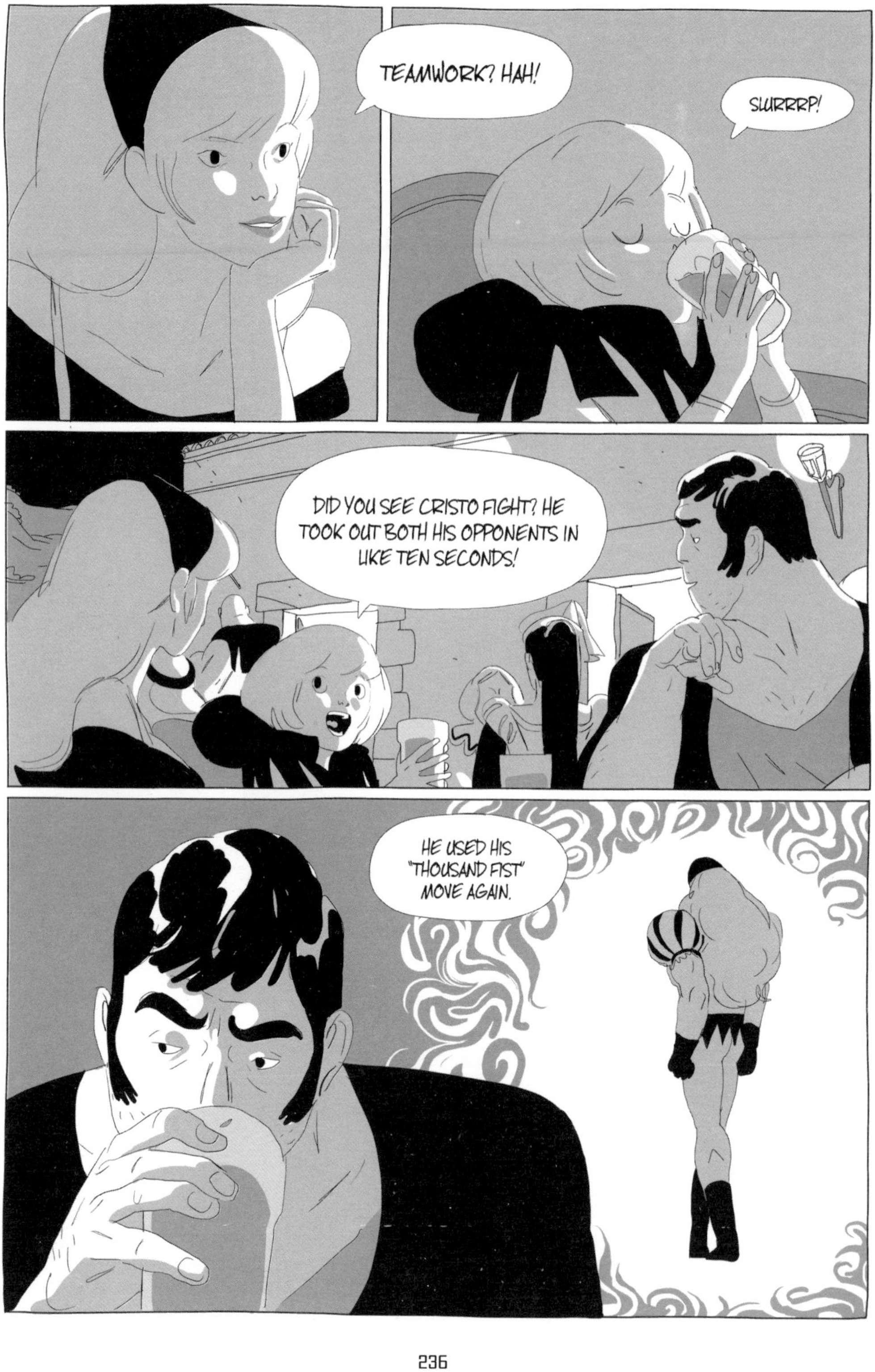
TEAMWORK? HAH!
SLURRRP!
DID YOU SEE CRISTO FIGHT? HE TOOK OUT BOTH HIS OPPONENTS IN LIKE TEN SECONDS!
HE USED HIS "THOUSAND FIST" MOVE AGAIN.

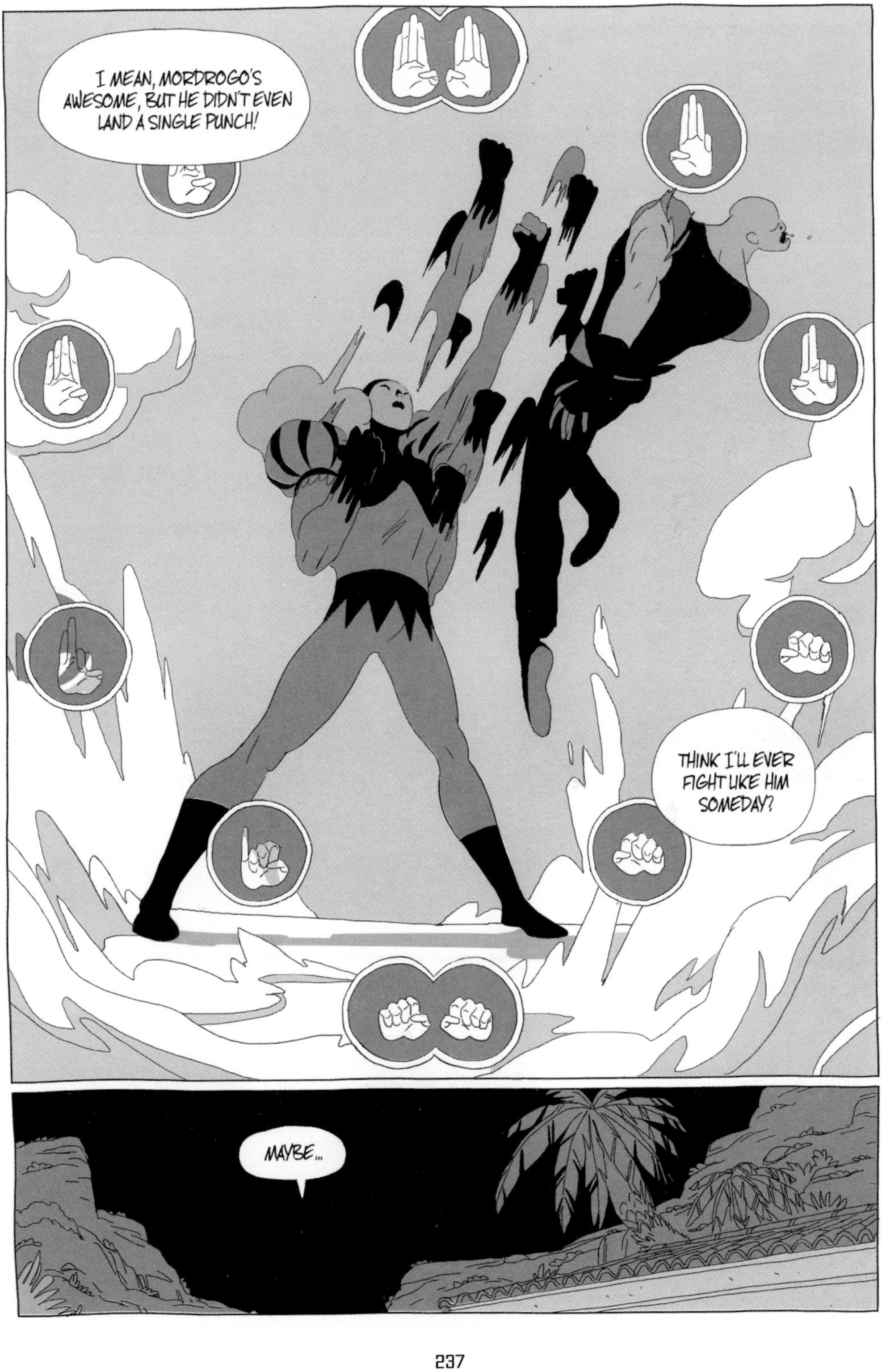
I MEAN, MORDROGO'S AWESOME, BUT HE DIDN'T EVEN LAND A SINGLE PUNCH!
THINK I'LL EVER FIGHT LIKE HIM SOMEDAY?
MAYBE...

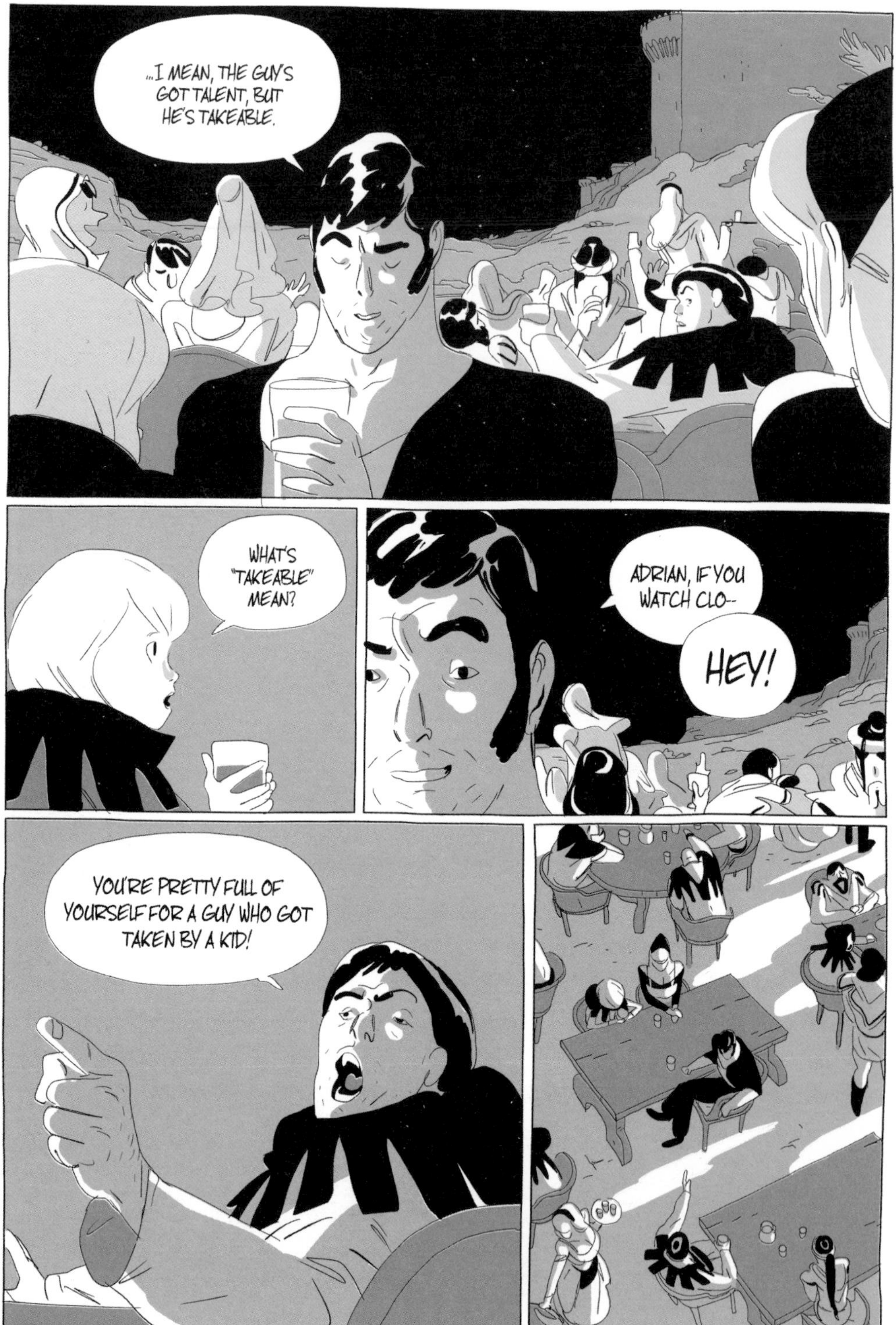
...I MEAN, THE GUY'S GOT TALENT, BUT HE'S TAKEABLE.
WHAT'S "TAKEABLE" MEAN?
ADRIAN, IF YOU WATCH CLO--
HEY!
YOU'RE PRETTY FULL OF YOURSELF FOR A GUY WHO GOT TAKEN BY A KID!

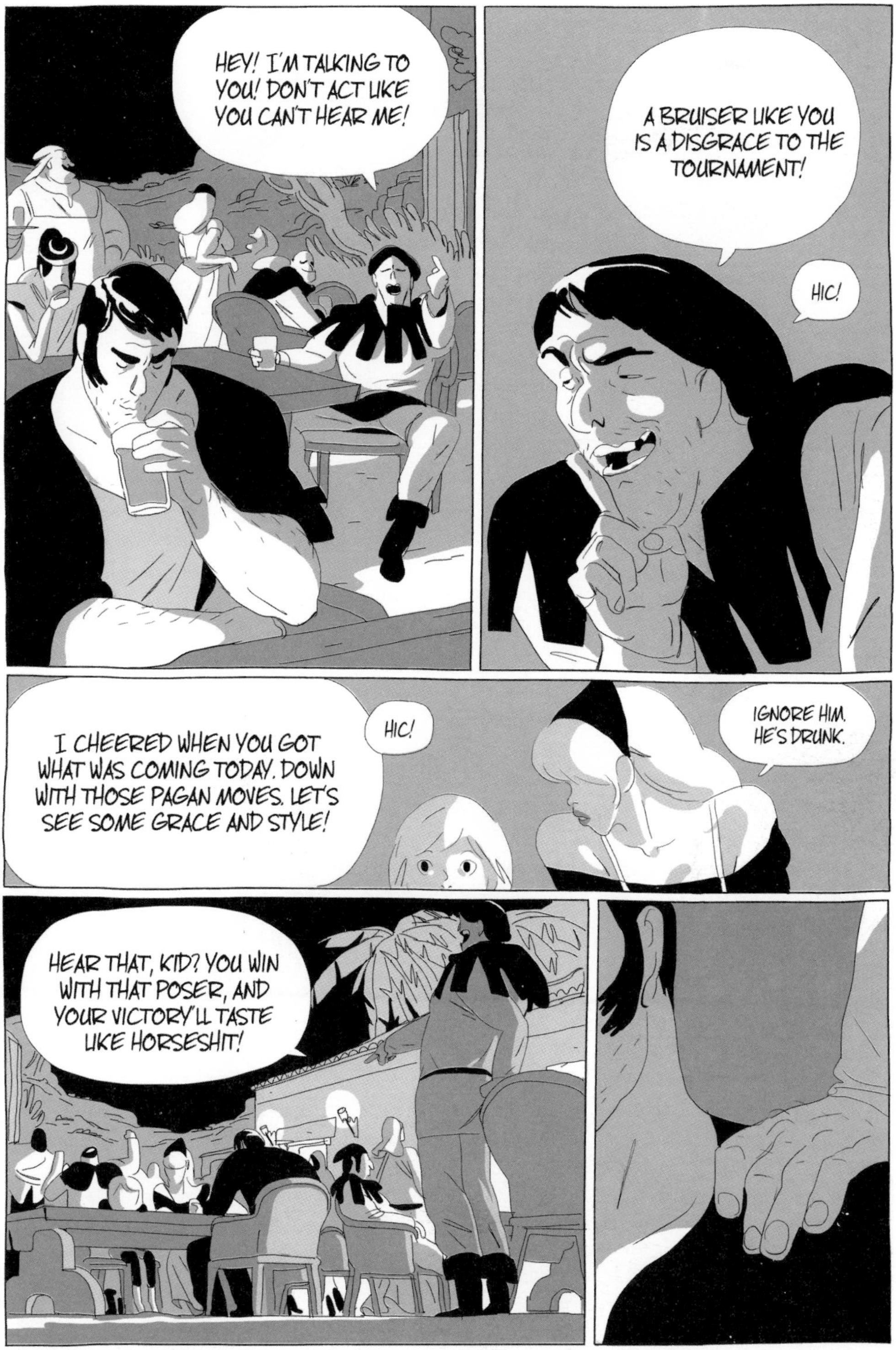
HEY! I'M TALKING TO YOU! DON'T ACT LIKE YOU CAN'T HEAR ME!
A BRUISER LIKE YOU IS A DISGRACE TO THE TOURNAMENT!
HIC!
I CHEERED WHEN YOU GOT WHAT WAS COMING TODAY. DOWN WITH THOSE PAGAN MOVES. LET'S SEE SOME GRACE AND STYLE!
HIC!
IGNORE HIM. HE'S DRUNK.
HEAR THAT, KID? YOU WIN WITH THAT POSER, AND YOUR VICTORY'LL TASTE LIKE HORSESHIT!

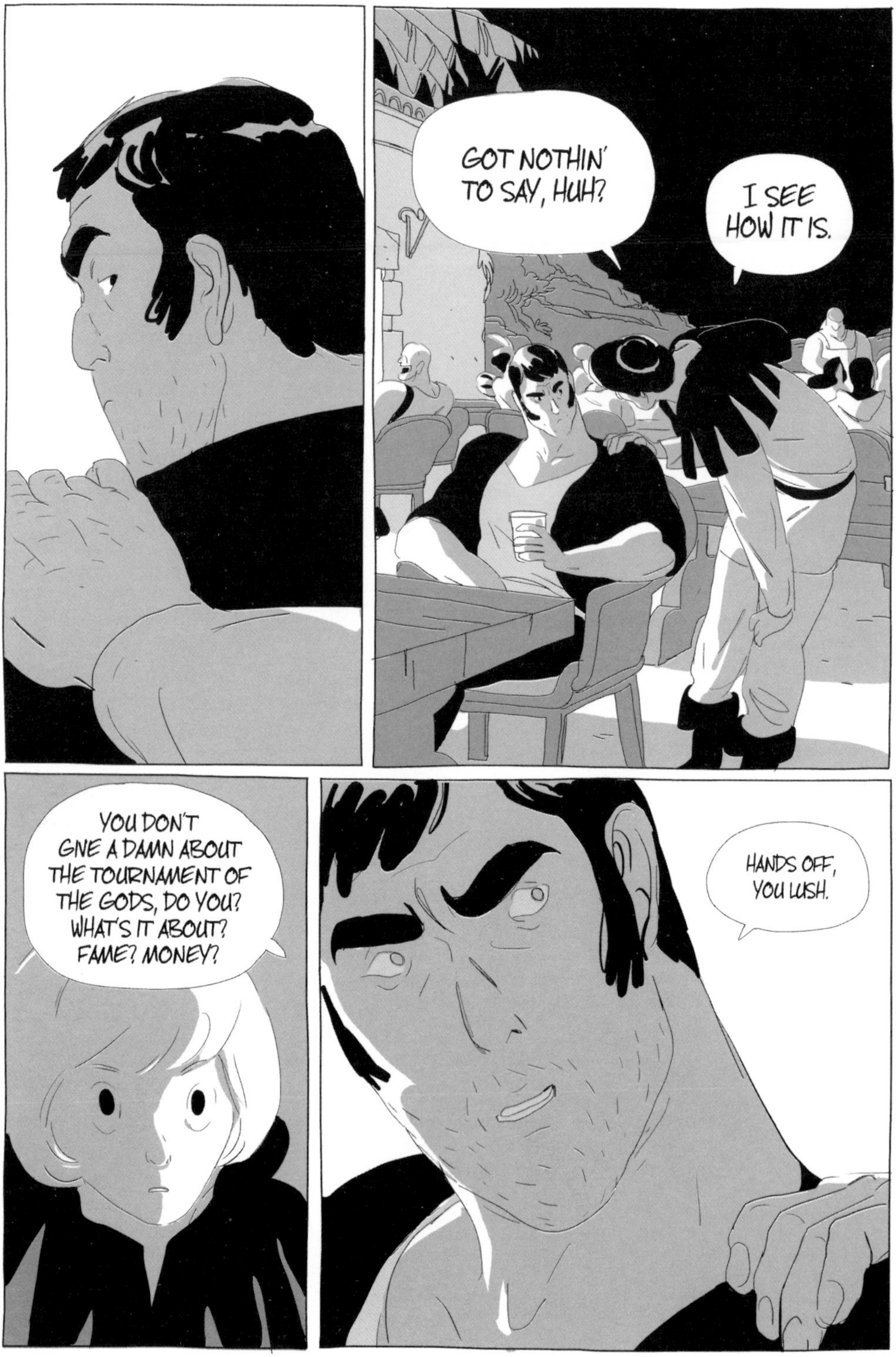
GOT NOTHIN' TO SAY, HUH?
I SEE HOW IT IS.
YOU DON'T GIVE A DAMN ABOUT THE TOURNAMENT OF THE GODS, DO YOU? WHAT'S IT ABOUT? FAME? MONEY?
HANDS OFF, YOU LUSH.

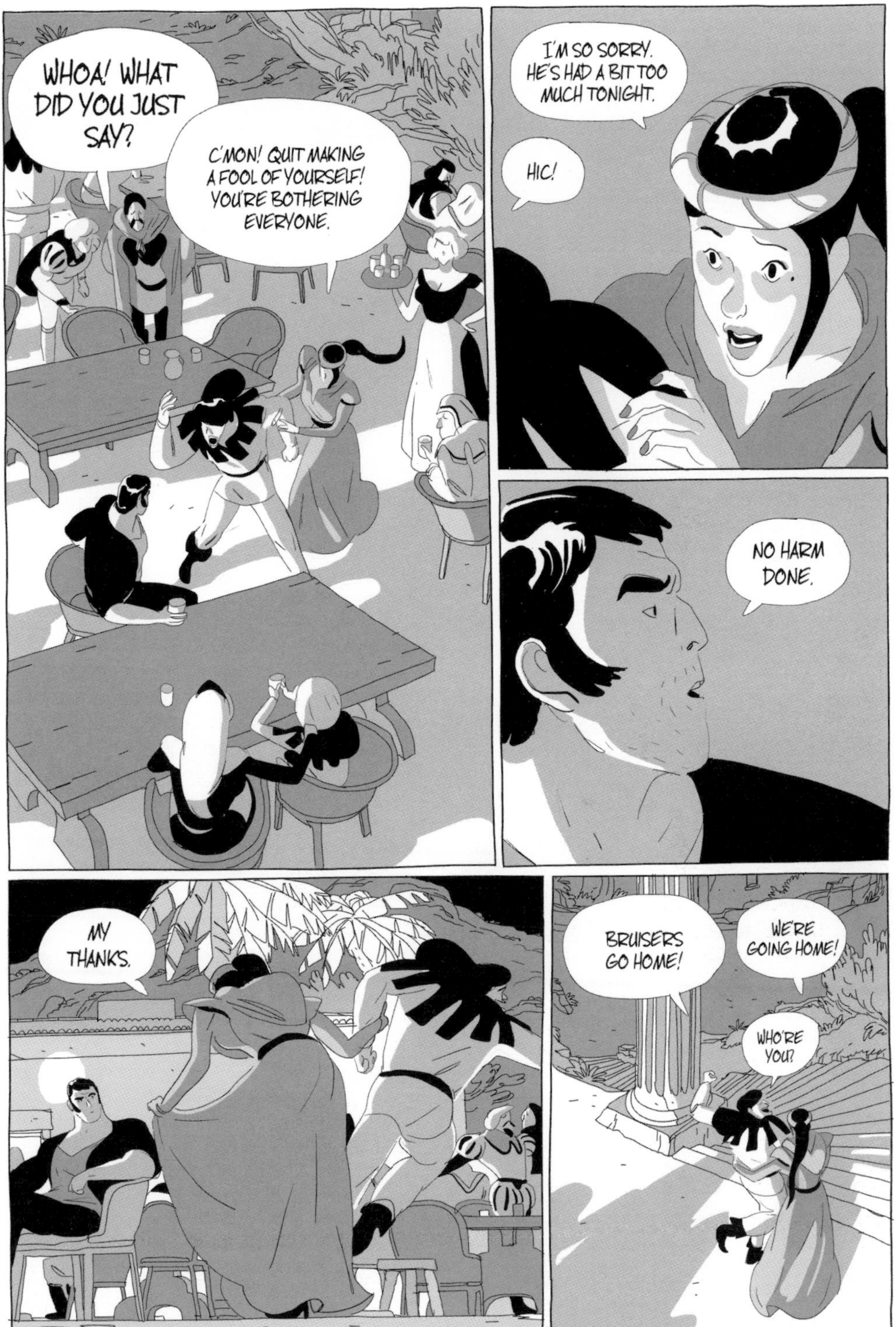
WHOA! WHAT DID YOU JUST SAY?
C'MON! QUIT MAKING A FOOL OF YOURSELF! YOU'RE BOTHERING EVERYONE.
I'M SO SORRY. HE'S HAD A BIT TOO MUCH TONIGHT.
HIC!
NO HARM DONE.
MY THANKS.
BRUISERS GO HOME!
WE'RE GOING HOME!
WHO'RE YOU?

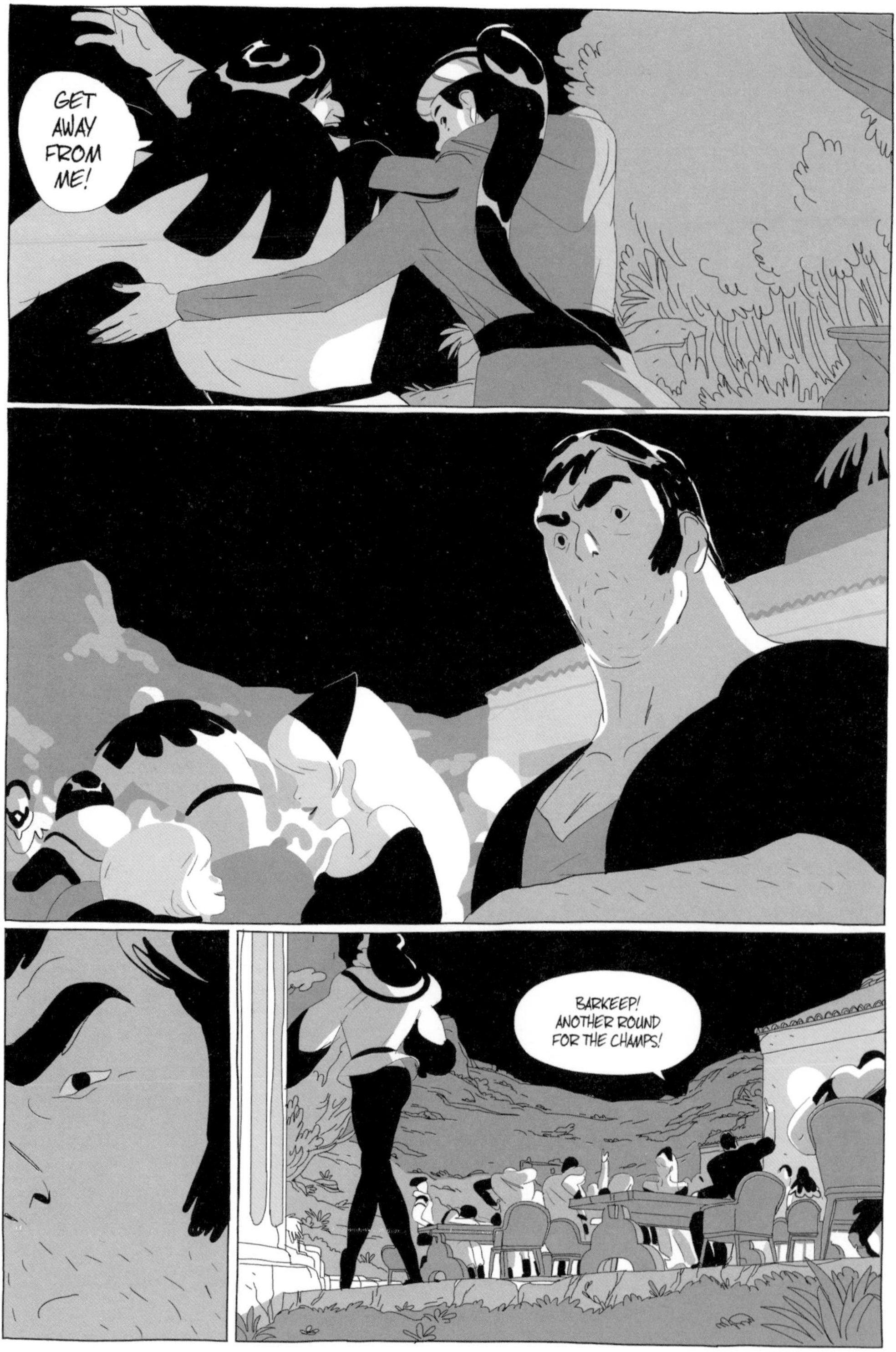
GET AWAY FROM ME!
BARKEEP! ANOTHER ROUND FOR THE CHAMPS!

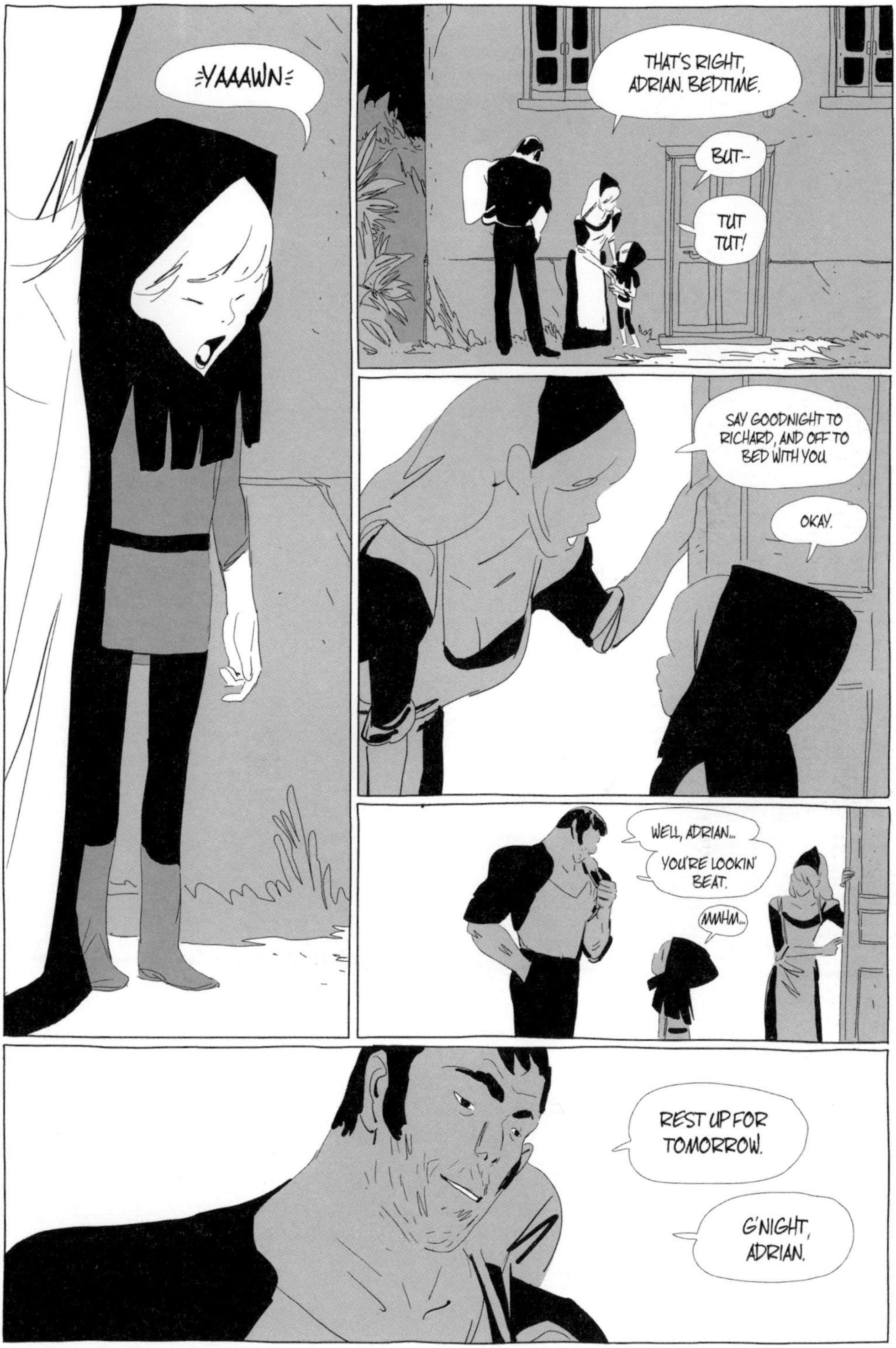
YAAAWN
THAT'S RIGHT, ADRIAN. BEDTIME.
BUT--
TUT TUT!
SAY GOODNIGHT TO RICHARD, AND OFF TO BED WITH YOU.
OKAY.
WELL, ADRIAN...
YOU'RE LOOKIN' BEAT.
MMHM...
REST UP FOR TOMORROW.
G'NIGHT, ADRIAN.

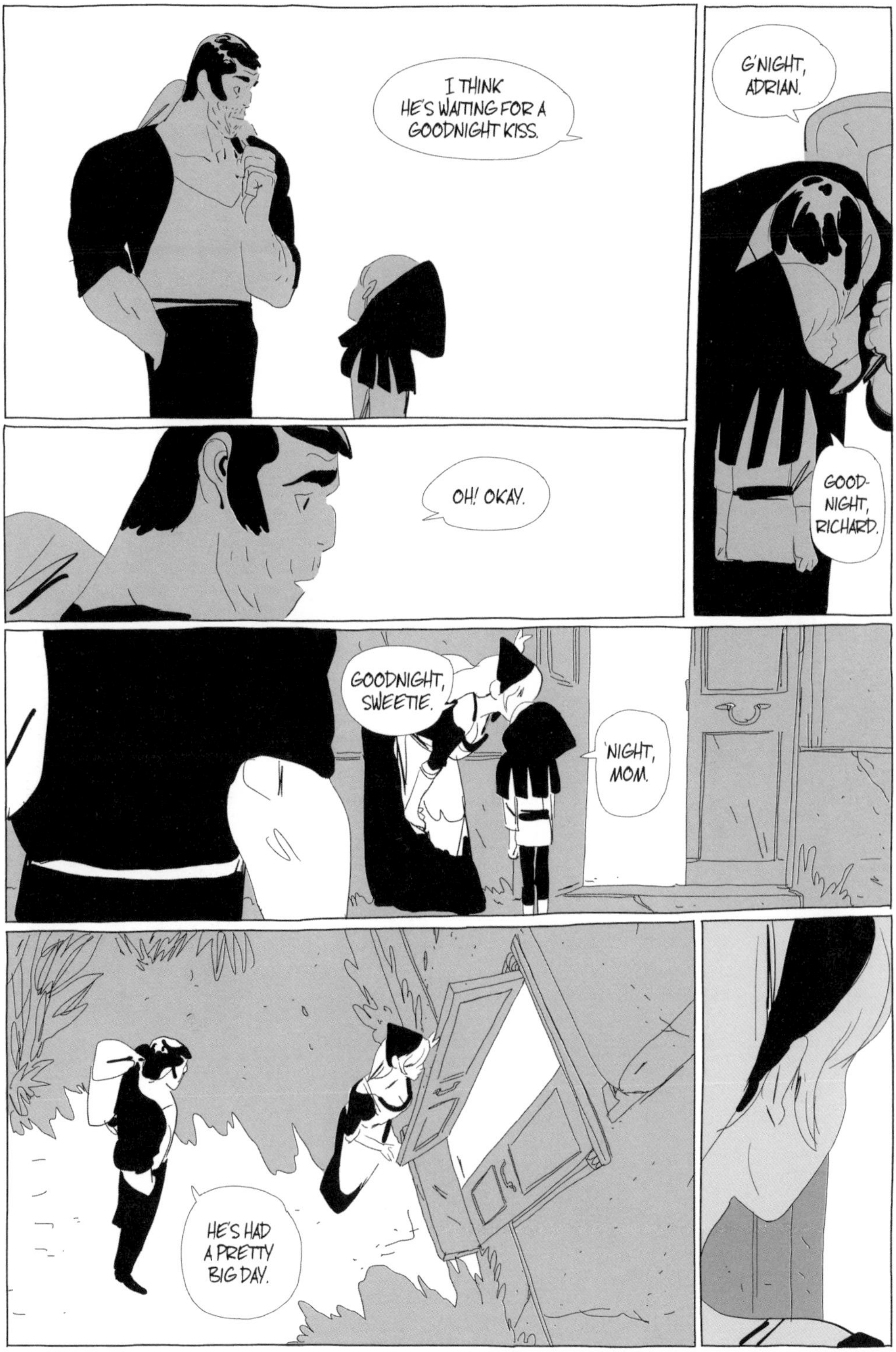
I THINK HE'S WAITING FOR A GOODNIGHT KISS.
OH! OKAY.
G'NIGHT, ADRIAN.
GOOD-NIGHT, RICHARD.
GOODNIGHT, SWEETIE.
'NIGHT, MOM.
HE'S HAD A PRETTY BIG DAY.

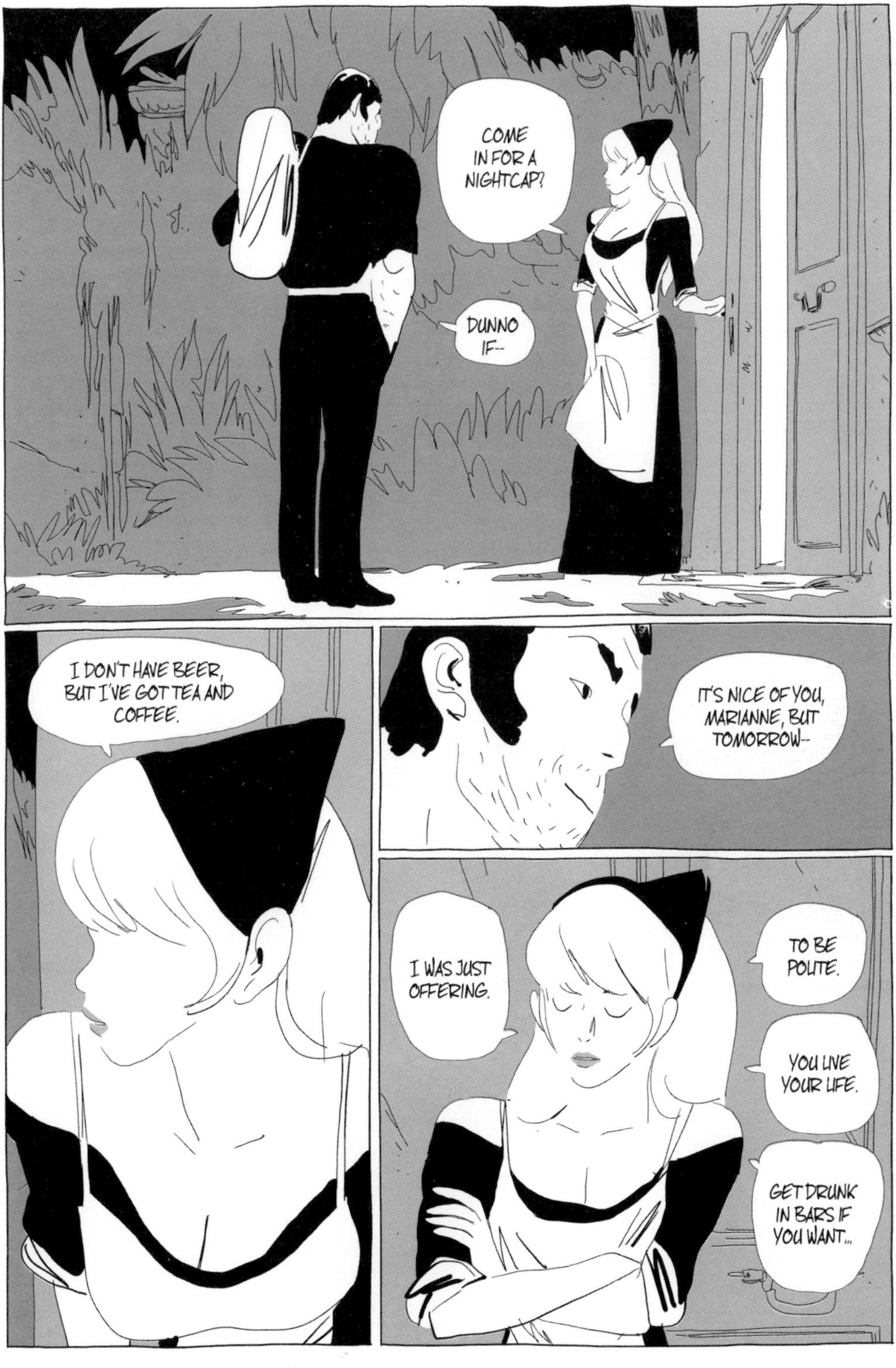

COME IN FOR A NIGHTCAP?
DUNNO IF--
I DON'T HAVE BEER, BUT I'VE GOT TEA AND COFFEE.
IT'S NICE OF YOU, MARIANNE, BUT TOMORROW--
I WAS JUST OFFERING.
TO BE POLITE.
YOU LIVE YOUR LIFE.
GET DRUNK IN BARS IF YOU WANT...

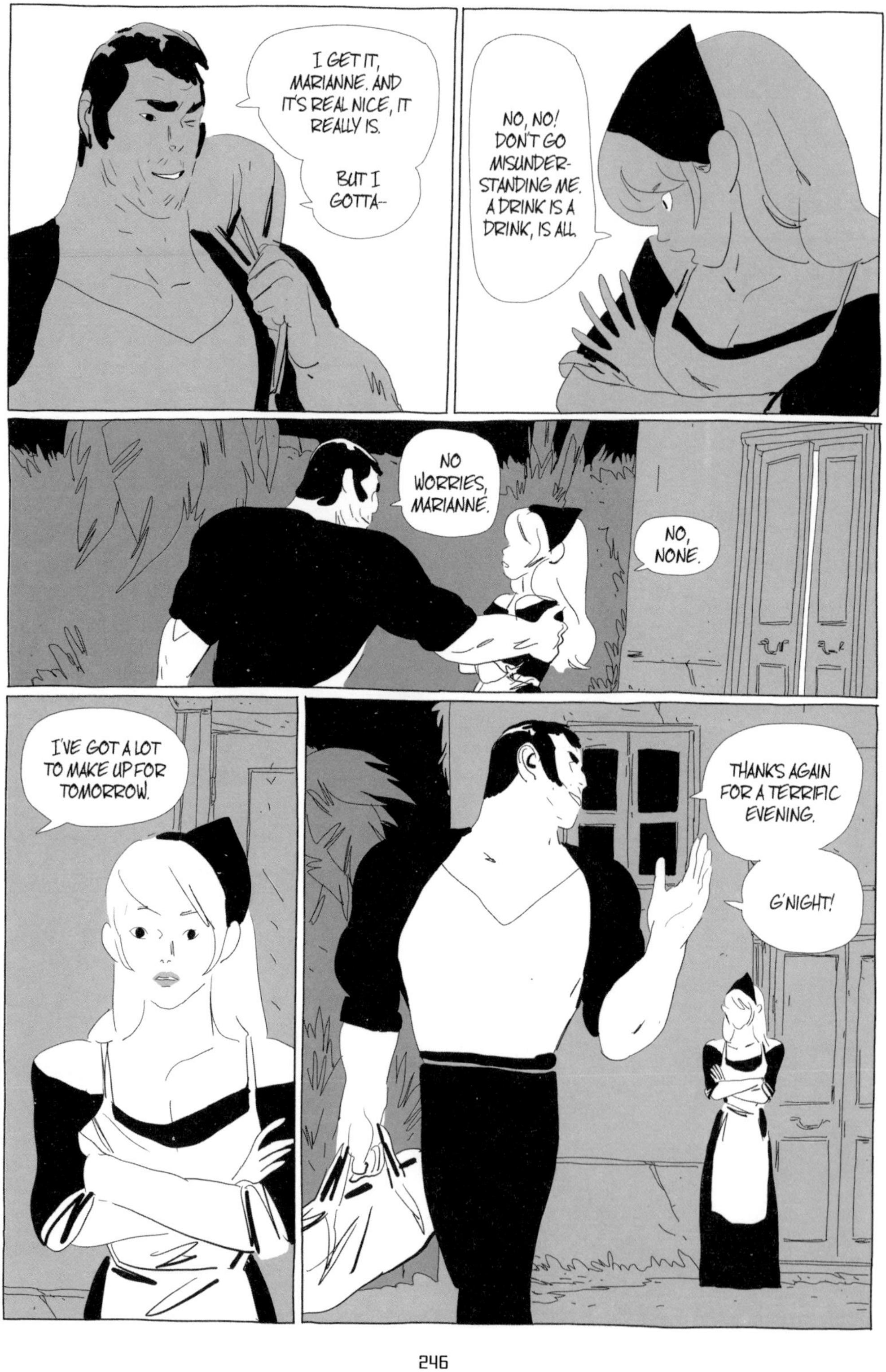
I GET IT, MARIANNE. AND IT'S REAL NICE, IT REALLY IS.
BUT I GOTTA--
NO, NO! DON'T GO MISUNDER-STANDING ME. A DRINK IS A DRINK, IS ALL.
NO WORRIES, MARIANNE.
NO, NONE.
I'VE GOT A LOT TO MAKE UP FOR TOMORROW.
THANKS AGAIN FOR A TERRIFIC EVENING.
G'NIGHT!

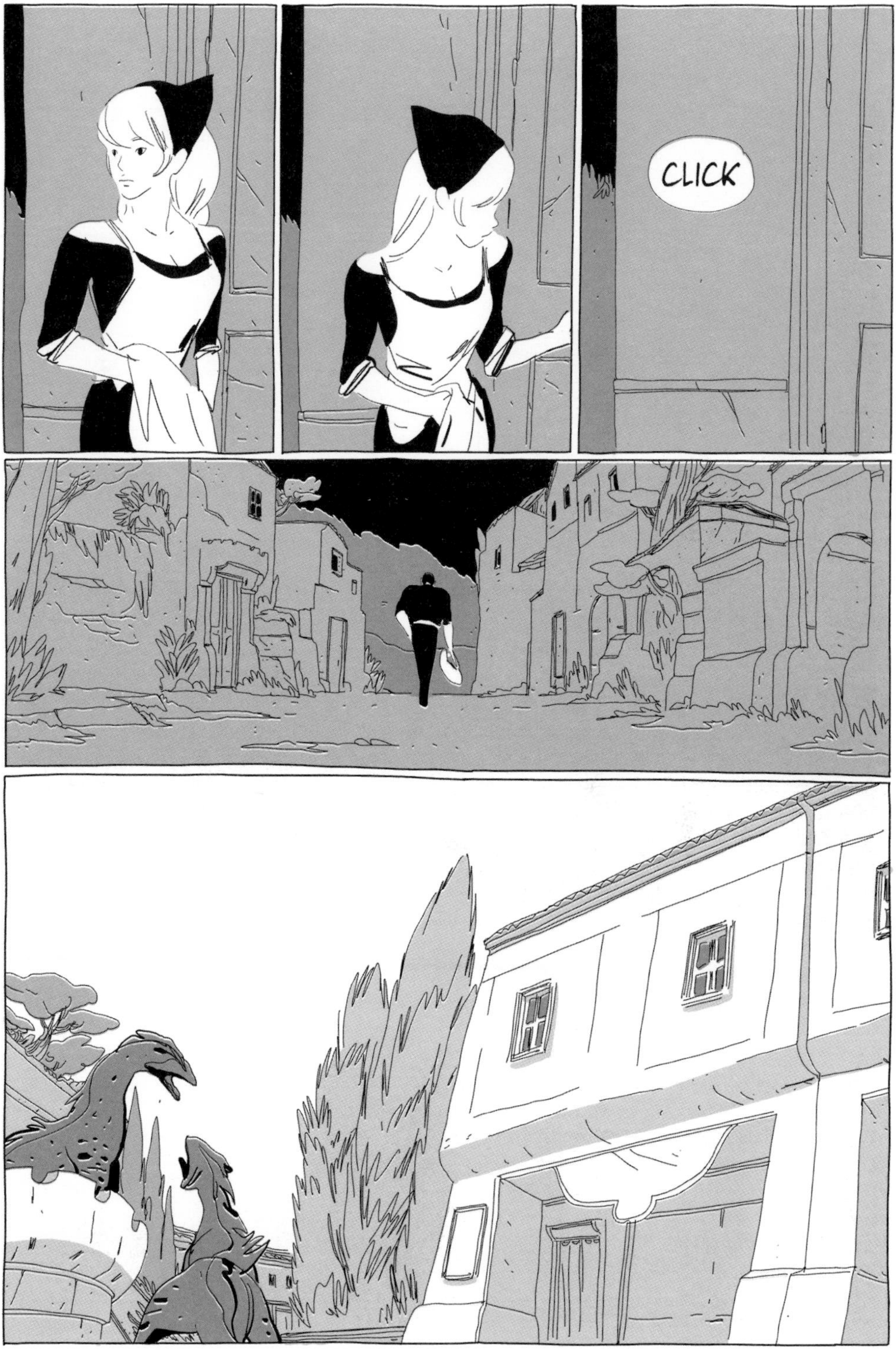
CLICK

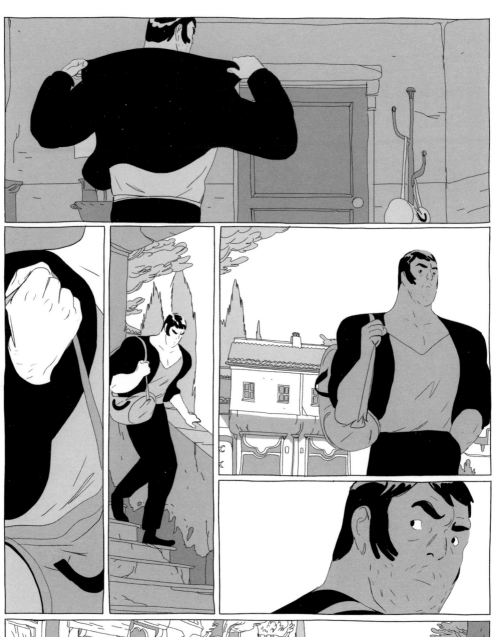

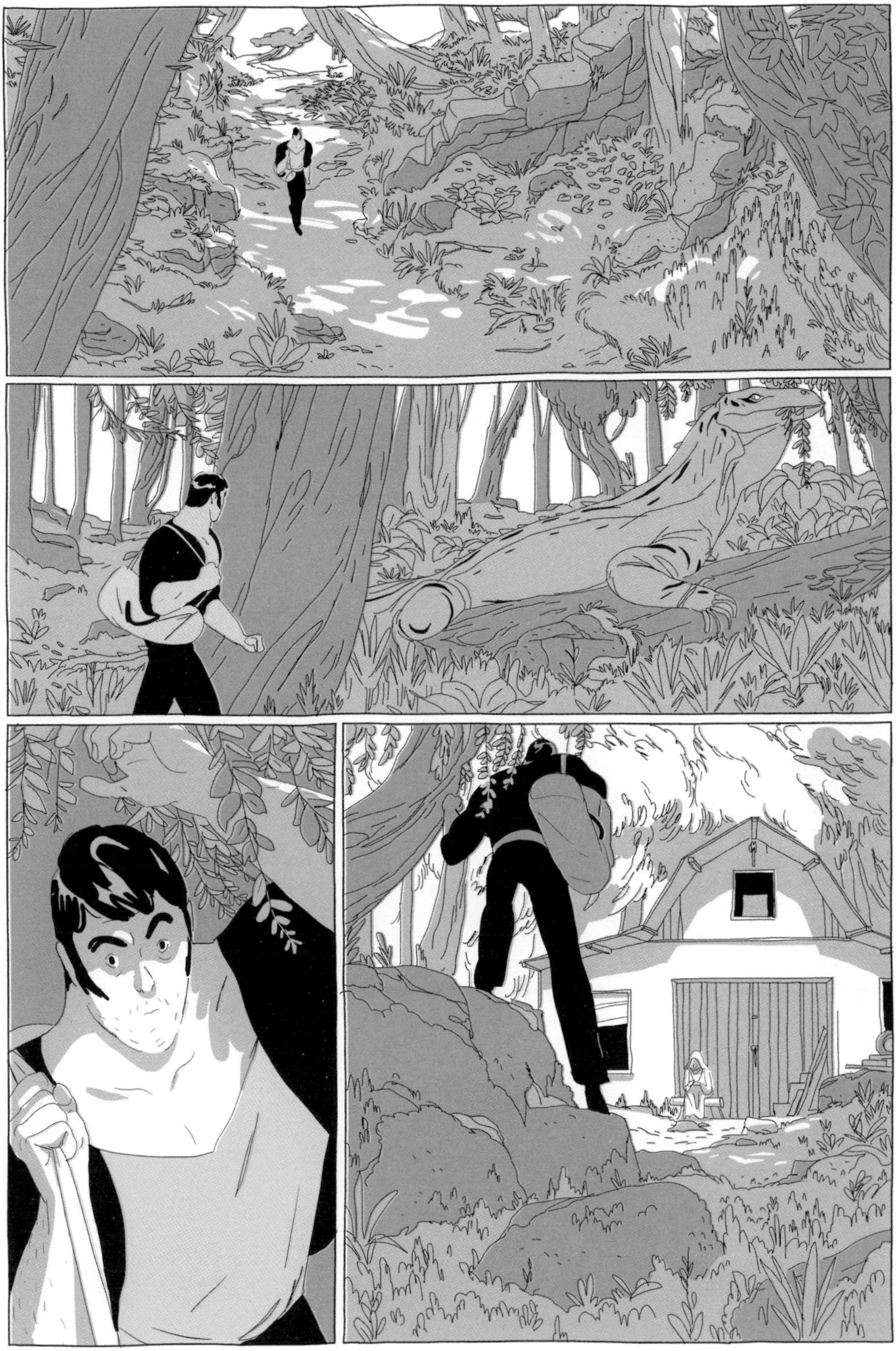

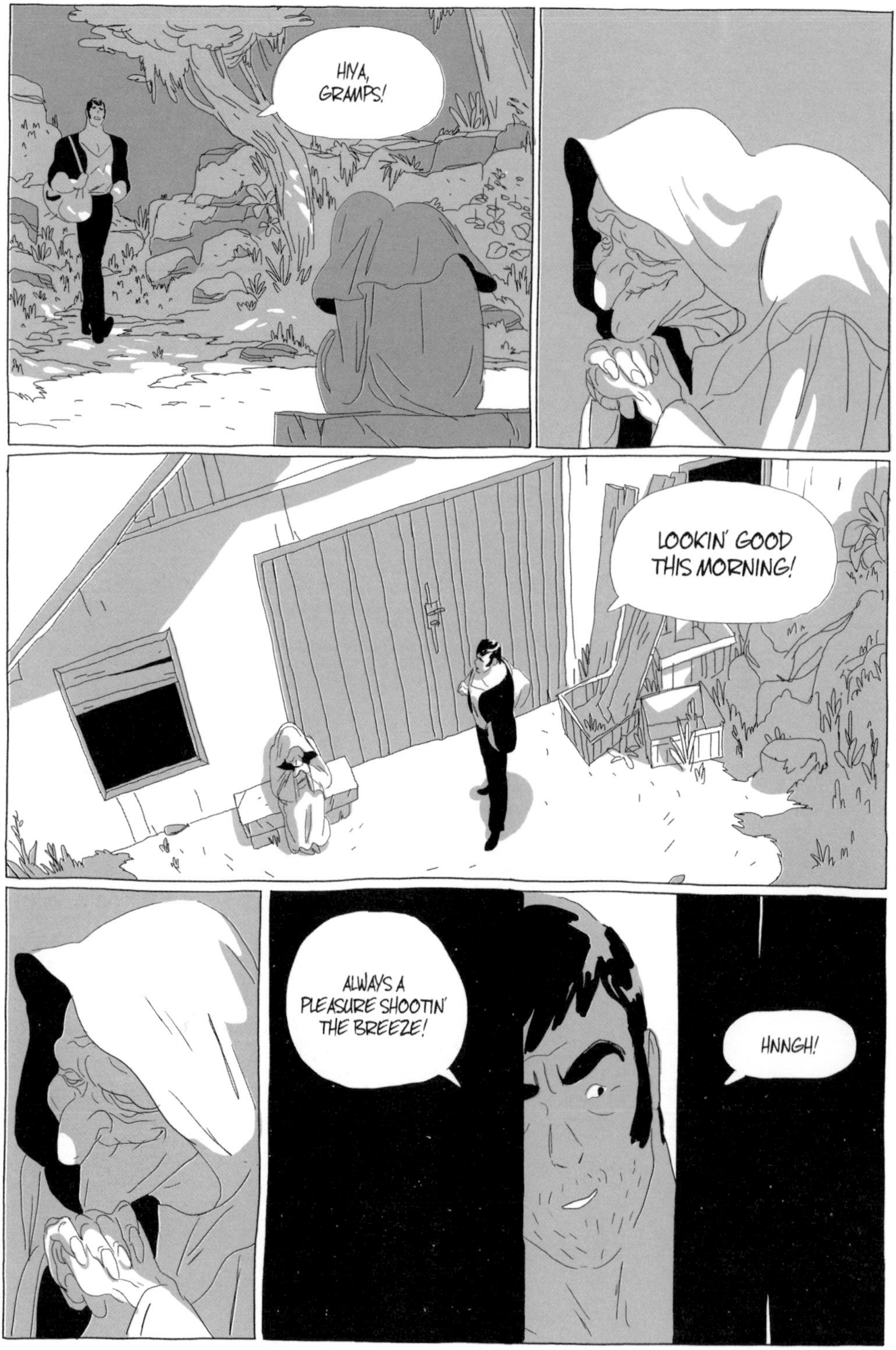
HIYA, GRAMPS!
LOOKIN' GOOD THIS MORNING!
ALWAYS A PLEASURE SHOOTIN' THE BREEZE!
HNNGH!

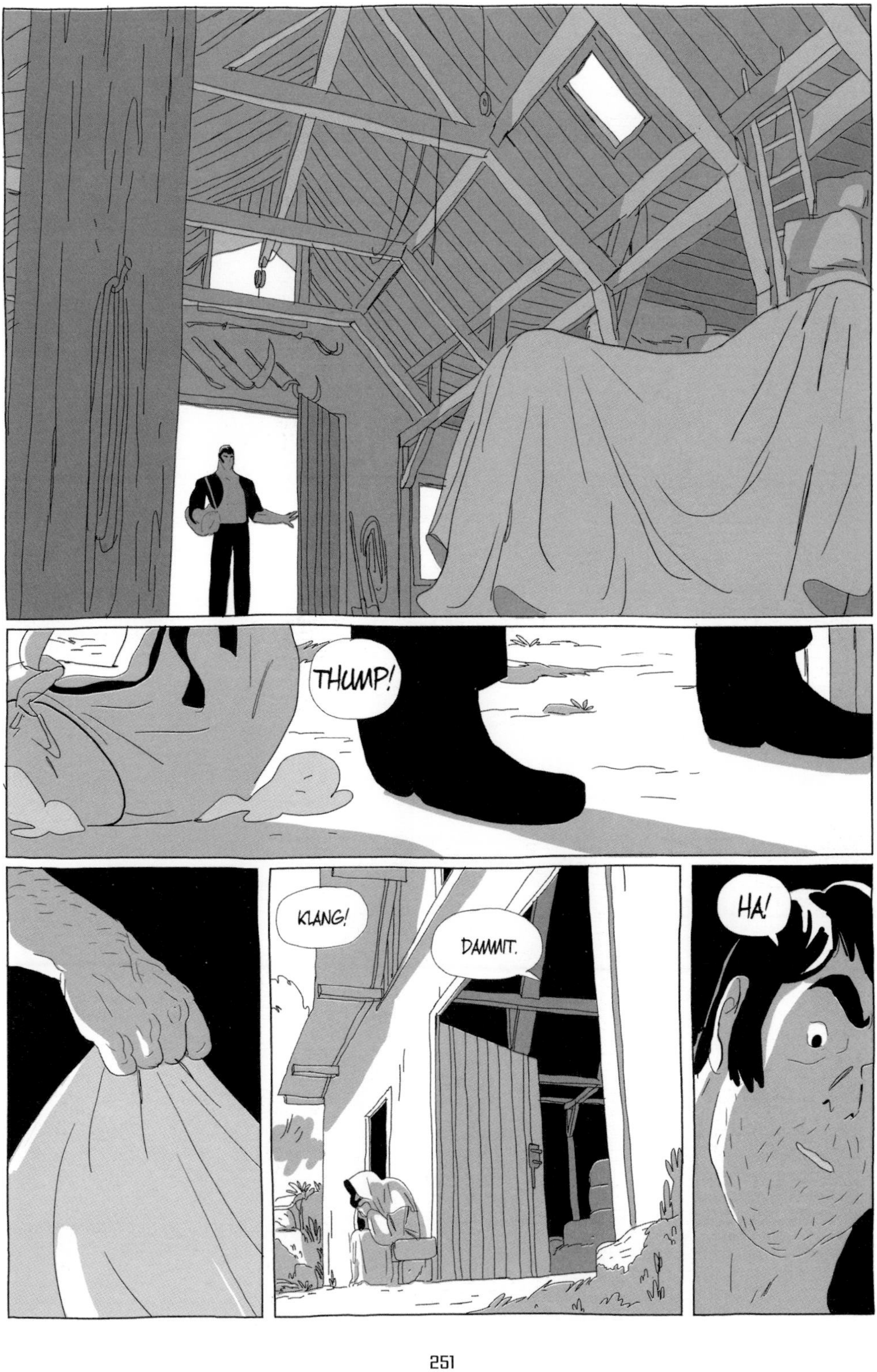
THUMP!
KLANG!
DAMMIT.
HA!

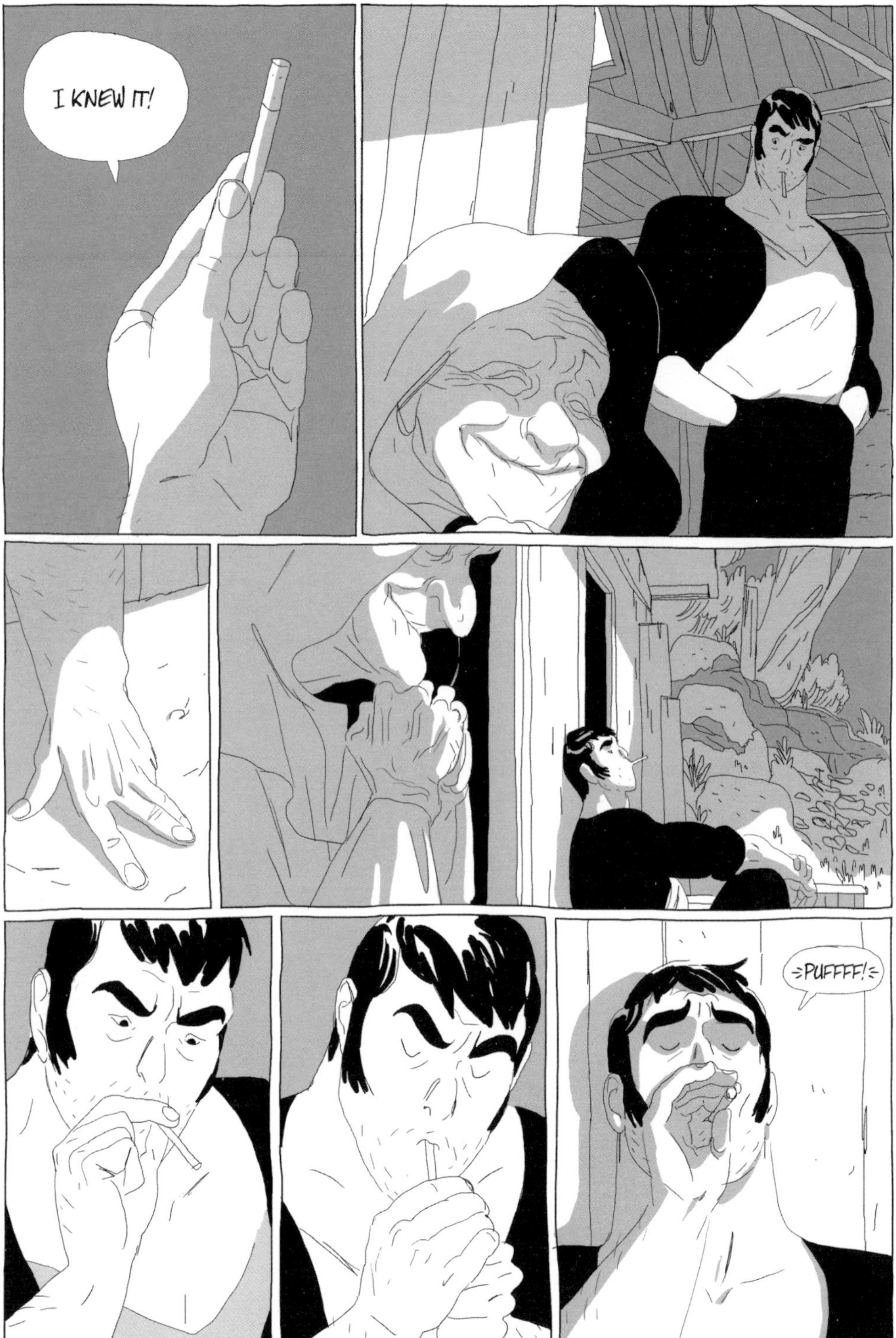
I KNEW IT!
PUFFFF!

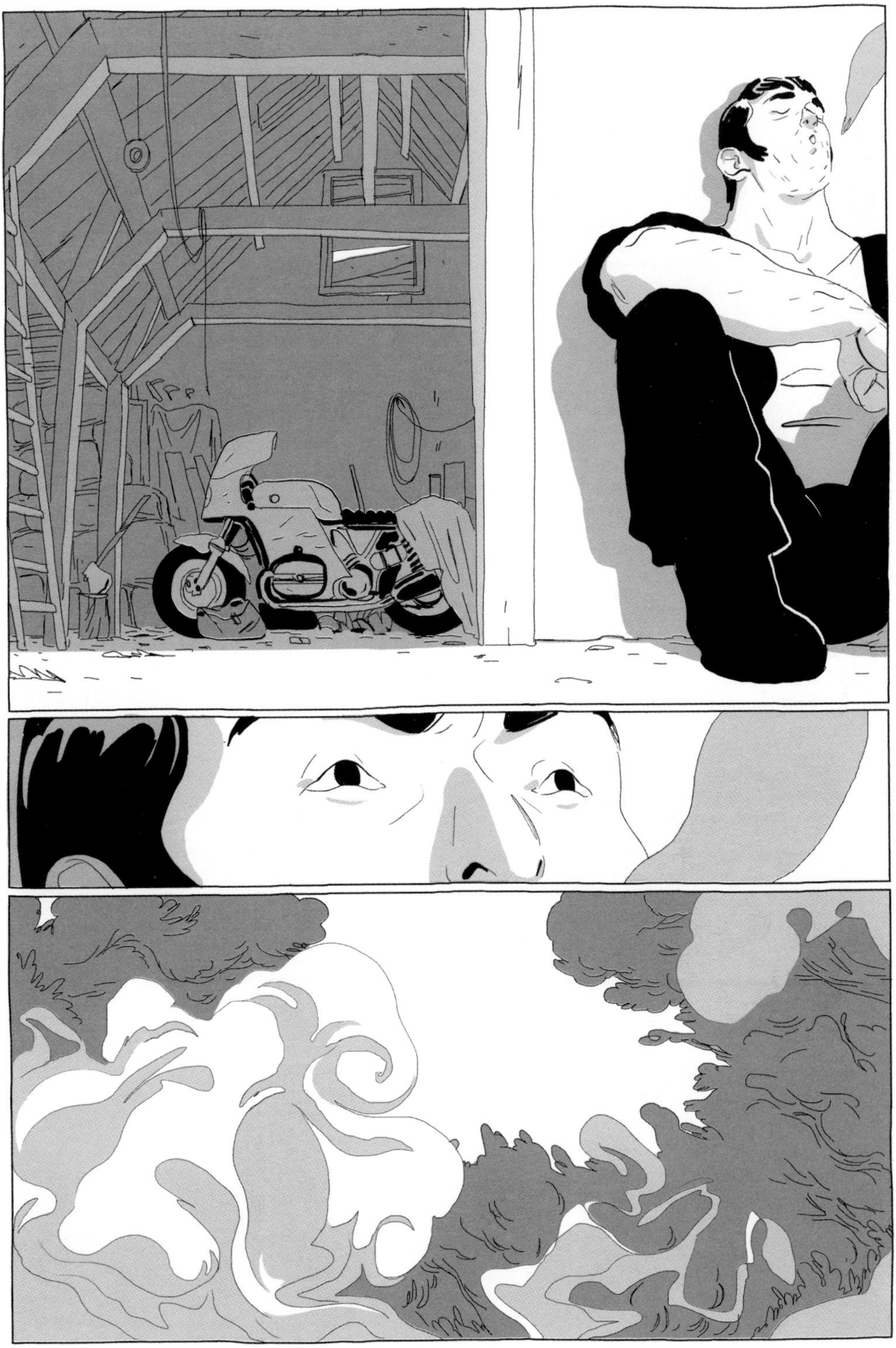

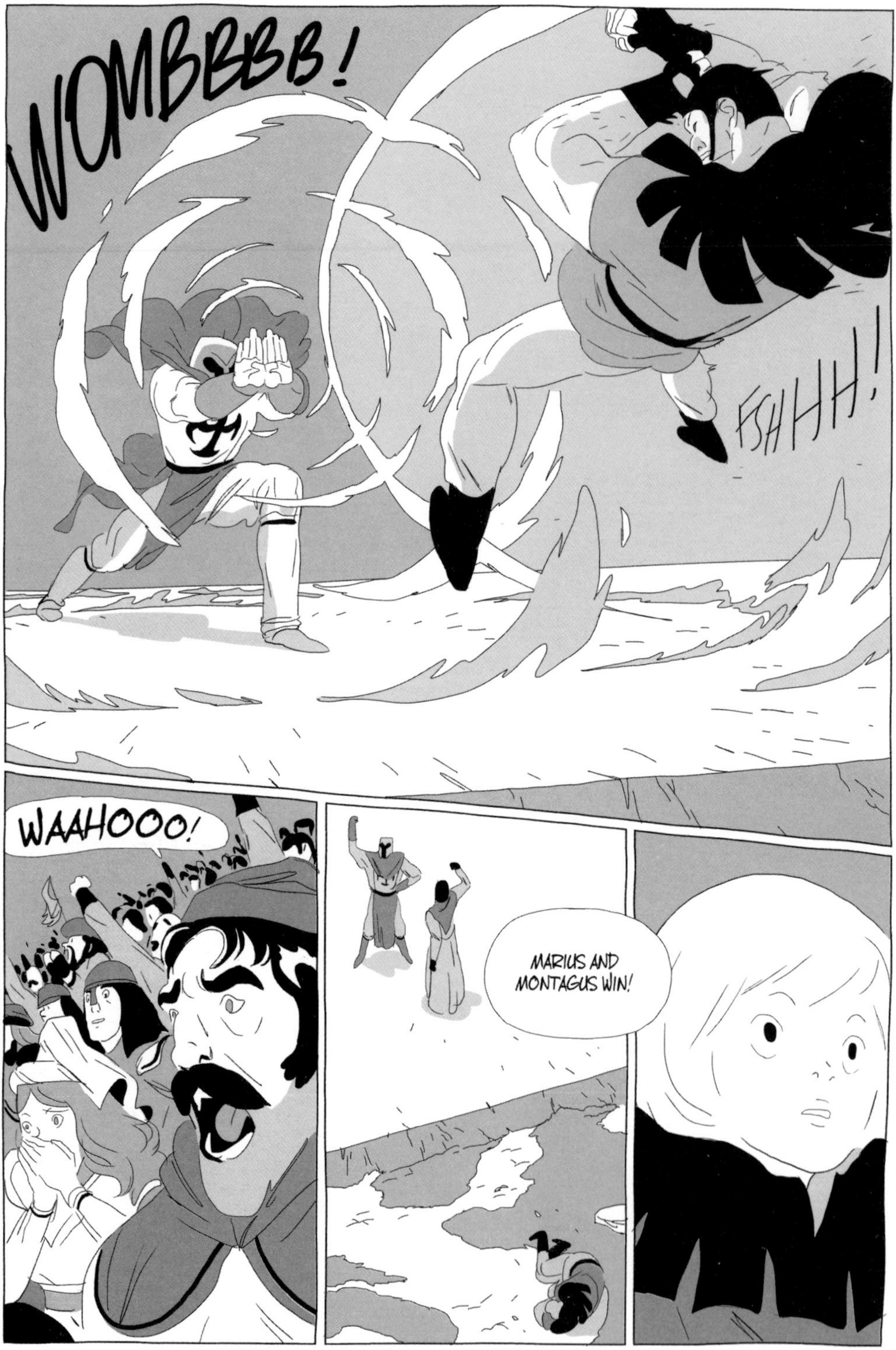
WOMBBBB!
FSHHH!
WAAHOOO!
MARIUS AND MONTAGUS WIN!

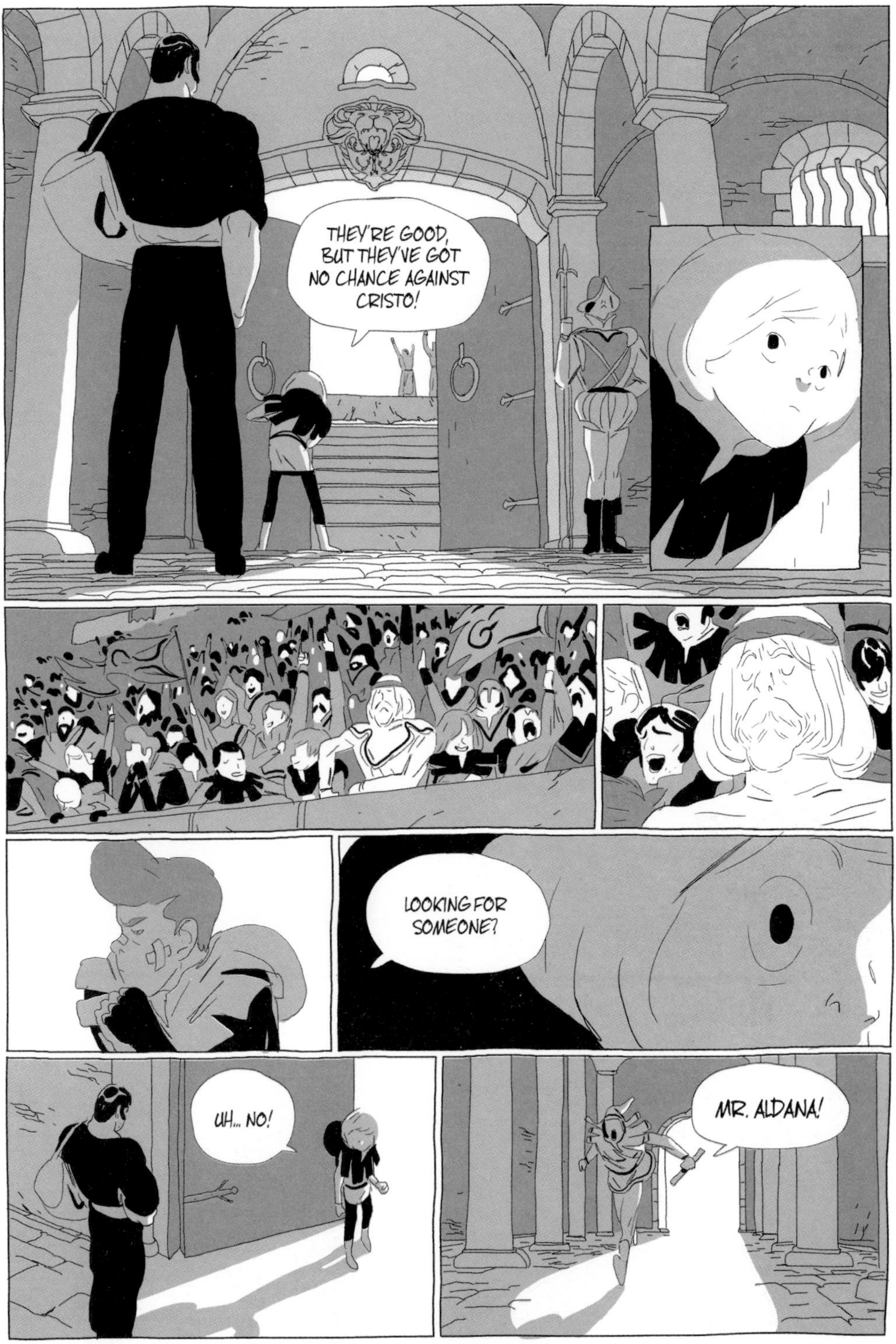
THEY'RE GOOD, BUT THEY'VE GOT NO CHANCE AGAINST CRISTO!
LOOKING FOR SOMEONE?
UH... NO!
MR. ALDANA!

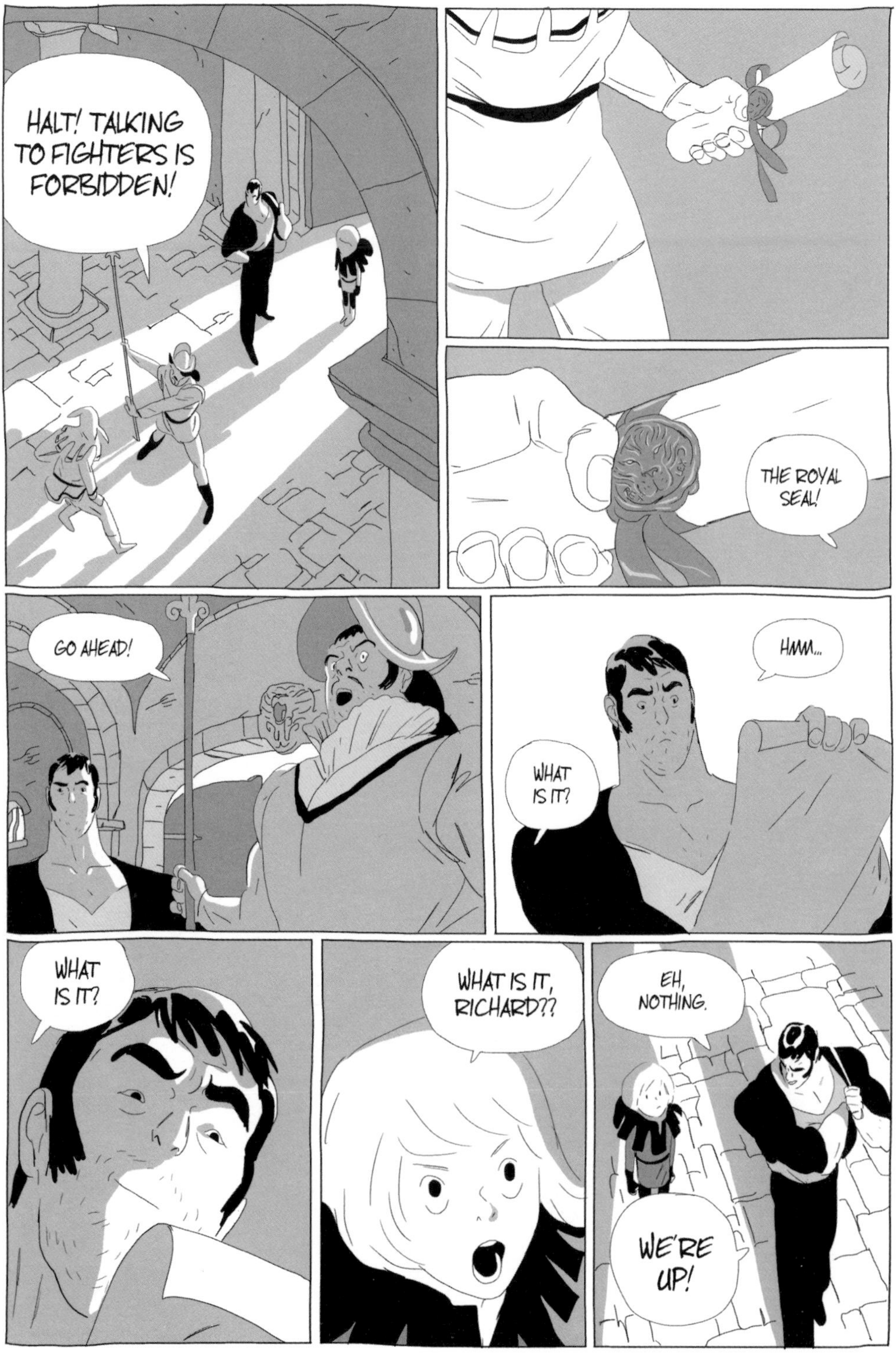
HALT! TALKING TO FIGHTERS IS FORBIDDEN!
THE ROYAL SEAL!
GO AHEAD!
HMM...
WHAT IS IT?
WHAT IS IT?
WHAT IS IT, RICHARD??
EH, NOTHING.
WE'RE UP!

LADIES AND GENTLEMEN!

PLEASE WELCOME...

HOURAAAA!

ALYSSA AND HALPES!

WHAAA

WHA AAAAA

CLAP CLAP CLAP CLAP CLAP CLAP CLAP CLAP CLAP CLAP CLAP

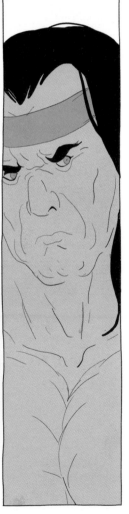

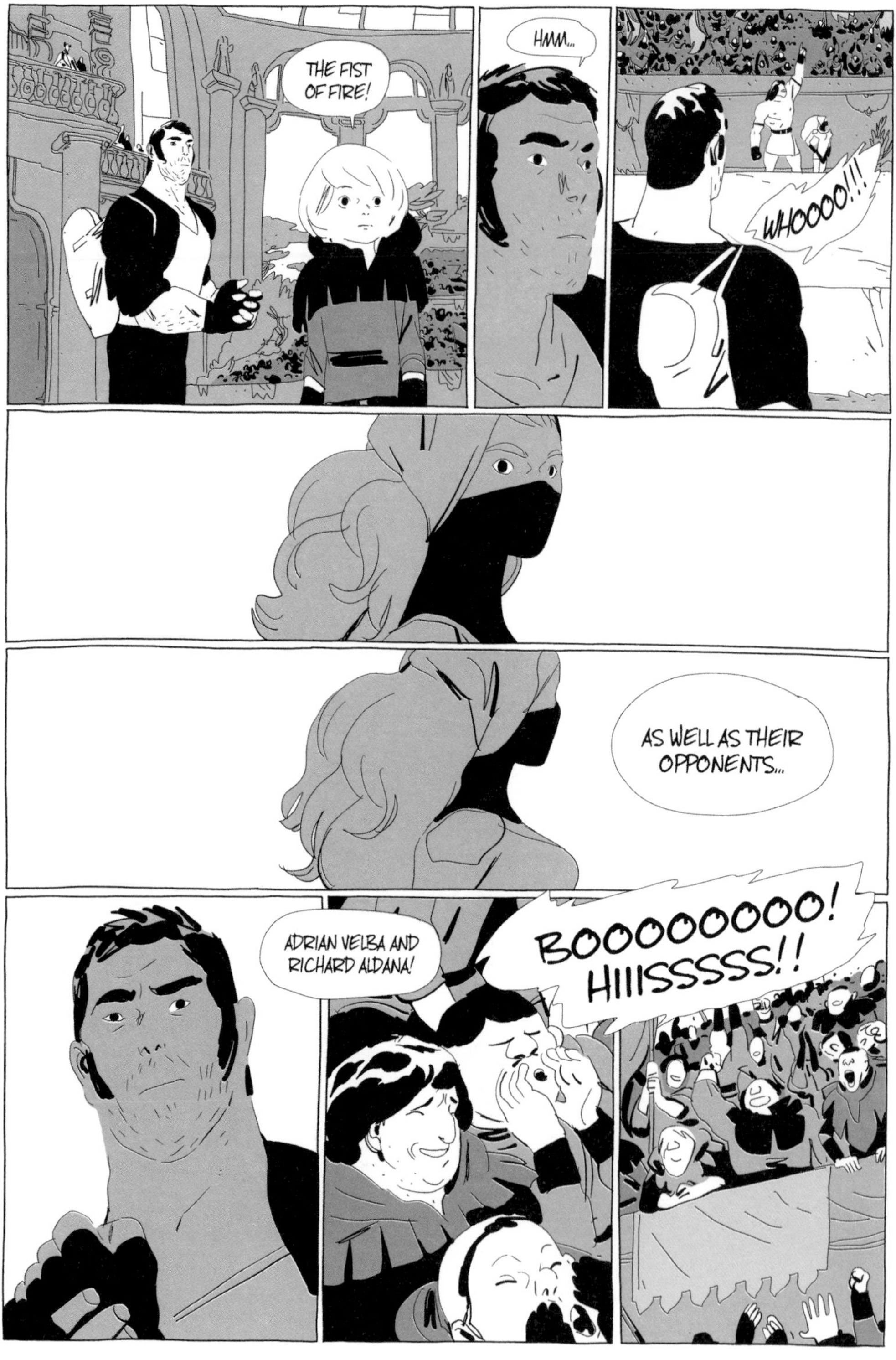
THE FIST OF FIRE!
HMM...
WHOOOO!!!
AS WELL AS THEIR OPPONENTS...
ADRIAN VELBA AND RICHARD ALDANA!
BOOOOOOOO! HIIISSSSS!!

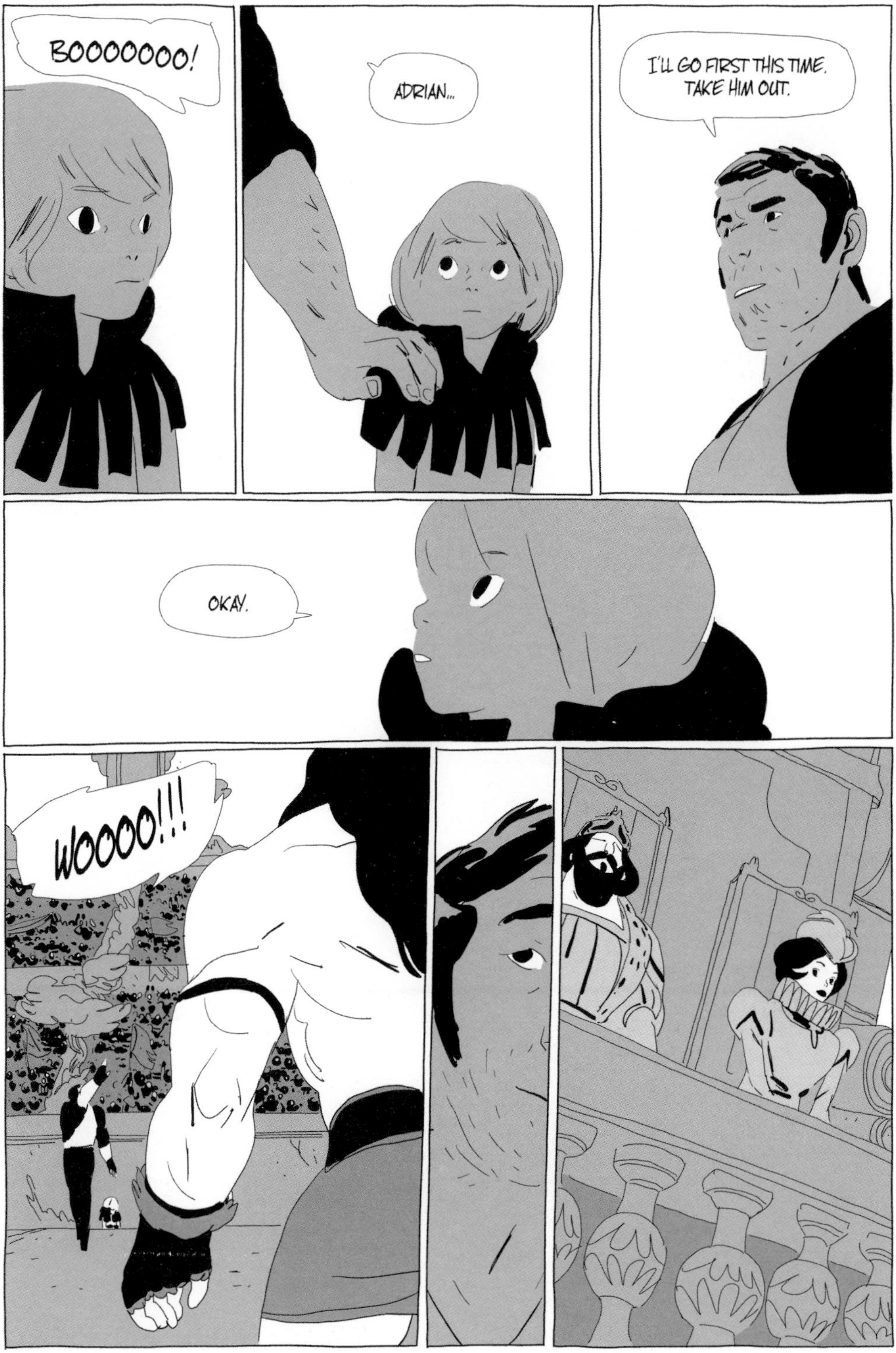
BOOOOOOO!
ADRIAN...
I'LL GO FIRST THIS TIME. TAKE HIM OUT.
OKAY.
WOOOO!!!

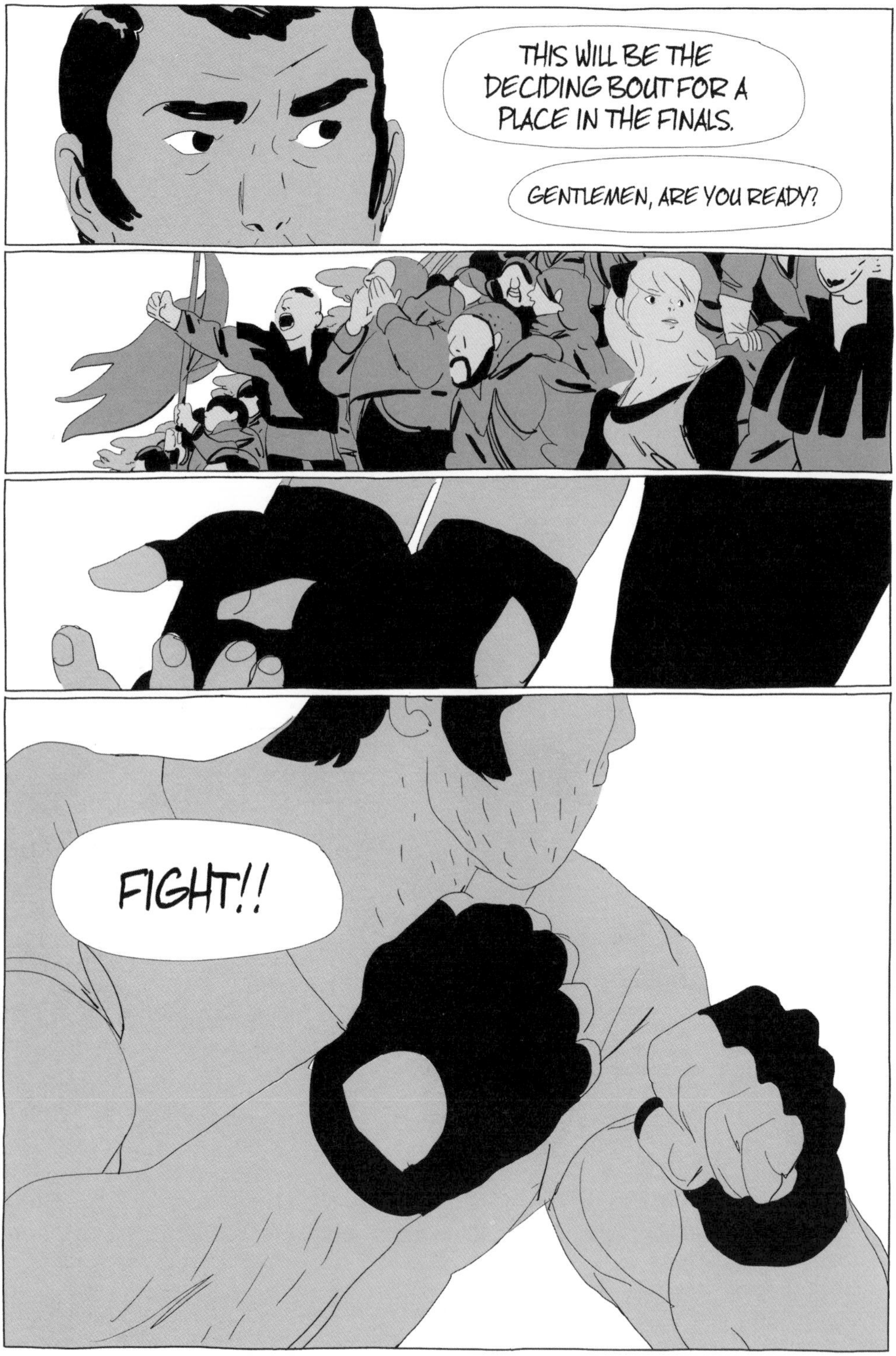
THIS WILL BE THE DECIDING BOUT FOR A PLACE IN THE FINALS.
GENTLEMEN, ARE YOU READY?
FIGHT!!

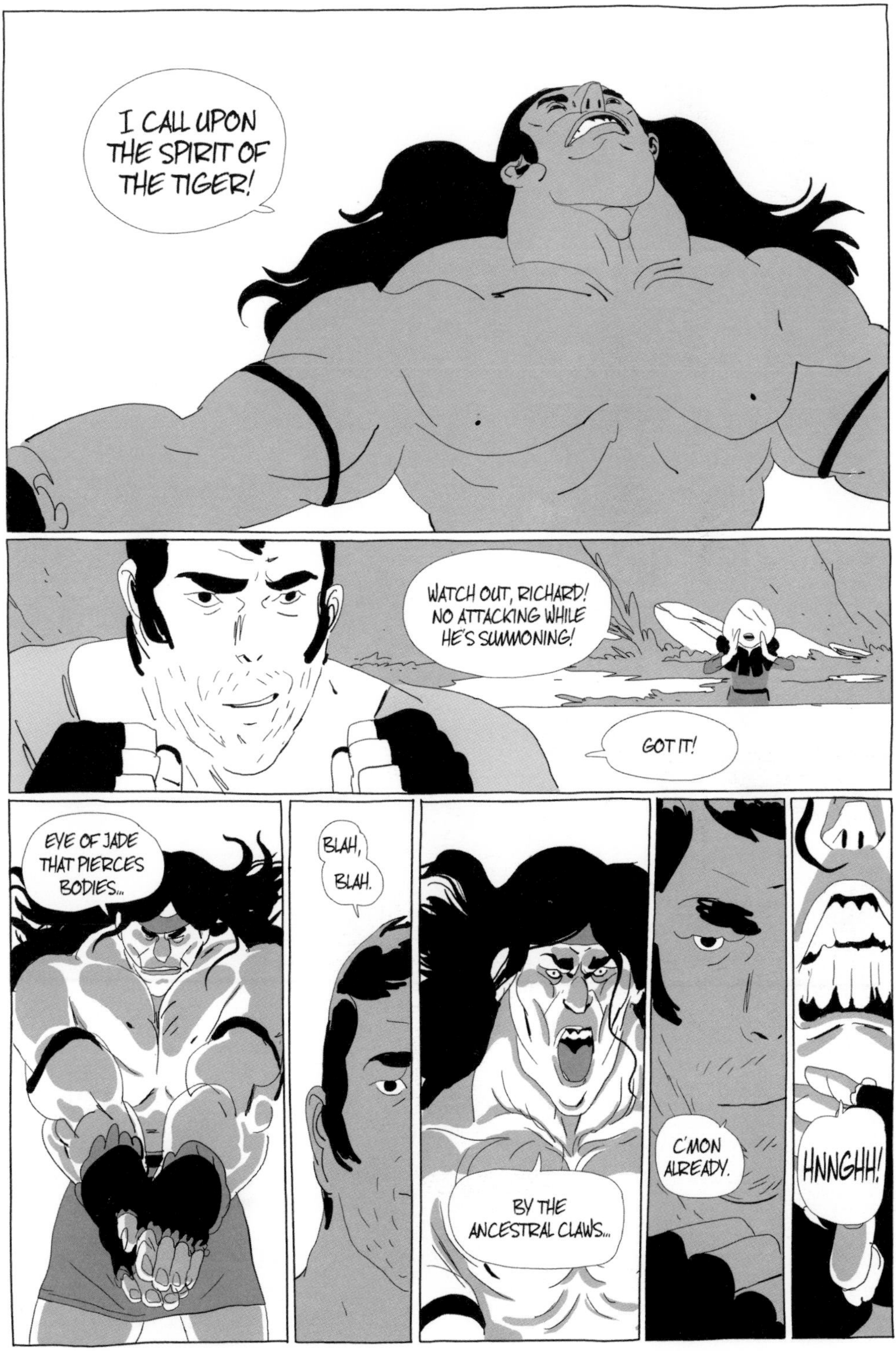
I CALL UPON THE SPIRIT OF THE TIGER!
WATCH OUT, RICHARD! NO ATTACKING WHILE HE'S SUMMONING!
GOT IT!
EYE OF JADE THAT PIERCES BODIES...
BLAH, BLAH.
BY THE ANCESTRAL CLAWS...
C'MON ALREADY.
HNNGHH!

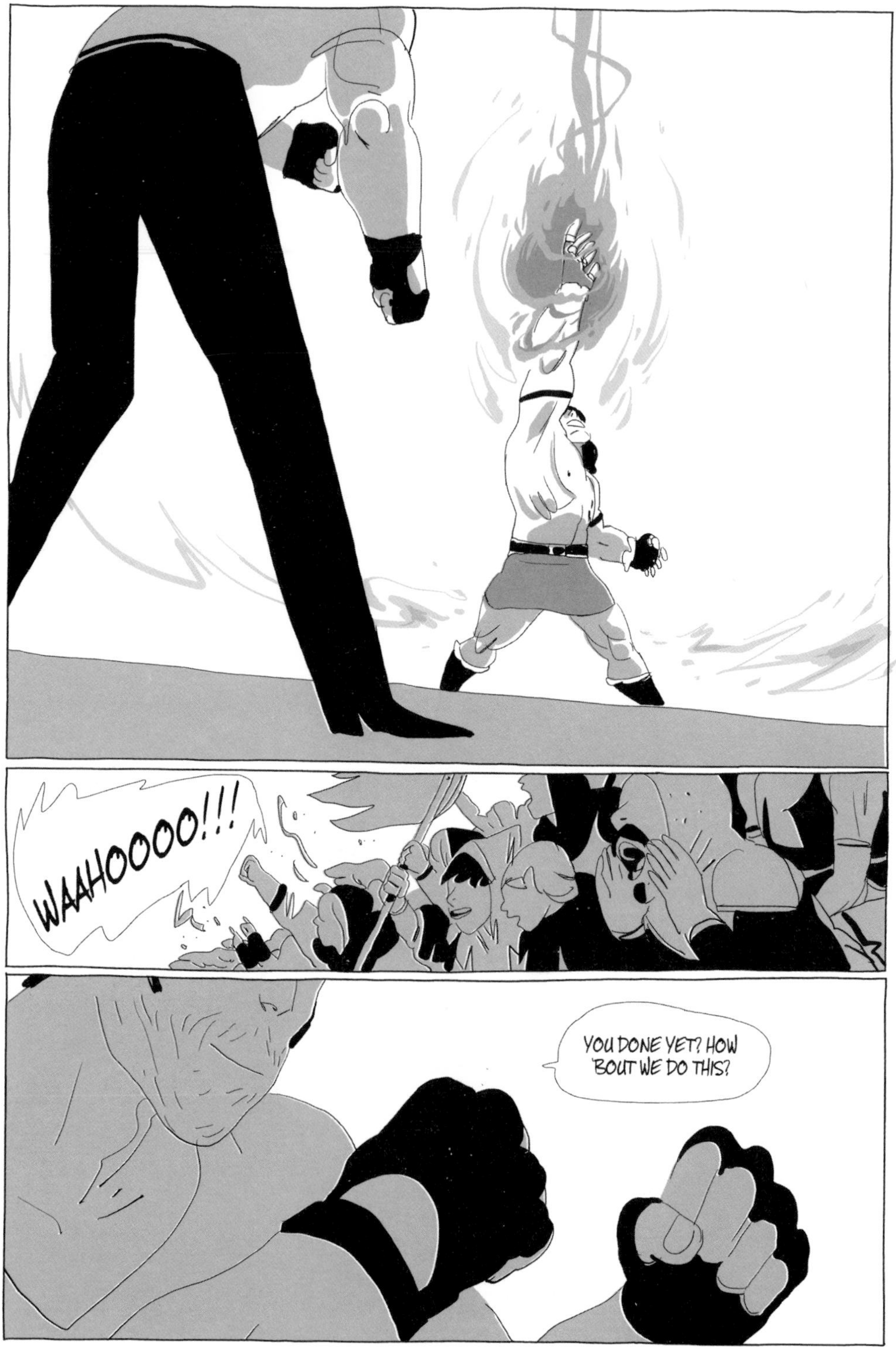
WAAHOOOO!!!
YOU DONE YET? HOW 'BOUT WE DO THIS?

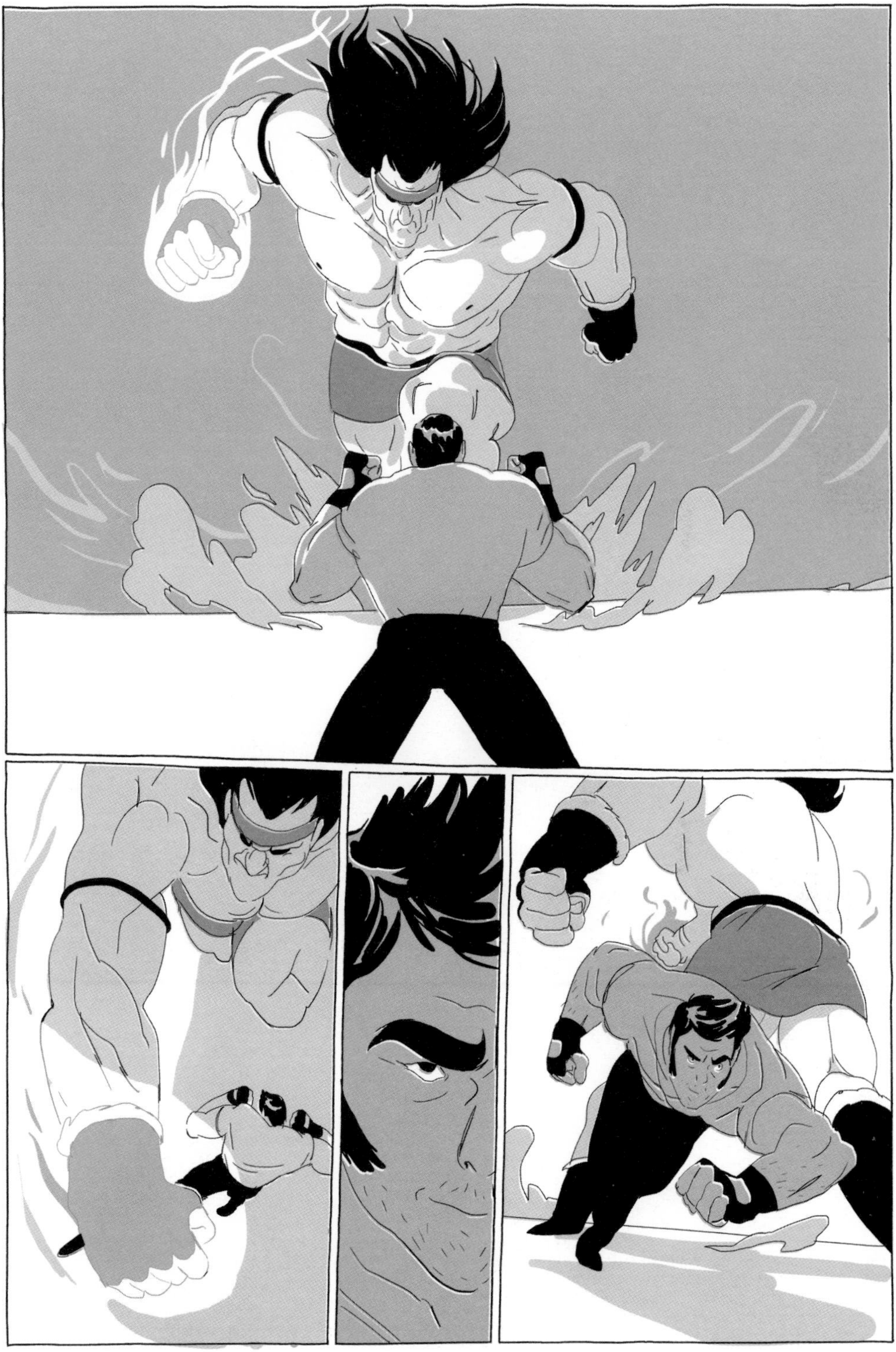

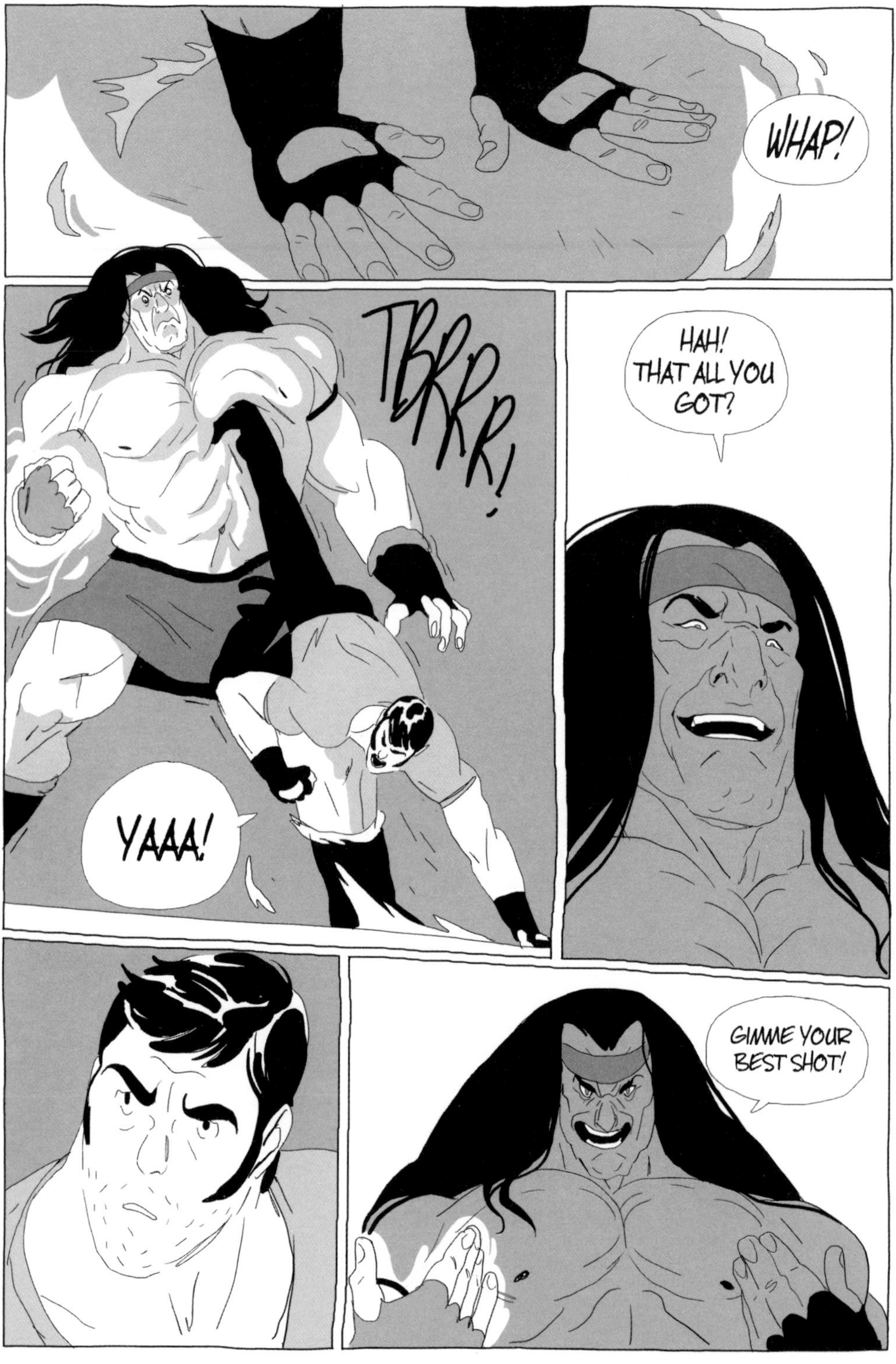
WHAP!
TBRRR!
YAAA!
HAH! THAT ALL YOU GOT?
GIMME YOUR BEST SHOT!

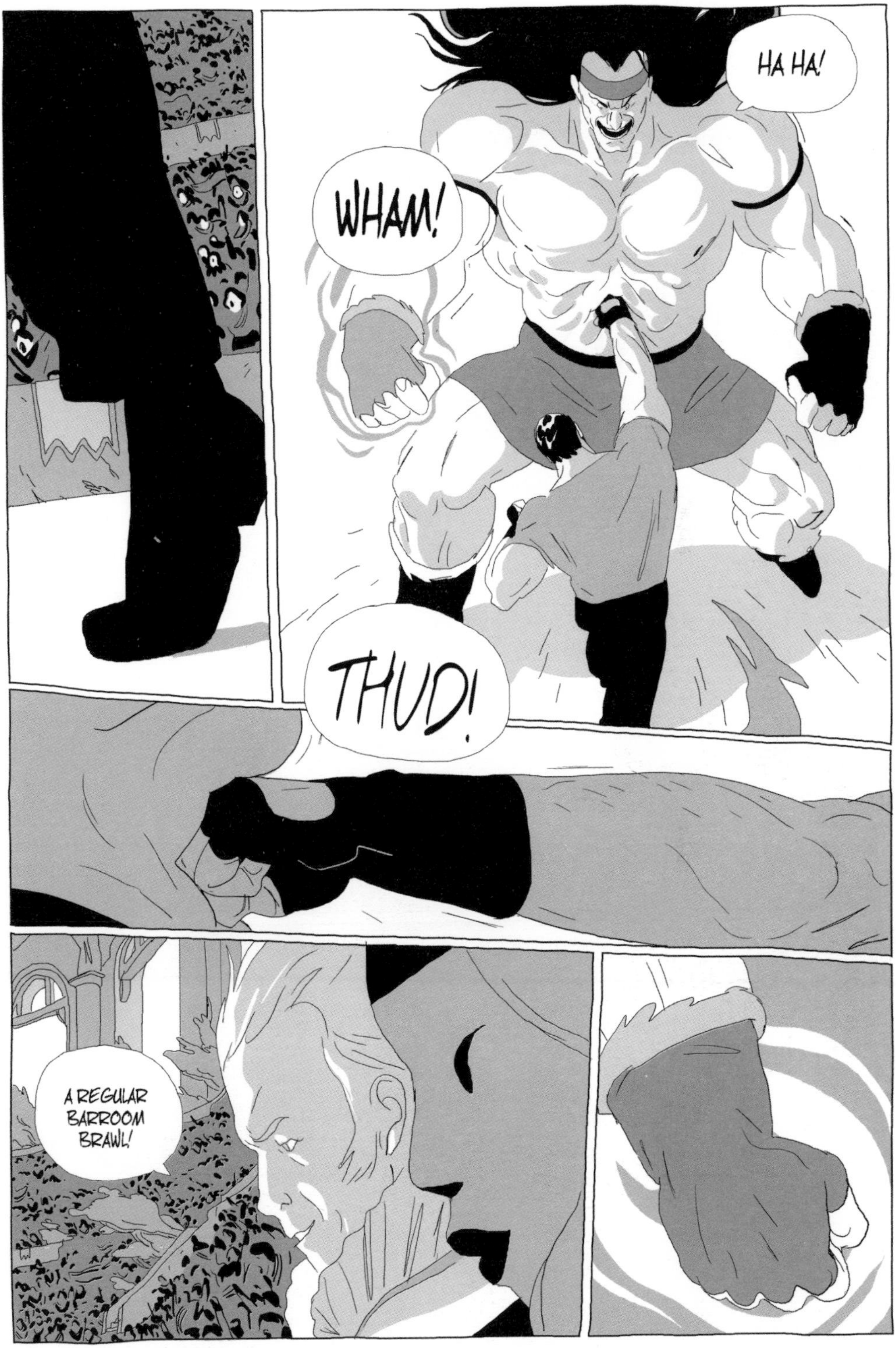
HA HA!
WHAM!
THUD!
A REGULAR BARROOM BRAWL!

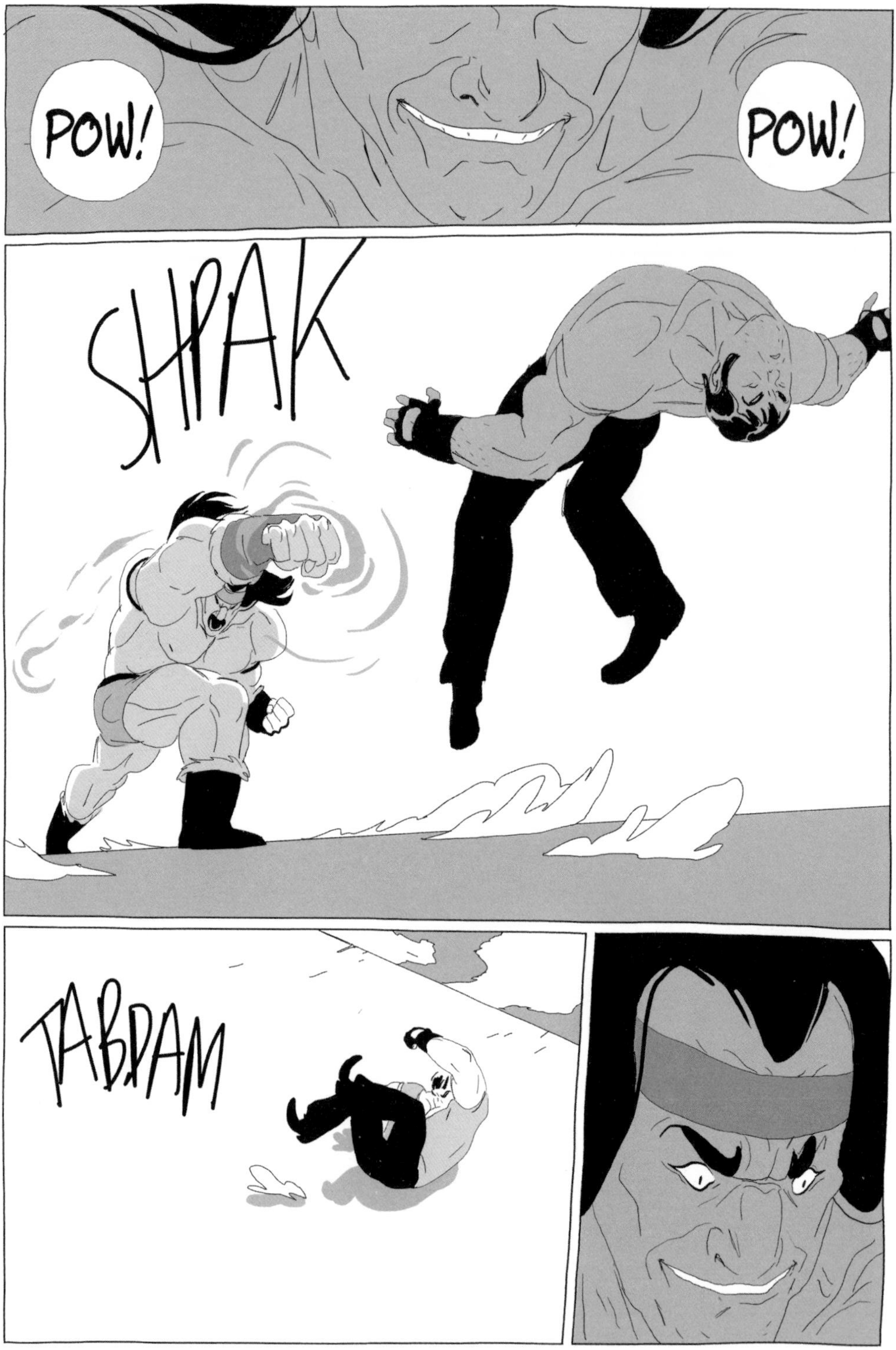
POW!
POW!
SHPAK
TABDAM

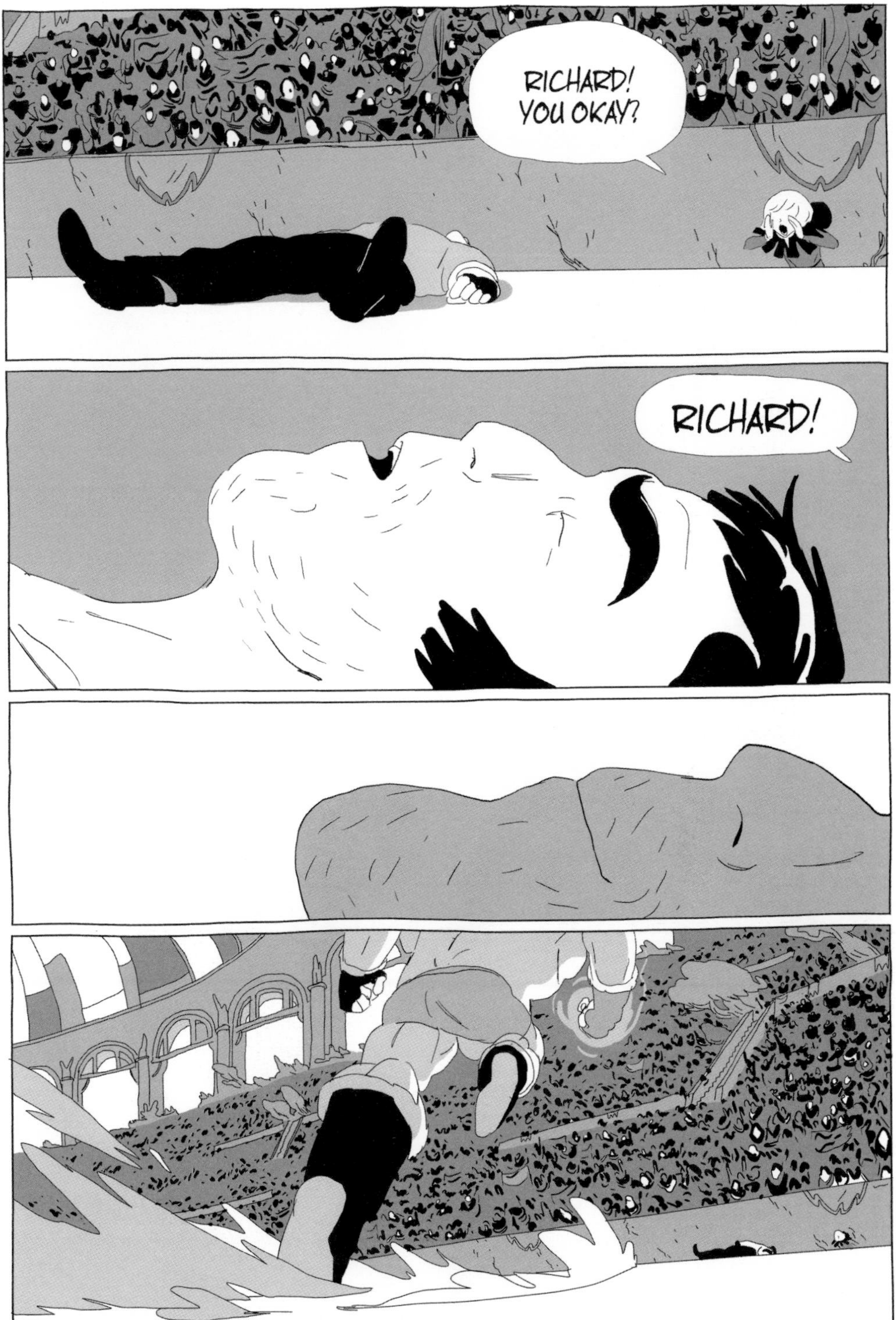
RICHARD! YOU OKAY?
RICHARD!

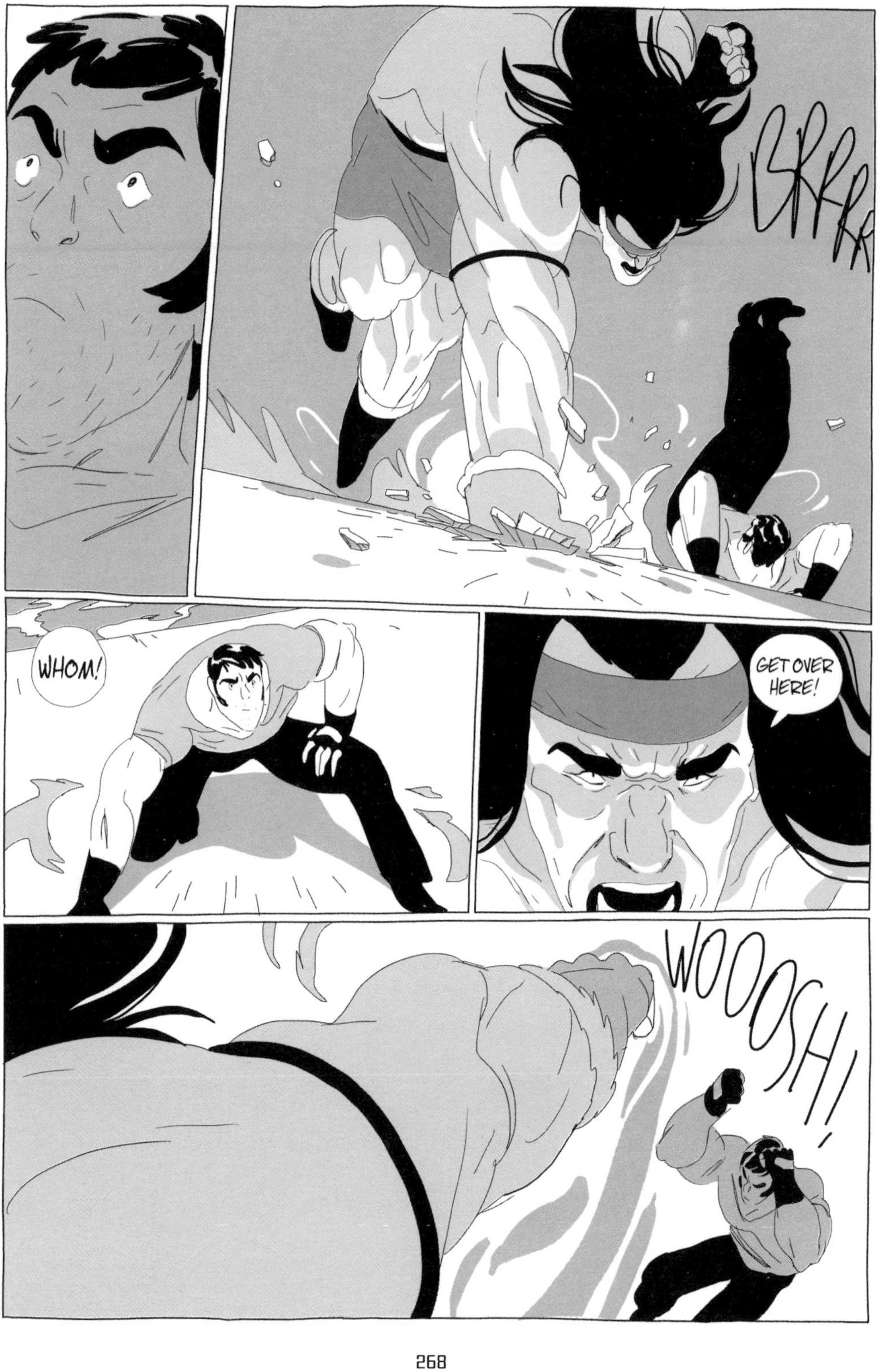
BRRRR
WHOM!
GET OVER HERE!
WOOOSH!!

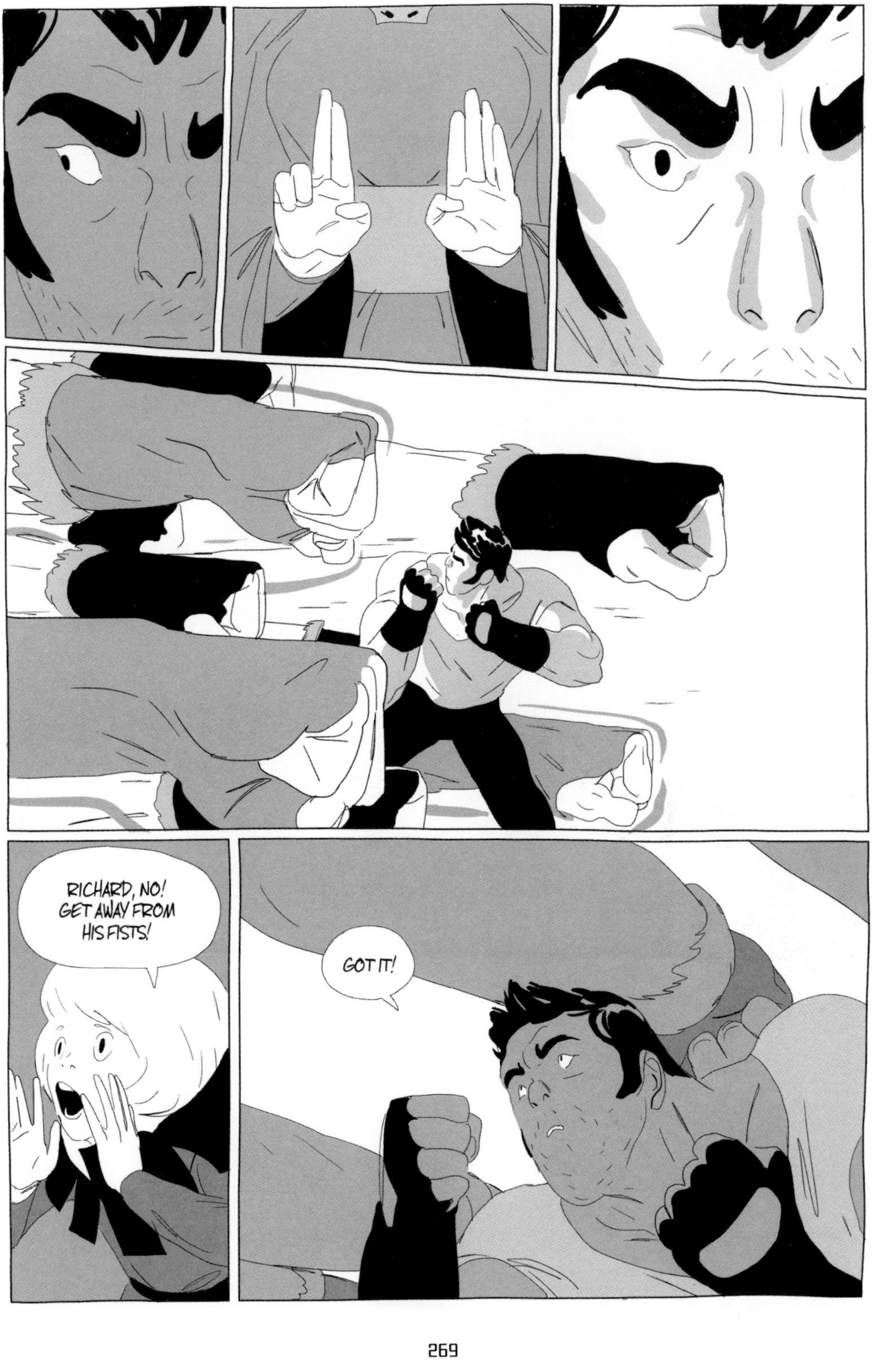
RICHARD, NO! GET AWAY FROM HIS FISTS!
GOT IT!

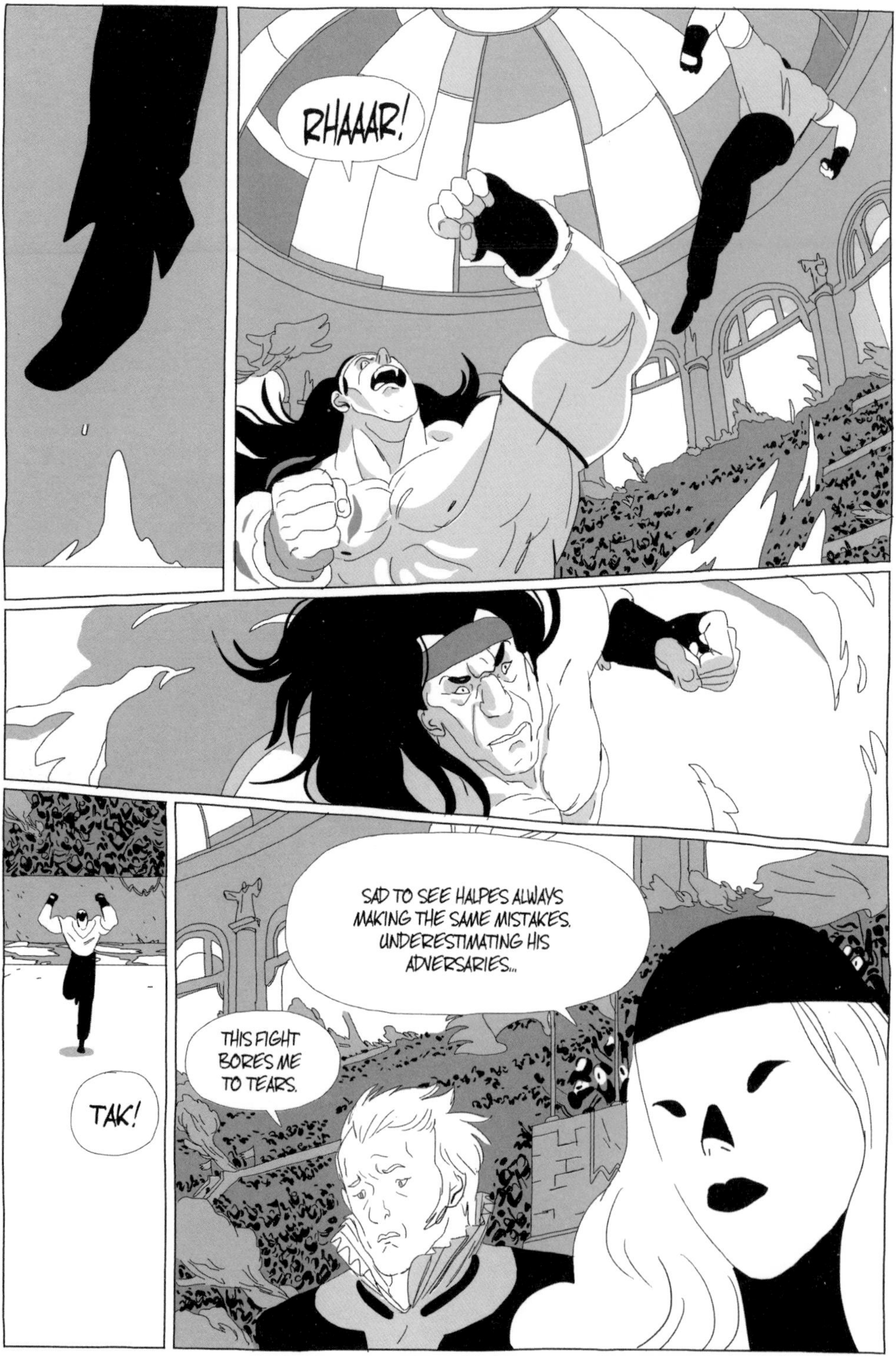
RHAAAR!
TAK!
SAD TO SEE HALPES ALWAYS MAKING THE SAME MISTAKES. UNDERESTIMATING HIS ADVERSARIES...
THIS FIGHT BORES ME TO TEARS.

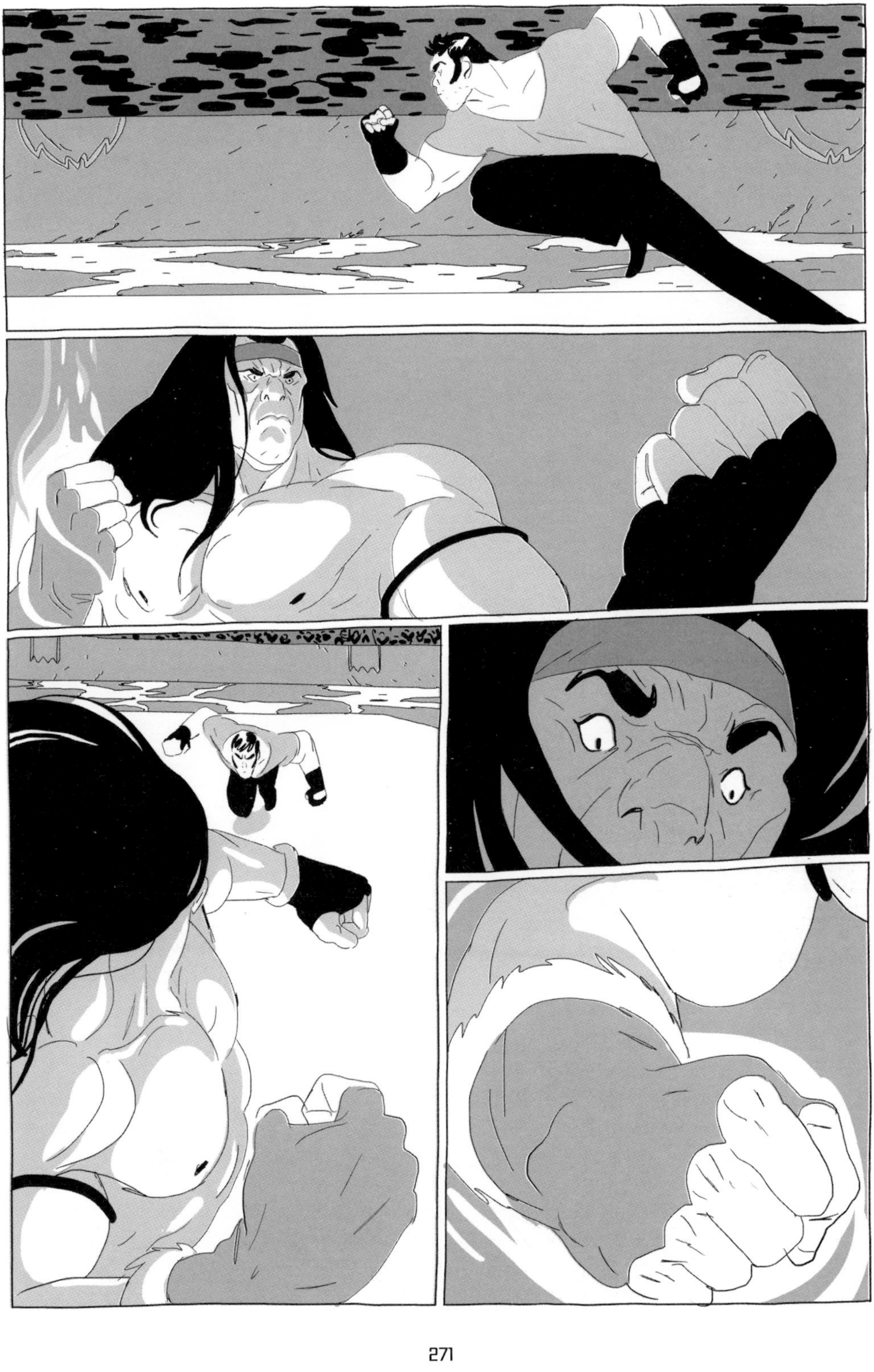

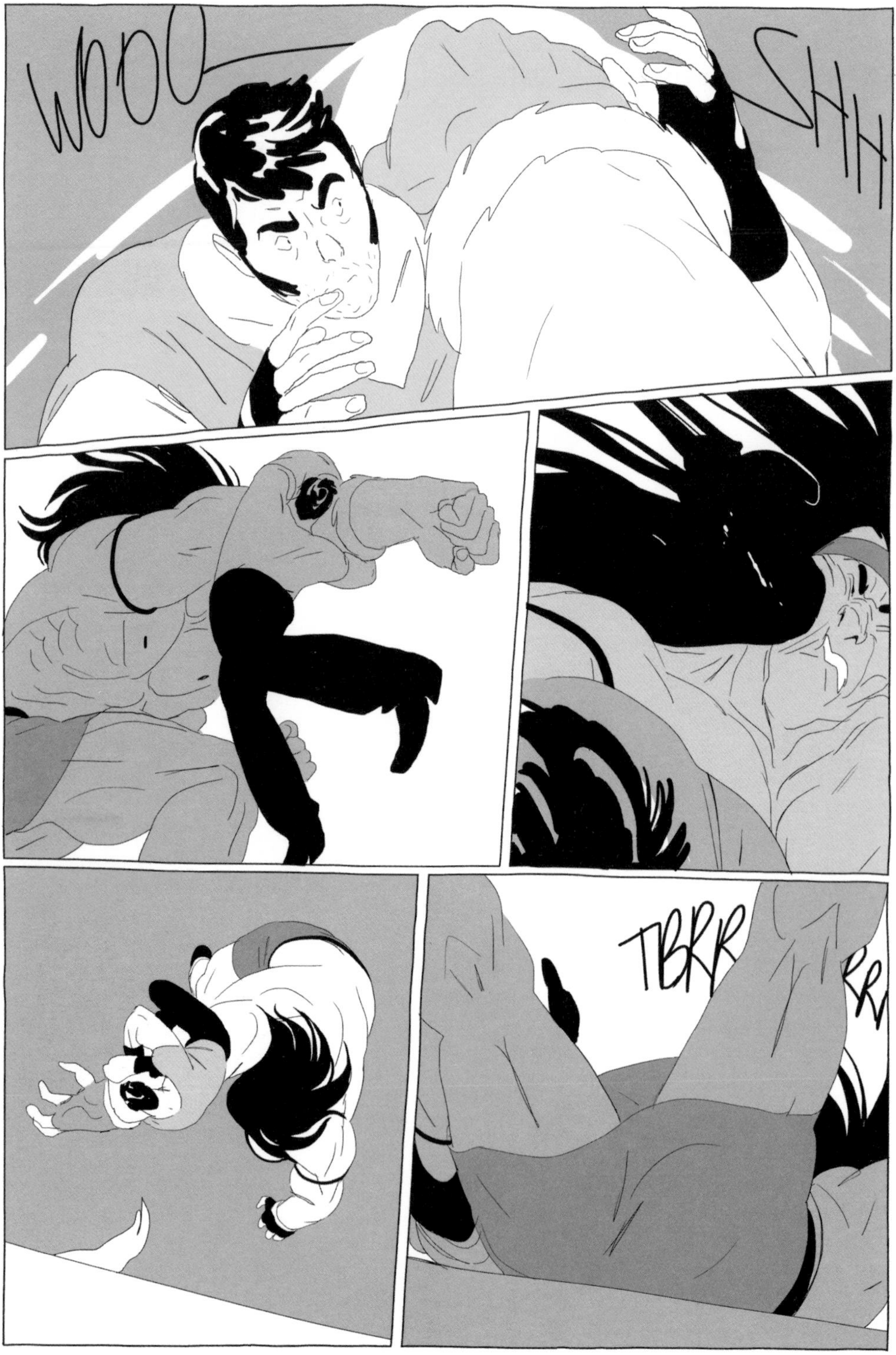
WOOO
SHH
TBRR

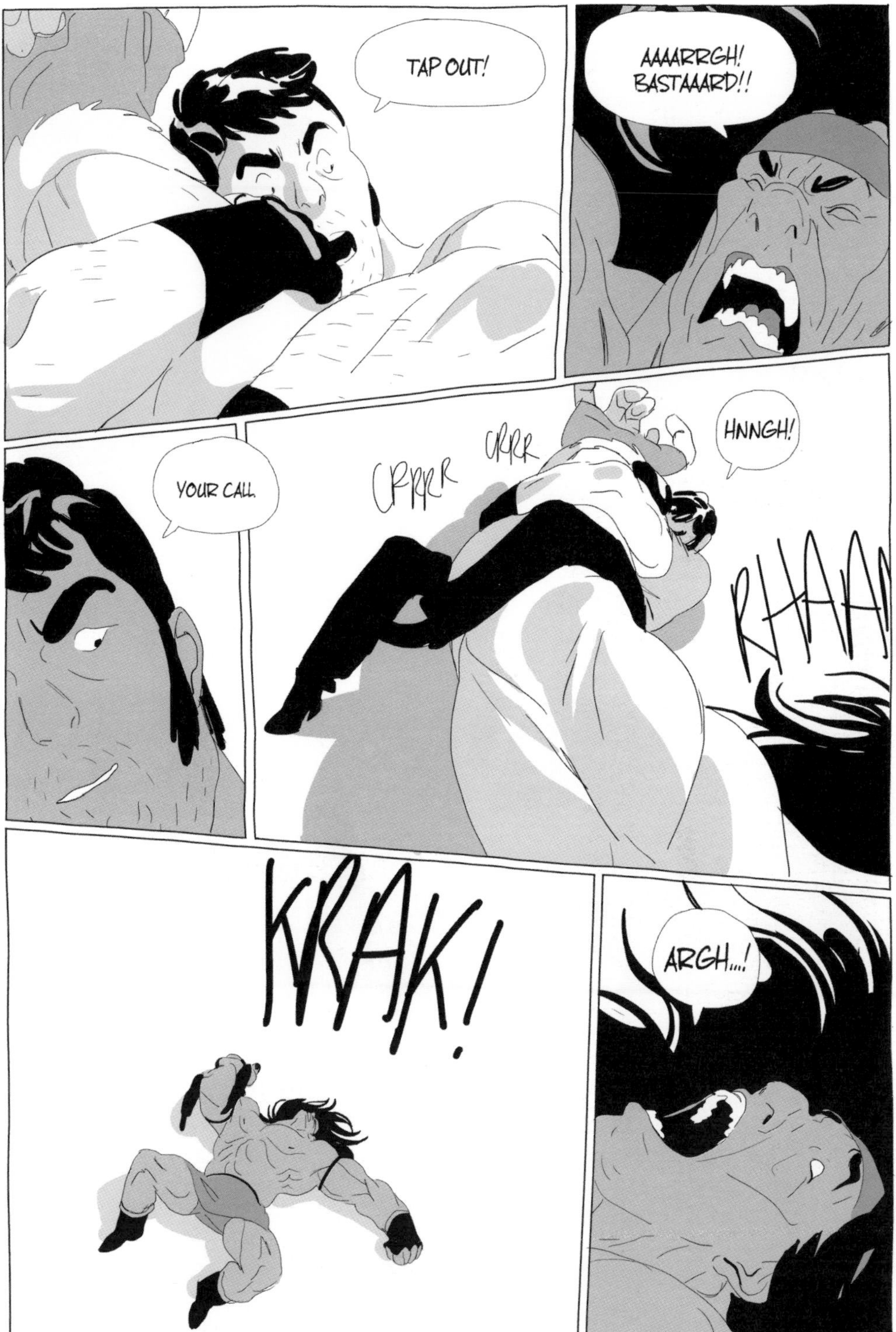
TAP OUT!
AAAARRGH! BASTAAARD!!
YOUR CALL.
CRRRR
CRRR
HNNGH!
KRAK!
ARGH...!

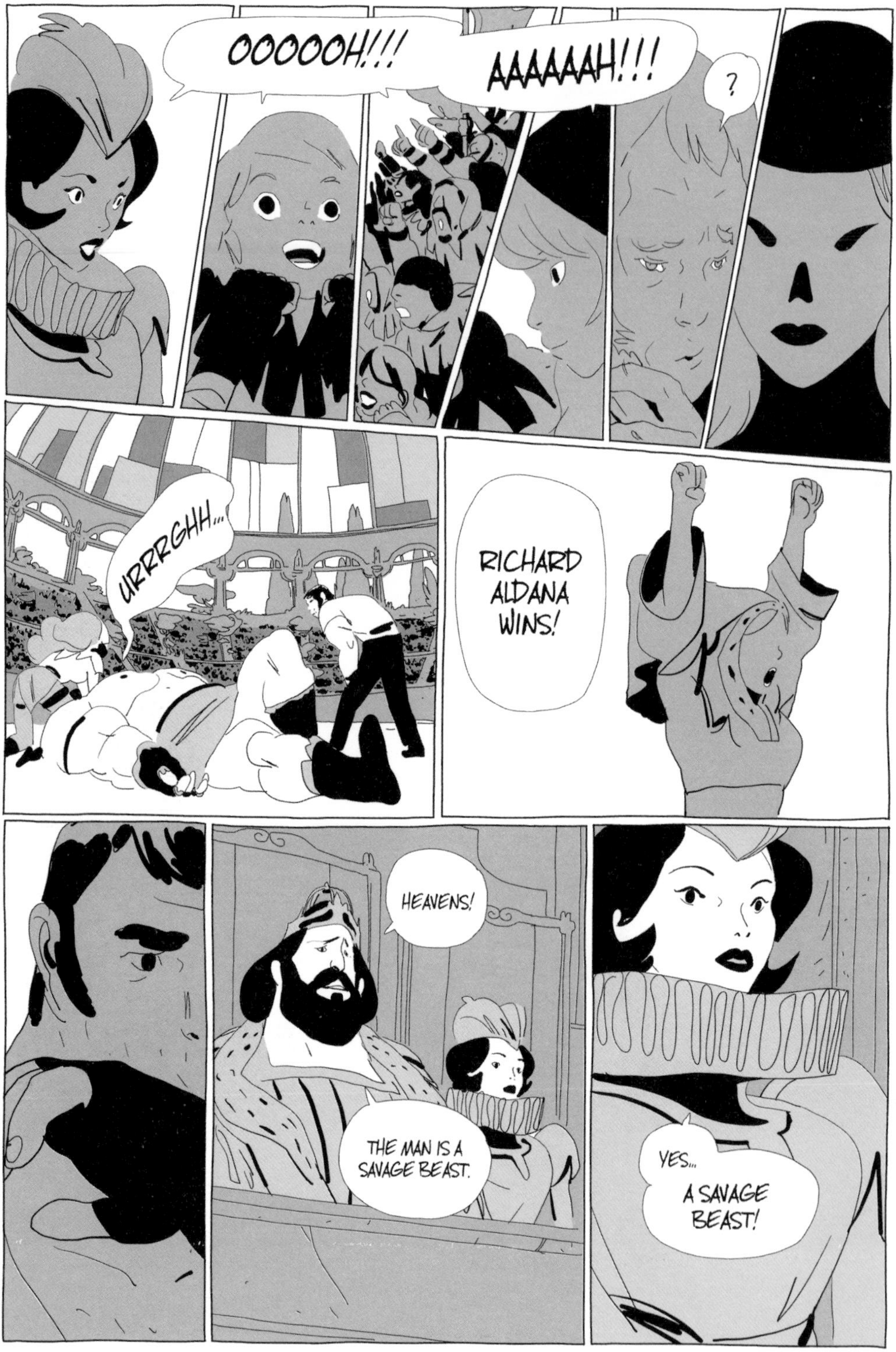
OOOOOH!!!
AAAAAAH!!!
?
URRRGHH...
RICHARD ALDANA WINS!
HEAVENS!
THE MAN IS A SAVAGE BEAST.
YES... A SAVAGE BEAST!

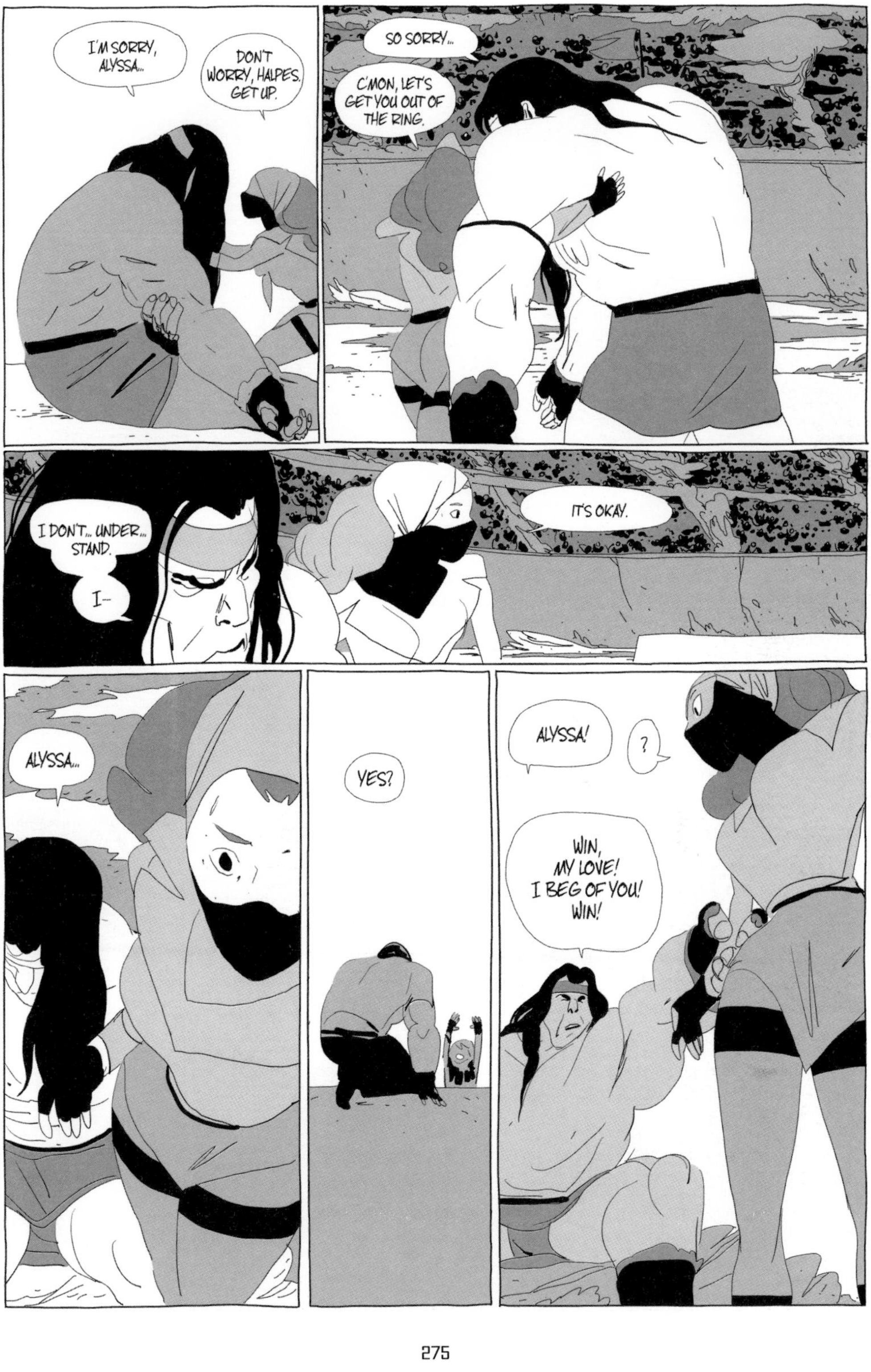
I'M SORRY, ALYSSA...
DON'T WORRY, HALPES. GET UP.
SO SORRY...
C'MON, LET'S GET YOU OUT OF THE RING.
I DON'T... UNDER... STAND.
I--
IT'S OKAY.
ALYSSA...
YES?
ALYSSA!
?
WIN, MY LOVE! I BEG OF YOU! WIN!

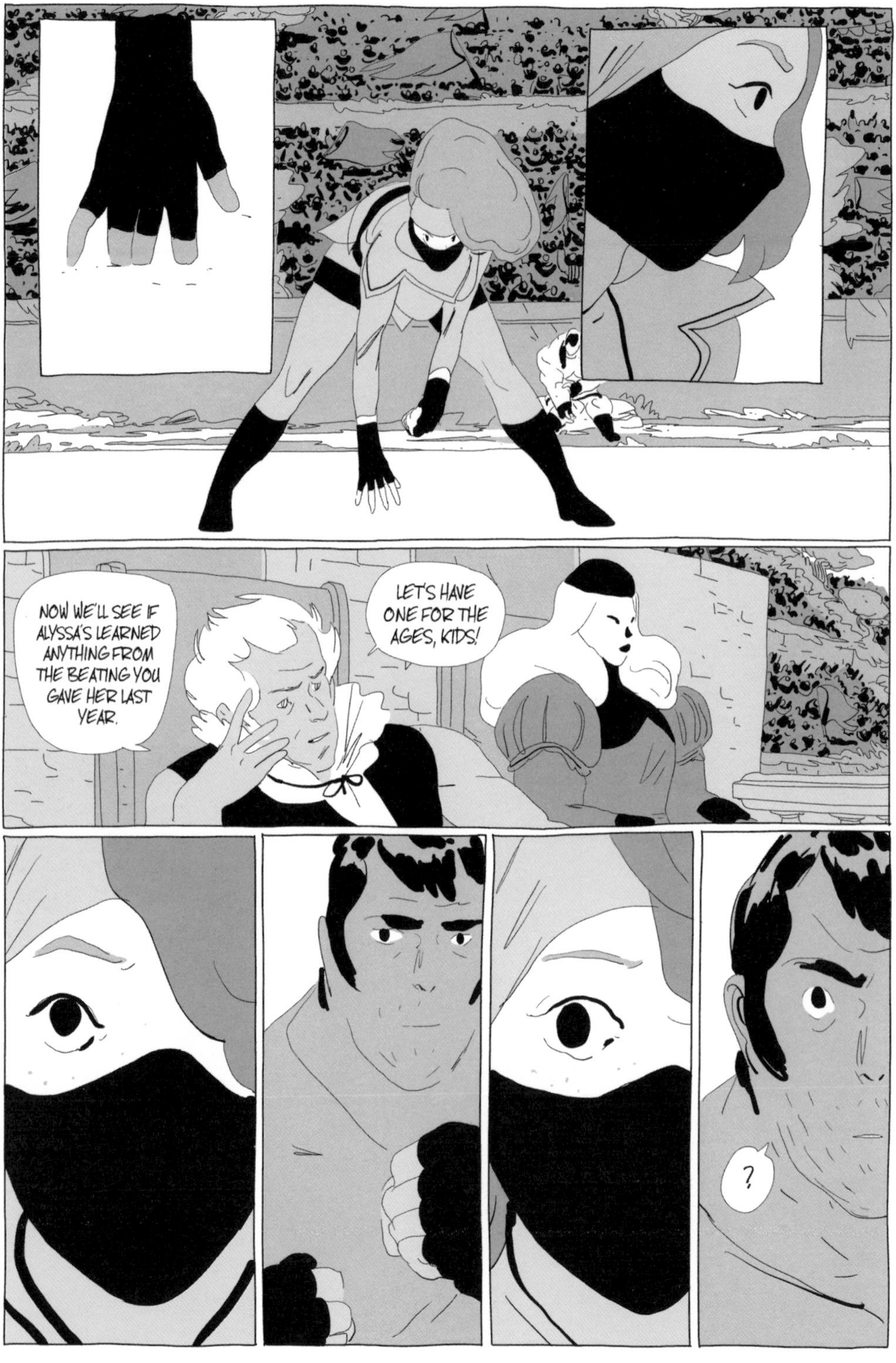
NOW WE'LL SEE IF ALYSSA'S LEARNED ANYTHING FROM THE BEATING YOU GAVE HER LAST YEAR.
LET'S HAVE ONE FOR THE AGES, KIDS!
?

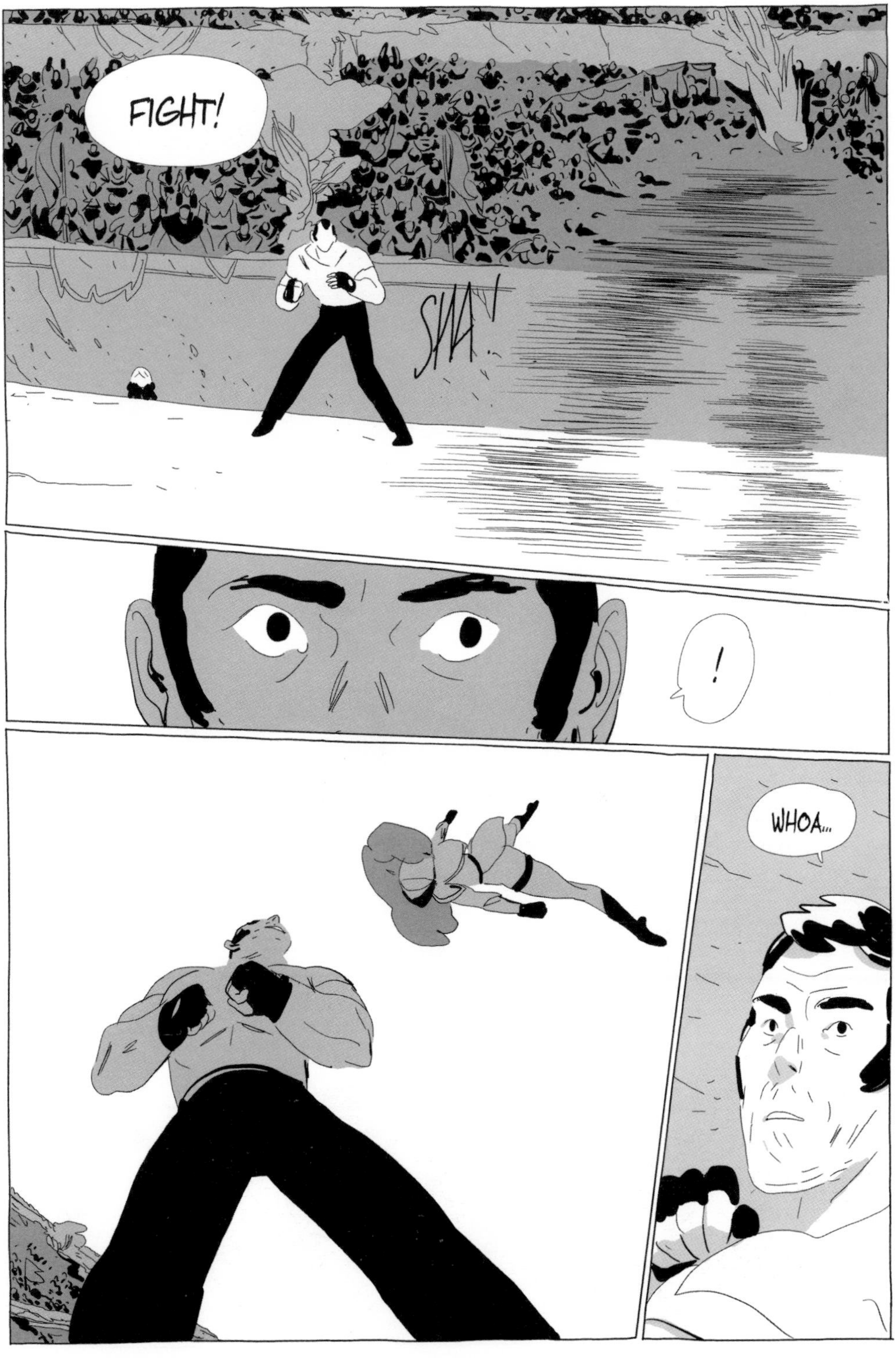
FIGHT!
SHA
!
WHOA...

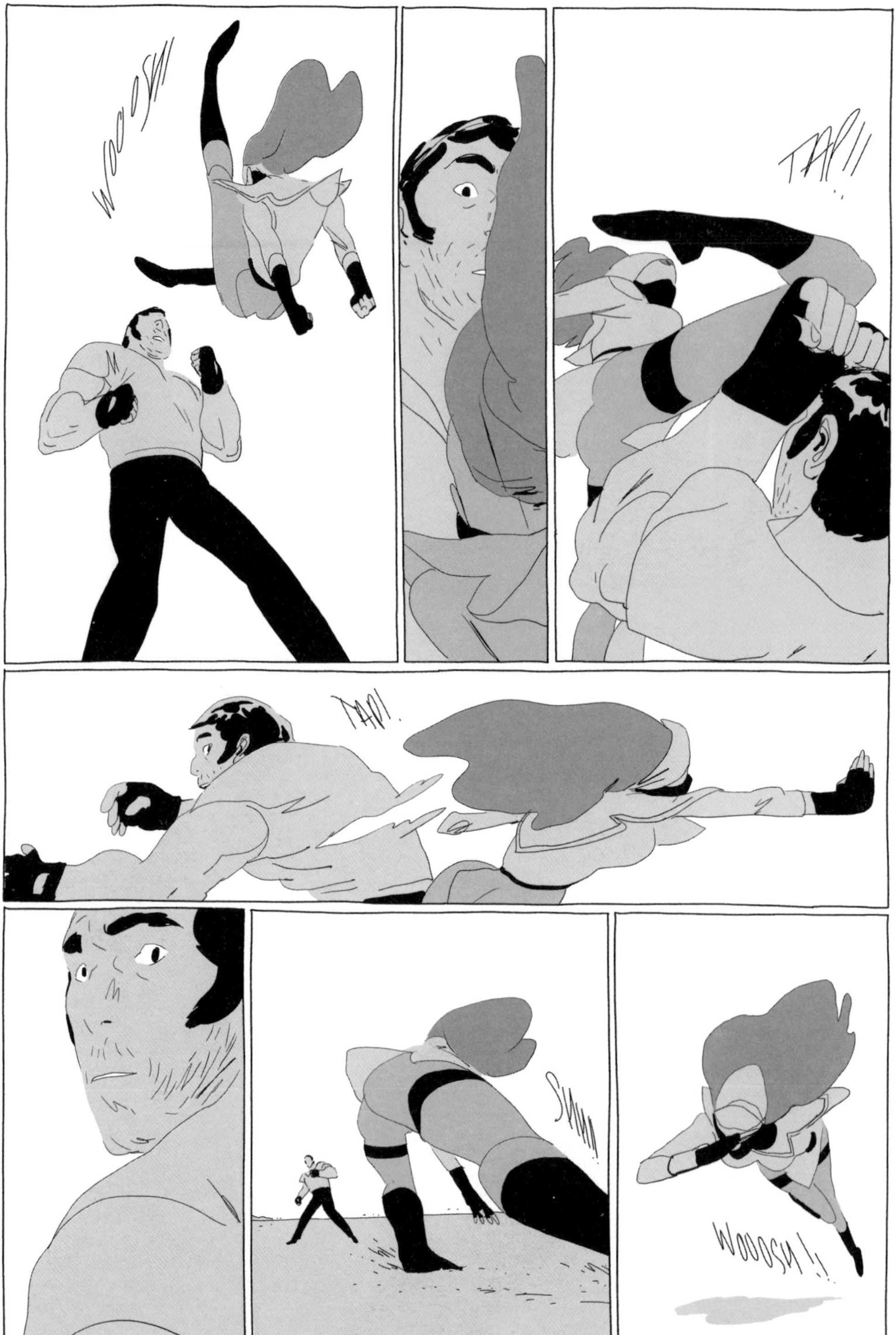
WOOOOSH
TAP!!
TAP!
SWHH
WOOOSH!!

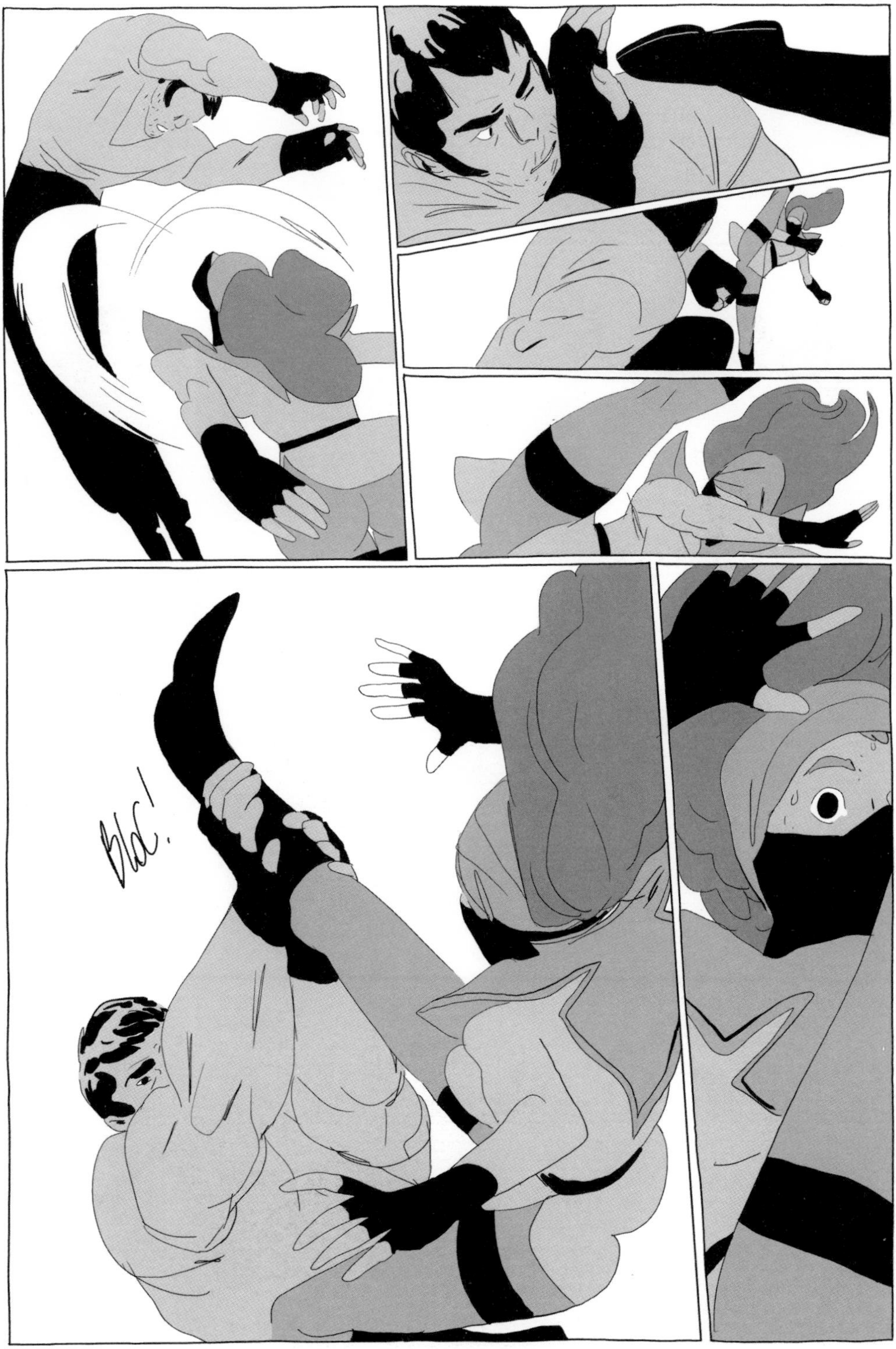
Blac!

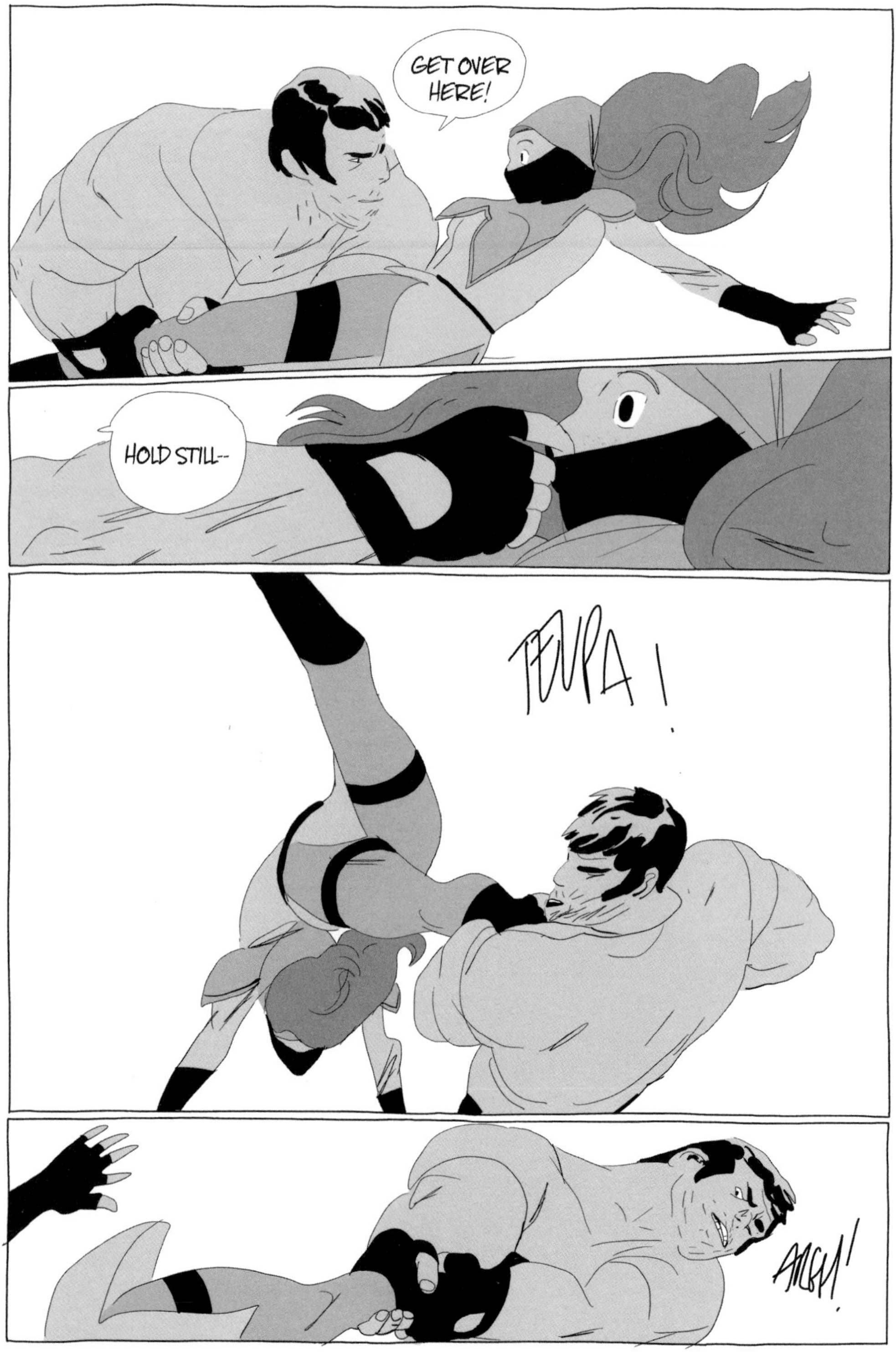
GET OVER HERE!
HOLD STILL--
ARGH!

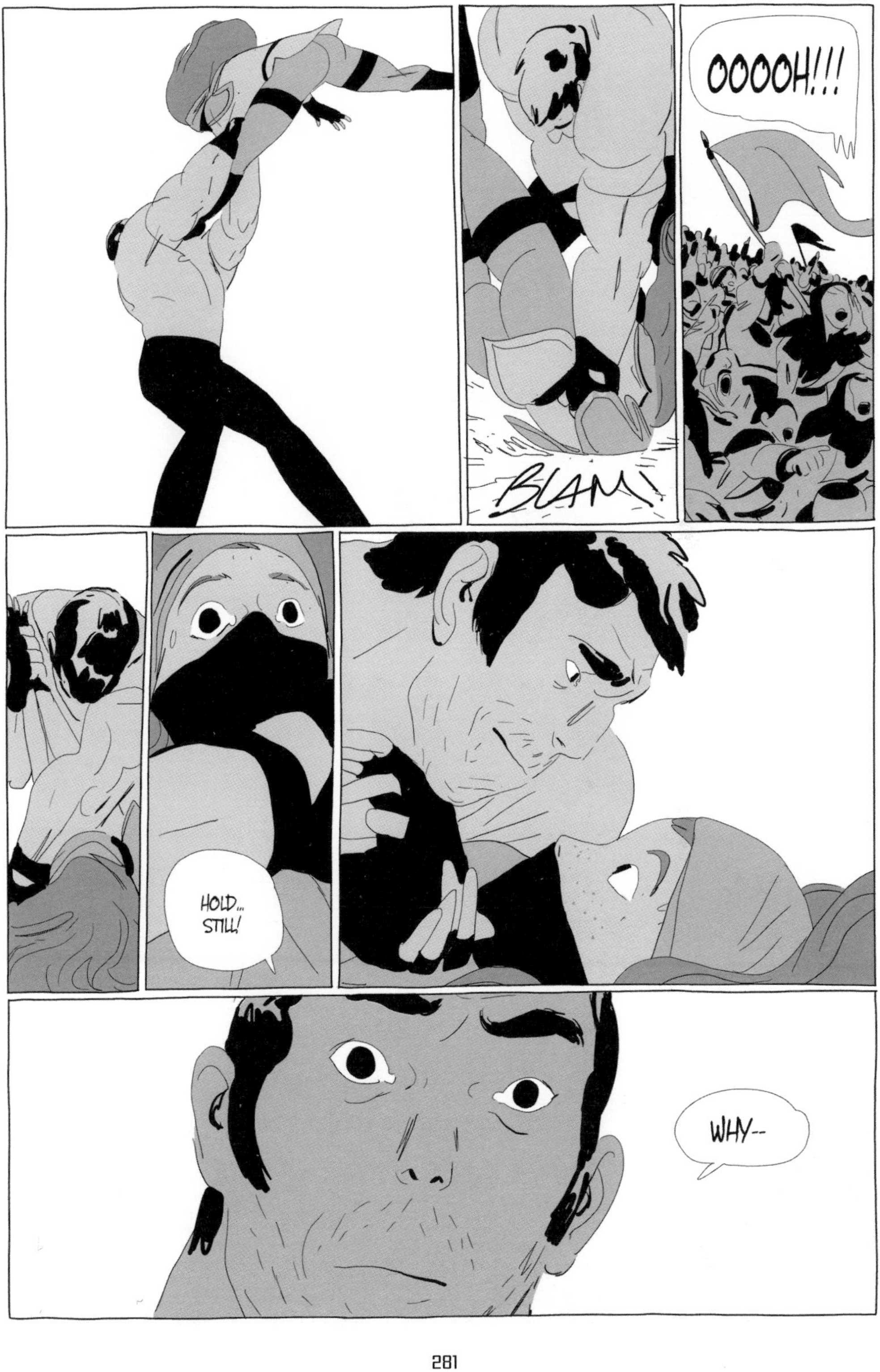
BLAM!
OOOOH!!!
HOLD... STILL!
WHY--

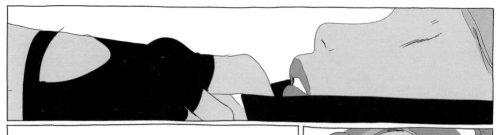

RRIP!

HNNNGH!!

AH HA!

WE'VE MET BEFORE...

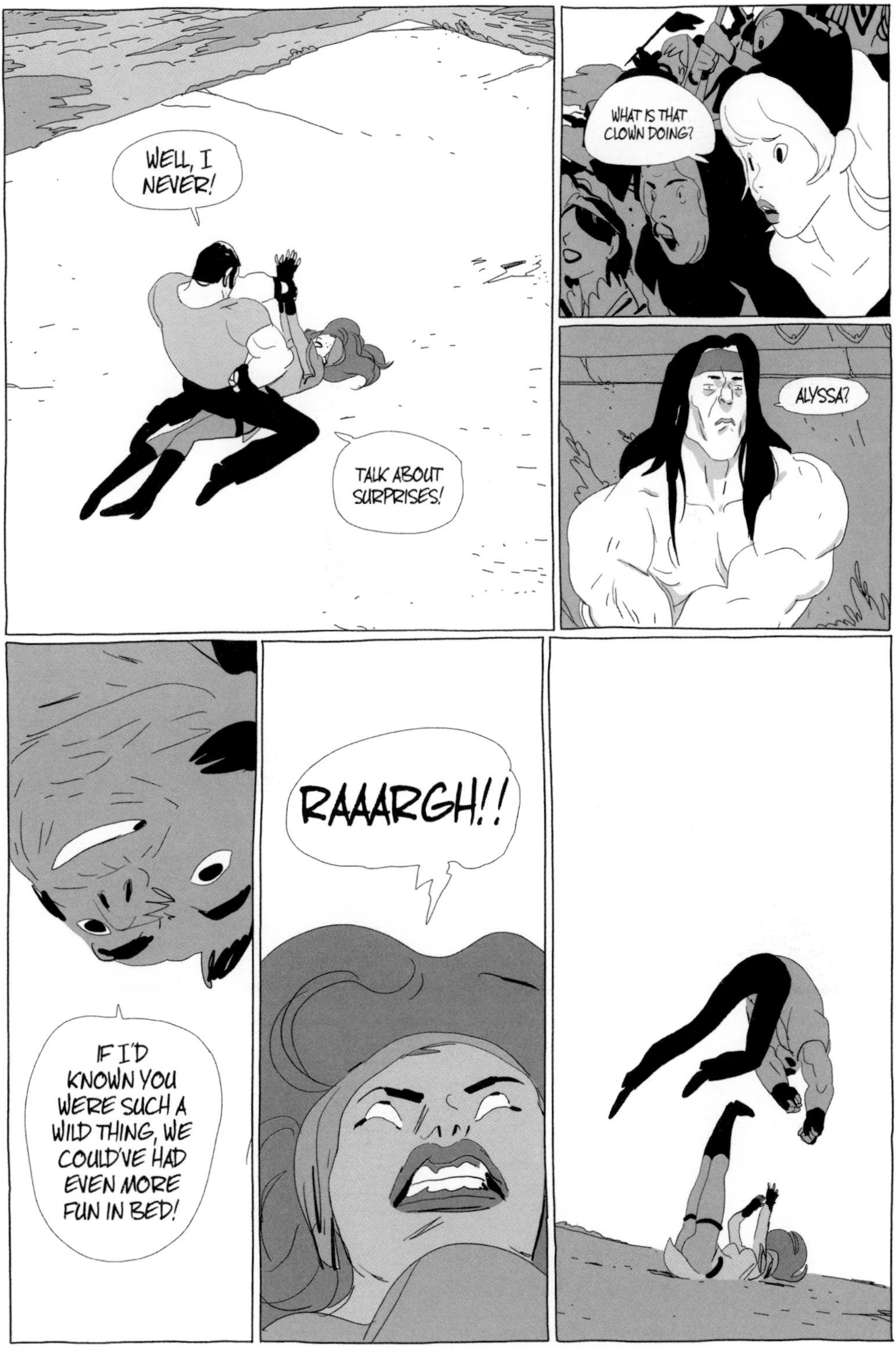
WELL, I NEVER!
TALK ABOUT SURPRISES!
WHAT IS THAT CLOWN DOING?
ALYSSA?
IF I'D KNOWN YOU WERE SUCH A WILD THING, WE COULD'VE HAD EVEN MORE FUN IN BED!
RAAARGH!!

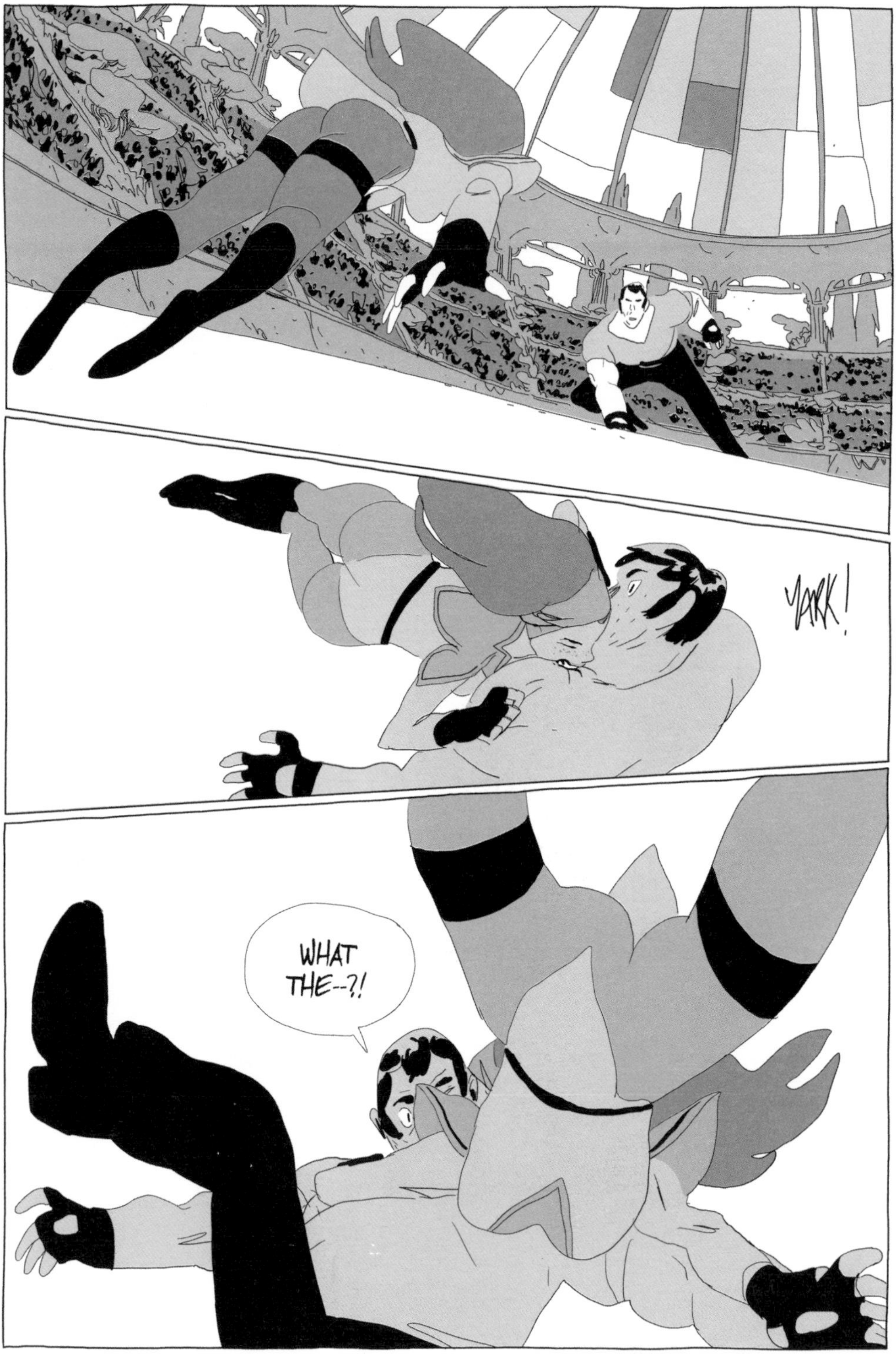
YARK!
WHAT THE--?!

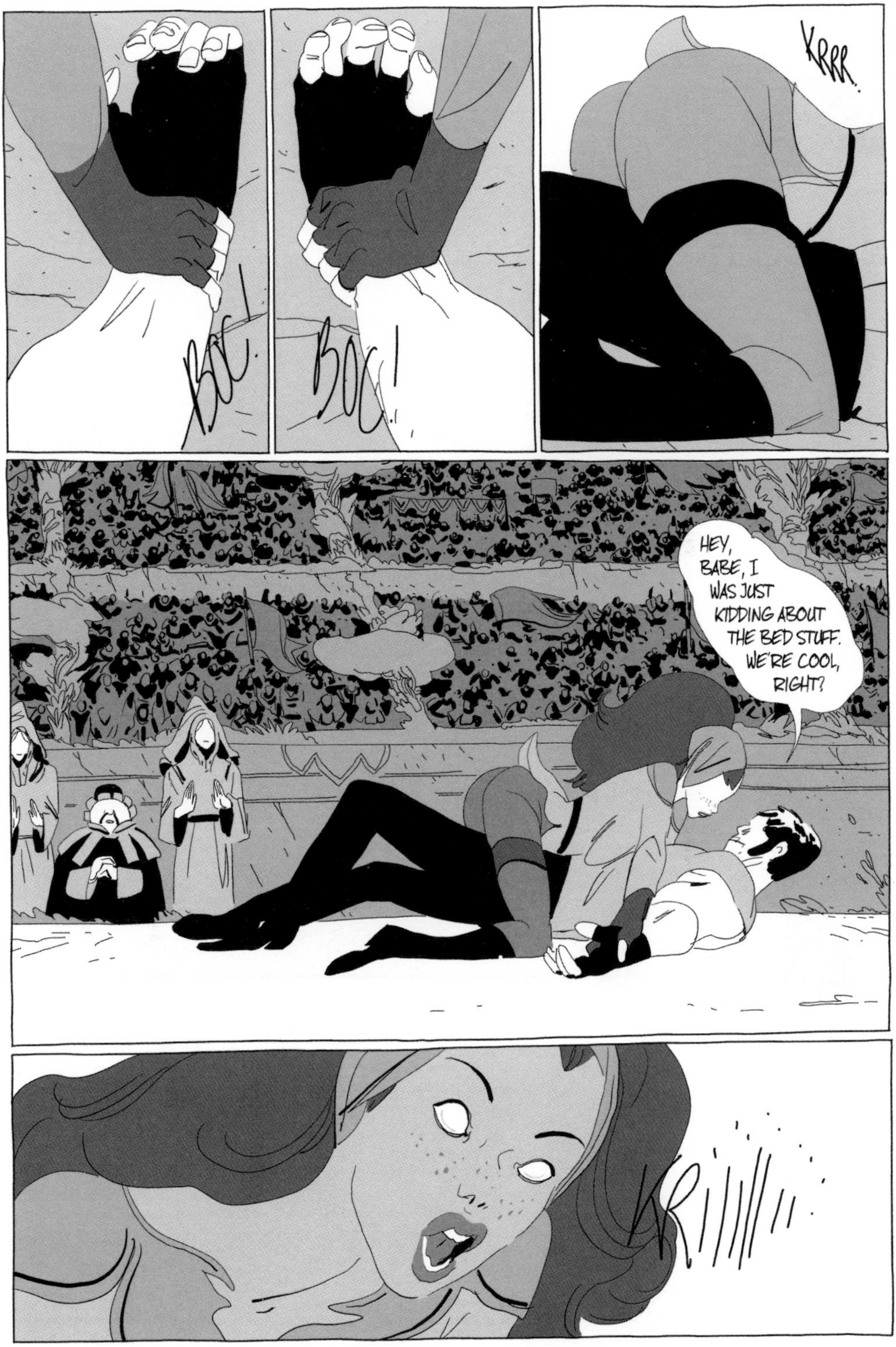
BOC!
BOC!
KRRR..
HEY, BABE, I WAS JUST KIDDING ABOUT THE BED STUFF. WE'RE COOL, RIGHT?
KRIIIII..

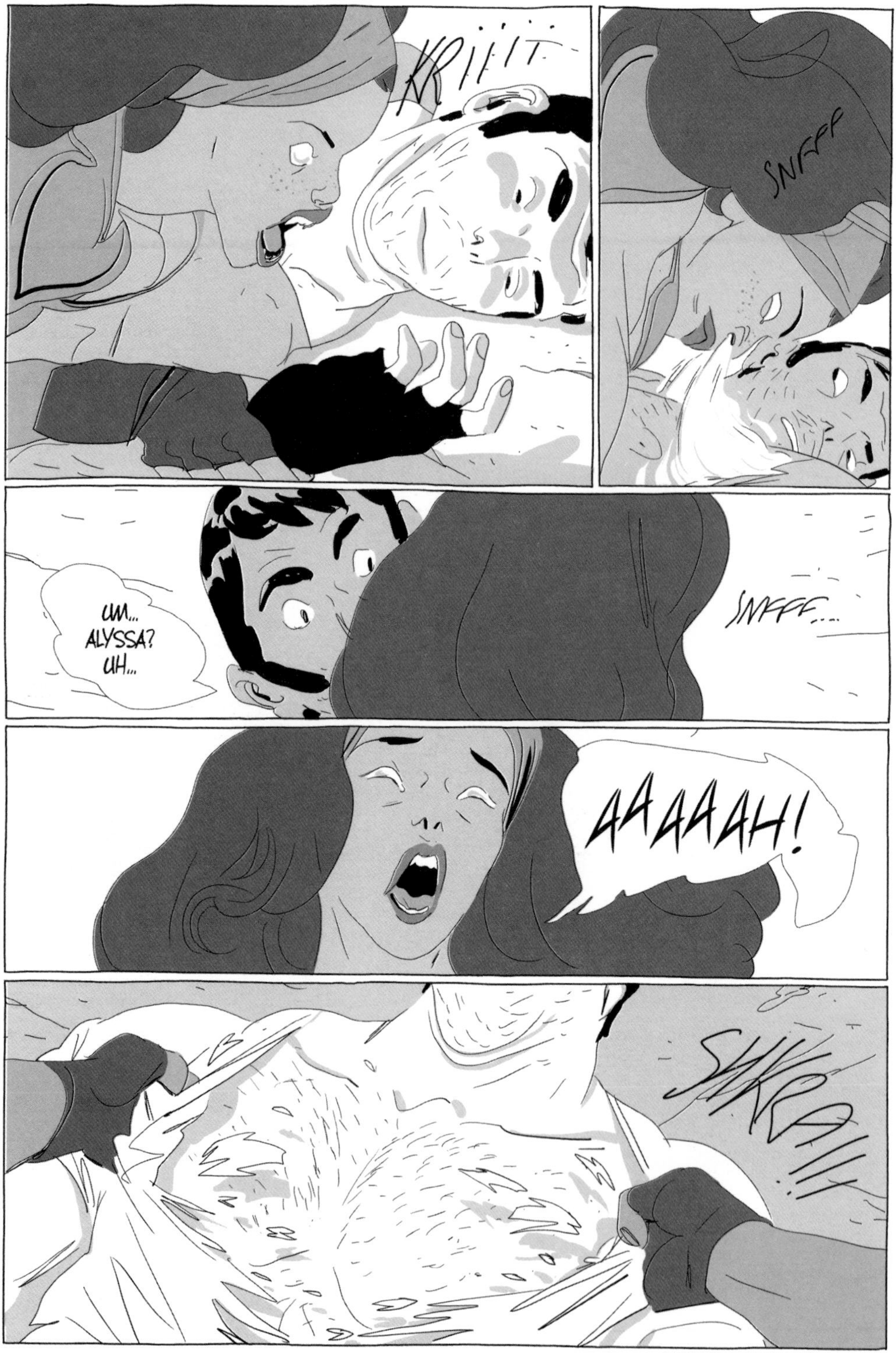
KRIIIT
SNIFFF
UM... ALYSSA? UH...
SNFFF....
AAAAAH!
SHRA!!!!

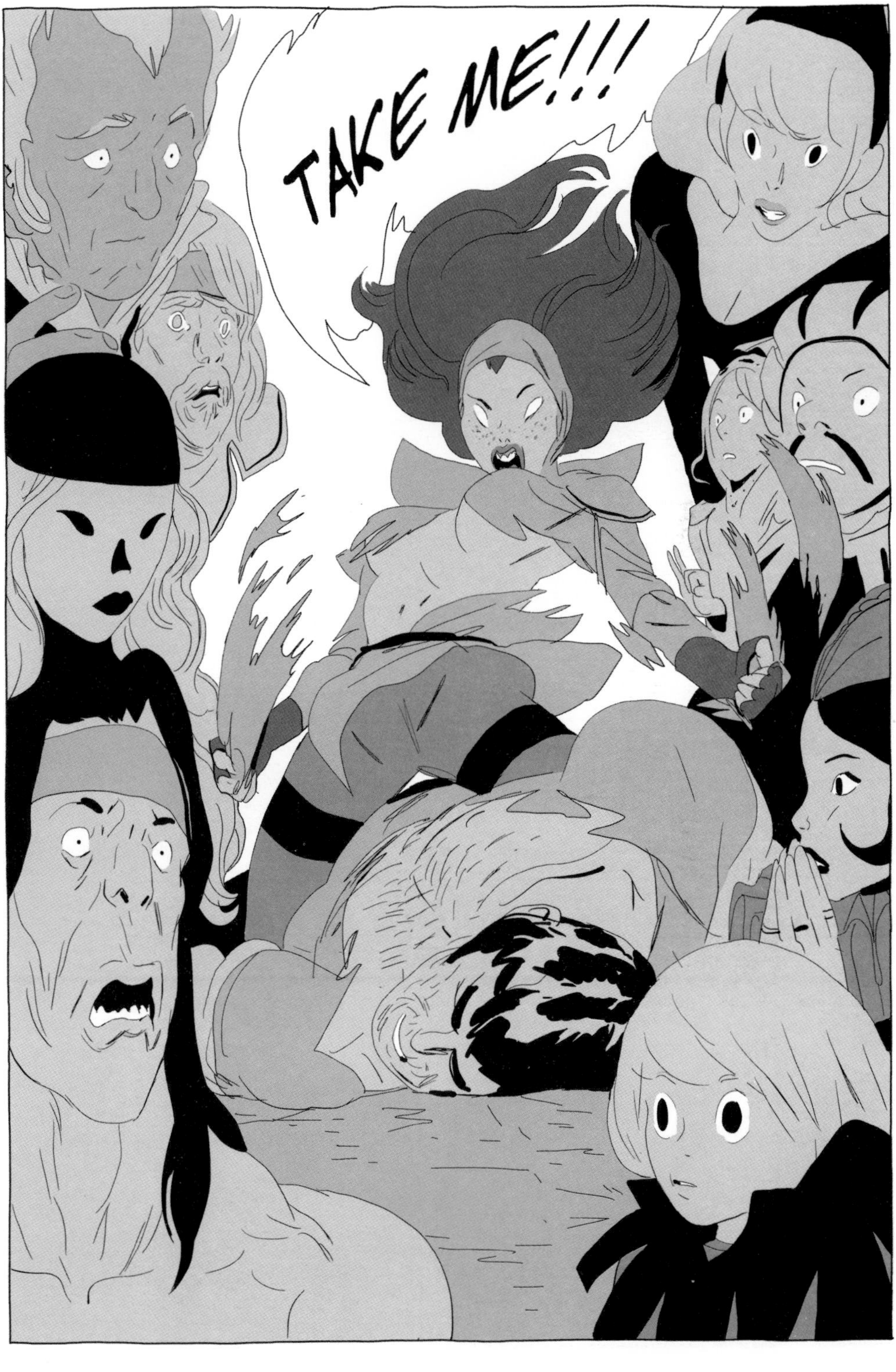
TAKE ME!!!!

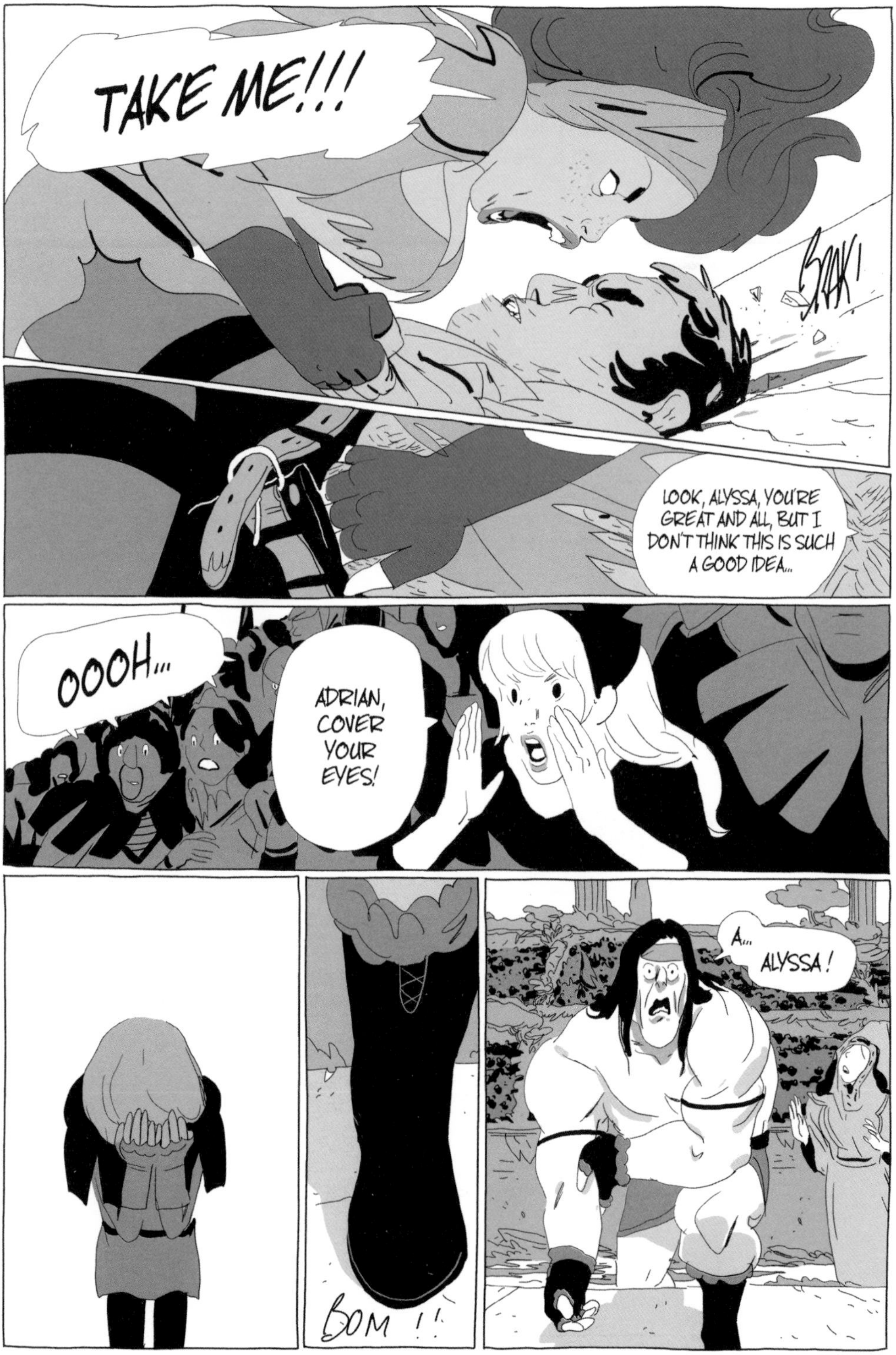
TAKE ME!!!
SRAK!
LOOK, ALYSSA, YOU'RE GREAT AND ALL, BUT I DON'T THINK THIS IS SUCH A GOOD IDEA...
OOOH...
ADRIAN, COVER YOUR EYES!
BOM !!
A... ALYSSA!

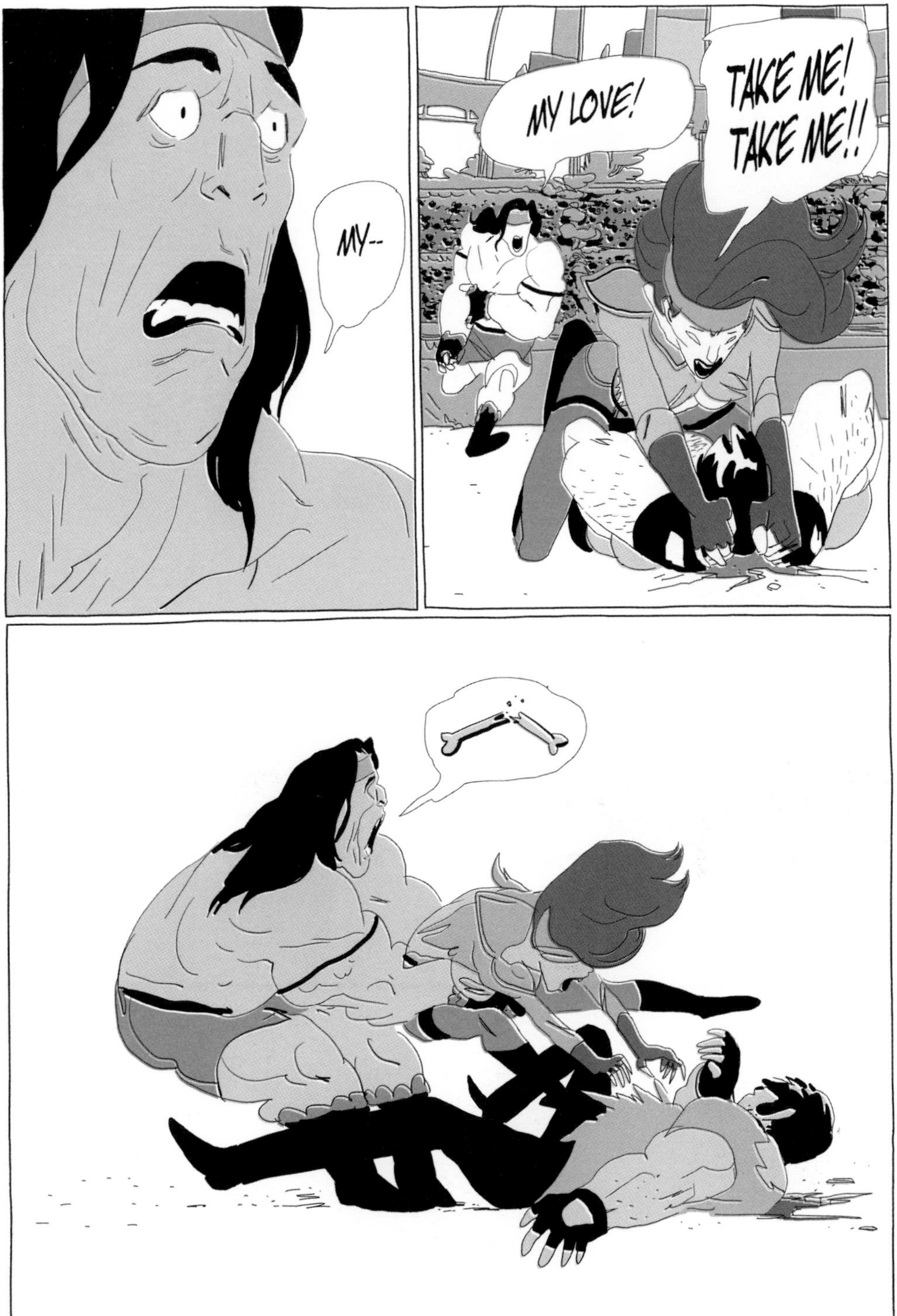
MY--
MY LOVE!
TAKE ME!
TAKE ME!!

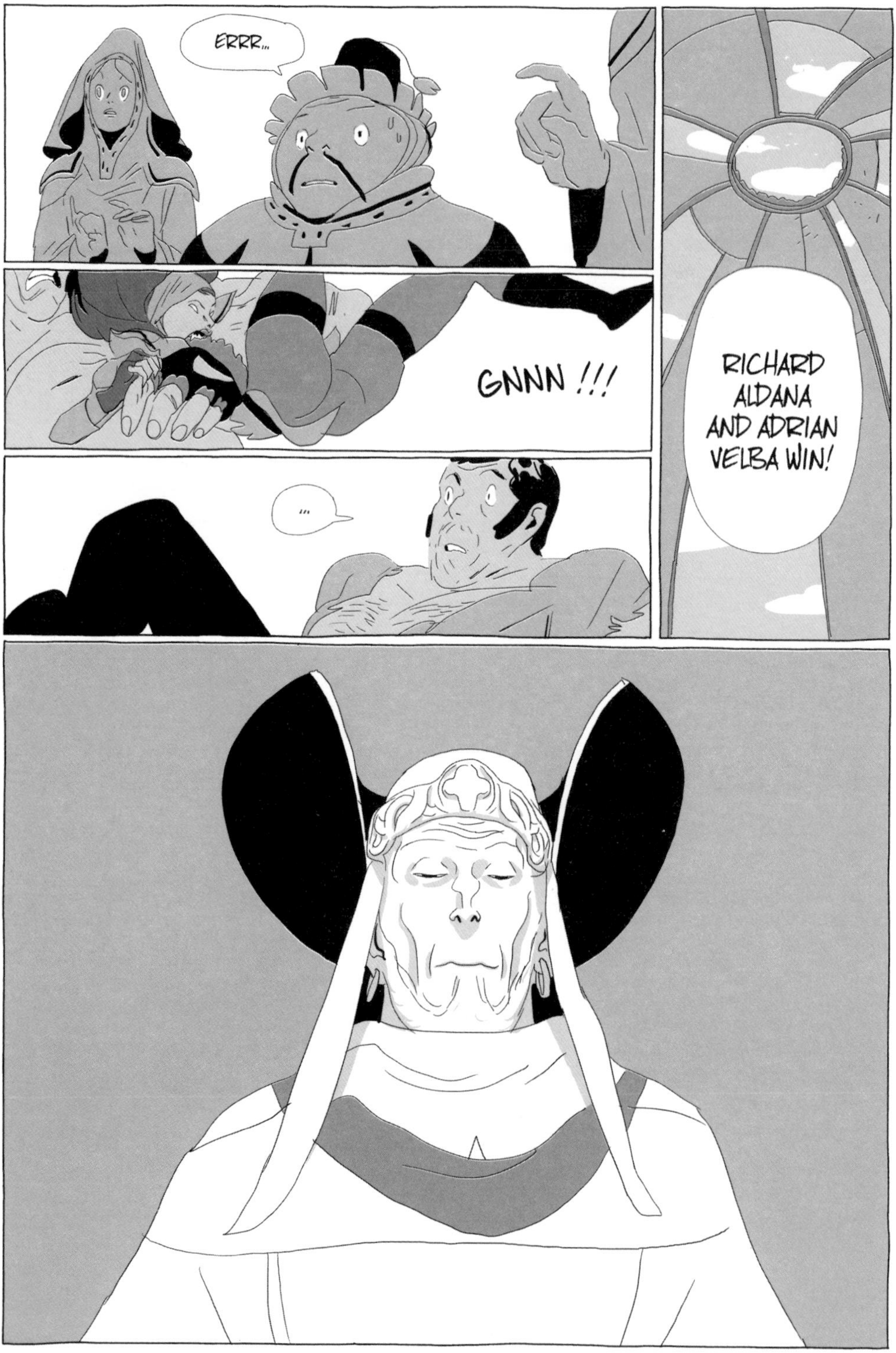
ERRR...
RICHARD ALDANA AND ADRIAN VELBA WIN!
GNNN !!!
...

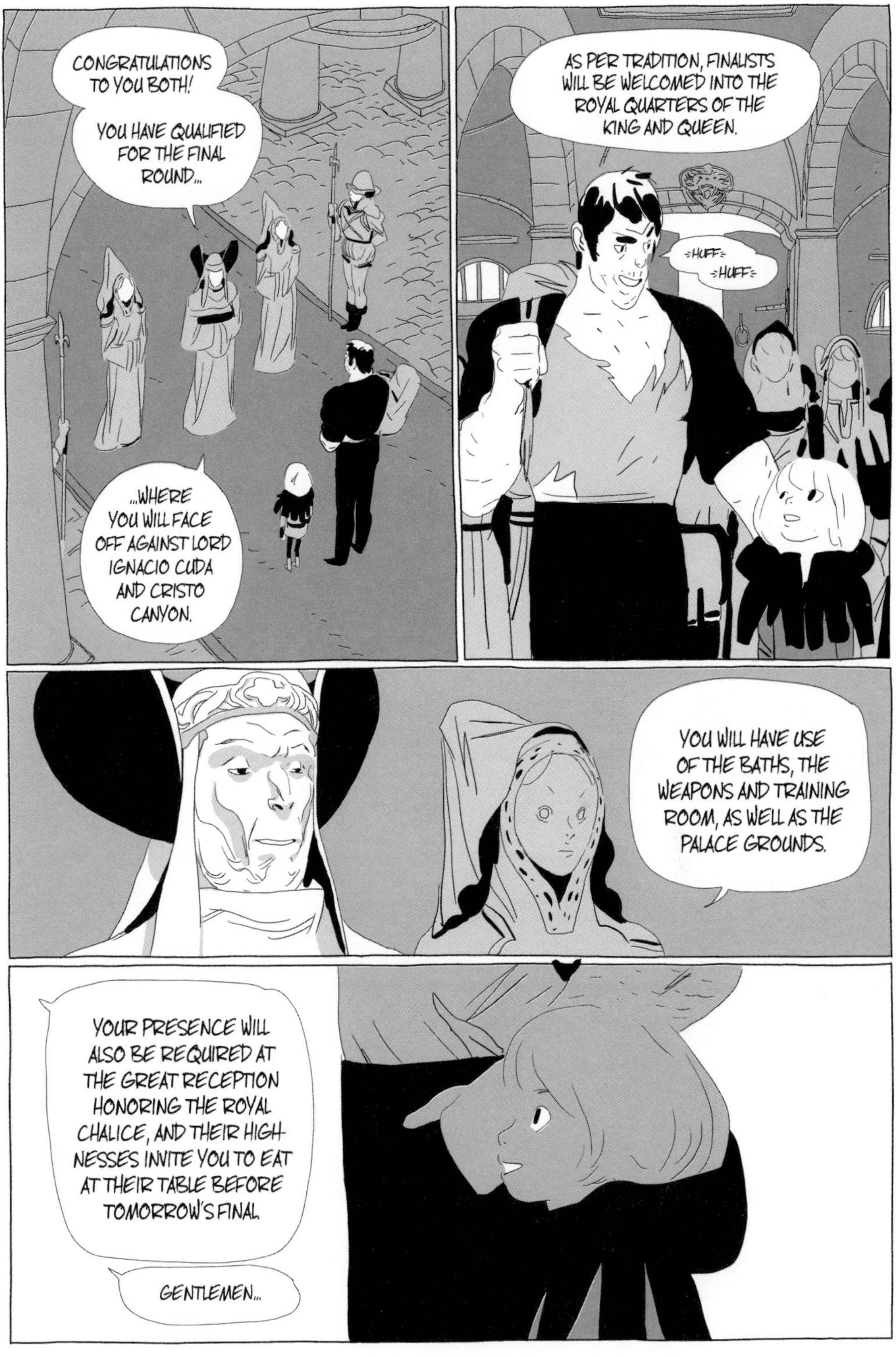
CONGRATULATIONS TO YOU BOTH!
YOU HAVE QUALIFIED FOR THE FINAL ROUND...
...WHERE YOU WILL FACE OFF AGAINST LORD IGNACIO CUDA AND CRISTO CANYON.
AS PER TRADITION, FINALISTS WILL BE WELCOMED INTO THE ROYAL QUARTERS OF THE KING AND QUEEN.
=HUFF=
=HUFF=
YOU WILL HAVE USE OF THE BATHS, THE WEAPONS AND TRAINING ROOM, AS WELL AS THE PALACE GROUNDS.
YOUR PRESENCE WILL ALSO BE REQUIRED AT THE GREAT RECEPTION HONORING THE ROYAL CHALICE, AND THEIR HIGH-NESSES INVITE YOU TO EAT AT THEIR TABLE BEFORE TOMORROW'S FINAL.
GENTLEMEN...

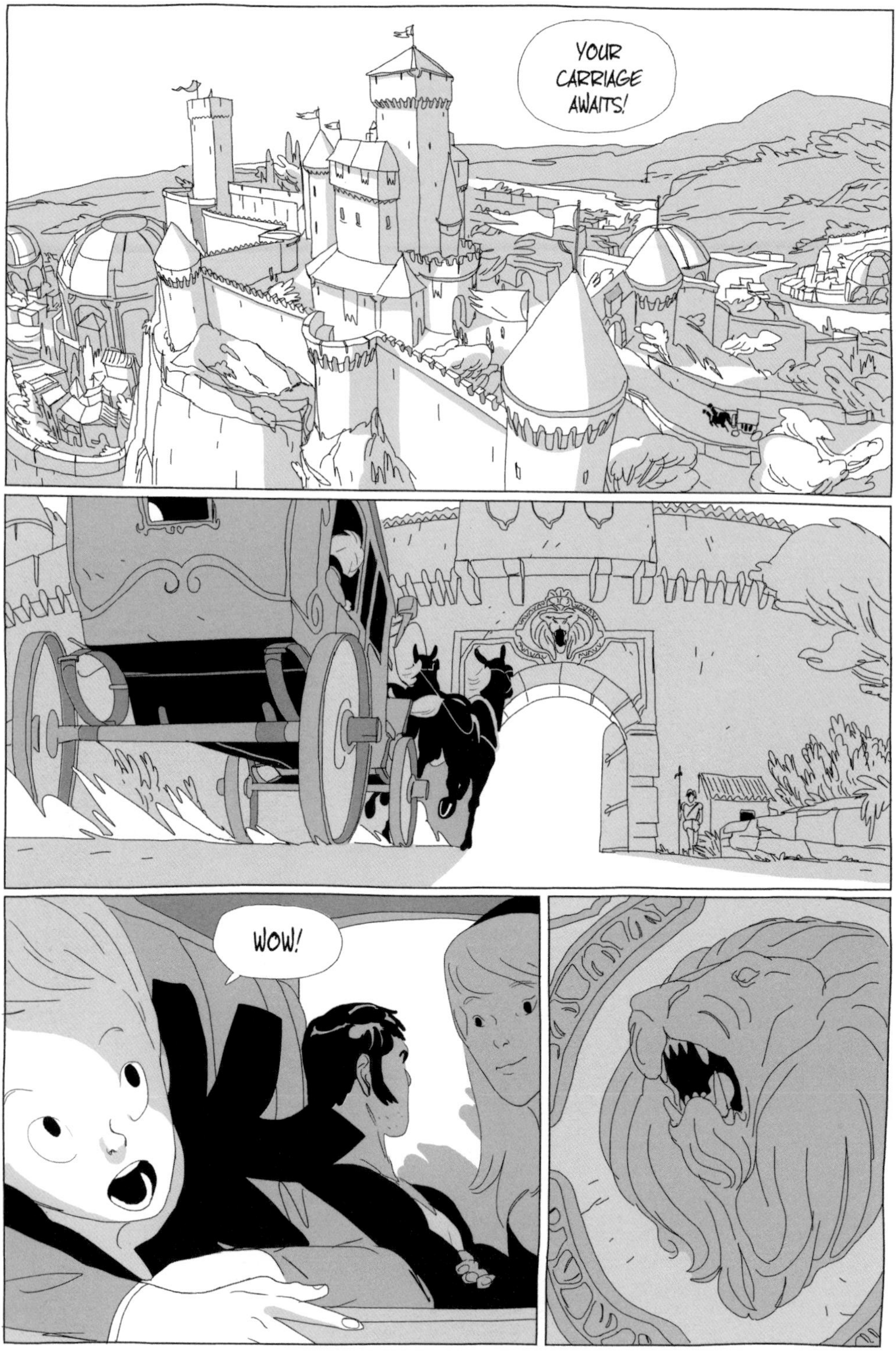
YOUR CARRIAGE AWAITS!
WOW!

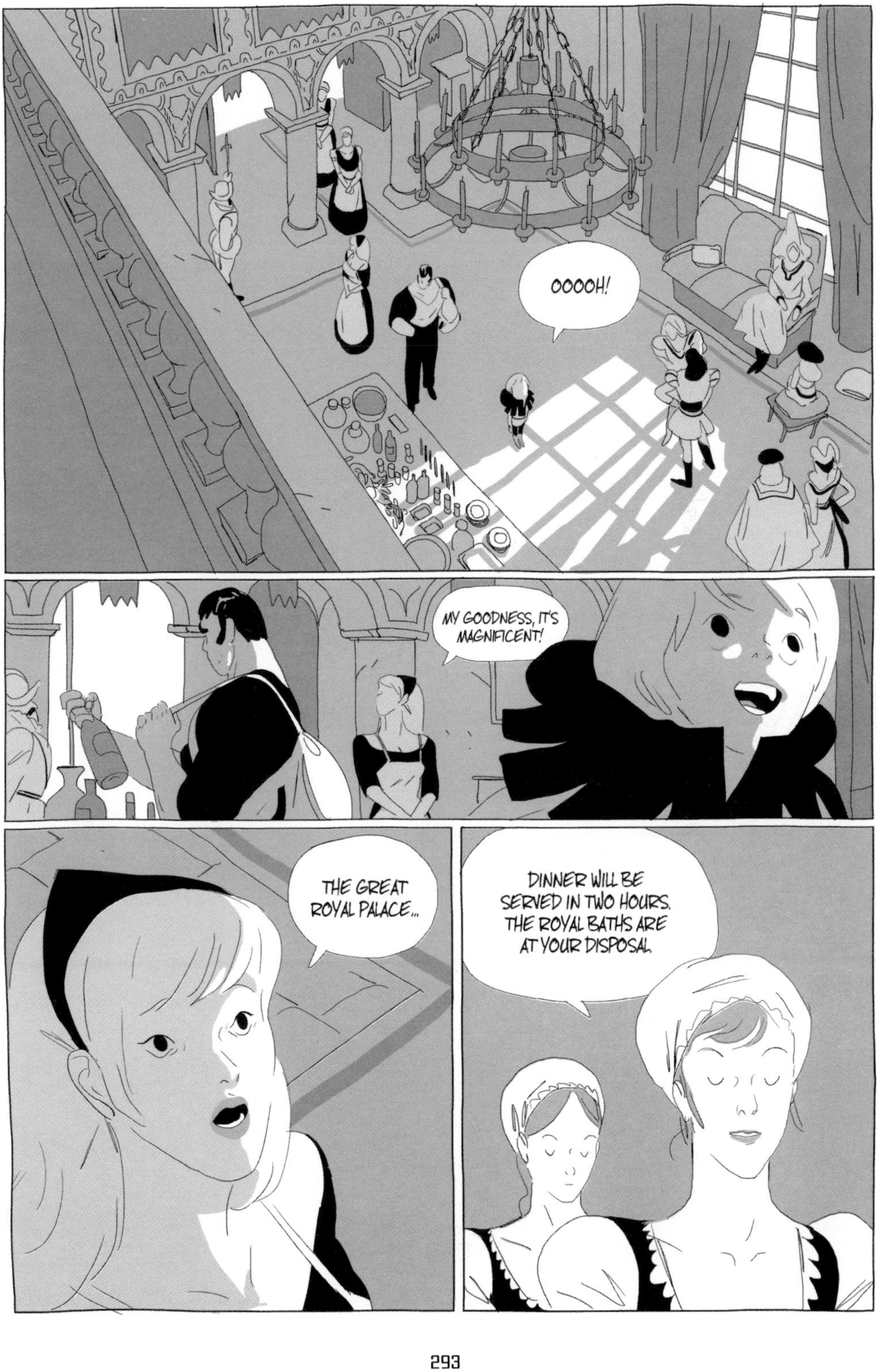
OOOOH!
MY GOODNESS, IT'S MAGNIFICENT!
THE GREAT ROYAL PALACE...
DINNER WILL BE SERVED IN TWO HOURS. THE ROYAL BATHS ARE AT YOUR DISPOSAL.

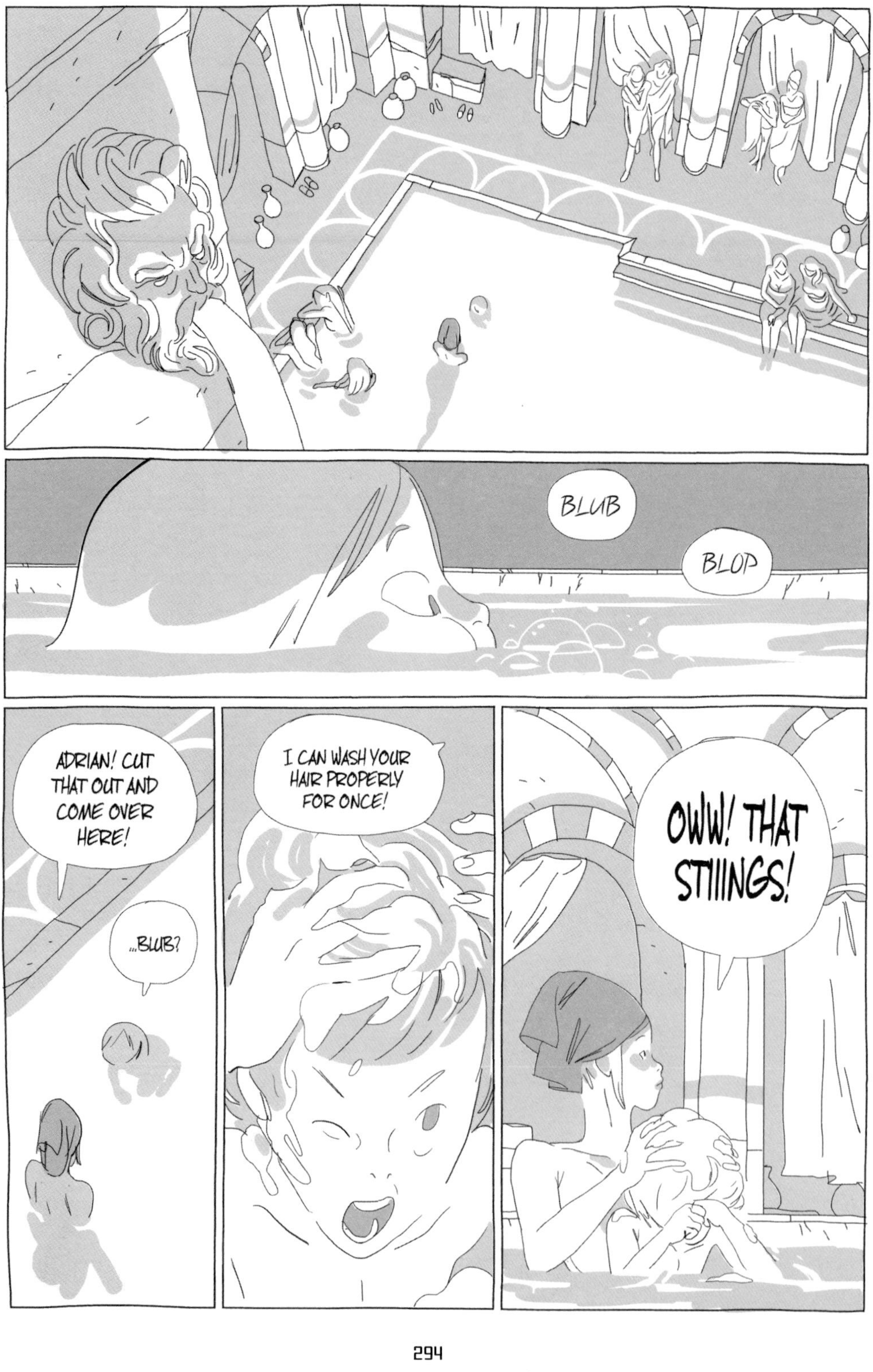
BLUB
BLOP
ADRIAN! CUT THAT OUT AND COME OVER HERE!
...BLUB?
I CAN WASH YOUR HAIR PROPERLY FOR ONCE!
OWW! THAT STIIINGS!

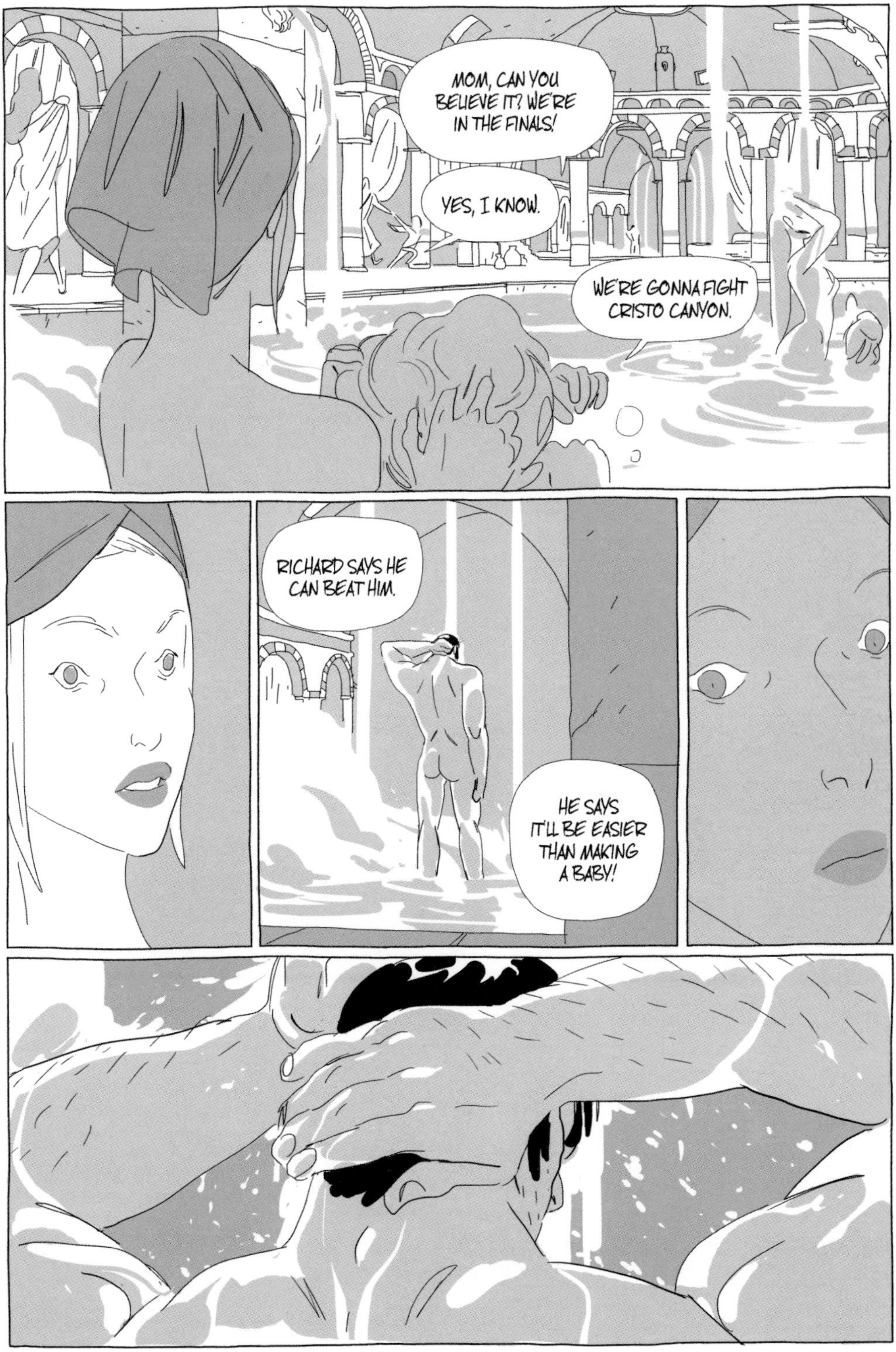
MOM, CAN YOU BELIEVE IT? WE'RE IN THE FINALS!
YES, I KNOW.
WE'RE GONNA FIGHT CRISTO CANYON.
RICHARD SAYS HE CAN BEAT HIM.
HE SAYS IT'LL BE EASIER THAN MAKING A BABY!

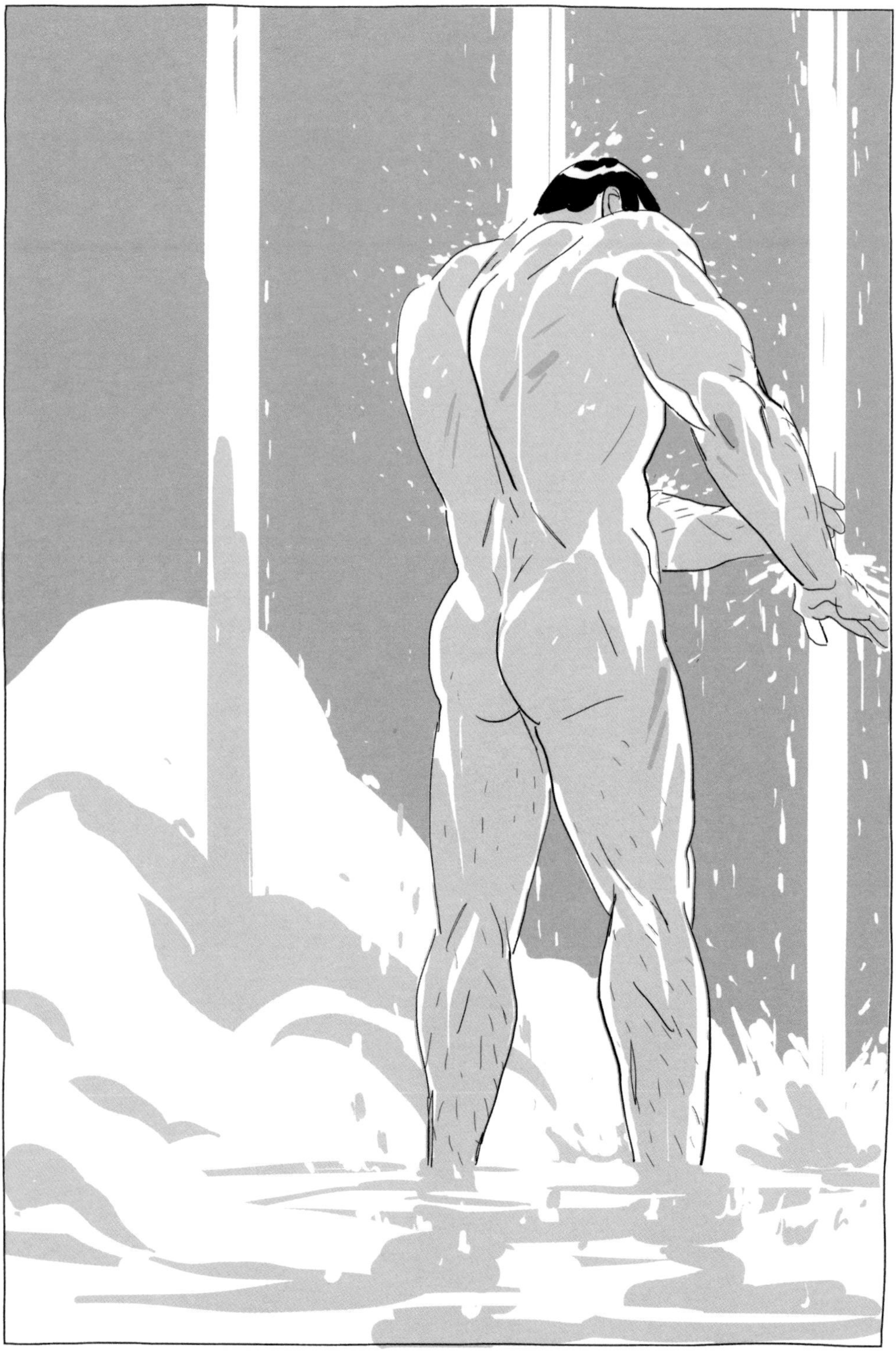

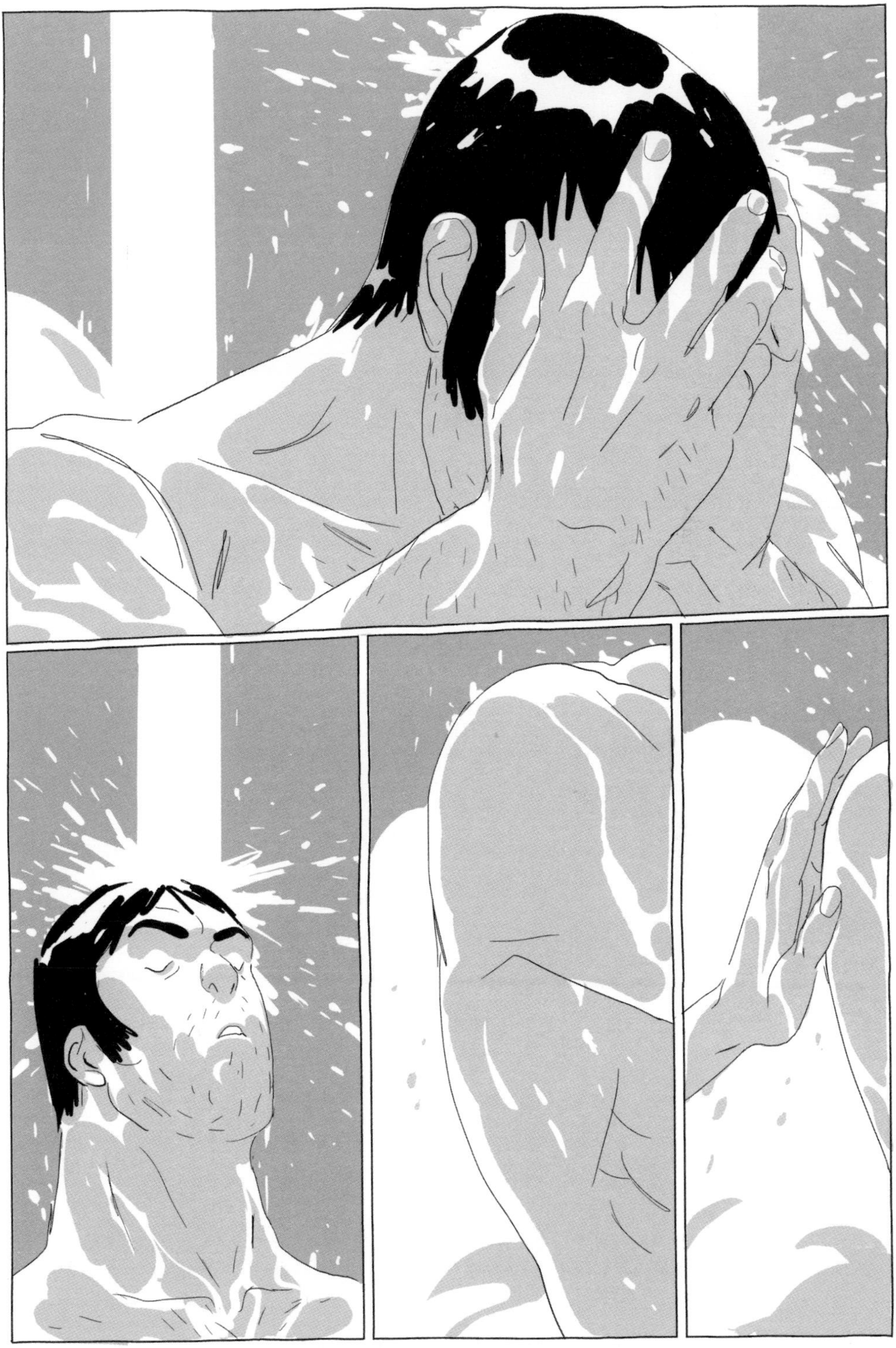

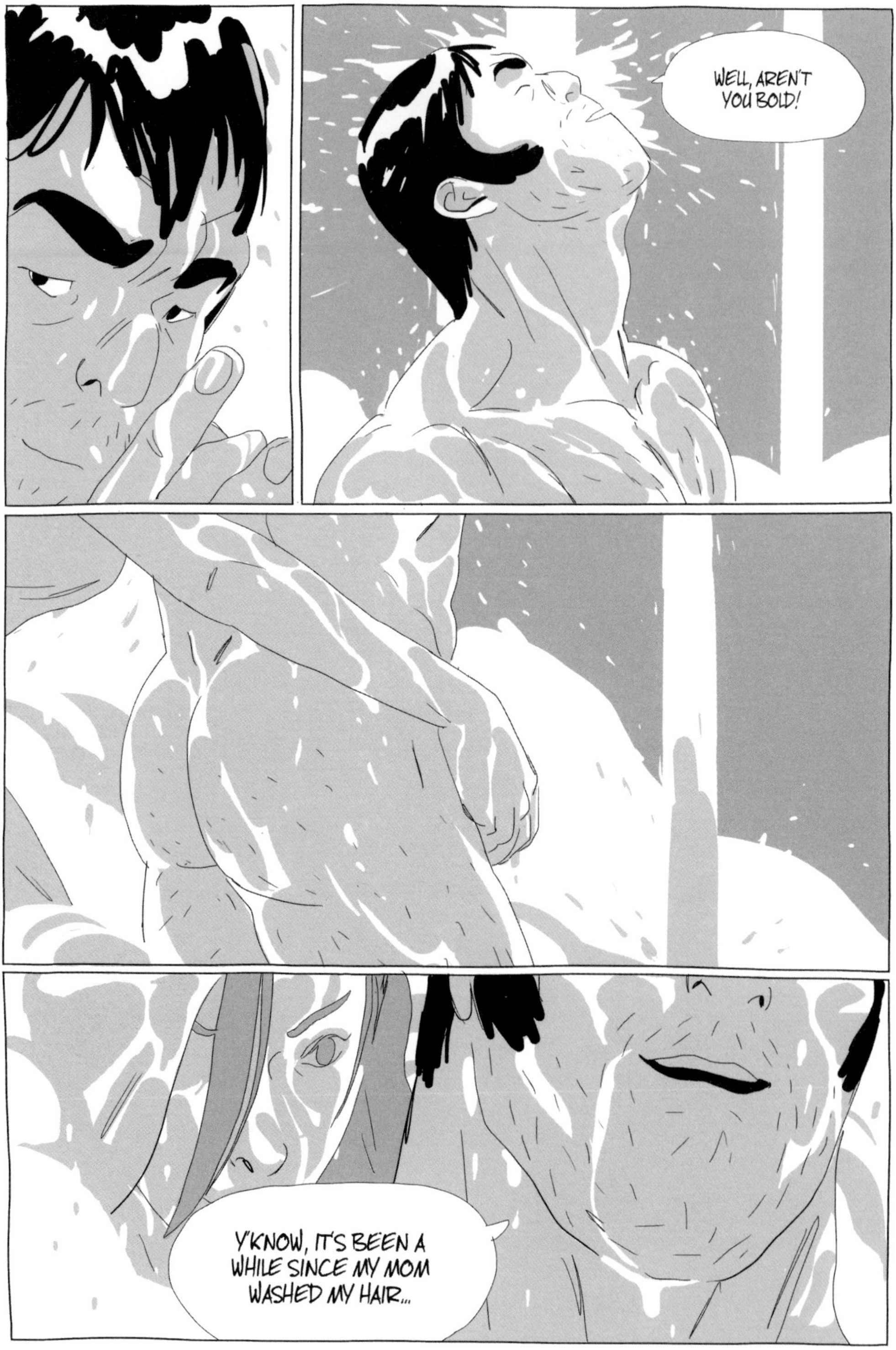
WELL, AREN'T YOU BOLD!
Y'KNOW, IT'S BEEN A WHILE SINCE MY MOM WASHED MY HAIR...

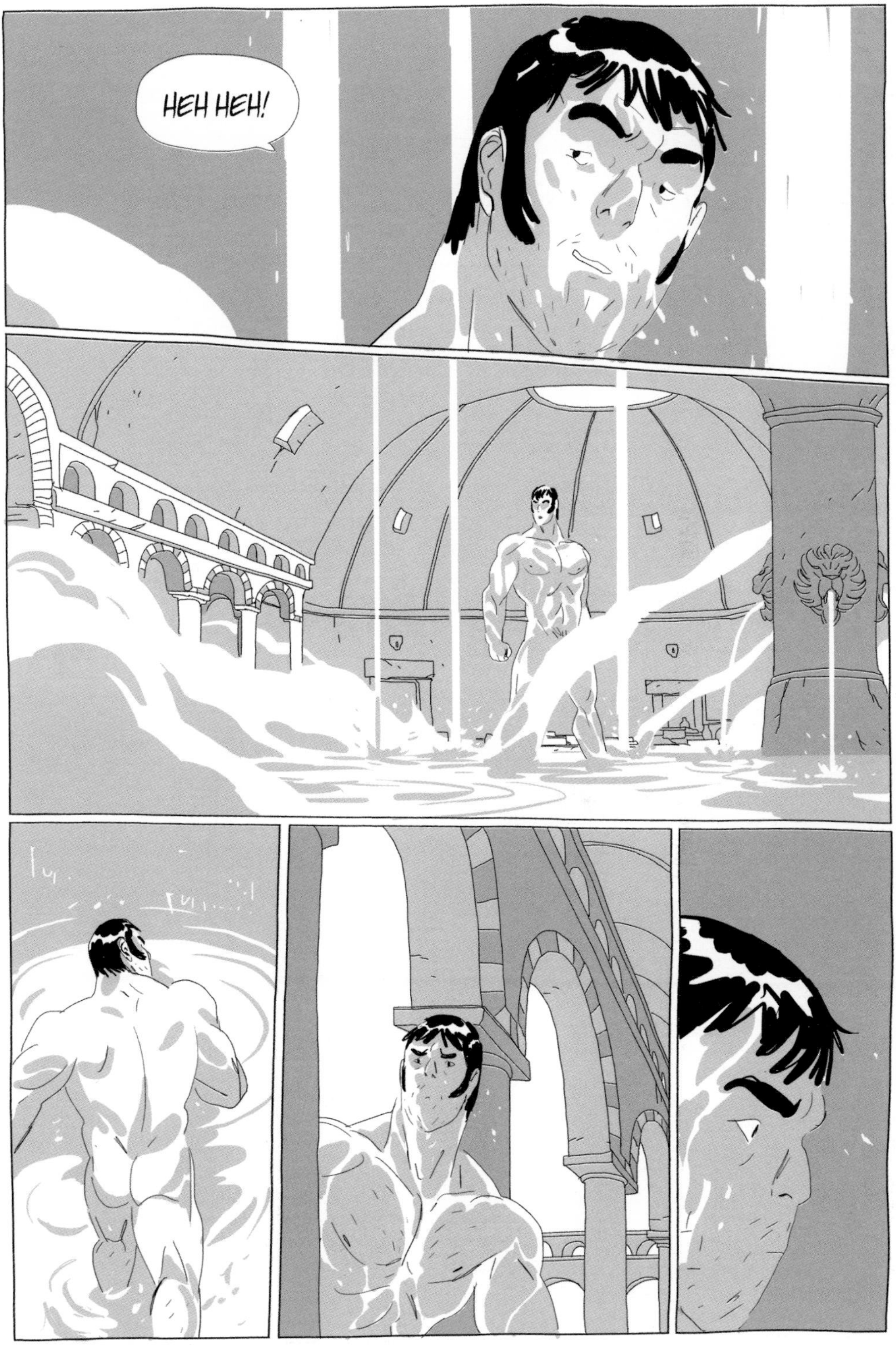
HEH HEH!

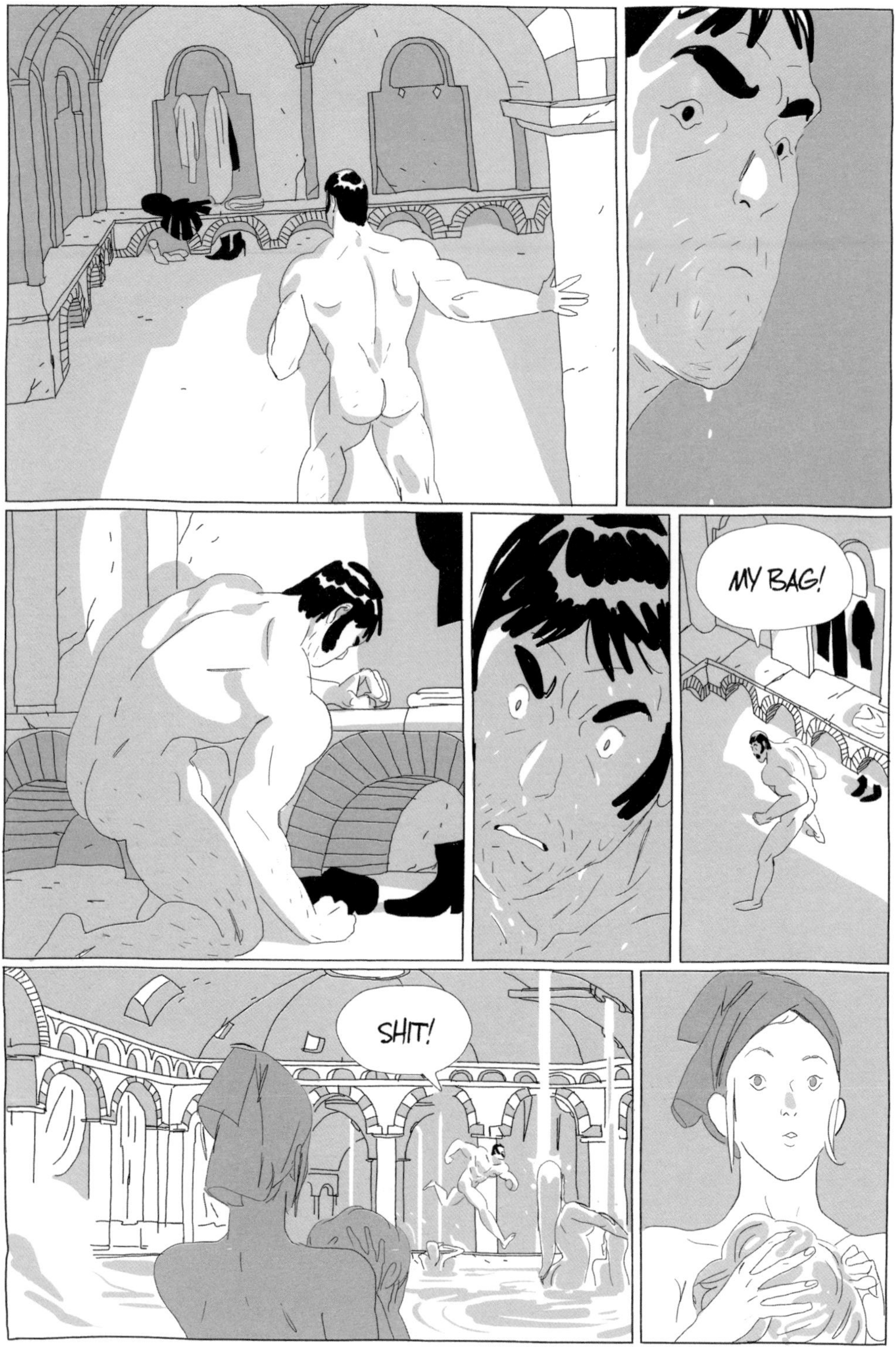
MY BAG!
SHIT!

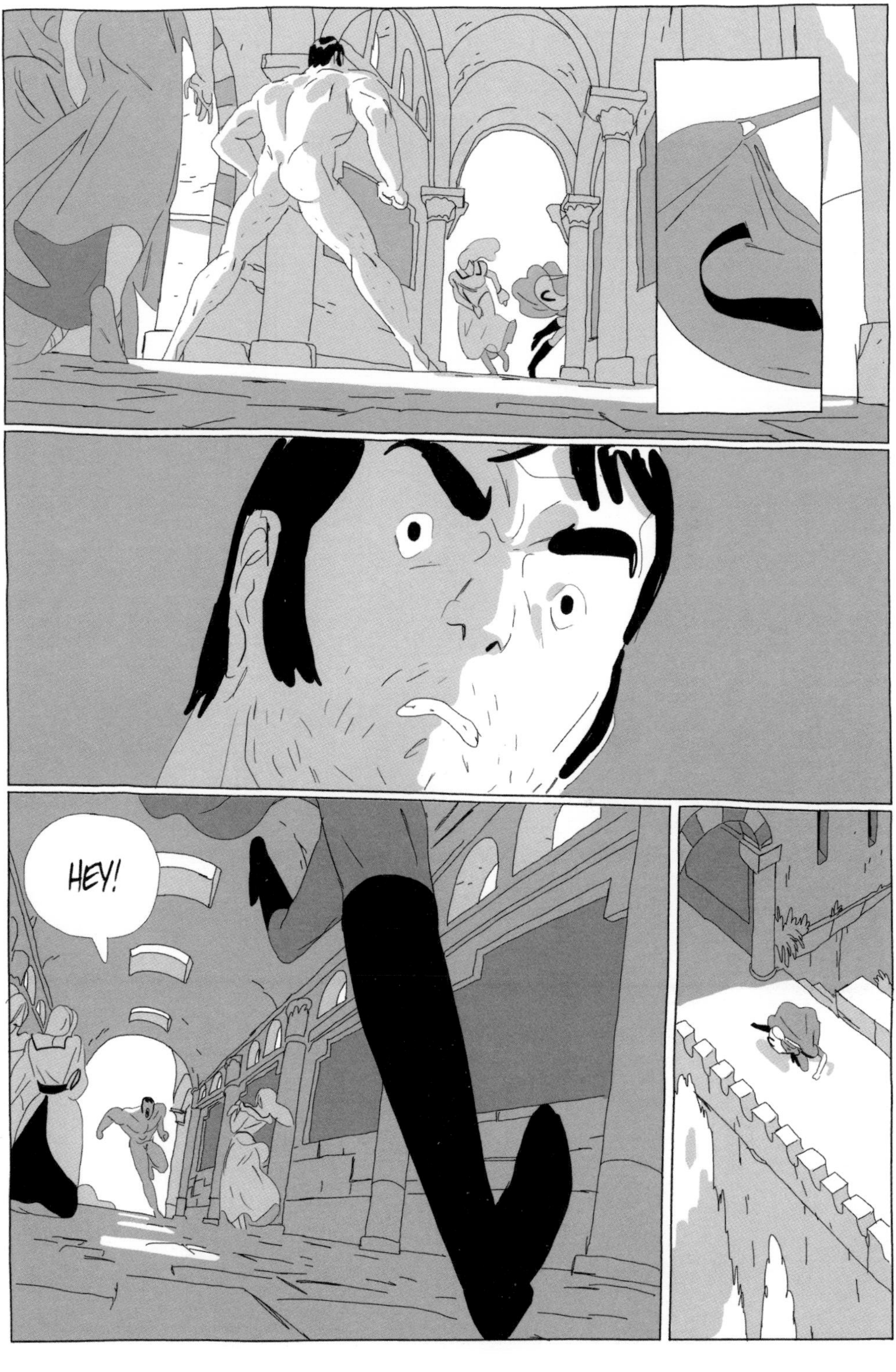
HEY!

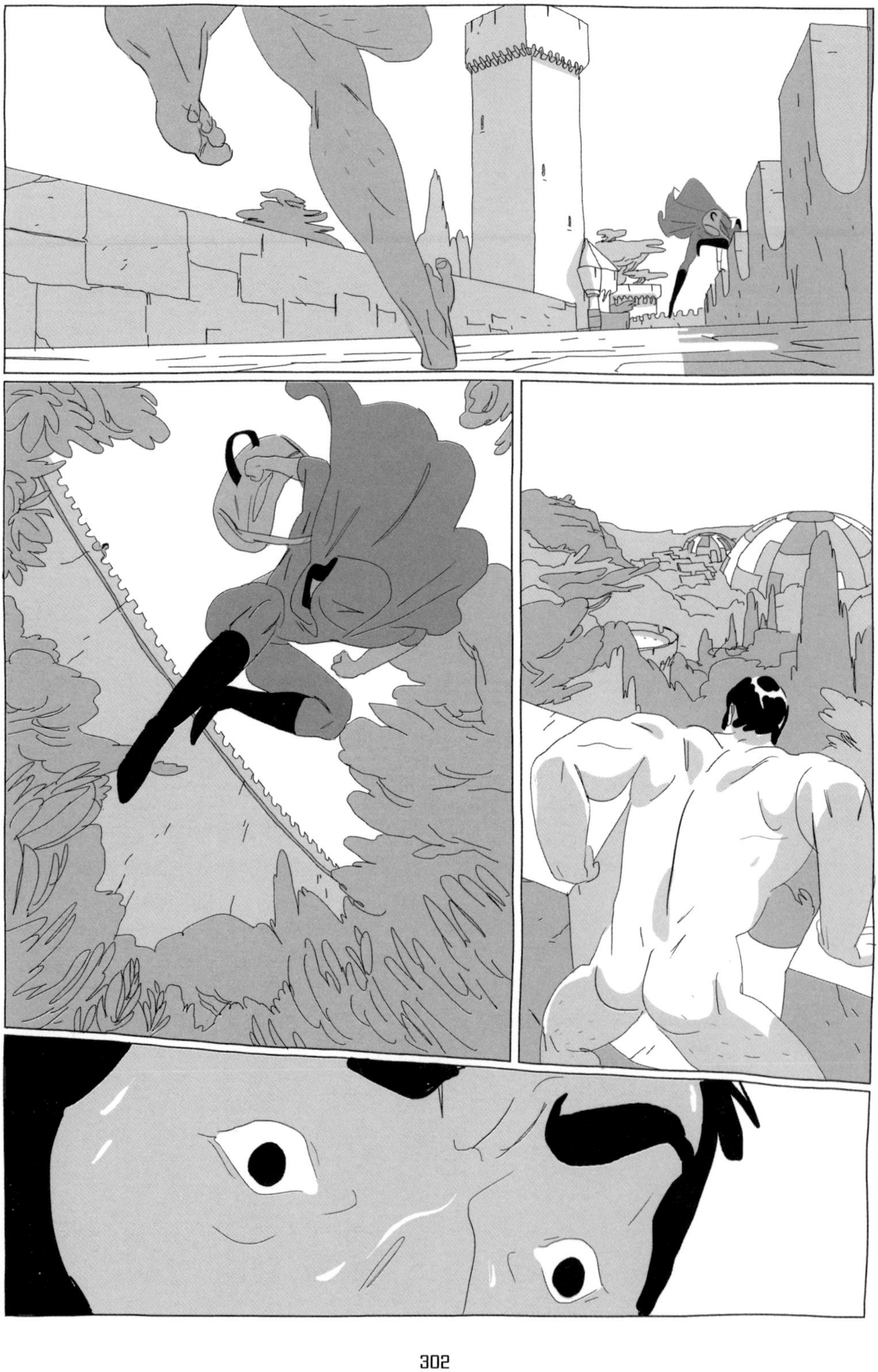

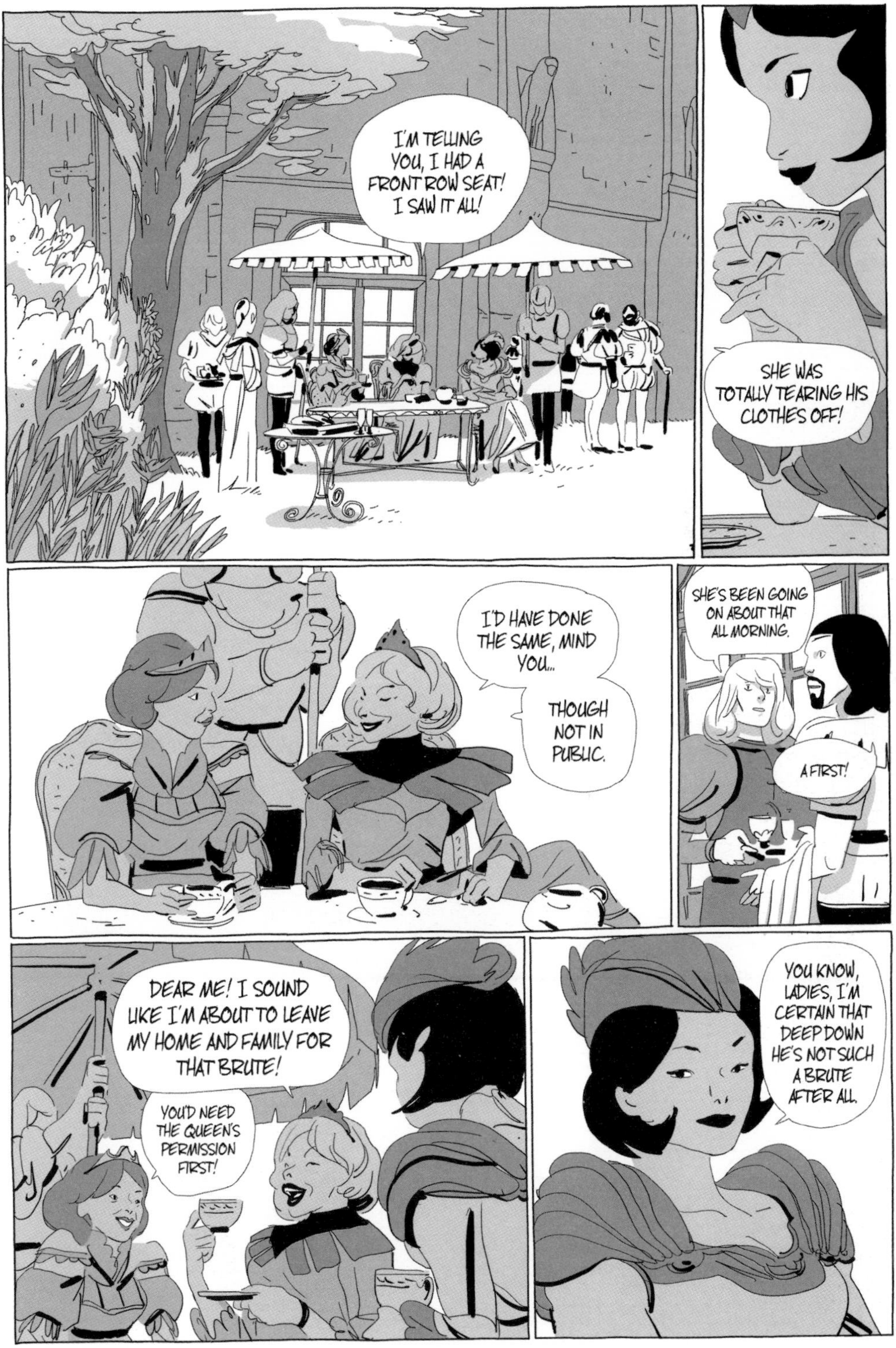
I'M TELLING YOU, I HAD A FRONT ROW SEAT! I SAW IT ALL!
SHE WAS TOTALLY TEARING HIS CLOTHES OFF!
I'D HAVE DONE THE SAME, MIND YOU...
THOUGH NOT IN PUBLIC.
SHE'S BEEN GOING ON ABOUT THAT ALL MORNING.
A FIRST!
DEAR ME! I SOUND LIKE I'M ABOUT TO LEAVE MY HOME AND FAMILY FOR THAT BRUTE!
YOU'D NEED THE QUEEN'S PERMISSION FIRST!
YOU KNOW, LADIES, I'M CERTAIN THAT DEEP DOWN HE'S NOT SUCH A BRUTE AFTER ALL.

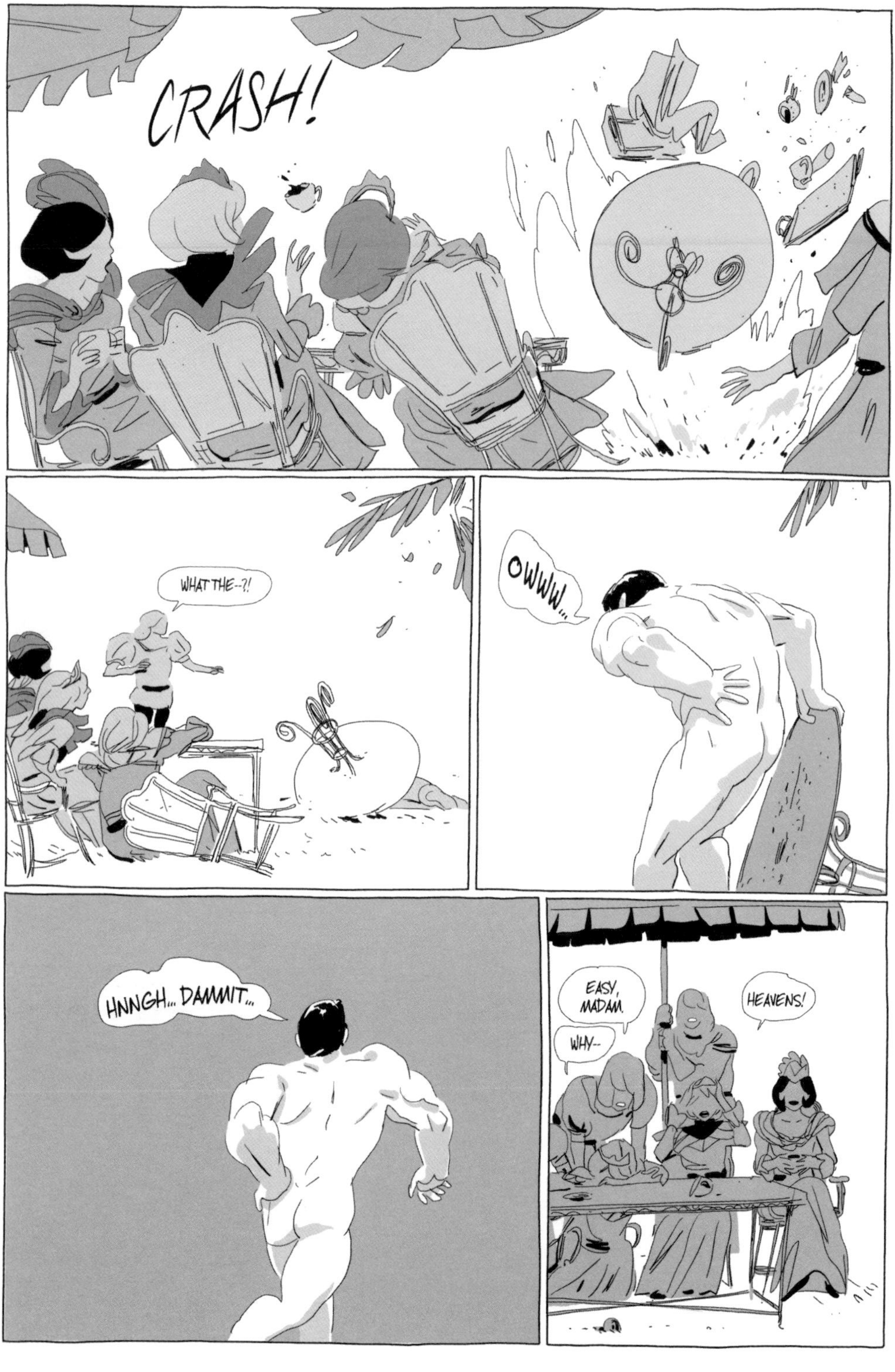
CRASH!
WHAT THE--?!
OWWW...
HNNGH... DAMMIT...
EASY, MADAM.
WHY--
HEAVENS!

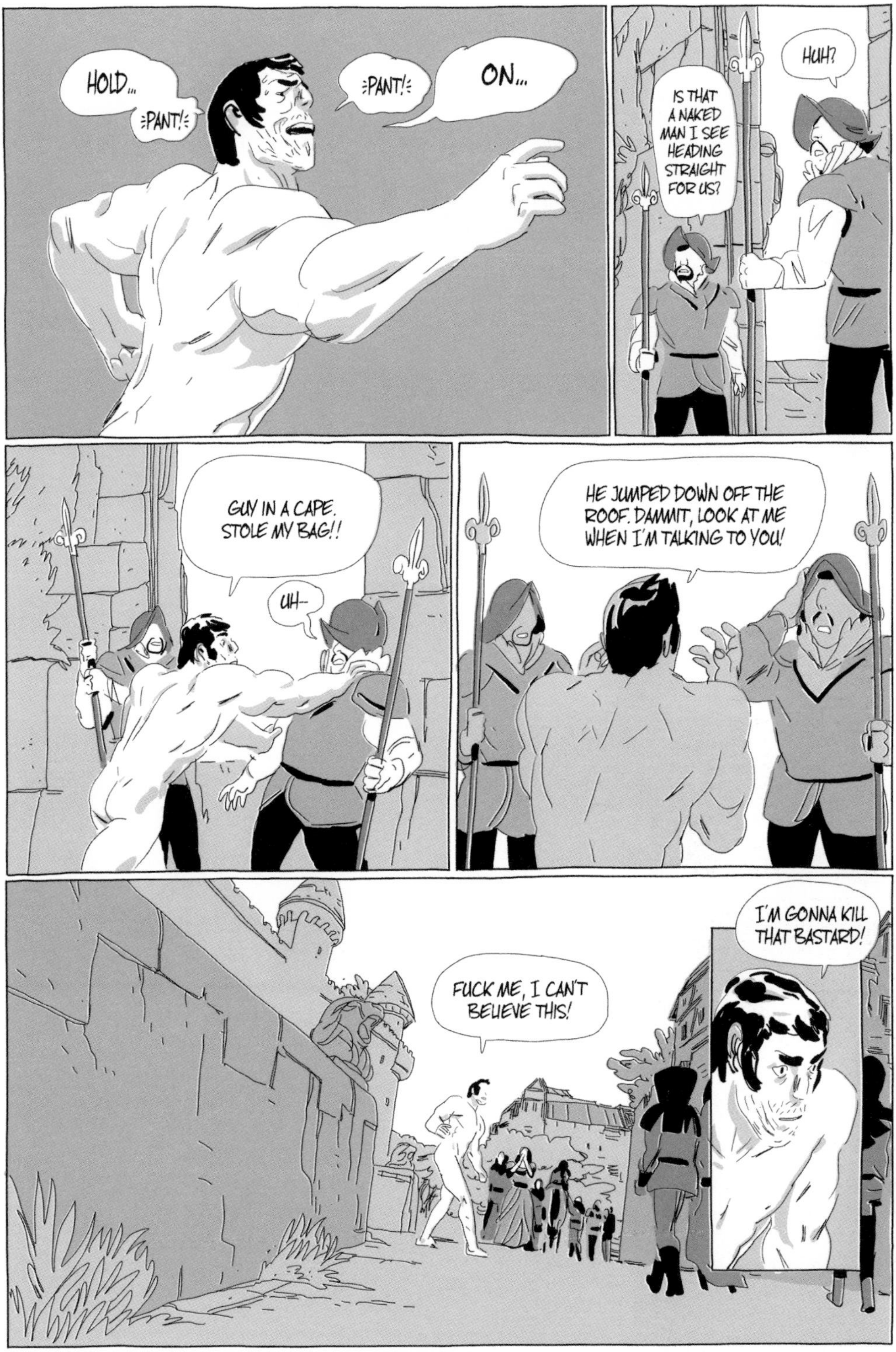
HOLD...
PANT!
PANT!
ON...
IS THAT A NAKED MAN I SEE HEADING STRAIGHT FOR US?
HUH?
GUY IN A CAPE. STOLE MY BAG!!
UH--
HE JUMPED DOWN OFF THE ROOF. DAMMIT, LOOK AT ME WHEN I'M TALKING TO YOU!
FUCK ME, I CAN'T BELIEVE THIS!
I'M GONNA KILL THAT BASTARD!

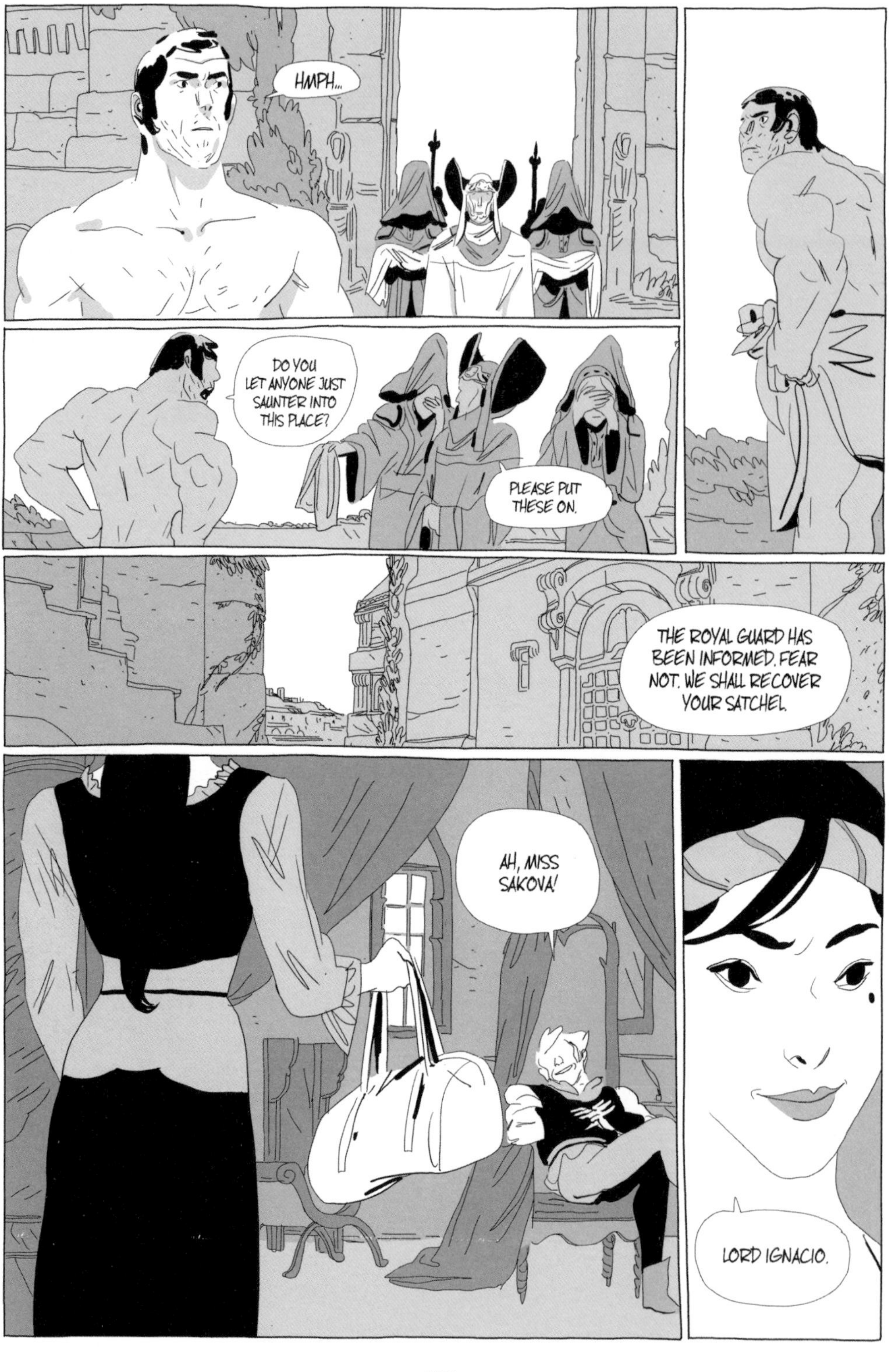
HMPH...
DO YOU LET ANYONE JUST SAUNTER INTO THIS PLACE?
PLEASE PUT THESE ON.
THE ROYAL GUARD HAS BEEN INFORMED. FEAR NOT. WE SHALL RECOVER YOUR SATCHEL.
AH, MISS SAKOVA!
LORD IGNACIO.

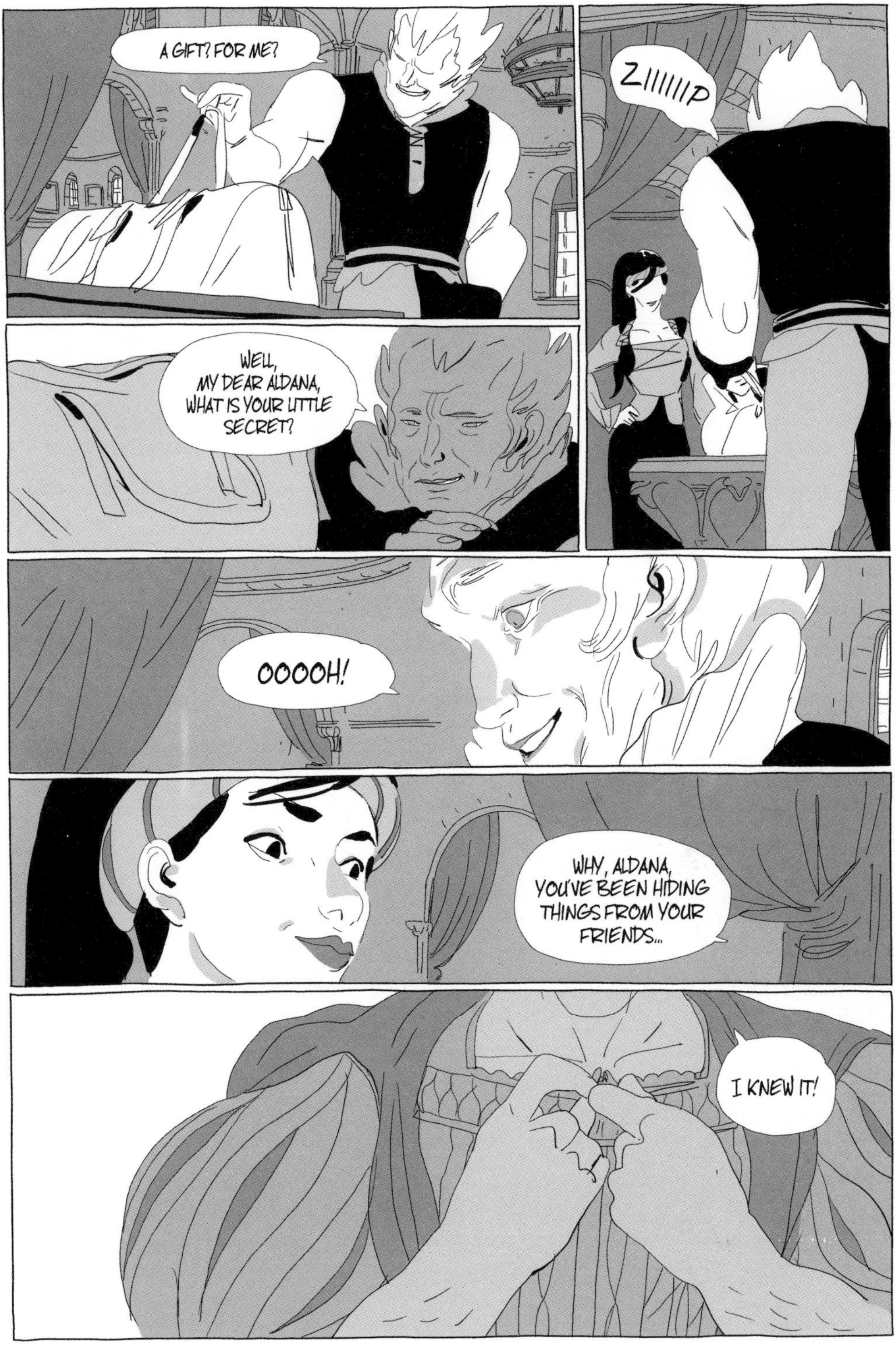
A GIFT? FOR ME?
ZIIIIIIP
WELL, MY DEAR ALDANA, WHAT IS YOUR LITTLE SECRET?
OOOOH!
WHY, ALDANA, YOU'VE BEEN HIDING THINGS FROM YOUR FRIENDS...
I KNEW IT!

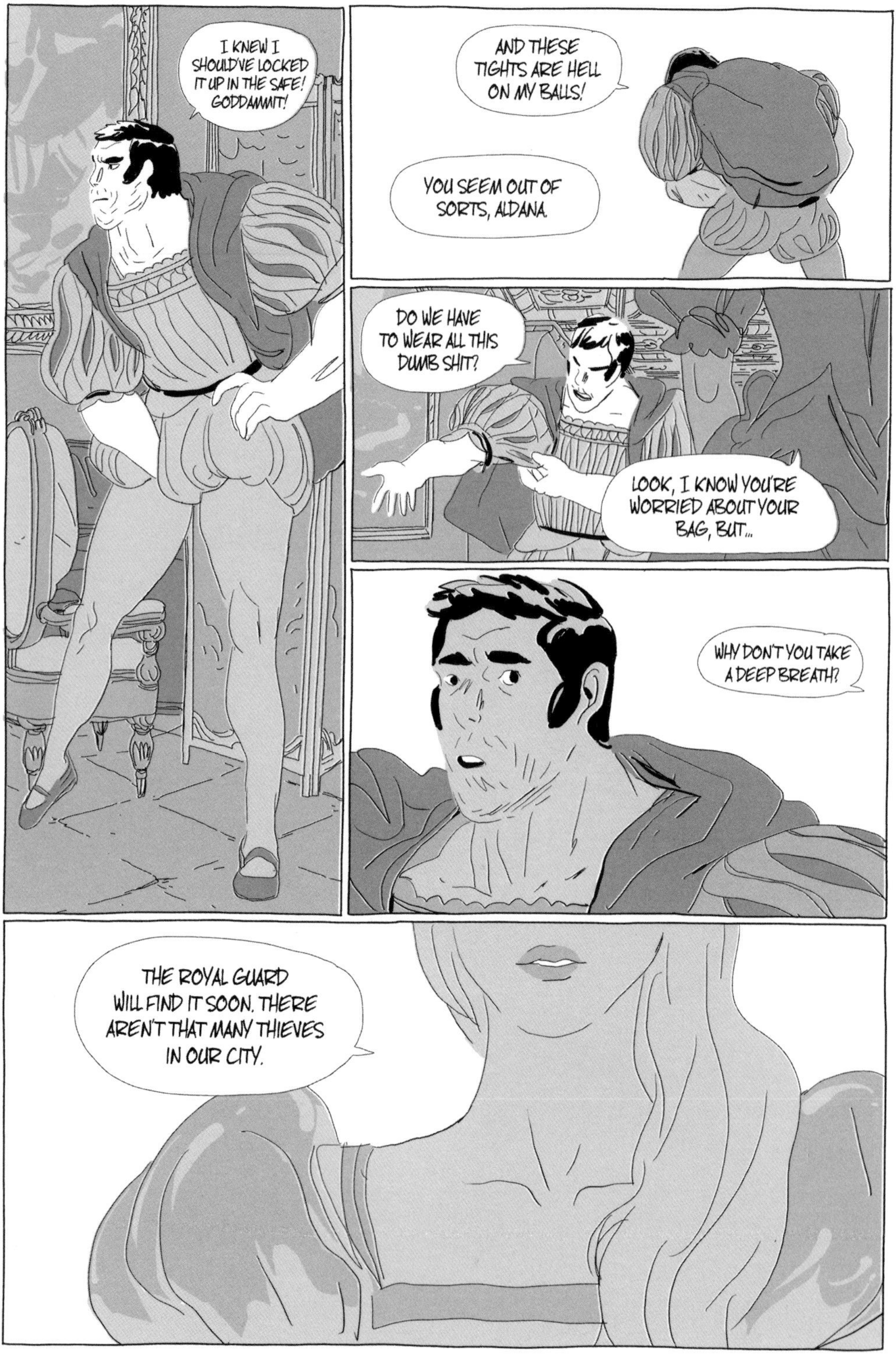
I KNEW I SHOULD'VE LOCKED IT UP IN THE SAFE! GODDAMMIT!
AND THESE TIGHTS ARE HELL ON MY BALLS!
YOU SEEM OUT OF SORTS, ALDANA.
DO WE HAVE TO WEAR ALL THIS DUMB SHIT?
LOOK, I KNOW YOU'RE WORRIED ABOUT YOUR BAG, BUT...
WHY DON'T YOU TAKE A DEEP BREATH?
THE ROYAL GUARD WILL FIND IT SOON. THERE AREN'T THAT MANY THIEVES IN OUR CITY.

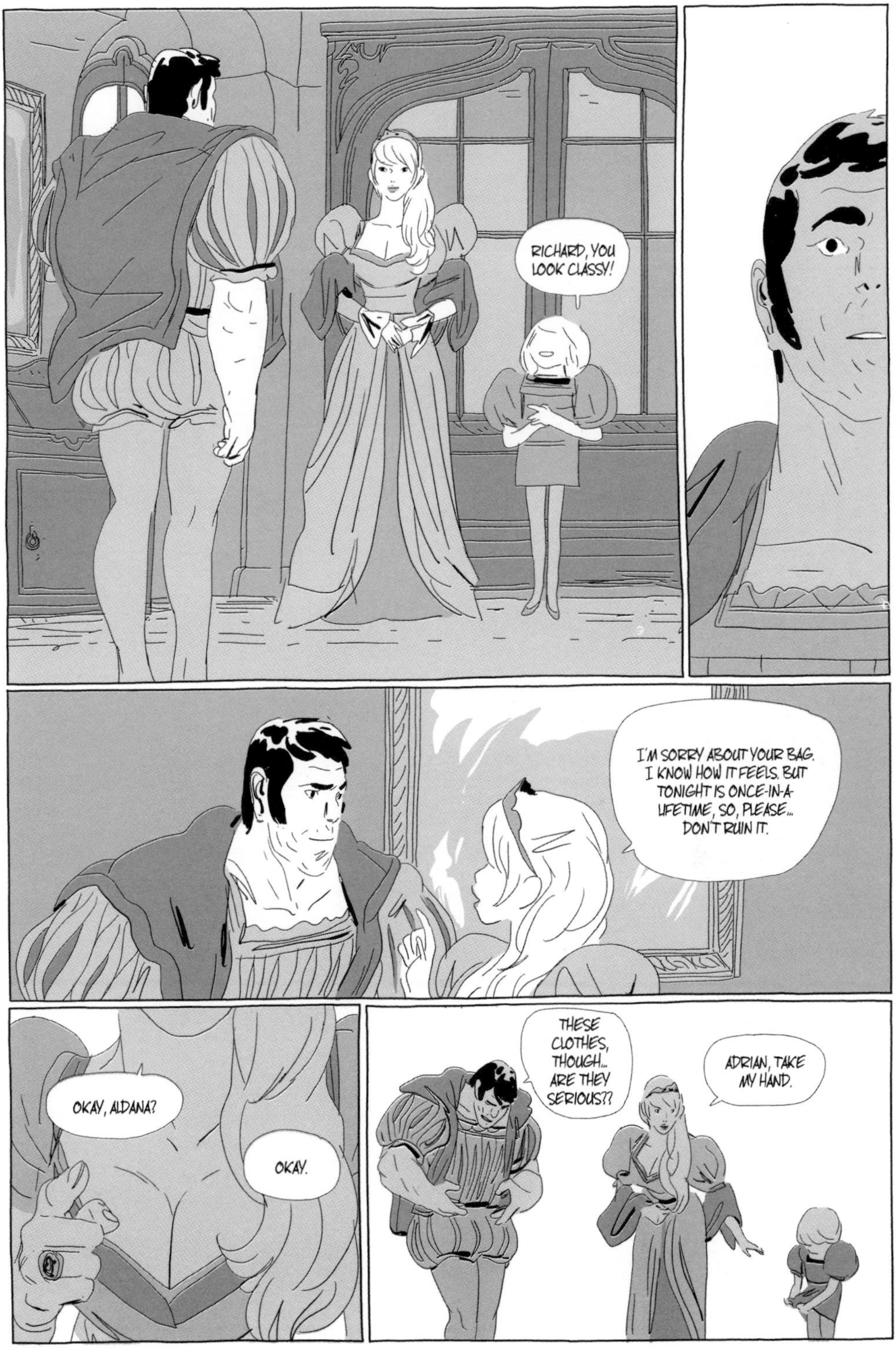
RICHARD, YOU LOOK CLASSY!
I'M SORRY ABOUT YOUR BAG. I KNOW HOW IT FEELS. BUT TONIGHT IS ONCE-IN-A-LIFETIME, SO, PLEASE... DON'T RUIN IT.
OKAY, ALDANA?
OKAY.
THESE CLOTHES, THOUGH... ARE THEY SERIOUS??
ADRIAN, TAKE MY HAND.

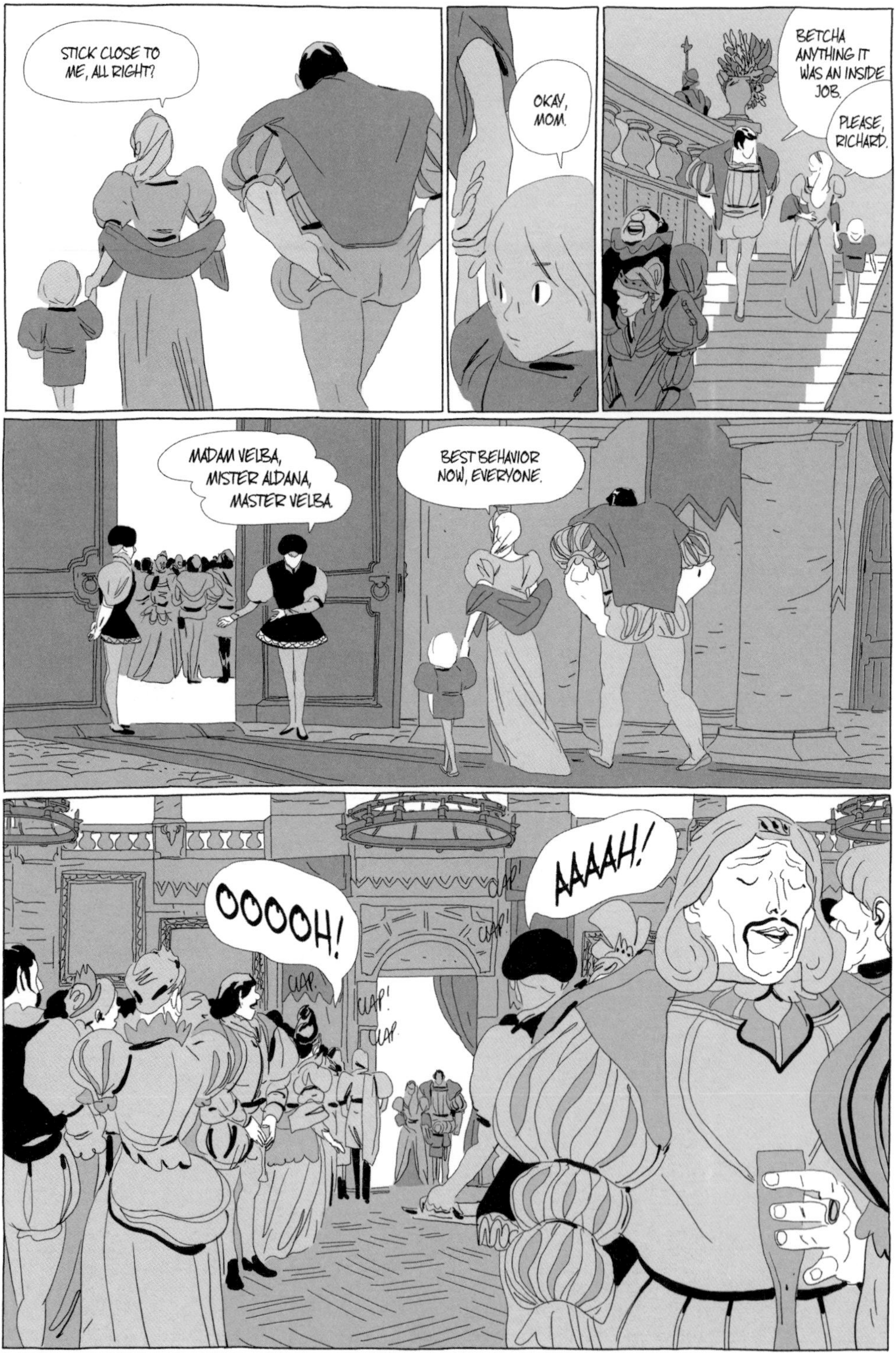
STICK CLOSE TO ME, ALL RIGHT?
OKAY, MOM.
BETCHA ANYTHING IT WAS AN INSIDE JOB.
PLEASE, RICHARD.
MADAM VELBA, MISTER ALDANA, MASTER VELBA.
BEST BEHAVIOR NOW, EVERYONE.
OOOOH!
AAAAH!
CLAP!
CLAP!
CLAP!
CLAP!
CLAP!

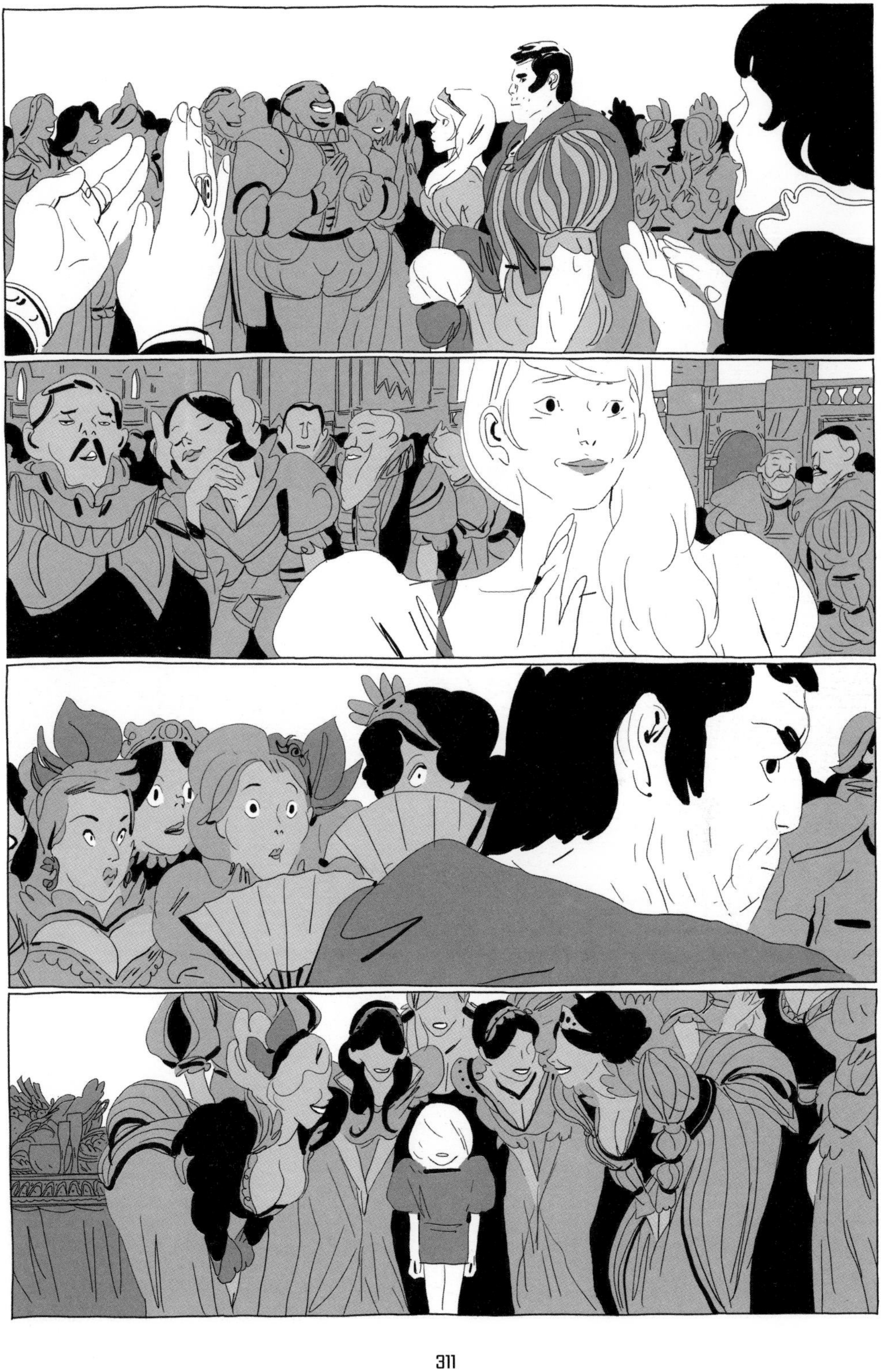

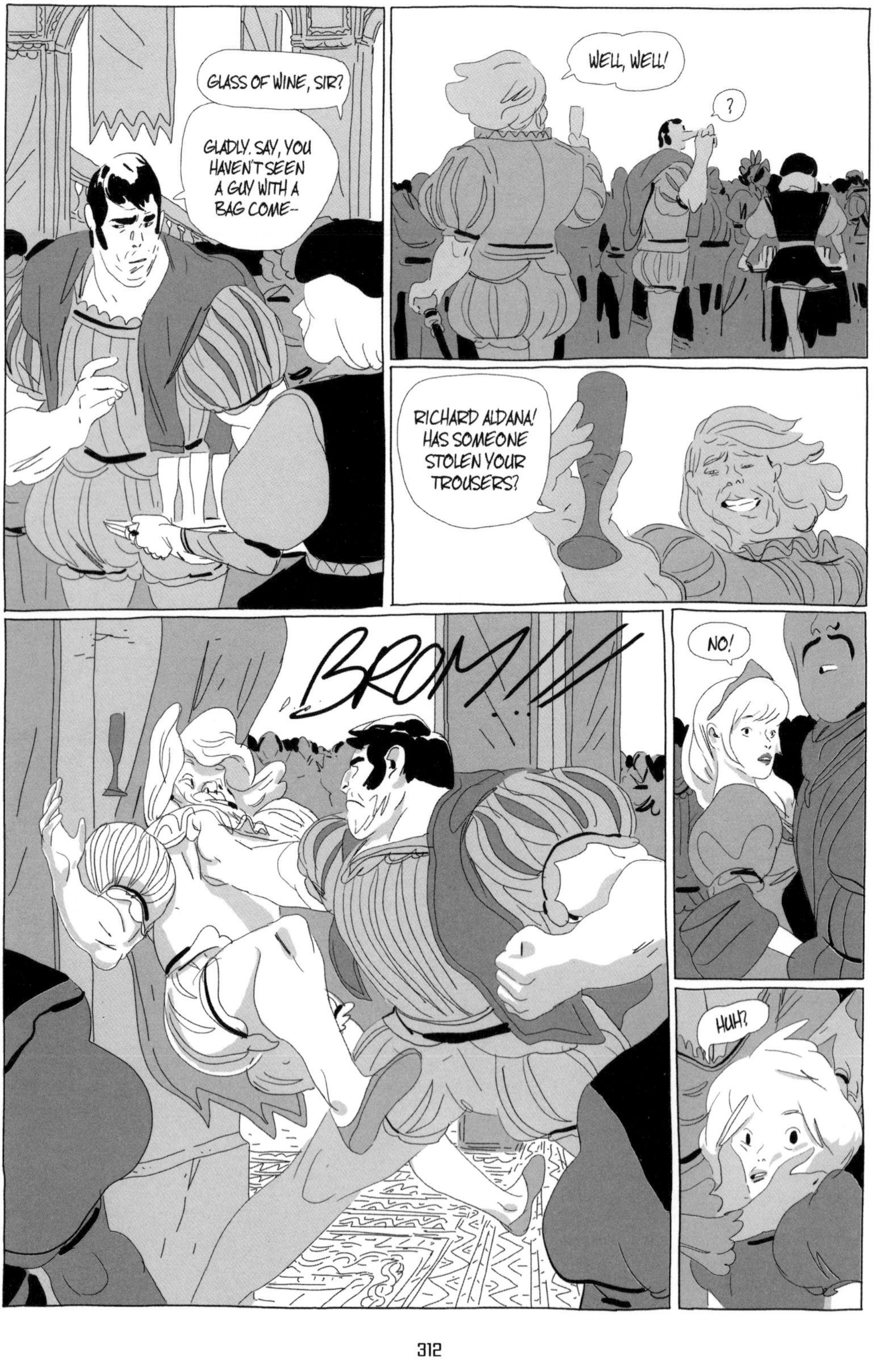
GLASS OF WINE, SIR?
GLADLY. SAY, YOU HAVEN'T SEEN A GUY WITH A BAG COME--
WELL, WELL!
?
RICHARD ALDANA! HAS SOMEONE STOLEN YOUR TROUSERS?
BROM!!!
NO!
HUH?

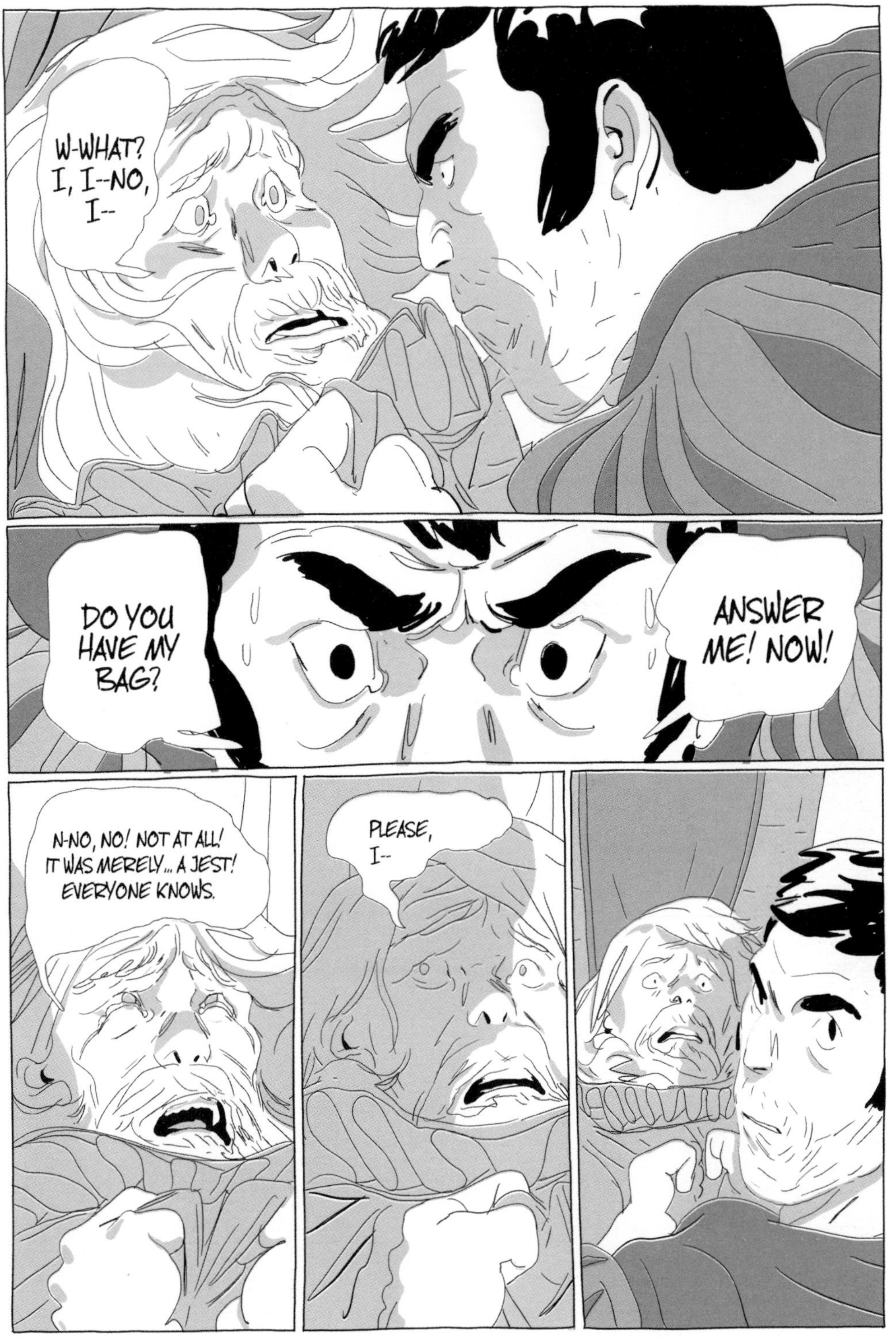
W-WHAT? I, I--NO, I--
DO YOU HAVE MY BAG?
ANSWER ME! NOW!
N-NO, NO! NOT AT ALL! IT WAS MERELY... A JEST! EVERYONE KNOWS.
PLEASE, I--

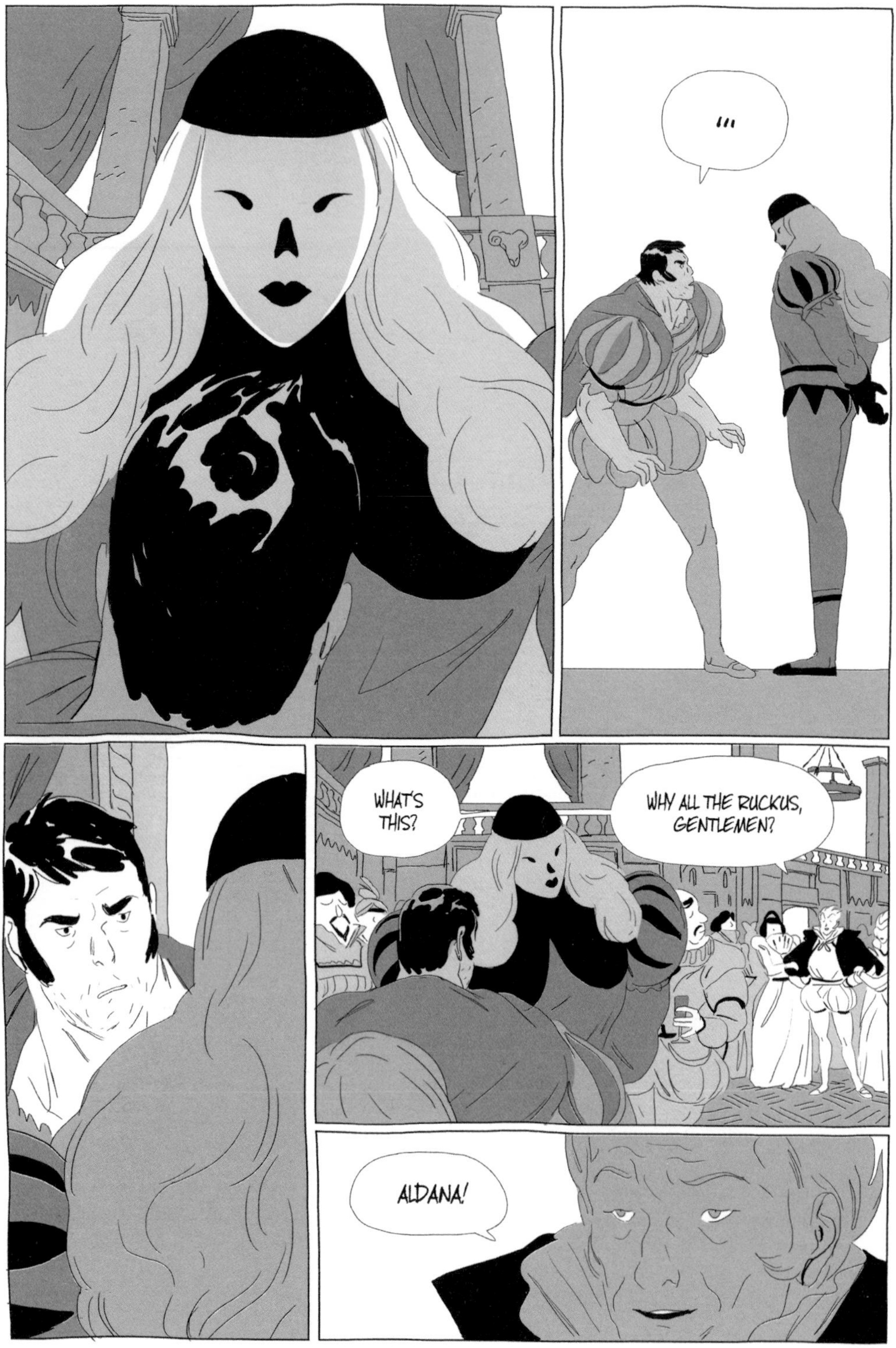
...
WHAT'S THIS?
WHY ALL THE RUCKUS, GENTLEMEN?
ALDANA!

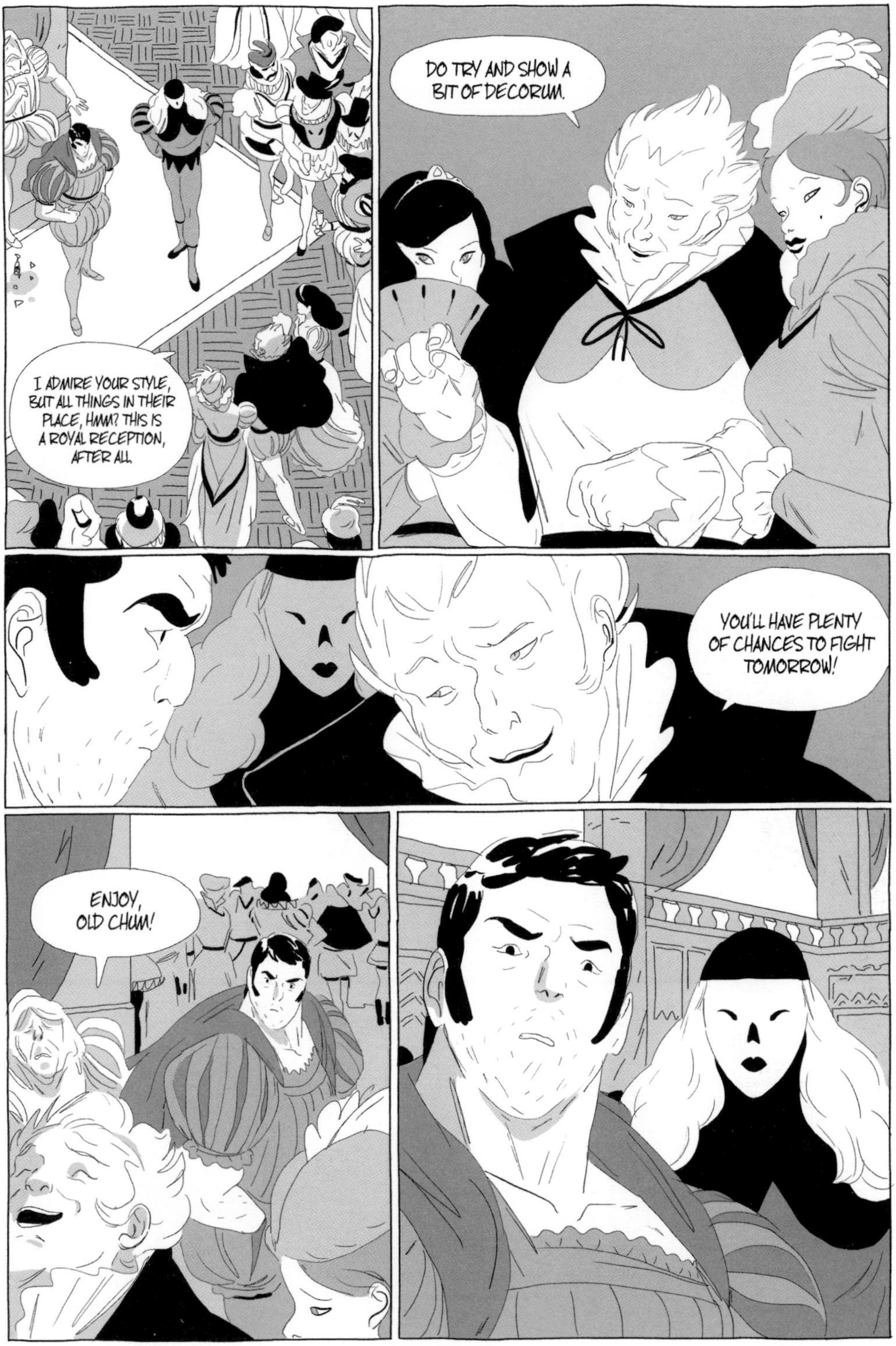
I ADMIRE YOUR STYLE, BUT ALL THINGS IN THEIR PLACE, HMM? THIS IS A ROYAL RECEPTION, AFTER ALL.
DO TRY AND SHOW A BIT OF DECORUM.
YOU'LL HAVE PLENTY OF CHANCES TO FIGHT TOMORROW!
ENJOY, OLD CHUM!

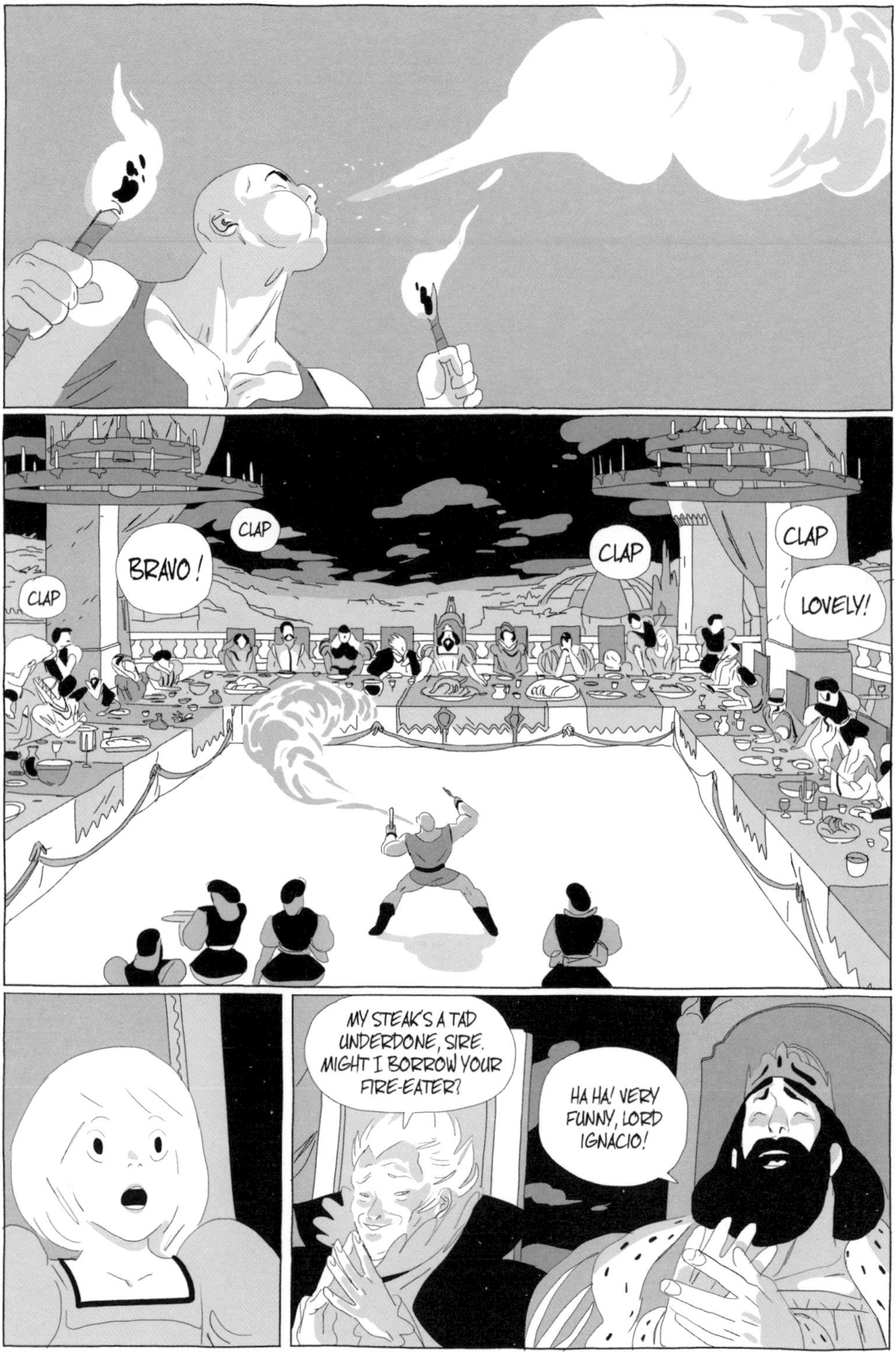
CLAP
BRAVO!
CLAP
CLAP
CLAP
LOVELY!
MY STEAK'S A TAD UNDERDONE, SIRE. MIGHT I BORROW YOUR FIRE-EATER?
HA HA! VERY FUNNY, LORD IGNACIO!

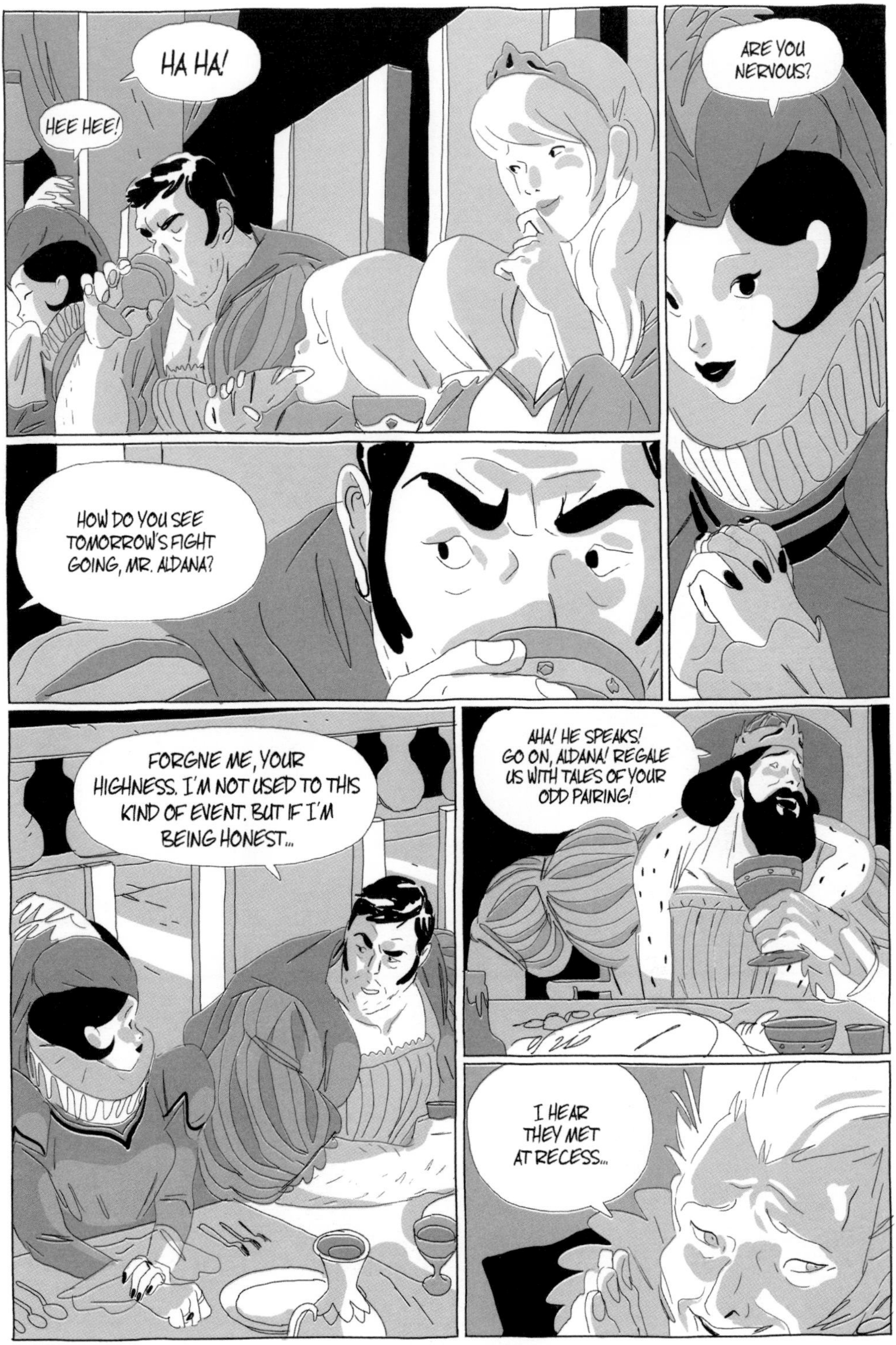
HA HA!
HEE HEE!
ARE YOU NERVOUS?
HOW DO YOU SEE TOMORROW'S FIGHT GOING, MR. ALDANA?
FORGIVE ME, YOUR HIGHNESS. I'M NOT USED TO THIS KIND OF EVENT. BUT IF I'M BEING HONEST...
AHA! HE SPEAKS! GO ON, ALDANA! REGALE US WITH TALES OF YOUR ODD PAIRING!
I HEAR THEY MET AT RECESS...

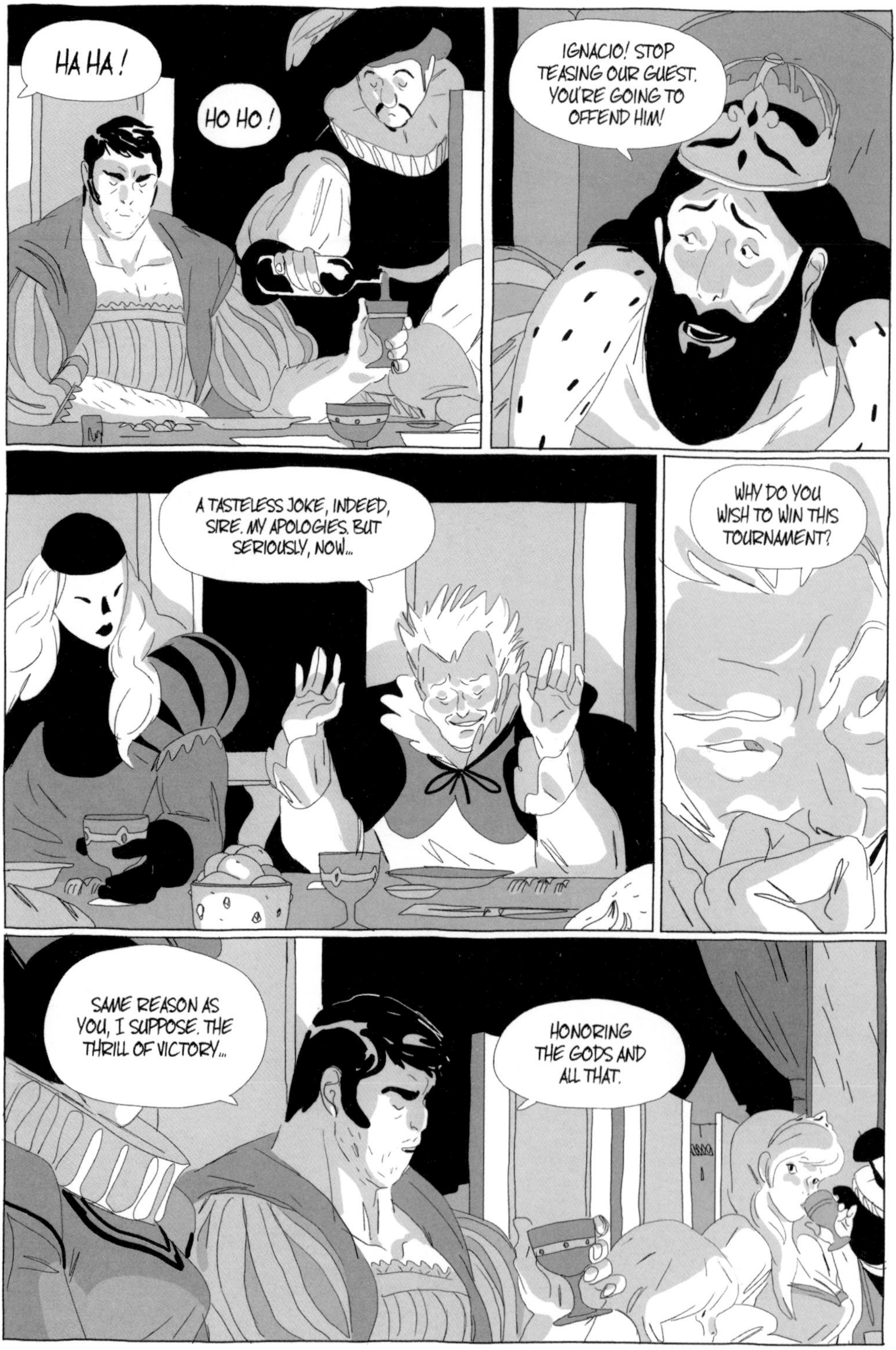
HA HA!
HO HO!
IGNACIO! STOP TEASING OUR GUEST. YOU'RE GOING TO OFFEND HIM!
A TASTELESS JOKE, INDEED, SIRE. MY APOLOGIES. BUT SERIOUSLY, NOW...
WHY DO YOU WISH TO WIN THIS TOURNAMENT?
SAME REASON AS YOU, I SUPPOSE. THE THRILL OF VICTORY...
HONORING THE GODS AND ALL THAT.

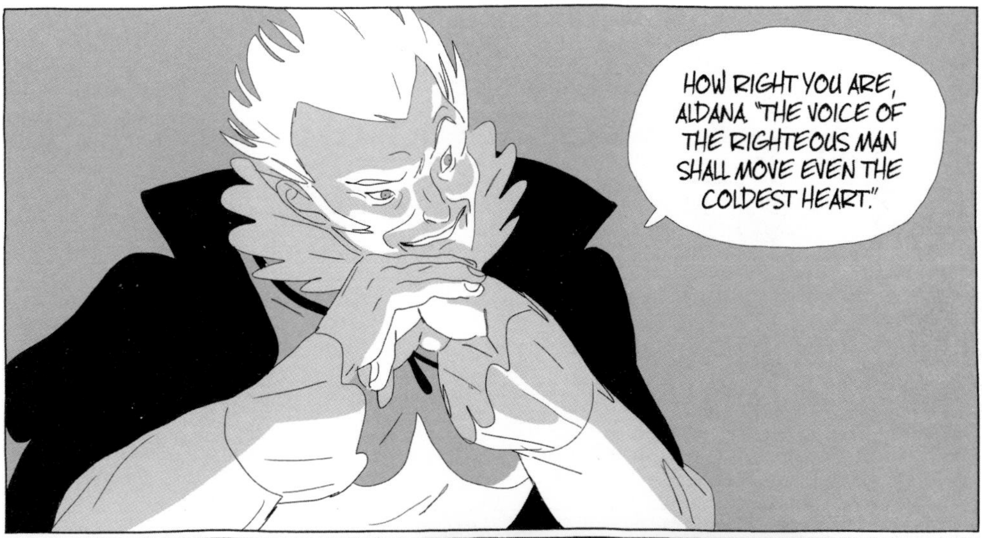
HOW RIGHT YOU ARE, ALDANA. "THE VOICE OF THE RIGHTEOUS MAN SHALL MOVE EVEN THE COLDEST HEART."

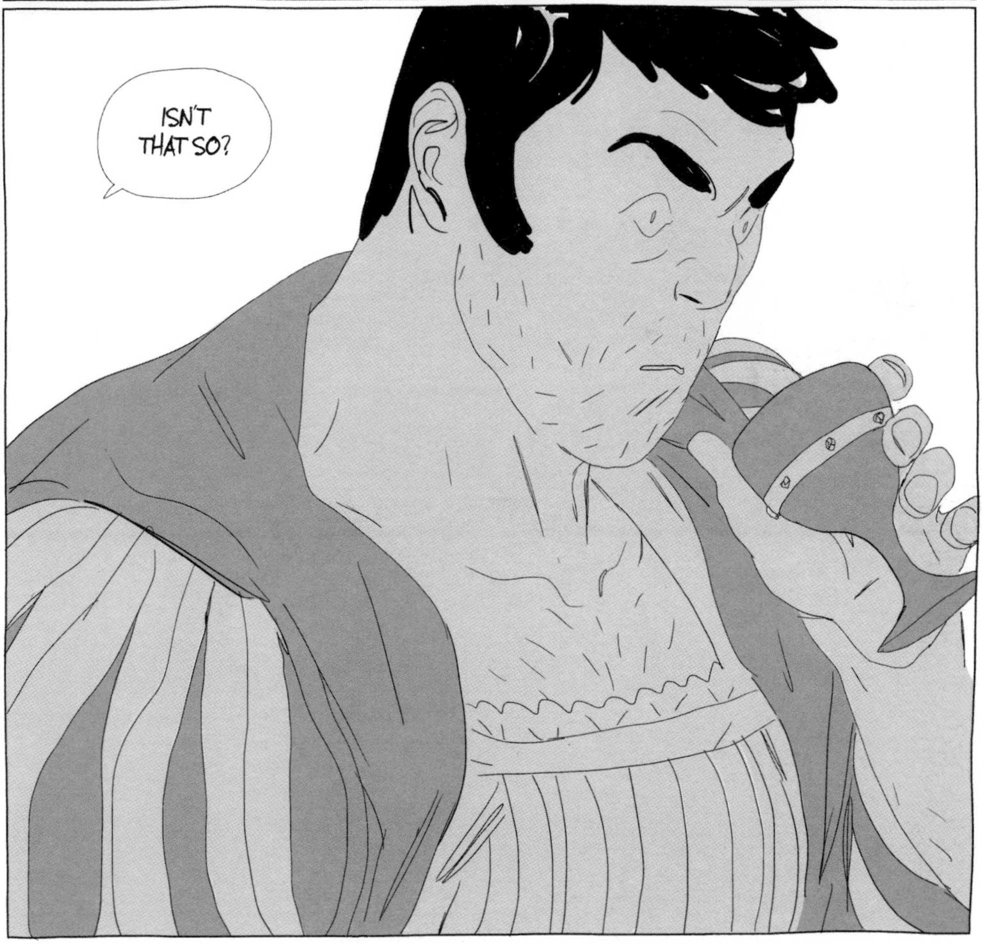
ISN'T THAT SO?

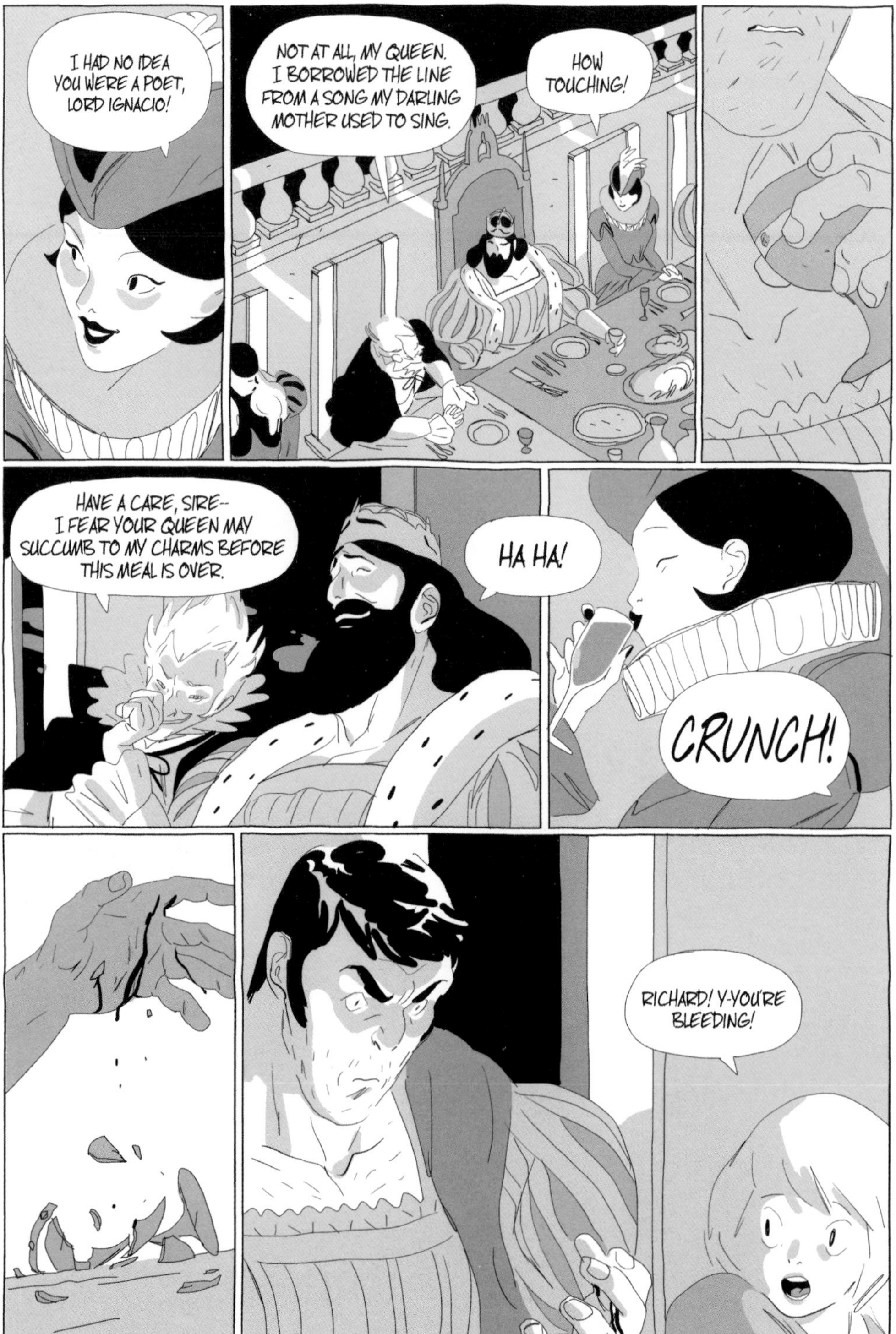
I HAD NO IDEA YOU WERE A POET, LORD IGNACIO!
NOT AT ALL, MY QUEEN. I BORROWED THE LINE FROM A SONG MY DARLING MOTHER USED TO SING.
HOW TOUCHING!
HAVE A CARE, SIRE-- I FEAR YOUR QUEEN MAY SUCCUMB TO MY CHARMS BEFORE THIS MEAL IS OVER.
HA HA!
CRUNCH!
RICHARD! Y-YOU'RE BLEEDING!

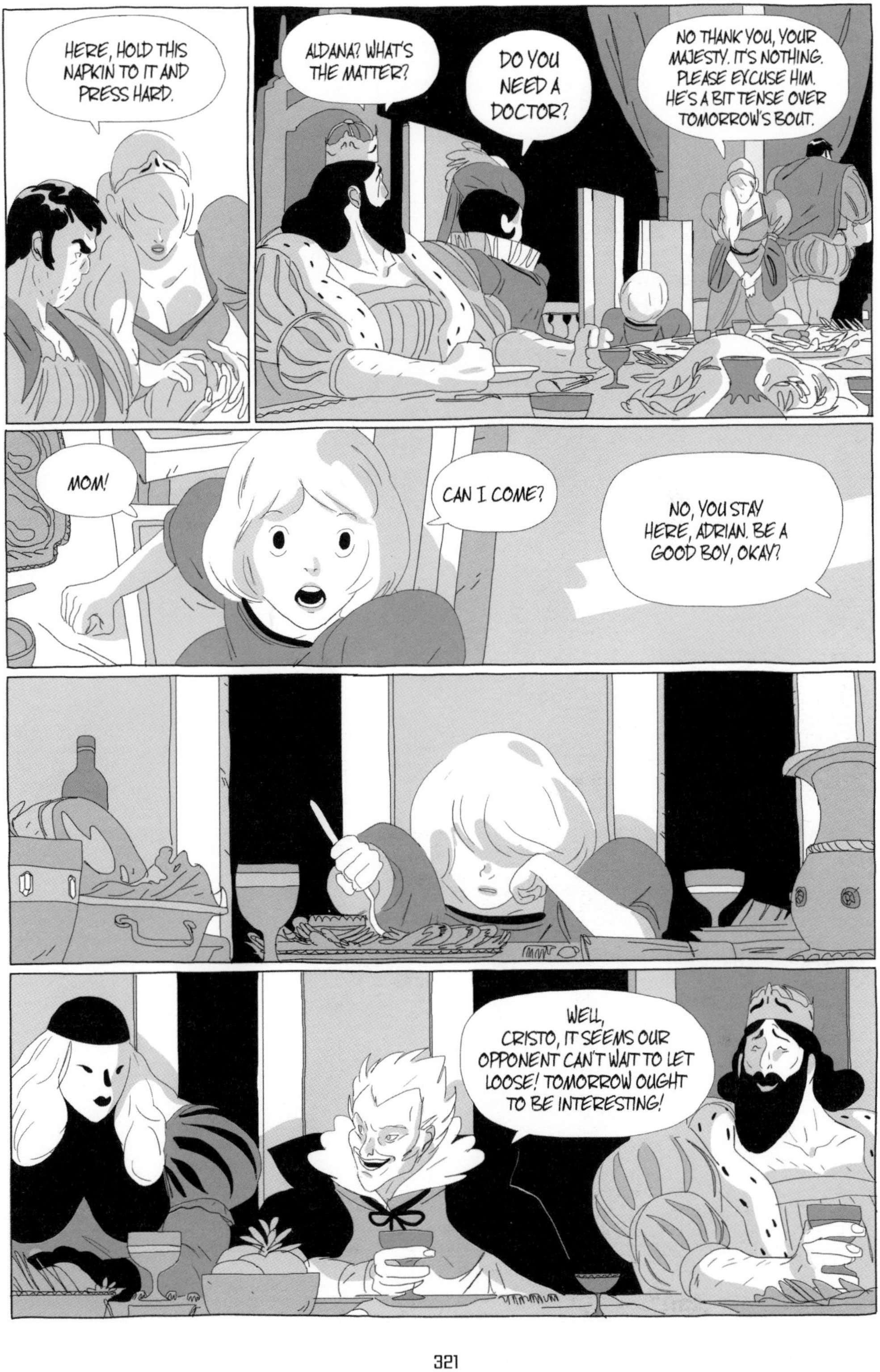
HERE, HOLD THIS NAPKIN TO IT AND PRESS HARD.
ALDANA? WHAT'S THE MATTER?
DO YOU NEED A DOCTOR?
NO THANK YOU, YOUR MAJESTY. IT'S NOTHING. PLEASE EXCUSE HIM. HE'S A BIT TENSE OVER TOMORROW'S BOUT.
MOM!
CAN I COME?
NO, YOU STAY HERE, ADRIAN. BE A GOOD BOY, OKAY?
WELL, CRISTO, IT SEEMS OUR OPPONENT CAN'T WAIT TO LET LOOSE! TOMORROW OUGHT TO BE INTERESTING!

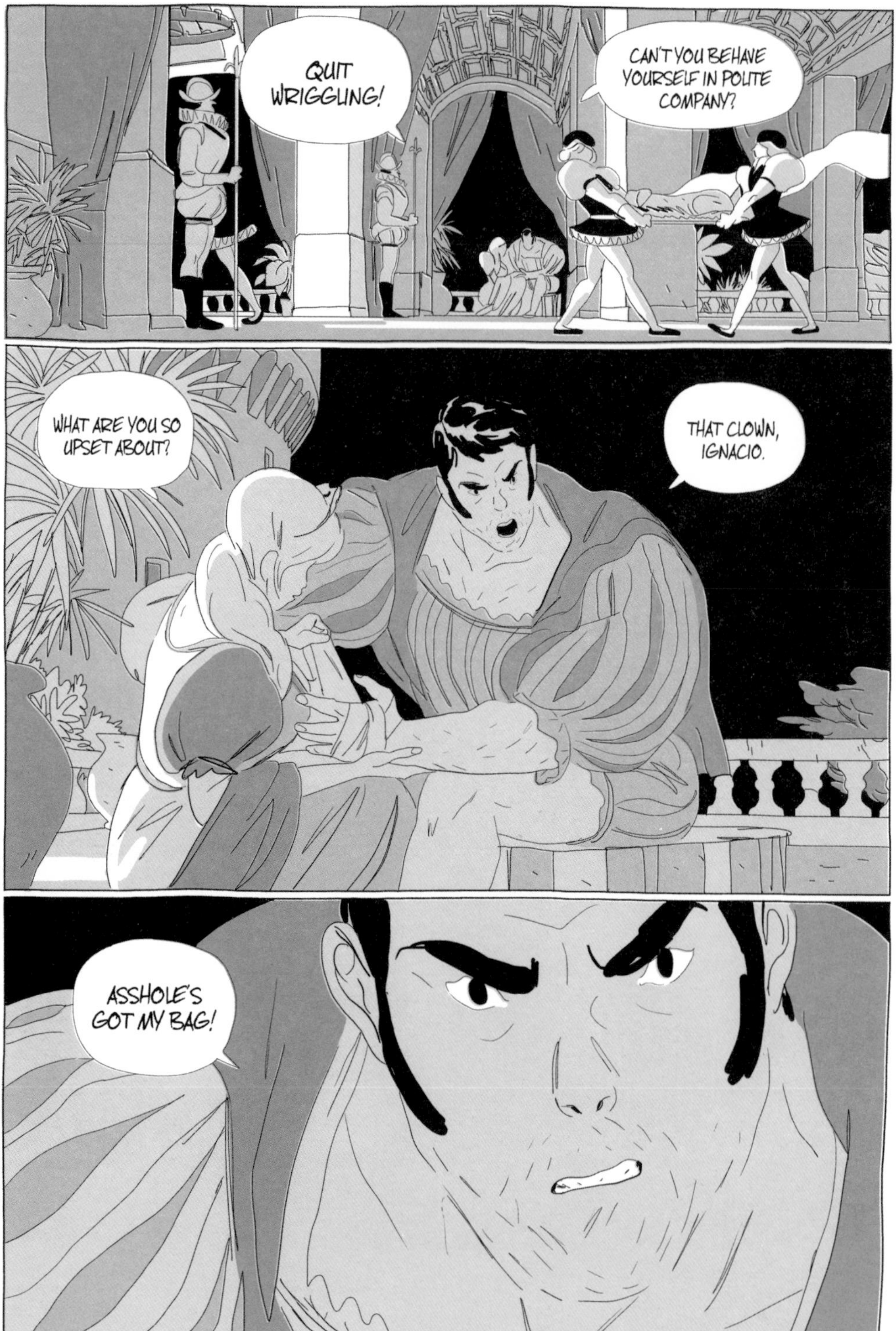
QUIT WRIGGLING!
CAN'T YOU BEHAVE YOURSELF IN POLITE COMPANY?
WHAT ARE YOU SO UPSET ABOUT?
THAT CLOWN, IGNACIO.
ASSHOLE'S GOT MY BAG!

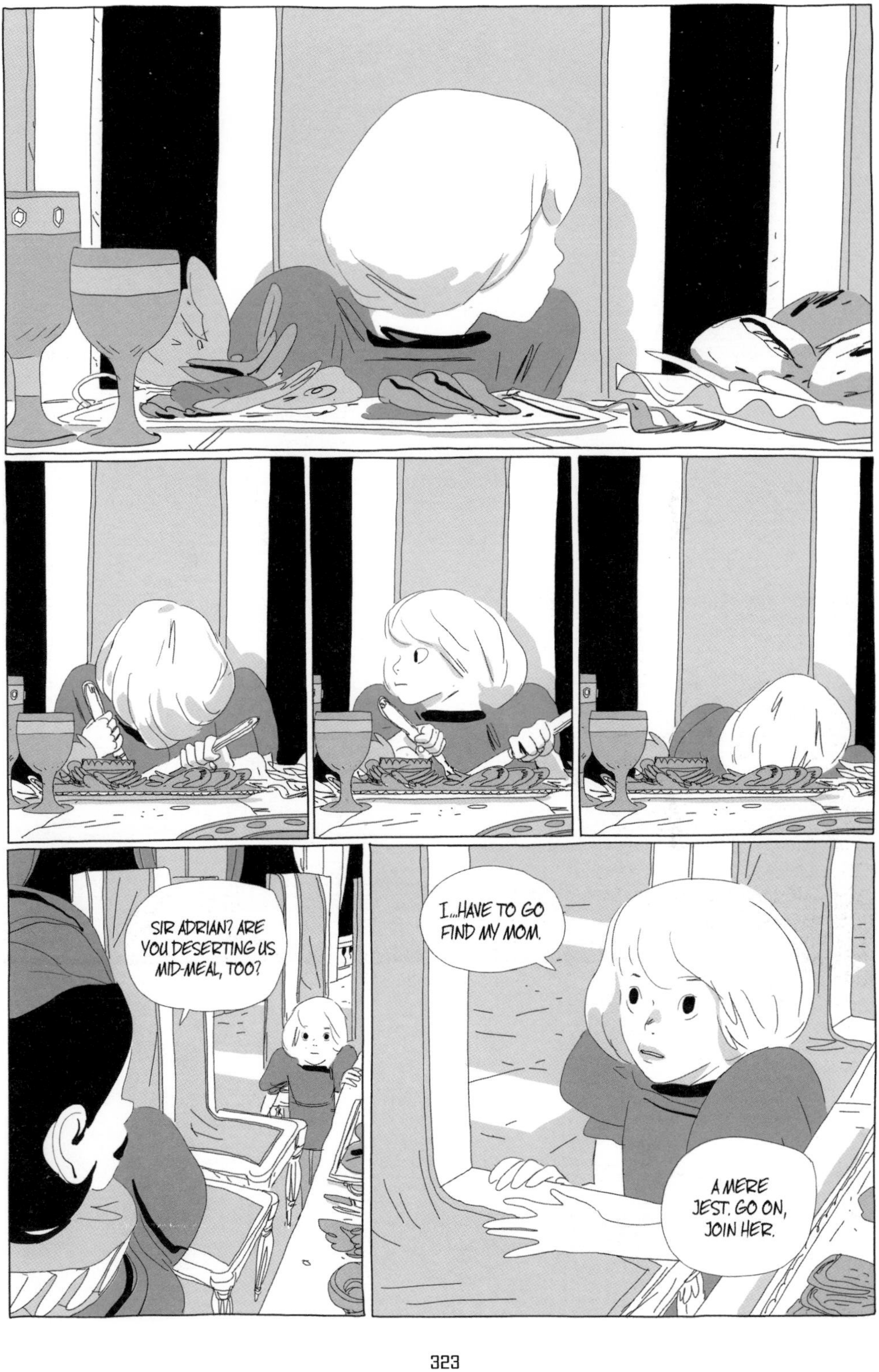
SIR ADRIAN? ARE YOU DESERTING US MID-MEAL, TOO?
I...HAVE TO GO FIND MY MOM.
A MERE JEST. GO ON, JOIN HER.

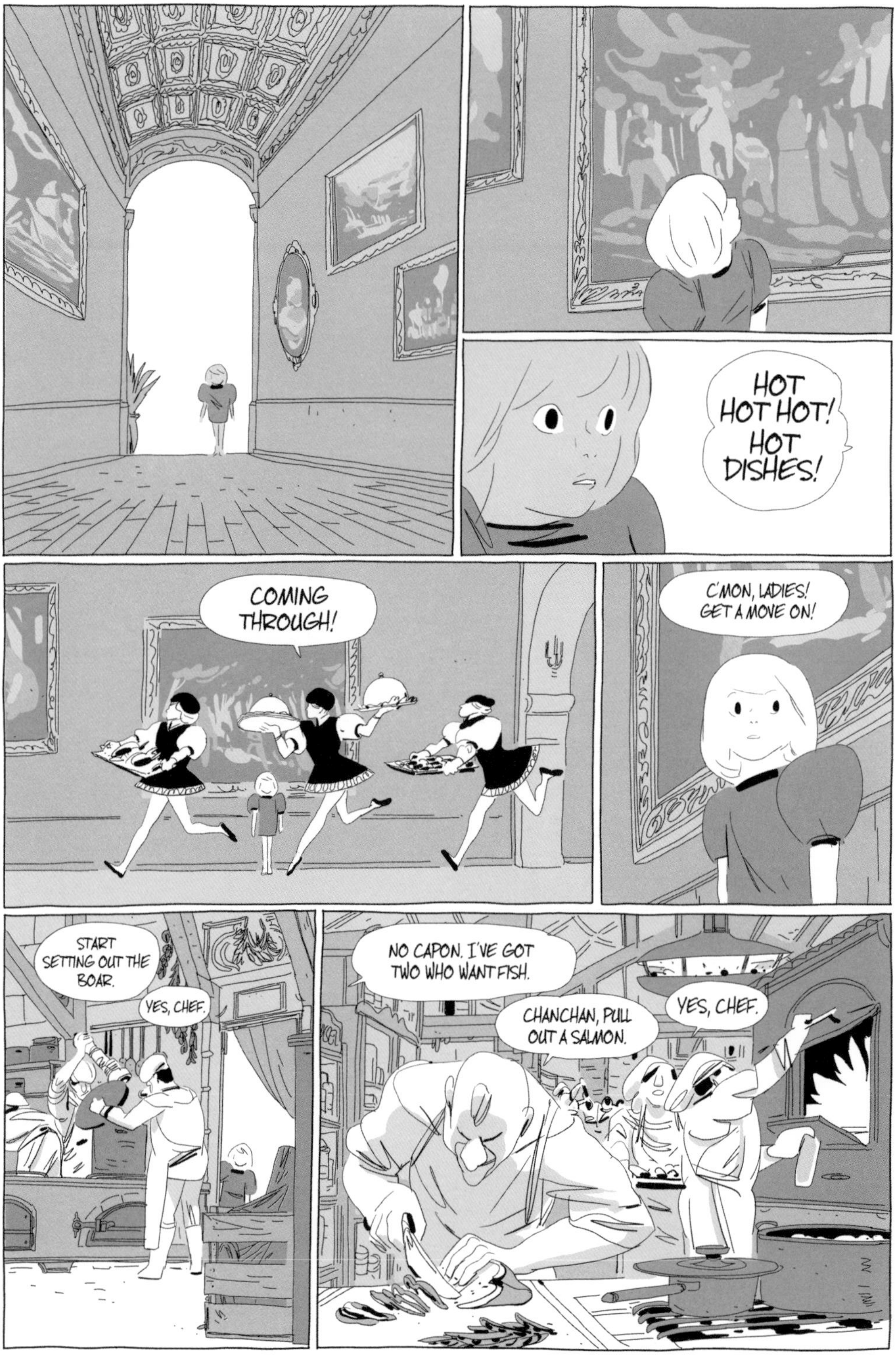
HOT HOT HOT! HOT DISHES!
COMING THROUGH!
C'MON, LADIES! GET A MOVE ON!
START SETTING OUT THE BOAR.
YES, CHEF.
NO CAPON. I'VE GOT TWO WHO WANT FISH.
CHANCHAN, PULL OUT A SALMON.
YES, CHEF.

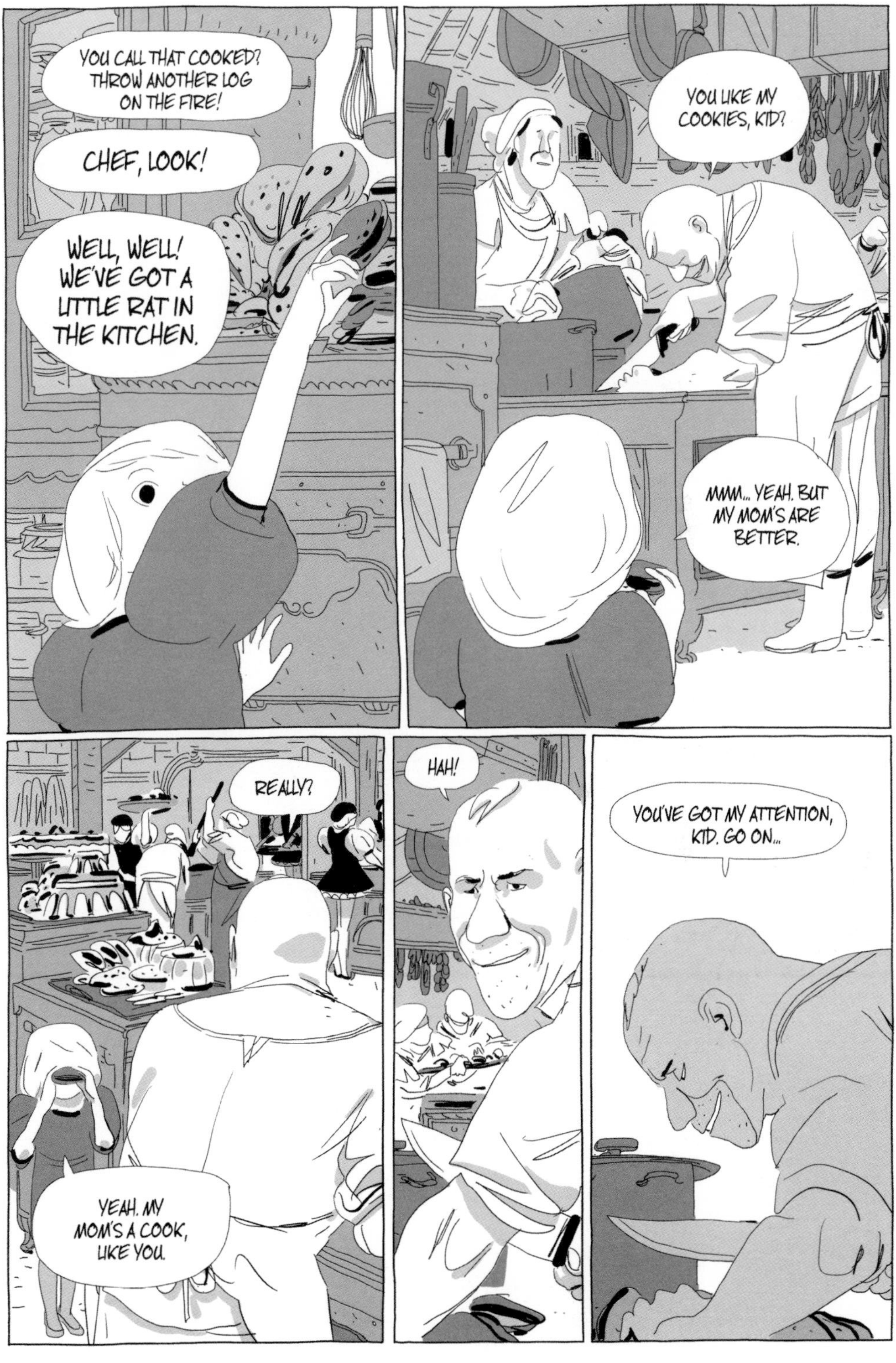
YOU CALL THAT COOKED? THROW ANOTHER LOG ON THE FIRE!
CHEF, LOOK!
WELL, WELL! WE'VE GOT A LITTLE RAT IN THE KITCHEN.
YOU LIKE MY COOKIES, KID?
MMM... YEAH. BUT MY MOM'S ARE BETTER.
REALLY?
YEAH. MY MOM'S A COOK, LIKE YOU.
HAH!
YOU'VE GOT MY ATTENTION, KID. GO ON...

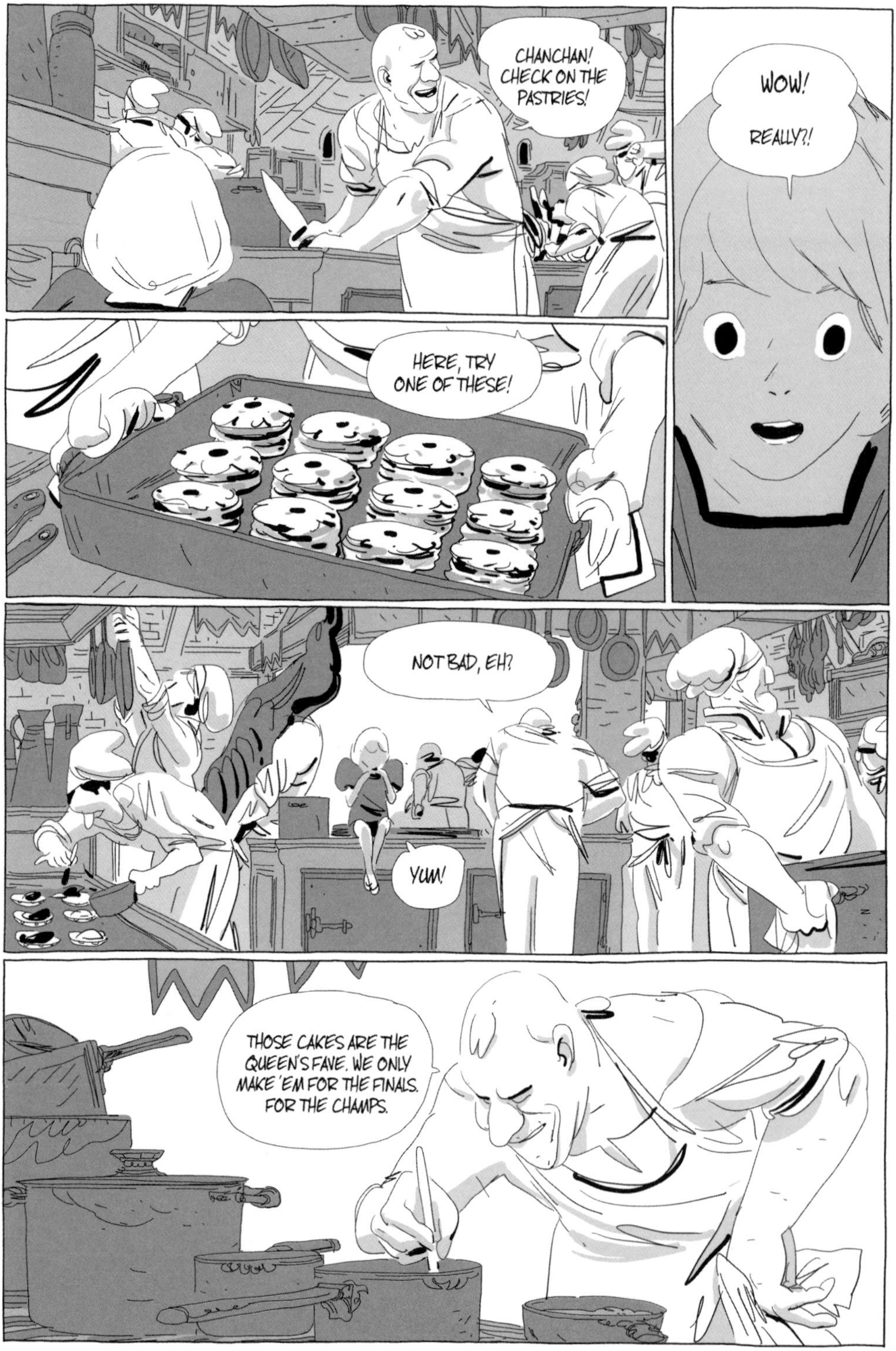
CHANCHAN! CHECK ON THE PASTRIES!
WOW!
REALLY?!
HERE, TRY ONE OF THESE!
NOT BAD, EH?
YUM!
THOSE CAKES ARE THE QUEEN'S FAVE. WE ONLY MAKE 'EM FOR THE FINALS. FOR THE CHAMPS.

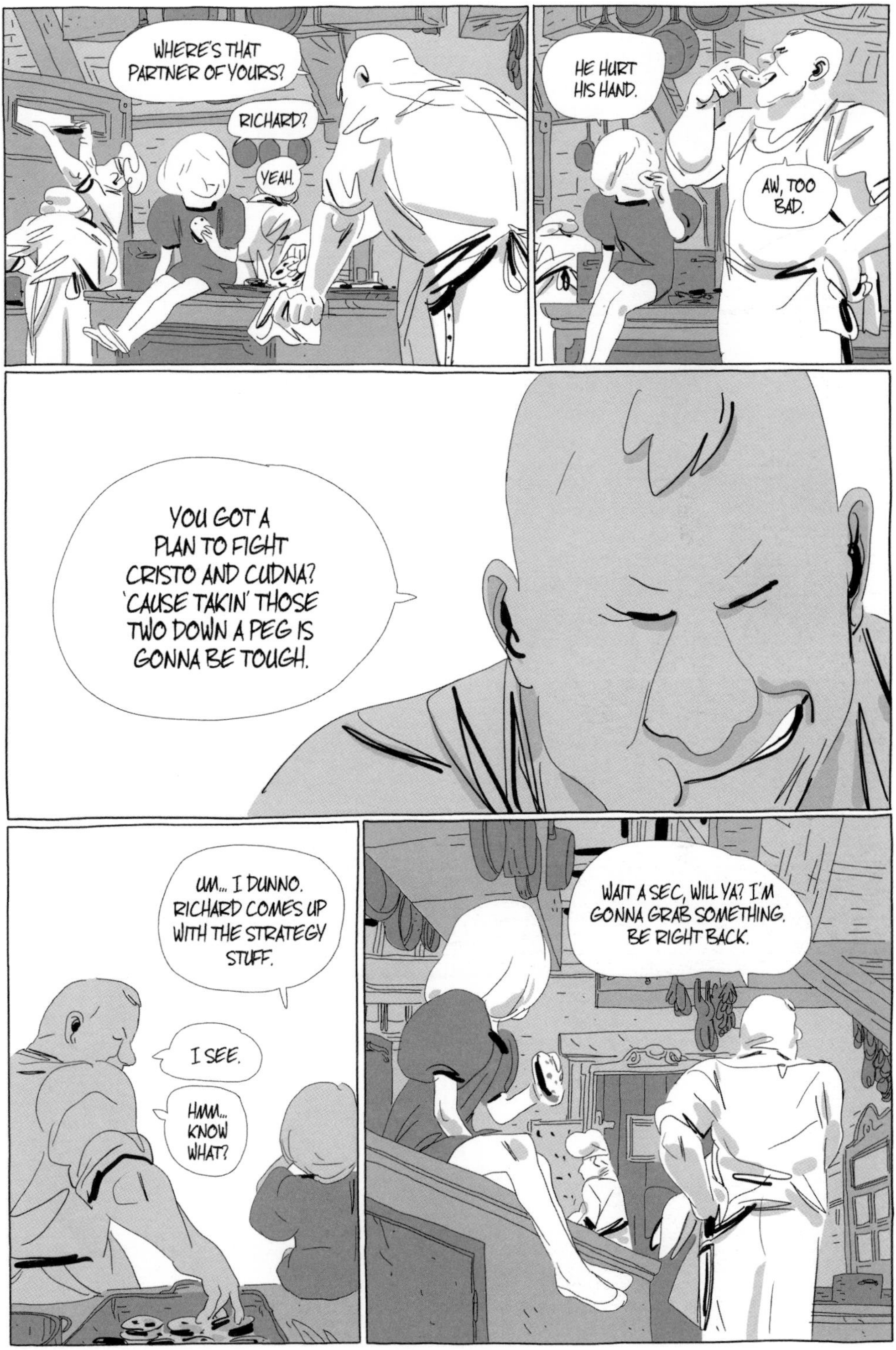
WHERE'S THAT PARTNER OF YOURS?
RICHARD?
YEAH.
HE HURT HIS HAND.
AW, TOO BAD.
YOU GOT A PLAN TO FIGHT CRISTO AND CUDNA? 'CAUSE TAKIN' THOSE TWO DOWN A PEG IS GONNA BE TOUGH.
UM... I DUNNO. RICHARD COMES UP WITH THE STRATEGY STUFF.
I SEE.
HMM... KNOW WHAT?
WAIT A SEC, WILL YA? I'M GONNA GRAB SOMETHING. BE RIGHT BACK.

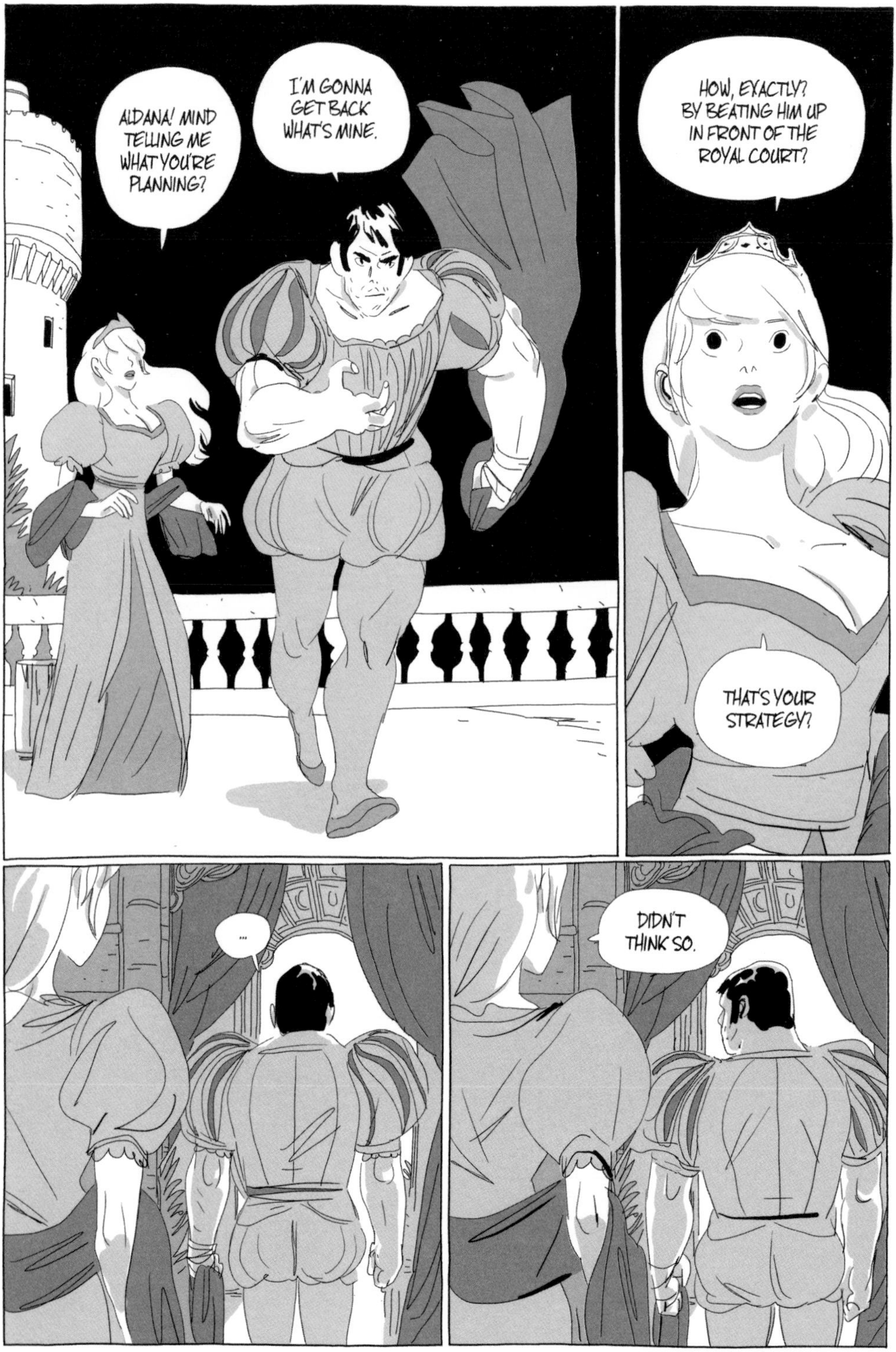
ALDANA! MIND TELLING ME WHAT YOU'RE PLANNING?
I'M GONNA GET BACK WHAT'S MINE.
HOW, EXACTLY? BY BEATING HIM UP IN FRONT OF THE ROYAL COURT?
THAT'S YOUR STRATEGY?
...
DIDN'T THINK SO.

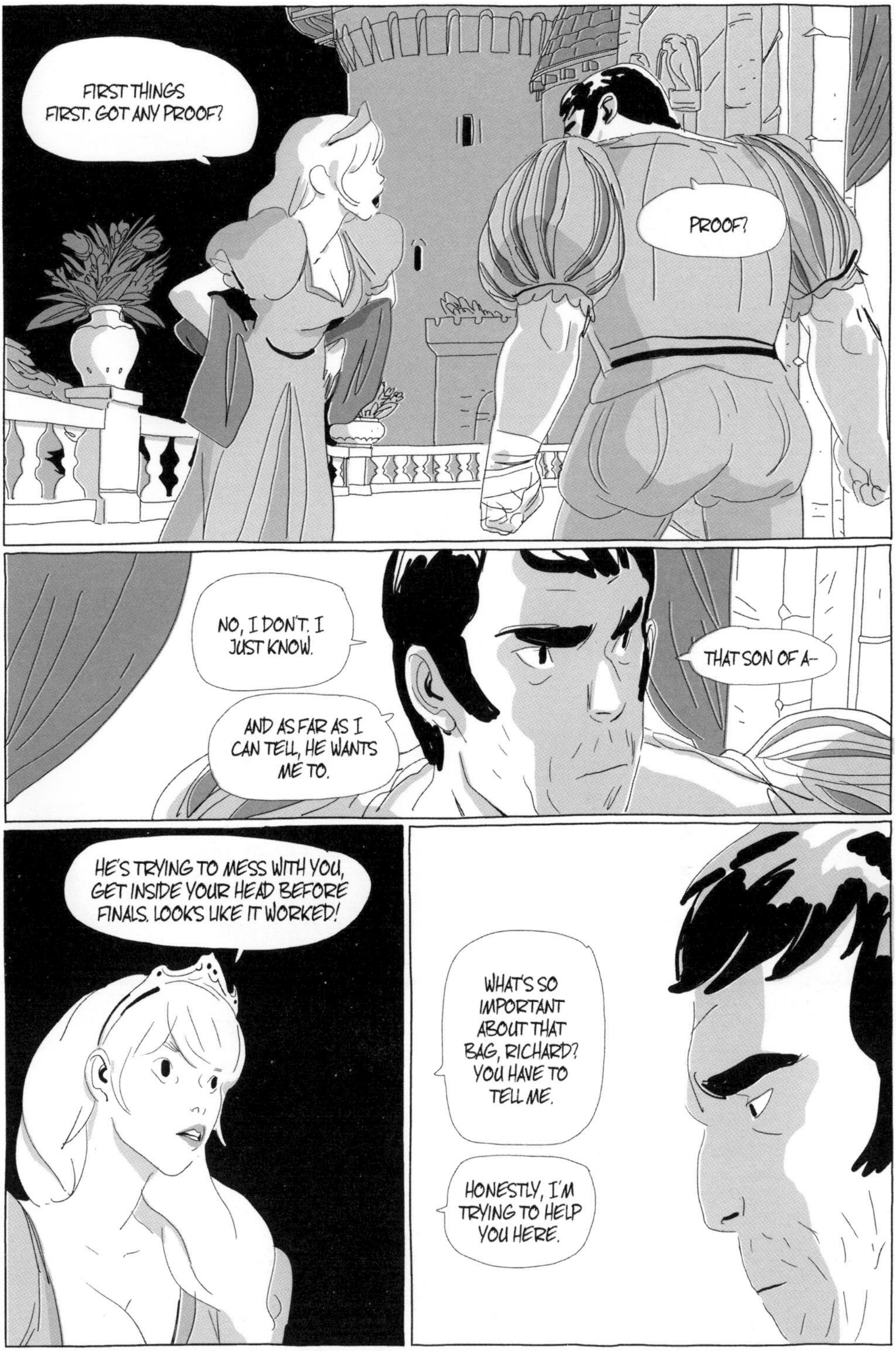
FIRST THINGS FIRST. GOT ANY PROOF?
PROOF?
NO, I DON'T. I JUST KNOW.
AND AS FAR AS I CAN TELL, HE WANTS ME TO.
THAT SON OF A-
HE'S TRYING TO MESS WITH YOU, GET INSIDE YOUR HEAD BEFORE FINALS. LOOKS LIKE IT WORKED!
WHAT'S SO IMPORTANT ABOUT THAT BAG, RICHARD? YOU HAVE TO TELL ME.
HONESTLY, I'M TRYING TO HELP YOU HERE.

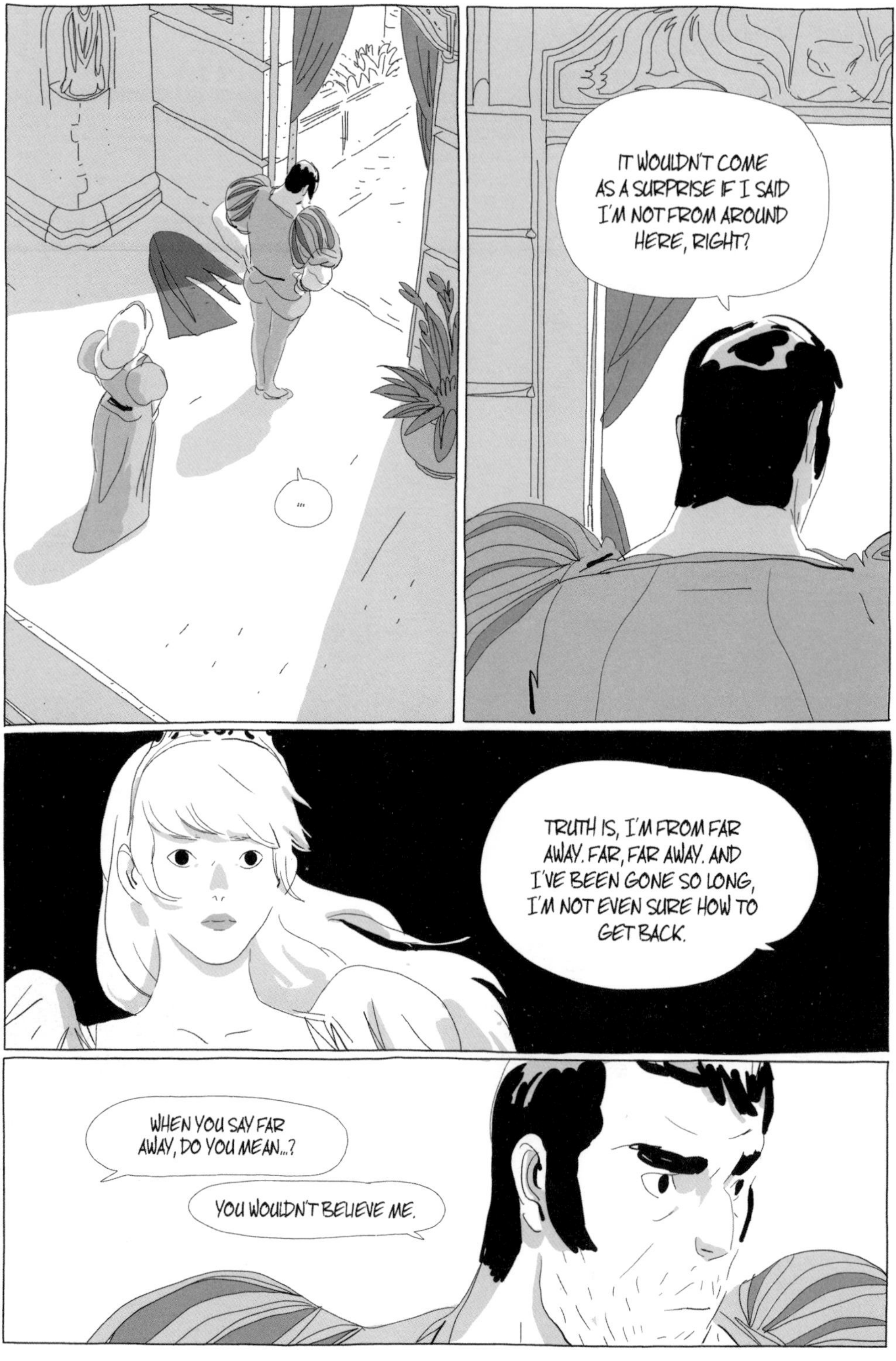
...
IT WOULDN'T COME AS A SURPRISE IF I SAID I'M NOT FROM AROUND HERE, RIGHT?
TRUTH IS, I'M FROM FAR AWAY. FAR, FAR AWAY. AND I'VE BEEN GONE SO LONG, I'M NOT EVEN SURE HOW TO GET BACK.
WHEN YOU SAY FAR AWAY, DO YOU MEAN...?
YOU WOULDN'T BELIEVE ME.

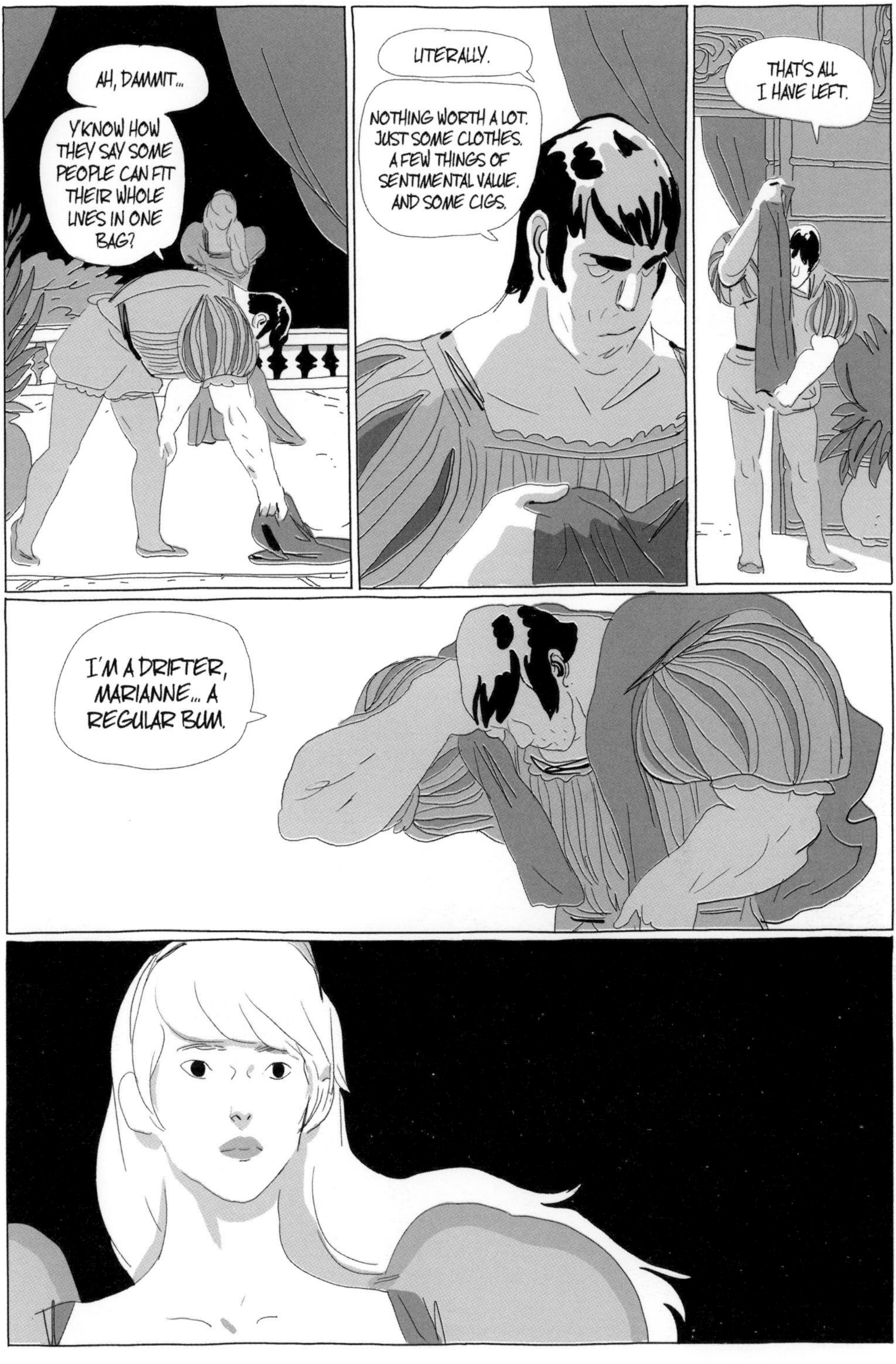
AH, DAMMIT...
Y'KNOW HOW THEY SAY SOME PEOPLE CAN FIT THEIR WHOLE LIVES IN ONE BAG?
LITERALLY.
NOTHING WORTH A LOT. JUST SOME CLOTHES. A FEW THINGS OF SENTIMENTAL VALUE. AND SOME CIGS.
THAT'S ALL I HAVE LEFT.
I'M A DRIFTER, MARIANNE... A REGULAR BUM.

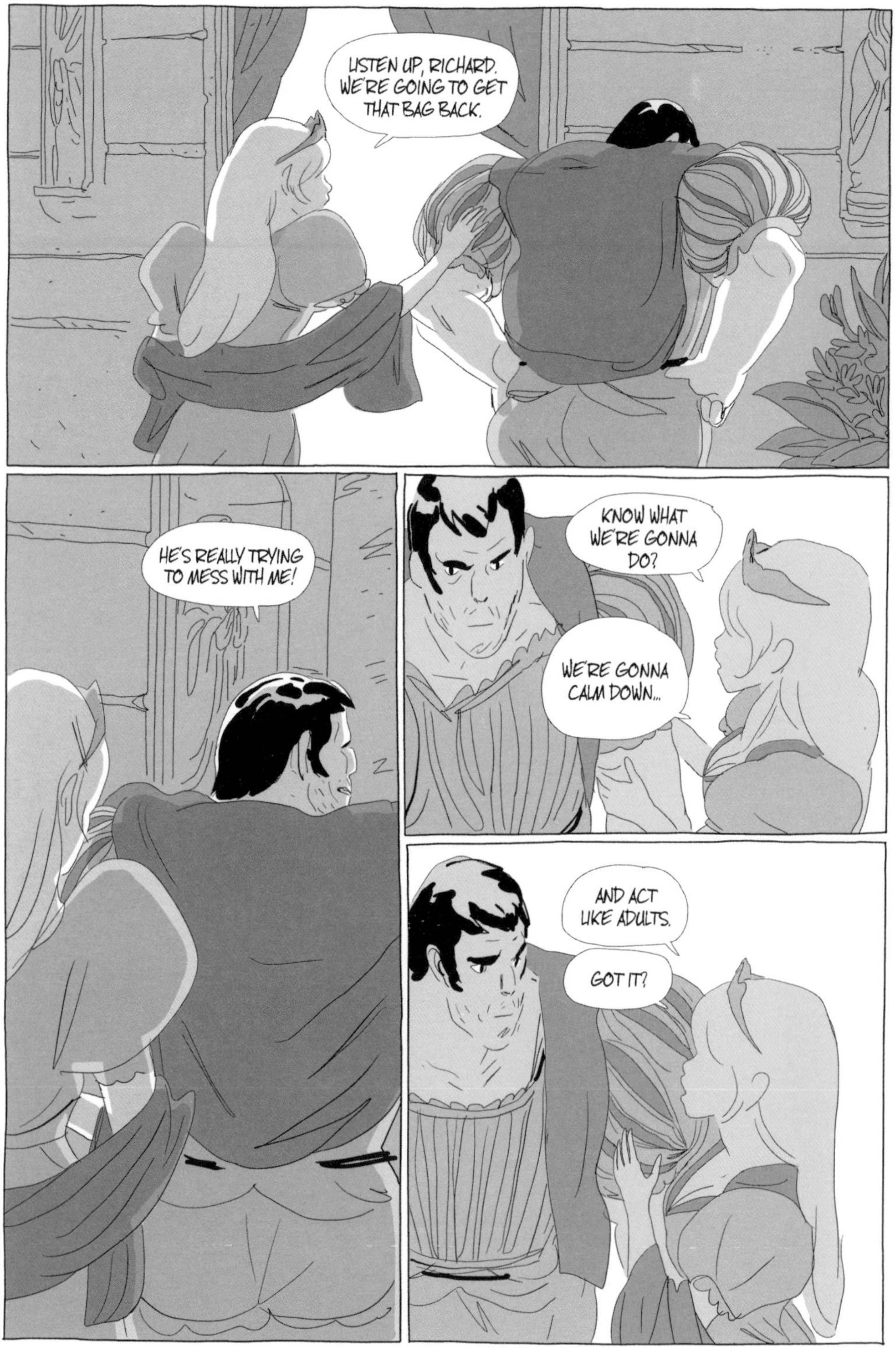
LISTEN UP, RICHARD. WE'RE GOING TO GET THAT BAG BACK.
HE'S REALLY TRYING TO MESS WITH ME!
KNOW WHAT WE'RE GONNA DO?
WE'RE GONNA CALM DOWN...
AND ACT LIKE ADULTS.
GOT IT?

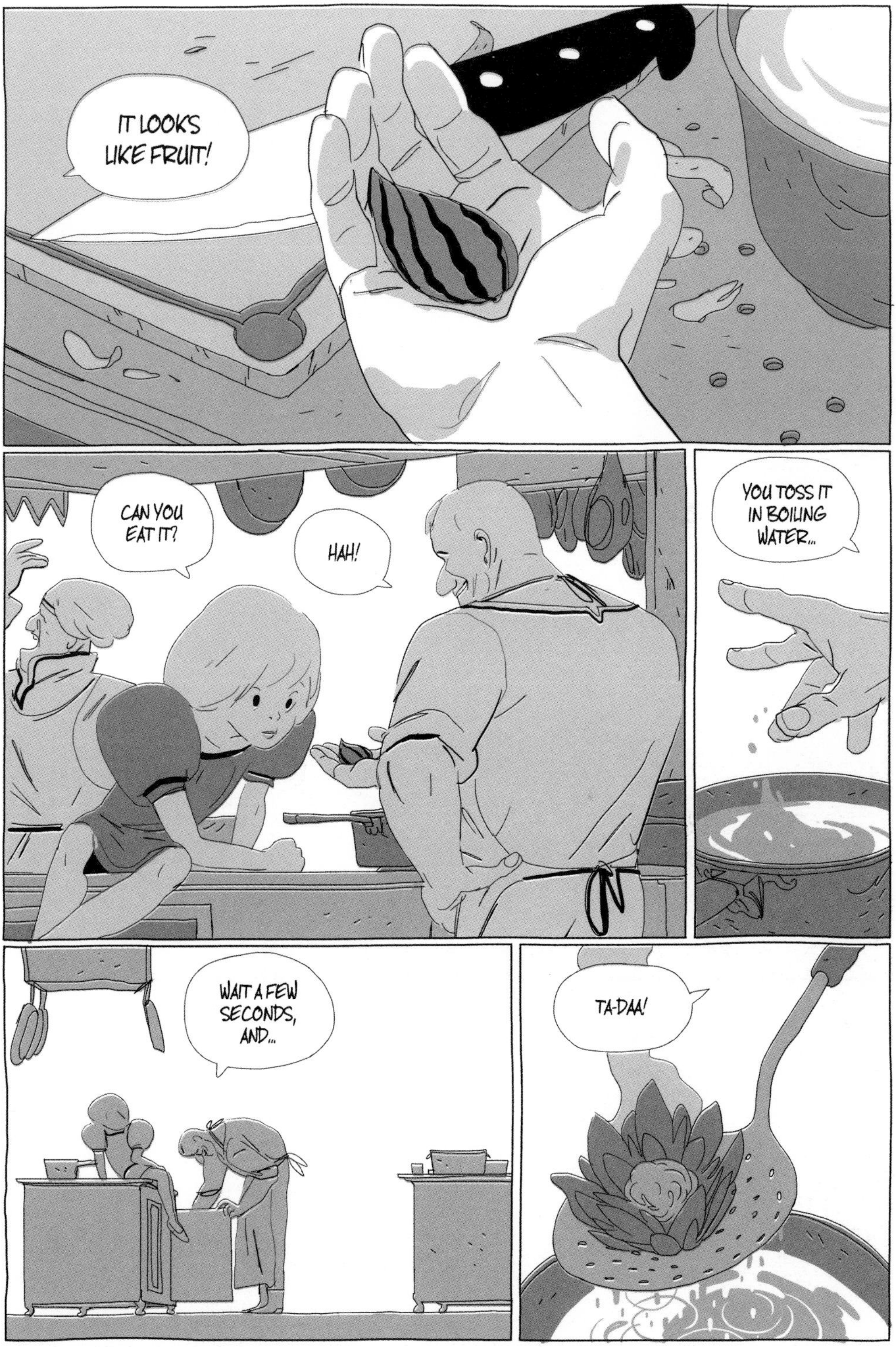
IT LOOKS LIKE FRUIT!
CAN YOU EAT IT?
HAH!
YOU TOSS IT IN BOILING WATER...
WAIT A FEW SECONDS, AND...
TA-DAA!

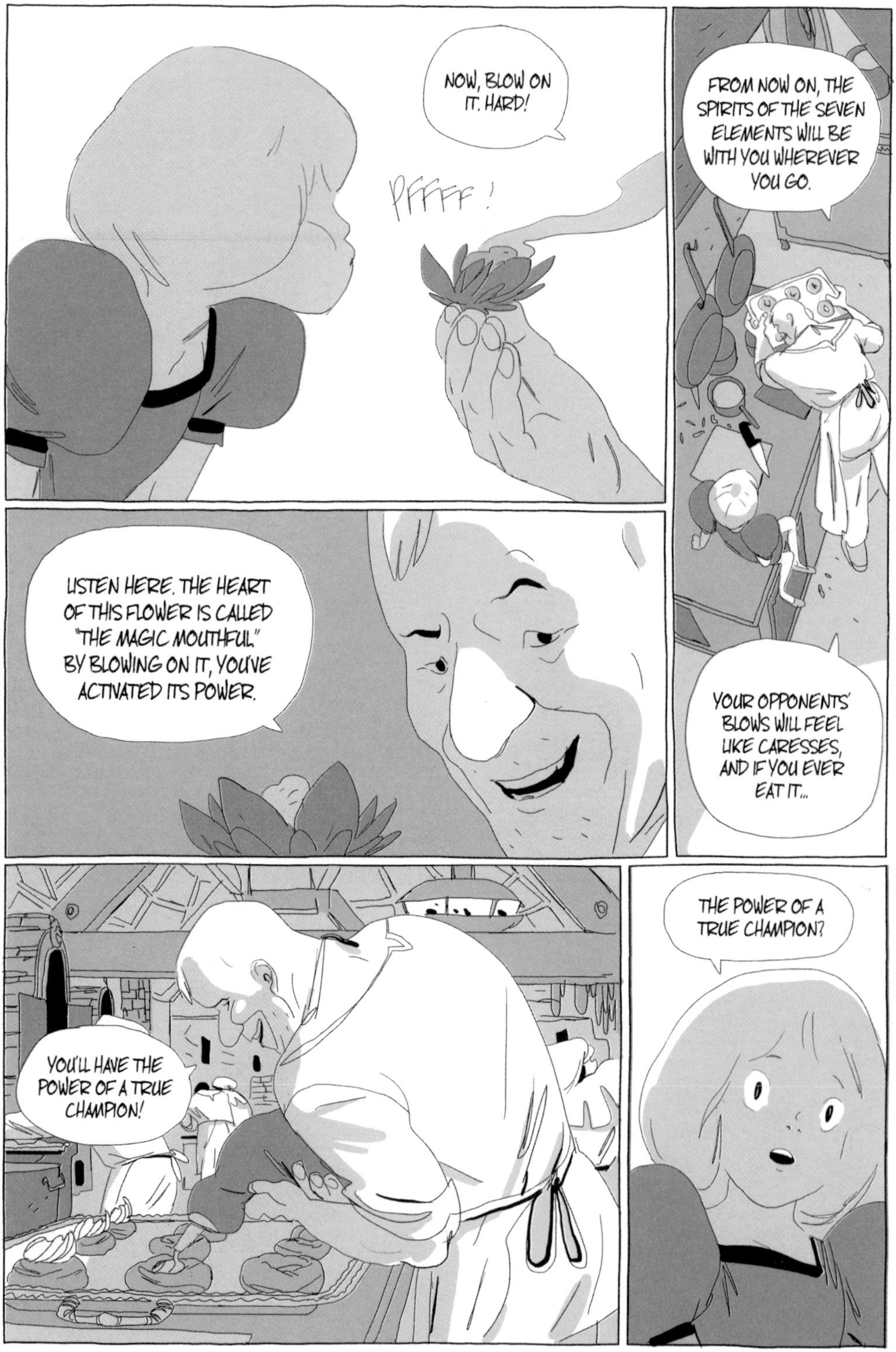
NOW, BLOW ON IT. HARD!
PFFFF!
FROM NOW ON, THE SPIRITS OF THE SEVEN ELEMENTS WILL BE WITH YOU WHEREVER YOU GO.
LISTEN HERE. THE HEART OF THIS FLOWER IS CALLED "THE MAGIC MOUTHFUL." BY BLOWING ON IT, YOU'VE ACTIVATED ITS POWER.
YOUR OPPONENTS' BLOWS WILL FEEL LIKE CARESSES, AND IF YOU EVER EAT IT...
YOU'LL HAVE THE POWER OF A TRUE CHAMPION!
THE POWER OF A TRUE CHAMPION?

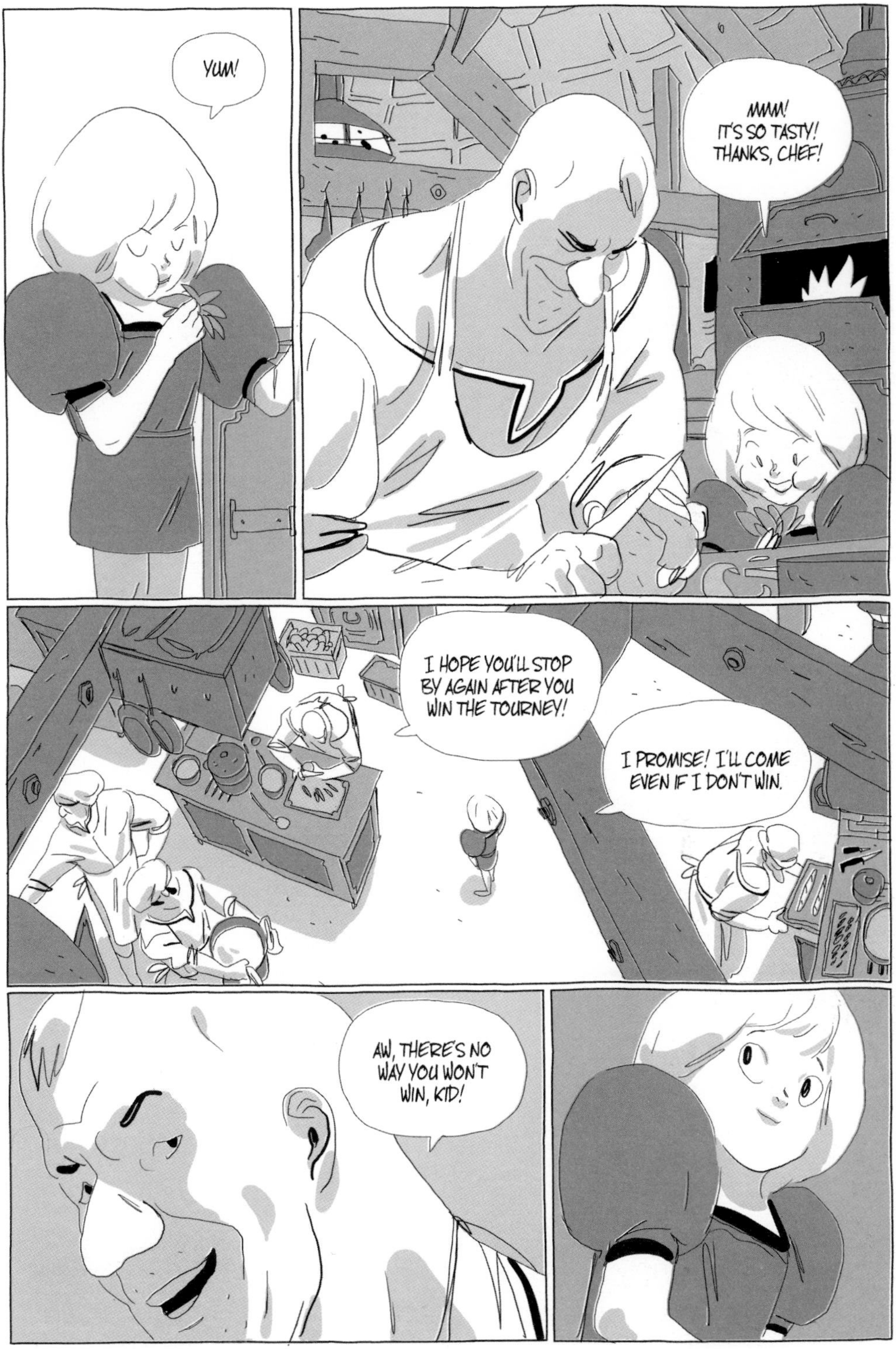
YUM!
MMM! IT'S SO TASTY! THANKS, CHEF!
I HOPE YOU'LL STOP BY AGAIN AFTER YOU WIN THE TOURNEY!
I PROMISE! I'LL COME EVEN IF I DON'T WIN.
AW, THERE'S NO WAY YOU WON'T WIN, KID!

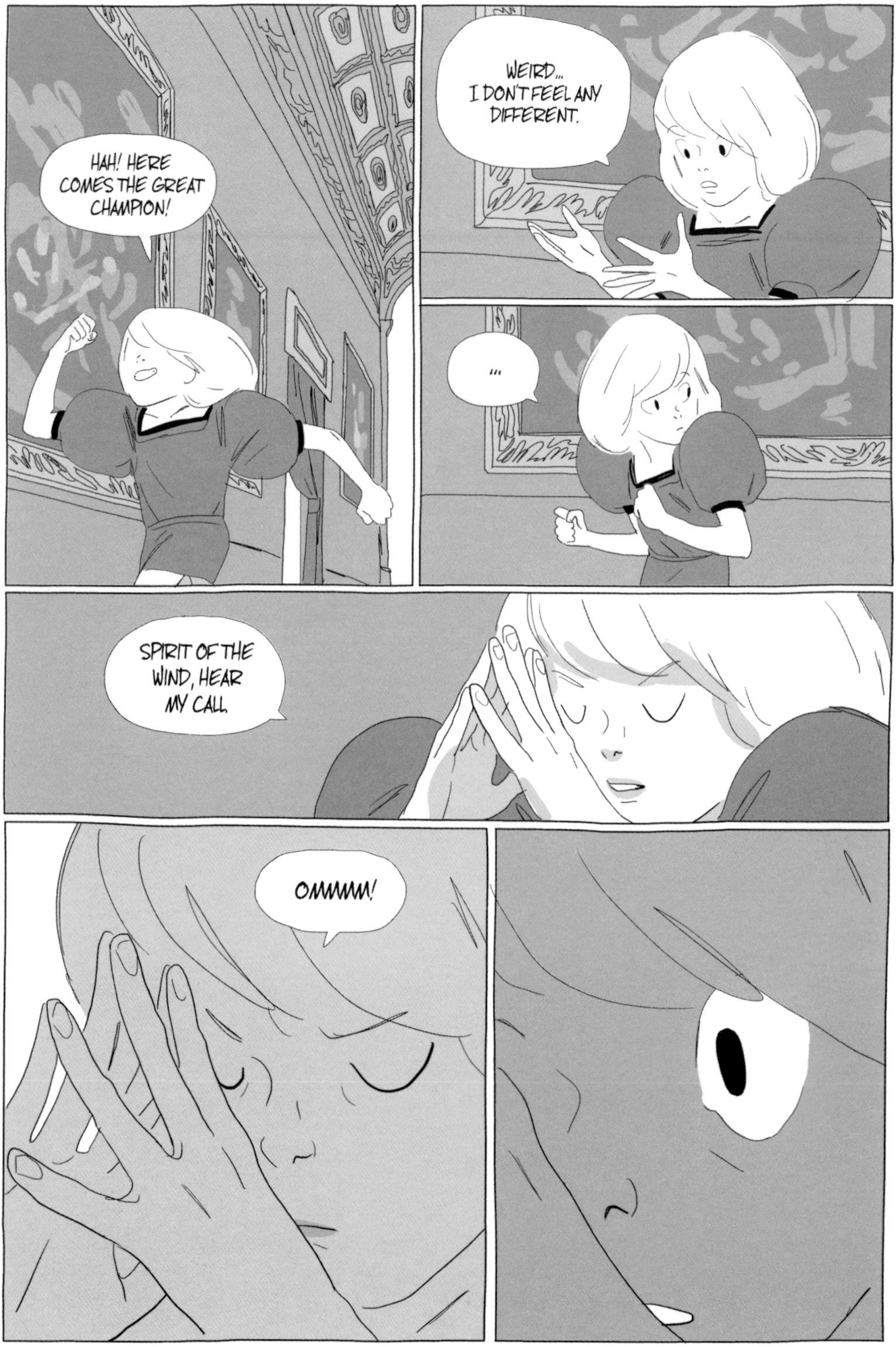
HAH! HERE COMES THE GREAT CHAMPION!
WEIRD... I DON'T FEEL ANY DIFFERENT.
...
SPIRIT OF THE WIND, HEAR MY CALL.
OMMMM!

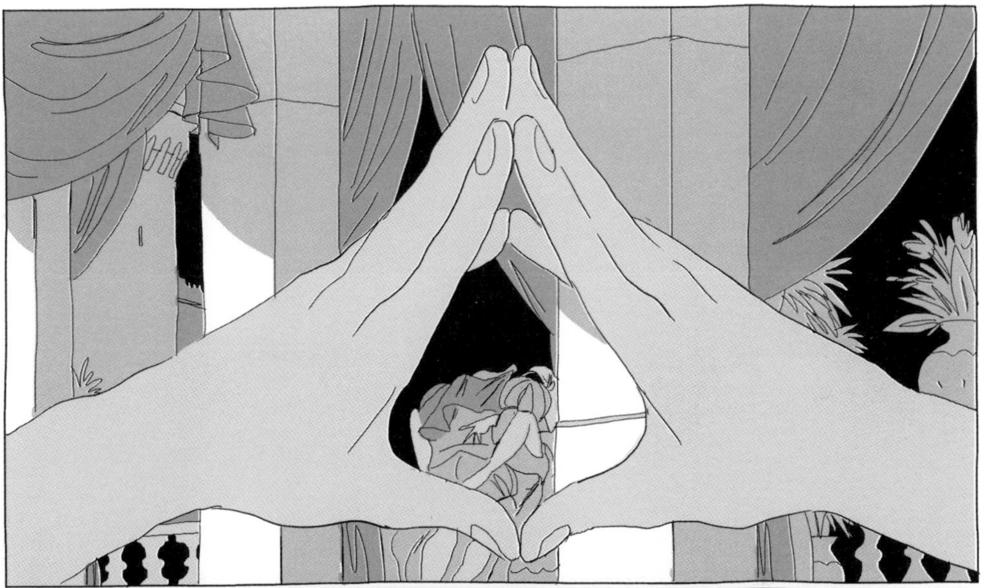

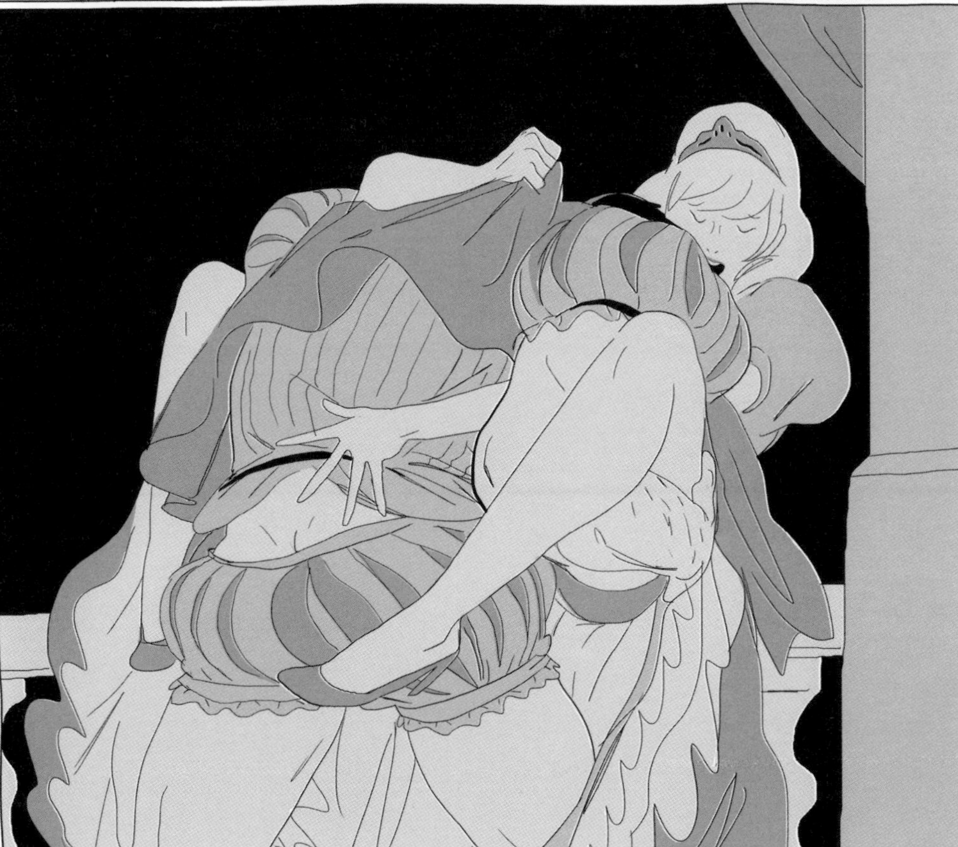

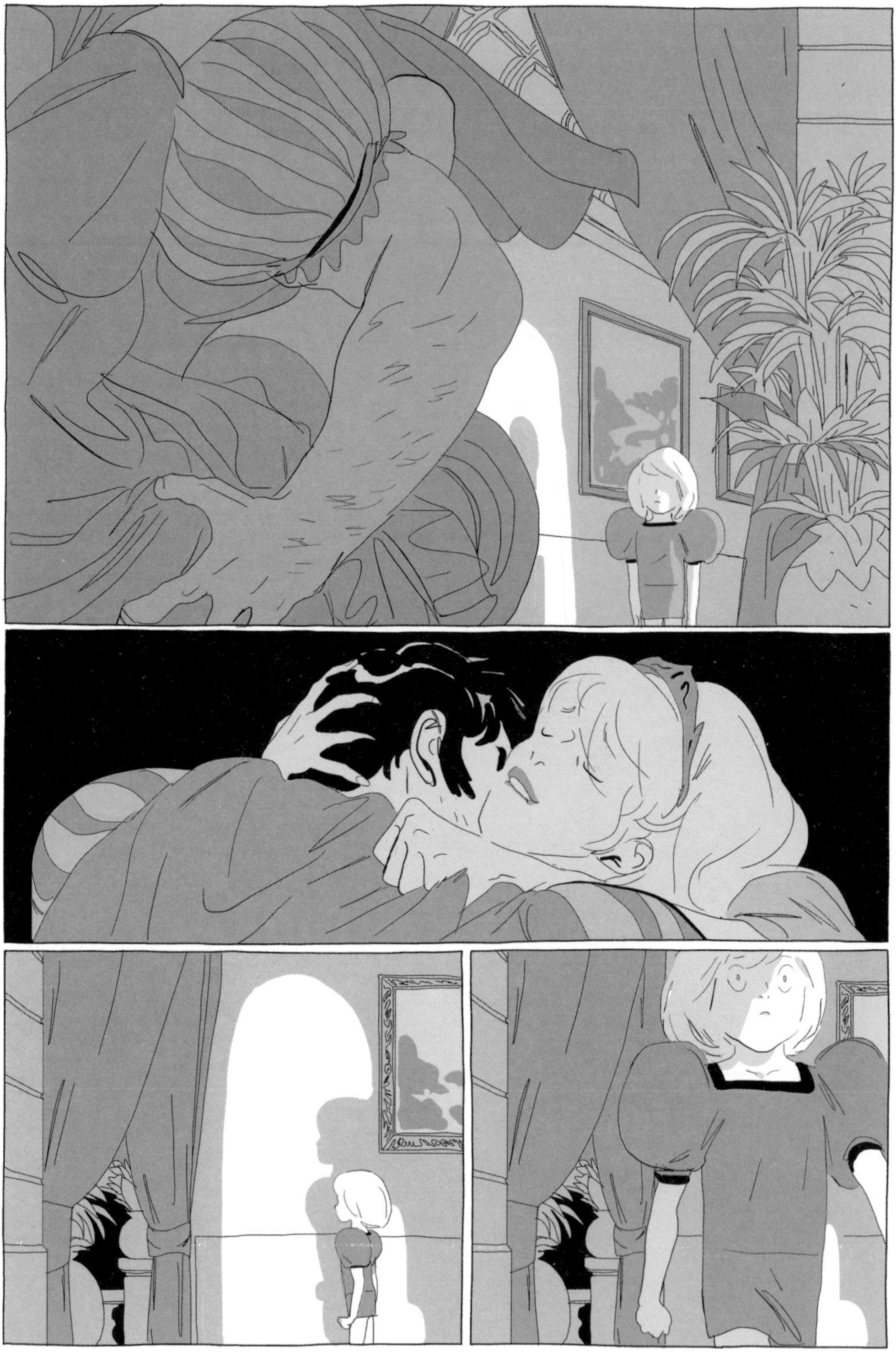

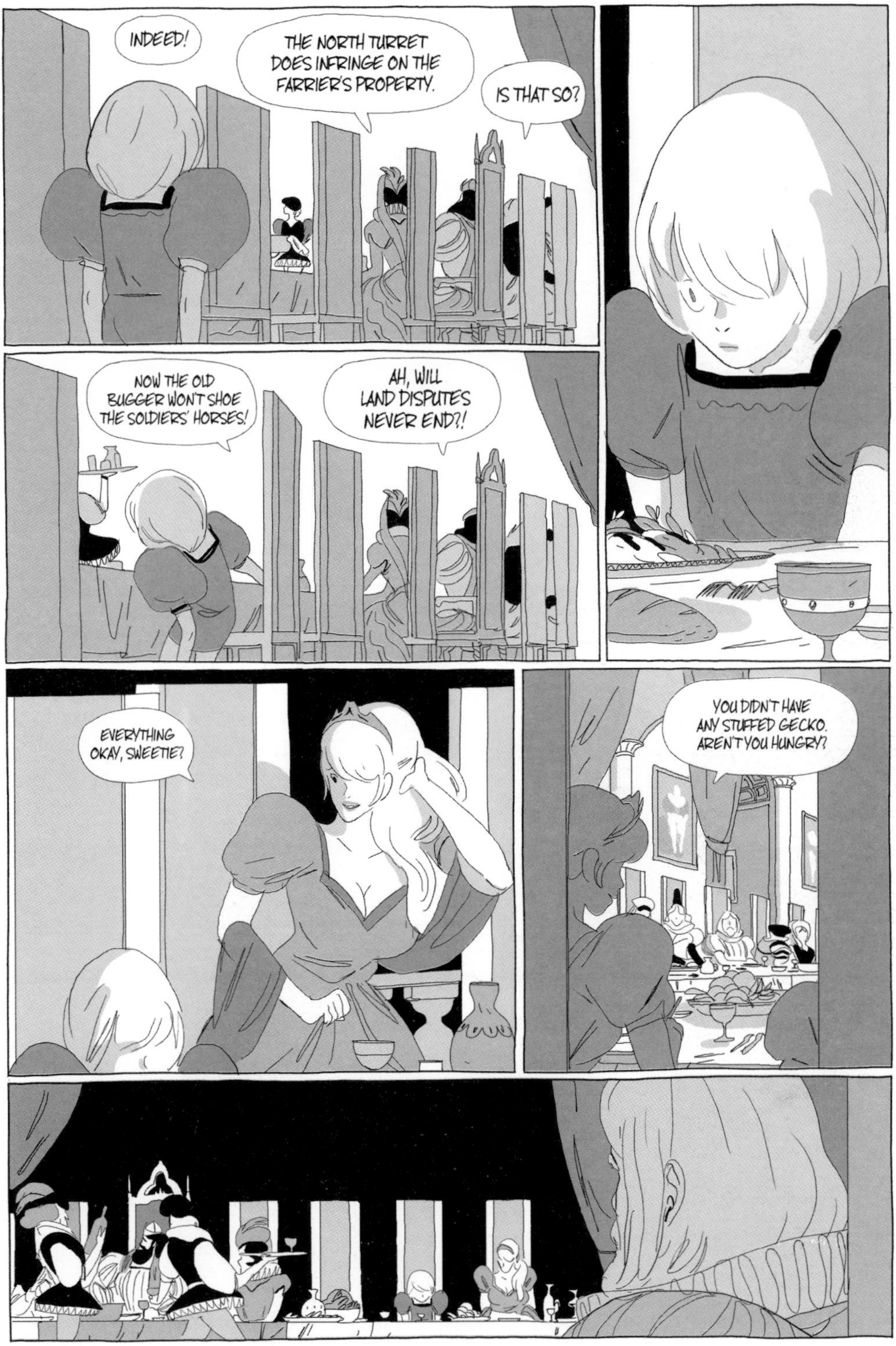
INDEED!
THE NORTH TURRET DOES INFRINGE ON THE FARRIER'S PROPERTY.
IS THAT SO?
NOW THE OLD BUGGER WON'T SHOE THE SOLDIERS' HORSES!
AH, WILL LAND DISPUTES NEVER END?!
EVERYTHING OKAY, SWEETIE?
YOU DIDN'T HAVE ANY STUFFED GECKO. AREN'T YOU HUNGRY?

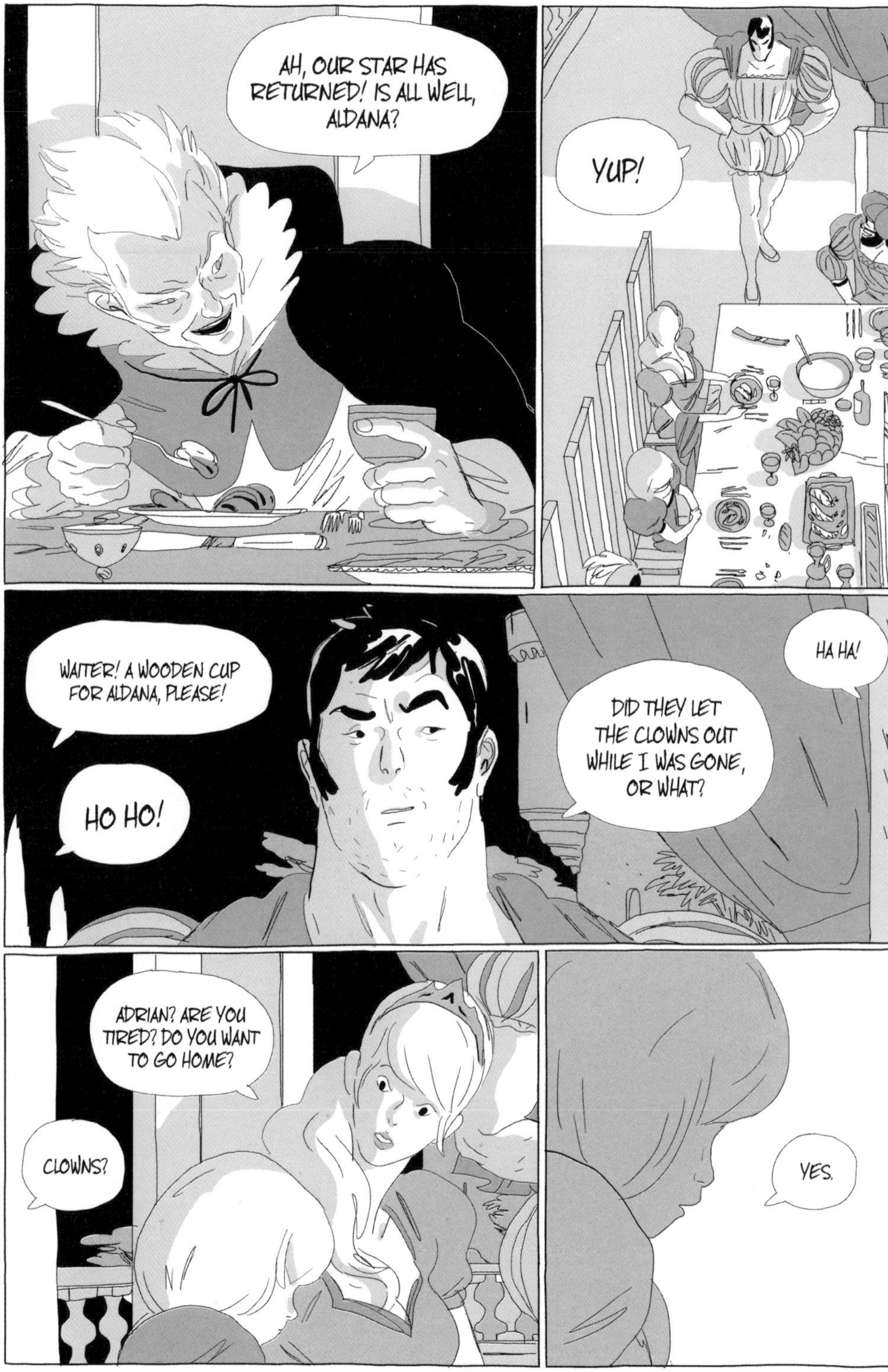
AH, OUR STAR HAS RETURNED! IS ALL WELL, ALDANA?
YUP!
WAITER! A WOODEN CUP FOR ALDANA, PLEASE!
HO HO!
DID THEY LET THE CLOWNS OUT WHILE I WAS GONE, OR WHAT?
HA HA!
ADRIAN? ARE YOU TIRED? DO YOU WANT TO GO HOME?
CLOWNS?
YES.

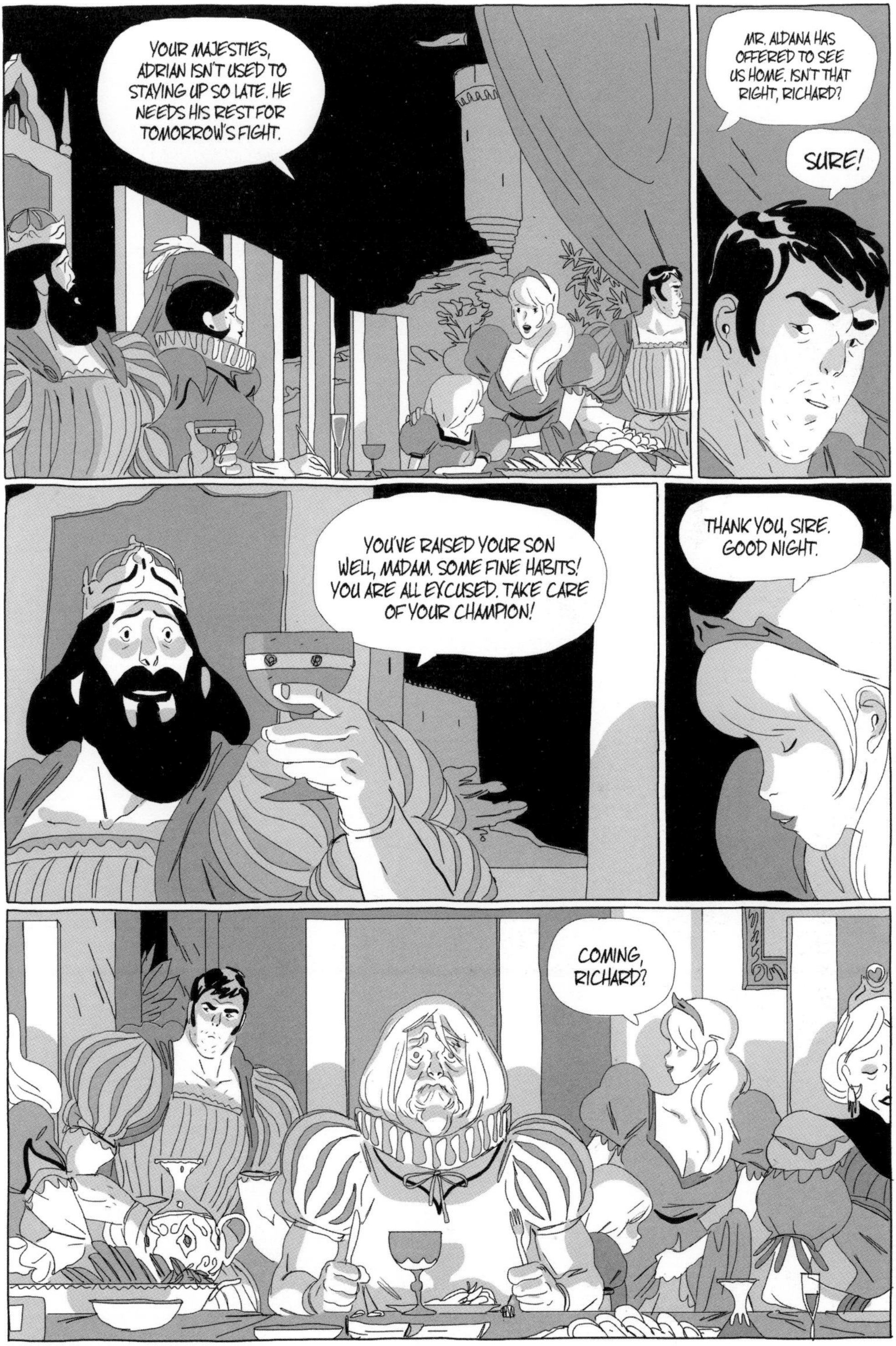
YOUR MAJESTIES, ADRIAN ISN'T USED TO STAYING UP SO LATE. HE NEEDS HIS REST FOR TOMORROW'S FIGHT.
MR. ALDANA HAS OFFERED TO SEE US HOME. ISN'T THAT RIGHT, RICHARD?
SURE!
YOU'VE RAISED YOUR SON WELL, MADAM. SOME FINE HABITS! YOU ARE ALL EXCUSED. TAKE CARE OF YOUR CHAMPION!
THANK YOU, SIRE. GOOD NIGHT.
COMING, RICHARD?

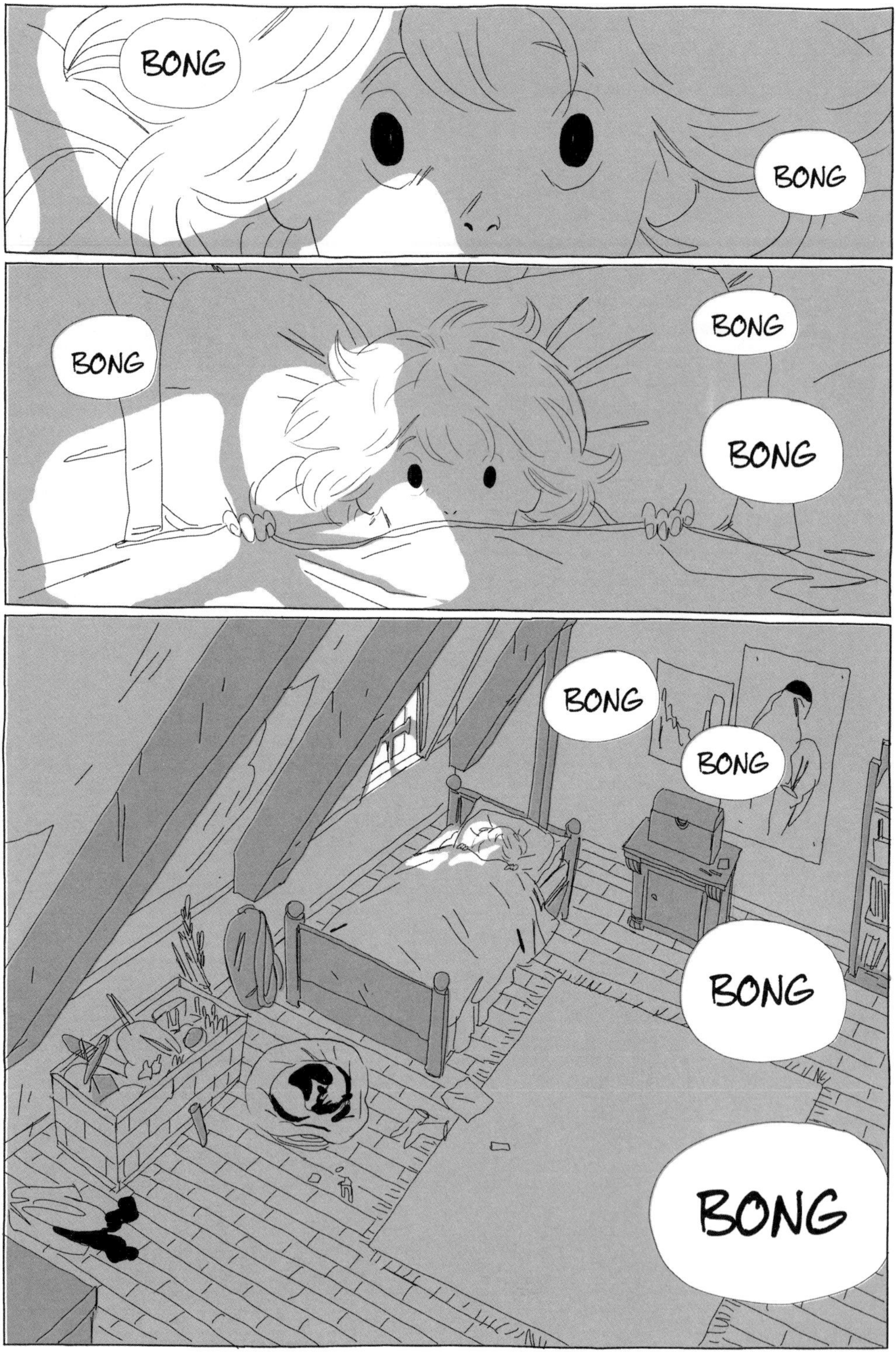
BONG
BONG
BONG
BONG
BONG
BONG
BONG
BONG
BONG

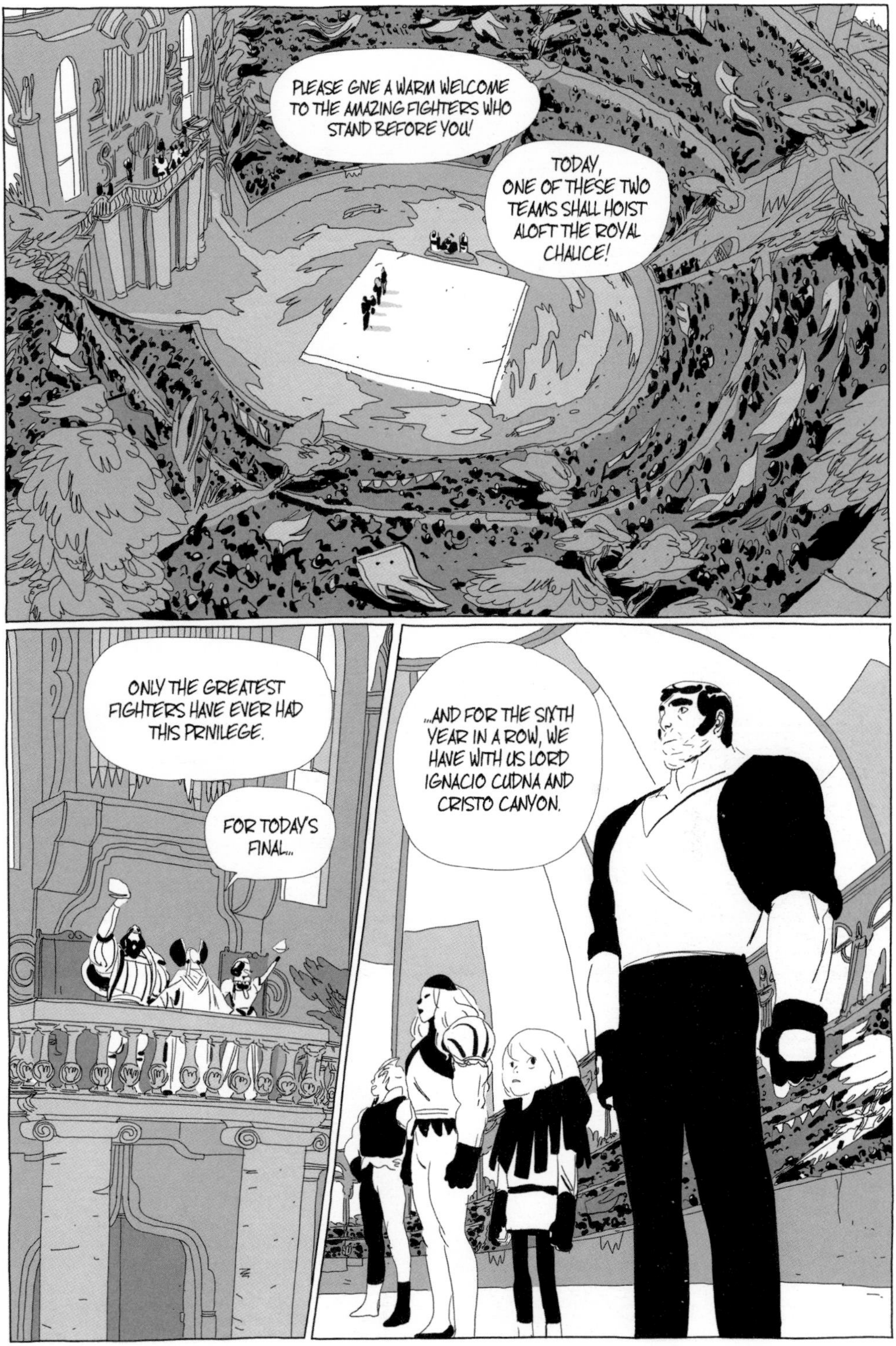
PLEASE GIVE A WARM WELCOME TO THE AMAZING FIGHTERS WHO STAND BEFORE YOU!
TODAY, ONE OF THESE TWO TEAMS SHALL HOIST ALOFT THE ROYAL CHALICE!
ONLY THE GREATEST FIGHTERS HAVE EVER HAD THIS PRIVILEGE.
FOR TODAY'S FINAL...
...AND FOR THE SIXTH YEAR IN A ROW, WE HAVE WITH US LORD IGNACIO CUDNA AND CRISTO CANYON.

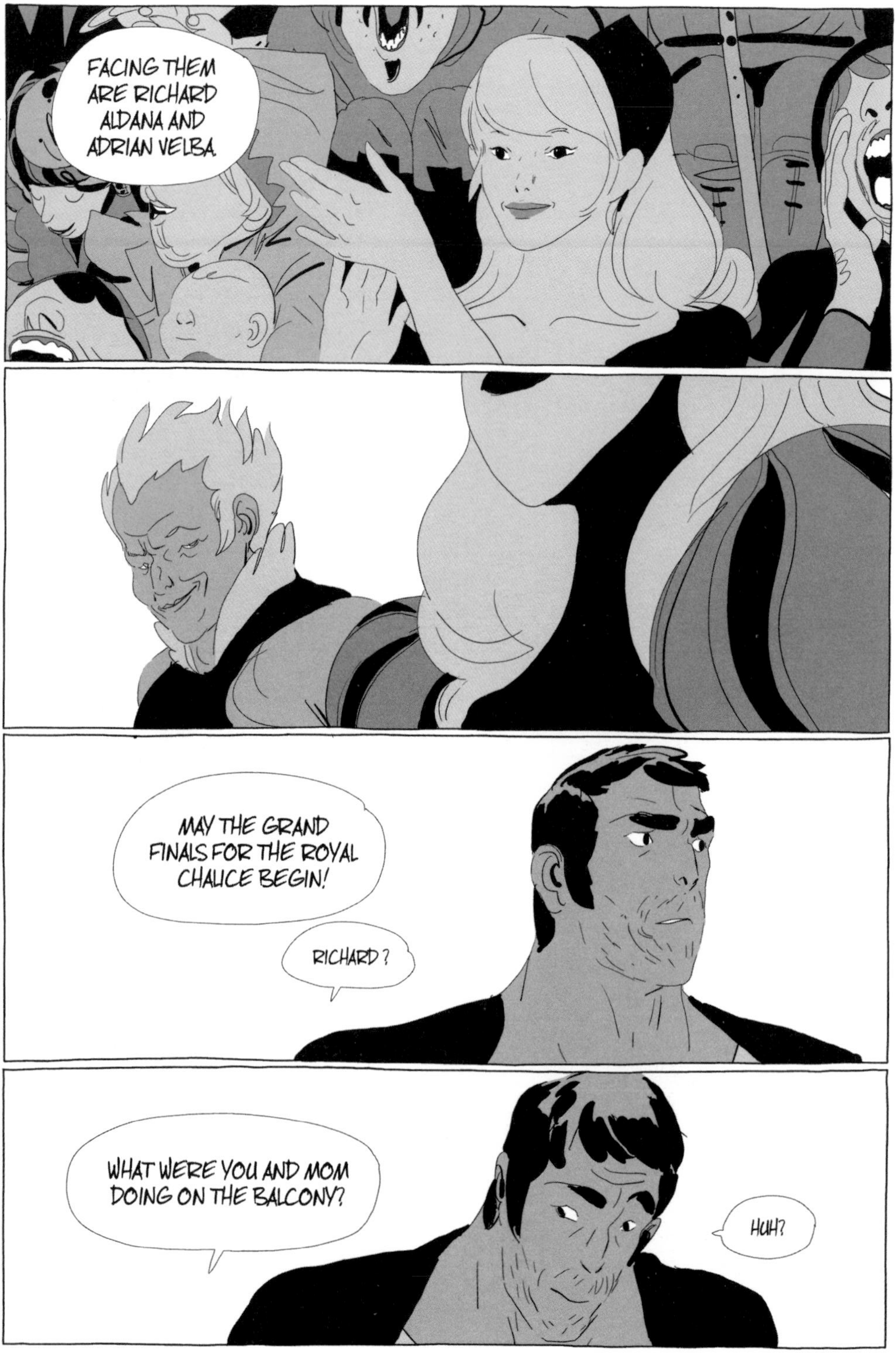
FACING THEM ARE RICHARD ALDANA AND ADRIAN VELBA.
MAY THE GRAND FINALS FOR THE ROYAL CHALICE BEGIN!
RICHARD?
WHAT WERE YOU AND MOM DOING ON THE BALCONY?
HUH?

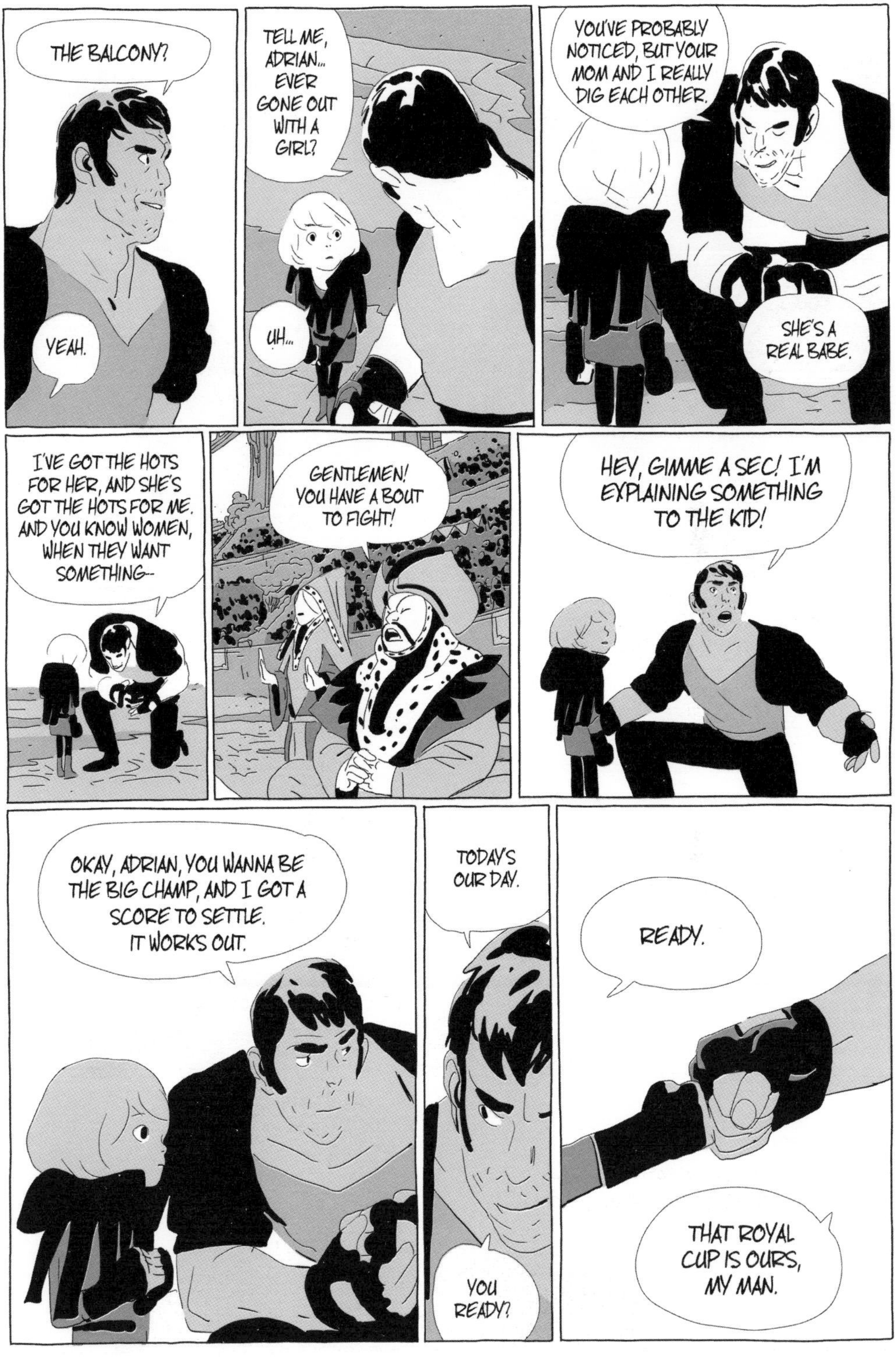
THE BALCONY?
YEAH.
TELL ME, ADRIAN... EVER GONE OUT WITH A GIRL?
UH...
YOU'VE PROBABLY NOTICED, BUT YOUR MOM AND I REALLY DIG EACH OTHER.
SHE'S A REAL BABE.
I'VE GOT THE HOTS FOR HER, AND SHE'S GOT THE HOTS FOR ME. AND YOU KNOW WOMEN, WHEN THEY WANT SOMETHING--
GENTLEMEN! YOU HAVE A BOUT TO FIGHT!
HEY, GIMME A SEC! I'M EXPLAINING SOMETHING TO THE KID!
OKAY, ADRIAN, YOU WANNA BE THE BIG CHAMP, AND I GOT A SCORE TO SETTLE. IT WORKS OUT.
TODAY'S OUR DAY.
YOU READY?
READY.
THAT ROYAL CUP IS OURS, MY MAN.

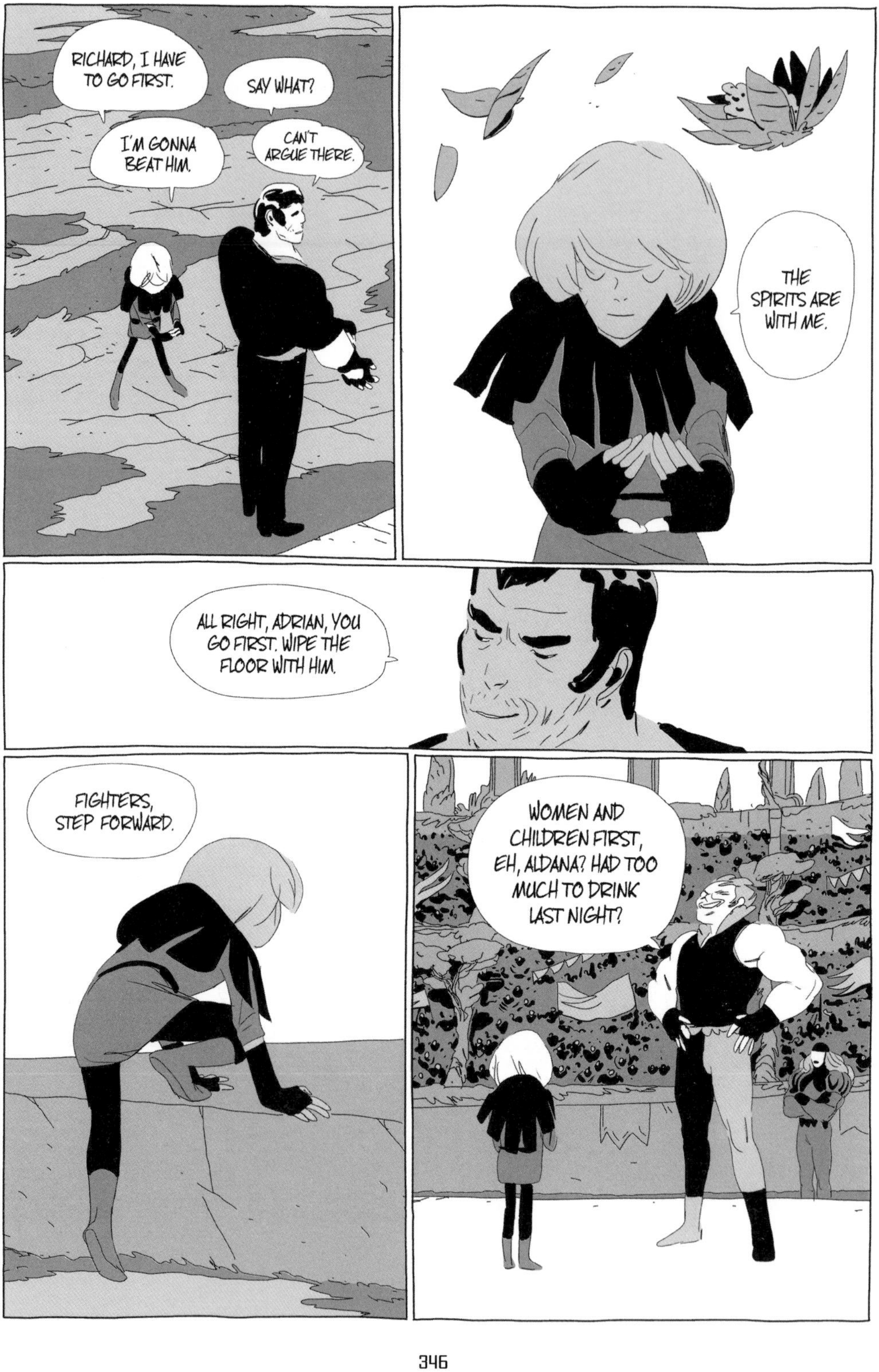
RICHARD, I HAVE TO GO FIRST.
SAY WHAT?
I'M GONNA BEAT HIM.
CAN'T ARGUE THERE.
THE SPIRITS ARE WITH ME.
ALL RIGHT, ADRIAN, YOU GO FIRST. WIPE THE FLOOR WITH HIM.
FIGHTERS, STEP FORWARD.
WOMEN AND CHILDREN FIRST, EH, ALDANA? HAD TOO MUCH TO DRINK LAST NIGHT?

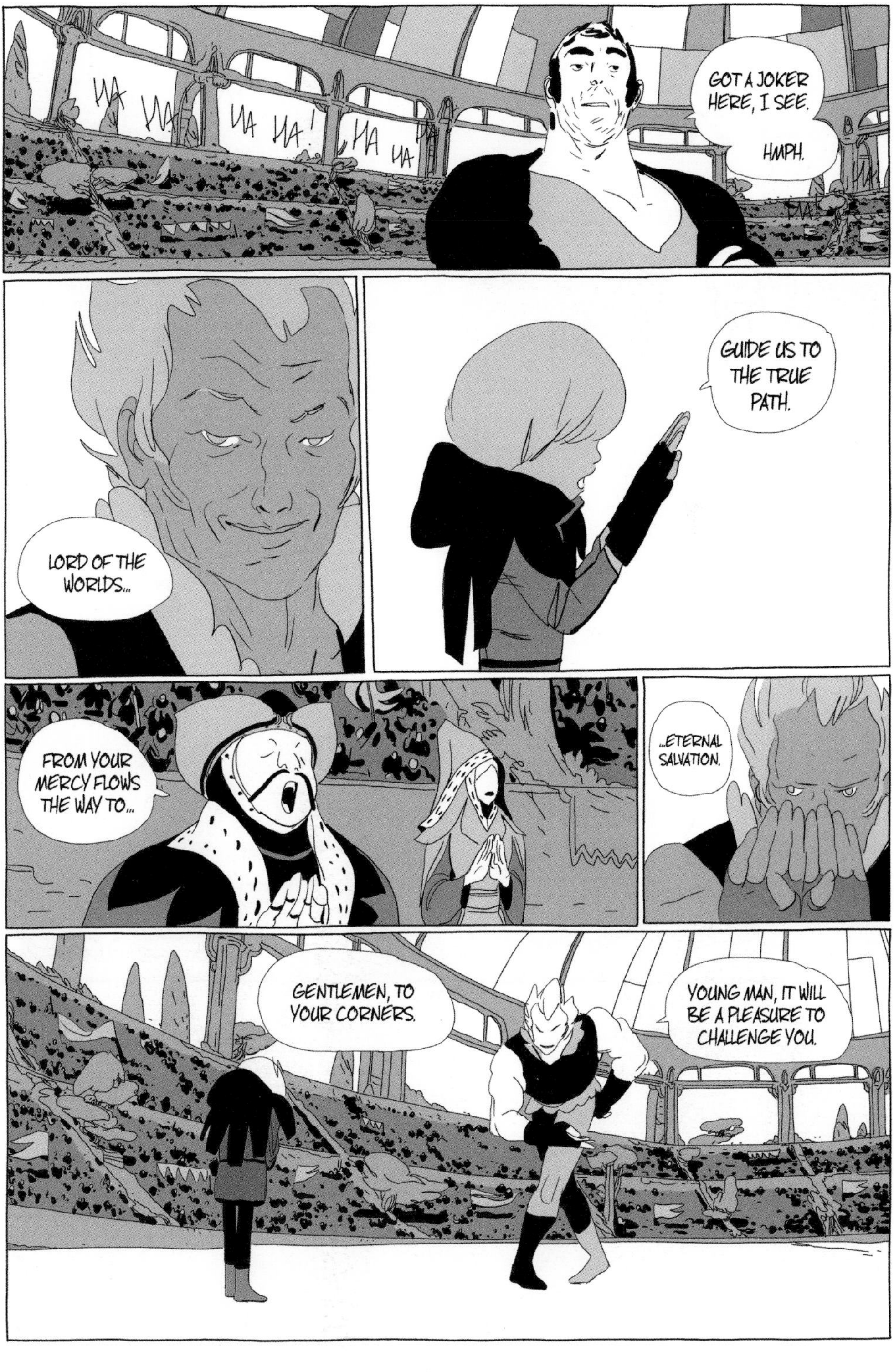
HA HA HA HA! HA HA HA
GOT A JOKER HERE, I SEE.
HMPH.
LORD OF THE WORLDS...
GUIDE US TO THE TRUE PATH.
FROM YOUR MERCY FLOWS THE WAY TO...
...ETERNAL SALVATION.
GENTLEMEN, TO YOUR CORNERS.
YOUNG MAN, IT WILL BE A PLEASURE TO CHALLENGE YOU.

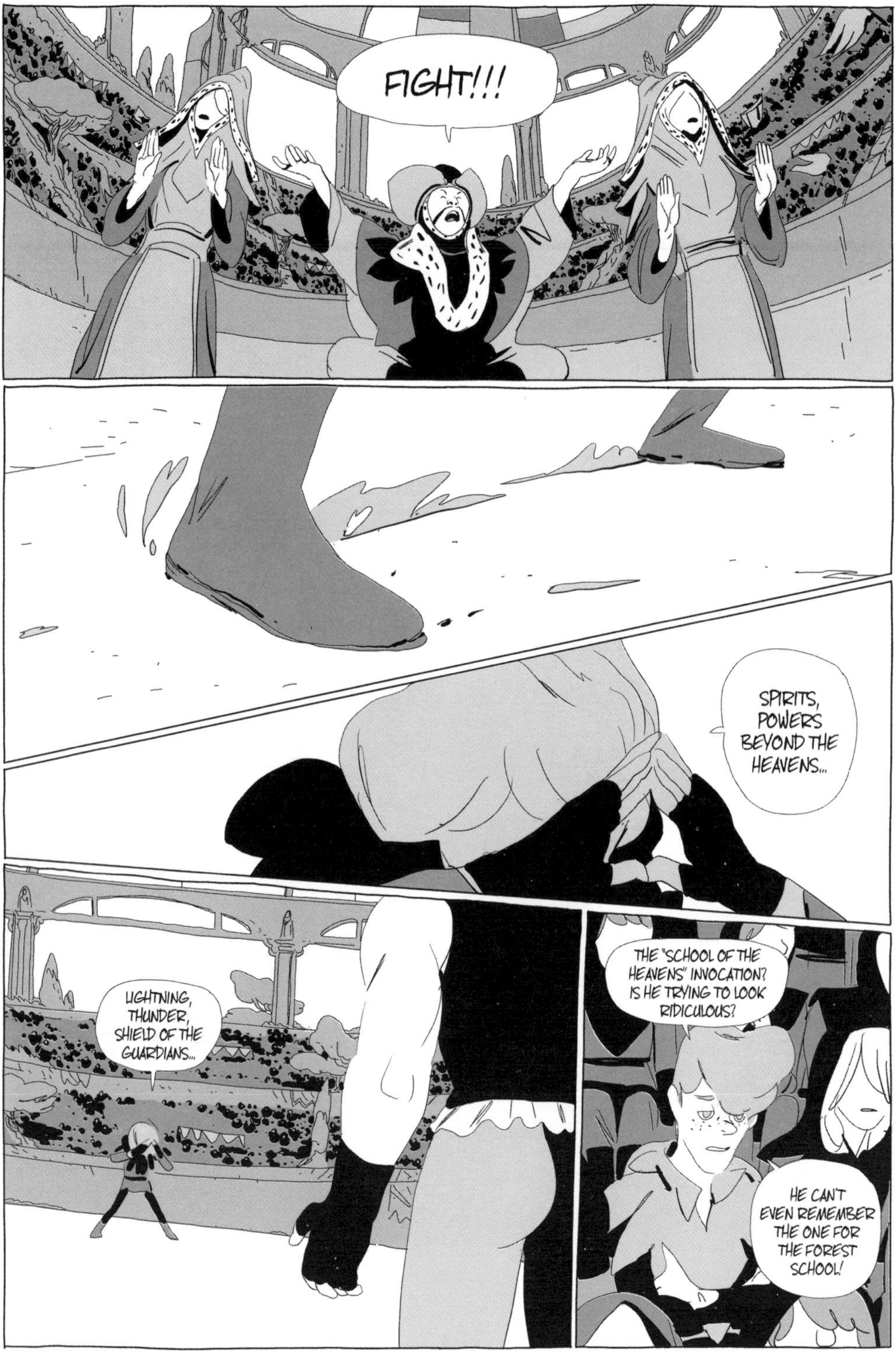
FIGHT!!!
SPIRITS, POWERS BEYOND THE HEAVENS...
LIGHTNING, THUNDER, SHIELD OF THE GUARDIANS...
THE "SCHOOL OF THE HEAVENS" INVOCATION? IS HE TRYING TO LOOK RIDICULOUS?
HE CAN'T EVEN REMEMBER THE ONE FOR THE FOREST SCHOOL!

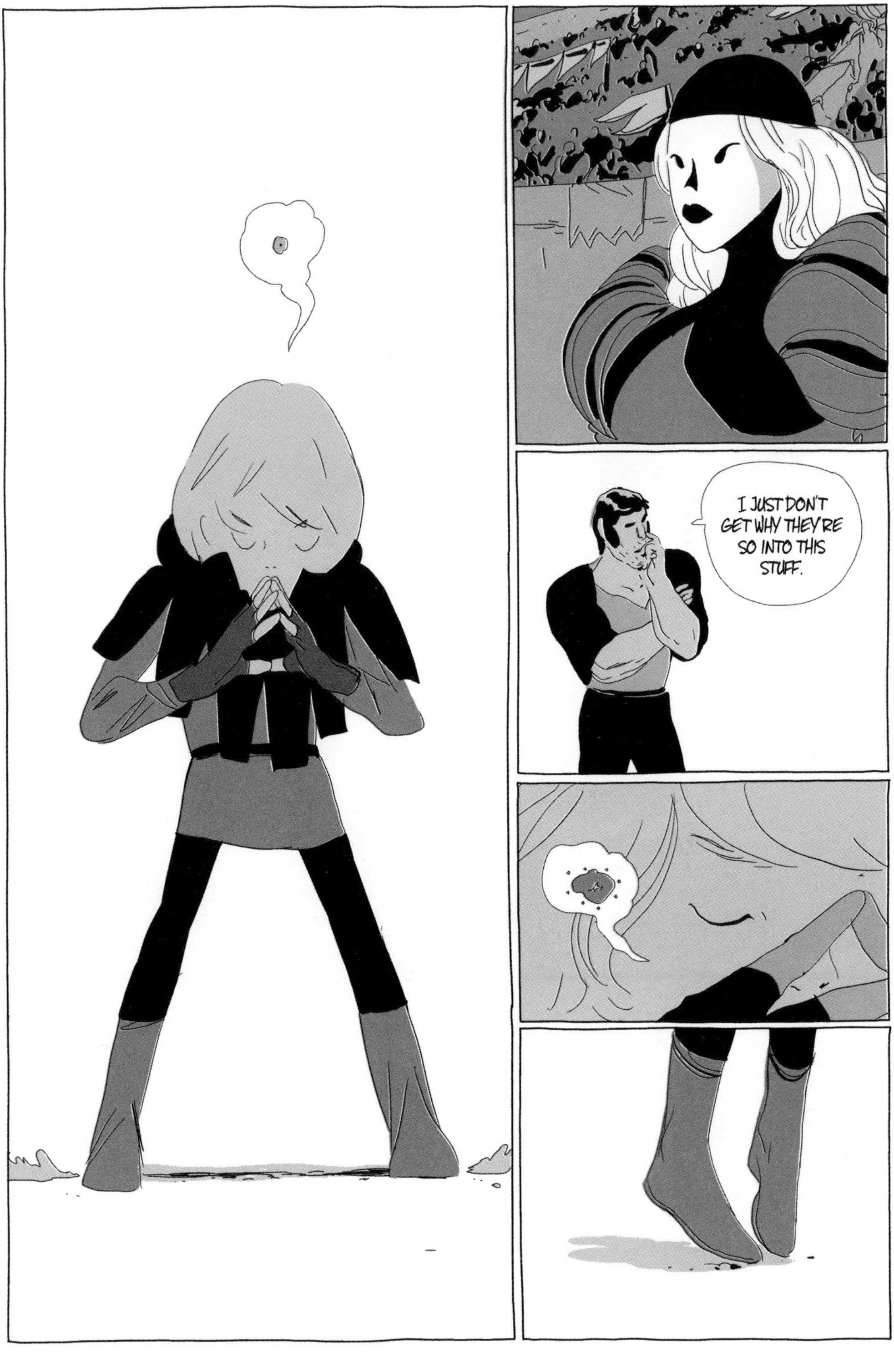
I JUST DON'T GET WHY THEY'RE SO INTO THIS STUFF.

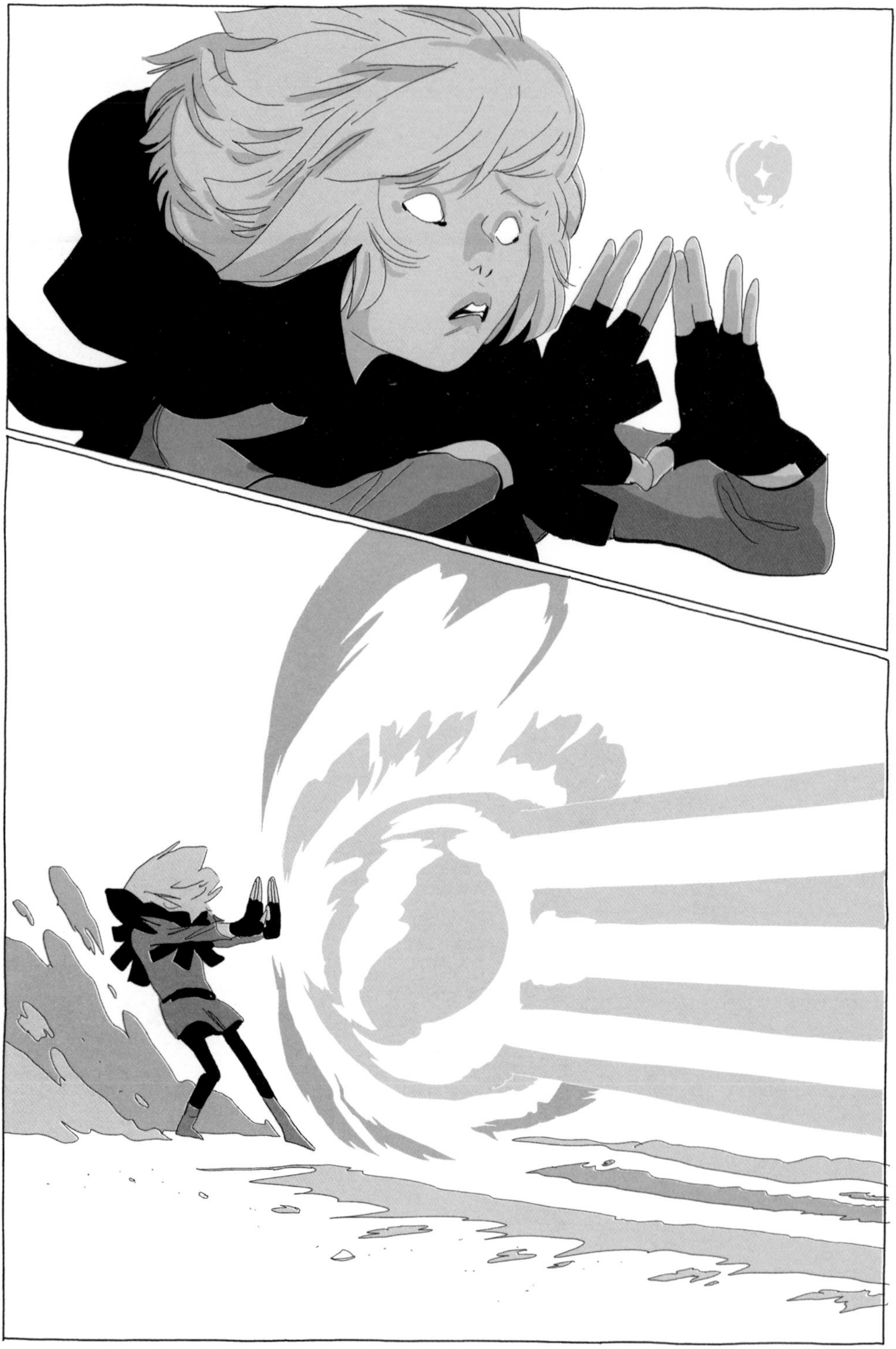

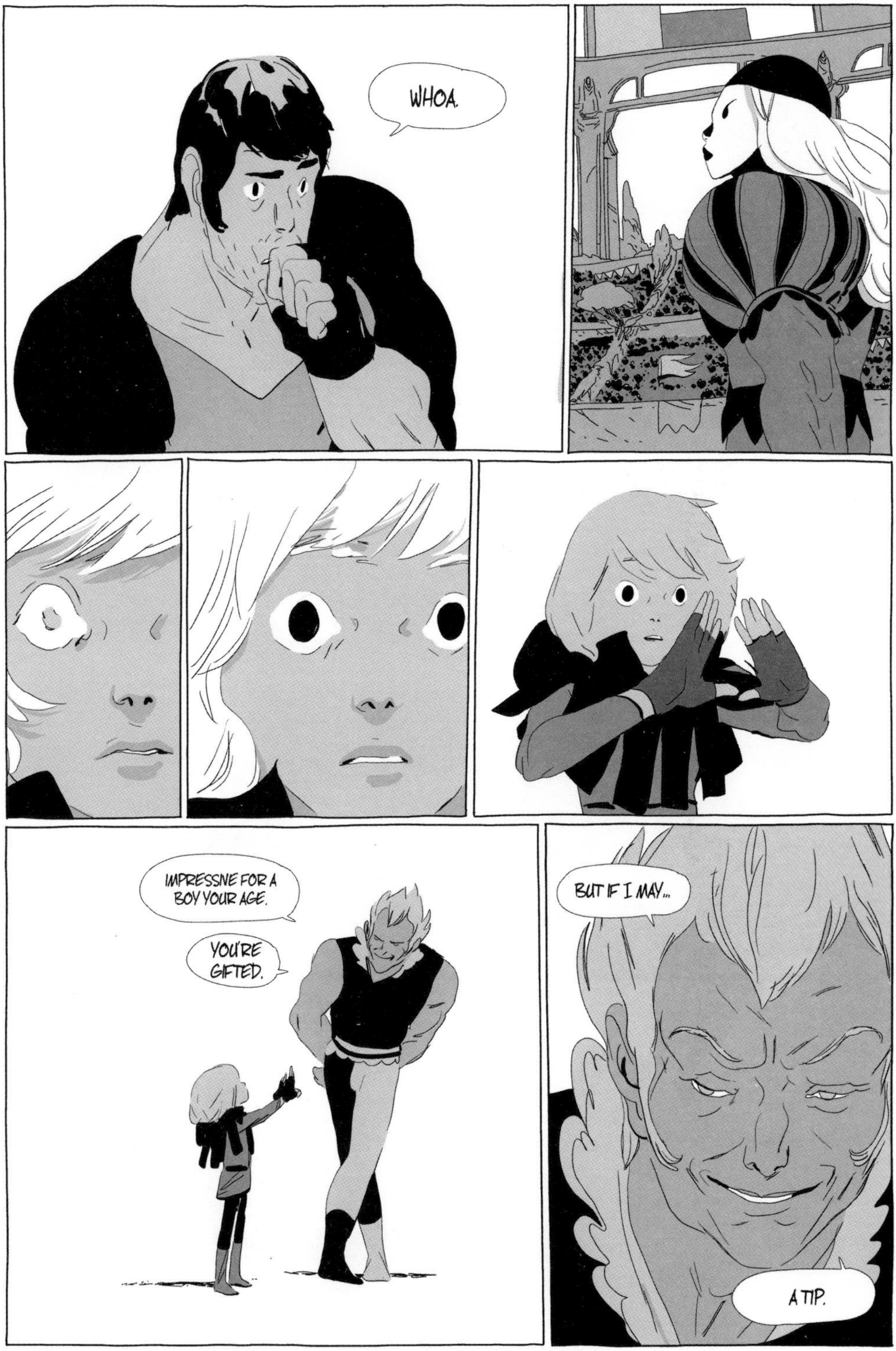
WHOA.
IMPRESSIVE FOR A BOY YOUR AGE.
YOU'RE GIFTED.
BUT IF I MAY...
A TIP.

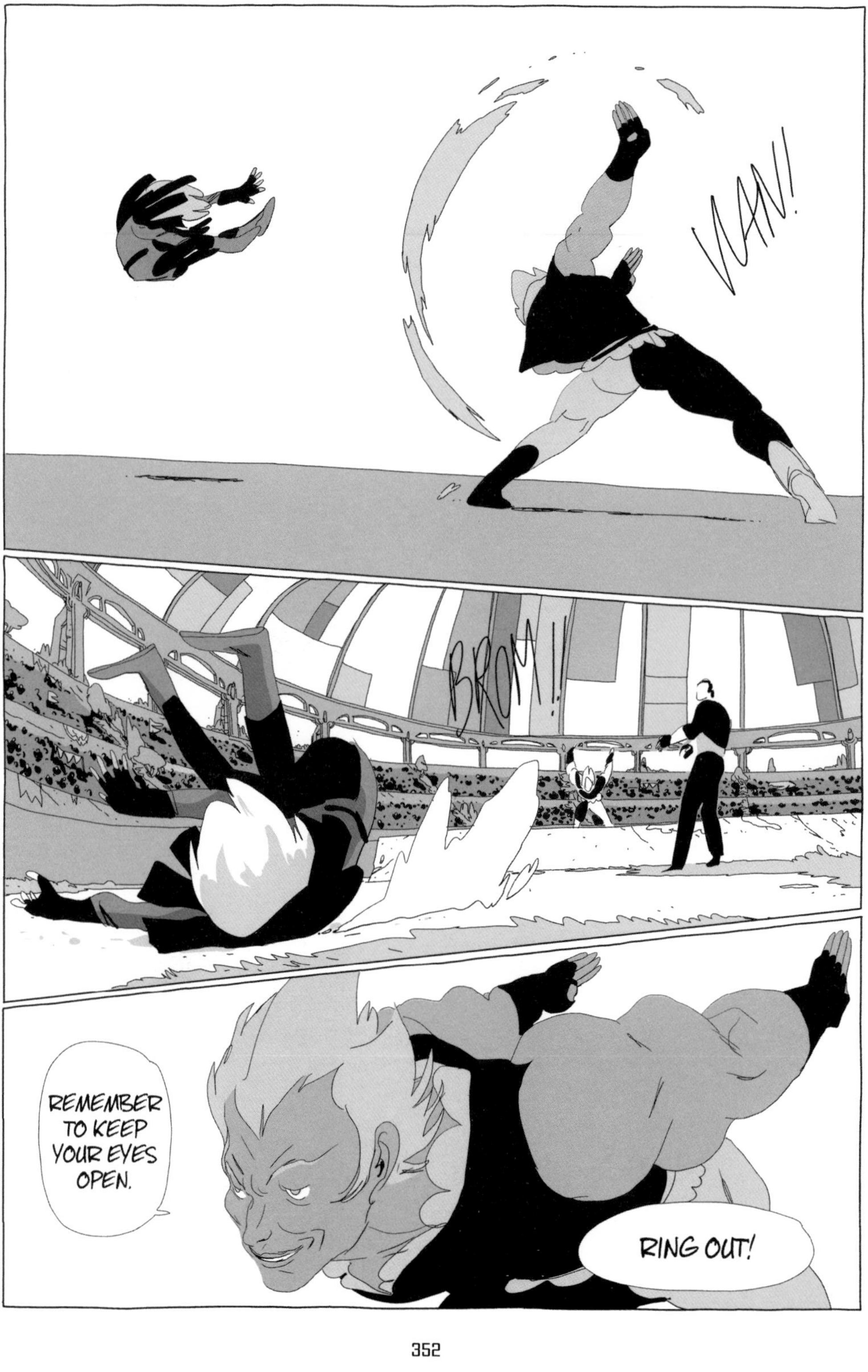
VLAN!
BROM!!
REMEMBER TO KEEP YOUR EYES OPEN.
RING OUT!

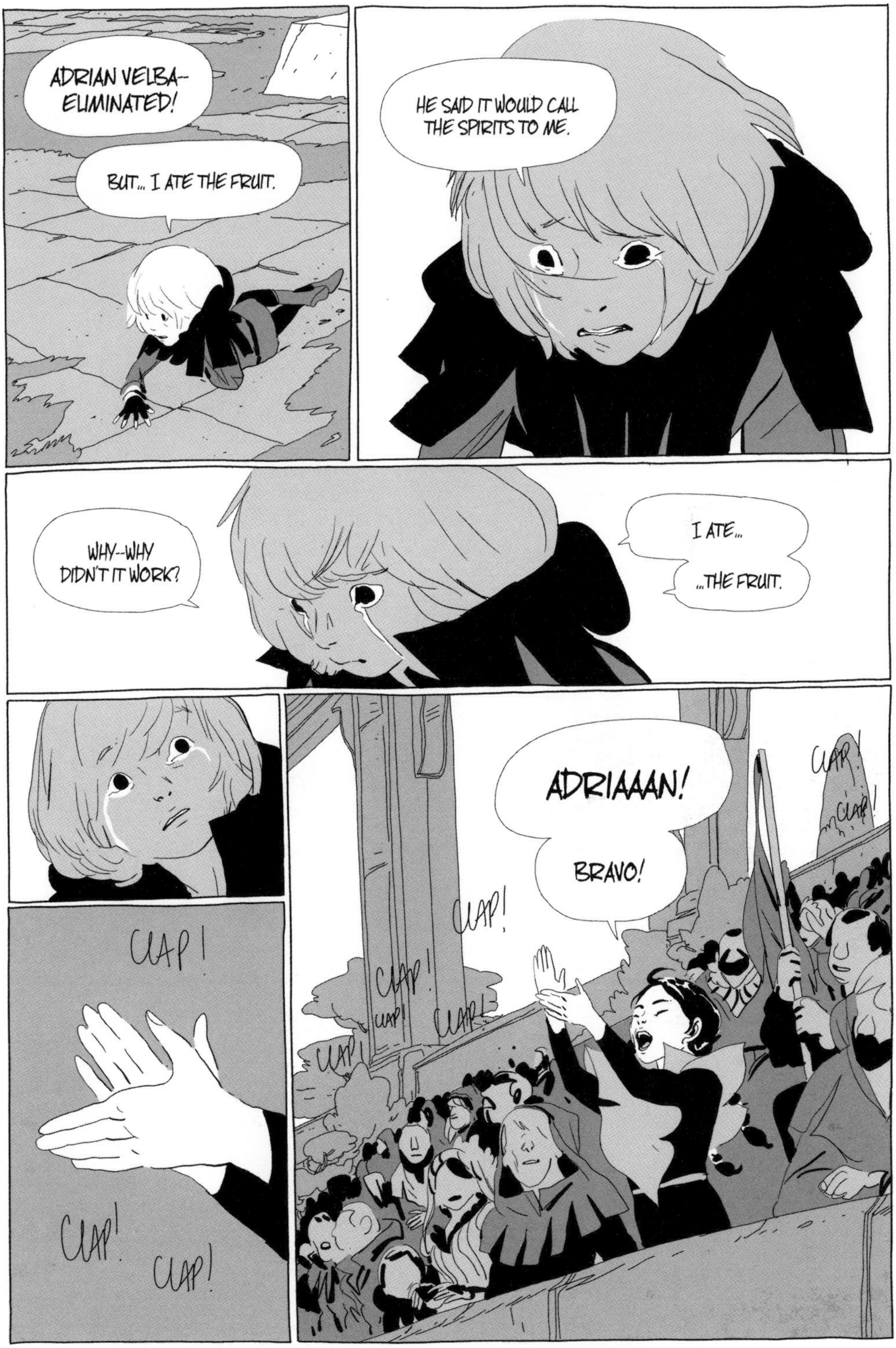
ADRIAN VELBA--ELIMINATED!
BUT... I ATE THE FRUIT.
HE SAID IT WOULD CALL THE SPIRITS TO ME.
WHY--WHY DIDN'T IT WORK?
I ATE...
...THE FRUIT.
ADRIAAAN!
BRAVO!
CLAP!
CLAP!
CLAP!
CLAP!
CLAP!
CLAP!
CLAP!
CLAP!
CLAP!
CLAP!
CLAP!

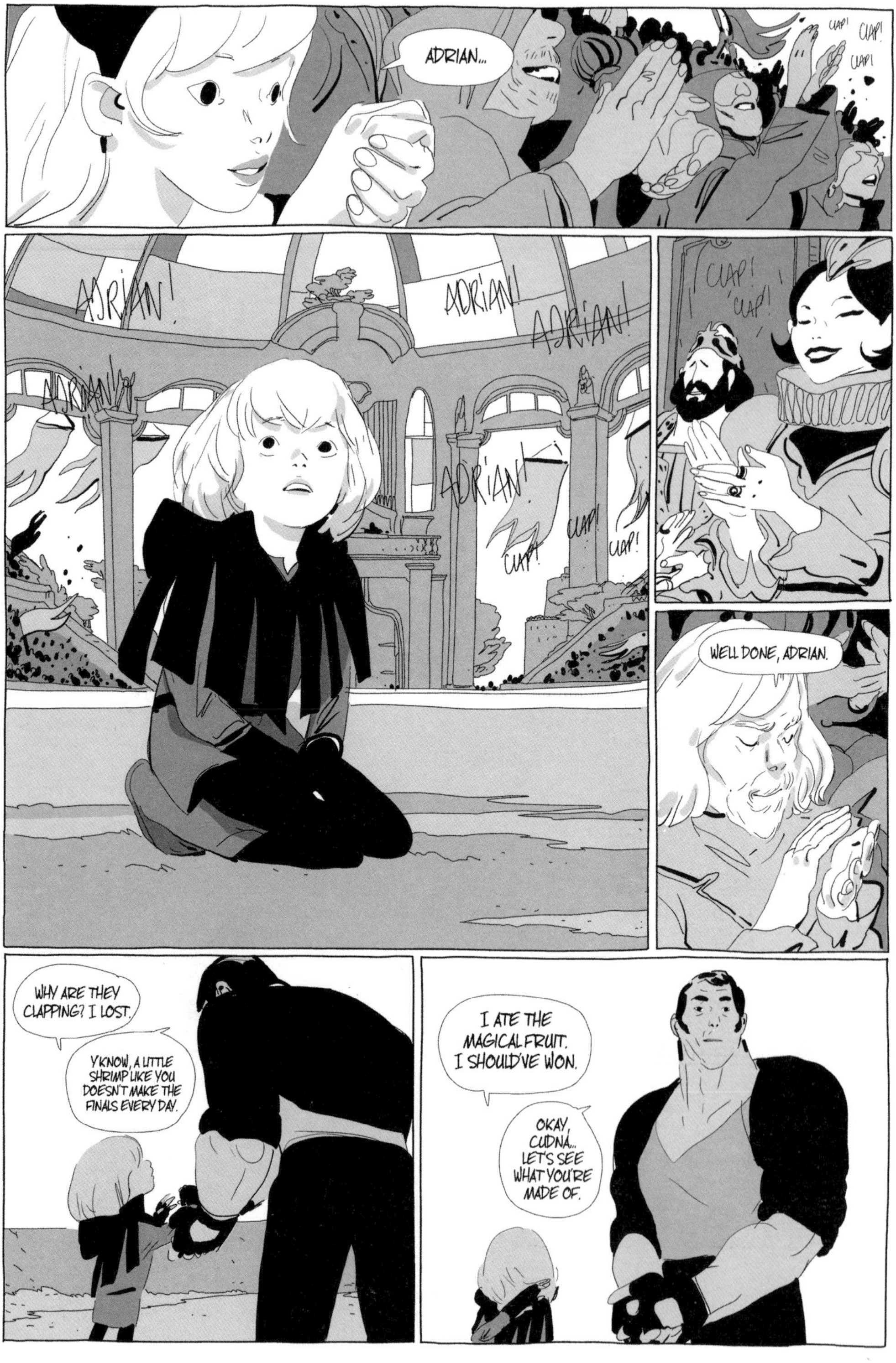
ADRIAN...
CLAP! CLAP! CLAP!
ADRIAN!
ADRIAN!
ADRIAN!
ADRIAN!
ADRIAN!
CLAP!
CLAP!
CLAP!
CLAP! CLAP!
WELL DONE, ADRIAN.
WHY ARE THEY CLAPPING? I LOST.
Y'KNOW, A LITTLE SHRIMP LIKE YOU DOESN'T MAKE THE FINALS EVERY DAY.
I ATE THE MAGICAL FRUIT. I SHOULD'VE WON.
OKAY, CUDNA... LET'S SEE WHAT YOU'RE MADE OF.

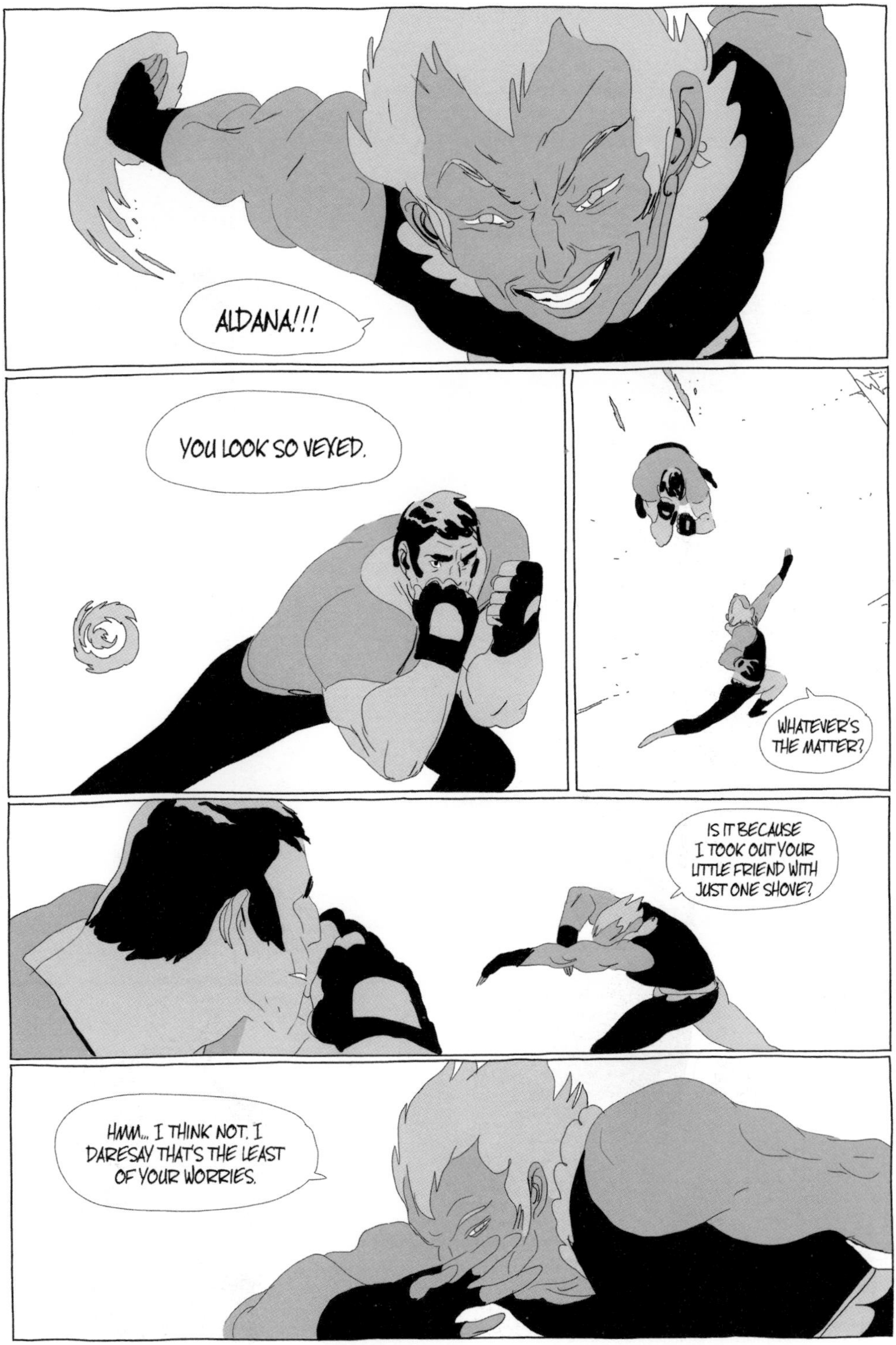
ALDANA!!!
YOU LOOK SO VEXED.
WHATEVER'S THE MATTER?
IS IT BECAUSE I TOOK OUT YOUR LITTLE FRIEND WITH JUST ONE SHOVE?
HMM... I THINK NOT. I DARESAY THAT'S THE LEAST OF YOUR WORRIES.

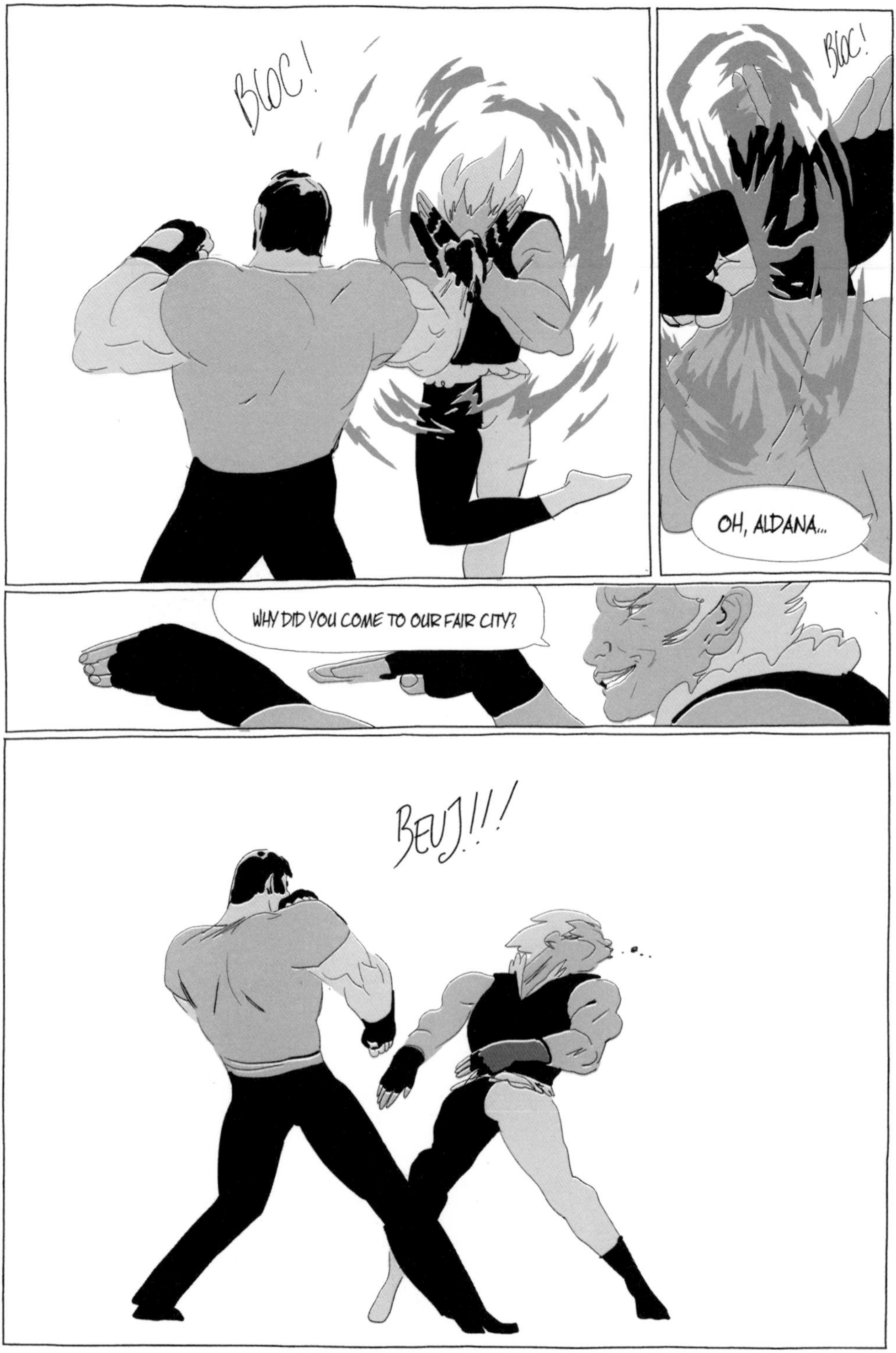
BLOC!
BLOC!
OH, ALDANA...
WHY DID YOU COME TO OUR FAIR CITY?
BEUJ!!!

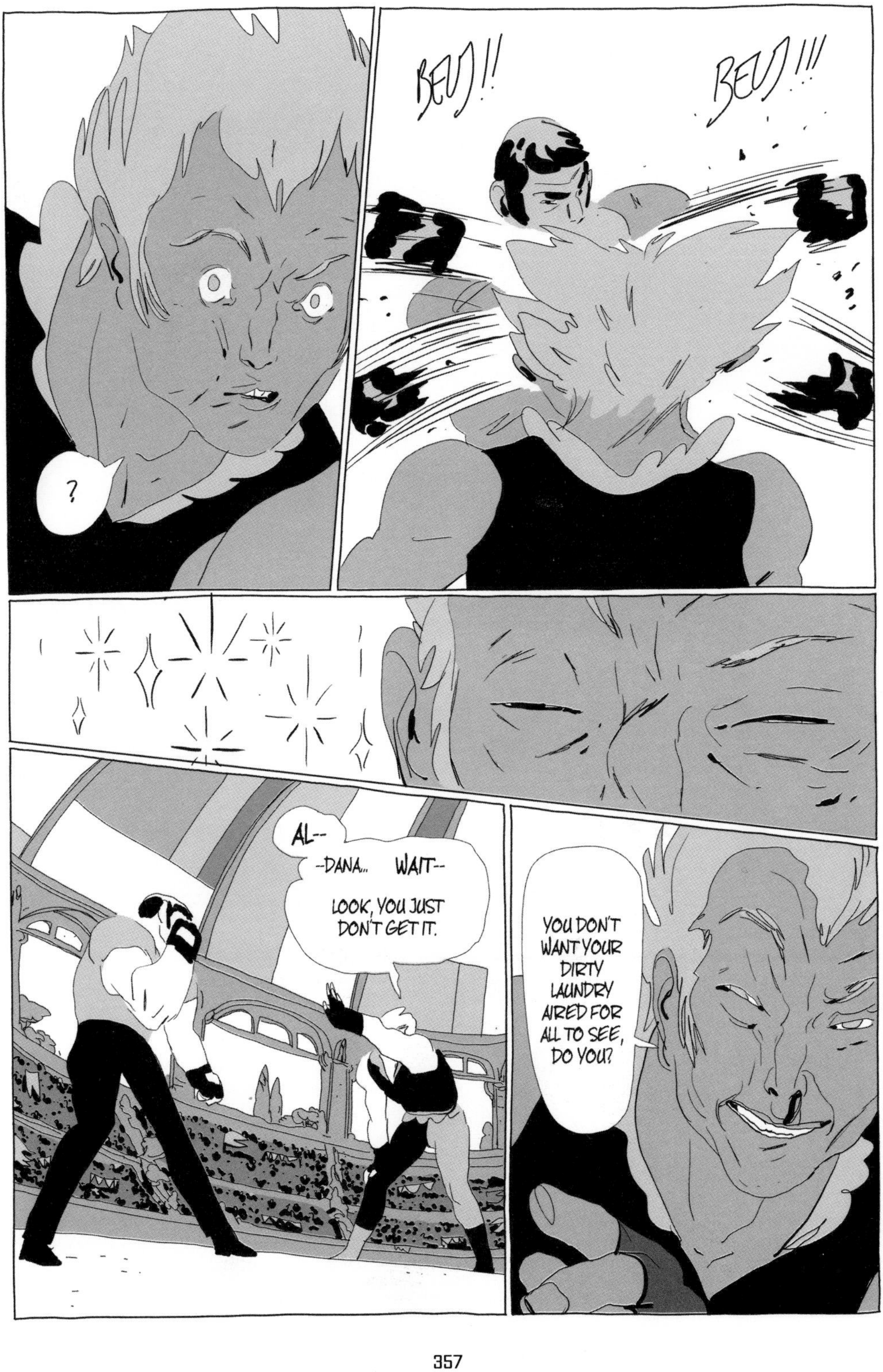
?
BEW!!
BEW!!!
AL--
--DANA... WAIT--
LOOK, YOU JUST DON'T GET IT.
YOU DON'T WANT YOUR DIRTY LAUNDRY AIRED FOR ALL TO SEE, DO YOU?

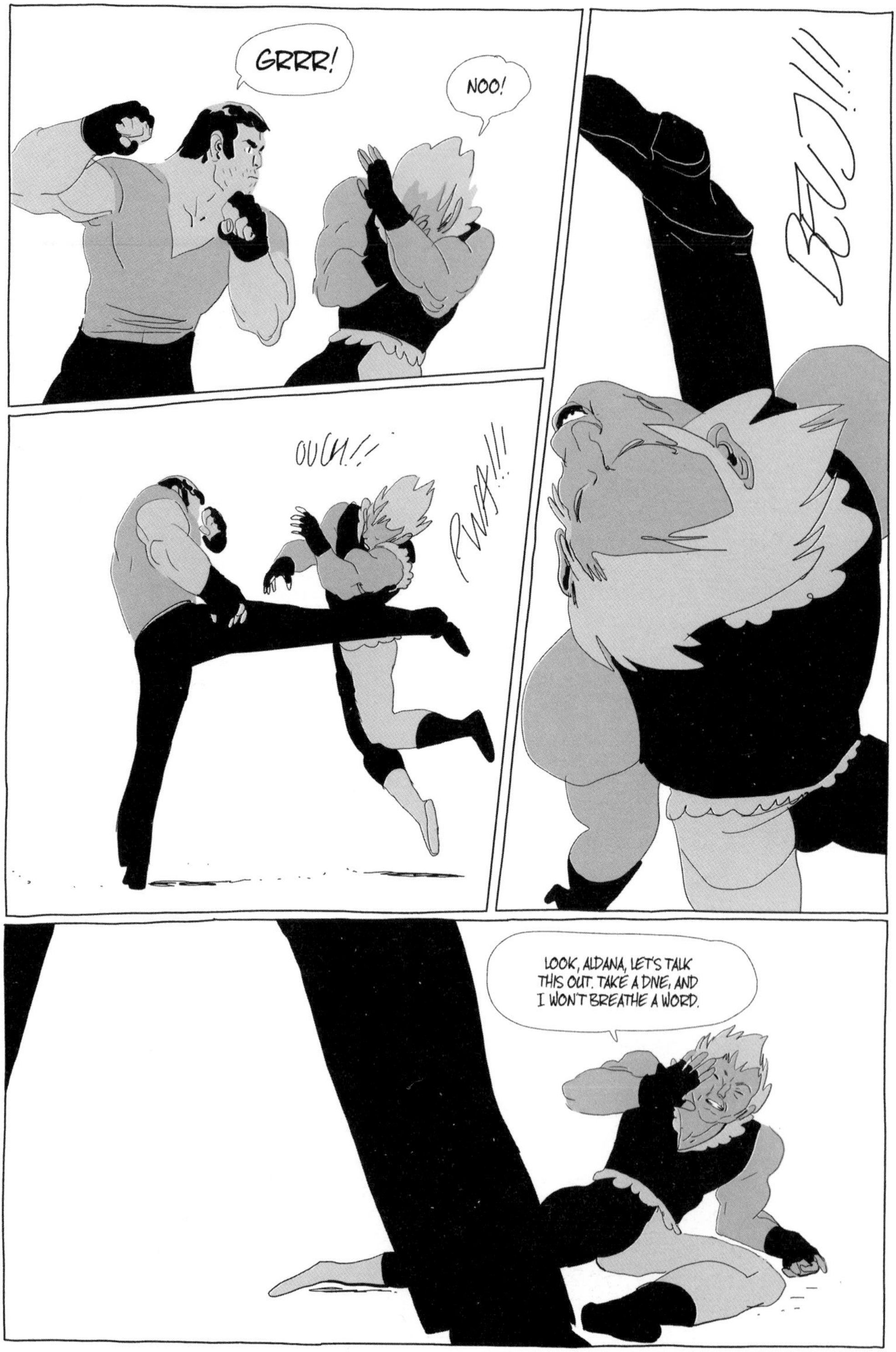
GRRR!
NOO!
BLAM!!!
OUCH!!
PWAP!!!
LOOK, ALDANA, LET'S TALK THIS OUT. TAKE A DIVE, AND I WON'T BREATHE A WORD.

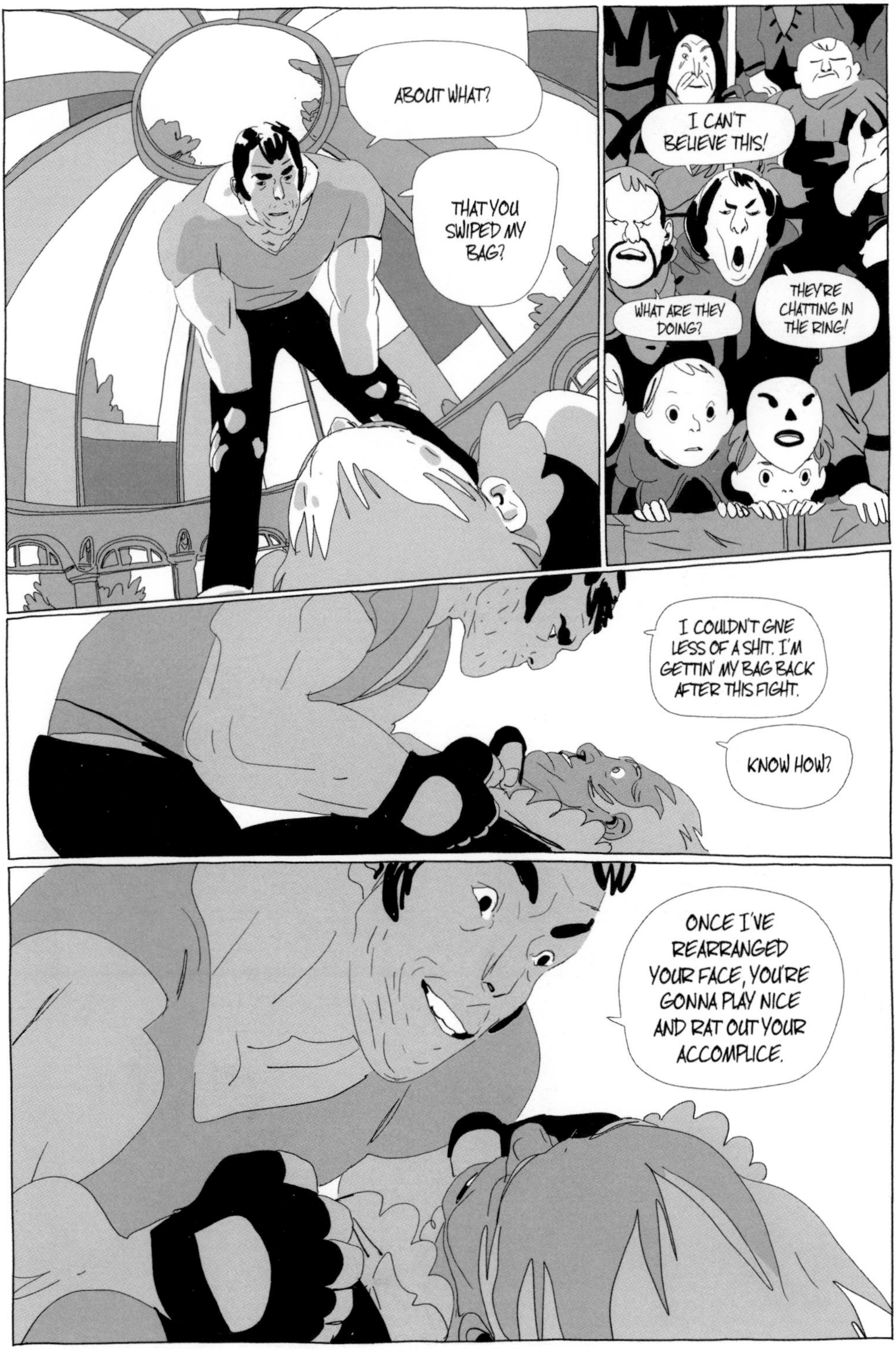
ABOUT WHAT?
THAT YOU SWIPED MY BAG?
I CAN'T BELIEVE THIS!
THEY'RE CHATTING IN THE RING!
WHAT ARE THEY DOING?
I COULDN'T GIVE LESS OF A SHIT. I'M GETTIN' MY BAG BACK AFTER THIS FIGHT.
KNOW HOW?
ONCE I'VE REARRANGED YOUR FACE, YOU'RE GONNA PLAY NICE AND RAT OUT YOUR ACCOMPLICE.

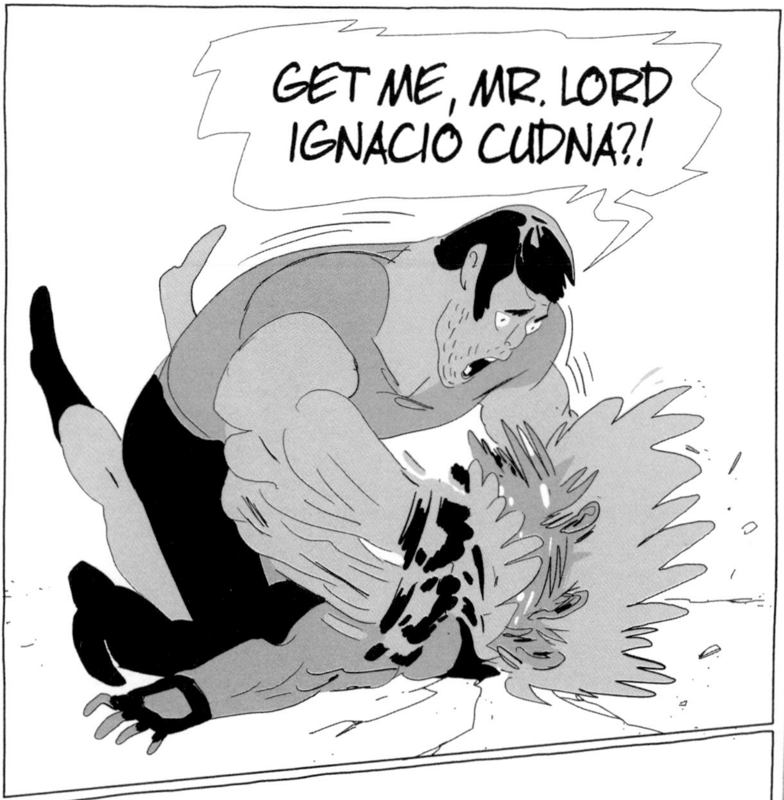
GET ME, MR. LORD IGNACIO CUDNA?!

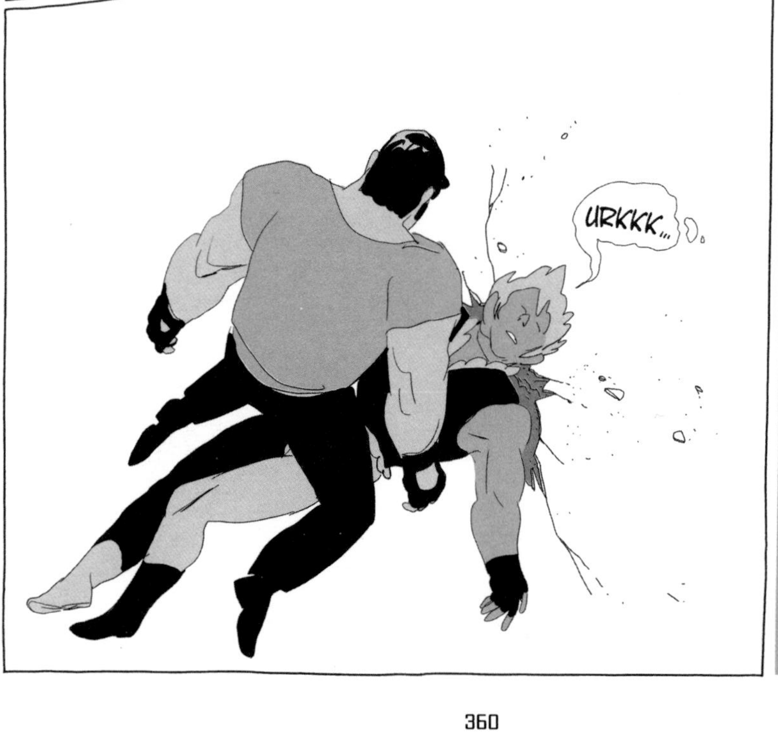
URKKK...

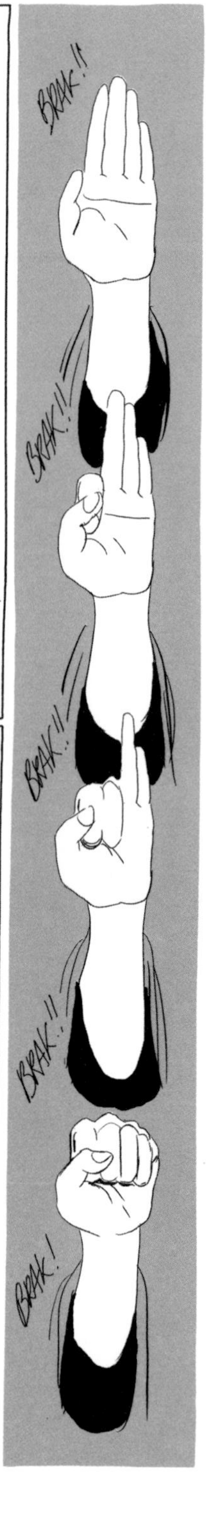
BRAK!!
BRAK!!
BRAK!!
BRAK!!
BRAK!

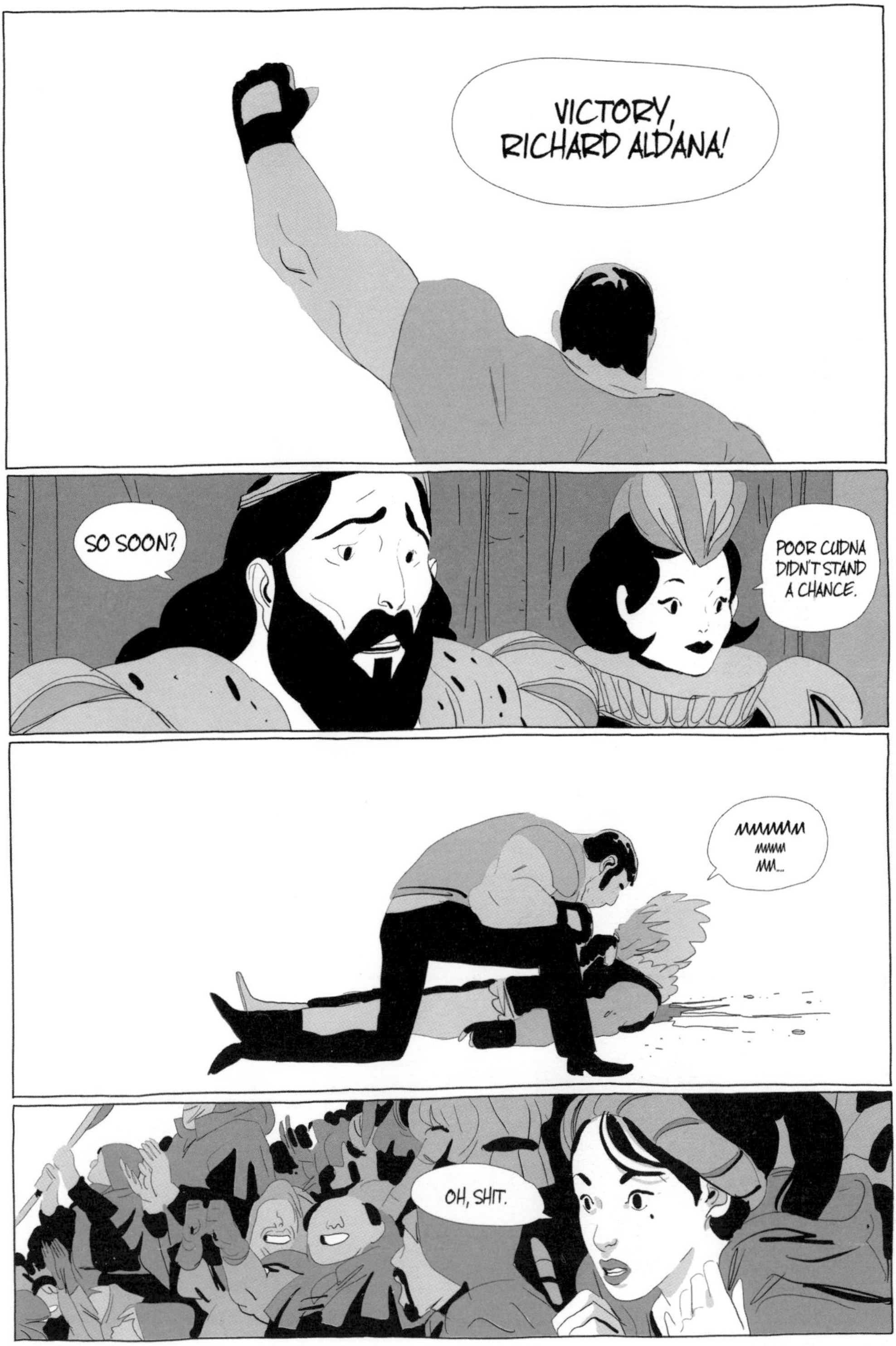
VICTORY, RICHARD ALD'ANA!
SO SOON?
POOR CUDNA DIDN'T STAND A CHANCE.
MMMMM MMMM MM...
OH, SHIT.

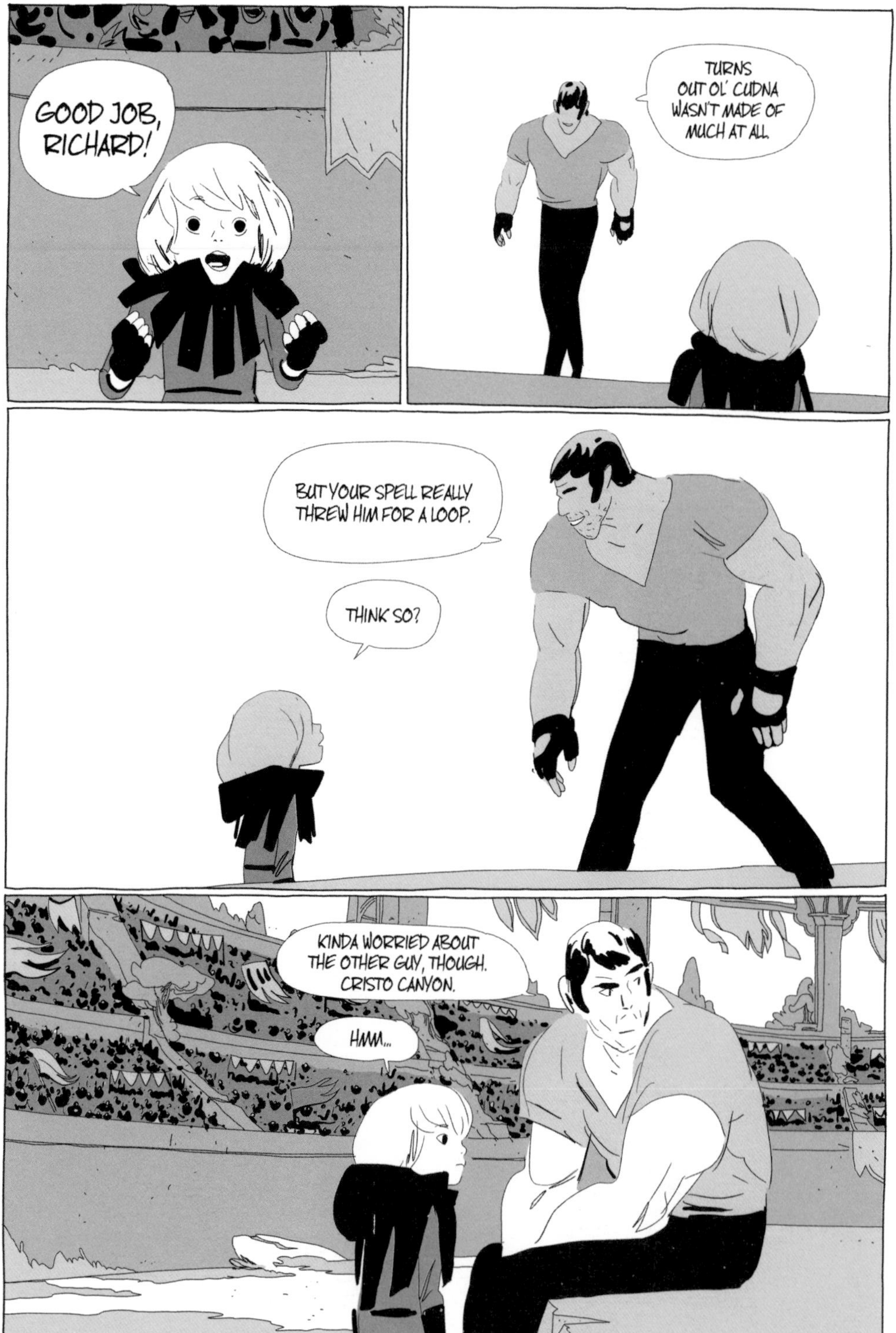
GOOD JOB, RICHARD!
TURNS OUT OL' CUDNA WASN'T MADE OF MUCH AT ALL.
BUT YOUR SPELL REALLY THREW HIM FOR A LOOP.
THINK SO?
KINDA WORRIED ABOUT THE OTHER GUY, THOUGH. CRISTO CANYON.
HMM...

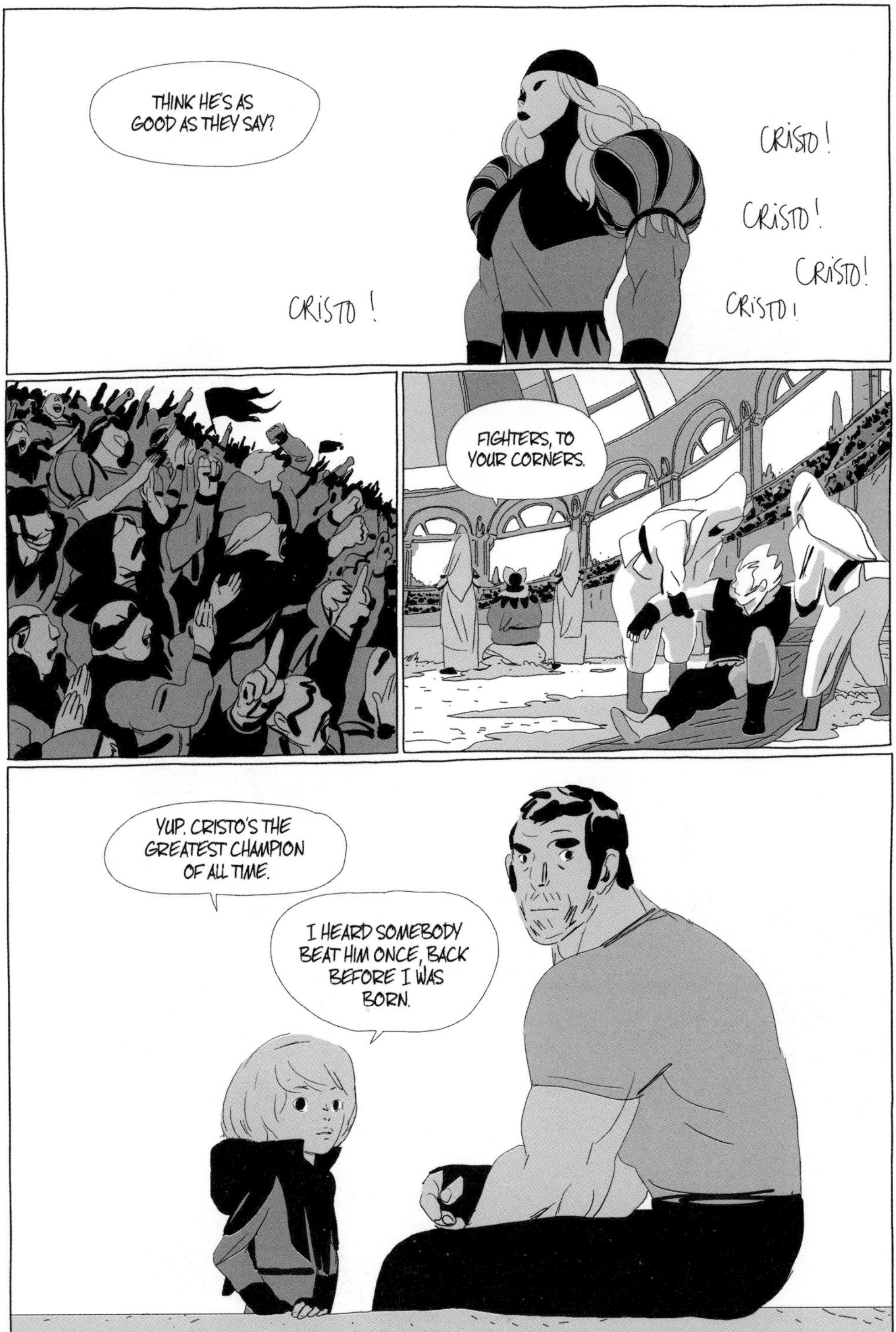
THINK HE'S AS GOOD AS THEY SAY?
CRISTO!
CRISTO!
CRISTO!
CRISTO!
CRISTO!
FIGHTERS, TO YOUR CORNERS.
YUP. CRISTO'S THE GREATEST CHAMPION OF ALL TIME.
I HEARD SOMEBODY BEAT HIM ONCE, BACK BEFORE I WAS BORN.

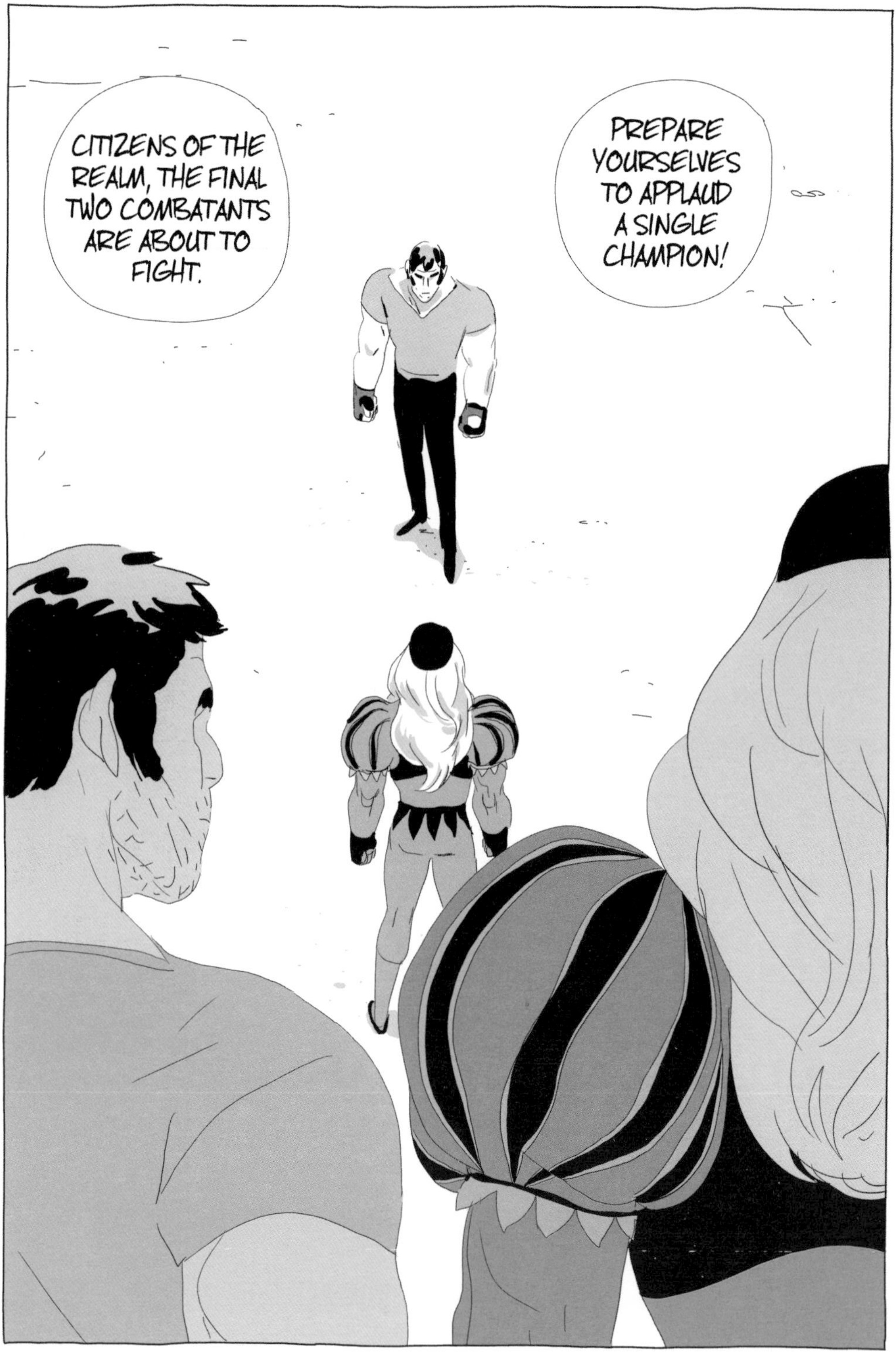
CITIZENS OF THE REALM, THE FINAL TWO COMBATANTS ARE ABOUT TO FIGHT.
PREPARE YOURSELVES TO APPLAUD A SINGLE CHAMPION!

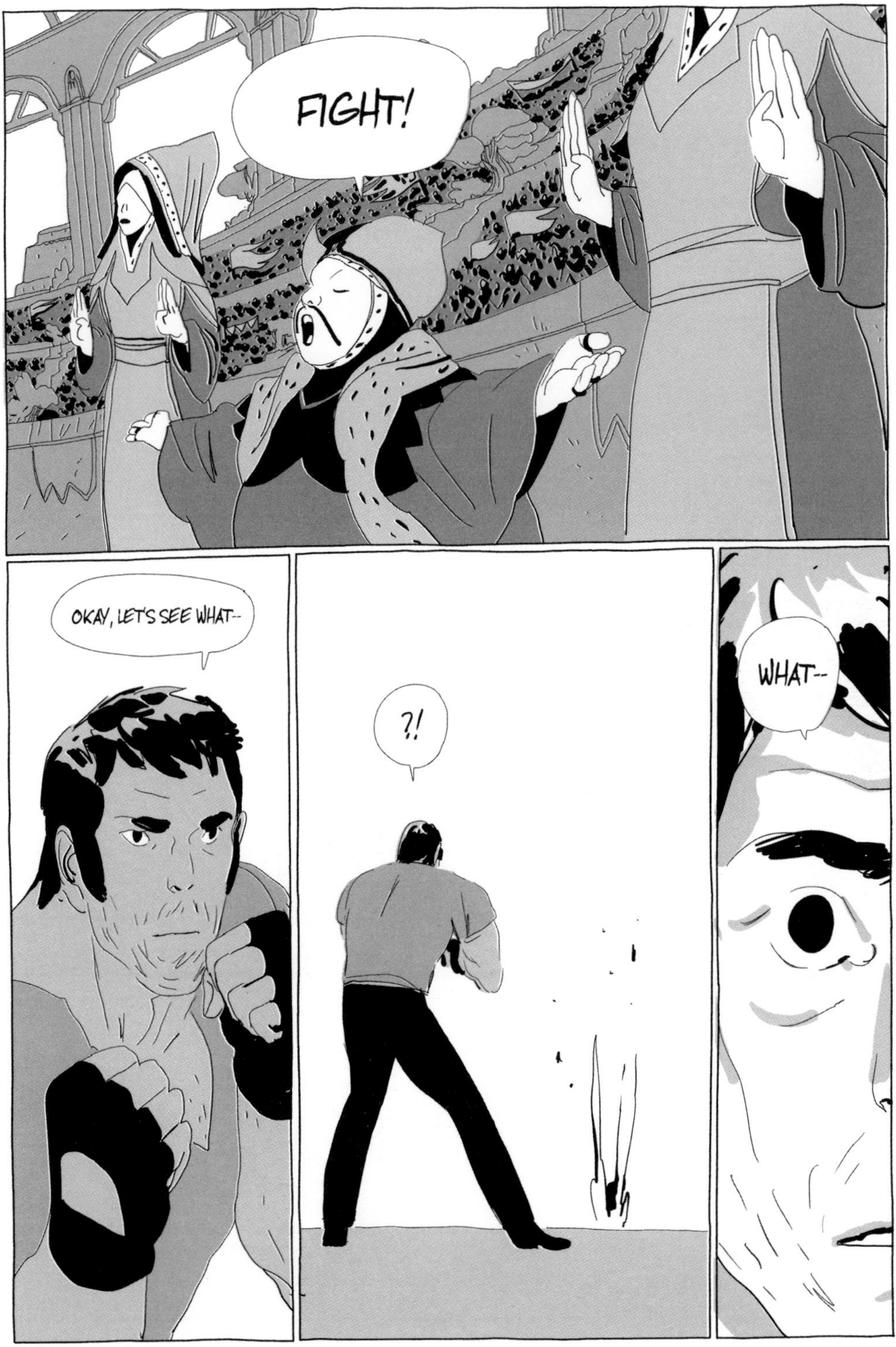
FIGHT!
OKAY, LET'S SEE WHAT--
?!
WHAT--

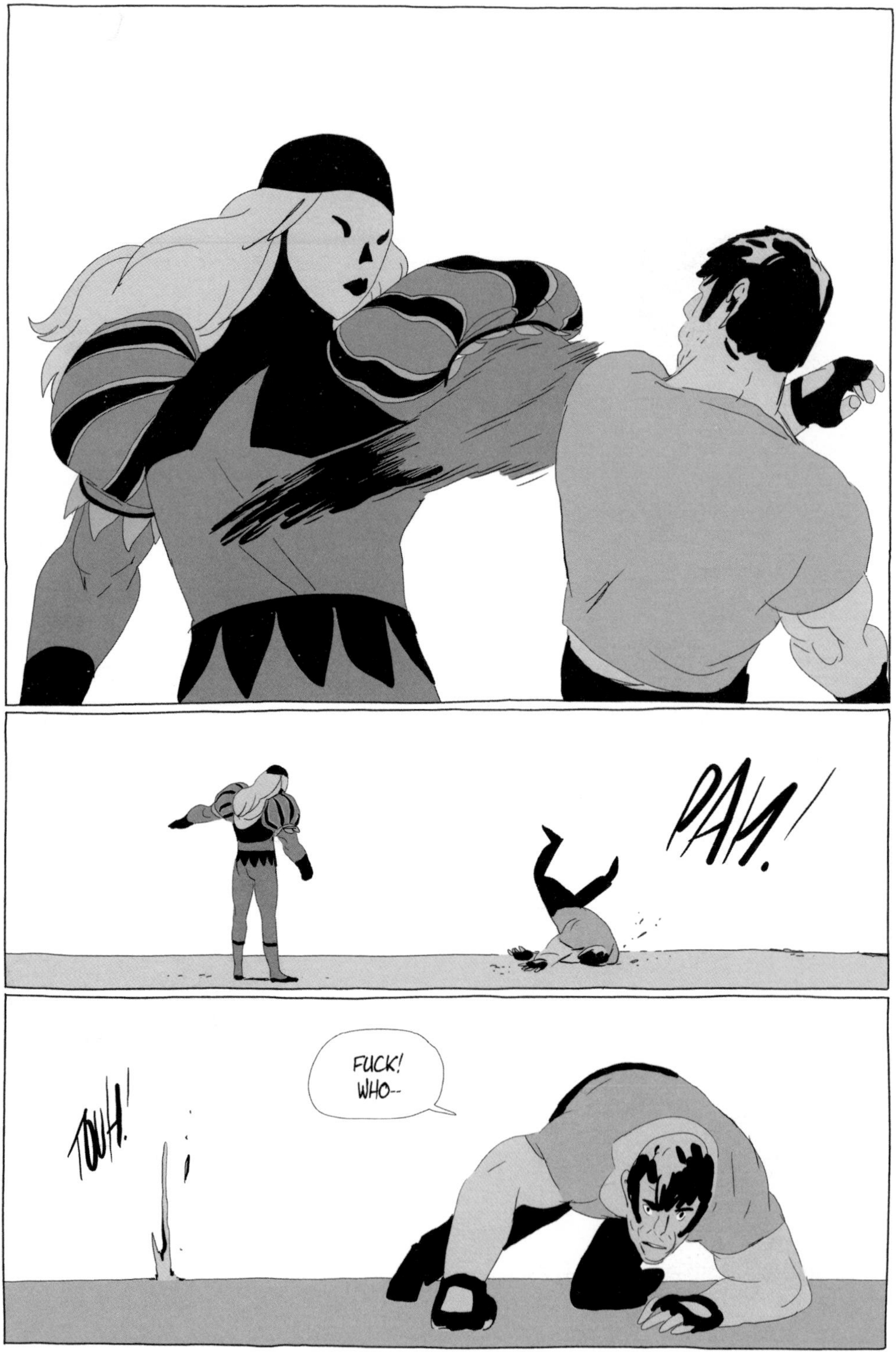
PAM!
TOWH!
FUCK! WHO--

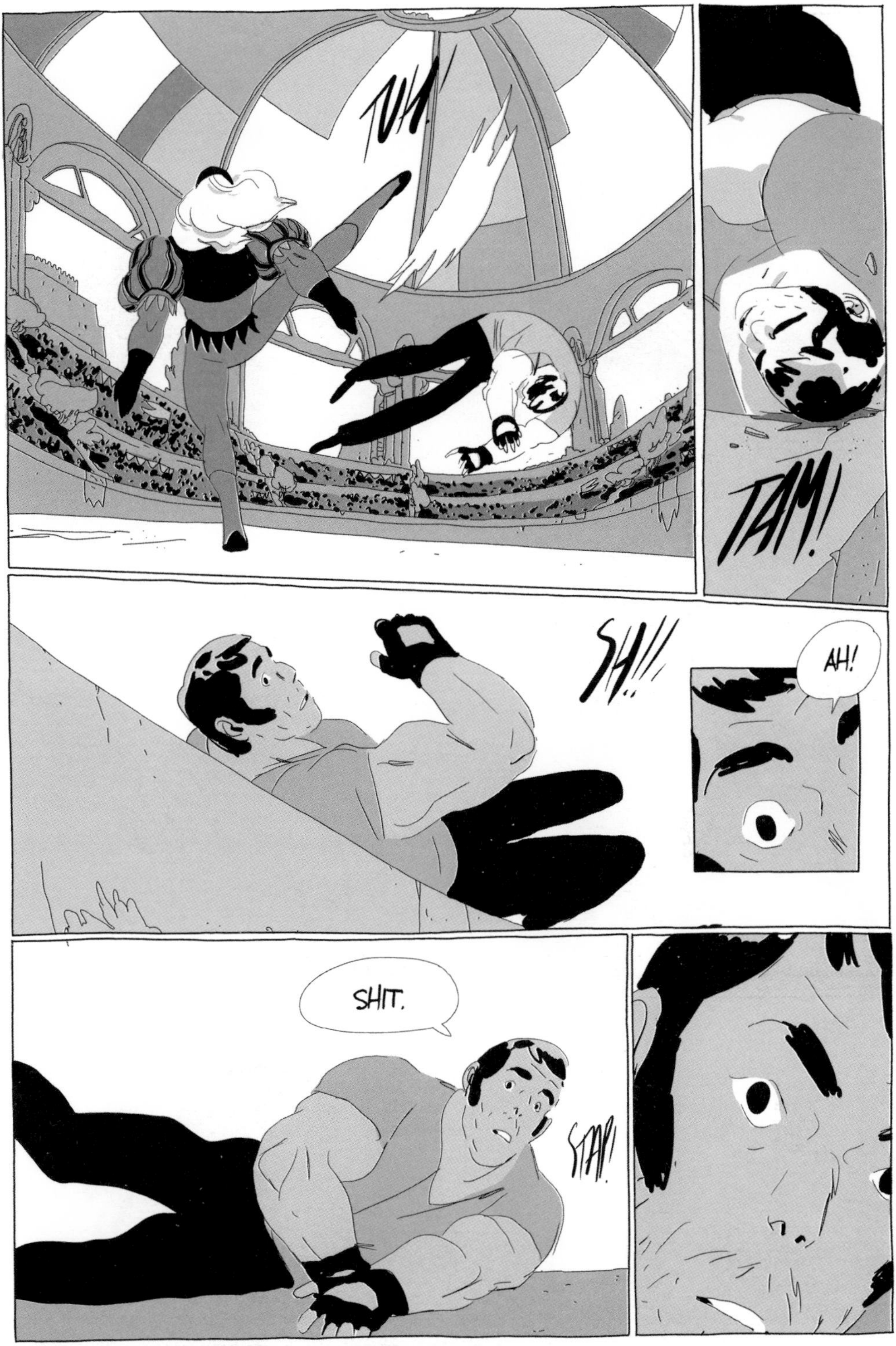
TUK!
TAM!
SH!!!
AH!
SHIT.
STAP!

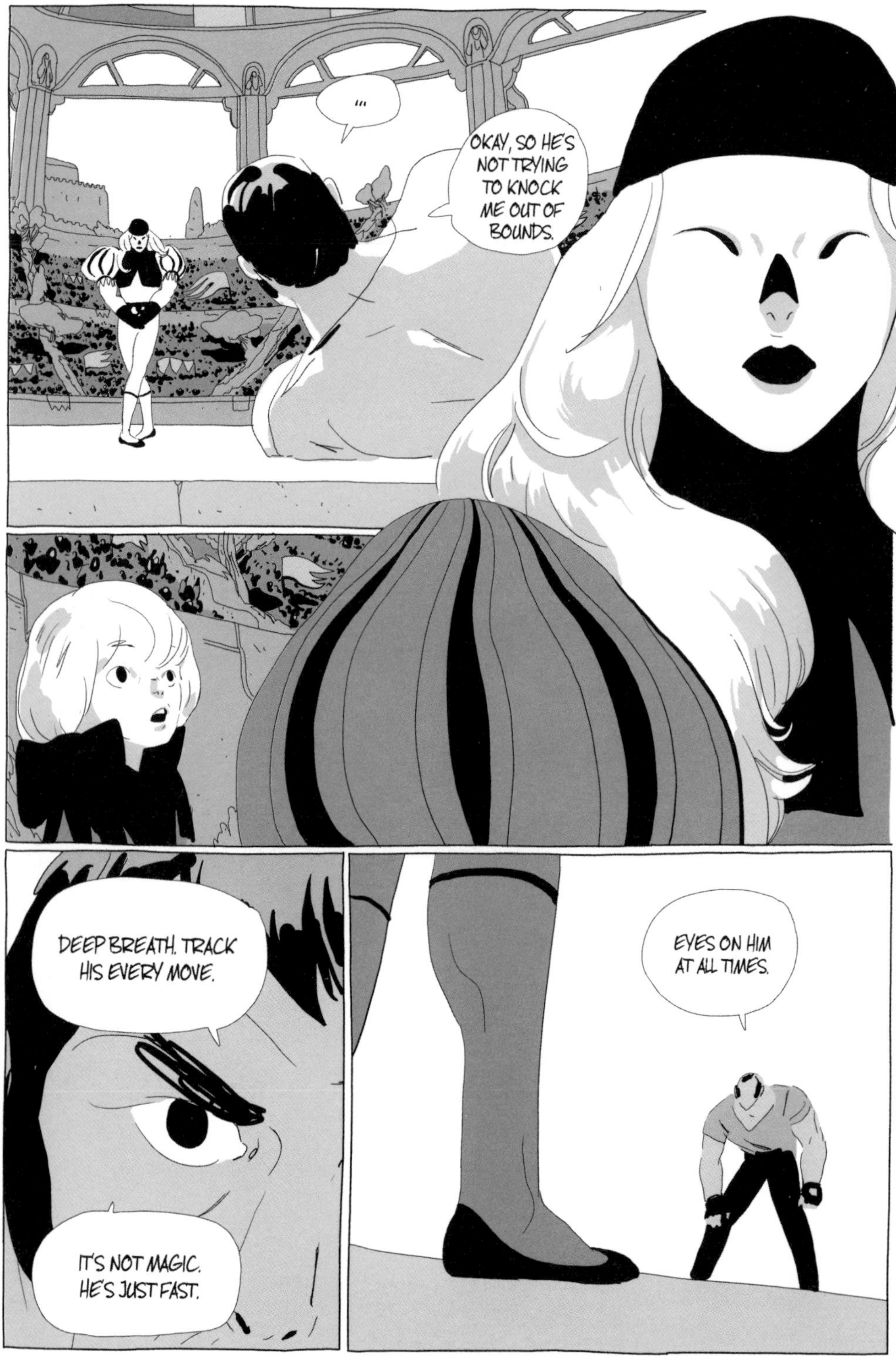
...
OKAY, SO HE'S NOT TRYING TO KNOCK ME OUT OF BOUNDS.
DEEP BREATH. TRACK HIS EVERY MOVE.
IT'S NOT MAGIC. HE'S JUST FAST.
EYES ON HIM AT ALL TIMES.

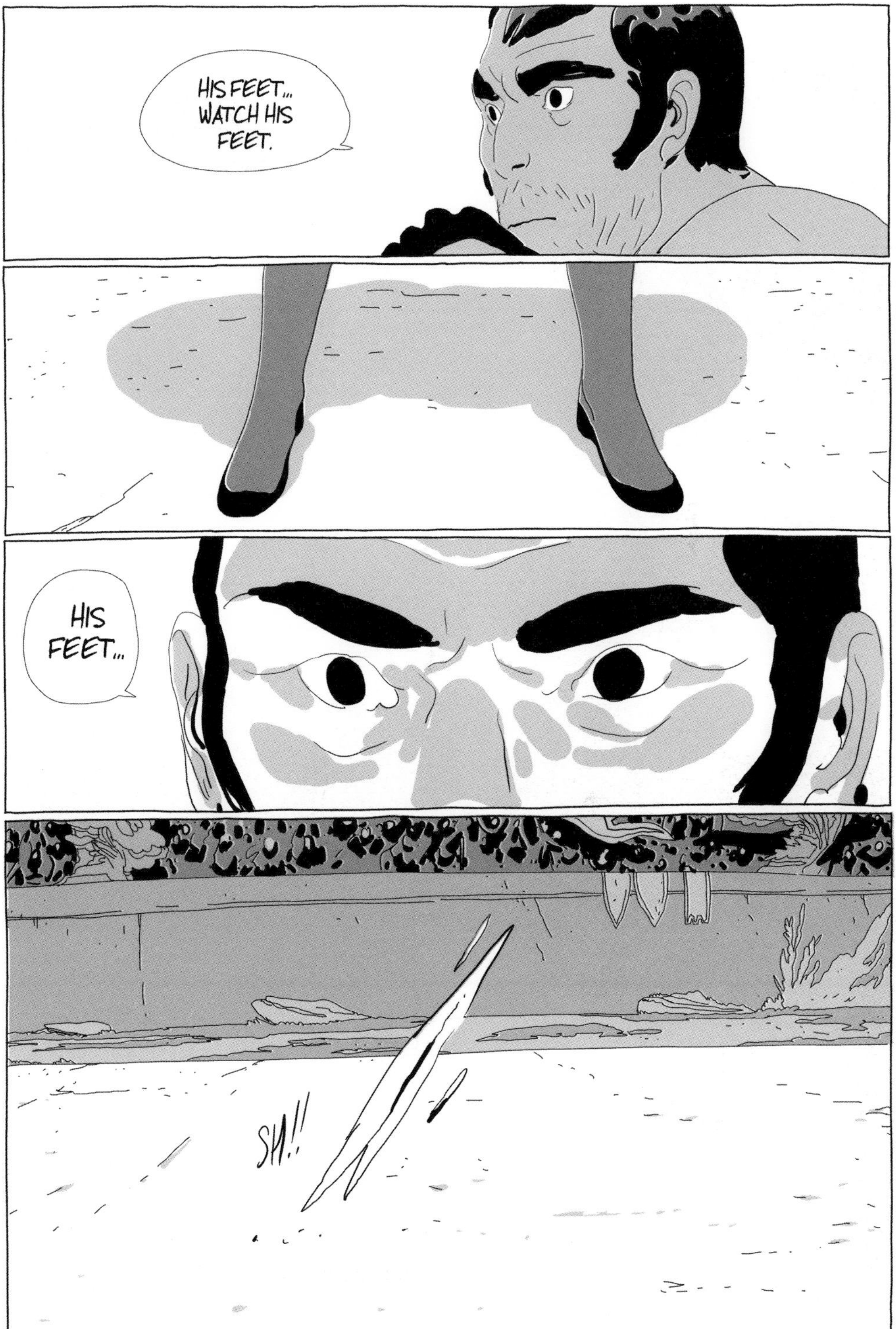
HIS FEET... WATCH HIS FEET.
HIS FEET...
SH!!

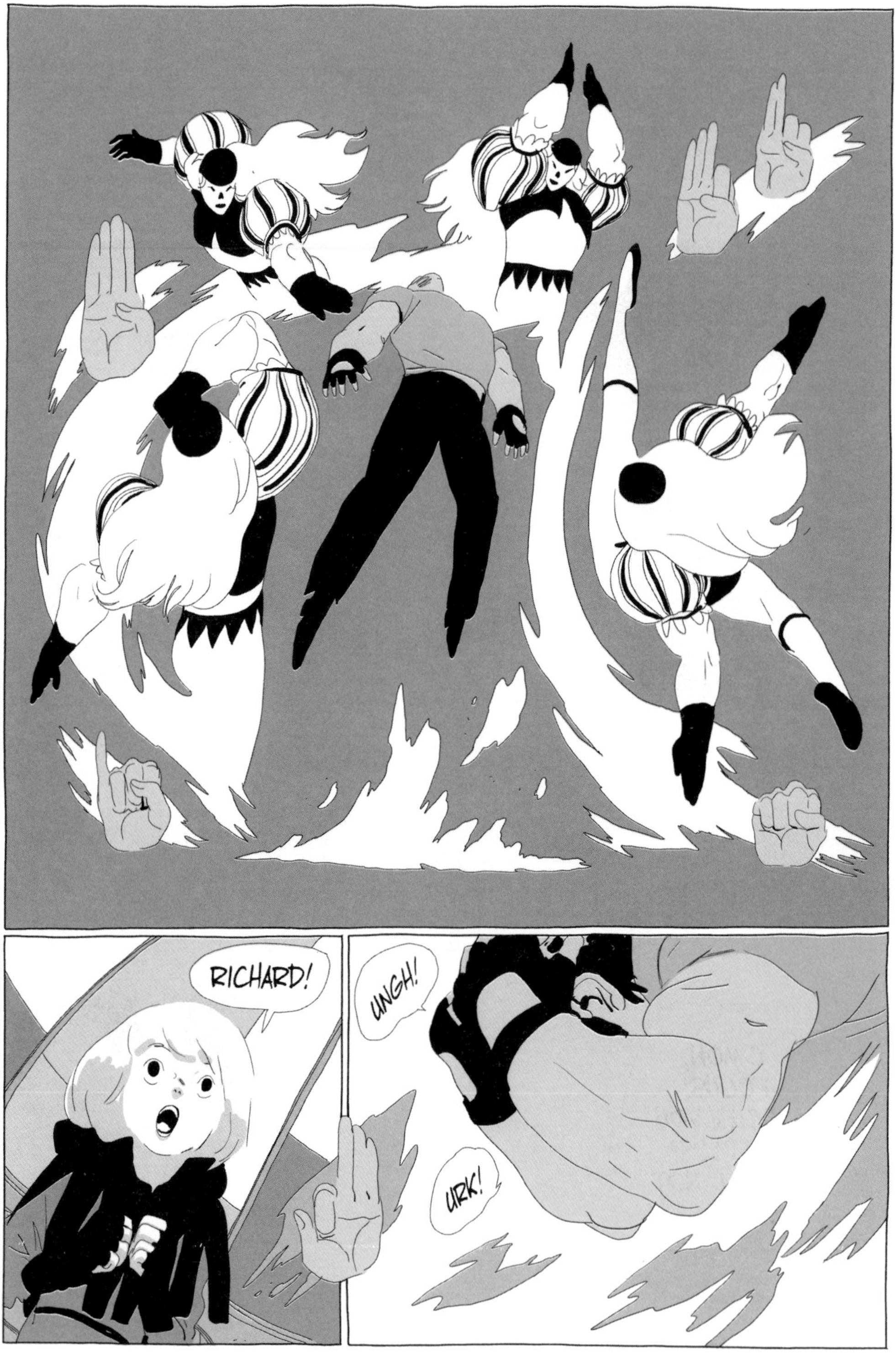
RICHARD!
UNGH!
URK!

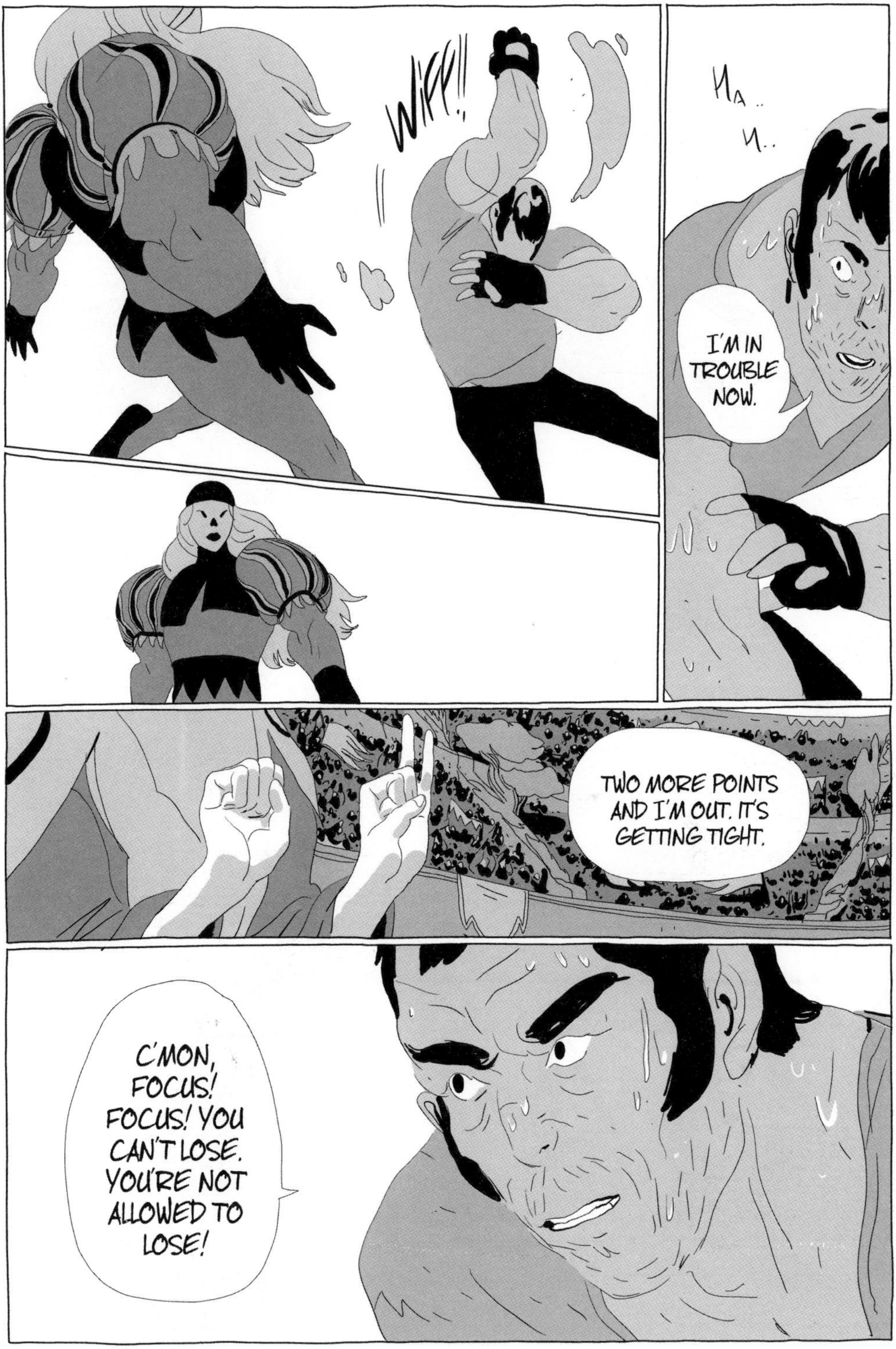
WIFF!!
HA..
H..
I'M IN TROUBLE NOW.
TWO MORE POINTS AND I'M OUT. IT'S GETTING TIGHT.
C'MON, FOCUS! FOCUS! YOU CAN'T LOSE. YOU'RE NOT ALLOWED TO LOSE!

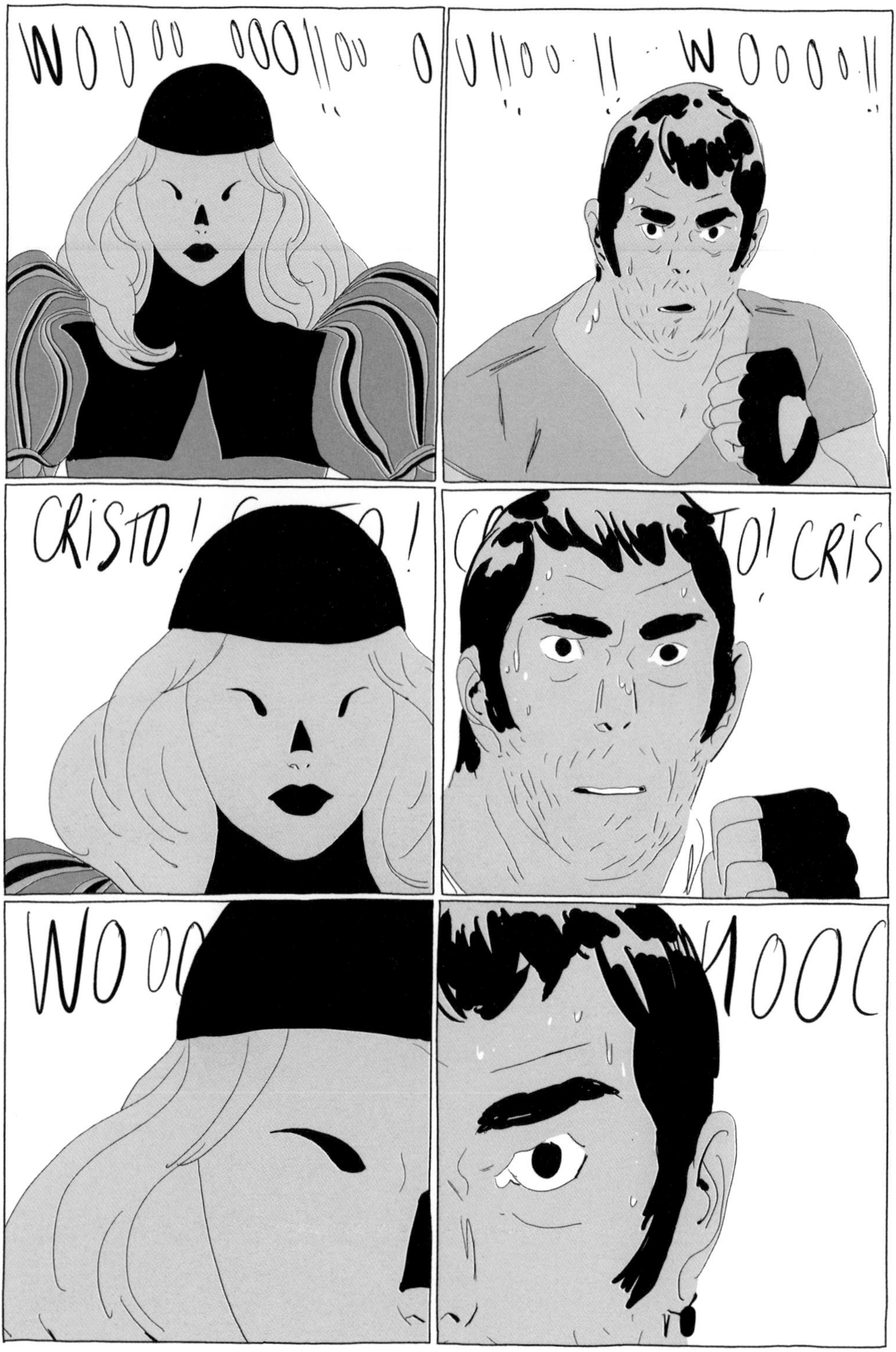
WOOOO!!
CRISTO!
CRIS

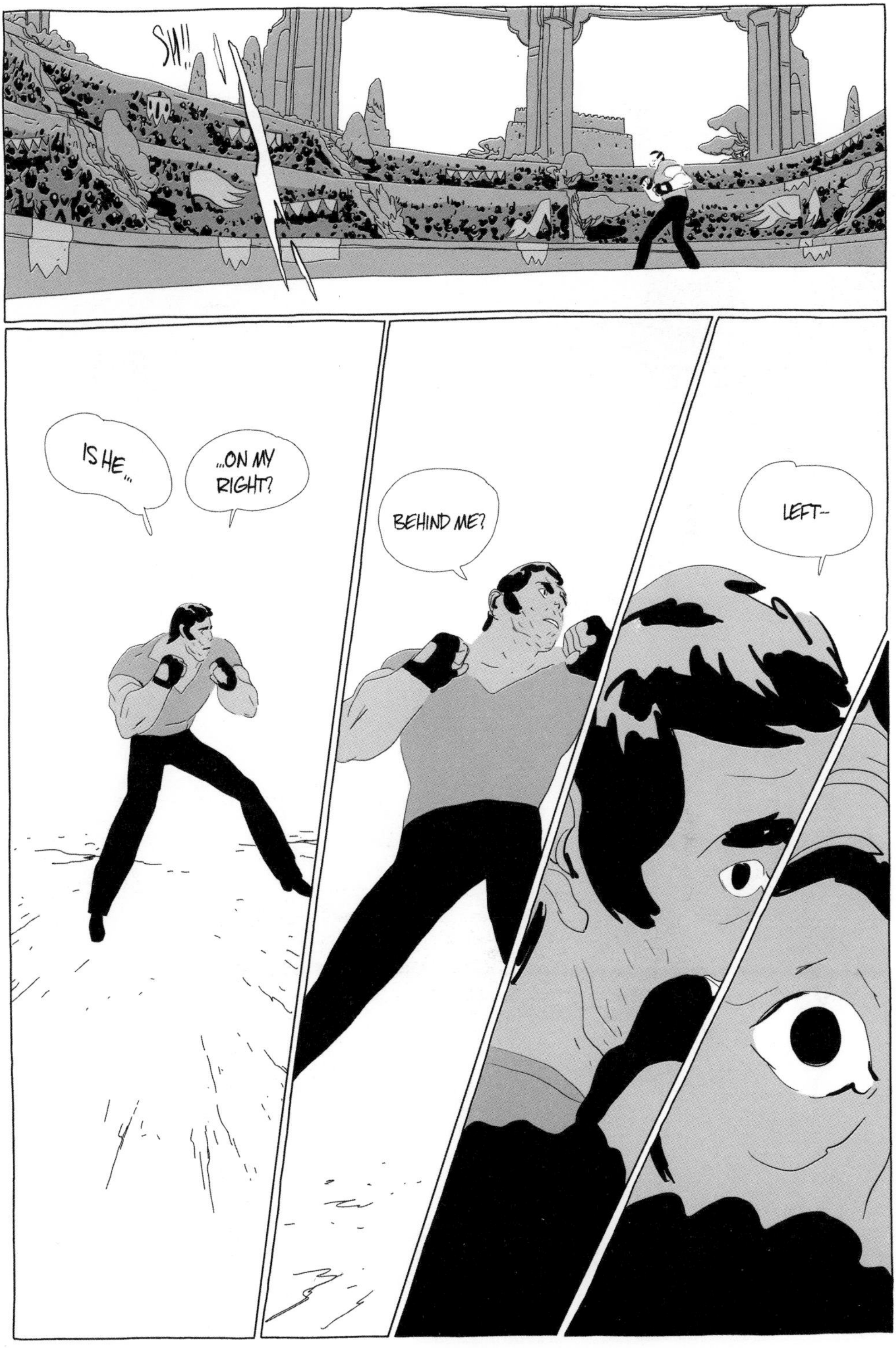
SWI!!
IS HE...
...ON MY RIGHT?
BEHIND ME?
LEFT--

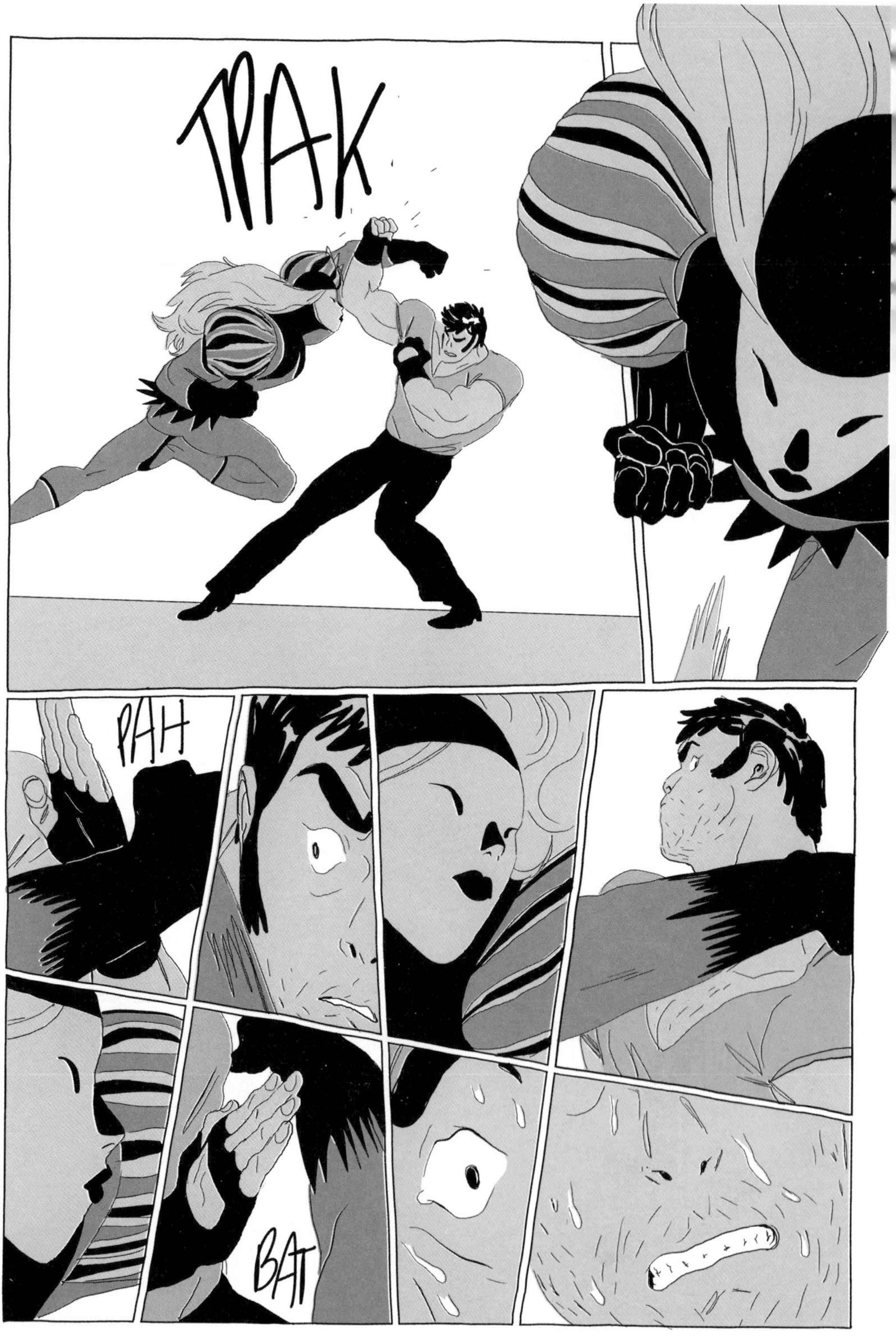
TPAK
PAH
BAT

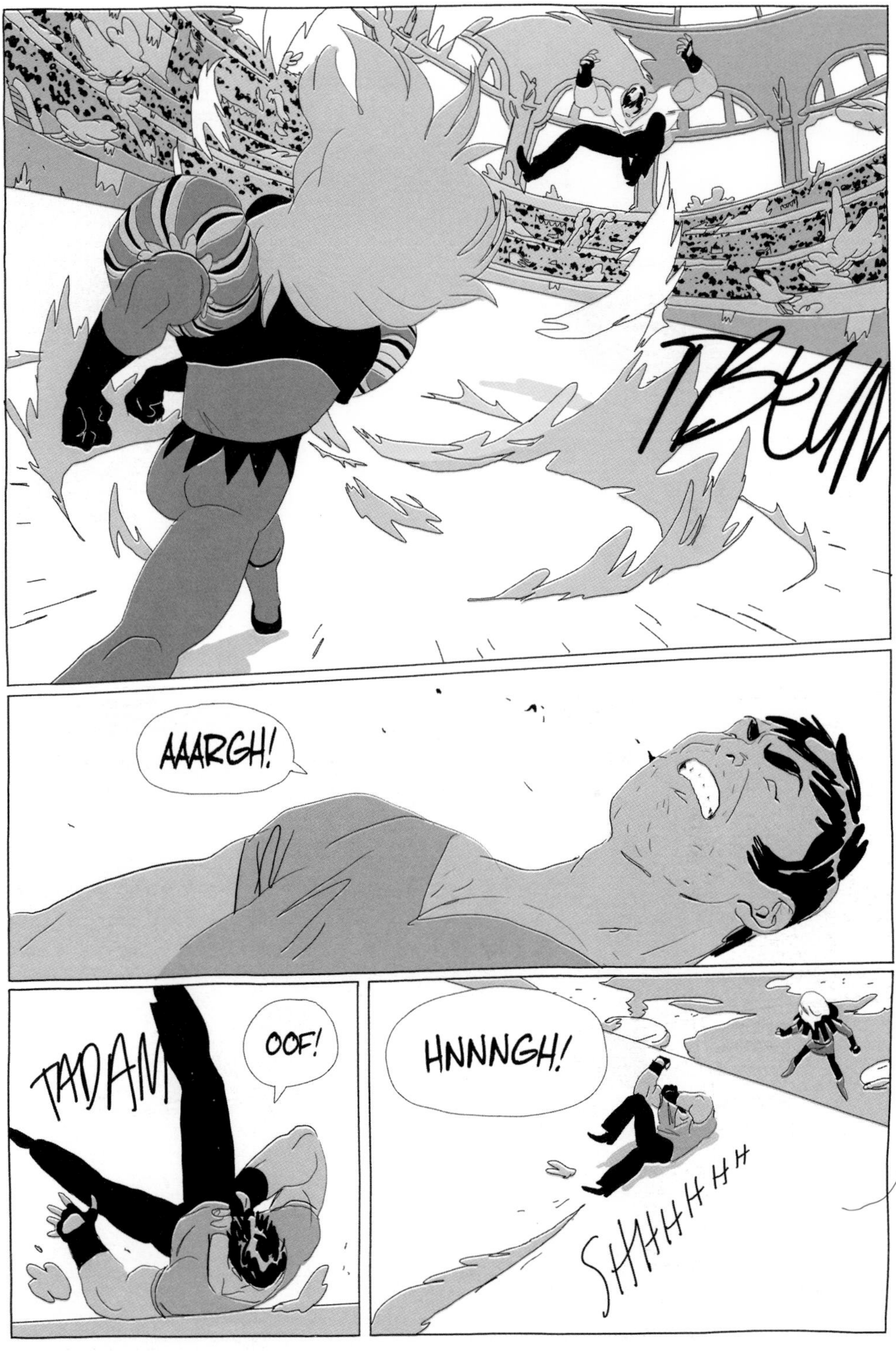
TBUM
AAARGH!
TADAM
OOF!
HNNNGH!
SHHHHHH

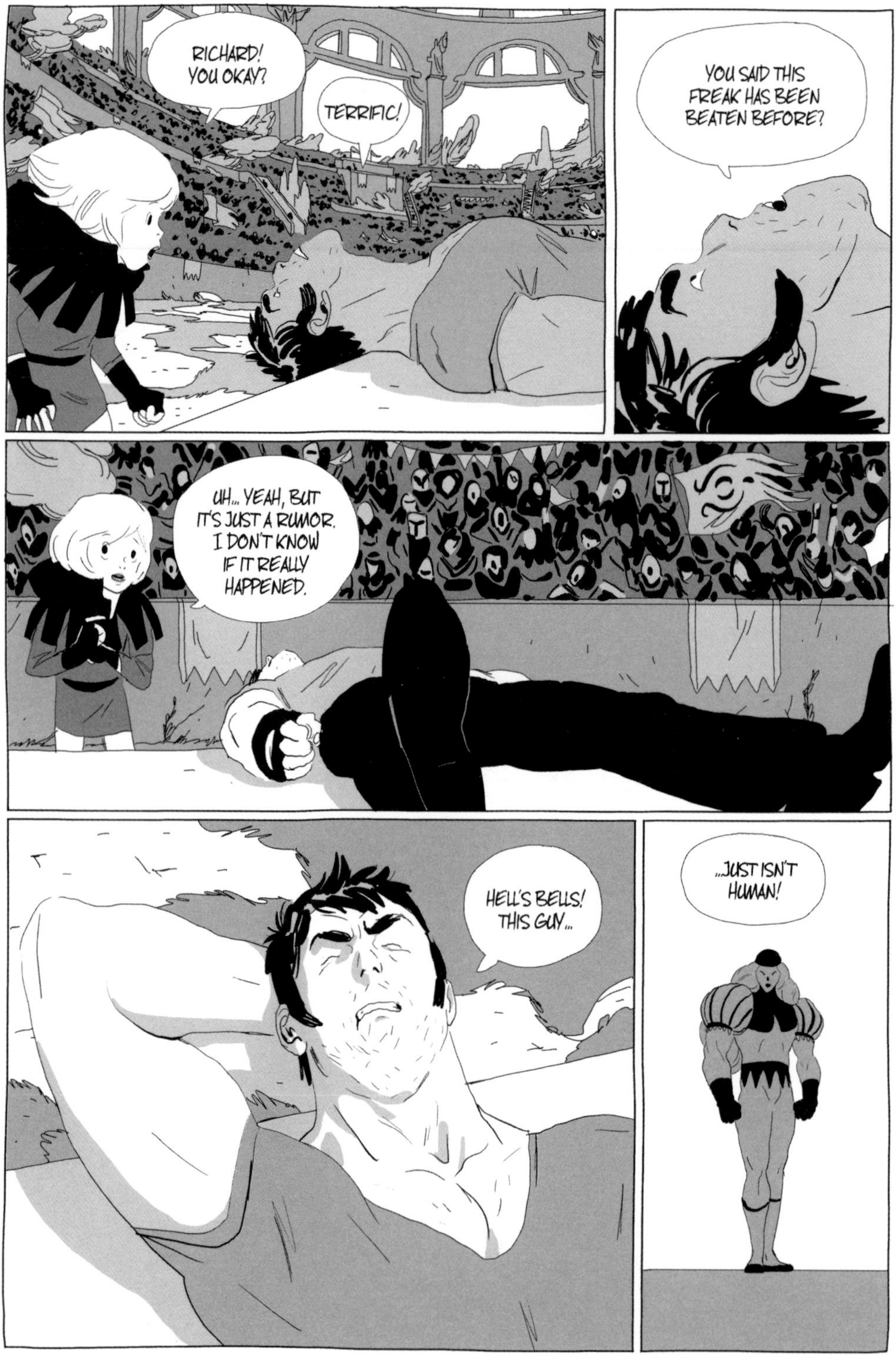
RICHARD! YOU OKAY?
TERRIFIC!
YOU SAID THIS FREAK HAS BEEN BEATEN BEFORE?
UH... YEAH, BUT IT'S JUST A RUMOR. I DON'T KNOW IF IT REALLY HAPPENED.
HELL'S BELLS! THIS GUY...
...JUST ISN'T HUMAN!

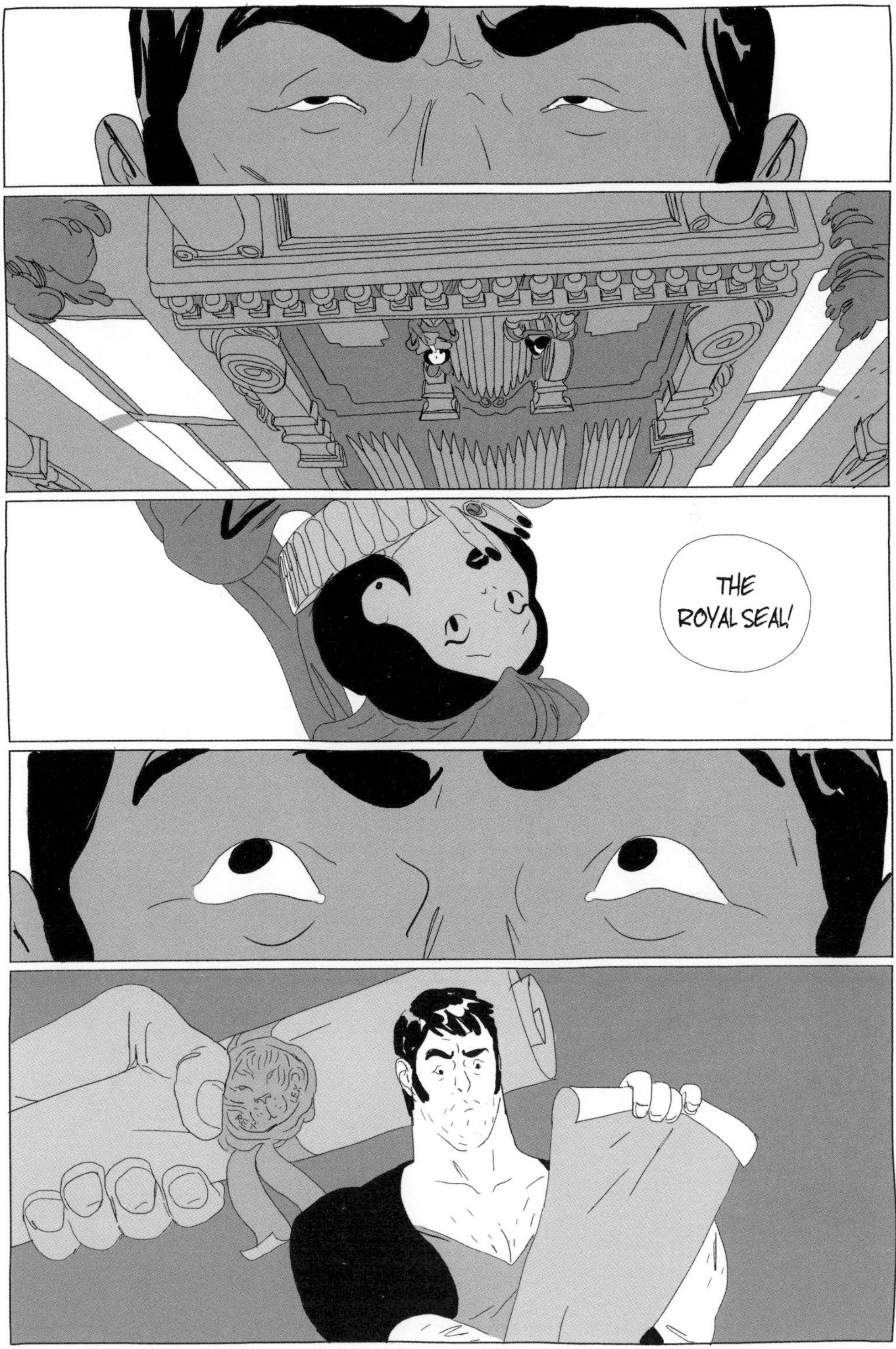
THE ROYAL SEAL!

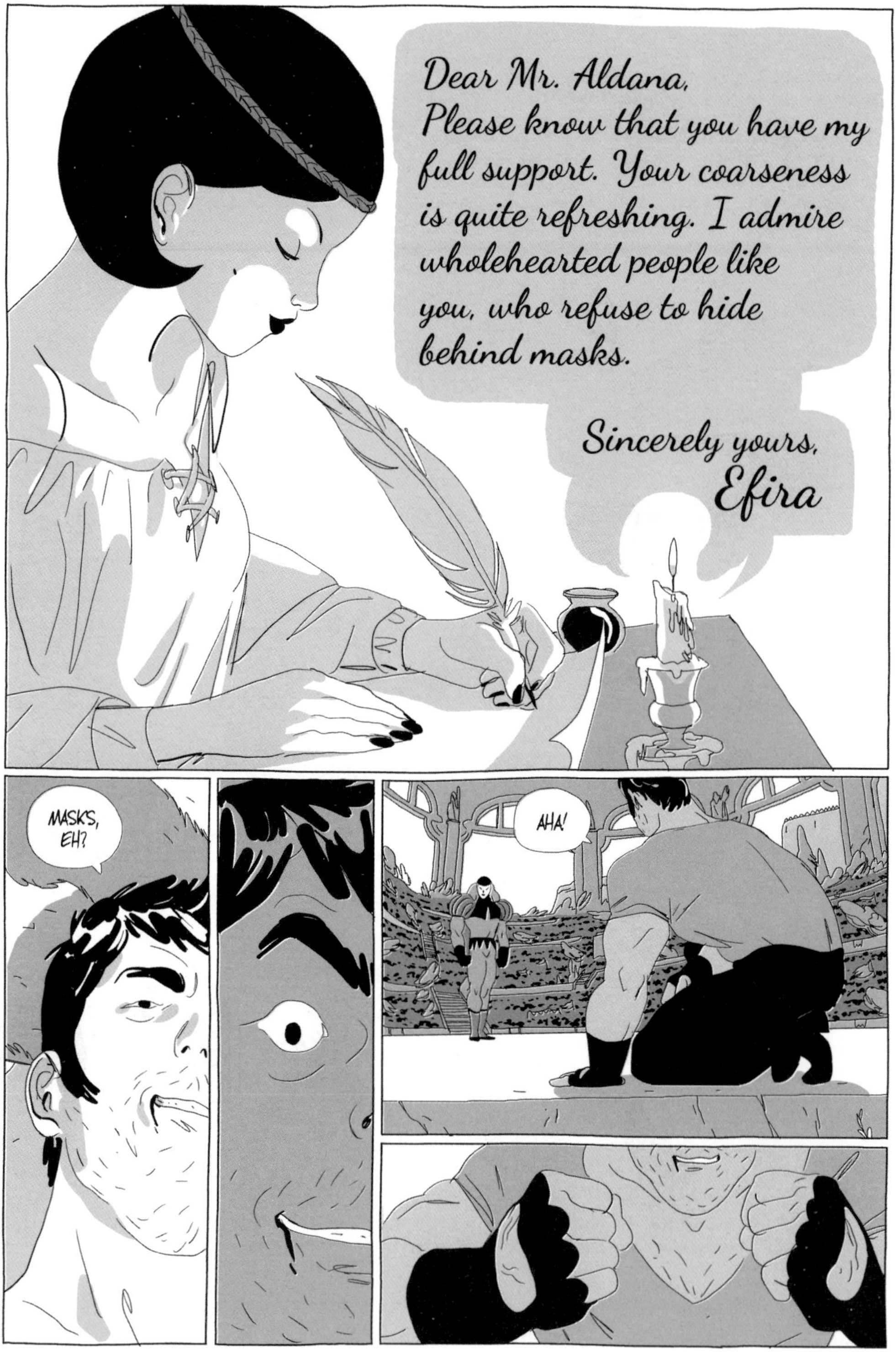
Dear Mr. Aldana,
Please know that you have my full support. Your coarseness is quite refreshing. I admire wholehearted people like you, who refuse to hide behind masks.
Sincerely yours,
Efira
MASKS, EH?
AHA!

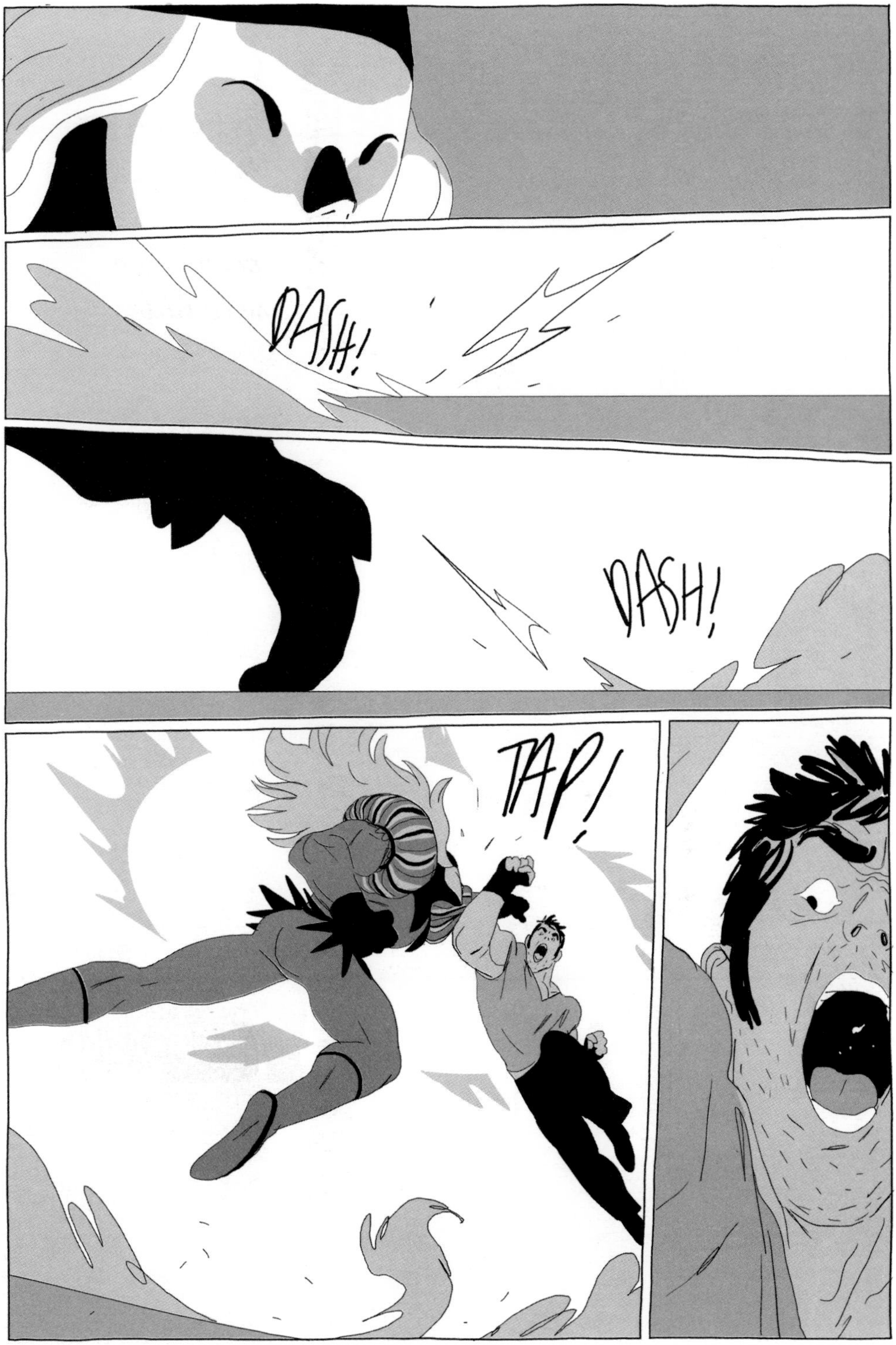
DASH!
DASH!
TAP!

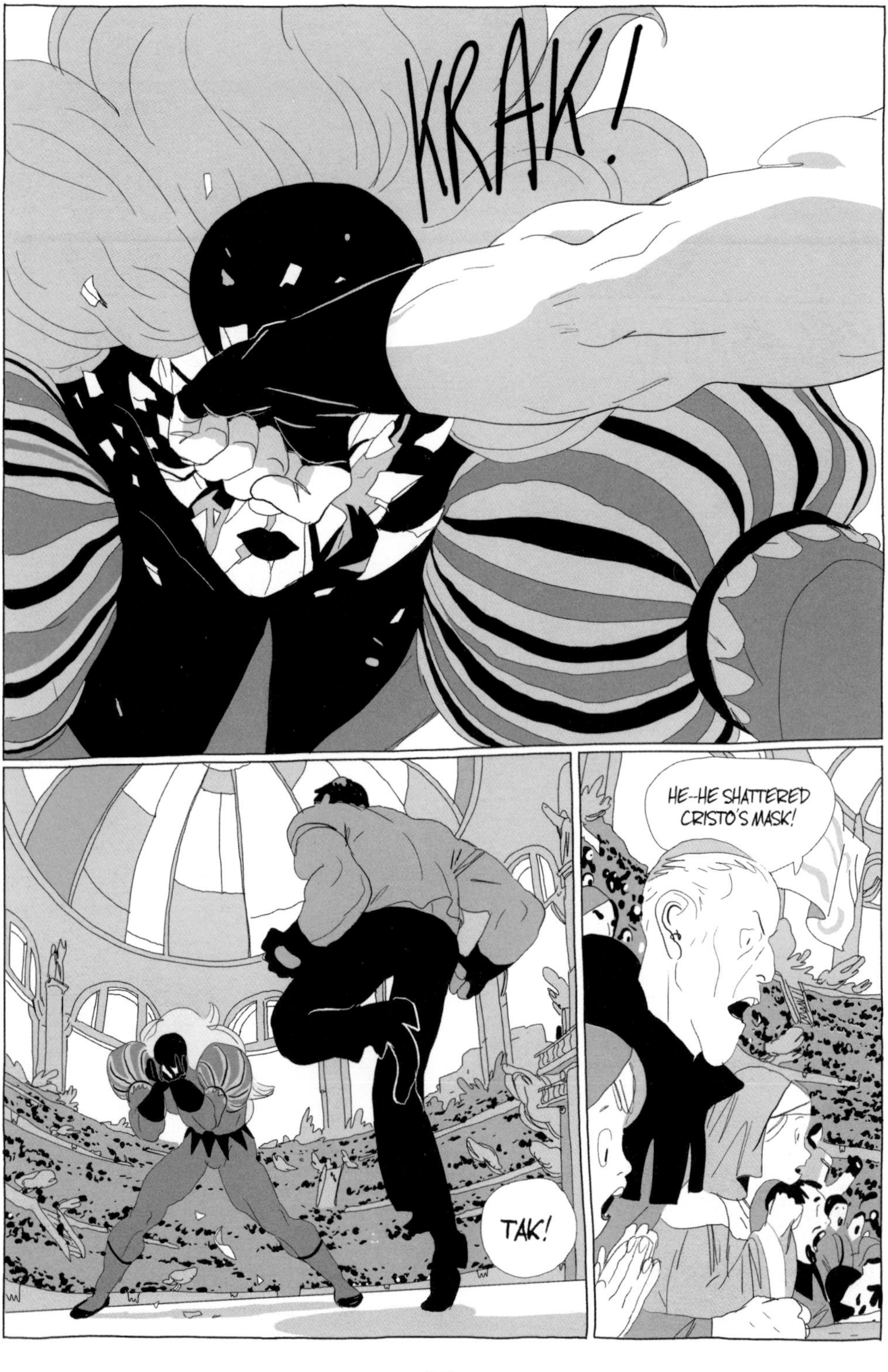
KRAK!
TAK!
HE--HE SHATTERED CRISTO'S MASK!

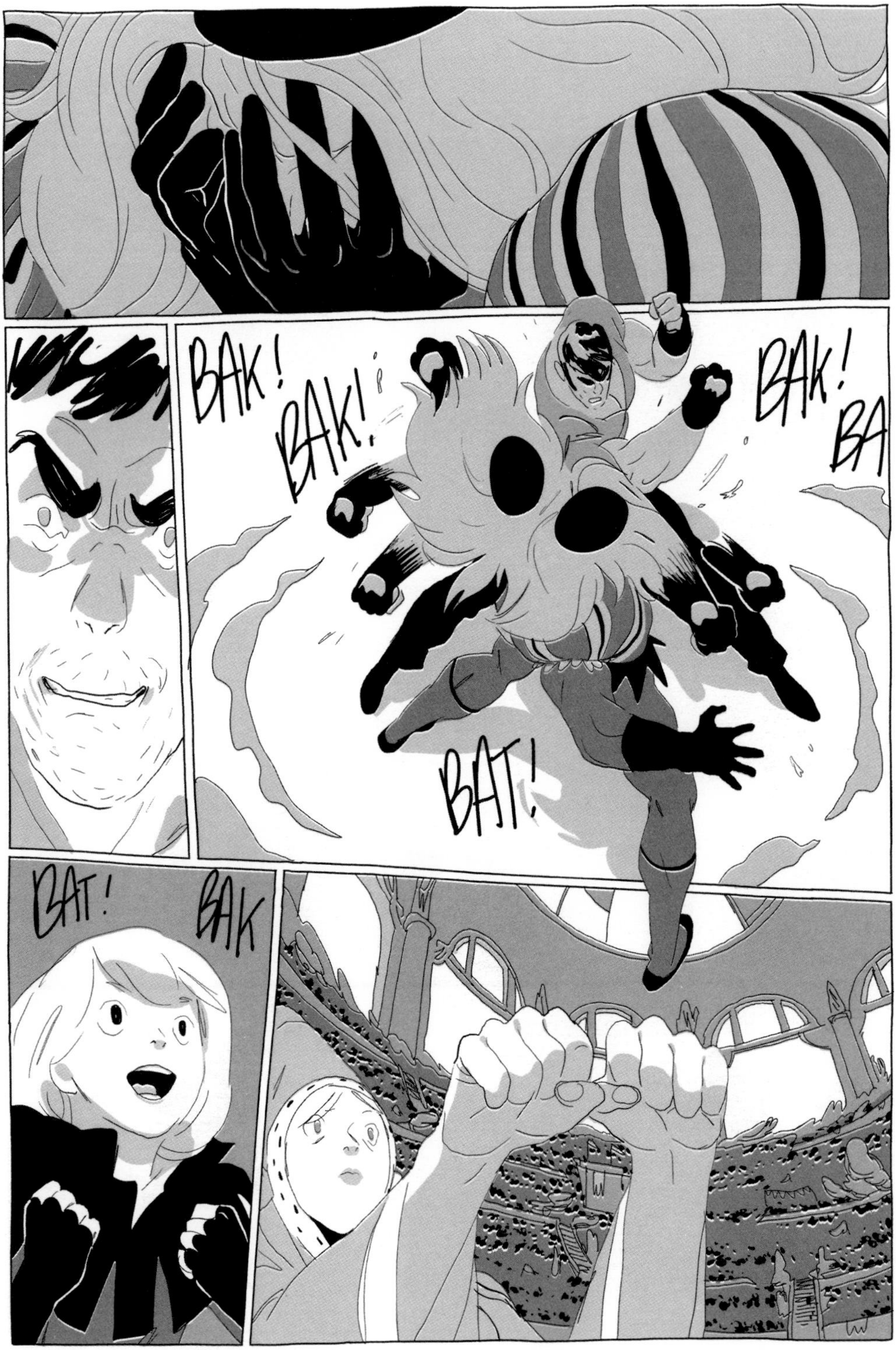
BAK!
BAK!
BAK!
BA
BAT!
BAT!
BAK

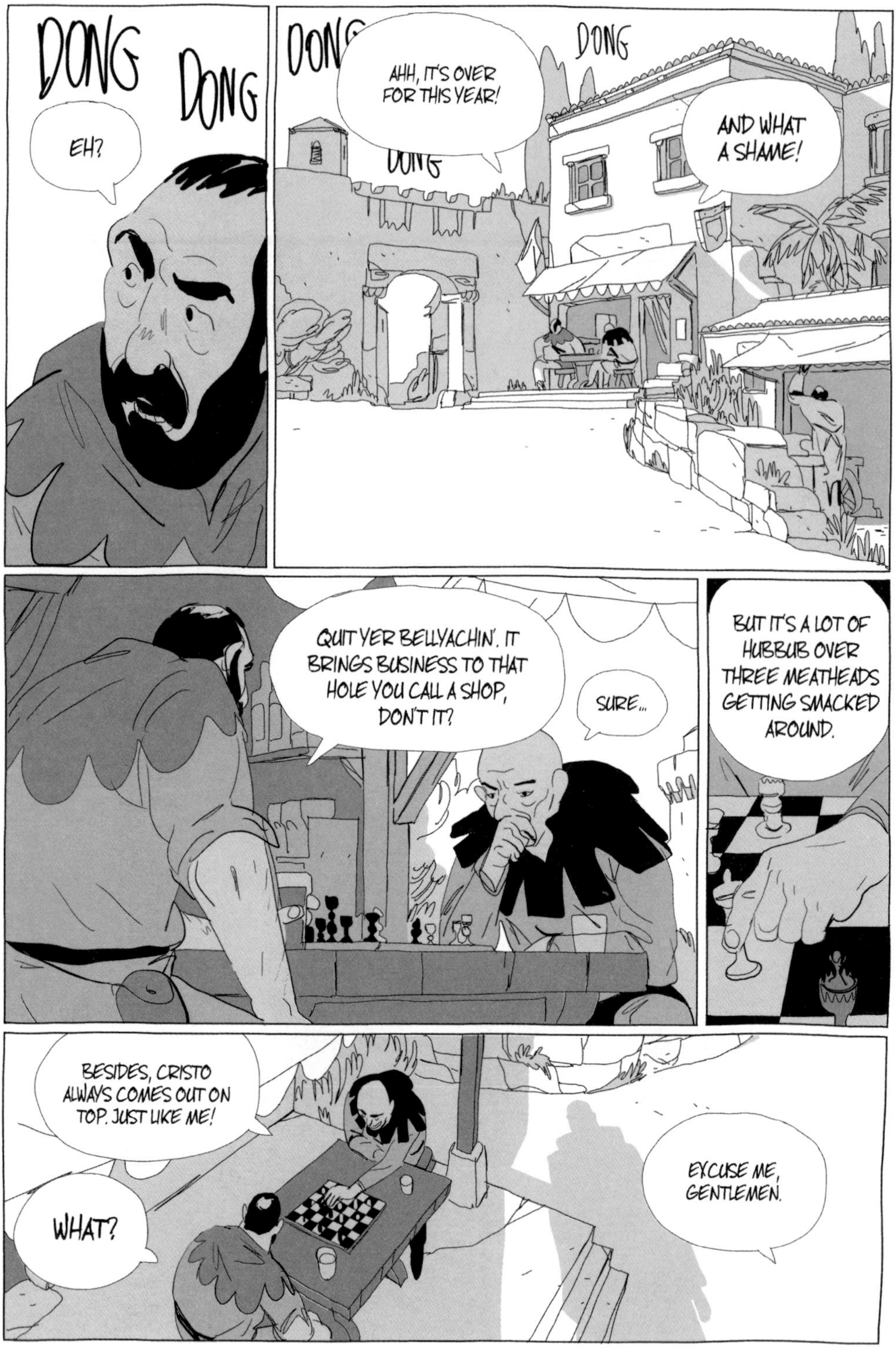
DONG
DONG
EH?
DONG
AHH, IT'S OVER FOR THIS YEAR!
DONG
DONG
AND WHAT A SHAME!
QUIT YER BELLYACHIN'. IT BRINGS BUSINESS TO THAT HOLE YOU CALL A SHOP, DON'T IT?
SURE...
BUT IT'S A LOT OF HUBBUB OVER THREE MEATHEADS GETTING SMACKED AROUND.
BESIDES, CRISTO ALWAYS COMES OUT ON TOP. JUST LIKE ME!
WHAT?
EXCUSE ME, GENTLEMEN.

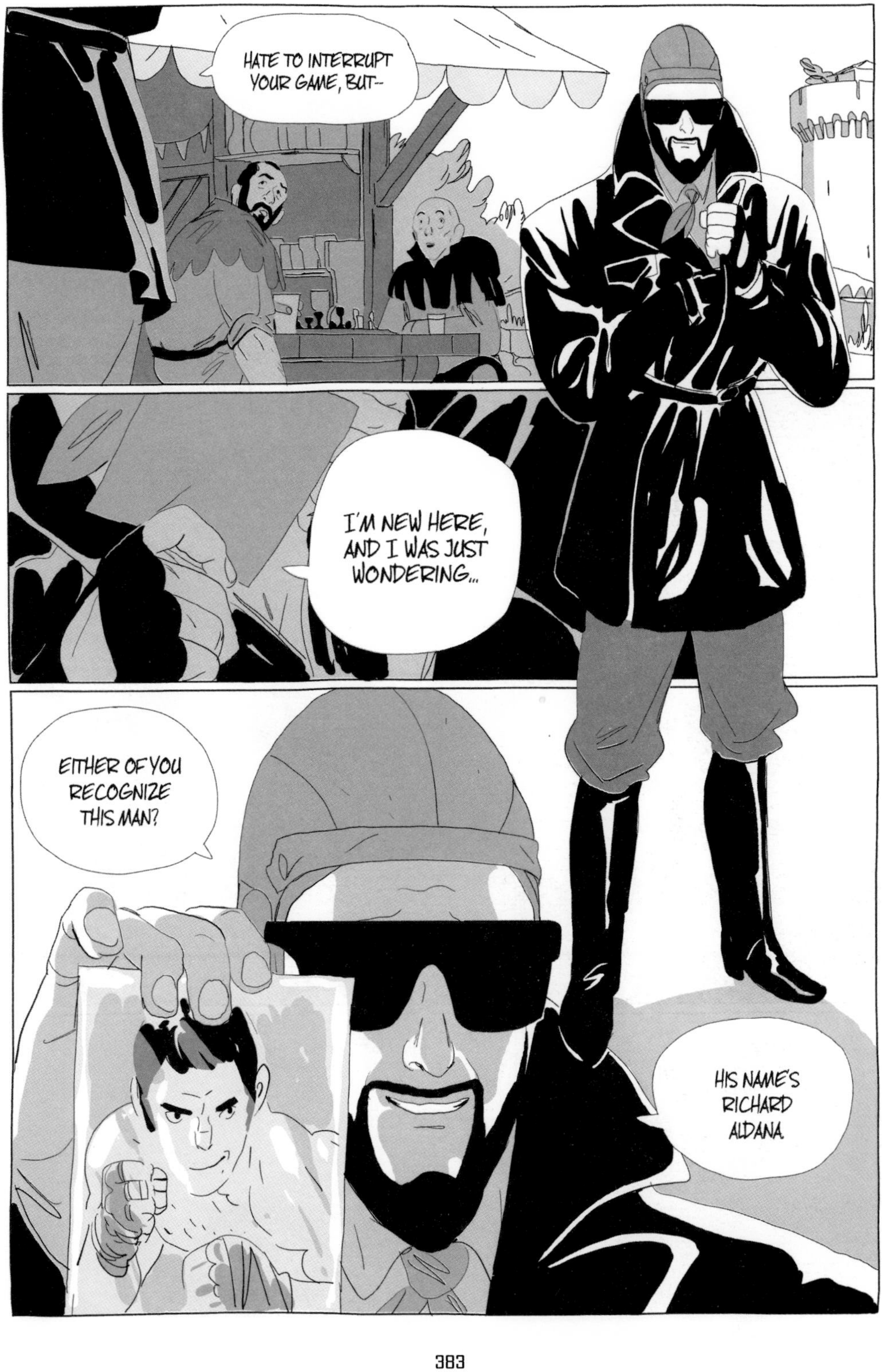
HATE TO INTERRUPT YOUR GAME, BUT--
I'M NEW HERE, AND I WAS JUST WONDERING...
EITHER OF YOU RECOGNIZE THIS MAN?
HIS NAME'S RICHARD ALDANA.

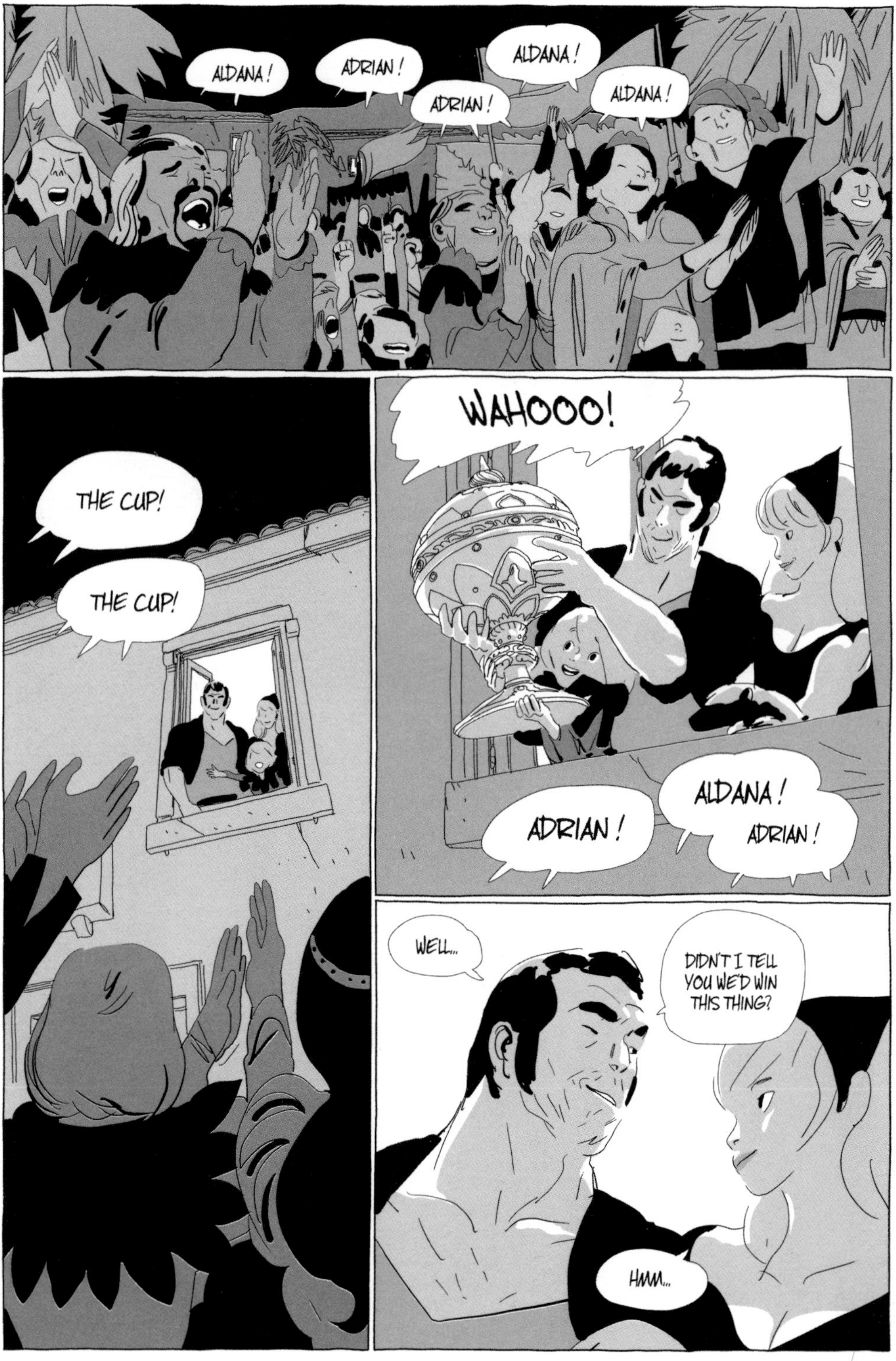
ALDANA!
ADRIAN!
ADRIAN!
ALDANA!
ALDANA!
THE CUP!
THE CUP!
WAHOOO!
ADRIAN!
ALDANA!
ADRIAN!
WELL...
DIDN'T I TELL YOU WE'D WIN THIS THING?
HMM...

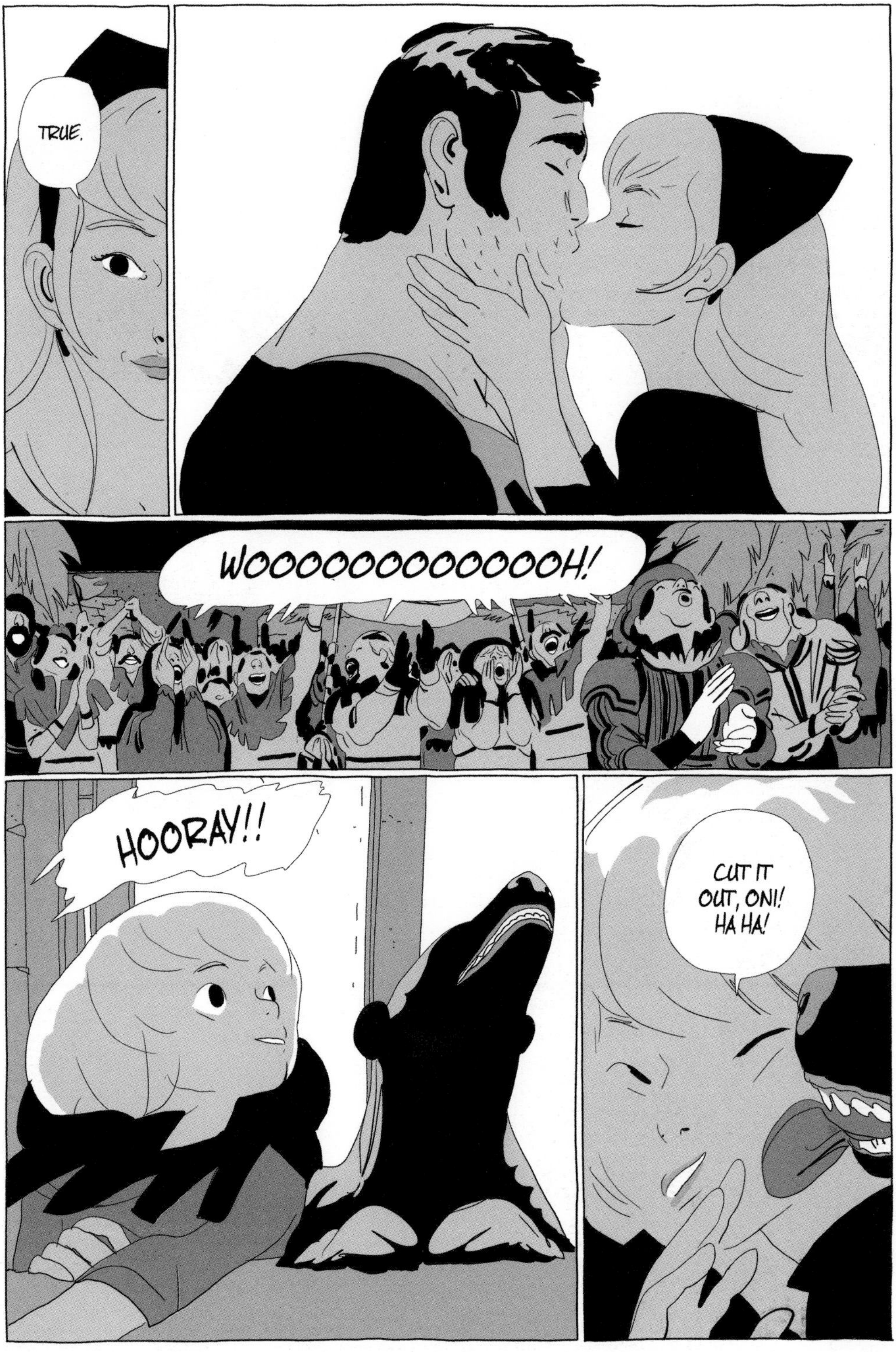
TRUE.
WOOOOOOOOOOOOOH!
HOORAY!!
CUT IT OUT, ONI! HA HA!

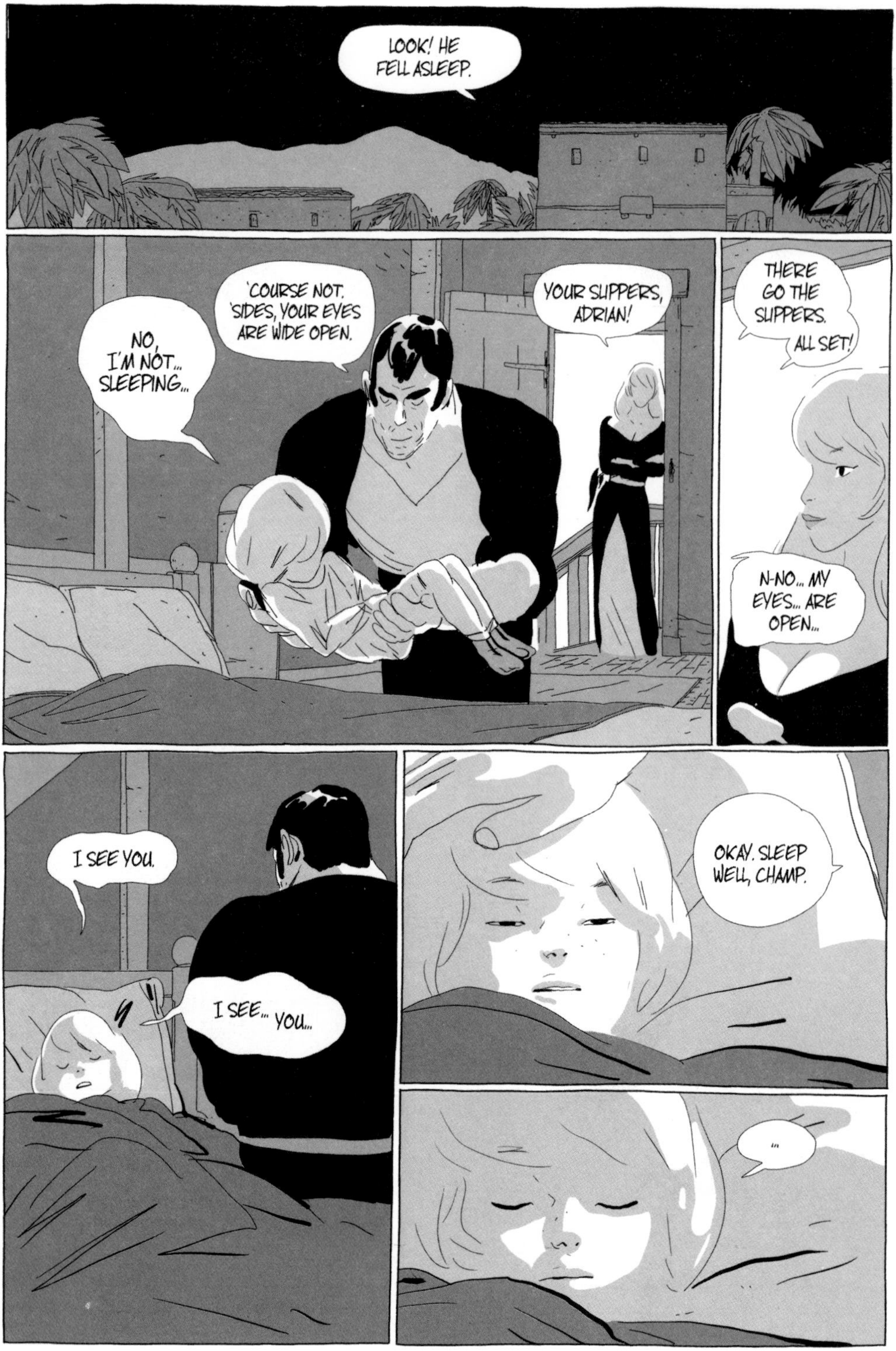
LOOK! HE FELL ASLEEP.
NO, I'M NOT... SLEEPING...
'COURSE NOT. 'SIDES, YOUR EYES ARE WIDE OPEN.
YOUR SLIPPERS, ADRIAN!
THERE GO THE SLIPPERS.
ALL SET!
N-NO... MY EYES... ARE OPEN...
I SEE YOU.
I SEE... YOU...
OKAY. SLEEP WELL, CHAMP.
...

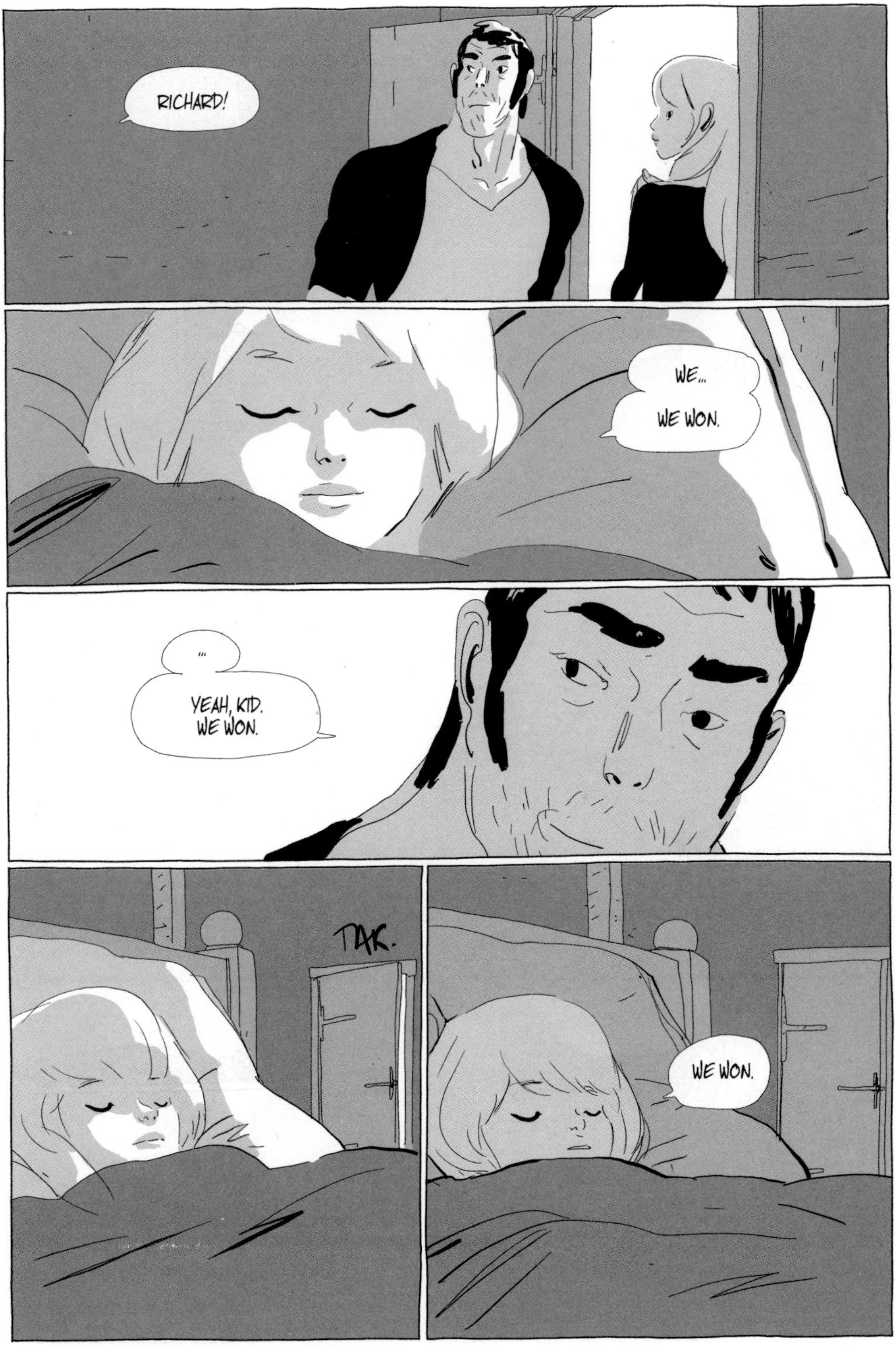
RICHARD!
WE...
WE WON.
...
YEAH, KID. WE WON.
TAK.
WE WON.

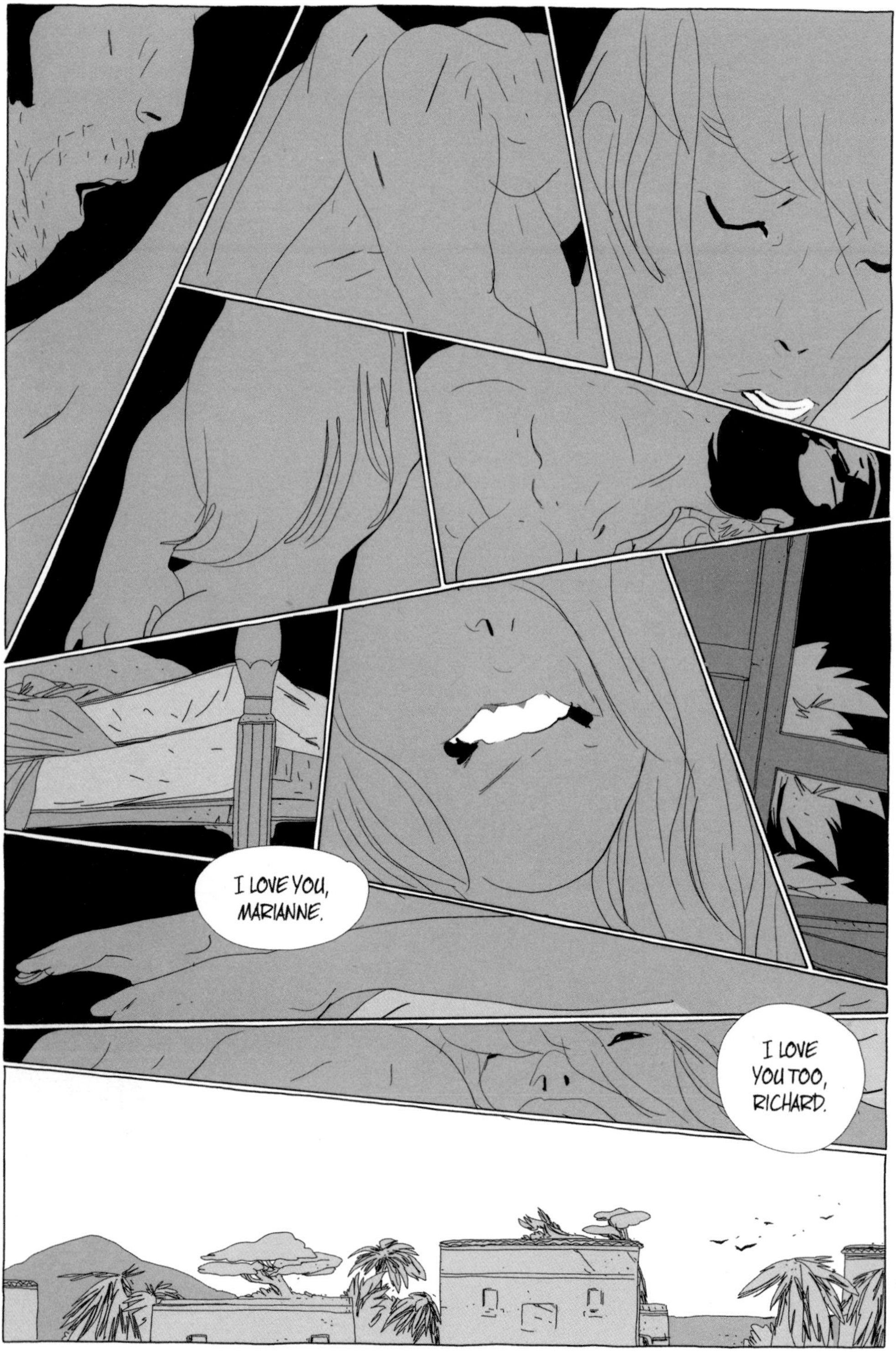
I LOVE YOU, MARIANNE.
I LOVE YOU TOO, RICHARD.

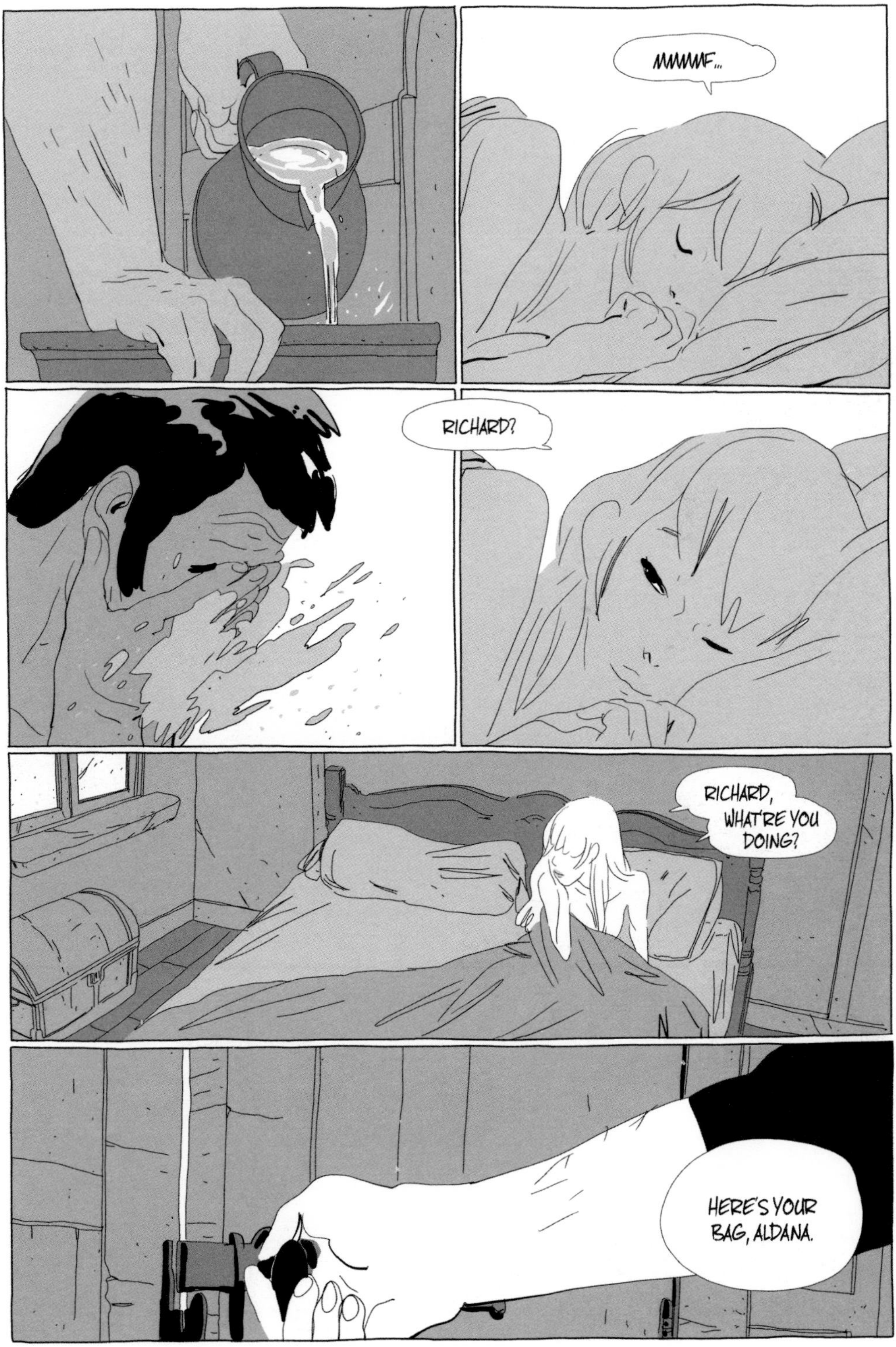
MMMMF...
RICHARD?
RICHARD, WHAT'RE YOU DOING?
HERE'S YOUR BAG, ALDANA.

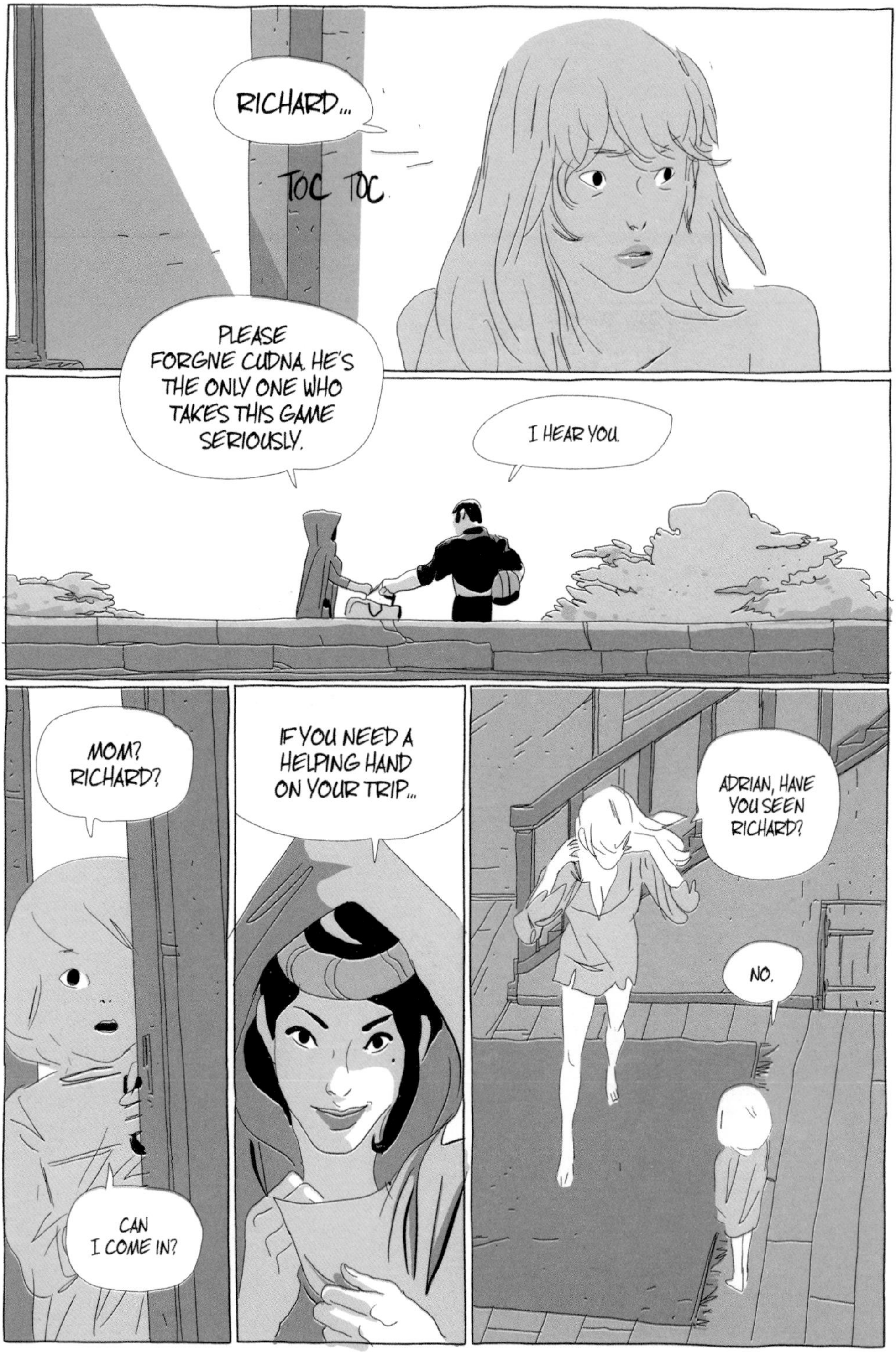
RICHARD...
TOC TOC
PLEASE FORGIVE CUDNA. HE'S THE ONLY ONE WHO TAKES THIS GAME SERIOUSLY.
I HEAR YOU.
MOM? RICHARD?
CAN I COME IN?
IF YOU NEED A HELPING HAND ON YOUR TRIP...
ADRIAN, HAVE YOU SEEN RICHARD?
NO.

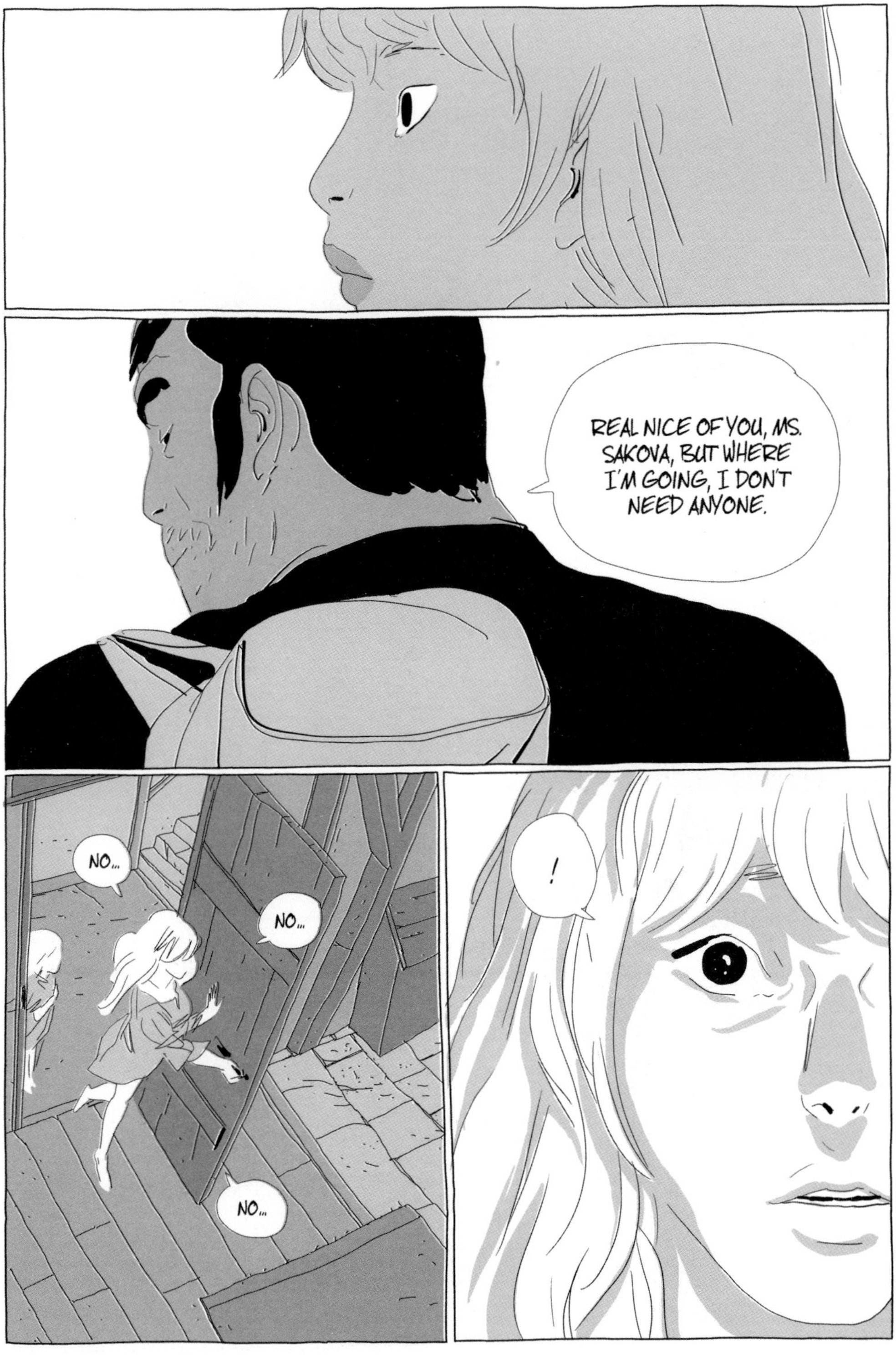
REAL NICE OF YOU, MS. SAKOVA, BUT WHERE I'M GOING, I DON'T NEED ANYONE.
NO...
NO...
NO...
!

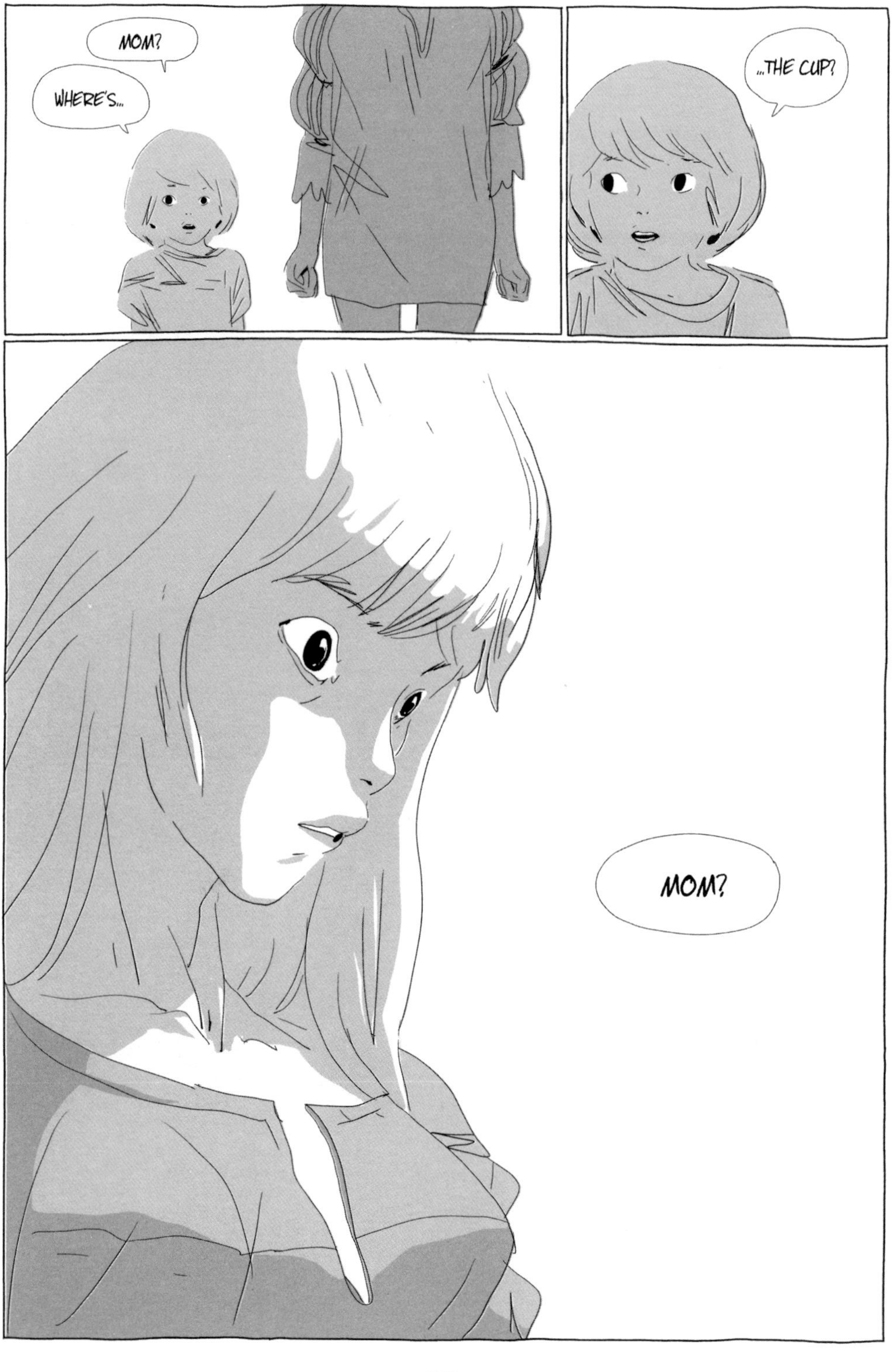
MOM?
WHERE'S...
...THE CUP?
MOM?

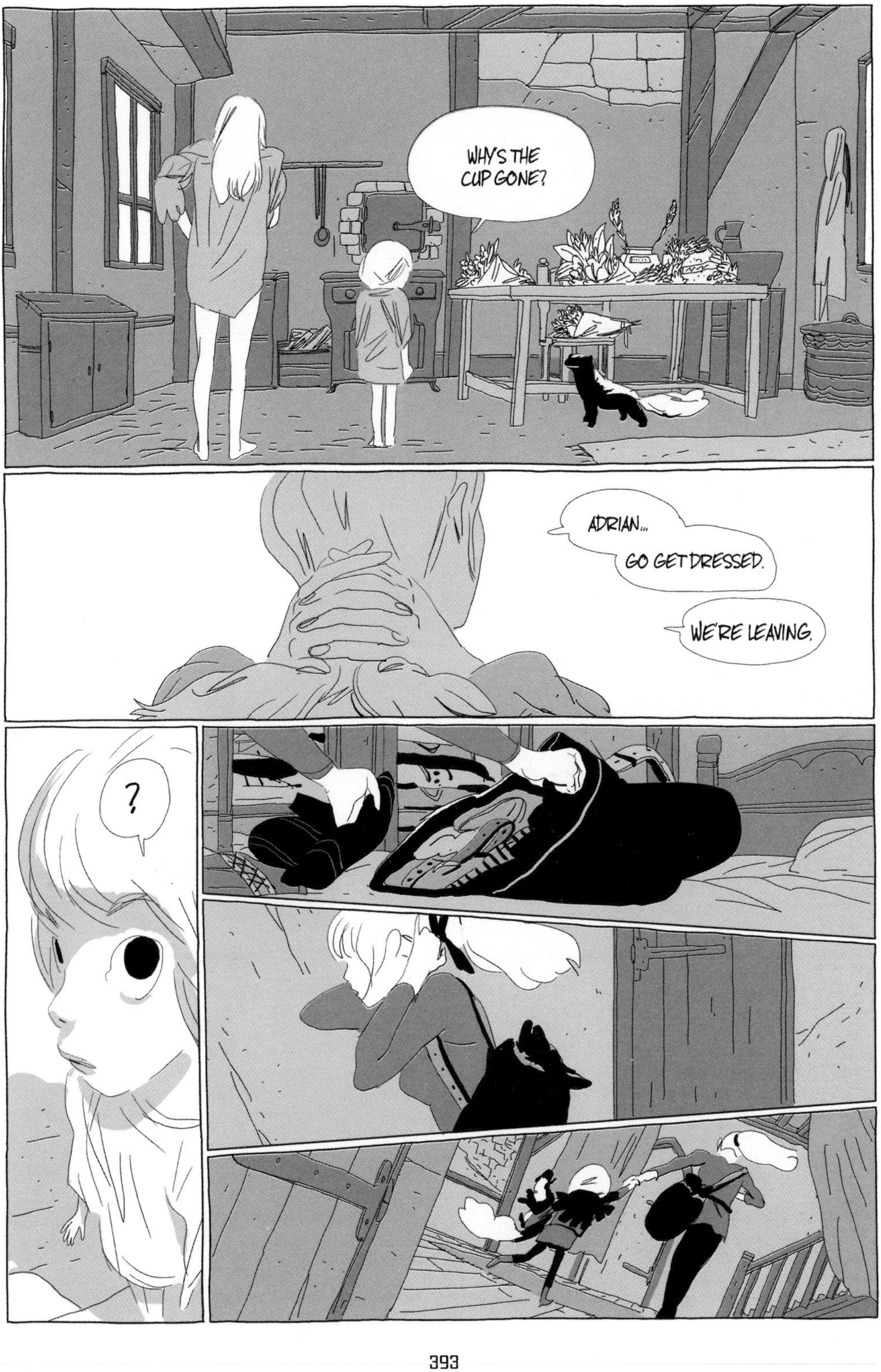
WHY'S THE CUP GONE?
ADRIAN...
GO GET DRESSED.
WE'RE LEAVING.
?

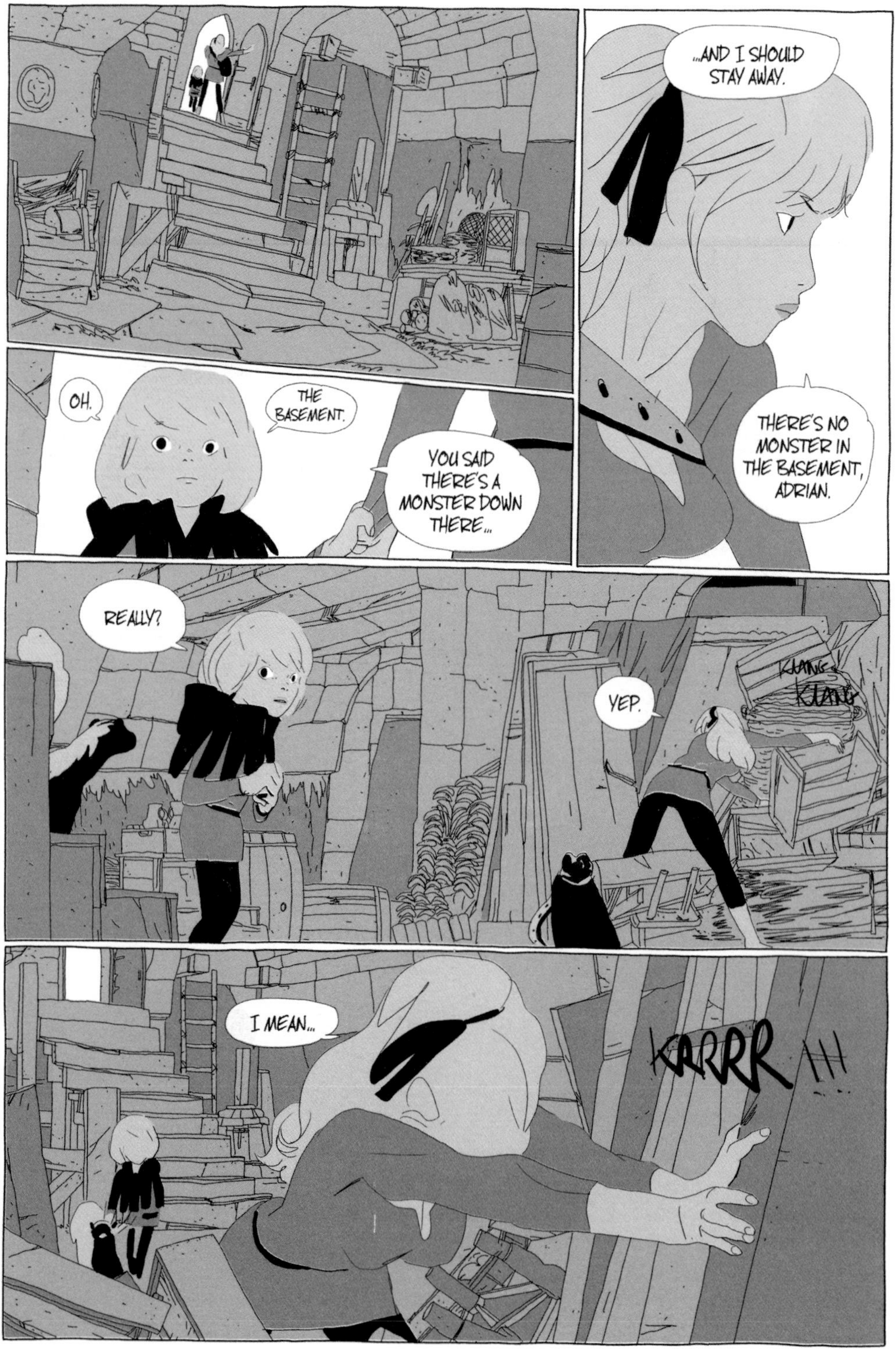
...AND I SHOULD STAY AWAY.
OH.
THE BASEMENT.
YOU SAID THERE'S A MONSTER DOWN THERE...
THERE'S NO MONSTER IN THE BASEMENT, ADRIAN.
REALLY?
YEP.
KLANG KLANG
I MEAN...
KRRRR !!!

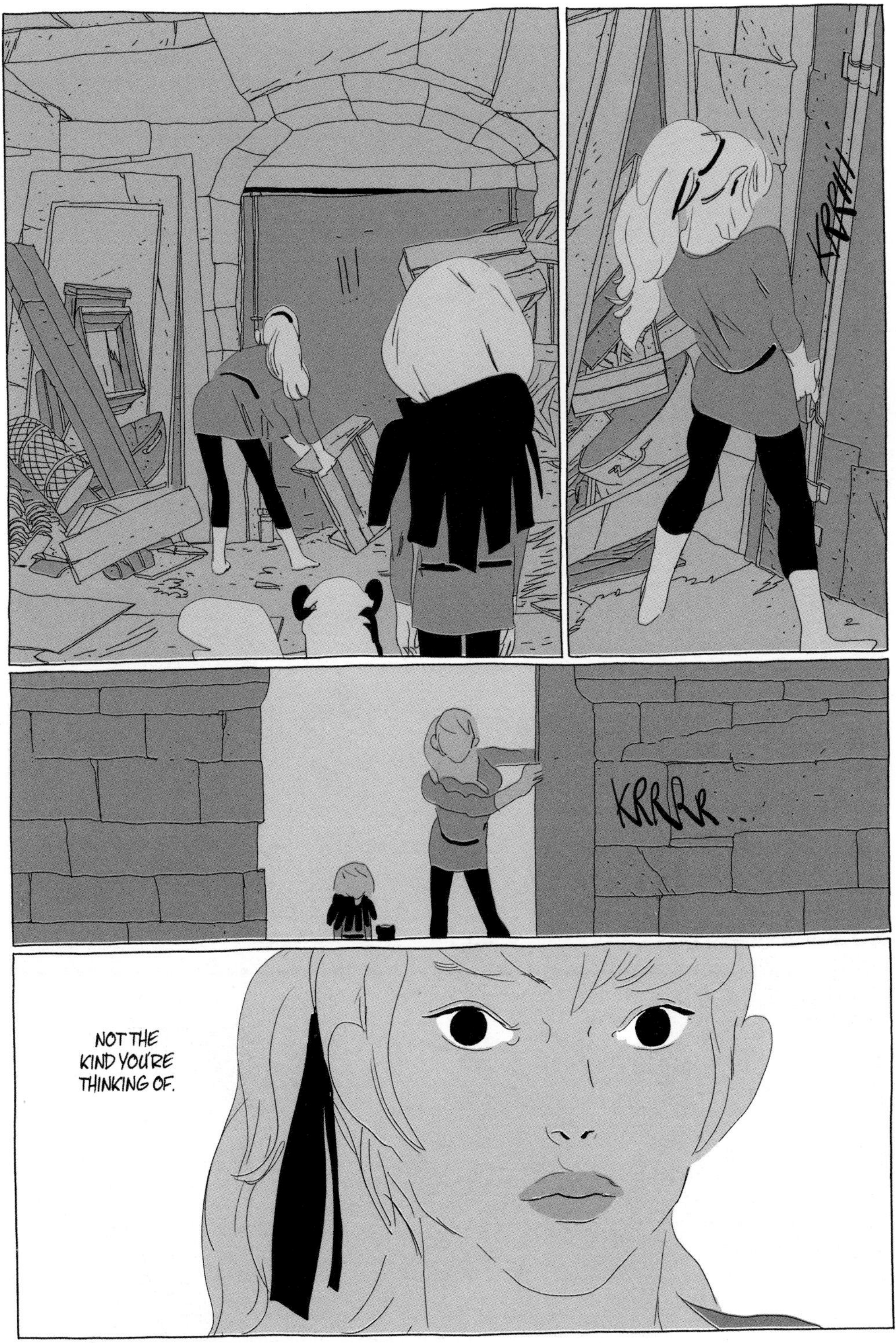
KRRH...
KRRRR...
NOT THE KIND YOU'RE THINKING OF.

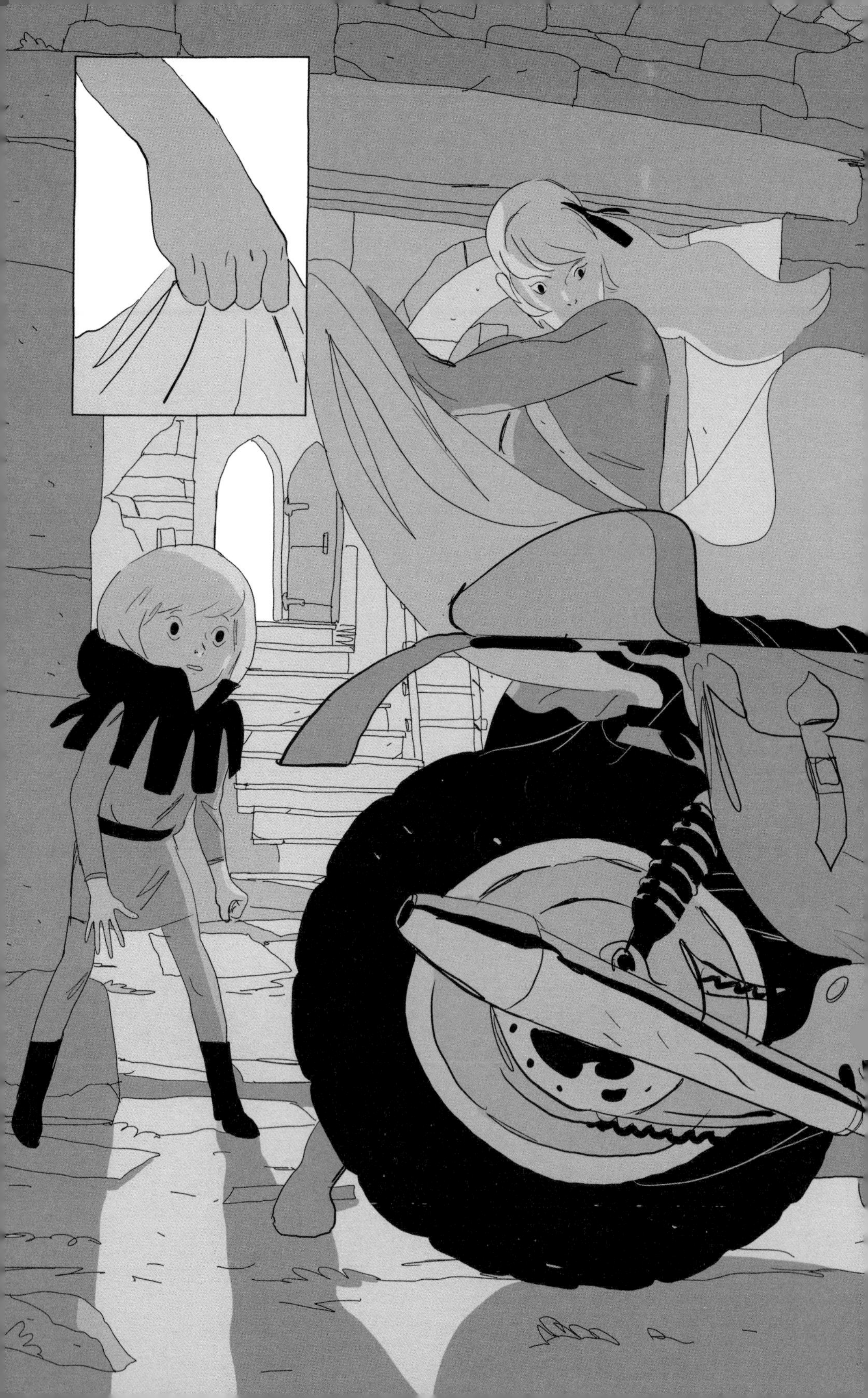

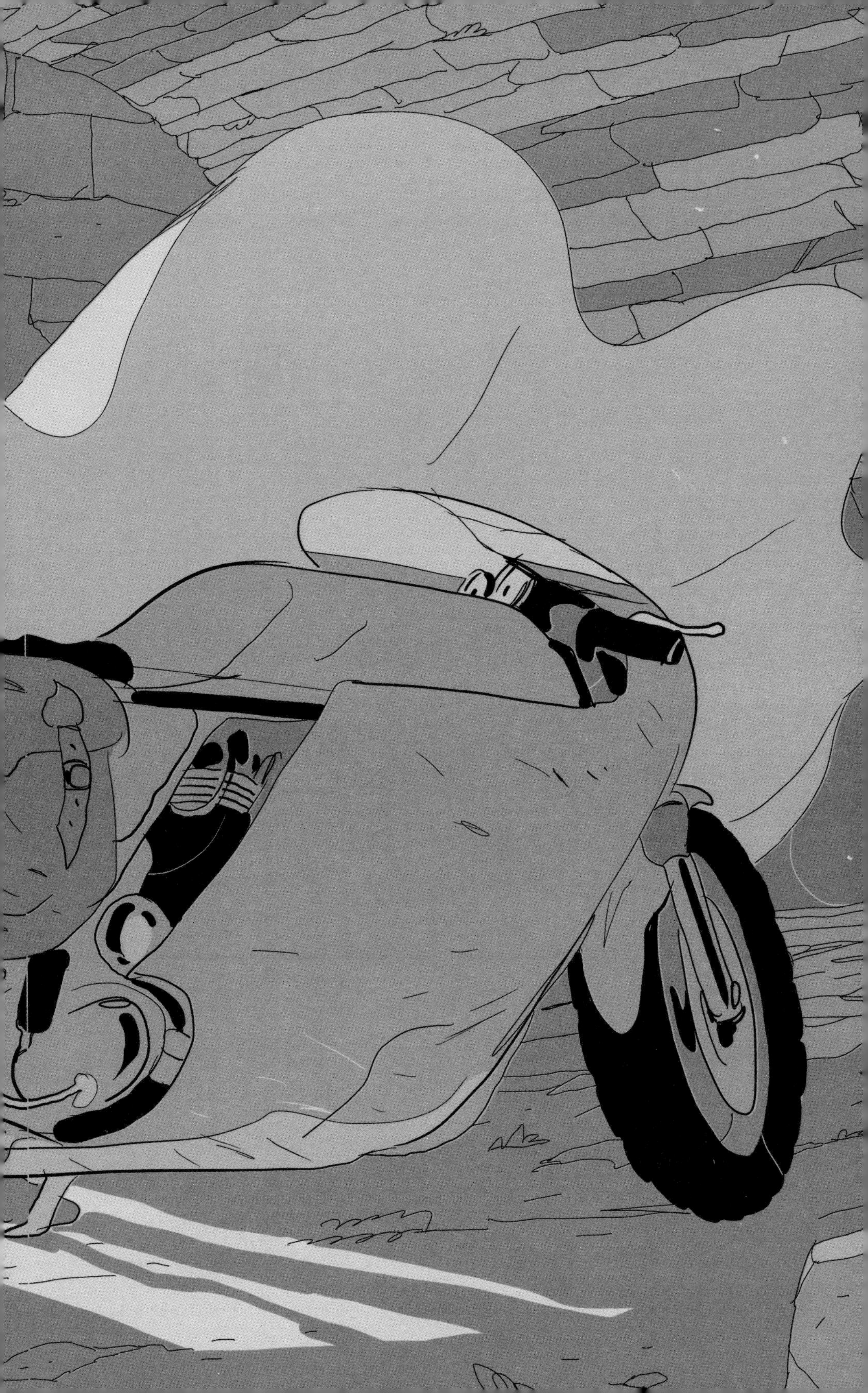

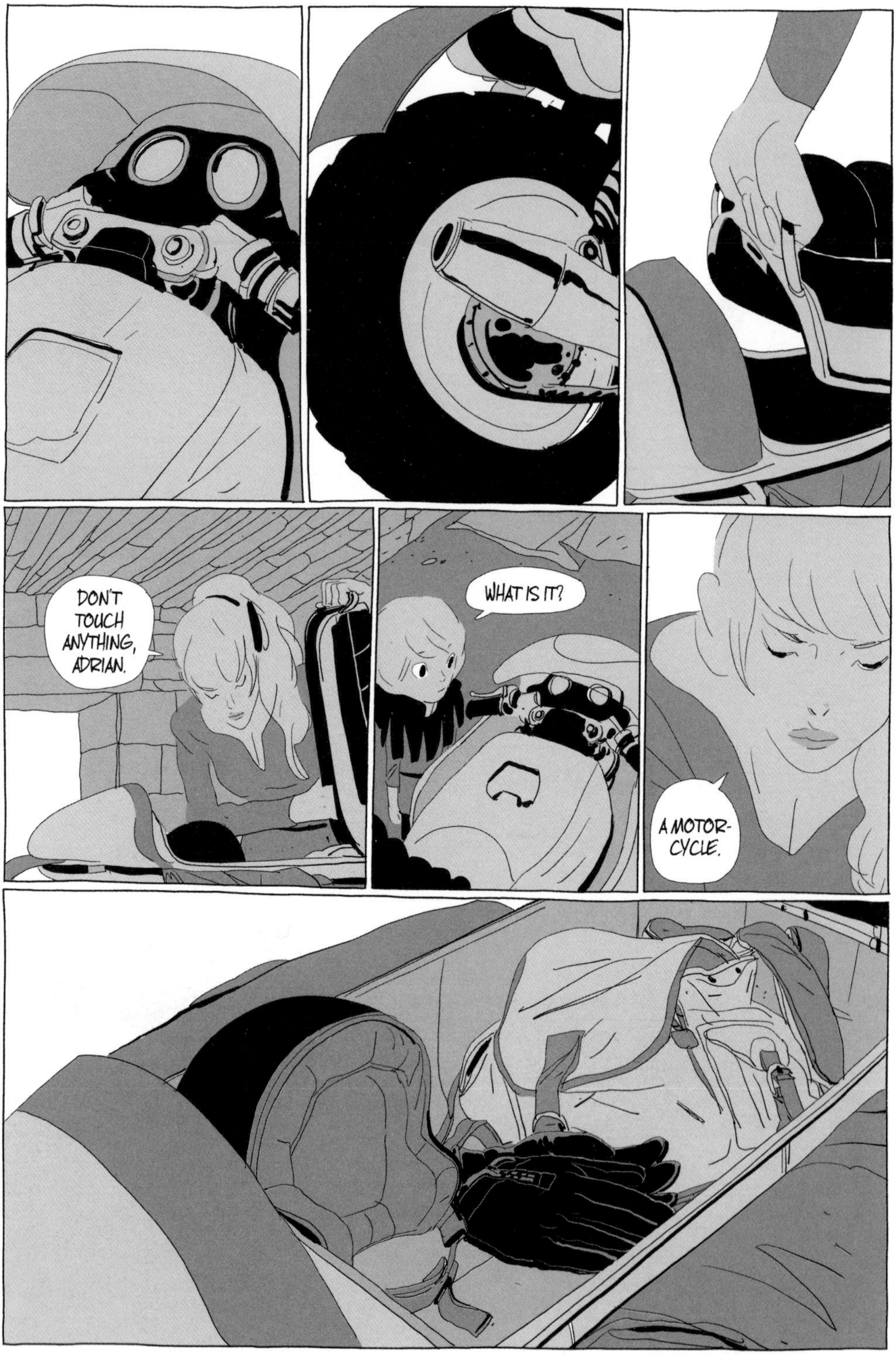

DON'T TOUCH ANYTHING, ADRIAN.
WHAT IS IT?
A MOTOR-CYCLE.

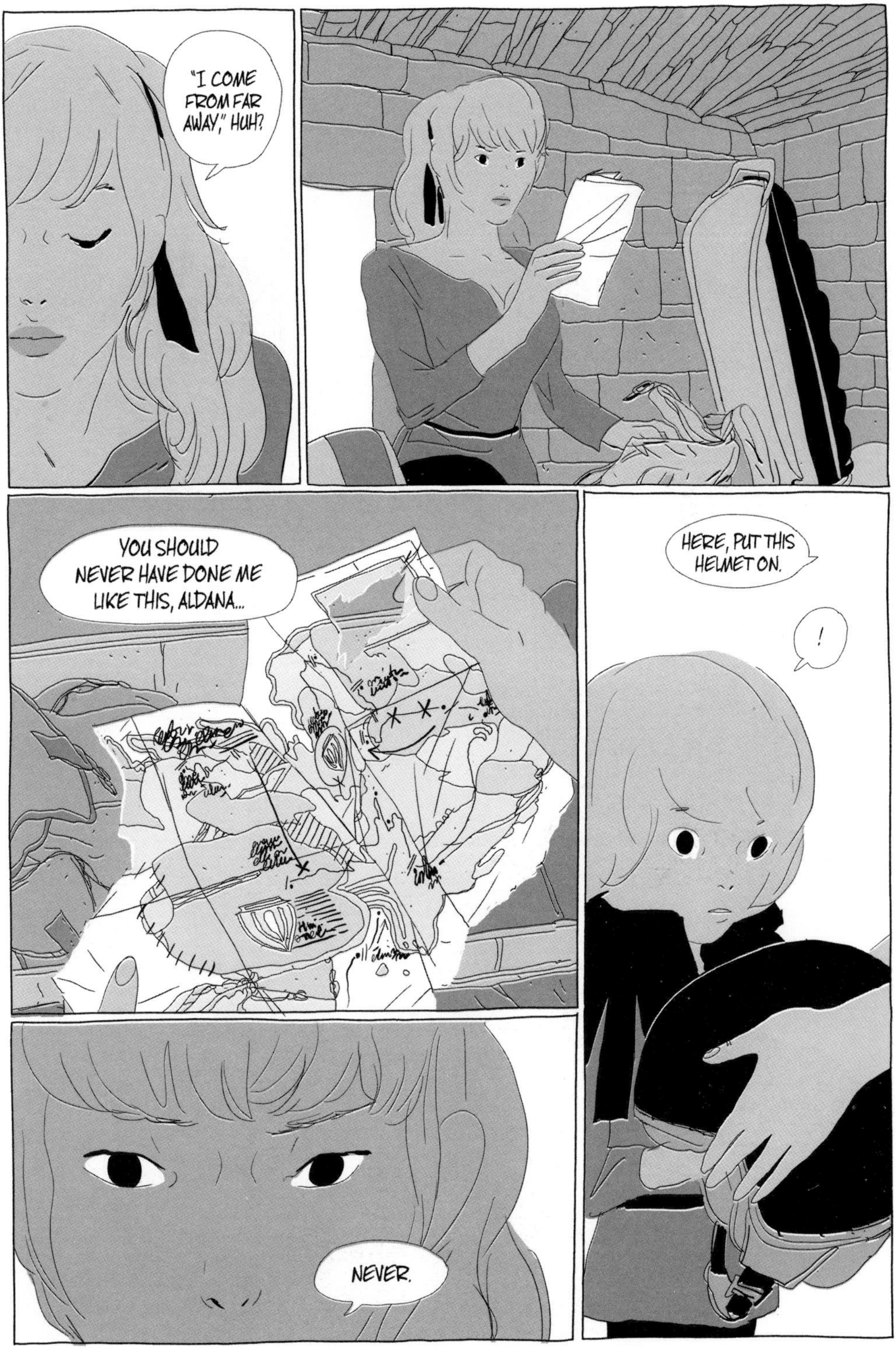
"I COME FROM FAR AWAY," HUH?
YOU SHOULD NEVER HAVE DONE ME LIKE THIS, ALDANA...
HERE, PUT THIS HELMET ON.
!
NEVER.

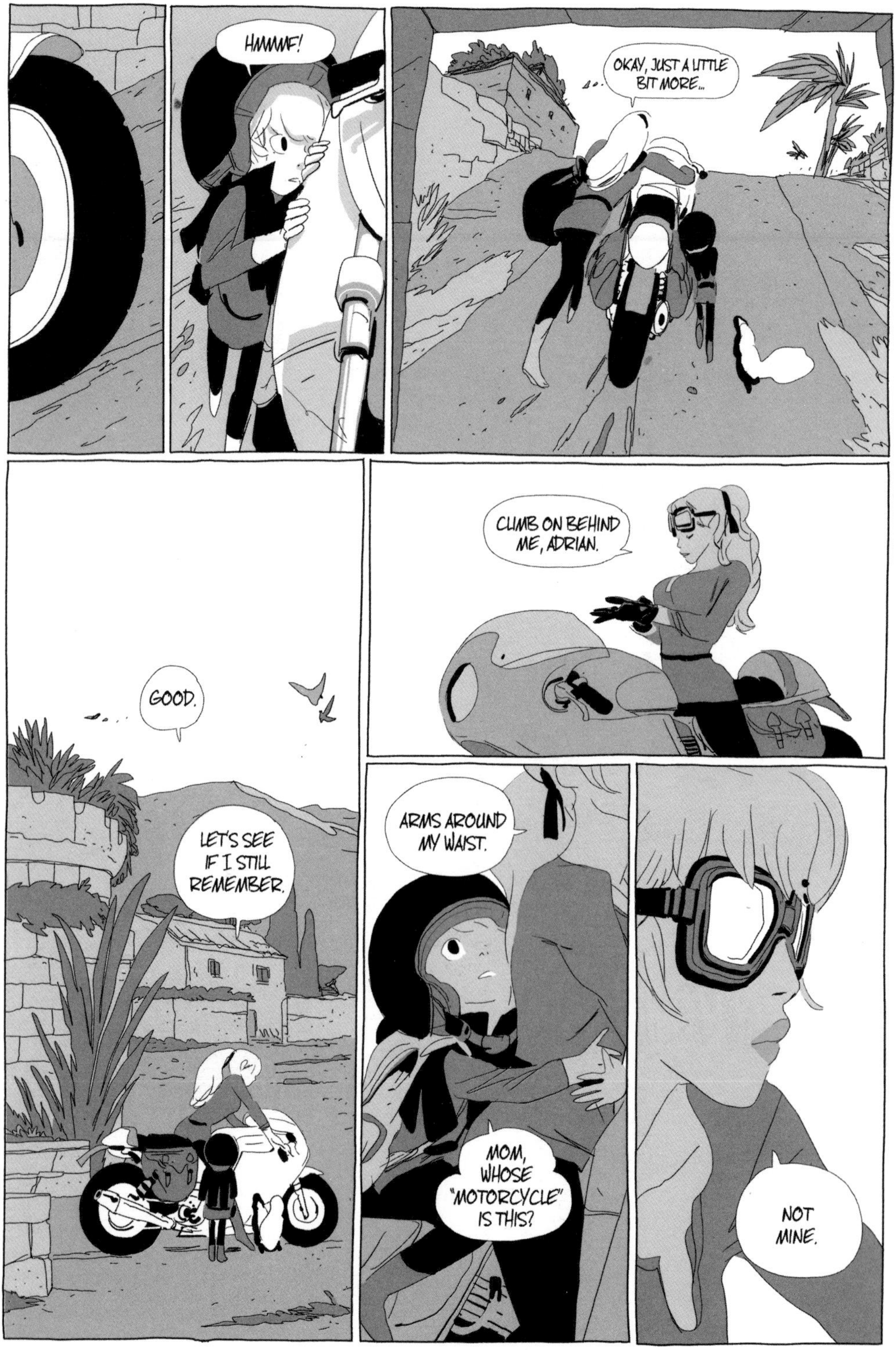
HMMMF!
OKAY, JUST A LITTLE BIT MORE...
CLIMB ON BEHIND ME, ADRIAN.
GOOD.
LET'S SEE IF I STILL REMEMBER.
ARMS AROUND MY WAIST.
MOM, WHOSE "MOTORCYCLE" IS THIS?
NOT MINE.

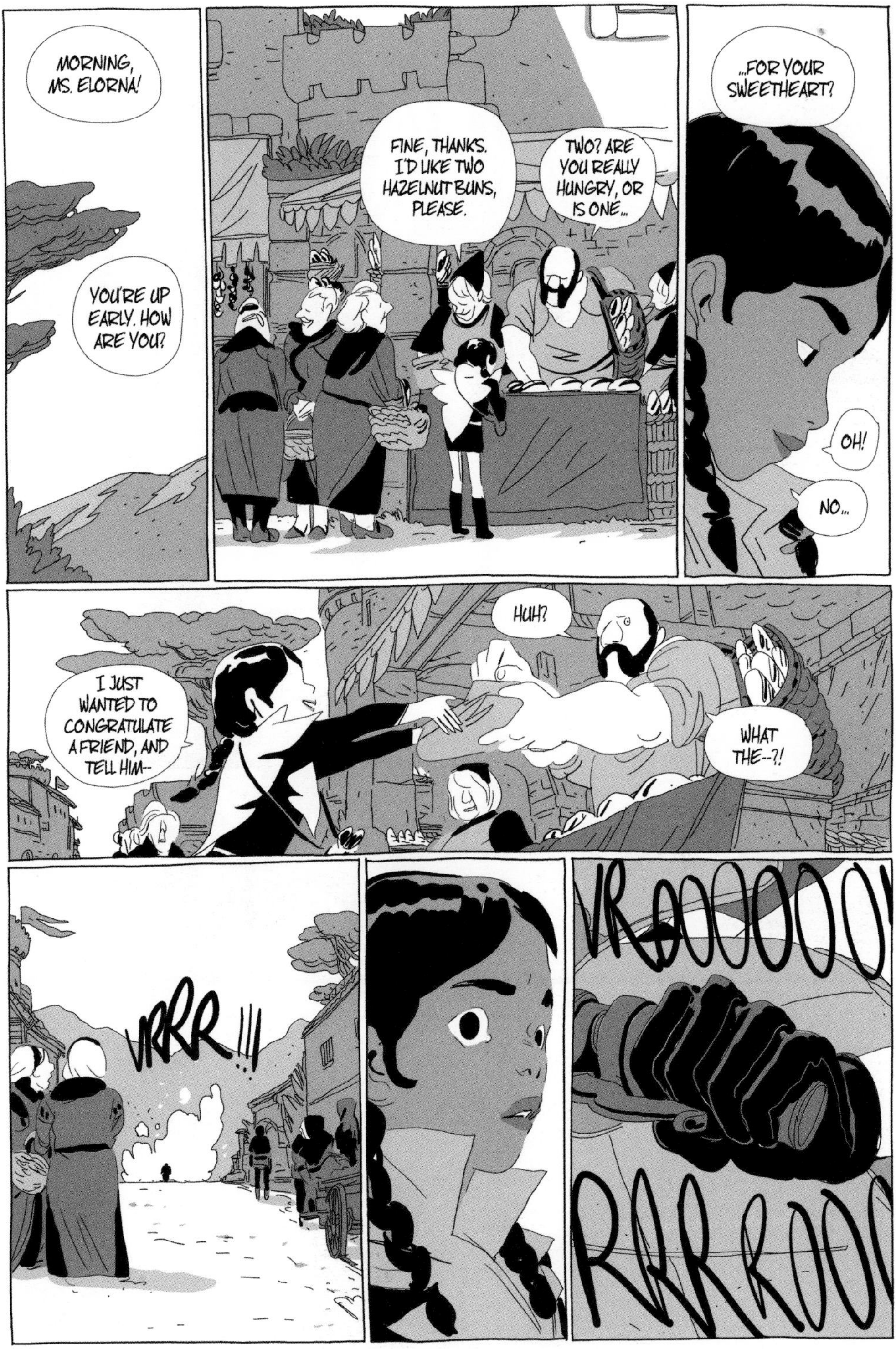
MORNING, MS. ELORNA!
YOU'RE UP EARLY. HOW ARE YOU?
FINE, THANKS. I'D LIKE TWO HAZELNUT BUNS, PLEASE.
TWO? ARE YOU REALLY HUNGRY, OR IS ONE...
...FOR YOUR SWEETHEART?
OH!
NO...
HUH?
I JUST WANTED TO CONGRATULATE A FRIEND, AND TELL HIM--
WHAT THE--?!
VRRR !!!
VROOOOOO
RRR ROO

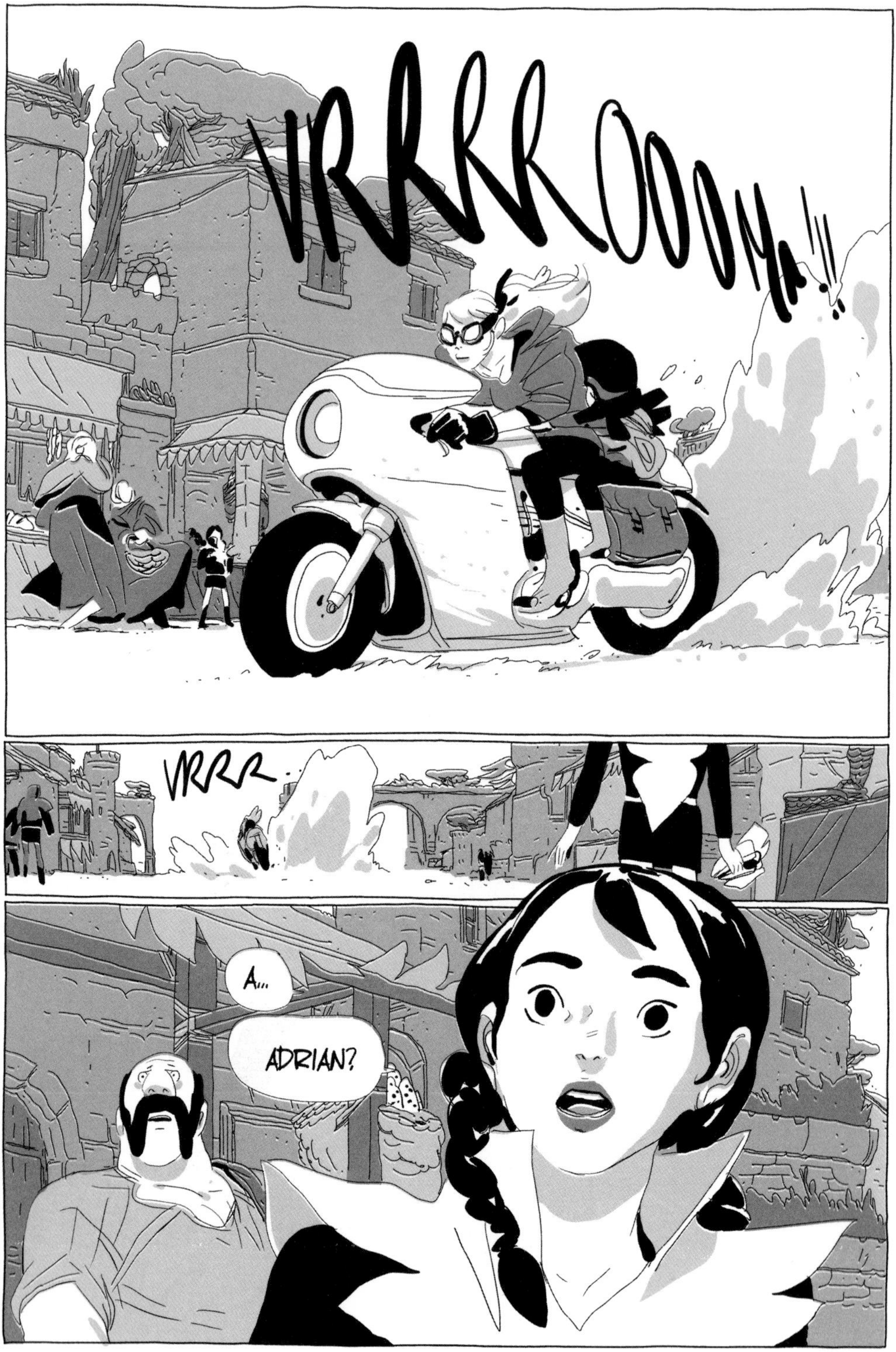
VRRRROOOM!!!
VRRR
A...
ADRIAN?

TO BE
CONTINUED

SKETCHBOOK GALLERY

ADRIAN VELBA

MARIANNE VELBA

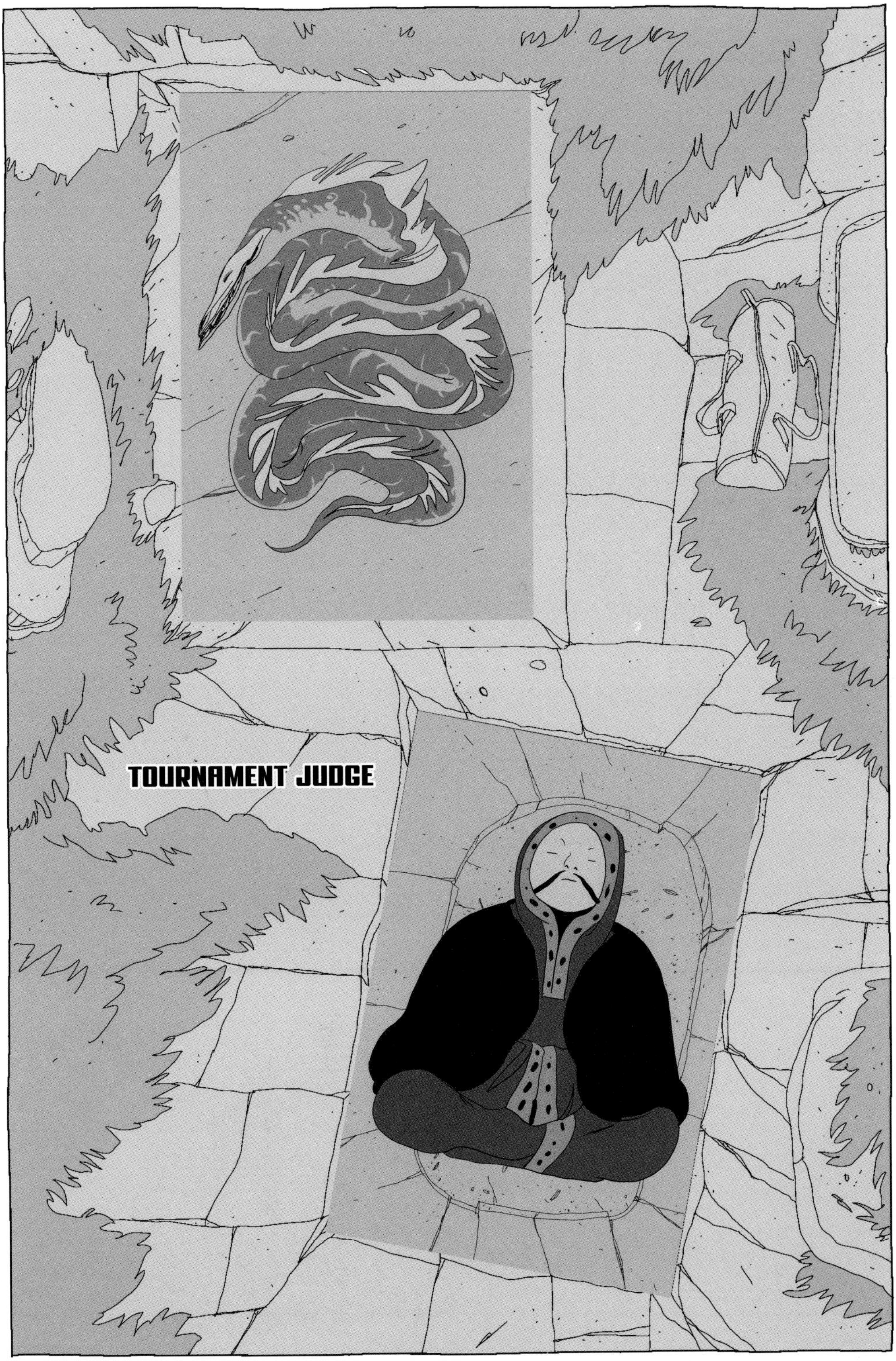
TOURNAMENT JUDGE

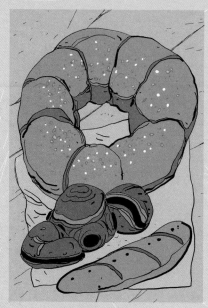

**PASTRIES FROM
MARIANNE'S BAKERY**

ONI

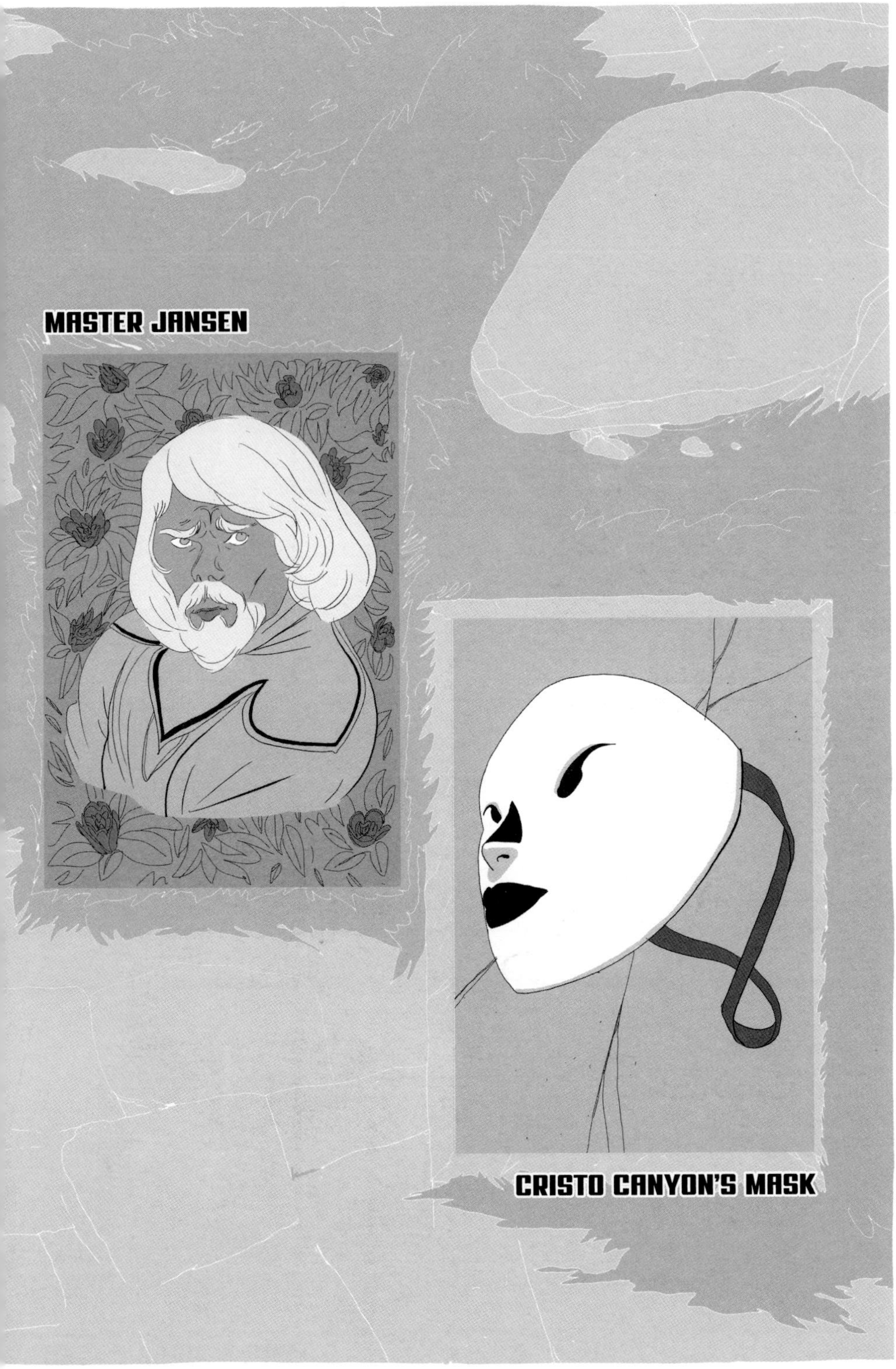
MASTER JANSEN
CRISTO CANYON'S MASK

ALYSSA

THE ROYAL CUP

LORD IGNACIO CUDNA

QUEEN EFIRA

THE SOARES BROTHERS

THE COMPLETE SERIES COLLECTED IN ENGLISH FOR THE FIRST TIME!

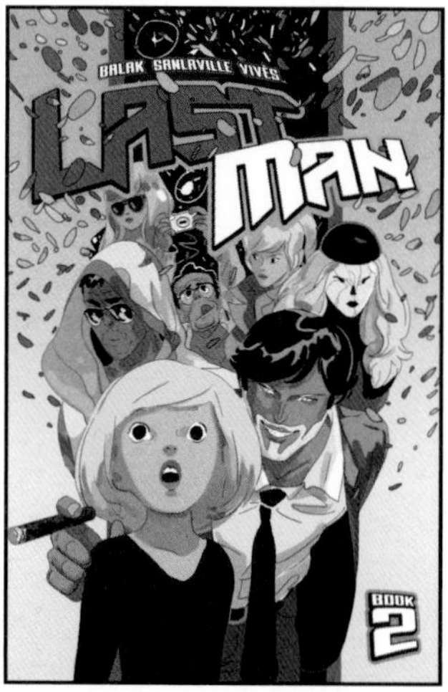
BALAK SANLAVILLE VIVÈS
LAST MAN
BOOK 2

ON SALE MARCH 2023
ISBN: 978-5343-2476-3 | $24.99

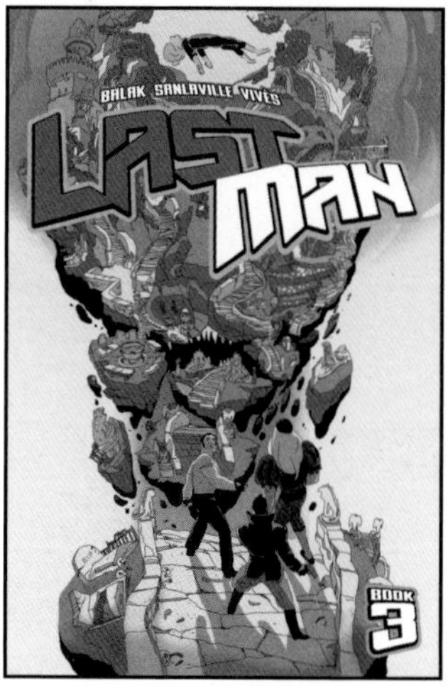
BALAK SANLAVILLE VIVÈS
LAST MAN
BOOK 3

ON SALE JULY 2023
ISBN: 978-5343-2581-4 | $24.99

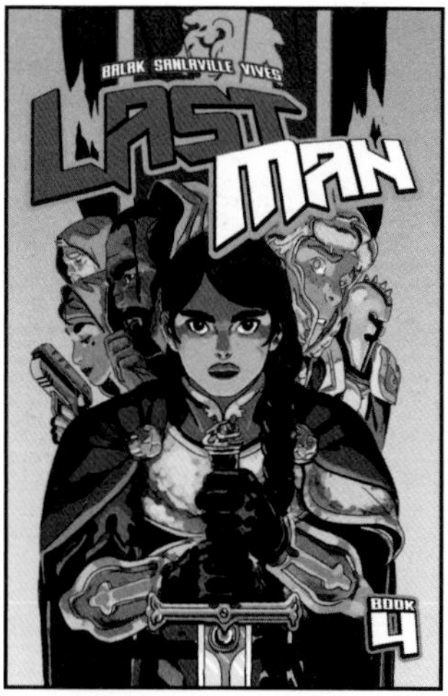
BALAK SANLAVILLE VIVÈS
LAST MAN
BOOK 4

ON SALE NOVEMBER 2023
ISBN: 978-5343-2582-1 | $24.99

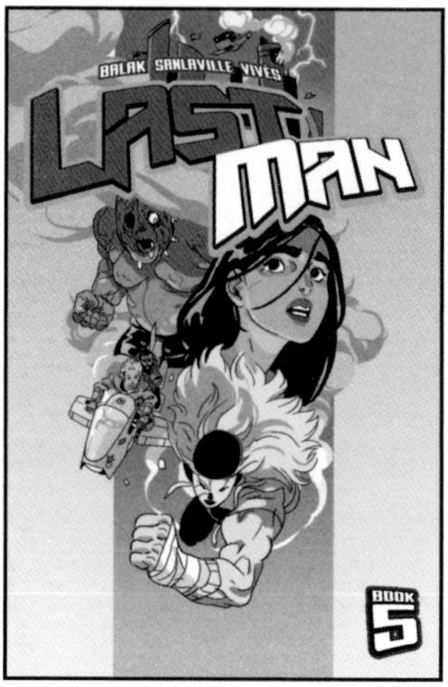
BALAK SANLAVILLE VIVÈS
LAST MAN
BOOK 5

ON SALE MARCH 2024
ISBN: 978-5343-2583-8 | $24.99

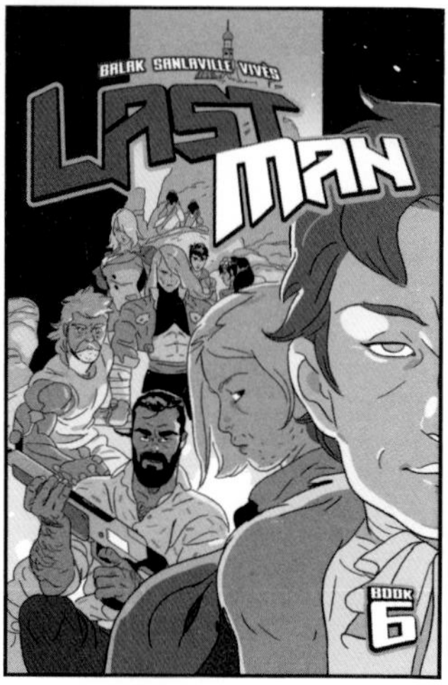
BALAK SANLAVILLE VIVÈS
LAST MAN
BOOK 6

ON SALE JULY 2024
ISBN: 978-5343-2584-5 | $24.99